CHRISTIAN PERSPECTIVES ON SEXUALITY AND GENDER

CHRISTIAN PERSPECTIVES ON SEXUALITY AND GENDER

Edited by

Elizabeth Stuart and Adrian Thatcher

Gracewing.

First published in 1996
jointly by

Gracewing		Wm B Eerdmans Publishing Co
Fowler Wright Books		255 Jefferson Ave SE
Southern Avenue	&	Grand Rapids
Leominster		Michigan 49505
Herefordshire HR6 0QF		USA

UK ISBN 085244 276 9   US ISBN 0 8028 4228 3

Typesetting by
Action Typesetting Limited, Gloucester, GL1 1SP

Printed by
The Cromwell Press, Broughton Gifford, Wiltshire, SN12 8PH

Contents

Introduction

Incarnational consciousness demands descent into the body: my personal
body, the body of my community, my earth, this cosmos. Not only do I
need to unlock the Word and Image hidden in me, personally, and
embody it; I need to be available for descent into that body of the
community.[1]

It is ironic that a religion which is grounded in what Weber calls
'incarnational consciousness' should have had so much trouble
with bodies. Western humanity still wrestles with ambiguous
attitudes to bodies – very few of us can say 'my body, my self'
or 'I am my body' with any conviction. We still understand
ourselves in dualistic terms. Our bodies are instruments of our
minds or spirits or souls. But they do not always feel like willing
servants, they are liable to get out of control and disobey us, or
worse revolt completely and take over our minds. We expend
enormous amounts of energy disciplining and taming our bodies
and when we fail we tend to be ashamed. We may live in a
permissive age and it may feel like the old ideals of virginity or
marriage have long passed away, but we still exhibit almost
neurotic uneasiness with being bodies. The AIDS pandemic
seemed to reinforce ancient subconscious connections between
the body, sexual activity and punishment and death. It is usually
only serious illness that finally forces us to acknowledge that
there is no radical distinction between ourselves and our bodies.[2]

Much of this discomfort has undoubtedly come from our
Christian culture. Despite the central proclamations that God is
the creator of matter, that the divine moves through human
history and, most importantly of all, that God has become a
body, much of Christianity ended up deeply suspicious of the
body. It has become customary to blame Greek philosophy for
this but the roots of the discomfort undoubtedly lie in some
aspects of the Judaism which brought Christianity to birth. The
culture of patriarchy into which both Judaism and Christianity
were born affirmed the normativity and superiority of men.
Women and their bodies were regarded as dangerous sources of
uncleanness. When this mentality met with Greek dualism which
associated the rational with the male and the non-material and

women with nature, corruptibility and matter, the stage was set for the emergence of a body-denying theology. Celibacy became the ideal, marriage the refuge for those who could not cope with celibacy. And yet we should not be misled into thinking that these views became orthodoxy overnight or that they were never challenged. Augustine's thesis that the transmission of 'original sin' is inextricably bound up with the sexual act and his conviction that sexual activity always involved some degree of concupiscence was vigorously challenged by several bishops including Julian of Eclanum who suspected Augustine of being more influenced by his Manichean past than the gospel. As articles in this volume attest, there have always been those within Christianity who have realised the full implications of incarnational theology and used their bodies as sources of knowledge about God.

Although Protestantism brought a much more positive attitude to sexual relations within marriage, discomfort with the body and sex remained, matters becoming more complicated by the birth of several new concepts in the post-enlightenment era. These included the idea that how one expressed oneself sexually had something to do with one's essential nature and that people could be categorised according to their sexual behaviour. The invention of sexual orientation or sexuality posed particular problems for Christianity. If it is possible to say that in every era there are one or two issues which force the Churches to ask uncomfortable questions about revelation and authority, then homosexuality has been one such issue in the modern era. Of course the Churches had always known that people engaged in same-sex sexual activity (which was regarded as sinful largely because it defied natural law), but this was regarded as a wilful perversion, like lying or stealing, and the matter was relatively straightforward. But once the existence of an essential sexual orientation became accepted as scientific orthodoxy, issues about the relative authority of the bible, tradition and contemporary experience emerged which had to be addressed and which most Churches are still wrestling with.

The rise of a feminist, womanist and mujerista consciousness within Christianity has done more than anything else to raise questions about the interaction between Christian faith and the body.[3] As Elisabeth Moltmann-Wendel has noted, 'Women are seismographs for change in culture, and their bodies are the places where conflicts become unmistakably evident.'[4] Women have been reclaiming their bodies and bodies in general from patriarchy's waste bin and have been attempting to do body theology for the twentieth century. The result as many articles in this reader testify is a theology which challenges some of the dominant tradition's most 'sacred' beliefs, for example, that sexual acts have one universal meaning – an expression of love commitment between a married man and woman and therefore must only take place within marriage or that marriage is the 'ideal' sexual relationship. Feminist theologians have been particularly concerned to expose the connection that exists in western culture between sexual activity and dominance and submission. The interconnections between sexuality and violence are ones which women and children have to live with daily but the churches have been remarkably slow and reluctant to address these issues. Feminist theologians have also drawn attention to the connections between the treatment of human bodies and the body of the earth or the bodies of communities.

What we are presently witnessing is the emergence of two divergent paths of theology. The official Churches are attempting to do what James Nelson labels 'a theology of (or about) sexuality' which

> tends to argue in a one-directional way: What do scripture and tradition say about our sexuality and how it ought to be expressed? What does the church say, what do the rabbis say, what does the pope say?...[5]

Feminist theologians, gay theologians and others, on the other hand, seek to develop what Nelson calls a 'sexual theology' which asks,

> What does our experience as human sexual beings tell us about how we read the scripture, interpret the tradition, and attempt to live out the meaning of the gospel?[6]

The articles which make up this reader generally represent the second approach. Together they give a good impression about what a radical difference doing sexual theology rather than attempting to build a theology of sexuality makes. Yet there is still much more work that needs to be done. The Churches are still wrestling with the idea that gender might be a social construction i.e. that what constitutes the 'feminine' and the 'masculine' is not biology but society. The wrestling has been very painful but soon they will have to begin to wrestle with the idea that sexuality may also be a social construction. What will a post-Foucaudian sexual theology look like? The signs are that it will focus on just behaviour, mutuality and reciprocity rather than on gender and orientation. Ironically, St Augustine's famous maxim, 'love and then do what you will' may become central.

Sexuality is still much of a mystery. There is no widespread agreement as to what it is or how it is formed in individuals. The parallels with spirituality are significant. What we can discern is that both are about relationships, about reaching out towards others and that both are essential to humanity. Human beings are sexual beings and spiritual beings. The challenge posed by the authors gathered together in this book is to see the sexual in the spiritual and the spiritual in the sexual. If we cannot then the incarnational heart of Christianity is no longer beating.

We were influenced in our choice of material by several criteria. First, as the title of the book and the majority of books in the *Perspectives* series suggests, the essays had to be Christian, i.e. their approach to sexuality and gender had to come from inside the traditions of Christian theology and faith, very broadly understood. Second, it was hoped that the essays would not simply theologise about sexuality, but that through them, theology and sexual experience would interact with each other. Third, the essays would be (several of our contributors urge) 'partial' (e.g. 11.2). We would not pretend to an impartiality which mimics the disinterestedness of patriarchy (see 6.1) or wilfully ignores the androcentric construction of theological knowledge. Given our wish also to be 'inclusive' (see below), just how partial were we able to be?

The partiality of the volume is influenced by two factors. We wished, fourth, to encompass people who have been marginalized by the patriarchal bias of traditional theological approaches to sexuality, e.g. lesbian women and gay men (ch. 7), the elderly (8.3), single people (ch. 10), and perhaps above all, victims of sexual violence (ch. 9). Traditional theology, however, is too important to be entrusted to traditionalists. We looked for theological work which, fifth, affirmed the tradition (and did not discard it) (ch. 1) while, sixth, engaging in far-reaching re-interpretation and revision. This re-interpretation is itself driven by the methods and insights of feminist and liberation theology. Particular manifestations of it are found in e.g. refashioning notions of power (ch. 3), re-examining *agape* and reinstating *eros* within a Christian theology of love (6.1 & 6.2), overcoming sexual dualism (ch. 8), and re-integrating sexuality and spirituality (ch. 5). This re-interpretation and revision is essential, we hold, to the well-being of theology and church. Without it, the good news of the gospel cannot be heard.

Seventh, within this committed framework we have been *inclusive*, or at any rate, as inclusive as possible. There are essays from Roman Catholics and the major Protestant churches, from liberal and evangelical perspectives, from men and women, single and married, lesbian, gay and straight. We are conscious that the third world is under-represented (but see 4.4). Essays vary greatly in length. Some are included because they convey single but important insights: others contribute originally to sexual theology and deserve greater space for more detailed arguments and claims to be heard. The essays deliberately vary in depth and so give the book the advantage of being accessible to different readerships at a variety of levels.

Eighth, we were pleased to let our selection be influenced by contemporary social and theological controversies. The current painful scrutiny of family and marriage as social institutions is reflected in our selection in chs. 4 & 11. These selections are strong enough to contribute, on their own terms, to the extensive and far-reaching conversations on family and marriage which usually take place outside theology. Theological contributions to Gender Studies are rare, yet our selections in ch. 2 deserve serious attention inside and outside theology, while being grounded in the experiences and dilemmas of Christian women and men. While the issues surrounding gender feature throughout the book, we decided early on to devote a specific chapter to gender as a topic. Every one of our chapters, we believe, contributes positively and strongly to contemporary controversies within the churches.

These criteria have been applied fairly loosely. Some areas covered by our chapters are supported by a meagre literature, while others are much richer and we have had to exclude excellent material for reasons of space. We were pleased to include one essay from a post-Christian perspective. While agreeing with many of the criticisms of the Christian tradition in this article, agreement with the editors was not a criterion of selection! We offer this book conscious of the oppression, exclusion, marginalisation and condemnation that the Christian faith still initiates, colludes with and actively supports. But the faith is also capable of being read and appropriated in redemptive, liberating ways, as many of the authors here testify. It is our hope that our readers will share the excitement of bringing together redemptive read-

ings of the faith with the totality of their own sexuality and
sexual experiences.

Notes

1.   Christin Lore Weber, *Woman Christ*, Harper and Row, San Francisco, 1987, p.
      46

2.   For a useful discussion of these issues see Elisabeth Moltmann-Wendel, *I Am My
      Body*, SCM, London, 1994.

3.   The term feminist theology applies primarily to theology done by white women
      from the northern parts of the world. Womanist theology refers to theology done
      from the basis of black women's experience and mujerista theology refers to
      theology done from the perspective of Spanish speaking women from the north
      and south. The point is that not all women are the same and we must not make
      the mistake of assuming that white women's experience is normative.

4.   Ibid., p. 9.

5.   James Nelson, *Body Theology*, Westminster/John Knox Press, Louisville, KT,
      1992, p. 21.

6.   Ibid.

1. Sexuality and the Christian Tradition

How do Christians interpret the Bible and the historical traditions of theology and faith bequeathed to us by every generation
of Christians since Jesus Christ? These issues assume acute
importance at a time when the authority of each is certain to be
questioned and assessed according to whether it is able to
empower and enlighten contemporary Christians who live in
vastly different historical, social, intellectual and cultural
circumstances from those of earlier generations. These issues are
particularly acute in sexual theology, because it is an area of
theology and tradition where the androcentrism and male bias
against women is painfully explicit.

In this opening section some of the issues posed by the Bible
and tradition for sexual theology are discussed, and tentative
solutions proposed. Stephen C. Barton argues that the polar
positions taken by conservative Christians and liberal biblical
critics towards the Bible are alike mistaken. He wishes to lay
aside the question posed by the title of his article, 'Is the Bible
Good News for Human Sexuality?', in favour of another, viz.
'What sort of people ought we to be and become, so that we are
enabled to read the Bible in ways which are life-giving in the
area of gender and sexuality?' This different question takes the
Bible out of the dock and puts the readers into it. Instead of
regarding the Bible as a quarry for digging out issues and proof-
texts, why not treat it, Barton asks, 'more like the text of a
Shakespearean play or the score of a Beethoven symphony,
where true interpretation involves corporate performance and
practical enactment...?'

Richard Price sets himself the question 'What was the origin
of the amazing concern with purity and sexual sin that came at
such an early date to characterize Christianity?' His article introduces readers to the immense effort required in order to enter
sympathetically into a thought-world which is largely closed to
us, while bequeathing to us beliefs and practices which are as
likely to exasperate as to inspire. Price argues that the distinctiveness of early Christian sexual ethics should be traced to the
New Testament and not blamed on Graeco-Roman influences.

The continued belief in an imminent Parousia, together with the desire both to avoid the precarious burdens of childbirth and to engage in *spiritual* as opposed to physical procreation, led to the high evaluation of celibacy and virginity. The (celibate) leadership of the Church was strict and unsparing in matters of sexual morality not least because 'Christians saw themselves as constituting a holy people, set apart as a distinct, third race from both Jews and pagans.' The early Church thus had a 'different ecclesiology' in the light of which alone, their strict disciplines may be understood. Price helps us towards a positive appreciation of some of the eccentricities of early Christian sexual ethics without suggesting that we have an obligation to emulate or reproduce them. Perhaps contemporary Christians can still stand in solidarity with the early Church by maintaining a radical distinctiveness between Christian and non-Christian understandings of sexual ethics, while living and expressing this distinctiveness in a different way? The remaining chapters of this book explore the foundations upon which a distinctive Christian sexual ethics may be built.

Daniel Doriani's essay, 'The Puritans, Sex, and Pleasure', casts valuable light on how, in one particular historical case and over one particular issue, viz. the enjoyment of sexual intercourse within marriage, Christians changed their minds. The Puritans openly disagreed with some Roman Catholic teaching, especially that the pleasure associated with sex within marriage was sinful. They held that purity before God was fully consistent (though to different degrees) with enjoyment of sexual pleasure, while backing off from several of the implications of such a view. Despite the restrictions the Puritans placed on married intercourse, they 'began to return the church to a more positive, indeed more biblical, concept of marital love,' and 'intended to radically reform Christian thinking on marriage and sexuality, in order to bring thought and practice into harmony with the Bible'. Their partial failure to achieve this harmony may have been due to their inability to distance themselves from 'the Greek and Catholic dualism with its denigration of and antipathy toward the body.' Perhaps we may add that they had underestimated the extent to which rigid patriarchal norms and celibate experience had shaped the tradition with which they were in partial conflict?

Stephen C. Barton is Lecturer in New Testament in the University of Durham, England. His article, 'Is the Bible Good News for Human Sexuality? Reflections on Method in Biblical Interpretation', was first published in *Theology and Sexuality*,

No. 1, 1994, pp. 42–54. Richard M. Price's article, 'The Distinctiveness of Early Christian Sexual Ethics' was first published in *The Heythrop Journal*, 1990, pp. 257–276. Daniel Doriani is Associate Professor in New Testament, Covenant Theological Seminary, St. Louis, Missouri, U.S.A. His article, 'The Puritans, Sex, and Pleasure', was first published in the *Westminster Theological Journal*, 53, 1991, pp. 125–143.

1.1 Is the Bible Good News for Human Sexuality? Reflections on Method in Biblical Interpretation

Stephen C. Barton

There can be little doubt that there is more disagreement than ever before over the question of the relevance of the Bible for understanding human sexuality. As in so many areas of Christian belief and practice, the consensus has broken down and is fiercely contested. For many, the Bible remains the touchstone and authoritative guide for how men and women are to understand and practise their sexuality and how life together in family, church and society is to be conducted.[1] For many others, the Bible has little or no authority because it belongs so obviously to a bygone age and its teaching is neither credible nor helpful.[2] Others, yet again, find themselves somewhere in the middle, caught between feelings of loyalty to the Bible and what it stands for on the one hand, and on the other, a firm conviction that modern people do not and cannot take the Bible seriously any more, especially when it is interpreted literally.[3]

One of the issues which often lies behind these disagreements is that of interpretation: what is the Bible for?, what does the Bible mean?, and is the Bible true? The aim of this essay is to discuss issues of method in interpretation with a view to showing that the original question is wrongly put. Instead of asking, is the Bible good news for human sexuality?, the question we should be asking is much more of the kind, what sort of people ought we to be and become, so that we are enabled to read the Bible in ways which are life-giving in the area of gender and sexuality? In other words, I wish to suggest that it is not the Bible that should be the main bone of contention. Rather, the focus ought to be on the readers: who it is who is reading the Bible and what it might mean for us to read the Bible well and wisely.

The Right Place to Start

Knowing the right place to start is the critical issue, often overlooked. One very common approach is to start with the Bible. Ironically, given their mutual antagonism, this tends to be the approach of both conservative fundamentalists and liberal historical critics. Both groups, faced with the question, is the Bible good news for human sexuality?, assume that the obvious and correct thing to do is to go 'back to the Bible', find the relevant texts, and see what they have to say. Many reports issued by church bodies and ecclesiastical authorities likewise

begin with opening chapters on 'what the Bible teaches',[4] the obvious
intention being to lay the firm foundations for what follows on interpretation and application. Here, the implicit assumption, of course, is
that interpretation and application follow the laying of the biblical
foundations rather than influencing it from the start! It is as if the
answers to this and any other question can be 'read off' the text in a
relatively straightforward way, either by 'stretching' history (in the
case of the fundamentalist) or by asserting historical distance (in the
case of the historical critic), with the matter of application following
on subsequently. The problem with this kind of approach is highlighted
well by Nicholas Lash in his critique of what he memorably depicts as
the 'relay-race' model of the relation between biblical criticism and
systematic theology:

> When the New Testament scholar has done his job, produced his
> completed package of 'original meanings', he hands this over to the
> systematic theologian, whose responsibility it is to transpose the mean-
> ings received into forms intelligible within the conditions of our
> contemporary culture. Systematic theologians who subscribe to this
> model are sometimes irritated by the fact that, because the work of New
> Testament interpretation is never finished, the baton never reaches them.
> The New Testament scholar appears to be 'running on the spot'; he never
> arrives at the point at which the baton could be handed over. The New
> Testament scholar, for his part, either ignores what the systematic theolo-
> gian is doing (it is not his business: he is only running the *first* leg of the
> race) or disapproves of the fact that the baton is continually being
> wrenched prematurely from his hands.[5]

Nevertheless, in some ways, starting with the Bible seems a common
sense and unobjectionable way of proceeding. Obviously, an important
ingredient of any Christian attempt to answer 'the question of human
sexuality' will be to try to find the relevant biblical material and see
what it says. Given that there are the two horizons in biblical interpretations, the horizon of the text and the horizon of the reader,[6] why not
start with that of the text? But there are problems lying not too far
beneath the surface of this apparently common sense, 'objective'
approach.

First, there is the problem of what model of the Bible and Bible
reading is being presupposed. To put it in the form of a question, what
is involved in using the Bible as a source of information or instruction?
Is the Bible understood best as a source, something to go back to or
dig into? Operating on the assumption that this is so, the conservative
fundamentalist quarries the Bible for the appropriate proof texts,
ascertains the plain (that is, literal) sense of the text and seeks then to
apply it in (what is believed to be) a straightforward, rational way to
everyday life. Operating on basically the same assumption, the liberal
historical critic also quarries the Bible, ascertains the plain (that is,
historico-philological) sense of the text and then, if he or she is religiously disposed, tries to weigh up rationally whether it is applicable

or not, taking its historically conditioned character into account.

But what if the Bible is something more than a source to be quarried and analyzed in the privacy either of the believer's 'quiet time' or of the academician's study? What if interpreting the Bible is not best understood in these decidedly positivist terms as a kind of archaeological dig for historical facts or revelatory propositions? What if the Bible is more like the text of a Shakespearean play or the score of a Beethoven symphony, where true interpretation involves corporate performance and practical enactment, and where the meaning of the text or score will vary to some degree from one performance to another depending on the identity of the performers and the circumstances of the performance? A number of writers have begun to explore this alternative model of interpreting the Bible.[7] Its advantage is that it brings the reading of the Bible back into the process of community formation, celebration and mission, and places responsibility on the community to read the texts in ways which are transforming and life-giving.

Related to the first problem is the problem of the 'Little Jack Horner' approach to the Bible. How adequate are approaches to the Bible which select out the 'purple passages' about gender and sexuality, or focus in a proof-texting way on those texts which support a particular understanding? This approach is very common, perhaps the most common. In an area of debate which is closely related to human sexuality, that of the status and role of women in Christian faith, think of the enormous attention devoted to New Testament texts like Gal. 3.28 ('neither male nor female ... in Christ Jesus'), or 1 Cor. 11.2–16 ('the head of a woman is her husband...'), or 1 Tim. 2.8–15 ('Let a woman learn in silence with all submissiveness...'). Even on single verses and single words within verses the scholarly and other literature can be enormous.[8]

There seems to be something fundamentally inadequate about this. For instance, there is the danger of trivializing the text, as if all that matters is whether or not selected texts (can be made to) speak for or against a particular conception of human sexuality.[9] I am not at all wishing to deny the general point that issues of human sexuality are important.[10] What I wish to question is the wisdom of so focusing the sexuality debate on Bible reading and interpretation that such issues become the dominant, sometimes almost exclusive agenda, and the Bible becomes little more than a battleground of competing special interest groups. Instead of being 'a lamp unto our feet and a light unto our path', the Bible is trivialized and at the same time the issue of human sexuality is trivialized as well. Our reading of the Bible becomes distracted from what might be regarded as more central, or at least equally legitimate, concerns – to do, for example, with faith in God and the pursuit of righteousness and justice. At the same time, the issues of gender and sexuality are marginalized: reduced to matters of exegesis, an exercise of which, in any case, only very few are equipped.

Then there is the danger that the Bible will not be allowed to speak as *one book*, but becomes fractured and fragmented instead into many isolated or even opposing parts. So, for example, the account of the creation of the man and the woman in Genesis 1 is played off against the account in Genesis 2–3, the celebration of sexual love in the Song of Songs is played off against the disciplinary emphasis of the Pentateuch, Jesus' attitude to 'prostitutes and sinners' is played off against Paul's, Paul the liberationist is played off against the apparent authoritarianism of the Pastoral Epistles, or more generally, the Old Testament is played off against the New.

Now I do not wish to deny that there are often very significant differences between one part of the Bible and another, not least on issues of gender and sexuality. Nor do I wish to encourage a simplistic harmonizing of one Bible passage with another. What I am concerned to point out, however, is the potential of these kinds of interpretative strategy paradoxically to cut off the scriptural branch on which they rest. For in the end, the Bible can be dispensed with altogether. Those who 'flatten out' the text of the Bible by a process of harmonization, so that it is always saying the same thing, undermine the Bible by making it monolithic, static and ultimately uninteresting. Those who divide up the Bible by setting one text over against another also undermine it, this time by divesting it of coherence and authority. What is needed instead is a way of reading the Bible which transcends these reductionist alternatives and allows the Bible to function as life-giving, revelatory scripture for the church.[11]

Also, there is the danger that the text becomes captive to tribal interests of one kind or another, whether conservative fundamentalism, liberal biblical criticism, feminism, gay liberation, or whatever. When this happens, the meaning of the text and even more the truth of the text tend to get confused with the question of whether or not the text can be used to support the identity and self-understanding of the group concerned. Kathleen Boone has shown recently how this happens in the way the Bible is used in Protestant Fundamentalism.[12] Anthony Thiselton, on the other hand, has also shown how this happens in the interpretation of the Bible by some feminists.[13] And, lest the historical critics think that their approach escapes this tendency towards tribalism, Stanley Hauerwas and Steve Long have argued with some force that historical criticism tends to serve the narrow interests of modern liberal individualism, and that the natives of this tribe are to be found most commonly in university departments of theology and religion![14]

The corollary of all this is a tendency towards scapegoating. So, for example, the Bible becomes the scapegoat for the anxieties of feminists and gay liberationists, or feminists and gays become the scapegoat for the anxieties of the loyalists, or the historical critics adopt an approach along the lines of 'a plague on both your houses' and withdraw to the apparently neutral and 'scientific' activity of the quest for the historical Jesus (or Mary or whoever).

Then there is the issue, what constitutes an appropriate set of expectations to bring to the biblical text? For some, it is essential to approach the text in a spirit of absolute trust, itself based upon a 'high' view of the Bible as the Word of God. For others, it is necessary to approach the text from a stance of systematic suspicion, on the assumption that the Bible is either outdated (so the modernist) or a weapon of oppression (so certain kinds of feminist). But it is rarely acknowledged that the loyalist position and the revisionist (or rejectionist) positions are two sides of the same coin, according to which the main issue is whether or not the Bible can be trusted. The Enlightenment tendency to put God in the dock for cross-examination is transferred here to the Bible. Now it is the Bible which is placed in the dock, with some quoting proof texts in its defence, and others quoting proof texts on behalf of the prosecution. Instead of allowing ourselves to be judged by Scripture as in some fundamental theological sense 'the book of God' – a stance advocated *inter alios* by Karl Barth and Dietrich Bonhoeffer – we become its judges. Instead of learning in community the kinds of skill and wisdom necessary to faithful interpretation and transforming enactment, we reify and absolutize the text either as a book to be obeyed or as a book to be dismissed.

Yet another problem is that of assuming that the text has only one meaning, the literal meaning, and that this is to be ascertained rationally using common sense in one form or another – that is, the common sense of the proverbial man or woman on the Clapham omnibus or the common sense arising out of the application of historical criticism. On this view, once the meaning of the text has been established, it is a matter simply of 'applying' it to the modern world, or of disregarding it as irrelevant to the modern world. But why assume that the meaning of the biblical text is univocal? It is one thing to resist the idea that 'anything goes' and that there are no limits to what a text may mean. It is another to go to the opposite extreme of saying that the text has one true meaning only (which usually happens to be the meaning my group holds to).

However, there is a more moderate position in between the extremes, with strong precedent in the Bible itself as well as in the exegesis of the Early Church and the Middle Ages. According to this view, and taking its hermeneutical cue from Paul's statement in 2 Cor. 3.6 that 'the letter kills but the spirit makes alive', a text may have meanings over and above that intended by the original author, meanings which the author was unable to see or which the author did not anticipate.[15] It is the character of the reading community, itself influenced by the history of the reception of the text in previous generations, which will determine in large measure in which direction the process of interpretation goes.[16] Once again, we are made to see the importance of the communal and practical dimensions of interpreting what the Bible says (and does not say) about gender and sexuality.

Finally, there is the problem which arises from a failure to address the difference between the meaning of a text and whether or not it is true. It is one thing to establish what the biblical text says. It is quite another to determine whether and how the text 'speaks'. To put it bluntly, questions like, was Jesus a feminist? – even if it could somehow be shown that the question was not meaningless (on the grounds of anachronism) and that, on the balance of historical probabilities, Jesus was a feminist – invite the rather deflating riposte, so what? What difference does it make to women suffering sexual abuse and political and economic oppression today to know that there happen to be historians who believe that Jesus was a feminist? Unless we have a broader theological and ecclesiological framework of understanding, experience and practice which enables us to see that Jesus' positive regard for the marginalized expresses something truthful about the inclusive nature of human salvation in Christ and about all humankind as made in the image of God, then the supposed attitude of the historical Jesus is of hardly more than (so-called) antiquarian interest.

To put it another way, unless we have an understanding of who Jesus is for us now and of how to be Christ-like in the way we as women and men conduct our relations, whether or not Jesus was a feminist (or gay liberationist or whatever) can be of only passing interest. This implies, in turn, that we cannot leave the task of wise readings of the Bible in the hands of historians, even historians who are Christian believers.[17] This is not to deny that the biblical text has an historical dimension which the methods of critical historiography will help to elucidate. Nor is it to deny the significance of the historian's contribution to a more nuanced and less anachronistic appraisal of (say) attitudes to gender and sexuality in Ancient Israel or in the Early Church.[18] It is, however, to assert that historical tools are not adequate on their own to the task of discerning the truth or otherwise of the biblical testimony, including the biblical testimony about human sexuality in relation to God and to one's fellow humans.

The same point needs to be made about the more recent 'literary turn' in biblical interpretation, including feminist biblical interpretation.[19] For while the methods of literary criticism in its various forms undoubtedly open up dimensions of the text and its power to communicate which might not otherwise be so evident to us, such tools on their own are not adequate to the task of discerning whether or not what the text says is true. Literary criticism helps us appreciate how the text speaks, but is mute when we come to ask, is what it says true? For the question of the truth of the Bible is above all a theological ecclesial and practical question. As Robert Morgan puts it: 'all Scripture has a literal meaning, but it does not all have a Christian theological meaning'.[20]

Starting Somewhere Else

If there is any force in the objections I have raised to approaches which start with the Bible, is there an alternative way of answering the question, is the Bible good news for human sexuality? I think that there is, and the alternative takes the form I stated at the beginning. It is that we start somewhere else. If we start with 'what the Bible says', the possibilities for disagreement are almost endless, and the answers we come up with – especially if they disturb beliefs and practices which we take for granted – can usually be postponed or kept at arm's length.

It is probably true to say, for example, that the attempt to resolve the ongoing and often highly charged debate over 'gay rights' and the legitimacy of the ministry of 'practising' gay priests by appeal to scriptural texts and exegetical inquiry has not proven conclusive and cannot do so.[21] It is not clear that the 'homosexuality' referred to in the Bible is what is meant by 'homosexuality' today. The texts themselves are opaque at crucial points and do not permit exegetical certainty. At the same time, it is possible to argue that it is not always the apparently most obvious texts which should count the most. Should our judgment in matters of sexuality be based on the story of Sodom in Genesis 19, or on the list of sexual prohibitions in 1 Cor. 6.9–10, or on the (at first sight irrelevant) parable of the Good Samaritan in Luke 10?

So, while by no means ignoring exegetical inquiry, we need to start instead with questions of a different kind, such as: what is our experience as men and women in church and society today? and, what kind of people do we need to be in order to interpret wisely what the Bible says, in a way which is life-giving in the realm of gender and sexuality? The point is powerfully made by Janet Martin Soskice in her recent essay, 'Women's Problems':

> What we must also ask ourselves as Christians, women as well as men, is, Has our Church made things any better, or have we colluded in silencing the already half-voiced, and in making the problems of women, 'just women's problems'? Bodies are being broken day after day on linked wheels of poverty, prostitution, sexual abuse and domestic violence. How can we map these sufferings on the broken and risen body of Christ?[22]

This approach has a number of significant benefits. For a start, it avoids the biblicism, both of a loyalist and of a critical kind, implicit in accepting the original question on its own terms. Now, it is no longer the Bible which is in the dock but we who ask the question or of whom the question is asked. Also, it makes possible the recognition that the Bible is the book of the church and that adequate interpretation of the Bible will be interpretation which is played out, crafted and honed in the practice, mission and perhaps especially in the suffering of the church in the world. Instead of remaining suspended at the theoretical level of either dogmatic literalist assertion or positivist historical inquiry, the issue of whether or not the Bible is good news becomes an invitation and a summons to show that it can be so by the way we live and the kinds of community we build.

Finally, I mention two consequences of this kind of approach. One consequence is that the way the Bible is interpreted by being lived out will be affected by considerations of context. In other words, the communities for whom the Bible is Scripture will have the demanding task of working out in practice how the Bible is and continues to be good news. They will do this each in their own way. But it will not be a case of 'anything goes'. The Church, as in a fundamental sense the privileged interpreter of the Bible, provides traditions of interpretation, social embodiment and liturgical action within which to work and upon which to build.

In addition, there are the important lines of insight and guidance provided by individuals, groups and movements outside the community of faith.[23] Indeed, in the area of gender relations in particular, it may for various significant reasons be the case that communities of faith have at least as much to learn about the will of God from outsiders or from those on the margins of the Church as from those within the Church. This point is well made by Ann Loades in her Scott Holland lectures:

> The person who did more than anyone else to clarify the troublesome use in her White Anglo-Saxon Protestant culture of selective and uncontextualized quotation from Pauline Epistles that had helped to bring women to the pass in which they were was Virginia Woolf.[24]

A second and related consequence of this approach is that individual groups and communities will have to accept responsibility for the way they interpret and 'perform' what the Bible says about gender and sexuality. This will involve making decisions (either explicitly or implicitly, consciously or unconsciously) of a theological and ethical kind – questions about who Christ is for us, who we are in the light of Christ, and what kind of people we want to be in relation to God-in-Christ and to our neighbours. Here, it will undoubtedly be the case that the communities who do this most wisely will be the ones whose members are training in the Christian virtues and who therefore have the traditions, skills and practice necessary to the task.[25]

The questions 'Is the Bible good news for human sexuality?' is, in other words, not best taken as a question first and foremost to put to the Bible. Rather, it constitutes a challenge to the church at the fundamental level of practical spirituality. It is those who know of what just and loving Christian practice consists who will be best equipped to read the Bible in a life-giving and liberating way. It is those who are themselves transformed and being transformed according to the image of Christ who will be best able to perform the scriptures in ways which bring life and Christ-like transformation to human sexuality.[26]

Notes
1. See e.g. L. Smedes, *Mere Morality* (Grand Rapids: Eerdmans, 1983); also, J.R.W. Stott, *Issues Facing Christians Today* (London: Marshall, Morgan & Scott, 1984), esp. part iv on 'Sexual Issues'.
2. This stance is particularly clear in Daphne Hampson's recent *Theology and Feminism* (Oxford: Basil Blackwell, 1990). In her discussion of the Bible in ch. 3, she says, e.g.:

'That the bible is deeply patriarchal may be taken as read.... The text is the product of a sexist, indeed misogynist, culture: the presuppositions of a patriarchal world are written into it. Moreover, such texts are the most dangerous in that they affect us at a subconscious level.... There is, one must conclude, little that can be done. Yet these texts are read as sacred texts' (pp. 85, 92).

3.   See e.g. J.S. Spong, *Living in Sin? A Bishop Rethinks Human Sexuality* (San Francisco: Harper & Row, 1988), esp. part ii on 'The Bible'.
4.   See, e.g. the recent document from the House of Bishops of the General Synod of the Church of England, entitled *Issues in Human Sexuality* (London: Church House Publishing, 1991). After a short introduction, the first major section addresses the biblical material, under the heading, 'Scripture and Human Sexuality', pp. 5–18.
5.   N. Lash, *Theology on the Way to Emmaus* (London: SCM Press, 1986), p. 79.
6.   See A.C. Thiselton, *The Two Horizons* (Exeter: Paternoster Press, 1980).
7.   See Lash, *Theology on the Way to Emmaus*, pp. 37–46; F. Young, *The Art of Performance* (London: Darton, Longman & Todd, 1990); also S.M. Schneiders, *The Revelatory Text* (London: Harper Collins, 1991), pp. 149–50.
8.   To take but one example, a recent article by Joseph Fitzmyer on the meaning of the word *kephale* ('head', according to the RSV and REB) in 1 Cor. 11.3, lists over twenty previous studies, most of which have been published since the early 70s – and the list does not even include works in languages other than English! See J.A. Fitzmyer, 'Kephale in I Corinthians 11:3', *Int* 47 (1993), pp. 52–59, with bibliography of other studies in n. 2.
9.   The way in which the same texts can be interpreted in diametrically opposed ways by people with (academically speaking) the same kinds of credentials is illustrated well in W.M. Swartley, *Slavery, Sabbath War and Women: Case Issues in Biblical Interpretation* (Kitchener, Ontario: Herald Press, 1983).
10.   Hence my earlier essay, 'Homosexuality and the Church of England: Perspectives from the Social Sciences', *Theology* 92 (1989), pp. 175–81.
11.   See further, D.L. Migliore, *Faith Seeking Understanding* (Grand Rapids: Eerdmans, 1991), pp. 40–55.
12.   K.C. Boone, *The Bible Tells Them So* (London: SCM Press, 1990).
13.   A.C. Thiselton, *New Horizons in Hermeneutics* (London: Harper Collins, 1992), esp. ch. 12.
14.   S. Hauerwas and S. Long, 'Interpreting the Bible as a Political Act', *Religion and Intellectual Life* 6 (1989), pp. 134–42.
15.   See the illuminating essay by the Reformation historian, D.C. Sainmetz, 'The Superiority of Pre-Critical Exegesis', *Ex Auditu* 1 (1985), pp. 74–82.
16.   See S.E. Fowl and L.G. Jones, *Reading in Communion: Scripture and Ethics in Christian Life* (London: SPCK, 1991).
17.   If I may venture a collegial comment at this point, it is, in my view, a weakness of J.D.G. Dunn's influential and otherwise very valuable approach to the art of biblical interpretation that, in practice, he places too one-sided an emphasis on historical criticism and reconstruction and does not acknowledge sufficiently the essential contribution to the interpretative process of both the tradition of faith which the reader brings to the text and the impact of the reader's own experience and community. See e.g. his essay, 'The Task of New Testament Interpretation', in *The Living Word* (London: SCM Press, 1987), pp. 3–24, where 'normative significance in all matters of interpretation' is assigned to the meaning intended by the original author (p. 22). Cf. also his essay, 'The New Testament as History', in A. Walker (ed.), *Different Gospels, Christian Orthodoxy and Modern Theologies* (London: SPCK, 1993), pp. 43–53.
18.   See e.g. S.B. Pomeroy, *Goddesses, Whores, Wives, and Slaves* (New York: Schocken Books, 1975); P. Brown, *The Body and Society: Men, Women and Sexual Renunciation in Early Christianity* (London: Faber & Faber, 1989); L.W. Countryman, *Dirt, Greed and Sex* (London: SCM Press, 1989).
19.   See e.g. P. Trible, *Texts of Terror, Literary-Feminist Readings of Biblical Narratives* (Philadelphia: Fortress Press, 1984).
20.   R. Morgan, 'Feminist Theological Interpretation of the New Testament', in J.M. Soskice (ed.), *After Eve: Women, Theology and the Christian Tradition* (London: Collins Marshall Pickering, 1990), p. 26. See also A. Thatcher, *Liberating Sex: A Christian Sexual Theology* (London: SPCK, 1993), pp. 15ff., where the distinction is drawn between a *biblical* sexual theology and a *Christian* sexual theology.
21.   The literature is enormous. Representative of various positions are the following studies: J. Boswell, *Christianity, Social Tolerance, and Homosexuality* (Chicago: Chicago University

Press, 1980); R. Scroggs, *The New Testament and Homosexuality* (Philadelphia: Fortress Press, 1983); M. Vasey, *Evangelical Christians and Gay Rights* (New York: Grove Books, 1991); D. F. Wright, 'Homosexuals or Prostitutes? The Meaning of ARSENOKOITAI (1 Cor. 6:9, 1 Tim. 1:10)', *Vigiliae Christianae* 38 (1984), pp. 124–53.

22. J.M. Soskice, 'Women's Problems', in Walker (ed.), *Different Gospels*, pp. 194–203.

23. Cf. Fowl and Jones, *Reading in Communion*, p. 111: 'If the people of God hope to read and enact the Scriptures faithfully in the various contexts in which we find ourselves, we will need to listen to (if not always follow) the words of the outsiders we encounter'.

24. A. Loades, *Searching for Lost Coins* (London: SPCK, 1987), p. 64. See also the valuable collection of essays by feminists of a very wide variety of faith perspectives and religious backgrounds, *Womanspirit Rising* (ed. C.P. Christ and J. Plaskow; New York: Harper & Row, 1979).

25. For further discussion along these lines, see S. Hauerwas, *The Peaceable Kingdom* (London: SCM Press, 1984).

26. I would like to acknowledge the helpful comments on this essay which I received from Ann Loades, Walter Moberly and Denys Turner, from the members of the Durham Centre for Theological Research and from the members of the Adults' Learning Group in Durham.

1.2 The Distinctiveness of Early Christian Sexual Ethics

Richard M. Price

The most exciting development of our time in the study of early Christianity has been the weakening of the departmental divisions between secular and ecclesiastical historiography.[1] As soon as the historian turns from such hoary topics of public history as the government and the army to the humbler but broader sphere of social relations, dissemination of ideas and personal self-identity, early Christian texts become too rich a source to be set aside, while in the post-Constantinian period the development of Christendom becomes a main part of the story.

Early Christianity is as valid a subject for antiquarian investigation as any other, and the corpse might seem to invite an unhurried and dispassionate examination on the dissecting table. Fortunately for the liveliness of the subject, the heritage of Christianity remains too important and too controversial to allow this to happen. Indeed, the more our Christian heritage is challenged, the more urgent it becomes to study its evolution. To an ecclesiastical historian for whom the ethical and social ideas of Christianity have a self-evident validity, research into their origins is no more than one of many feasible acts of homage. But for the secular historian to whom Christian attitudes come to appear more and more bizarre, it is a matter of the liveliest concern to unearth why and how so curious a system of values attained dominance in our European culture. Since the Enlightenment placed a question-mark against the Christian heritage, the scholar who turns his critical gaze on early Christianity is bound to feel that he is touching on a raw nerve, and will be tempted to enjoy the delicious combination of insinuating his own prejudices while simulating the strict impartiality of the scientific historian.

In no area is this more true than in that of sexuality – our attitude towards our sexual nature and the moral problems it gives rise to. The extremely demanding teaching of the Church on the subject of marriage, and the attendant repression of sexuality outside marriage, is a part of our Christian heritage that is still potent even where it is outwardly rejected. It is this that provokes denunciation from the ideologist and the subtler barbs of the hostile historian. The detached, acerbic style was already developed to perfection by Edward Gibbon, who wrote on the early Church's attitude to marriage:

The historian of the orthodox casuists on this interesting subject betrays the perplexity of men, unwilling to approve an institution which they were compelled to tolerate. The enumeration of the very whimsical laws, which they most circumstantially imposed on the marriage-bed, would force a smile from the young, and a blush from the fair.[2]

In both attitude and tone, Gibbon has had no lack of successors. Most recently, Robin Lane Fox's *Pagans and Christians* devotes the greater part of a chapter to early Christian sexual morality, with a fullness and relish that almost make up for the total lack of sympathy. It is disconcerting to find in so full a treatment a judgement as simplistic as the *obiter dictum* that virginity 'is nothing but the most selfish of human ideals'.[3] When so precise and self-effacing an historian as Wolfgang Liebeschuetz specifies asceticism and intolerance as the two main contributions that Christianity has made to European culture, the allegations of Gibbon have come to appear established facts of history.[4]

In this context the work of Peter Brown, from his essays on early Christian monasticism to *The Body and Society*, his new *magnum opus* on sexual renunciation in the early Church, takes on its full significance.[5] He too is one of those secular historians with no personal loyalty to the Christian Church who will increasingly dominate the study of the subject. But Brown's approach has a breadth and tolerance that is strikingly different from the heavy legacy of Gibbon. His perspectives are not dominated by the moral absolutes of the Enlightenment, with its open or masked hostility towards traditional Christianity. It is not simply that he is concerned to understand rather than judge. For him history has to be broken down into the experience of individuals who made free choices with an understanding of what was at stake and had, often, the courage to abide by them. As we accompany Peter Brown, we attain an imaginative empathy with a whole series of ancient men and women who tried to realize and enflesh their Christian faith in their own contexts. The sneering from a distance of Gibbon and his modern *epigonoi* begins to appear facile and less than interesting.

I

This new closeness has as its shadow a certain loss of perspective. Peter Brown's leisurely survey of sexual renunciation in the six centuries from St Paul till John Climacus leaves us with rather too many individuals making their own decisions in different settings and from subtly different motives. For a broader starting point let us begin with his essay on the late antique period in the five-volume *History of Private Life* initiated by Philippe Ariès and now in process of publication in a variety of European languages.[6] Writing for a broad audience, Brown sets out the Christian stance with a certain manly boldness:

On the surface the Christians practised an austere sexual morality, easily recognizable and acclaimed by outsiders: total sexual renunciation by the few; marital concord between the spouses; strong disapproval of remarriage. This surface was presented openly to outsiders. Lacking the clear ritual boundaries provided in Judaism by circumcision and dietary laws, Christians tended to make their exceptional sexual discipline bear the full burden of expressing the difference between themselves and the pagan world.

If this for Brown was 'the surface' of early Christian sexual morality, the kernel of the matter was the concern with single-mindedness, or purity of heart, a reorientation of the will so that it would cease to serve the complex and warring impulses of the natural man and respond instead with unreserved openness to the will of God.[7] As Brown notes, it is scarcely surprising that the ideal of singleness of heart led to the commendation of virginity, and that leadership in the Christian communities became increasingly reserved to a celibate élite.[8]

Admittedly, talk of early Christian discipline may suggest a penitential system more dominant and all-embracing than the early Church ever developed. The rules of the Christian communities, with their broad-ranging and unnuanced condemnation of all adultery, fornication and homosexual activity, might appear to leave little room for pastoral flexibility; the same could be said of the rules for canonical penance, with their insistence on a period of public humiliation and abstention from the sacraments, terminated by the bishop alone, in an equally public act of absolution that, once received, could never be repeated.[9] But the inflexibility of rules and procedures can only have meant that often they could not be applied. Our evidence on the actual working of canonical discipline is limited. It is sufficient to exclude any assumption that it only applied in cases of public scandal, or as a penalty for sinful relationships rather than isolated acts; but we have to presume that few bishops would have been so unwise as to impose public penance on a young male (who might easily fall back into sin) or a young woman (who could not afford public exposure).[10]

The discipline, of course, did not apply to those who were not baptized, and it is a familiar observation that late antique Christians tended to postpone baptism. But in a world of high infant and adolescent mortality many a child or young person must have been baptized in danger of death, only to live on subject (in theory) to the full rigours of ecclesiastical discipline. In his *Confessions* Augustine writes of a childhood illness:

> The mother of my flesh was in heavy anxiety, since with a heart chaste in Your faith she was ever in deep travail for my eternal salvation, and would have proceeded without delay to have me consecrated and washed clean by the sacrament of salvation, while I confessed You, Lord Jesus, unto the remission of sins; but I made a sudden recovery. This caused my baptismal cleansing to be postponed; for it was argued that if I lived I

should inevitably fall again into the filth of sin; and after baptism the guilt of sin's defilement would be in itself graver and put the soul in graver peril.... Why do we constantly hear such phrases as: 'Let him alone, let him go on as he is, he is not yet baptized'?[11]

The anguish of Monica over whether to baptize the young Augustine (thereby threatening his salvation if he lived) or not to baptize (thereby damning his soul if he died) must have been shared by many early Christian mothers. It is painful to think that this was the Church's contribution to the anxious world of children's sick-beds.

But to return to penitential discipline, the system of public penance was too rigid and awesome to be the right instrument for the disciplining of individuals. Its main power was declarative: the humiliation of public penance, the disabilities imposed during penance and even after reconciliation, the fact above all that penance was not a routine procedure that could be repeated but an extraordinary provision that no one could avail himself of more than once, all these features expressed most forcibly that the Church was a community of saints, not a refuge of sinners. The limited practicability of the system brought home to all that the Church was holy and undefiled, that its true members necessarily reflected this holiness in their own lives, and that to make generous provision for backsliders would simply compromise these truths. As a result, the system deterred rather than attracted penitents. Most Christians who had the misfortune to fall into mortal sin after baptism prudently postponed confession till they were on their deathbeds, when public exposure and the performance of penance could no longer be imposed.

It is a familiar fact that the modern discipline of private penance, which involves no public exposure and can be endlessly repeated, was introduced as normative in the Catholic world by the Fourth Council of the Lateran in 1215.[12] It was the same council that imposed annual penance on each of the faithful. It is a mistake to view this as a relaxation of discipline. In fact, its effect was to subject all Christians to penance for the first time; the Church was no longer to turn a blind eye to such standard features of medieval *mores* as fornication and concubinage. Moreover, the repeatability of penance made it feasible to lengthen the list of mortal sins requiring sacramental absolution. It was the development of private penance that led the confessor to take an interest in the frequency and mode of marital intercourse, and to interrogate adolescents on their solitary sins.[13] The need to determine the most intimate details of one's life by obedience to a spiritual father had been restricted in the late antique world to monastic society; it was now extended to, potentially, the entire Catholic population.[14] This impetus given by the Fourth Lateran Council to the development of an earnest lay Christianity was intensified by a change of character that Christendom underwent in the early modern period. A recent work of John Bossy has as its theme the replacement of the strong communal emphasis in medieval Christendom by a new stress in the Churches of the Reformation and Counter-Reformation alike on the spirituality of the individual.[15] A consequence was that the holiness that had always been attributed to the Church as a body was now seen with a new urgency to require the sanctification of each individual member. Earnest Catholics had now no alternative but to impose on themselves, with the help of regular private confession, the sexual restraint that the penitential system of the early Church had more proclaimed to all than imposed on each. The rebellion of the permissive society against sexual discipline in our own age is a rebellion against the changes initiated by the medieval introduction of private penance and perfected by the individualism of the early modern world.

II

It remains true, however, that a heavy emphasis on sexual restraint goes back to the early Church; and quest for the origins of the glory or the shame of Christianity takes us back there. This emphasis finds striking expression in the canonical legislation that proliferated from the fourth century. Take, for instance, the Canonical Epistles of Basil of Caesarea, which list a variety of sins with appropriate penances for each.[16] Violation of oaths is treated in two canons, theft in two, participation in pagan or magical rites in five, murder or manslaughter in twelve, and sexual offences in no less than forty-one. The length of penance is also indicative. Adultery and homosexual acts receive 15 years, which is more than the 10 years for abortion and only slightly less than the 20 years for wilful murder.[17] We find the same emphasis on sexual morality if we turn to what on the positive side was deemed to earn special divine favour. In the ascetical literature of the second and third centuries – the Apocryphal Acts and the Pseudo-Clementine Epistles – it is clear that sexual renunciation is the royal road to divine favour and spiritual gifts, while renunciation of wealth is generally demoted to the status of an optional extra. Keeping the body pure appears as a condition both necessary and sufficient for a spiritual marriage with Christ.[18]

All this contrasts markedly with what we find in the writings of the New Testament (with the exception of the Apocalypse of John).[19] Our Lord's own celibate state is in the Gospels an unremarked corollary of his prophetic role. Sexual morality receives a distinctive treatment in the dominical forbidding of divorce and the Pauline encouragement of virginity, but remains a subordinate theme, without any of the emphasis that accrued to it a century later. The question is inescapable: what was the origin of the amazing concern with sexual purity and sexual sin that came at such an early date to characterize Christianity?

A favourite answer among those who both deplore this conern and wish to uphold Christianity is to place the blame on contamination from outside, notably from Hellenism. If (as *must* have been the case) the first Christians had a thoroughly positive attitude towards sex and marriage, the replacement of this by its opposite has to be attributed to alien influence – and what can that be, if not the dualism of Platonism, with its denigration of the body and its pleasures? At this point Peter Brown's exemplary patience gives way:

> To be frank: I have frequently observed that the sharp and dangerous flavour of many Christian notions of sexual renunciation, both in their personal and their social consequences, have been rendered tame and insipid, through being explained away as no more than inert borrowings from a supposed pagan or Jewish background. [20]

To attribute whatever one dislikes in historical Christianity to alien influences, and thereby exclude it from the authentic deposit of faith, is so obviously a tendentious device to preserve the truth and distinctiveness of Christianity that it scarcely needs the refutation of the historian. The contrast between originally body-affirming Christians and bleakly otherworldly Platonists is no less crude and absurd than its once popular opposite – the contrast between body-hating Christians and pleasure-loving pagans that was so dear to decadents of a century ago such as Swinburne and Merezhkjovsky. [21]

It remains of interest, however, to inquire into the dominant attitudes towards sex and marriage in the Graeco-Roman world of the Church's most successful missions. On this subject Peter Brown exhibits commendable caution. The literary evidence relates directly to the attitudes of aristocrats and philosophers; the task of discerning the currents among the great mass of the population is a delicate one, that has still to be performed. We must beware of a crude and contrived comparison between a Christian stereotype and a pagan stereotype both of our own concoction. Peter Brown steers clear, with perhaps excessive caution, of one lively current debate, sparked off by a stimulating hypothesis of the leading French expert on Roman sexuality, Paul Veyne. [22] Veyne argued, from epigraphic as well as literary evidence, that the first few centuries of the Christian era saw not so much the replacement of Graeco-Roman sexual *mores* by Judaeo-Christian ones as the development within both paganism and Christianity of what he calls the 'bourgeois' notion of marriage, with its stress on fidelity and stability. That this was a novelty of the imperial period is the weakest claim in Veyne's thesis. [23] But it is likely that more and more historians will turn away from attributing a host of developments in late antique culture to the victory of Christian over pagan values, in favour of a subtler scenario where universal personal needs and a common social experience are seen as more decisive than clashes of ideology.

The truth is that it is vain to seek to compare the values and attitudes of the 'average' pagan and the 'average' Christian. Apart from the dangers of generalization, there is the problem of juggling with two unknowns. Our evidence is primarily literary, made up of a range of texts – philosophical, medical, theological – which present the sexual discourse of an educated élite rather than the *vox populi*. Peter Brown's attempts to map the experience of a gallery of individuals, from the great salons of Rome to the villages of rural Syria, are inevitably imaginative and impressionistic. The first task of the sober historian must be to compare the texts we have precisely for what they are – exercises in sexual discourse. For this reason the *History of Sexuality* that is Michel Foucault's *magnum opus* (though sadly *imperfectum*) represents the most solid advance in recent scholarship.[24] Foucault has been criticized for concentrating on a small body of literary texts, as if they can be presumed to be representative of the attitudes of their day. His presupposition that discourse shapes rather than reflects experience is a philosopher's claim that will not impress historians. But we may still concede that he was right to see that the novel element that Christianity introduced into the sexuality of the ancient world was precisely a new variety of sexual discourse. At first this discourse was the preserve of a small class of literary celibates; its stress on sexual purity, on the horrendous nature of any sexual sin and on the superiority of celibacy to marriage may have appeared almost as alien to many a Christian layman of the first few centuries as to his pagan neighbour. But gradually over the centuries, through the teaching of the clergy and the development of penitential discipline, this discourse came to shape the values and attitudes of the Christian faithful.

How did the sexual discourse of early Christian writers differ from that of their pagan contemporaries? Sexual ethics did not loom large in the philosophy of the time. The ethics of Platonists and Stoics alike laid stress on rational self-control, on the dominance of the intellect over the will, and the subjection of emotions and physical impulses. This teaching was related to a widespread and popular ideal of 'macho' masculinity, in which unrestrained emotion and enslavement to physical passions were considered to be feminine and despicable, especially if these led a man to be emotionally dependent on some other person.[25] For instance, Suetonius tells how Lucius Vitellius, three times consul, 'was of very ill repute because of his passion for a freedwoman, which went so far that he used her spittle mixed with honey to rub on his throat and jaws as a medicine'.[26] A consular was allowed a mistress but was not supposed to fall in love with her; in striking contrast to modern attitudes, it was love not sex that was problematic. This denigration of passionate feeling was reinforced in Platonism by professions of other-worldliness; we read in the *Didaskalikos* of Alcinous, for instance, that 'we must use reason and doctrine in such a way as to detach ourselves for the most part from human affairs and to attend always to things intelligible'.[27] We might expect that this ethic of self-control would have led to a negative attitude to sex. But the evidence is against this. The Stoics accepted the sexual drive as natural and strongly encouraged procreation as public-spirited, though their disapproval of all activity that was merely for the sake of pleasure rather than some ulterior goal led to a restrictive sexual ethic, where sexual acitivity was considered laudable only when it took place within marriage and was aimed at procreation. To fornicate was to show a lamentable lack of self-discipline; but Stoics, unlike Christians, did not condemn it as being, like adultery, contrary to the natural, i.e. the moral, law.[28] Young men who remained chaste before marriage (an unusual feat in the Graeco-Roman world) were told to keep quiet about it and not despise those who were less selfcontrolled.[29] Meanwhile in the Platonic camp, Alcinous defends the desire for pleasure on condition it is not inordinate and, on the subject of homosexuality (so horrendous to Christians), accepts a sexual element in masculine friendship as natural and unproblematic. This positive evaluation of sexual activity as serving to cement the relationship between two persons reappears in the treatment of marriage, where Plutarch advises regular intercourse between spouses as a means of 'freeing marriage from the complaints that pile up from everyday living'.[30]

In all, the sexual discourse of the philosphers of the first two centuries is quiet and unemphatic, with a refusal either to commend sexual activity as a constitutive part of true happiness or to condemn it as a hindrance. To deduce that pagans of the early imperial period had a remarkably relaxed attitude to the whole subject would be to miss, however, the distinctive character of the philosophical discourse of the time, which concentrated so heavily on the goods of the soul that the needs of the body could not be adequately attended to. For a fuller picture of Graeco-Roman sexual discourse we need to turn to the writings of the medical men, who unlike the philosophers accorded sexual activity serious and detailed treatment. There is a full discussion of sexual abstinence in an admirable textbook of the early second century, the *Gynaecology* of Soranus.[31] Chapter Seven, entitled 'Is permanent virginity healthy?', presents arguments for and against. On the one hand, 'All excretion of seed is harmful in females as in males. Virginity, therefore, is healthy, since it prevents the excretion of seed.... Men who remain chaste are stronger and bigger than others.... Women who have renounced intercourse are less susceptible to disease'. On the other hand, 'Neither in males nor in females is excretion of seed harmful, but only in excess.... Many people after intercourse have been more agile and carried themselves more nobly'. Soranus concludes that in his own view 'permanent virginity is healthy, in males and females alike; nevertheless, intercourse seems consistent with the general principle of nature according to which both sexes have to ensure the succession of living beings'.[32] One may suspect that behind such studiously neutral and scientific discourse lay deeply rooted intuitions connecting chastity of the body and integrity of the person, intuitions that Christians clearly shared. But here too we find no potential influence that might account for the peculiar strictness and intensity of the Christian sexual code. The Church's concern with sexual conduct as a matter of prime moral and spiritual importance is not paralleled in pagan texts, which view sex within marriage as unproblematic, sex outside marriage as sometimes harmless and rarely gravely wrong, and sexual conduct as a matter to be regulated by considerations more of health than of spirituality.

At the same time, it is undeniable that these patterns of sexual discourse in Greek philosophy and medical writing, and their broader social context, facilitated the development and dissemination of the sexual ethic of the early Christians. A rejection of pleasure as an end in itself and a stress on rational self-control were adopted by most Christian writers, and employed with confidence in support of a sexual ethic that was likewise restrictive. A world used to hearing that the moral ideal was one of the domination of appetite by reason and that sexual abstinence preserves one's vitality was not going to react to Christian virginity and celibacy with disgust or contempt. Galen will have been typical of fair-minded pagans when he wrote:

> [Christians] include not only men but also women who refrain from cohabiting all through their lives; and they also number individuals who, in self-discipline and self-control in matters of food and drink, and in their keen pursuit of justice, have attained a pitch not inferior to that of genuine philosophers.[33]

But although Christian writers were able to appeal to the higher paganism in support of their views and make some use of pagan arguments in propagating them, Christian sexual ethics were not substantially indebted to Greek thought. To account for their particular features – the stress on the spiritual fruits of sexual abstinence, on strict monogamy, and on the horrendousness of sexual sin – we need to turn to the themes of sexual discourse that arose from the distinctive content of the Christian Gospel.

III

The distinctive sexual discourse of early Christianity, as I have observed, is in large part of second-century origin and post-dates the New Testament. But it would be a mistake to deduce that its source must lie outside the biblical canon. A careful reading of the letters of St Paul, in particular, may show how this discourse was fed by a whole range of specifically biblical themes. It is for the exegete to fathom the intentions of St Paul himself and for the philosopher to determine which ideas are a logical development of his teaching. The mere historian may, however, observe without presumption that St Paul's letters provided plentiful inspiration for advocates of sexual renunciation. It may be true that Paul intended 1 Corinthians 7 to moderate rather than encourage sexual renunciation, but what in effect he does is to damn marriage with faint praise.[34] Leaving aside the question whether his advocacy of virginity as enabling single-minded attention to the affairs of the Lord is simply a psychological truism (of very doubtful truth) or depends on notions of ritual purity, it is striking that St Paul makes no mention of what for the Jew, Christian or pagan of his day would have appeared the main reason for marriage – the need to maintain the human species.

It is correct to observe that this omission followed from Paul's belief in the imminence of the Parousia. But it is incorrect to deduce that it was therefore no more than an accidental and temporary aberration. The meaning of the proclamation of the nearness of the End in so many books of the New Testament, and of the renewal of this proclamation in so many Christian writers of the following centuries, needs more extensive treatment than it can receive here. Suffice it to say that not even the New Testament writers appear to have intended the proclamation so literally that it was open to empirical disproof; Paul, for instance, combined the most unambiguous proclamation of the nearness of the End with a pattern of mission dominated less by the need for the speedy evangelization of the known world than by the careful laying of foundations in individual Christian communities. We may say that he intended his churches to continue indefinitely to expect an imminent parousia, and this is indeed what the Church proceeded to do. There were few generations in the early centuries when belief in Christ's imminent return did not find forceful expression.[35] In consequence, throughout the early centuries Christian ascetics remained indifferent to the charge that sexual renunciation threatened the continuance of the species and was therefore contrary to the will of God: the true Christian looked ahead to the end of this age and the inauguration of the age to come, and viewed physical procreation as an ultimately futile attempt to secure that everlasting continuity assured only by the spiritual birth of baptism and the perfect preservation of the baptismal seal through the unsullied purity of the virgin state.[36]

Those elements of Pauline spirituality summed up by exegetes as 'realized eschatology' reinforced this theme. Christ himself had taught that there is no marriage in heaven. Paul taught his converts to interpret baptism as entry into the risen life of Christ and to live their lives as in the day of the Lord's coming. It seemed to follow that the true Christian would renounce marriage even in this life. In addition, Paul preached a strong doctrine of the holiness of the body, as the temple of the Holy Spirit and destined to enjoy the resurrection, while sexual misconduct severed the body from Christ.[37] Those in the second century who embraced his stress on bodily holiness and its link to union with Christ soon developed the notion that the risen Christ offered each human being a nuptial union that excluded as bigamous a simultaneous union to a human spouse.[38] The warmth and physicality of this spirituality makes the old charge of hating the body singularly inapposite.

The Church of the second century, as we all know, was rocked by heresy, and the whole notion of a strict orthodoxy upheld by episcopal authority and secured by biblical canon developed as a remedy. But it is worth noting how much the Church took over from the heretics. Irenaeus crushed Gnosticism by appeal to the notion of apostolic tradition, preserved both in writing and in the continuity of authoritative oral teaching; but this notion had first been developed by the Gnostics themselves.[39] Likewise, the Church came to condemn as 'encratites' those who championed virginity and condemned marriage.[40] But it took over from the encratites the notion that sexual renunciation was a prerequisite for the highest spiritual graces and could reasonably be expected of the leaders of the Christian community.

We must never forget that our evidence consists almost exclusively of the writings of clerical celibates. Few Christian laymen could read, and the evidence does not suggest that calls to sexual renunciation were prominent in preaching. A theme that crops up as a leitmotif in Peter Brown's *The Body and Society* is that the exaltation of virginity remained at odds with the rights and status of the Christian household, dominated by its *paterfamilias*. The latter wanted his sons to marry and continue his line, and had no wish to see his daughters leave his authority for some convent of virgins. He was sufficiently imbued with the respect for marriage universal in the ancient world to be genuinely shocked when some imprudent spiritual guide obtruded the ideal of virginity into the salons and bedrooms of the everyday world.[41]

To view sexual renunciation as self-denial *in excelsis*, as an unhealthy rejection of natural impulses, as we moderns tend to do, is to miss its social implications. Sex meant marriage, and marriage meant submission to the heavy expectations and demands of society. Roman girls married young, at puberty, and were immediately caught in the painful cycle of childbearing, and in all the social restrictions imposed on women by their menfolk's terror of adultery.[42] Escape from marriage gave members of both sexes their freedom, and enabled the creation of ascetic communities which were not tied to the repetitive treadmill of procreation, but anticipated here and now the abiding spiritual community that would be the destiny of all the saints in heaven. This liberation was all the more marked in the case of women. The apocryphal Acts of the Apostles, which, however fictional, reflect social realities, narrate again and again how female converts rejected the marriage bed, to the fury of their menfolk, who took their revenge on the Christian missionaries. What the women were rejecting, and the menfolk defending, was not so much the sanctity of sex as the subjugation of women to their husbands. This was still the issue in the fourth century, when the Council of Gangrae condemned the ascetical movement of Eustathius. The Eustathians taught women to abhor marriage and leave their husbands; they dressed men and women, slaves and free, in the same garb. The equality of the women was further expressed by cutting off their long hair; the good bishops of

Gangrae were horrified at this rejection of the sign 'which God gave to every woman as a reminder of her subjection, thus annulling, as it were, the ordinance of subjection' (Canon 17).

This tension is already present in the Pauline epistles. The First Letter to the Corinthians encourages celibacy, but at the same time firmly discourages the separation of spouses. The principle that 'everyone should lead the life which the Lord has assigned to him' (1 Cor 7:17) is used to enforce the subjection of wives to husbands, as of slaves to their masters. The spiritual equality proclaimed in Galatians 3:28 ('There is neither slave nor free, there is neither male nor female') is, according to Paul, to be kept firmly out of the sphere of real social relations.[43] The Deutero-Paulines enforce still further the traditional hierarchy of the married household:

> I permit no woman to teach or to have authority over men; she is to keep silent. For Adam was formed first, then Eve; and Adam was not deceived, but the woman was deceived and became a transgressor. Yet woman will be saved through bearing children.[44]

The same text proceeds in a later chapter to condemn those 'who forbid marriage.... For everything created by God is good'.[45] The sentiment is unimpeachable, but in the context the defence of marriage means the enslavement of women.

Peter Brown takes us step by step through the debate of the following centuries, where the defence of marriage in such Fathers as Clement of Alexandria and Tertullian continued to be a defence of the established social order, and the renunciation of marriage expressed a nostalgia for that more free and equal society that was believed to have existed before the Fall.[46] By the time Brown's survey comes to the end, in the age of Jerome and Augustine, we find already what was to remain the medieval compromise – government of the Church by a celibate élite, unique respect accorded to monks and nuns safely shut away in monasteries, while the traditional family under its male head remained the basic social unit in the outside world.[47]

IV

The strengthening of the marriage bond remained the other plank in the sexual discourse of early Christian writers. Their stress on the value of virginity excluded positive promotion of matrimony, even in reaction to the excesses of encratism; Clement of Alexandria's delightfully backhanded commendation of marriage as more virtuous than celibacy since it is more exposed to temptation was quite exceptional.[48] But in a society where marriage remained firmly the norm, the institution of the family could not be shaken by the advocacy of celibacy, however enthusiastic. On the positive side, Christian writers were much concerned to uphold monogamous marriage in the face of excesses in the opposite direction, that of sexual indulgence.

St Paul in the course of his advocacy of celibacy in 1 Corinthians 7 generously allows a man to marry if otherwise his passions will drive him into fornication. The implication is that marriage, and marital intercourse in particular, has as its prime function the satisfaction of the sexual urge. Here is the origin of the Catholic theme of marriage as a remedy for concupiscence. But the early Fathers were too attracted to the ideal of virginity to consider the satisfaction of physical urges a justification for anything.[49] Instead, they applied as the criterion for lawful sexual intercourse the presence of an intention to procreate. In the words of Athenagoras (*Plea for Christians*, 33), 'Each of us thinks of his wife with a view to nothing more than procreation. For as the farmer casts seed into the ground and waits for the harvest without further planting, so also procreation is the limit we set on desire'. J.T. Noonan has pointed out the paradox that the Christian writers of the first five centuries combined stress on procreative purpose with a marked lack of interest in actual procreation: it was spiritual not physical generation that peopled the Church, man's eyes should be fixed not on an earthly future but on the age to come, and in any case the world is already densely populated.[50] Procreative purpose was promoted as providing a rational control of marital intercourse and its only possible justification in a Christian context, not because Christians had any duty to have children.

Here again the question arises of a possible debt to contemporary pagan thought. Noonan characterizes this ethic as a Christian 'adoption of the Stoic rule', since we find in Stoic writers such as Musonius Rufus a similar restriction of lawful sexual activity to procreative intercourse within marriage.[51] But this may be a case of '*plus c'est la même chose, plus ça change*'. Christians and Stoics alike insisted that intercourse must be linked to procreation; but while Christians did so not out of a love for procreation but in order to defend intercourse against encratite attack, Stoics and other pagan writers could take marital intercourse for granted, while stressing that every married man had a duty to beget children for the good of his city and fatherland. It is therefore misleading to talk of Christians 'adopting the Stoic rule'. Rather, the great Christian themes of single-mindedness and purity of heart, of the superiority of spiritual to merely physical procreation, of expectation of the Parousia and a consequent otherworldliness – themes that were a powerful spur to the renunciation of marriage – played a part even within marriage, in promoting a restrictive ethic materially close to Stoicism but distinct in its ideology and motivation.

Christian disapproval of sex for pleasure surfaced also in another area where Christian distinctiveness is more generally admitted – the question of remarriage.[52] The Church upheld and repeated the dominical prohibition of divorce and remarriage. There was admittedly room for casuistry in the case of adultery by the wife, where divorce was universally allowed and sometimes insisted upon; but even here the Church forbade the remarriage of divorcees. The contrast between this strict Christian discipline and the ease of divorce in both Jewish and pagan society has often been pointed out, and rightly. What was the reason for the Church's hostility to remarriage? The great majority of texts repeat Our Lord's somewhat laconic prohibition without further discussion. But the treatment of the theme in the *Shepherd of Hermas* deserves special mention, as an example of the particularity and coherence of Christian moral discourse: Hermas bases the prohibition of remarriage on the duty of Christians to forgive the repentant. In the case of divorce after adultery, the innocent partner must remain faithful to his unfaithful spouse in order to keep open the possibility of reconciliation (*Mandate* IV.1).

Monogamy in its strictest sense (dear to the Vicar of Wakefield) was part of the Christian ideal: a number of Fathers forbid remarriage even after the death of one's spouse. This scruple did not arise from the need to await reunion with one's original spouse in the world to come, since the teaching of Christ that there is no marriage in heaven (Lk 20:35) was taken seriously. It arose rather from the high valuation of the single state. To have married in one's youth, when blood was strong and family pressure irresistible, was unimpeachable. But for a mature and independent widower or widow to seek a second marriage was evidence of less than Christian priorities. The Church called widows in particular to a special ministry of intercession, as a spiritual 'altar' of God. To prefer remarriage was to reject an important ecclesial role.[53]

The sacramental status of marriage in the early Church was akin to what pertains today in most non-Catholic Churches. Christian marriage was not compared to baptism and the eucharist, but was acknowledged to be a solemn compact before God and a channel of grace. As Origen wrote,

> When it observes measure, marriage is fragrant with a charism, the one that results from harmony.... But that the marriage of a believer with a pagan is a charism from God is something I would not say. A charism of God cannot reach pagans; when the pagan partner begins to believe and attains salvation, then he or she begins to receive the charism.[54]

Origen likewise reaffirms the teaching of Ephesians 5 on the duty of Christian spouses to imitate the love of Christ for his Church, as Ignatius of Antioch had before him.[55] This gave marriage spiritual significance, and made the wedding of a Christian couple a matter of concern for the Church; it is only in the fourth century that it became normal for a Christian wedding to be blessed by a priest – to the disgust of Jerome, who exclaimed, 'A preacher of continence should not celebrate weddings' – but as far back as the begining of the second century Ignatius of Antioch had urged Christian couples to marry only with the approval of the bishop, 'in order that the marriage should be according to the Lord and not according to desire'.[56] In the *Acts of Peter* (ch. 2) one Rufina is struck with paralysis for trying to receive holy communion after committing adultery. The story illustrates how the Christian's sacramental life powerfully reinforced the moral duty of sexual purity and marital fidelity. In all, the Christian commendation of the single state did not exclude a high theology of marriage; and specific teaching was offered on how even marriage could contribute to a spiritual goal. Loving and stable matrimony was not, of course, a Christian invention, and Christian marriage shared many features with pagan marriage. But Christian discourse was concerned to bring out certain novel emphases – on the curbing of concupiscence, the ideal of strict monogamy, the imitation of the love of Christ – in order to develop a specifically Christian doctrine of marriage linked to the central themes of the Gospel.

V

It has been an aim of this article to show that early Christian sexual ethics owed little to Graeco-Roman paganism, whatever the points of convergence. Everyone admired strict control of the fleshly appetites, but the Christian emphasis on sexual purity, both outside and inside marriage, had an intensity that was all its own, and requires its own explanation. We have seen how it developed from certain New Testament themes. This makes the development comprehensible, but falls short of explaining why development occurred in this particular direction.

The answer is surely to be found in the peculiar situation of the Church in the Roman Empire. Christians saw themselves as constituting a holy people, set apart as a distinct, third race from both Jews and pagans.[57] The boundaries between themselves and surrounding society needed to be variously affirmed, if the Church was not to feel contaminated by its environment. This apartness and purity of the Church found expression and reinforcement, as we saw, in her strict penitential discipline, which, before the medieval development of private confession and repeated absolution, was more concerned to maintain the holiness of the Church than to deal compassionately with human weakness. If in both penitential discipline and general moral teaching the Church insisted on strict control of the sexual appetites, this was surely because of a keen sense that the purity of the Church as the body of Christ required that her members should strive to maintain the purity of their own bodies. The use of the word 'body' for a social as well as a physical organism is more than a convenient metaphor, but reflects an intimate connection between our experience of the two. In the words of a distinguished social anthropologist:

> The social body constrains the way the physical body is perceived. The physical experience of the body, always modified by the social categories through which it is known, sustains a particular view of society. There is a continual exchange of meanings between the two kinds of bodily experience in that each reinforces the categories of the other.[58]

The interconnection of the two is well and powerfully expressed in a text of the middle of the second century:

> The Church, which is spiritual, was manifested in the flesh of Christ, showing us that, if any of us guard her in the flesh and do not corrupt her, he will receive her again in the Holy Spirit. For this flesh is the anti-type of the Spirit, and so no one who corrupts the antitype will receive the reality. So what this means, brethren, is that you must guard the flesh in order to receive the Spirit.[59]

It was therefore natural enough that the great Christian theme of the holiness of the Church created an emphasis on maintaining purity of the body.

There were other considerations, of course, that contributed to the development of a distinctive Christian sexual ethic. Reference was made above to the early Christian ideal of a perfect response to God through a single-minded purity of heart. This ideal drew attention to the sexual urges as a prime example of the divisions within the human will that generated man's chronic contentiousness with his neighbour and resistance to the will of God. The inability of the will to direct the sexual drive, whether to stimulate or to extirpate it, provided the clearest of many pointers to the fact that man's resistance to the will of God went deeper than the conscious choices of the individual. The teaching of St Paul on the inveterate battle between the spirit and the flesh (where 'flesh' is not restricted to bodily impulses but certainly draws attention to them) echoed and re-echoed in the continuing tradition of the Church before being fully developed in Augustine's exhaustive analysis of the radical disorder in man's sexual drive.[60] Nevertheless, we may well conclude that at least until Augustine the dominant factor in the development of a distinctive Christian sexual ethic was the need to express and preserve the purity of the Church as the body of Christ through the purity of the bodies of its members. To maintain her own integrity as a heavenly society that was only sojourning on earth, the Church needed members whose own bodies stood apart from the blurring and contamination, the loss of personal integrity and bodily vigour, brought about by easy sexual relations. It was this ecclesial concern that gave the sexual ethic of the early Christians its distinctive edge, its sharp clarity, its reiterated emphases. Modern Christians who feel that traditional Christianity attached undue importance to sexual morality and made it too restrictive need to be aware that their own lack of sympathy with the traditional discipline arises not only from sexual liberation but also from a different ecclesiology, from a lowering of the boundaries between the Church and the world. The broad questions of the relationship between the Church and its human environment, of the precise sense in which the Christian should be in the world but not of it, need to be pondered and resolved before the sexual ethic of traditional Christianity can be rightly understood and fairly judged.

Notes

1. See Alexander Murray in *Journal of Roman Studies* 73 (1983), p. 191.
2. Edward Gibbon, *The Decline and Fall of the Roman Empire*, ch. 15 (ed. Bury, vol. II, p. 36).
3. R.J. Lane Fox, *Pagans and Christians* (London, Viking, 1986), pp. 340–374. The quotation is from p. 360.
4. J.H.W.G. Liebeschuetz, *Continuity and Change in Roman Religion* (Oxford U.P., 1979), p. 293.
5. P.R.L. Brown, *The Making of Late Antiquity* (Harvard U.P., 1978), ch. 4; 'The Rise and Function of the Holy Man in Late Antiquity', *JRS* 61 (1971), pp. 80–101; *The Body and Society: Men, Women and Sexual Renunciation in Early Christianity* (Columbia U.P., 1988; London, Faber & Faber, 1989). The best general introduction to Brown's contribution and significance is A. Murray, 'Peter Brown and the Shadow of Constantine', *JRS* 73 (1983), pp. 191–203.
6. P. Brown, 'Late Antiquity', in P. Ariès & G. Duby (eds.), *A History of Private Life*, vol. 1 (ed. P. Veyne), *From Pagan Rome to Byzantium*, (Harvard U.P., 1987), pp. 237–311. My quotation is from p. 263.
7. On the ideal of singleness of heart, and the threat to it that sexual urges were seen to pose, see Brown, *The Body and Society*, pp. 34–39, 70–71.
8. *A History of Private Life*, vol. 1, pp. 266–270. R. Cholij, *Clerical Celibacy in East and West* (Leominster, Fowler Wright, 1989) is a recent defence of the thesis that total sexual abstinence for the clergy was the primitive discipline of the Church from the time of the Apostles. It is certainly true that from the second century the influence of the Levitical model of the priesthood, on the one hand, and of encratism, on the other, will have created a strong pressure in this direction, even if formal canonical rules were a later development.
9. For the early history of penance see the selections of texts with excellent introductions provided by C. Vogel, *Le Pécheur et la pénitence dans l'église ancienne* (Paris, Ed. du Cerf, 1966) and H. Karpp, *La Pénitence* (Neuchâtel, Delachaux, 1970).
10. Canon 15 of the Council of Agde (506) and Canon 24 of the Council of Orleans (538) forbade subjecting the young to penance, because of the rigours of the penitential state, which included sexual renunciation even after reconciliation. Basil, Canon 34 (*Ep.* 199), lets adulteresses off the exposure that would follow from the full sequence of penitential discipline.
11. *Confessions*, I.11.17, tr. F.J. Sheed.
12. For the gradual evolution of private penance see *Dictionnaire de Théologie Catholique*, XII.1 (Paris, 1933), cols. 845–948.
13. See M. Bernos, *Le Fruit défendu* (Paris, Le Centurion, 1985), pp. 101–113; J.-L. Flandrin, 'Sex in Married Life in the Early Middle Ages', in P. Ariès & A. Béjin (eds.), *Western Sexuality* (Oxford, Blackwell, 1985), pp. 114–129.
14. The minutiae of sexual conduct appear already in the early medieval penitentials: see P.J. Payer, *Sex and the Penitentials* (University of Toronto Press, 1984). But it was the Council of 1215 that led to the extension of a detailed sexual casuistry to all dutiful Christians.
15. J. Bossy, *Christianity in the West 1400–1700* (Oxford U.P., 1985).
16. Basil, *Epp. 118, 199, 217.*
17. Canons 2, 56, 58, 62.
18. Orthodox writers (Ps-Clement, *Ad virgines*, I.8, Clement of Alexandria, *Stromata*, III. 4 & 59) had constantly to remind the celibate that there were other virtues than sexual continence. The renunciation of wealth appears as a condition for charismatic gifts in *Acts of John*, Latin Version, XVI; but this passage is less typical than Aphrahat, *Demonstratio*, VI.8, where the continent need to be told not to practise usury.
19. Rev. 14:4 ('those who have not defiled themselves with women') has obvious encratite overtones, even if the meaning may be partly allegorical.
20. *The Body and Society*, p. xvi.
21. Swinburne's *Hymn to Proserpine* – 'Thou hast conquered, O pale Galilaean,/The world has grown grey from thy breath' – puts in the mouth of the ascetical Julian the Apostate Swinburne's own hedonistic creed. Equally preposterous is Pt I, ch. 20 of Merezhkovsky's *The Death of the Gods* (St Petersburg, 1896), where Julian rapes a nun in front of a crucifix in order to give her a practical lesson on the sanctity of sex. Yet more curious is the interpretation of Christianity in Vasily Rozanov's *The People of the Moonlight* (St Petersburg, 1911), which sees as the kernel of Christianity 'spiritual sodomy' – and innate revulsion towards sexual differentiation, relations with the opposite sex, and consequently the family. Rozanov's treatment is indebted to contemporary psychology rather than to the

early Gnostic texts which view sexual differentiation negatively, for which see J.T. Noonan, *Contraception* (Harvard U.P., 1965), pp. 67–68.

22. P. Veyne, 'La Famille et l'amour sous le haut empire romain', *Annales, E.S.C.*, 33.1 (1978), pp. 35–63.

23. See especially R.P. Saller & B.D. Shaw, 'Tombstones and Roman Family Relations in the Principate', *JRS* 74 (1984), pp. 124–146.

24. Michel Foucault, *Histoire de la sexualité* (3 vols., Paris, Gallimard, 1984). The fourth projected volume, which was to have covered early Christian texts, was uncompleted by the time of the author's death and has not appeared. One chapter of it ('The Battle for Chastity') is available in *Western Sexuality* (see note 13, above). An outstanding discussion of the work is provided by A. Cameron, 'Redrawing the Map: Early Christian Territory after Foucault', *JRS* 76 (1986), pp. 266–271.

25. See Bernos, *op. cit.* (note 13), pp. 22–26; P. Veyne, 'Homosexuality in Ancient Rome', in *Western Sexuality* (note 25, above), pp. 26–35: Brown, *The Body and Society*, pp. 9–11.

26. *Life of Vitellius*, 4 (tr. J.C. Rolfe).

27. Alcinous (or Albinus), *Didaskalikos*, 28.4.

28. Musonius Rufus (ed. O. Hense, Leipzig, 1905), *Fragment 12*, of which an English translation is available in A.J. Malherbe, *Moral Exhortation. A Greco-Roman Handbook* (Philadelphia, 1986), pp. 152–154.

29. Epictetus, *Enchiridion*, 33.8. For a young man to frequent prostitutes was accepted as a matter of course (as implied by Achilles Tatius, *Cleitophon and Leucippe*, II.37.5). Where such conduct was criticized, it was for prodigality rather than licentiousness.

30. Alcinous, *Didaskalikos*, 32.4, 33.4; Plutarch, *Amatorius*, 769AB. Neoplatonism valued sexual abstinence more highly, but without really approaching the Christian attitude. As Brown puts it (*The Body and Society*, p. 181). 'Porphyry and his pagan colleagues took sexual austerity for granted. They saw no peculiar symbolic value in sexual renunciation when practised by their male peers; and they thought that it was positively inappropriate, if not impious, that young women of marriageable age should renounce their duty to society and to the "gods that preside over generation" by vowing their bodies to perpetual virginity'.

31. I use the translation of Soranus by O. Temkin (Baltimore, 1956). Admirable use is made of him by A. Rousselle, *Porneia* (Oxford, Blackwell, 1988), pp. 24–77.

32. On the Graeco-Roman attitude to marital sexuality *Gynaecology*, ch. 10 is also notable, as when Soranus asserts that 'as food swallowed without appetite and with some aversion is not well received and fails in its subsequent digestion, neither can the seed be taken up or, if grasped, be carried through pregnancy, unless urge and appetite for intercourse have been present'. At the same time, a gentleman was supposed to show decorum and remember his social status in bed (Brown, *The Body and Society*, p. 21); to be lascivious was appropriate with one's mistress, disgusting with one's wife (Plutarch, *Coniugalia Praecepta*, 140B; Athenaeus, *Deipnosophists*, XIII, 573B). One trusts that ancient spouses did not feel inhibited by this barrage of divergent requirements when embarking on their marital duties.

33. R. Walzer, *Galen on Jews and Christians* (Oxford U.P., 1949), p. 65.

34. For able treatments of 1 Cor. 7 that bring out Paul's lack of enthusiasm for marriage and the variety of his reasons, see H. Conzelman, *Commentary on 1 Corinthians* (Philadelphia, Fortress, 1975), *ad loc.*, and P.A. Gramaglia, *Il matrimonio nel cristianesimo preniceno* (Rome, Borla, 1988), pp. 7–37.

35. Pre-Nicene texts that reiterate the imminence of the Parousia include *Epistle of Barnabas* (4.3), *2 Clement* (16.3), Tertullian, *De oratione* (5), Cyprian, Ep. 67, Eusebius, *Demonstr. evang.* (1.9).

36. See Brown, *The Body and Society*, pp. 184–185, 298–299.

37. Lk. 20:35; Col. 2:12; Rom. 12:13; 1 Cor. 6:13–20.

38. E.g. *Acts of Judas Thomas*, 117, 124.

39. E.g. Ptolemy, *Letter to Flora*, in Epiphanius, *Panarion*, 33.7.

40. The term 'encratite' to describe a distinct heresy first appears in Irenaeus (*Adv. haer.*, I.28) and Clement (*Stomata*, VII.108).

41. Highly indicative is the contemporary Christian reaction to Jerome's tract *Against Jovinian*. Jovinian argued against attaching value to celibacy or fasting in themselves. The main lines of Jerome's reply, with its insistence on the biblical teaching on the superiority of the virgin to the married state, were orthodox enough, but the vehemence with which he obtruded his theme causes revulsion among the pious laity of Italy. See J.N.D. Kelly, *Jerome* (London, Duckworth, 1975), ch. XVII.

42. See Brown, *The Body and Society*, pp. 6, 24–25.

43. See the trenchant discussion in G.E.M. de Ste. Croix, *The Class Struggle in the Ancient Greek World* (London, Duckworth, 1981), pp. 104–111, 419.
44. 1 Tim. 2:12–15a.
45. 1 Tim. 4:3.
46. Brown, *op. cit.*, pp. 79–82, 122–139, 169–171, 205–209.
47. See E. Patlagean, *Pauvreté Économique et Pauvreté Sociale à Byzance* (Paris, 1977), pp. 114–143. Monastic literature laid an exaggerated stress on the danger to monks of propinquity to women as part of a strategy to keep monks cooped up and thereby insulate society from the radical challenge of their renunciation, as Brown notes (*op. cit.*, pp. 241–244).
48. Clement, *Stromata*, VII.70.
49. For the few exceptions see J.T. Noonan, *Contraception* (Harvard U.P., 1965), pp. 77–78, 249, 312–313.
50. Noonan, op. cit., pp. 75–85.
51. Noonan, op. cit., pp. 75–77. Musonius Rufus, *Fragment 12* (see note 28, above).
52. See C. Munier, *Église et Cité* (Paris, Cujas, 1979), pp. 35–55.
53. For strict monogamy see Munier, *op. cit.*, pp. 55–57; for the status and role of widows, G. Friedrich (ed.), *Theological Dictionary of the New Testament*, vol. IX (Michigan, Eerdmans, 1974), pp. 459–465; for widows as a spiritual altar, Polycarp, *Ad Philippenses*, 4.2 and *Didascalia Apostolorum*, ii. 26.
54. Origen, *Fragment 34*.
55. Origen, *Hom. in Cant.*, 2.1; Ignatius, *Ad Polycarpum*, 5.1.
56. Jerome, *Ep. 52*.16; Iganatius, *Ad Polycarpum*, 5.2.
57. See A. von Harnack, *Die Mission und Ausbrietung des Christentums* (4th ed., Leipzig, 1924), pp. 226–237, 259–271.
58. Mary Douglas, *Natural Symbols* (London, Cresset, 1970), p. 65. Equally suggestive for our understanding of the early Church are the following sentences a few pages later (70–71): 'If there is no concern to preserve social boundaries, I would not expect to find concern with bodily boundaries.... Furthermore, there is little prospect of successfully imposing bodily control without the corresponding social forms'.
59. *2 Clement*, 14.3.
60. See Brown, *The Body and Society*, pp. 47–49, 70–71, 402–427, and E. Pagels, *Adam, Eve and the Serpent* (London, Weidenfeld, 1988), pp. 127–150.

1.3 The Puritans, Sex, and Pleasure

Daniel Doriani

It has long been customary in some circles to vilify the Puritans for legalism, joylessness, an ascetic capitalism, and prudery. But their vigor, bravery, and accomplishments have continued to draw scholars' attention, so that a fairer picture of the Puritans has, with resistance, been emerging.

Old accusations still flow from newer pens. Lyle Koehler claims the Puritans condemned the 'toys' of material existence such as fine food and entertainment and had a 'moral distaste for sensual pleasure.'[1] Lawrence Stone accused English Protestants and Catholics of believing that 'sensuality itself, the lust of the flesh, is evil.' Christianity as a whole, he continued, and the Puritan ethic in particular, maintains that 'the pleasures of the flesh were peculiarly sinful.'[2]

Since the 1930s Christian and non-Christian scholars have been laboring to exonerate the Puritans of such charges. The Puritans, they maintain, were disciplined and principled, but not legalistic. They favored moderate enjoyment of food, drink, and recreation, but did not endorse asceticism. The Puritans, their defenders declare, had a healthy attitude toward marital love, including sex, and must not be confused with the Victorians, who were indeed prudish.

Some Christian researchers and writers, however, have passed from the necessary task of rehabilitation to the dubious one of hagiography. The Puritans' accusers were entirely wrong, they claim. Percy Scholes, already in 1933, argued that the appearance of Puritan opposition to pleasure stemmed from their sabbatarianism, and especially their resistance to King James' *Book of Sports*, which virtually required Englishmen to engage in games and recreation on Sunday. Scholes, after researching Puritan social habits, concluded, 'I have failed to find evidence of their opposing any kind of pleasure as such.'[3]

Ronald Frye wrote that classical Puritanism 'inculcated a view of sexual life in marriage as the "crown of all our bliss"' such that Puritan divines educated England in a more liberal view of marital love.[4] More recently Leland Ryken has credited the Puritans with rejecting medieval attitudes toward sex. 'Married sex was not only legitimate in the Puritan view; it was meant to be exuberant.' Sex was good, created by God for human welfare and even pleasure, and the Puritans were not squeamish about it, Ryken claims.[5]

The reader puzzles: how can two diametrically opposed views of the Puritans both attract scholarly defenders? Who is right? Or does the truth lie somewhere between the extremes? This article will attempt to give and substantiate answers to these questions while examining the Puritans' teaching on sex and pleasure from their first hundred years in England.[6] It evaluates the Puritan teaching on the basis of their own standard and intention: to change their society by proclaiming biblical ideas on sex in marriage.

I. The Context for Puritan Teachings on Marital Relations

We can best understand the Puritans' teachings on physical love if we compare them with the teachings of the Roman Church, which they consciously opposed.[7] Asceticism had a long and varied history since almost the beginning of the church's life.

From the second century on, many considered virginity superior to marriage. Second marriages were sins, third marriages signs of unbelief. To avoid sexual temptation some early Christian men chose desert dwellings that kept them miles and years away from even a glimpse of a woman. A few slept innocently with women to strengthen themselves by enduring temptation. Others applied Christ's words, 'If your hand causes you to sin, cut it off,' too literally. The marriage of priests was discouraged, then forbidden; finally, the prohibition was enforced. The church fathers allowed Manichee, Gnostic, and other dualistic varieties of Greek thought to influence their reading of Scripture and their conclusions about the role and value of marriage and sexuality. Generally, the fathers had an emotional embarrassment and a visceral aversion toward coitus. They feared sexual passion and pleasure, especially the powerful, scarcely controllable sexual impulse. The animal-like aspect of sexuality repelled them and they condemned the loss of rational control which accompanied sexual activity. The whole affair seemed shameful and lustful.[8]

Several consequences followed. Augustine, Tertullian, Jerome, and others concluded that even in marriage, even when man and wife act in order to beget children, concupiscence so attends the procreative act that there is always at least venial sin.[9] Many theologians restricted coitus even within marriage and nearly all exalted virginity.

On the other hand, they had to affirm that God created all things, including marriage and the human way of procreation. Since all his creations are good, no orthodox theologian could condemn matrimony and sexuality without qualification. They judged it merely a lesser good, virginity being the greater. But the church did seriously maintain the goodness of marriage, exalting it as a sacrament and condemning its unrestrained critics. So Augustine could even affirm that before the fall Adam and Eve were a married man and woman and that they would have reproduced sexually even if they had remained sinless. In God's plan 'the procreation of children [was] ... part of the glory of marriage, and not of the punishment of sin.'[10]

These ideas, however, are more concessions than main themes. The fathers held that lust (hence sin) taints all sexual activity. Hence it should be as restrained and infrequent as possible, even in marriage.[11] Theologians judged virginity superior to marriage, in general, not only for those with 'the gift.' Finally, and with much resistance, they required the 'counsel' of chastity for all clergy.

Medieval Catholic theologians adopted the outlook of the early church. Taking Thomas Aquinas as their representative, we find the same qualified respect for God's institution of marriage, limited by praise of virginity and fear of concupiscence and pleasure. The capacity to give pleasure was a problem that threatened to condemn the sex act even in marriage. Even in marriage Aquinas thought the sex act a dangerous thing, precisely because it was so enjoyable. Aquinas conceded that the marriage act is not always sinful, but, before he concluded his argumentation, he affirmed that (1) the marriage act is 'always shameful' because always 'connected with concupiscence,' (2) 'there is always excess of pleasure in the marriage act' which absorbs the reason and separates one from God, (3) God forbids enjoyment as a last end, and (4) 'the marriage act is evil in itself' although it is an evil connected 'only' with punishment and concupiscence and not necessarily sin.[12]

Bound to accept the force of texts such as 1 Cor. 7:3, 28 and 1 Tim. 5:14, Aquinas admitted that the 'marriage act' is not 'altogether unlawful.' It is lawful only if it is performed out of a sense of duty to beget children or to render one's debt to his spouse: 'For if the motive for the marriage act be a virtue, whether of justice that they may render the debt, or of religion, that they may beget children for the worship of God, it is meritorious. but if the motive be lust ... it is a venial sin.'[13] That is, if the motive is *duty* to God (children) or man (spouse) the marriage act is meritorious. If the motive is desire, even for one's wife, it is sinful.

The views of Augustine and Aquinas remained the orthodox standard until the Reformation and beyond and actively competed with Protestant teachings in the marketplace of ideas. For example, the sixteenth-century Spanish Catholic humanist Ludovico Vives had his *Instruction of a Christian Woman* published in London in 1557. In it Vives exalted virginity and chastity, asserting that chastity is a woman's chief virtue, saying, 'There is nothing that our Lord delighteth in more than virgins.' Indeed, Vives so esteemed these virtues that he praised them even in marriage. He lauded one woman who lay with her husband but once a month and then only when certain she was not pregnant, approved another who bore one child and then ceased marital relations, and praised Mary and others who perpetually remained virgins in marriage. He concluded, 'bodily pleasure is unworthy [of] this excellent nature of ours ... and therefore every body despiseth it ... the more he hath of that excellency of the soul.... Neither will [he] use this pleasure often except it be such as have but beastly vile and abject minds.'[14]

II. Early Puritan Teachings on Marital Relations

The Puritans, like all Protestants, rejected several of the Roman Catholic principles enumerated here. They affirmed that marriage is intrinsically as good as virginity and hinted that it might be better. They rejected clerical celibacy and with it the notion that there are 'counsels of perfection,' such as virginity, for which all should strive. They opposed Catholic views because they believed they caused fornication, 'whoredom,' and even infanticide as priests and nuns attempted to destroy the evidence of their sin.[15] Protestant thinkers declared matrimony good because it prevented such sins and produced a holy seed. But such affirmations do not necessarily entail the idea that sex and pleasure are good in themselves. The theologians of the early and medieval church rejected the idea. Contemporary Christian teachers affirm or assume it; but the Puritans' view is more elusive.[16]

From the first, the Puritans accepted the continental Protestant view that faithful married couples are chaste, that the chaste love of matrimony is a 'second sort of virginity.'[17] Thomas Becon, writing in the mid-sixteenth century, said, 'Wedlock is honorable among all persons and the bed undefiled.... The very act of matrimony ... is also pure and clean in the sight of God.'[18] Becon also refuted an interesting Roman Catholic argument for celibacy. The church had reasoned that the sacraments are holy and pure and must not be touched by an unclean person such as a man (a priest) rising from his wife's side. Since a priest touches the sacraments daily and may not defile them, he would not be free to fulfil his sexual duty to his wife. Hence priests should not marry. Becon replied that because the marriage bed is undefiled, 'A priest in the fear of God lying with his wife, and having her company may with a good conscience rise from his wife's side and do whatsoever pertaineth unto his office.'[19] While Becon asserted the honor and chastity of marriage and the marriage bed and critiqued Roman teaching, he failed to develop his simple affirmation that, within marriage, the sex act is pure.

The next generation, writing in the late sixteenth century and represented by Robert Cleaver and William Perkins, began to propound a fuller sexual ethic. While still affirming the purity of sex in marriage, they initiated a partial return to Catholic attitudes and restrictions governing marital sex. Cleaver advocated a period of betrothal before marriage to differentiate men, who can restrain their desire for sexual satisfaction, from brute beasts, who cannot. He warned that couples can pollute and defile their marriage if they use their privilege 'without prayer and soberness.'[20] Perkins considered the rendering of 'due benevolence' an essential duty of marriage, adding that it must be performed with a 'singular and entire affection.' But he judged the marriage bed 'indifferent – neither good nor bad.' He amplified, 'This coming together of man and wife, although it be indifferent, yet by the holy usage thereof it is made a holy and undefiled action.' 'Holy usage' entails three things: first, moderation, 'for even in wedlock, excess in lusts is no better than plain adultery before God'; second, occasional abstinence, such as during fasts and menstruation; and third, prayer, that God would bless their action with a blessed seed.[21]

The outlook and advice of Cleaver and Perkins carried over into the early seventeenth century. In that period a variety of Puritan spokesmen published sermons or longer studies on the family. Their thought attained both maturity and consensus in most areas. They struggled, however, with the topic of marital relations. They followed Becon's assertion that marriage and the marriage bed are pure. They also believed marital relations have good ends or purposes: the prevention of fornication and the birth of a godly seed. But did they believe marital relations are good in themselves? Did they think God created sexuality, in part, for the enjoyment or pleasure of husband and wife? The Puritans made statements that support either a positive or a negative answer, but the next sections intend to show that frequent warnings about the dangers of sex virtually annulled their affirmations of the goodness of sexuality.

III. Puritan Appreciation of Marital Love and Sexuality

Several Puritan writers show that the Reformation started to create a new attitude toward love among the godly in England. John Dod, profoundly revered in his life time, typifies the genuine but oblique praise of love in the early seventeenth century. Dod began his discussion of married love by saying that if we cannot control lust, 'then God hath called us to the estate of matrimony.' Yet marriage alone will fail to subdue lust:

> Every married person must labor for pure and fervent love to his yokefellow.... If married persons get fervent and pure love one to the other, this will keep them safe. For it is not the having of a wife, but the loving of her that makes a man live chastely: but if she have him, and yet hate him ... she is in danger every day to be defiled. Fervent love must then be sought for. Not such as flesh can yield ... but pure love is a gift of God.[22]

So Dod suggested that fervent sensual love helps the married avoid adultery. As he put it, those who partake of 'holy delights' will not seek 'ungodly pleasures.'[23] Positive as Dod's remarks are he still praised marital love more for its ability to prevent sin than for its intrinsic merits.

Thomas Gataker, author of four popular marriage sermons,[24] could be more direct. Among the duties of love a man has toward his wife, Gataker said the fifth duty was to take physical delight in her. Quoting Prov. 5:15, 18–19 in full and taking it at face value, he told the listening husband:

'Joy and delight in her. Drink,' saith the wise man, 'the water of thine own cistern. Let thy fountain be blessed: ... and rejoice in the wife of thy youth: let her be unto thee as the loving hind, and the pleasant roe: let her breasts or her bosom content thee at all times: and delight continually, ... even dote on the love of her.' As if the Holy Ghost did allow some such private dalliance and behavior to married persons between themselves as to others might seem dotage: such as may be was Isaac's sporting with Rebekah.[25]

Gataker believed that it is a tactic of the demonic to misrepresent Christianity as a damper placed upon the joys of living, or to portray it as opposed to human happiness. This false picture of Christianity, says the Puritan Gataker, is

an illusion of Satan, whereby he usually persuades the merry Greeks of the world; that if they should once devote themselves to the service of Jesus Christ, that then they must bid an everlasting farewell to all mirth and delight; that then all their merry days are gone; that in the kingdom of Christ, there is nothing, but sighing and groaning, and fasting and prayer. But see here the contrary: even in the kingdom of Christ, and in his house, there is marrying and giving in marriage, drinking of wine, feasting, and rejoicing even in the very face of Christ.[26]

Several Puritans implicitly addressed the physical aspect of marriage when they described the love husband and wife share. Daniel Rogers said the finger of God effects a 'secret sympathy of hearts' between some men and women. Marital love is therefore more than the spiritual affection Christians share and more than the physical attraction even brute animals experience. It is a 'sweet compound of both, religion and nature.'[27] Rogers evoked the emotional and tactile aspect of marriage in a tender description of the devoted wife. 'She joys in his presence, mourns in his absence, reposes herself in his bosom, being asleep, watcheth his waking, follows after him, hangs upon him in his departing, longs for his return.'[28]

Along with Becon, William Gouge probably did the most to promote a positive outlook toward marital relations. The context for Gouge's longest discussion of marital relations was the prevention of the heinous sin of adultery. To stay pure, husband and wife must diligently guard their heart, eyes, ears, tongues, lips, hands, feet, company, diet, apparel, and time, for misuse of any can lead to sin. Speaking more broadly of marriage, Gouge continued:

One of the best remedies [for adultery] that can be prescribed to married persons is that husband and wife mutually delight each in the other, and maintain a pure and fervent love betwixt themselves, yielding that 'due benevolence' one to another which is warranted and sanctified by God's word, and ordained of God for this particular end. This 'due benevolence' (as the Apostle stileth it), is one of the most proper and essential acts of marriage: and necessary for the main and principal ends thereof: as for preservation of chastity in such as have not the gift of continency, for increasing the world with a legitimate brood, and for linking the affections of the married couple more firmly together. These ends of marriage, at least the two former, are made void without [sic] this duty be performed.

As it is called 'benevolence' because it must be performed with good will and delight, willingly, readily and cheerfully; so it is said to be 'due' because it is a debt which the wife owes to her husband, and he to her.[29]

We have quoted at length because there are three breakthroughs, for the Puritans at least, in these paragraphs. First, Gouge has at last openly granted 'due benevolence' a vital *independent* role in marriage. He has broken with Aquinas, and surpassed Luther and many of his brothers, by saying that due benevolence is 'an essential act of marriage,' not just something necessary because of its good results (progeny and the prevention of sin). Thus, Gouge was consistent when he later reasoned against Augustine and Ambrose (his chosen representatives of Catholicism) that a man may 'know' his pregnant wife, for 'conception is not the only end of this duty.'[30]

Second, Gouge, albeit with some hesitation, introduced a new end of marital relations: the increase of affection between husband and wife. (The idea that sexual relations can aid in 'linking the affections' is alien to classic Catholicism and at best implicit in a few earlier Protestants.) Third, although Gouge still called marital relations a duty he believed it should be a delightful duty for both partners. With that perspective Gouge was free to cite Prov. 5:19 adding a liberal qualification: 'As the man must be satisfied at all times in his wife, and even ravished with her love; so must the woman.'[31]

It appears, then, that the Puritans began to return the church to a more positive, indeed more biblical, concept of marital love. To be accurate, however, we must emphasize the word 'began.' While Puritan thinking does restore important, previously neglected facets of biblical thought, even the most progressive writers emphatically qualified their most liberated remarks. So Gouge urged his audience to remember that Prov. 5:18-19 is metaphorical and hyperbolic. He said that Christians with ardent affection will 'exceed not the bounds of Christian modesty and decency.' He condemned the insatiable spouse whose demands are 'provoking rather than assuaging lust' and who insists upon his due at all times, even on days of religious fasting, illness, or menstruation.[32] Likewise, the same Gataker who encouraged husbands to take physical delight in their wives also had profound reservations about the sexual impulse. Several authors surprise us both with their commendations *and* their reservations about sex. Old Catholic ideas and unassimilated biblical ideas contested for control of their minds.

IV. Puritan Restrictions of Marital Love and Sexuality

The Puritans affirmed that God created human sexuality, that sex potentially has certain God-pleasing results, and that the marriage bed is pure. We have seen that they even began to appreciate the physical and romantic aspects of married love. But they formulated so many warnings and restrictions that their protestations of the goodness and purity of sexuality lost their force.

Let us consider three restrictions the Puritans placed on sexual activity within marriage. First, they warned against lustful, intemperate, and animal-like sex. John Robinson asserted that, though marriage can prevent adultery, that benefit can be lost through abuse:

> As a man may surfeit at this own table or be drunken with his own drink; so may he play the adulterer with his own wife, both by inordinate affection and action. For howsoever the marriage bed cover much inordinateness this way: yet must modesty be observed by the married, lest the bed which is honorable, and undefiled, Heb. 13:4, in its right use become by abuse hateful, and filthy in God's sight.[33]

Robert Bolton also gave then took away. He said the marriage bed is undefiled, but added that married couples have a duty to preserve their conjugal chastity and their marriage bed as follows:

> It ought by no means to be stained with sensual excesses, wanton speeches, foolish dalliance, and other incentives of lust, which marriage should quench, not inflame. Even in wedlock, intemperate and unbridled lust, immoderation and excess is deemed, both by ancient and modern divines, no better than plain adultery before God.

He cited several authorites including Augustine who said: 'As a man may be a wicked drunkard with his own drink; and a glutton, by excessive devouring of his own meat; so likewise, one may be unclean in the immoderate use of the marriage bed.' Not that Bolton absolutely opposed pleasure, but the pleasure of marriage, he taught, 'must be mingled with some severity ... and serious pleasure.... It ought to be a delight conscientious and circumspect.'[34]

In one passage Gataker evinced a view of marital sexuality akin to Aquinas. He conceded that the human inclination to 'nuptial conjunction' is not 'at all evil simply in itself,' but added that since the fall 'this affection is not only tainted and mixed generally with much filth, but it is grown so violent, impetuous and headstrong ... with the most that it is ready to break forth into grievous inconveniences.'[35]

William Whately also opposed excess passion and even resisted approving pleasure:

> The married must not provoke desires for pleasure's sake, but allay desires when they provoke themselves. They must not strive by words and gestures to inflame their passions, when they are cool. But when

such passions are of themselves moved, then must they take the benefit
of their estate to assuage them, that they may not be troublesome to them
in the duties of religion and of their callings.[36]

Excess, he warned, weakens the body and shortens life, enflames
passion, and disposes to adultery. It breeds satiety, disables, and
hinders fruitfulness. So Christian prudence requires the temperate
enjoyment of God's ordinance.[37]

The Puritans often said that passionate lusts and lustful deeds reduce
man to the level of a beast. Nicholas Byfield linked 'excesses of concupiscence' with 'brutish sensuality.' Rogers railed against men who live
like 'brute beasts' in that 'their will is their law.'[38]

Second, Puritan preachers restricted the times of sexual relations.
Fear of bestial behavior led some to advocate a period between
betrothal and marriage to demonstrate that man does not copulate like
an animal. The Puritans also restricted the times of sexual activity in
marriage. They asked their hearers to adhere to the Levitical restrictions against sexual relations during menstruation.[39] The Puritans also
advised listeners about the frequency of marital relations. Whately said
the marriage bed 'must be used as seldom and sparingly as may stand
with the need of the persons married.'[40] Daniel Rogers, observing that
some Greek philosophers set numerical guidelines for frequency,
suggested:

> I say not as they say once weekly or thrice monthly ... because I know
> there can be no set rule for all persons, seasons of marriage and varieties
> of bodies ... but ... if heathens could rove at such a mark ... I should
> think it rather meet that Christians, especially in years, should rather aim
> at being under the line than above it.

Rogers qualified himself at length, emphasizing Christian freedom and
the impossibility of a 'punctual' decision, but the impression remains
that Rogers sided with the Greeks and Catholics rather than Luther
who thought twice a week was ideal.[41]

Third, the godly brethren limited the spontaneity of sex by requiring
the married to pray before intercourse. Bolton advised newly married
couples that they should 'for two or three days ply prayer, that they
may have good children, and please the Lord in their marriage
duties.'[42] Whately said that before relations husband and wife must
consider that their action is lawful, then thank God for it.

> As therefore it were a brutish profaneness, for any man to sit down to his
> table, as a horse to the manger, and cram himself with viands, without
> craving the blessing of God first ... so it is likewise a great licentiousness
> for married people ... to come together in marriage, forgetting or
> neglecting to receive the Lord's blessing and to give him due praises.[43]

Rogers, Cleaver, and Hieron also told married couples to pray before
sexual activity and consider the legality, purpose, and need of blessing

for their activity.[44]

Some historians have said the chief motive behind the Puritans' interest in governing sexual relations was their desire to prevent adultery and the disturbance of the social order through bastardy or ill-advised marriages. But if we take the Puritans at their word, their chief goal was to please God and to be pure before him. They give no credit to those who remained clean only through lack of opportunity to sin or fear of the consequences.[45]

Bolton observed that some use the marriage bed intemperately, knowing they are free from human censure. Yet, he solemnly warned they should not think this gives them license for any behavior, for 'assuredly God's pure eye cannot look upon them; but without repentance will certainly plague them.' The 'plague' that Bolton threatened would fall on children begotten during uncontrolled sexual activity. He warned husbands and wives who abused the marriage bed with carnal love or excessive passion that 'divine justice doth many times deservedly chastise it ... with miscarriages, barrenness, bad children.'[46] Hieron agreed that 'God usually punisheth men's distempered, unbridled, and disordered lusts, in their posterities.'[47] Cleaver was most explicit and terrifying:

> Christians therefore must know that when men and women raging with boiling lust meet together as brute beasts, having no other respect than to satisfy their carnal concupiscence when they make no conscience to sanctify the marriage bed with prayer, when they have no care to increase the church of Christ ... it is the just judgment of God to send them either monsters or fools, or else such as ... one most wicked, graceless and profane persons.[48]

Whately agreed that God has the power to give monstrous, wicked, or cursed or diseased children to punish parents for prayerless or lustful conjunctions. Indeed he said that a child conceived through an 'unseasonable [menstrual] conversation ... must needs inherit numerous diseases.'[49]

The Puritans intended their warnings to motivate Christians to crave God's blessing for their reproductive activity. And, happily, Richard Greenham uttered the balancing word of encouragement that children sought of God by their parents often excel in natural and supernatural gifts.[50] Nonetheless, the unintended consequences of the Puritans' teaching make one shudder. *If* their hearers took it seriously, it surely brought helpless and unassuaged guilt, remorse, and recrimination when handicapped children were born or babies died in infancy.

To summarize, the Puritans never attacked sexual activity in itself, but they rarely praised its intrinsic value. Further, they so restricted sexual activity that, if the man in the pew believed the preachers, spontaneous, passionate, physical love would be almost impossible. To complete the portrait of Puritan attitudes toward sex, we need only describe their attitude toward extramarital sexual activity.

V. The Condemnation of Extramarital Relations

The Puritans' denunciations of extramarital sexual sin showed an unprecedented virulence and volubility. Becon opened our era with a diatribe against whoredom which called it a sin, an abomination, a capital offense, and an act which brings God's most extreme temporal and eternal judgment.[51] Rogers closed it with a sixty-page appendix to *Matrimoniall Honour* 'discovering the just vengeance of God upon all ... defilers of marriage.'[52] The adulterer, Rogers warned, 'is drowned in his own perdition and cannot get out.... Your damnation sleeps not! He shall come upon you.... Hell fire and all do smell sweet in his nostrils.'[53] Byfield said the sin of whoredom 'consumes men's strength, wastes men's substance, compasseth men with evil in the midst of the congregation; is worse than theft; destroys the soul, both by making men without understanding, and sending them to hell.'[54]

Gouge found no sin to be so notorious and heinous in all Scripture. Adultery attacks God the Father, Son, and Holy Ghost, the spouses of the adulterers, the children, the friends, the town, the nation, the church, and the guilty parties themselves. Perhaps worst, adultery ruins marriages. 'For by it husband's and wife's affection ... is so alienated, as seldom it is reconciled again.' God hates, denounces, and condemns adulterers. 'Whoremongers, and adulterers God will judge. Now consider what a fearful thing it is to fall into the hands of the living God.'[55] Such strong words arouse our curiosity. Why did the Puritans have such animus toward sexual sins? Why did they deem them worse than all others? What do their protestations reveal as we evaluate Puritan attitudes toward sex and pleasure?

VI. Analysis

The Puritans intended to radically reform Christian thinking on marriage and sexuality, in order to bring thought and practice into harmony with the Bible. They and their most ardent supporters believe they succeeded. Their critics believe they modified but continued to maintain oppressive Greek or Christian ideas of sexuality and pleasure.

The preceding exposition has attempted to show that neither the Puritans' detractors nor defenders accurately portray the Puritans' theology of sex and pleasure in marriage. They neither judged sexual life as the crown of married bliss nor expressed an exuberant attitude toward sex in marriage. But it is not quite right to say they believed sensuality is evil either.

There are several ways to account for the contradictory interpretations of the Puritans' views of sex and pleasure. Some appear to have read the Puritans tendentiously, looking for and seizing upon evidence to confirm a preconceived thesis. These scholars disregard counterevidence and falsely (not to say deliberately) claim statements for their case. The writer who depends on tendentious secondary sources is, obviously, doomed.[56]

But even if problems with method and integrity were solved, it would be difficult to describe the Puritans' views. Their views resist generalizations because they struggled with an internal tension or inconsistency in their own thought.

The godly preachers accepted several ideas that, if failing to contradict, at least conflict with each other. First, the Puritans maintained that God created marriage and sex. Both are pure and holy because created by God, even before the fall. Second, due to the strength of human sexual appetites (as well as God's desire for progeny), God makes it a duty for couples to communicate their bodies to each other, except for occasional, brief, and mutually agreeable separations. Sexual activity is, therefore, pure and an ongoing part of a normal marriage. Third, sexual relations have beneficial products: offspring, the prevention of fornication, and, a few said, the promotion of love and communion between man and wife. But fourth, the Puritans could not rid themselves of the Greek and Roman Catholic idea that lust taints the procreative act so that it is shameful. They feared the power of sexual desire, its spontaneity, its capacity to resist the will, and its pleasure, so intense that it overwhelms the consciousness. Human sexuality reminded theologians of man's separation from God. (It is impossible to contemplate God during intercourse, they said.) Mankind's rebellion against God and internal disorder were centralized in human sexuality.

The Puritans never fully articulated such Greek and Catholic ideas; they might even have rejected them if presented for their scrutiny. But the preachers' writings show that they at least subconsciously adopted them. Since the first of the three ideas enumerated above clash with the fourth, Puritans authors contradict themselves, or at least make incompatible remarks. Therefore even honest and skilled researchers can formulate Puritan views differently.

Two critical questions must be answered in order to make a just critique of the Puritans. To evaluate the preachers on their own terms, to judge them according to their own agenda and standards we must ask: How did their teachings on sexuality measure up against the Bible's? If they promoted unbiblical ideas, why did they do so? In choosing this agenda we do not deny that other valid critical approaches exist. A scholar might, for example, examine the social consequences of Puritan ideas and discover that Puritan notions promoted social order. But the exposition of God's word and judgments stood foremost in their minds. We see this in their references to God's judgment of secret acts and in their relative disregard for social norms concerning the age of marriage. (For example, they said parents should arrange marriages for their children when sexual needs require it and basically ignored the possible results of poverty and overpopulation.)[57]

How then do the Puritans measure up against their own rule, fidelity to the Bible? First, the godly brethren gave undue prominence to extra-marital sexual sin. Unlike the Puritans, biblical writers do not declare sexual sins to be peculiarly soul-threatening. To be sure, habitual sexual offenders will not enter the kingdom of God, but then neither will idolaters, thieves, drunkards, slanderers, or swindlers (1 Cor. 6:9–11; cf. Rom. 1:26–32).

Second, the Puritans' warnings against sexual sin in marriage are fundamentally unbiblical. The Bible does not regulate sex in marriage, except through general principles such as love and self-sacrifice. The Bible only commands that relations continue (1 Cor. 7:1–5). The preachers' advice about the quantity and quality of marital sex probably had two sources. From Catholicism they had a lingering discomfort with sex and passion; from the entire European intellectual world they inherited an emphasis on sobriety, moderation, and temperance.

Moderation was a universal ethical principle applied by theologians and moralists of every persuasion to the use of all kinds of earthly or physical goods: sex, food, drink, sleep, recreation, celebrations, clothing, and even familial affection. Among non-Puritan moralists John Bodenham said temperance is 'of all the virtues the most wholesome.'[58] Richard Brathwaite added, 'there is no virtue which doth better adorn or beautify man than temperance or moderation.'[59] English physicians also extolled the virtue of moderation.[60] The Puritans also used the principle of moderation extensively. For example, Robinson said: 'And he that is not sober in himself, using and desiring moderately, the good things of this nature life, as meat, drink, apparel, sleep, pastime, credit, and the rest: will neither converse righteously with men, nor piously with God.'[61] Perkins often used the principle of moderation in his casuistry and called it the first principle for the right use of the marriage bed. 'This is the judgment of the ancient church, that intemperance, that is, immoderate desires even between man and wife, are fornication.'[62] Bolton concluded a fifty-page discussion of moderation that warned against excess in meat, drink, apparel, recreation, and sleep this way: 'Christians are in more danger of being spiritually undone by a sly insinuation ... and immoderation in ... lawful things than by gross assaults of four sins.'[63]

In commending moderation, therefore, the godly brethren conformed to prevailing ideas. The idea of moderation seems to have gone from Greek thought to Aquinas through Aristotle. Through Aquinas it became part of the mental furnishings of the ethical mind of Europe. Broadly speaking, the advocates of moderation believed it required self-limitation and the avoidance of extremes. Their discussions show that they commended several forms of moderation: (1) self-control with regard to the senses and sensual pleasures including clothes and sleep as well as food, drink, and sex; (2) modesty or dignity in conduct, so that one does not show extreme emotion, enthusiasm or devotion to anything, whether it be work, play or loved ones;

(3) the general avoidance of passion.

Several questions can lead us into an evaluation of the Puritans' concept of moderation. Is moderation a biblical concept? If so, what does the Bible mean by moderation? If moderation is a biblical notion, is it a great, general principle for life or a relatively minor one that must fit under more important ones? Further, how might the concept of moderation apply to sexuality in marriage?

Even though most modern translations lack the term 'moderation' and the *KJV* uses it but once, the concept is biblical. Self-control is a fruit of the Spirit, and a mark of righteousness and maturity that Proverbs and the letters of Peter and Paul often require. The wicked and the foolish, on the other hand, fail to restrain their anger, their tongues, and their passions for physical pleasures. The Puritans rightly observe that even familial love can be immoderate, as David's indulgent devotion to Absalom proves. So the concept of moderation, in the first sense, is biblical.

The second and third senses of the Puritan concept of moderation must be questioned, however, for the bible approves some instances of extreme emotion, devotion, or even passion. For example, Michal despised David's passionate dance of joy before the Lord in 2 Samuel 6. But the Lord, Samuel's author lets us know, approved David's 'immoderate' celebration (2 Sam. 6:23). Jesus and Paul both praise 'immoderate' generosity (Luke 21:4; 2 Cor. 8). The book of Numbers praises the zeal, the passion, of Phinehas, grandson of Aaron, who ran his spear through an Israelite man and a Moabite woman while they sinned (Num. 25:1-13). Zeal for the house of God consumed David, and his greater Son, Jesus (Ps. 69:9, John 2:17).

Moreover, the authors of the Bible require believers to have a zealous, single-minded (i.e. passionate) devotion to God's kingdom that will often lead to immoderate action (Luke 12:31-34; 14:25-27; Rom. 12:11). Finally, Prov. 5:18-19 and the Song of Solomon appear to approve and even command the very *marital* 'immoderation' that the Puritans so frequently denounced. These and other similar texts demonstrate that Scripture sees nothing intrinsically wicked about extremes in emotion, devotion, or passion. Moderation, in other words, is not an absolute value. We must deny moderation the standing of an absolute ethical principle. The moderation of passion may be good, bad, or indifferent, depending on the object of the passion, the manner of its expression, and the nature of the situation in which the passion might be expressed.

The Puritans' belief in the necessity of moderation contributed to their striking assertion that marital lusts cause the birth of deformed or evil children. We must bear in mind that, although the idea may seem repugnant or foolish today, it was 'scientifically' sound and theologically accepted then. Men reasoned that if lust deforms the soul during conception, that deformity can be pased on to the soul or body of a child conceived in that meeting. It is as irrelevant for our critique to observe that the preachers had good intentions as it is to say they were wrong. Just this matters: the Puritans' insistence on moderation as a general principle for behavior is unbiblical, as are their threats regarding the consequences of passion.

This conclusion compels us to ask why the godly brethren insisted on moderation and restraint of passion. Ronald Frye has argued that they attacked lust in marriage because immoderate love had a violence which precluded it from maintaining the stability necessary for marriage. The Puritans feared immoderate love could degenerate into jealousy, satiety, or a self-centered displeasure. Frye shows that the Puritans viewed lust as a destructive perversion that ruins marriages and offends God.[64] Frye's answer is incomplete, however. The most telling quotations he adduces for his answer condemn lust as the ground for choosing a spouse and entering marriage. The Bible certainly teaches, with the Puritans, that physical or sexual attraction is no basis for marriage. But the fundamental issue is not passion as a *basis* for marriage but the legitimacy of passion *within* marriage. The question is, assuming a couple marries for companionship, partnership, and progeny, can they go on to enjoy 'immoderate,' passionate, sensual love?

When Frye draws his conclusions he says the Puritans treated physical love as good and pure in itself, no matter how ardent it might be, while repudiating lust defined as 'immoderate, unstable affection and degrading idolatry.'[65] But the problem cannot be solved by a definition: 'ardent love' is good; 'immoderate affection' is bad. Does ardent love include ardent *sexual* love or is sexual passion always immoderate? In other words, while the Puritans have biblical grounds for guarding against lust, especially as a basis for marriage, they never specified what constitutes lust within marriage. They failed to distinguish the two senses of lust: (1) strong desire, as a neutral thing depending on its object; and (2) inordinate passion, especially for something forbidden. To be sure, one can lust for his or her own spouse. When a man treats his wife as an object for his selfish pleasure or gratification, or when a woman controls her husband, keeping him for her own use, there can be lust. But does that mean all strong sexual desires are sinful? Or is there still a place for healthy passion in marriage? The Puritans never addressed that precise question but their treatment of the Song of Solomon and Prov. 5:18–19 suggest they would not endorse passion in marriage. They dismissed the passions of the Song of Solomon by accepting the idea that it is an allegory of Christ and the church, not a love song. Further, they added a dozen glosses to Proverb 5, all eroding its plain sense. Finally, they insisted, citing 1 Tim. 4:3–5, that sexual relations be consecrated with prayer. It is one thing to assert that sexual relations always may be consecrated with prayer; it is another to say or imply that they always must be. One needs only a little imagination to see how this precept, if obeyed, would restrict marital passions.

To summarize, the Puritans' vague discomfort with passion and pleasure descends from the Greek and Catholic dualism with its denigration of and antipathy toward the body. The godly brethren found it very difficult to make a complete break with that tradition, even over several generations.

But we must put the Puritans' shortcomings in perspective. Although they failed in the explication, they did reestablish and defend the essential purity of marital relations. Their views, though imperfect, were more healthy and biblical than those of the Catholic Church from Jerome to Aquinas to Vives. For example, while they imposed sundry limits on sexual expression in marriage, the Roman Church forbade relations during menstruation, pregnancy, and lactation; during seasons of fasting and on certain festival days; for forty days before Easter, Pentecost, and Christmas; and for three to seven days before communion. Further, casuists recommended abstinence 'on Thursday in memory of Christ's arrest, on Friday in memory of his death, on Saturday in honour of the Virgin Mary, on Sunday in honour of the Resurrection and on Monday in commemoration of the departed.'[66]

By contrast the Puritans were sexual realists and liberators. They too forbade sex during fasts but they recognized no annual fasts, only extraordinary fast days for special purposes. Another questionable prohibition, that against sex during menstruation, can at least claim biblical warrant. On that, the Puritans can be criticized for failing to apply the already known concept of the ceremonial law to annul the Levitical dictum. Still the Puritans granted far more freedom than the Catholics.

Furthermore, the Puritans stayed closer to the Bible than other Protestant Englishmen. There is a remarkable instability in much of the writing of the latter, far surpassing that of the Puritans' vacillation between biblical and Catholic ideas. For example, Richard Brathwaite praised chastity and virginity yet left room for discreet extramarital affairs in his *English Gentlewoman*.[67] They also mixed serious marital advice with bizarre sexual tales and titillating stories, while others entertained readers with vapid poetry and misogynist ravings.[68]

Autobiographies, court records on sexual offenses, and demographic studies of bastardy and prenuptial pregnancy prove that the biblical position needed English spokesmen. Fornication and adultery were common, while desertion, spontaneous divorce, and bigamy were not too rare.[69]

When compared to continental Protestants, the Puritans do not fare badly either. Luther and Lutherans stressed the negative role of marital sex, the remedy for fornication. Calvin was more successful at freeing himself from antipathy to pleasure in itself. Yet he shared the universal belief that excess passion amounts to lust, hence sin, even in the marriage bed.[70] Neither Luther nor Calvin emphasized that pleasure or even the enhancement of marital affection was a purpose of sex. The Puritans, also silent except for Gouge, were preparing the way for such thoughts by relaxing the fear of pleasure, stressing cohabitation and companionship in marriage, and requiring spouses to perform their sexual duties. Soon enough Milton was asserting the intrinsic benefits of marital relations.

We have found, therefore, that neither the Puritans' detractors nor their champions are entirely right. We have ascribed the difficulty in interpreting Puritan sexual thought to the Puritans themselves, who strove to restore pure scriptural teaching to England but could not break free from all their cultural and intellectual bonds. While readers may find flaws – some of them frightening – in Puritan thinking easily enough, there is room for charitable judgment. Puritan preachers successfully attacked the worst errors from the Middle Ages and began to restore biblical thinking about sexuality to Reformation and post-Reformation England.

In conclusion, then, the Puritans intended to bring radical reformation of Christian thinking on marriage and sexuality. While they failed in that goal, they did achieve a real, if incremental, advance toward restoring biblical teaching in the Christian community.

Notes

1. Lyle Koehler, *A Search for Power* (Urbana, IL: University of Illinois Press, 1980), 10.
2. Lawrence Stone, *The Family, Sex & Marriage in England, 1500–1800* (New York: Harper & Row, 1977), 499, 523.
3. Percy Scholes, *The Puritans & Music* (London: Oxford University Press, 1934), 304–12.
4. Ronald Frye, 'The Teachings of Classical Puritanism on Conjugal Love,' *Studies in the Renaissance 2* (1955), 149, 153–55.
5. Leland Ryken, *Worldly Saints* (Grand Rapids: Zondervan, 1986), 43–45.
6. This article uses sources to represent the Puritan position on the basis of the definition articulated by Patrick Collinson in *The Elizabethan Puritan Movement* (Berkeley: University of California Press, 1967), 13, 22–27, and Peter Lake in *Moderate Puritans and the Elizabethan Church* (Cambridge: Cambridge University Press, 1982), 1–12, 279–92. Both deny that the Puritans should be defined as a party opposed to the Anglicans. They were, instead, fervent believers, 'the hotter sort of Protestant,' men and women who actively strove for godliness and were personally convinced of the truths of Protestant Christianity. This article confines itself to English Puritans before the civil war, specifically from Thomas Becon's work on matrimony published in 1542 to Daniel Rogers', published in 1642.
7. For a thorough, balanced, and meticulously documented overview of Roman Catholic attitudes toward sex from the Patristic age to the Council of Trent, see Derrick S. Bailey, *Sexual Relation in Christian Thought* (New York: Harper & Brothers, 1959), 19–166, 179–80. The following five paragraphs depend somewhat on pp. 19–102 of his book.
8. See e.g. Augustine, *The City of God* (New York: Random House, 1950), 14.16–18, 23, 26.
9. Bailey, *Sexual Relation*, 44–58.
10. Augustine, *City of God* 14.21.
11. Some praised marriages in which husband and wife agreed to remain virgins permanently.
12. Thomas Aquinas, *Summa theologica* (New York: Benziger Brothers, 1922), Q41, A3; Q49, A4.
13. Ibid., Q41, A3–4.
14. Ludovico (or Juan) Vives, *The Instruction of a Christian Woman* (London, 1557), D4, H4, Aa3.
15. Thomas Becon, *The Worckes of Thomas Becon* (London: J. Day, 1563), 585r. Becon inveighed against clerical celibacy for over eighty pages (575v–616r).
16. See Ed and Gaye Wheat, *Intended for Pleasure: New Approaches to Sexual Intimacy in Christian Marriage* (Old Tappan, NJ: Revell, 1977), 19–23 passim. The title says enough.
17. John Calvin, *Institutes of the Christian Religion* (LCC; Philadelphia: Westminster, 1960), 4.12–28 and 3.19.7–11.
18. Thomas Becon, *The Catechism of Thomas Becon with Other Pieces* (The Parker Society

Publications 3; Cambridge: Cambridge University Press, 1844), 103-4. Throughout this article spelling has been modernized in quotations but not in titles.

19. Becon, *Worckes*, 609v.

20. Robert Cleaver, *A Godley Forme of Household Government* (London: T. Creede, 1603), 140, 158, 182.

21. William Perkins, *The Workes of William Perkins* (3 vols; Cambridge: J. Legatt and Cantrell Legge, 1616-18), 3.689.

22. John Dod, *A Plaine and Familiar Exposition of the Ten Commandments* (London: F. Kingston, 1612), 287, 290-91.

23. Ibid., 291.

24. The length of two sermons indicates that he inserted additional material for publication.

25. Thomas Gataker, *Certaine Sermons* (2 vols.; London: J. Haviland, 1635), 2.206.

26. Thomas Gataker and William Bradshaw, *Two Marriage Sermons* (London: W. Jones, 1620), 14.

27. Daniel Rogers, *Matrimoniall Honour* (London: T. Harper, 1642), 146-50.

28. Ibid., 188-89.

29. William Gouge, *Of Domesticall Duties* (London: J. Haviland, 1622), 221-22.

30. Ibid., 224.

31. Ibid., 217.

32. Ibid., 360-61, 223.

33. John Robinson, *The Works of Robinson, the Pilgrim Father* (London: John Snow, 1851), 3. 241-42.

34. Robert Bolton, *Some Generall Directions for a Comfortable Walking With God* (London: Legatt, 1634), 242-44.

35. Gataker, *Sermons* 2.165.

36. William Whately, *Directions for Married Persons* (ed. John Wesley; Christian Library; London: T. Cordeux, 1821), 12, 265. This edition is Wesley's abridgement of *A Bride Bush: Or a Direction for Married Persons* (2d expanded ed.; London: B. Alsop, 1623).

37. Ibid.

38. Nicholas Byfield, *A Commentary on the Three 1st Chapters of the 1st Epistle General of St. Peter* (London: M. Flesher and R. Young, 1637), 600; Rogers, *Honour*, 178, cf. 164, 177.

39. Robert Cleaver, *A Godly Forme of Household Government* (London: T. Creede, 1603), 157; Gouge, *Duties*, 224, inter alia.

40. Whately, *Directions*, 265.

41. Rogers, *Honour*, 177-80. Luther, for contrast, suggested biweekly relations as a guide; see Steven Ozment, *When Fathers Ruled: Family Life in Reformation Europe* (Cambridge, MA; Harvard University Press, 1983), 119.

42. Bolton, *Walking*, 384.

43. Whately, *Directions*, 262-63.

44. Cleaver, *Godly Form*, 158; Rogers, *Honour*, 179; Samuel Hieron, *The Sermons of Master Samuel Hieron* (London: J. Legatt, 1624), 410.

45. Rogers, *Honour*, 173.

46. Bolton, *Walking*, 243-44.

47. Hieron, *Sermons*, 410.

48. Cleaver, *Godly Form*, 301.

49. Whately, *Directions*, 263, 266.

50. Richard Greenham, *The Works of Richard Greenham* (London: H.H., 1605), 277.

51. Becon, *Catechism*, 643-50. The text is from a sermon, 'An Homily Against Whoredom.'

52. Rogers, *Honour*, 327 ff.

53. *Ibid.*, 344, 351, 348 respectively.

54. Nicholas Byfield, *An Exposition upon the Epistle to the Colossians* (London: James Nisbet and Co., 1868), 359-60 (first published in London, 1615).

55. Gouge, *Duties*, 219-21.

56. For example, both Frye and Ryken, on the basis of brief remarks open to different interpretations, claim Whately, who probably had the most negative attitude toward sex, for their case that the Puritans were liberators. both also quote a statement from Gataker permitting playful and pleasurable contact betwen couples, but neither cites an equally powerful and vivid (hence quotable) admonition against lust and license in marriage. I believe Frye, Stone, and Koehler fell into the first error mentioned. Ryken surely committed the second.

57. For God's judgment of secret acts, see Bolton above (note 46). For marriage at the time of sexual need, see Gouge, *Duties*, 564-65.

58. John Bodenham, *Politeuphuia or Wits Commonwealth* (London: J. Flesher, 1647), 74.

59. Richard Brathwaite, *English Gentleman* (London: J. Haviland, 1630), 305-6.
60. See Stone, *Family*, 512.
61. Robinson, *Works* 3,128.
62. Perkins, *Workes* 3.689.
63. Bolton, *Walking* 154-206.
64. Frye, 'Love,' 156-58.
65. Ibid., 159.
66. Bailey, *Sexual Relation*, 133-34.
67. Richard Brathwaite, *The English Gentlewoman* (London: B. Alsop and T. Fawcet, 1631), 1-26, 138, 147.
68. See, respectively, Richard Brathwaite, *Ar't Asleepe Husband?* (London: R. Bishop, 1640); Thomas Overbury, *His Wife with Additions of New Characters and Many Other Witty Conceits* (London: I.I., 1627); and Thomas Swetnam, *The Arraignment of Lewde, Idle, Forward & Unconstant Women: or the Vanitie of Them, Choose You Whether* (London: T. Norris, 1645).
69. Stone, *Family*, 546-622.
70. Calvin, *Institutes* 2.8.44; 3.10.2.

2. Sexuality and Gender

The chief impetus for re-examining and reconstructing Christian notions of sexuality has come from the Christian feminist and womanist movements. In exposing the androcentric fallacy at the heart of most Christian theology and the connections between the marginalisation and disempowerment of women, gay men, and black people, feminist theology gives notice of the complete rethinking of Christian doctrine and practice that will be necessary when attempting to do theology from a body-affirming, women-affirming perspective.

Astri Hauge in 'Feminist Theology as Critique and Renewal of Theology' provides a useful introduction to and analysis of feminist theologies and their exposure of and challenge to androcentric theologies.

Carter Heyward addresses a question with which every Christian feminist struggles: 'Is a Self-Respecting Christian Woman an Oxymoron?' Can Christianity be ultimately liberating for women, gay men, black people, disabled people and all those who have been deprived of a sense of self-respect by the body-hating, misogynistic, dualistic tradition within Christianity? Heyward believes that it can, that it is, but always 'in spite of its own institutional sin', and only because minorities within the Church, with their 'epistemological privilege', have the ability and courage to challenge patriarchally constructed theology and offer an alternative hermeneutic. Heyward makes it quite clear that many in the Church fear self-respecting (i.e. feminist) women and gay men because in their own persons they shake the foundations of the theological system, particularly the systems of authority, and threaten the political system too. As Heyward's article illustrates there has been a turning of the tide – many Christian women, gay men and members of other minorities have ceased to look to a Church institution which has marginalised and oppressed us for legitimation of our lives. They have learnt to trust their own experience of God, not merely as private individuals, but as communities.

One of the most important responses to feminist theology has been theological reflection by men on masculinity. Where this has been an attempt to defend contemporary notions of masculinity from the 'attack' of feminism it has been an unhelpful and dangerous phenomenon, but where men have attempted to acknowledge the truth of much of the feminist critique and engage in theological reflection upon it from the perspectives of maleness the result has been constructive and healing. As J. Michael Hester notes, 'many wives and children bear the burden of men's difficulty with relationships often leaving them starving for attention'. In his article 'Men in Relationships: Redeeming Masculinity' Hester reflects upon men and their problems with intimacy. He details the way in which western constructs of masculinity associate intimacy with femininity. Hester suggests that they need to replace the Conquering Hero image of masculinity with the Healer 'who cares for the environment and relationships', the Soldier with the Mediator, the Breadwinner with the Companion, the Expert with the Colleague and the Lord with the Nurturer. Hester finds a model for such a redeemed masculinity in the biblical story of the friendship between David and Jonathan and ultimately in the person of our brother Jesus Christ. What Hester overlooks is the tragic outcome of both these stories: these men suffered for their rejection of contemporary constructs of masculinity. Concepts of masculinity are enforced structurally and politically, and there is a limit to the effectiveness of individual 'conversions'.

One of the most important tasks of feminist theology has been the deconstruction of the 'biology is destiny' arguments of natural theology by the unmasking of the androcentric bias of such arguments. Men and women may speak with different voices, to use Carol Gilligan's phrase, but these voices do not derive from inherent, essential biological differences but from being born and nurtured in a world which imposes rigid concepts of gender differences upon them. James Ashbrook, in 'Different Voices, Different Genes: "Male and Female Created God Them"', examines the genetic, hormonal and physiological evidence for differences between the sexes arguing that 'we hear different voices because of different genes' and that 'the cultural contrasts are derived from biological substrata'. Using this scientific data Ashbrook constructs a theology of complementarity. The theological concept of complementarity is not very old but has quickly been adopted by authors of official Church documents as an argument against the affirmation of lesbian and gay relationships. Men and women, it is argued, are created fundamentally different and when in relationship they complement each other and reflect the full image of God. Although undoubtedly challenging to the feminist approach Ashbrook's argument has some important flaws. For example, he fails to acknowledge the non-neutrality of the scientific project. He also ignores the legitimation his argument may be seen to give to unjust and violent behaviour between men and women and lastly he fails to acknowledge that the heart of Christian tradition has always affirmed that biology is not destiny – it is possible and desirable to be 'born again' into a new way of relating and being, defined not by biology but by grace and love.

Roland Martinson, in 'Androgyny and Beyond', also asks questions about the origins of differences between men and women but acknowledges that there are as yet no clear answers. His concern is the call that some make for the adoption of 'androgyny', that is the embodiment of so-called masculine and feminine characteristics in all people. Martinson questions the value of this vision, noting the social construction of notions of masculinity and femininity, and asking whether all such qualities (most clearly and influentially listed by C.G. Jung) are in fact desirable. He also exposes the inherent dualism behind the whole concept of androgyny. Instead he argues that Christian faith should seek to establish justice, mutuality and equality for men and women and 'enfranchise a broader range of constructive human potentialities'.

Astri Hauge is a researcher at the Norwegian Lutheran College and Hospital, Oslo, Norway. Her article 'Feminist Theology as Critique and Renewal of Theology' was first published in *Themelios*, Vol. 17.3, April/May 1992, pp. 8–11.

Roland Martinson teaches Theology at the Luther Northwestern Theological Seminary, St Paul, Minnesota. His article 'Androgyny and Beyond' was first published in *Word and World: Theology for Christian Ministry*, vol. 5, Fall 1985, pp. 370–79.

James Ashbrook is Senior Scholar in Religion and Personality at the Garrett-Evangelical Theological Seminary. His article 'Different Voices, Different Genes: "Male and Female Created God Them"' was first published in *The Journal of Pastoral Care*, vol. 46, no. 2, Summer 1992, pp. 174–83.

J. Michael Hester's article 'Men in Relationships: Redeeming Masculinity' was first published in *Review and Expositor*, vol. 87, Winter 1990, pp. 107–19.

Carter Heyward is Howard Chandler Robbins Professor of Theology at the Episcopal Divinity School, Cambridge MA. Her article 'Is a Self-Respecting Christian Woman an Oxymoron?' was first published in *Religion and Intellectual Life*, vol. 3. no. 2, Winter 1986, pp. 45–62.

2.1 Feminist Theology as Critique and Renewal of Theology

Astri Hauge

The Background of Feminist Theology

It is impossible to separate Christian theology from the social context and nature of the church in any era in which the theology is produced. We need to recognize that while the Bible is our final and permanent authority, theology, like the church itself, is in constant need of reform and renewal. The church's teaching on the relation between men and women could be argued to have historically owed more to the social nature of the church than to biblical revelation. It seems to many observers that traditional Christianity has taught the *equality of souls* for God and in the world to come, and the *inequality of the sexes* in this world and in the church. Throughout most of its history, the major part of the church has been a patriarchal institution based on an anthropology which defined the male as superior and 'head' and the female as inferior and subordinate. Through its sexually distinguished 'doctrine of man' it has for centuries legitimated laws and structures in society which secured male rule and demanded female obedience.[1]

Within the Christian church, however, there have been several women and men who have discovered the seeds of equality within the Bible and have perceived the equal status of man and woman as an idea intrinsic to the gospel. Many Christian women have experienced a discrepancy betwen the *gospel* from which they have drawn strength and inspiration and the male-dominated *church* which has restricted their life and ministry. In a sense, then, feminist theology has existed as long as there have been women who have reflected upon their Christian faith and their Bible in a way that differed from the dominant patriarchal tradition of interpretation. Very often, however, the egalitarian interpretations were ignored and forgotten or criticized and rejected and then sank into oblivion.

Modern feminist theology emerged in the USA at the end of the 1960s. It is rooted primarily in Christian women's experience of living under the pressure of patriarchal ideology and structures claimed to be the eternal will of God. The modern feminist movement has provided a better climate than earlier times for the growth of feminist theology: the general consciousness-raising among women, the greater awareness of women's issues in society and, not least, the experience that 'sisterhood is powerful' have been ideological and social factors giving women inspiration and courage to take on the hard task of critical reconsideration of church life and theology.

What is Meant by 'Feminist Theology'?

Feminist theology at present is both a critical voice *within* the church and a revolt *against* the church from women outside who are determined to develop religious alternatives. In the USA, where the major part of feminist theology has been published so far, 'theology' usually has a much wider meaning than in Europe. The notion comprises any systematic reflection upon questions of the foundation and meaning of life, whether connected to a religious tradition (Christianity, native American religion, *etc.*) or not. The boundaries between general philosophy of religion, religious studies and theology related to a particular religion are often indistinct.

There is no one feminist theology that can represent the whole, but rather a multitude of feminist theologies. They not only diverge in style and content but also conflict with each other with regard to the positions they hold, *e.g.* in their assessment of the Christian tradition.[2] One should therefore abstain from making general judgments on feminist theology. In spite of the differences, however, it is possible to point out some distinct methodological tendencies and common feminist convictions.

I will define feminist theology as *reflection on the content and meaning of religion with particular regard to women's status and situation, which recognizes the use and misuse of religion in the past and the present for the oppression of women and has as its aim to contribute to the liberation of women*. This is a descriptive definition which can apply to various feminist theologies, both within and outside Christianity. These various theologies have some basic feminist assumptions in common:

1. *Patriarchy* is the big problem that has given rise to feminist movements that struggle for women's liberation. 'Patriarchal' refers to institutions, social structures and ideologies that implicitly assume or explicitly claim the superior status of males and their 'natural' right to exercise authority and leadership in society, family and church. (Some prefer 'sexism' as characterization of the sexual hierarchy and gender ideology in contemporary societies where traditional patriarchal ideology and structures have waned.)
2. Feminist theology, as feminism in general, is based on an *egalitarian anthropology*, claiming the full equality of male and female (equal dignity, equal and full humanity, entitled to equal rights, *etc.*).[3]
3. The corollary of this anthropological stance is the *commitment to social and political struggle* against specific forms of oppression

and for the liberation of women, in order to create a society with equality and freedom for all.

Some readers might be unfamiliar with the usage of the key concepts *sex* and *gender* in modern feminist literature: (i) *Sex* is a *biological designation* and corresponds to *male* and *female* as biological/sexual definitions. (ii) *Gender* is a *social designation* referring to sociocultural consequences or implications of sex, *i.e.* the particular cultural shape of sex (biological nature) into different roles, status and normative patterns of behaviour attributed to men and women in a given culture. (iii) *Gender* can also be distinguished as a *symbolic, ideological category* referring to sexual myths, ideas about female and male nature, polarized philosophical and ideological definitions of *masculine* and *feminine*; these provide the foundation for sociocultural inequality.

These distinctions of the notions 'sex' and 'gender' are by and large shared by feminist writers. The main point is the claim that differences between men and women concerning attitudes, values, thinking, *etc.* are not naturally given, but predominantly determined by culture. This view is held by the majority of feminists.

Feminist Critique of Traditional Theology

In Western societies (as in nearly all societies) the cultural hegemony has rested in the hands of men. The right to define and describe reality, including the 'nature' and 'proper role' of female and male, has been a prerogative of the sciences, philosophy and theology in which men held the authority positions. Feminist scholars in all fields seek to explore the implications of this fact.

First of all, feminists emphasize that theology has been developed not simply by males, but by males within a patriarchal culture and church. In mainstream theology this has not been recognized as a problem deserving consideration. Though contemporary philosophy and theology recognize the significance of a person's preunderstanding in the process of interpretation, theology has paid little attention to the wider sociocultural context in which the interpreter's preunderstanding has been shaped. Like other liberation theologies, feminist theology criticizes the predominant Western academic theology for its lack of awareness about the significance of socioeconomic context and social class for theological work. Consequently, according to feminists, theology has legitimated oppressive social structures or, at least, been insensitive to injustice and structural evil. Feminists add that male scholars take sexual hierarchy for granted, support it ideologically, or fail to discover the phenomenon at all. In a patriarchal context the tacit preunderstanding of males (and often of females, too) is normally a patriarchal understanding of reality, except for individuals who somehow have developed a critical attitude toward the existing order.

Furthermore, in a social system where sex has been (and still is, in part) the most basic criterion for the distribution of social roles and functions, the typical life experience of males and females respectively becomes very different. Nevertheless, most male scholars have not recognized the hermeneutical significance of gender and apparently assume that their perspective is universally human. Therefore they have not been able to discover or willing to accept women's perspective, as a different approach from a different preunderstanding, as a legitimate and necessary perspective.

The critique raised by feminist theologians against the male-dominated theological traditions is paralleled by feminist critique of other academic studies. It can be summed up in the notion *androcentrism* (male-centredness): sociologically, men are at the centre of both the religious and the secular community, whereas women live on the periphery and are therefore often outside men's scope. Women's world, as well as the whole human world, has been described from men's perspective and interpreted by means of men's concepts and thoughts, if it has been seen at all. Often women and women's issues are neglected, marginalized or blotted out altogether. This is a result of gender-biased presuppositions and androcentric answers to methodological questions: What is the object (or subject matter) of this discipline? What are the important issues and problems? Which sources are important, and which data are relevant in dealing with this problem? Very few, if any, would explicitly exclude women's issues or gender issues when answering such questions. Nevertheless, the major part of male studies implicitly shows the impact of androcentric priorities. The prevalent silence in mainstream theology about sexism and patriarchalism in church and society, past and present, is striking evidence of the non-priority of issues which are crucial to women.[4]

And just here is the dividing line between feminist and non-feminist theologies: Is *sexism* a serious problem? And if so, is it a problem for which theology has some responsibility, a problem which should be on the theological agenda? Feminists say yes, pointing to the pervasive impact of a long patriarchal tradition on church life and on our culture in general. Feminist theologians agree that androcentrism is an adequate general characterization of traditional theology, but diverge in their assessment of the range and profundity of the distortions brought upon theology by an androcentric orientation and patriarchal assumptions. As a result of the long-term struggle of the women's movement, clear-cut patriarchal ideology and power structures in society have waned and egalitarianism has made progress in the Western world. This has also had an impact on contemporary theology. In my opinion, one should not simply talk of mainstream theology as 'patriarchal' or 'androcentric', but discern between three levels of androcentrism in theology:

1. Overtly patriarchal theologies, which are based on a

conscious/explicit patriarchal ideology (defining male-female as respectively superior and subordinate/inferior) and explicitly legitimize a patriarchal ordering of society.

2. Implicitly patriarchal theologies, which have a lot of subtle (perhaps unconscious) patriarchal assumptions without propagating patriarchal ideology; they function to support traditional attitudes.

3. 'Egalitarian' theologies, which in principle recognize the equality of the sexes but have little insight into the androcentric presuppositions and priorities built into their methodologies and traditions. In practice they are unable to discover gender issues and deal adequately with them.

Feminist Theology as Methodological Renewal

The feminist critique of traditional academic theology naturally leads to a reconsideration of methodological issues.[5] However, often methodological reflections are scanty, perhaps lacking altogether. Nevertheless, there is always an implicit methodology which can be analysed. I will roughly indicate the methodological distinctiveness of feminist theology in a few points:

1. Contrary to mainstream theology, which is assumed to be 'gender neutral', feminist theology claims to be developed out of women's perspective or feminist perspective. Its scholarly ideal is not the 'impartiality' or 'objectivity' of established scholarship, but the conscious 'advocacy stance' of liberation theologies in favour of the oppressed. Feminist theology aims at providing a contribution to the liberation of women and other oppressed groups, seeing itself as a part of the wider feminist struggle for liberation.

    The notions 'women's perspective' and 'feminist perspective' need some clarification. 'Women's perspective' seems to imply that women have a common perspective which males do not and cannot have. However, this biologically defined group comprises women adhering to traditional womanliness as defined by patriarchy (=*femininity*) as well as women revolting against it (=*feminism*). 'Women's perspective' is therefore, in my opinion, an indistinct notion which easily blurs the existing ideological conflicts among women. 'Feminist perspective' is a more stringent notion because it points to a feminist understanding of reality (*i.e.* patriarchy or sexual hierarchy as an unjust reality, legitimated by ideologies and religious beliefs, *etc.*). A feminist perspective conflicts naturally with a patriarchal perspective, which considers the sexual hierarchy the right and natural order of things. It also conflicts with any kind of perspective which lacks awareness of sexism as a problem in our culture.

2. Many feminist theologians emphasize that feminist theology is not created by isolated individuals, but is developed in a community doing theology together in a communal process of reflection.

3. Traditionally, the various theological disciplines (except pastoral theology) have mainly been concerned with the theoretical aspects of religion (like holy scriptures, dogmas, theological concepts, *etc.*), their traditioning, adaptation, and the mutual influence of religious and philosophical *ideas* throughout history. Feminist theology extends its field of interest beyond the ideas to the *sociopolitical* and *psychological consequences* of religious ideas and Christian practices. Their impact on laws, social structures, popular attitudes and beliefs has determined the framework of women's (and men's) lives and, hence, formed individual women's experiences to a high degree. This broad scope makes a bridge from feminist theology to women's studies in other fields, like history, sociology, psychology, social anthropology, *etc.* Theories and findings are adopted and employed to shed new light on various issues in theology.

4. The most important and distinctive methodological novelty in feminist theology is the principal claim that *women's experience provides important data and insight for theological work.*

'Women's experience' is in itself an ambiguous concept and is rarely defined. Is there a common women's experience across cultural, religious and political borders, or do we talk about experience related to a particular group, or some individual women's experience? From the contents of numerous contributions one can infer that the concept comprises the totality of women's experience in everyday life, in the private as well as in the public sphere, 'secular' experience as well as religious experience, or experiences related to religious institutions. In practice it is used with different contents or emphases by different writers. Many writers, perhaps a majority, emphasize women's social experience (determined by sociocultural factors),[6] while others primarily focus upon bodily experience (determined by biology).[7]

'Women's experience is the source and norm of feminist theology' is a frequently used slogan in the US. What is really the status and function of women's experience in doing theology? Is it the source not only of new *questions* and perspectives, but also of the new *answers* women are searching for? There is no consensus upon these fundamental issues. Radical feminist theology clearly tends to regard women's experience as a normative *'text'* and gives it status as an independent source of knowledge of the divine. Others give it mainly the status of *context*, from which new, existential questions emerge. Of course, this is a simplification of the various positions actually taken on a very complex issue.

In brief: Women's various experience of oppression throughout history and in our time is the basic experiential impetus for doing theology from a feminist perspective. This implies usually both a critical analysis of the ways in which religious beliefs, institutions and practices have overtly legitimated oppression or in subtler ways supported sexism, and also the development of a viable alternative, a non-sexist theology. Since mainstream theology has ignored women's experience and the questions and challenges emerging from it, feminists recognize the relevance of Mary Daly's advice: women must 'begin asking non-questions and start discovering, reporting, and analyzing non-data'.[8]

Feminist Theology: Reform or Replacement of Christian Theology?

The claim that women's experience of oppression is a basic presupposition for feminist theology does not imply that all feminist theologians have strong experiences of being oppressed in their churches or in their social life. However, we have an important common ground in the knowledge and consciousness of women's sufferings past and present in the name of God. Many women still suffer or protest because their churches promote patriarchal teachings which place women in a subordinate and restricted role because of their sex. Although many churches have abandoned theologies of women's subordination and even ordain women, sexism is not abolished as an ideological and structural reality.

The undeniable link between Christianity and the patriarchal order of Western societies gives rise to a fundamental question: Is Christianity essentially oppressive to women, or has Christian faith been misused to legitimize patriarchal systems contrary to its intentions? Is it possible to reform or convert a patriarchally stamped theology into an egalitarian theology which is liberating to women? Or do convinced feminists have to reject this tradition and create a theology for women on quite another basis?

Feminist theologians give diverging answers to these essential questions. A frequently used typology employs two main categories of feminist theology: (i) the *reformist* one, wanting to cleanse Christian theology from patriarchalism and transform it into an egalitarian theology; and (ii) the *revolutionary* one, considering Christianity as inherently and essentially misogynous and therefore working to develop a new feminist theology on a different basis. Those belonging to the first category emphasize the egalitarian and liberating elements of the Christian tradition (primarily in the Bible). Patriarchy, in their view, is the historical and cultural framework which has impacted Christianity, but it is not an essential part of the gospel. The revolutionary feminist theologians consider it a waste of time to search for liberating pieces in a religion permeated by patriarchal ideology.[9]

However, this categorization is a bit too simple and inadequate to comprise the recent developments within feminist theology. Still taking the attitude to the Christian tradition as the basis for the typology, one should distinguish between at least three main categories, in my opinion:

1. *Moderate reformist feminist theology* will criticize and replace patriarchal interpretations of biblical texts, dogmas, *etc.*, and include issues related to women's experience in the various theological disciplines. The Bible is the most basic source, but there are different views on the relation between revelation and Scripture, biblical authority, *etc.* The moderate reformists are apologetic, defending the relevance of the Christian tradition and its compatibility with crucial aspects of feminism. Such theologies can take the form of a feminist version of some existing theological direction, *e.g.* liberation theology, process theology, various confessional theologies. [10]

2. *Radical reformist feminist theology* differs from the moderate one primarily on two basic issues. The radical reformists also find something usable in the Bible, but have a very critical stance to its central message (the biblical witness to the triune God, the gospel of the crucified and risen Jesus Christ). It is considered a collection of religious experiences of the past which in principle should not be bestowed with greater truthfulness and authority than other religious experiences. There is a clear tendency to syncretism, *e.g.* in making a selection of sources from the Christian tradition and from other religious traditions to meet the religious and psychological needs of feminists. [11]

3. *Revolutionary, radical feminist theology* departs from the two former types in its total rejection of the Christian tradition and in its programme of developing an alternative feminist religion and theology (or *thea*logy, as some Goddess theorists put it). However, there is no one alternative, but rather a multitude of post-Christian and non-Christian feminist theologies founded on various theoretical bases and drawing upon diverse sources (in addition to 'women's experience', of course): contemporary feminist philosophy and analysis of culture, religion and society, psychological theory in feminist reinterpretations, ancient religious traditions, *e.g.* Goddess religions and witchcraft, and living 'primitive' religions, *e.g.* shamanism. [12]

Evangelical Feminist Theology: No Contradiction in Terms

It is my firm conviction that an evangelical and biblically rooted feminist theology is not only possible but also necessary for the health of the Christian church and its life and mission in the world. In the following I will briefly give some reasons for this position. It should be understood, therefore, that in the remaining paragraphs of this article, I am discussing the role of a feminist theology that is based upon evangelical presuppositions.

1. Like numerous other Christian feminists I hold the view that the egalitarian elements of the Bible have priority over the patriarchal ideas in terms of theological significance though not in terms of quantity. Space does not allow in-depth arguments for this view, only some brief suggestions. According to Genesis 1–3, male and female have equal status in *creation*; male dominion is a consequence of sin. (Most Christians have not perceived the judgment upon Adam as a prohibition against combating 'weeds and thorns' by means of agricultural technology, a position inconsistent with the claim that male dominion is the eternal law of God.) *Jesus'* attitude to women was remarkably egalitarian and liberating. *Redemption* implies a freedom from the bondage caused by the fall; partly and anticipated in this era, fully in the era to come. Through *salvation* and *baptism* male and female have equal status (Gal. 3:28). The church has seen it as a corollary of the gospel to fight the social and ecclesiastical inequality between Jews and Gentiles (in Paul's time) and later on the social inequality between slaves and free human beings; thus it is in accordance with the gospel to abolish the social inequality betwen men and women. *Paul's prescriptions* of women's subordination should primarily be understood as a consequence of his missionary principles: for the sake of the gospel, Christians should adapt to current customs when possible and avoid unnecessary stumbling blocks. (It is noteworthy that the domestic codes do not tell husbands to rule over their wives. Thus the patriarchalism of the NT is limited and toned down.) In brief, though the Bible was written in a patriarchal culture and reflects patriarchal customs and attitudes, it contains remarkably non- and anti-patriarchal elements connected with central aspects of its content.

2. Protestant theology has some basic assumptions which provide a link to aspects of the feminist critique. The majority of Protestants agree upon the *reality of sin* also in reborn Christians and recognize *human limitation* in understanding God's will (*cf.* also 1 Cor. 13:9–12). Hence, although theology has normative pretensions, one should admit that theology is always a partial and limited interpretation of the word, acts and intentions of God. As such it cannot be wholly untainted by human sinfulness and self-assertion. The combination of selfishness (of individuals and groups) and limited understanding (which often is claimed to be the full truth) can result in theologies that legitimate existing unjust power structures and the exploitation of the poor by the privileged ones.[13] Christian theology should understand itself as a type of human intellectual enterprise which is always in need of self-criticism as well as criticism from outside. An adequate response from the theological establishment to the feminist critique is not rejection or neglect, but rather the self-critical question: *What truth* does this feminist critique contain?

3. Most Protestants hold the view that 'the priesthood of all believers', *i.e.* the community of faith, is assigned the ultimate responsibility for teaching and preaching the Word of God in the world. Therefore theology should be seen as *the continual reflection of the whole people of God upon its faith and upon its witness to the gospel in words and deeds in the world, founded upon the biblical testimony of God's revelation as its normative source of knowledge about God.* The theological task requires not only the skills of theological experts. The particular perspectives, experiences, insights and concerns of Christians living in various cultural contexts and life situations are contributions needed to illuminate the situation in which the people of God live and bring their witness.

4. The different experiential contexts of women and men provide a sufficient argument for a theology incorporating women's experience. The reflection of God's people upon their faith and witness is biased and partial when the majority of God's people are practically excluded from it. The typical traditional women's experience of childcare and housework as well as the 'feminist' experience of struggling against various kinds of oppression both provide significant insights that until recently have had no place in theology. However, a feminist theology should not be regarded as a completion of male-authored theology considered as basically right, though limited. An 'equal but different' (complementarity) model of men's and women's experience fails to address the problems of androcentism and patriarchalism within predominant theology. A feminist theology must be critical, liberating and constructive. The pervasiveness of androcentric thought within the established theological tradition urges clearing up in the attic of theology. Feminist theology must explore critically the ramifications of androcentrism in theology and its effects in church and society.

5. Feminist theology must not only demand for itself the right to deal with the problems of sexism and androcentrism. These problems need also to be taken seriously and put on the agenda of established male-dominated theology. As long as its silence about sexism continues, and as long as androcentric thought goes on unrecognized, the predominant theology will continually reproduce its inherent biases. It is not enough that women's engagement in feminist theology is tolerated as a kind of special interest, or that feminist challenges to androcentric methodology and interpretations are accepted as interesting new viewpoints. Such responses are insufficient to bring about changes in the way mainstream theology is done by the theological establishment. Therefore it is an important task to analyse further the institutional conditions and the hindrances for doing feminist theology and for transforming androcentric theology into a truly inclusive theology.

6. Feminist theology intends to bring about a renewal of theology, not

only to criticize. Its constructive task is to reflect upon the whole of Christian faith and praxis from a feminist perspective. Taking women's experience seriously and making women's issues visible is an important dimension of this constructive work. It is an urgent task to develop a methodology for a feminist theology which is consciously and definitely *Christian* and *feminist* at the same time. This requires, in my opinion, both *a fundamental commitment to the gospel and to Jesus Christ as the centre of faith,* and *a commitment to women's liberation and to combating the evil of sexism as its particular centre of concern.* The methodology of a biblically rooted feminist theology will share basic principles with traditional theology, while others will be challenged. The concern for women's liberation calls for a creative transformation of methodology which can enable theology to integrate insights from women's experience and feminist scholarship. For the sake of its own insight, and for the sake of its tasks toward the church and the world, it must stay in a two-way critical and informative dialogue with non-feminist Christians as well as with non-Christian feminists. A Christian feminist theology must therefore live in a double context, the Christian church and the community of women.

Notes

1. *Cf.* Elizabeth Clark and Herbert Richardson (eds.), *Women and Religion. A Feminist Sourcebook of Christian Thought* (New York, 1977); George Tavard, *Woman in Christian Tradition* (Notre Dame, Indiana, 1973); Rosemary R. Ruether (ed.), *Religion and Sexism: Images of Woman in the Jewish and Christian Traditions* (New York, 1974); Rosemary Ruether and Eleanor McLaughlin (eds.), *Women of Spirit. Female Leadership in the Jewish and Christian Traditions* (New York, 1979).
2. *Cf.* the anthology *Womanspirit Rising* (eds. Carol P. Christ and Judith Paskow, San Francisco, 1979), with contributions from Christian, Jewish and non-Christian feminist theologians.
3. It is disputable whether some of the radical feminist theologians hold a position of female superiority, *e.g.* Mary Daly's *Gyn/Ecology* (Boston, 1979).
4. As one of the exceptions can be mentioned Paul K. Jewett, *Man as Male and Female* (Grand Rapids, 1978) and *The Ordination of Women* (Grand Rapids, 1980).
5. Rosemary Ruether's *Sexism and God-Talk: Toward A Feminist Theology* (Boston, 1983) has a lengthy methodological account. In addition, biblical scholars like Elisabeth Schussler Fiorenza and Phyllis Trible also have extensive methodological contributions.
6. *E.g.* Rosemary Ruether, Letty Russell, Mary Daly (see notes 5, 8, 10–12).
7. *E.g.* Penelope Washbourn, *Becoming Woman: The Quest for Wholeness in Female Experience* (San Francisco, 1977).
8. Mary Daly, *Beyond God the Father: Toward a Philosophy of Women's Liberation* (Boston, 1973), pp. 11–12.
9. *Womanspirit Rising*, pp. 9–11.
10. Some representatives of this position are: Letty M. Russell, *Human Liberation in a Feminist Perspective – A Theology* (Philadelphia, 1974), *The Future of Partnership* (1979), *Growth in Partnership* (1981); Virginia R. Mollenkott, *Women, Men, and the Bible* (Nashville, 1977), *The Divine Feminine* (New York, 1983); Patricia Wilson-Kastner, *Faith, Feminism and the Christ* (Philadelphia, 1983).
11. Ruether's books *Sexism and God-Talk* and *Womanguides: Readings Toward a Feminist Theology* (Boston, 1985) are typical representatives of this position.
12. Mary Daly's later books (*e.g. Gyn/Ecology: The Meta-Ethics of Radical Feminism*, 1979, and *Pure Lust: Elemental Feminist Philosophy*, 1984) represent the more philosophical orientation within this category. Starhawk is a well-known theorist of feminist witchcraft religion which includes elements of ancient Goddess religion and contemporary shamanism. She is the author of *The Spiral Dance: A Rebirth of the Ancient Religion of the Great*

Goddess (San Francisco, 1979), *Dreaming the Dark: Magic, Sex and Politics* (Boston, 1982), *Truth or Dare: Encounters with Power, Authority and Mystery* (San Francisco, 1987). Naomi Goldenberg represents a Goddess theology based on a feminist reinterpretation of Jungian psychology: *Changes of the Gods. Feminism and the End of Traditional Religions* (Boston, 1979).

13. *Cf.* W.S. Swartley, *Slavery, Sabbath, War and Women: Case Issues in Biblical Interpretation* (Scottdale, 1983).

2.2 Is a Self-Respecting Christian Woman an Oxymoron?

Reflections on a Feminist Spirituality for Justice

Carter Heyward

Thank you for inviting me. I'm honored to be in this company – to be with Katie Finney again; to have learned so much from your responses, questions, and workshops; and also to have received gifts from my sister-lecturers: Rosemary Ruether's astute leadership in envisioning the future work of Christian feminists; Carol Christ's courage and passion in opening to many of us new vistas of womanpower; Kathy Green's challenging probing of Jewish feminist experiences and questions; and my colleague at the Episcopal Divinity School, Elisabeth Schüssler Fiorenza's brilliant discerning of possibilities for textual interpretation which does justice to women's lives.

The planners of this conference have put together a provocative agenda. There is however a major omission from the speakers' roster. None of us is Black, Hispanic, Asian, or native American. In late 20th Century U.S.A., we should be aware, at least, that any conversation about 'Feminism and Religious Experience' which takes place in the context of a nearly all-white group is a very limited conversation indeed and a testimony to the roots and effects of a racism which continues to plague us all.

Tonight I'm doing something I've only done two or three times before: singing and chanting a little in the course of my presentation. I do this for two reasons: First, to try to bring you into the composition of this written piece. As I worked on it, I found myself spontaneously humming and singing old hymns, chants, and songs by Holly Near and Meg Christian. The music became a source of the presentation itself. Second, I believe that art, music, and other nonexpository forms of communication often convey a more wholistic spirituality than the spoken word. I hope that the music may add a dimension to what I'm going to say and that it will round out some of the flatness of my words, which may otherwise seem tiring, especially here at the end of a very good – and very long – day. Please sing or hum with me, and do not worry that our tunes may be different. Feminism is, after all, a cacophony of diversity!

(*Chant*)
There is nothing sweet here
and nothing bitter
tonight today
only the pungent odor
of salty faith
rooted watered opening
turning and turning
opening and rooted
we are making
revolutions.[1]

It is fashionable today, in much of the Christian church, to immerse oneself in 'spirituality' *instead* of in work on behalf of justice. The fruits of the Spirit are relished by individuals as special gifts which can be enjoyed most fully in the privacy of one's own prayer-life. The political clutter and clamor of justice-making is portrayed as the special interest of those who are still stuck in the 60's. More and more 'spirituality' denotes the lofty aims of God and 'justice' the grubby work of human beings. Even religious feminists are apt to stumble into this dualistic pitfall, in which such aims as wholistic health and psychospiritual growth are set apart from, and take precedence over, any serious involvement in the collective work, struggle, and conflict which is vital to social transformation.

My presentation is rooted in the tension between the individual person's spiritual pilgrimage and the historic, now global, liberation movement for justice. In particular, I am concerned here with *justice for women – feminist justice.* I am interested in a *feminist spirituality*, in which individual women and men, who are committed to the daily well-being of *all* women, may be more fully empowered to struggle for, and celebrate the small changes which enhance the survival and dignity of every woman as well as the larger vision of justice. This global vision beckons us into solidarity with all women and other marginalized people, which means men who are oppressed on the basis of race, ethnicity, religion, class, sexual preference, disability, nationality, or age. Lest this vision appear so broad as to be beyond our capacity to view in concrete, daily terms, we should keep in mind that it is precisely *in* the small places of our lives and those of others that the vision is seeded. We cannot envision 'justice' if we set our sights pretentiously and arrogantly on what 'the whole world' ought to look like. For surely as U.S. history should make abundantly clear, we do not and ought not all look alike, act alike, believe alike. The people of Iran, China, Nicaragua, South Africa and the United States are different people with various cultures, languages, and gods. And so may it be forever in the multi-textured tapestry of creation and history.

Justice does not mean 'oneness' or 'unity' in the sense of 'sameness.' It does mean the creation of the conditions for mutual respect among all persons; hence justice involves, concretely, the creation of religious, national and cultural societies in which every person has ready access to food, shelter, medicine, education, work, and leisure time. Every woman, as well as every man, is entitled by birth to respect – the respect of others as well as self-respect. Thus, justice-making is, by definition, a feminist movement.[2]

'Respect' is, in fact, a synonym for non-sentimentalized 'love.' I employ the term 'respect' here in order to give substance to the meaning of 'love' as something more than simply 'affection' and something altogether other than 'charity.' In order to clarify connections between the individual's spirituality and the feminist liberation movement for justice, I want to focus my remarks on *self-respect*, which I take to be a primary psycho-spiritual aim of any authentic spirituality.

What does self-respect involve? In what ways does our prevailing cultural ethos support, or impede, self-respect – for women, and for men? As a Christian, I am particularly interested in the role of the church in creating or abrogating the conditions for self-respect – especially women's self-respect. I invite you to join me in exploring this terrain, which, I trust, may carry us on toward places in which we will be able to envision horizons of justice.

> *(Chant)*
> We shall respect our neighbors
> Just as we respect ourselves
> And in so doing
> We shall respect our God
> Which is an honest way
> Of stating the sacred truth
> Which men have obfuscated
> By telling us
> That we must love the Lord
> Our King and Master
> And, still, if we are able
> Our neighbors as ourselves.

A self-respecting woman is one whose life is rooted in a sense of her own positive value. She acts in a knowledge that she is as valuable a member of the human family as anyone else, and no more so. She acts on the basis of cooperative, rather than competitive expectations. She has nothing to prove. She owes no explanation, no defense, certainly no apology for her strong self-love. A self-respecting woman is one who has come into a creative liberating power, and she knows that this power which many feminists call God is in fact ours, not simply hers. A power which is shared, collaborative, common. A self-respecting woman lives among us as someone proud, someone humble, a woman grounded and vulnerable, able to be touched. A sister whose resources are available to us, a woman reserved, able to withold as well as to give, able to receive or to reject whatever is given to her. A self-respecting woman knows that whatever genuinely enhances her own well-being enhances us all, and whatever does her no good, pays her no true respect, is bad for the whole human family.

A self-respecting man could be characterized in the same way. Thus, in an important sense there is little difference between a self-respecting woman and a self-respecting man. To be either is difficult in our society. Neither women nor men are rewarded for living on the basis of a radical awareness that each and every person is valuable. Each person's creativity, and work, and relationships. No more and no less than any others. Any man or woman whose way of being among us reflects such an assumption is perhaps an anomaly in the vast, increasingly impersonal social order which has been constructed over 200 years as the stage in which the drama of advanced patriarchal capitalism is to be played out. Ours is a far cry from the world in which Adam Smith offered his vision of capitalism as a just socio-economic order in which every man, that is to say, every white, ostensibly heterosexual, propertied male, had a right to his own little castle, his house, his family, his trade, a chicken in his pot. Capitalism, Smith and other enlightened philosophers in Europe and the United States believed, would create the conditions for self-respect among white men with access to economic privilege. Few then or now seemed to grasp the ways in which community would be broken, and human responsibility obfuscated, by the presupposition that every man has certain inalienable rights: specifically freedoms of mind and movement, which must remain unfettered by, and take precedence over, all other possible goods including the basic social conditions for a humane society.

And so it is that the rights of 'man' – the white propertied male – take precedence over the civil rights of black people, the equal rights of women, the dignity of sexual nonconformists, the economic rights of the working classes, and most basically, the ready accessibility of survival resources for the whole human family. The failure, and I think it was a failure, of the white male architects of the United States Constitution, to foresee the fundamental flaws in a society founded essentially on freedom as a privilege for individual white men, rather than on justice as our arena of collective responsibility to one another, has been compounded in our century by the effects of a phobia which has held us in its grip: the doctrine of anti-communism. Those who continue to this day to shape our nation have been so hamstrung by this doctrine that the basic conditions for self-respect have been all but eliminated in our society, even for privileged white men.[3]

Self-respect is not a personal virtue, something which anyone can somehow find or create, if she or he turns inward and tries. Self-respect is a spiritual pilgrimage which cannot be made easily, if it can be made at all, without certain basic conditions for the journey. Food, shelter, education, medical care, meaningful work, leisure-time, and the encouraging of open minds are basic conditions for self-respect. As such, they are human rights which should be available to all. No one should have to earn them. No one should have to prove that he or she deserves them or is eligible for them. I am describing basic conditions for a just and decent human world.

> *(Sing)*
> 'Why are our history books so full of lies?
> No word is spoken of why the Indian dies.
> Or that the Chicanos love the California land
> Why do our books all say it was discovered by one white man?
> That's just a lie, one of the many,
> And we've had plenty
> I don't want more of the same.
> No more genocide in my name.'[4]

It's difficult for a man, regardless of his race, his religion, or his sexual preference, to be a self-respecting person in this society: similarly difficult for a woman of any color or culture. But there is a difference, and those who tell you that there is not speak lies. For example, that a woman can do anything she wants. That any woman who really wants to can make it in our society. That the Equal Rights Amendment is redundant. That women have it good. Or that any woman can have self-respect. Those who deny or downplay the pervasive effects of sexism and heterosexism in our society are running from something. Those who say that they don't have an opinion on women's rights. Or that they're neutral. Or that it doesn't make any difference to them, have aligned themselves *de facto* with the mighty forces which are intent upon keeping women of all colors, classes, cultures, and patterns of relational bonding, in our various subordinate places. As Bishop Desmond Tutu said recently in New York City, 'Whenever people say to you, "In this situation, we are neutral," you can always know that they have taken a decision to side with the powerful.'[5] A self-respecting man, be he black or white or brown or red or yellow, is swimming against strong patriarchal currents – what Mary O'Brien calls 'the male-stream' of competitive hegemony,[6] the public world of profit-oriented expectations, in which a gentle, open-minded man, who is committed to a more fully human society as the condition for his and others' self-respect, is likely to be dismissed, treated as if he were not a real man, trivialized, held in contempt, red-baited, fagbashed, jailed, otherwise brutalized. But the one thing he has going for him, especially if he is white, is a tenet built into the civil and religious structures of the United States: that a real man has not only a right, but moreover a responsibility, to work as hard as he can in full public view for himself – his livelihood, his family, his own well-being. As I've noted, this male prerogative is interpreted still today by legislators and judges as largely a white privilege, something that can be earned by those people, usually white males, with access to economic resources. Nowhere is this clearer than in the current Administration's efforts to turn back the clock on the small positive gains in affirmative action which have been made over the last 20 years.

A self-respecting woman today, regardless of her race, culture, class, or sexual preference, does not merely swim against the male-stream: by the very fact of her self-respect in sexist society, the self-respecting woman's activities and ideas generate such turmoil, cause such serious disturbance in the male-stream, that it is likely to become a drowning pool, an undertow which will most certainly suck down and destroy even the most able female contender, if she attempts to ford these mighty currents by herself, alone. The difference between a self-respecting man and a self-respecting woman in our society, is that unlike the man, the woman has no civil or religious mandate to struggle in full public view for herself. Within the limits of any particular political regime, whether it's Roosevelt's, Carter's, or Reagan's, for example, a woman is welcome to work publicly on behalf of others – husbands, employers, students, children, patients, refugees, or the massive corporate entities peculiar to advanced capitalism. But a woman is not encouraged by any dominant civil or moral custom to work, struggle, or speak publicly on her behalf. Since self-respect goes hand-in-hand with the person's commitment to act on behalf of her own well-being, as vital to the public good, a self-respecting woman represents, quite literally, a contradiction to the general public consensus of what constitutes the good society. She represents its demise, and is actually, for that reason, the bad woman. Thus the feminist movement, increasingly a movement for all women of all races, classes, cultures, and religions is, I believe, the most fundamentally threatening social force in this nation today. Not because it signals equal pay for equal work, the drafting of women, homosexual marriages, unisex bathrooms, or the undoing of discriminatory insurance policies, but because each of these bits and pieces is but one in a whole tapestry which is our society, our life together, our economic system, our political sensibilities, our religious assumptions and beliefs.

Please fantasize with me for a minute. Suppose all affluent, or economically relatively secure women, most of us white, were to step down publicly from the pedestal which has been used not to protect us from the world of white men, but rather the white men's public world from us. Suppose we were to say to the men in our lives, 'To hell with your sexist, racist, classist privilege. We don't want to be your ladies or your queens. We don't want our daughters and sons to be your princesses and princes. We don't want your money, your silent or your not-so-silent rage, your anxiety, your ulcers. We want our own lives (which is not to say, necessarily, that we don't want you, or that we don't love you or that we don't want to be with you).' Suppose also that poorer women, white women, many black racial/ethnic women as well, were to insist publicly upon the conditions which would enhance their self-respect and that of their children. Suppose all these mothers, lovers, workers, sisters, daughters and friends were to state publicly that they will live and work neither beneath nor above men of whatever race, ethnicity, or class. Suppose lesbians and straight women were to begin publicly to set the conditions for how and with whom we will love, live, marry or not, have sex or not, procreate or not, and raise children or not. Suppose that every woman were to announce publicly that she will not bring children into this world until they are guaranteed the conditions which will enable them to grow and thrive in self-respect. Suppose too, that every female worker, every nurse or doctor, secretary or executive, maid or lady of the house, caretaker of someone else's children or of her own, student or teacher, parishioner or priest, inmate or warden were to say publicly to our congresspeople, senators, courts, and president that we will no longer be privatized nor divided among ourselves. No longer women set against women, no longer women unable to share stories, secrets and dreams. No longer women kept from organizing on behalf of our own lives and the lives of those who will inherit the earth from us. Suppose that each and every battered woman were actually to leave the house. Each abused child actually to be given refuge. Each victim of racial or sexual harassment actually to be given comfort and advocacy rather than blame. Suppose all such women and children, whose numbers are legion, were actually to organize themselves publicly to fight back. Suppose, finally, all of these women and children, women-workers, women-lovers, wives, mothers, sisters and daughters, poor and more affluent women, were to march on Washington. Suppose we were to come without guns or sticks or stones. Suppose our only weapon was our passion for justice. Suppose we were marching, singing for our lives, moving slowly down Pennsylvania Avenue towards the barricades which protect the White House from the public. Suppose we came singing, publicly declaring our celebration of a God in whom women's creative liberating power is steeped.

> *(Chant)*
> 'God is our shepherd, we shall not want. She
> maketh us to lie down in green pastures.
> She leadeth us beside the still waters. She
> restoreth our soul. Yea, though we walk
> through the valley of the shadow of death, we
> will fear no evil, for she is with us. She
> prepareth a table before us in the presence
> of our enemies. She annointeth us with
> oil. Our cup runneth over. Surely goodness
> and mercy will follow us all the days of our
> life and we will dwell in the presence of our
> God forever.'

What do you suppose would happen if we came? I am clear that such womanpower would not be met kindly. We would be seen correctly as a subversive, terrorist, revolutionary movement, because we would together embody an unspeakably terrible assault on the 'rights of man' upon which the nation has been built. If we were to refuse to leave until we had a concrete, unequivocal guarantee of justice for all in this society, we would be either carried off to asylums, mowed down by horses, dogs, sticks, or guns, or we would have to become the new government of the United States. A fantasy indeed, but it is in fact what the feminist movement is all about. It is also what self-respecting men and women in our society, including its religious institutions, are all about: movement toward a transformed social order, a just world, a time and a space in which the conditions which generate the possibility for self-respect for all people are basic human rights, available to all.

> *(Sing)*
> 'I have dreamed on this mountain since first I was my
> mother's daughter,
> and you can't just take my dreams away.
> Not with me watching, no you can't just take my dreams
> away.'[7]

Feminism has been rooted historically in women's self-respect. Self-respect is itself rooted in an awareness that every other person is as valuable as we are – that is, in our love for others, those most unlike us as well as those most like us. Feminism is a commitment to participate in creating justice for all people of different races and cultures and classes and religions. It was not coincidence that the early feminist movement in this country in the nineteenth century was also an abolition movement. Such women as Angelina and Sara Grimke and Sojourner Truth pressed relentlessly for abolition of slavery and its effects, as well as for the equal rights of women, black and white. It should not surprise us that, as years wore on, amidst fierce resistance among white men to the aims of both abolition and suffrage, some white feminists abandoned the movement for black rights to work on behalf of white female privilege, thus allowing themselves to be co-opted by the white male agenda, which divides all oppressed people in order to defeat all oppressed people.[8] This is still today an issue in the feminist movement, though less so now than ten years ago, as white feminists have begun to acknowledge and attempt to deal with our racist and classist behavior. The more honest we are with one another across race, ethnic, and class lines and the more inclusive feminism is of *all* women's well-being, the more potent a social force we will become. The current Administration, with its broadside attacks on all races, classes and cultures of women: on black, Hispanic, other racial and ethnic groups; and on gays and lesbians has begun to radicalize the feminist movement. We are today a less white, less affluent, less college-educated, less upwardly-mobile movement than even five years ago. We are also necessarily both underground at times, and involved frequently in political movements which have not been particularly feminist in the past. I refer to such movements as peace work, the struggle to get the United States off the back of Nicaragua, and out of the way of the liberation movements in South Africa, El Salvador, Guatemala, the Philippines, Chile, and the list goes on.... These liberation efforts are stengthened increasingly by participation and leadership of feminist women and men. Audre Lorde, in a presentation in Cambridge last year, asked, 'What does it feel like to be a citizen of a country which is on the wrong side of virtually every liberation movement in the world?'[9] It feels outrageous to me. It feels exhausting. And it feels good to be connected to women and men throughout this nation and this world who are committed to living our lives, which may mean dying our deaths, on behalf of that justice in which many of us first learned to believe from this nation's ideals, however flawed, and from our various religious heritages. Thus, I stand here in historical continuity with both the American Revolution of 1776, and my particular religious community, the Christian Church, as I witness to the power and presence of a God whose thirst for justice is unquenchable. It is she who moves the struggle. She who demands a voice

> *(Sing)*
> 'God of grace and God of justice,
> On Thy people pour Thy power,
> Grant us wisdom, grant us courage,
> For the facing of this hour.
> For the facing of this hour.[10]

What's happening around us today may not be too far from what was happening some 50 years ago in Germany. Hitler is not likely to return to planet Earth as a little goosestepping man with a moustache. He is more likely to come to us in the shape of our own social, including our religious, institutions in which we are led to believe that only those who think right, act right, look right, and believe in the right god are deemed worthy of respect and life. I am not as frightened of Jesse Helms, contemptuous of both God and humankind as he is, as I am of the Democratic Party's efforts to clean up its image by keeping women on the bottom, gays in the closets, racial/ethnic minorities on the street, and 'God' safe in the church. I am not as scared of Jerry Falwell, bowing as he does before the idols of our generation, as I am of mainline Christian churches' preoccupation with a privatistic, individualistic spirituality which signals a quiescent attachment to a God who will not disturb us. Were I to chronicle the fall of this nation, writing of these things 200 years from now, I suspect I would conclude that the first and final enemy of the U.S. people was not communism, nor militarism, nor even nuclear bombs or the greed upon which advanced capitalism is built, but rather the passivity, the sense of utter powerlessness which the church engenders among its people by preaching and teaching bad theology, and which renders our numbers virtually impotent in the face of mounting evil.

How, then, can a self-respecting man or woman be a Christian? This is not a rhetorical question, nor a simple one. I am happy to say that many of the seminary students whom I am privileged to come to know in my work wrestle profoundly with this question, and the most compassionate and courageous among them do not find easy answers. More to the point is the question of how a self-respecting person can participate willingly in an institution which historically has not taught its people self-respect. To the contrary, Christian people have been taught to be self-effacing, self-negating, self-emptying, *especially if we are women*. The most notable Protestant theologians of the past generation – for example, Reinhold Niebuhr and Paul Tillich – reinforced the self-denying character of the historical tradition by insisting, with the early Fathers, that pride is a sin. As Valerie Saving and Judith Plaskow, two feminist theologians, have noted: for most women, pride in one's self and one's work is something we need to seek.[11] Pride is a moral good. Our lack of pride may well be our most egregious sin. Good Christian men throughout Christian history, have lifted a theological assumption – that pride is wrong and loss of self, right – out of its social-historical context and spoken of it as if it were the eternal Word of God, the Truth. We must lose ourselves in order to find ourselves? This is Gospel? The Good News? For a battered woman or gay man, an abused child or hungry black citizen? Good news for Nicaraguan peasants and Ethiopian children? Until the human social order generates the basic conditions for self-respect, it is an unfair, unrealistic, immoral expectation for us to lay upon persons the mandate that they should give themselves away, lose themselves or live for others. Like Reinhold Niebuhr, good Christian gentlemen have failed to perceive the extent to which pride is a sin specifically of those who shape and govern religion and society, those who do indeed posit themselves at the center of the world of God. This is pride: putting oneself at the center, around whom everyone and everything else must revolve. It is a sin, but it is specifically *not* the sin of those who must struggle at the margins for their own names, dignity, rights or lives. No theological truth can be simply created in the minds of white propertied men and laid on everyone else. All theological truth, all teachings about God, salvation, sin, and so forth, must be determined *by* those *about* whom and *to* whom it is meant to speak. White straight, Euro-American men can speak only for themselves. White men and women cannot theologize for people of color. Men cannot theologize for women. The Vatican cannot theologize for the poor of Brazil or Nicaragua.[12]

Those on the bottom – historically, those least empowered in the church and the world – are called by God to lead the way in discovering theological truths for our generation: theological truths and moral imperatives. It is not that women can speak for men. Or black people for whites. It is simply that poor people, people of darker shades and ethnic groups, women, lesbians and gay men, and members of religious minorities have what liberation theologians call an 'epistemological privilege' – the privilege of actually *knowing* God first, and therefore the ability to lead others to God. Knowing God first, because God lives and moves always at the bottom of the heap. God is *with* the poor and marginalized. God struggles in prisons, closets, and on the streets. Those who are at the bottom of the barrel in any culture, religion, nation, society or economic situation have the privilege of naming God because *only they* know the name of the God who struggles to resist oppression. God groans for breath and life and self-respect with and among those who have been cast out, marginalized, in every situation, from the center of our public life together. When met by the God of the margins, those who hold religious and civil power can, and usually do, reject this God as a phony or a lie. But they cannot take her away from those who know and love her. We speak our own theological truths. This is the heartbeat of feminist liberation theology.[13]

The Vatican and other patriarchal religious voices are correct in their perception, that such theology threatens traditional hierarchical church structures. Whenever the poor are taken seriously, the policies and privileges founded upon the accumulation of private capital are most assuredly threatened. Whenever women's lives are taken seriously, the policies and principles which are dedicated to the perpetuation of white male control are indeed challenged. Whenever the real daily lives and dreams of common folk are taken seriously as authoritative in the knowledge and love of God, traditional hierarchical arrangements of ecclesiastical power are in serious trouble.

If I thought for a moment that the Pope, the Archbishop of Canterbury, or any single person, group, or convention of Christians had the power either to ask or answer my most urgent moral, spiritual questions, I would not stay in the church for five more minutes, for I regard such mind-body control-tactics as fundamentally immoral precisely because they disempower us. They trivialize our capacity to stand and be counted on behalf of God's creation. To relinquish our moral agency and the critical necessity of becoming self-affirming, self-respecting people who can assume responsibility for shaping our lives in the world is to give up the purposefulness and creative power of being human in God's world. It is in fact to lose our souls. And so, we must, if we are self respecting, say no to the wielding of moral and spiritual authority over us. This does not mean that each of us is accountable to no one but him or herself. God forbid. It *does* mean that for every human person, our communities of moral and spiritual accountability include, but are not limited to, the religious institutions to which we belong.

I am, for example, no more accountable, by my ordination vows, to the Bishop and the Episcopal church, than I am by my baptism to all those many women and gays who no longer go to church because they feel as if their lives do not matter, in no small part because men with ecclesial authority don't know what to make of feminists or self-affirming lesbians and gay men. I am no more accountable by my baptism to Christian women and men than I am by my birthright as a citizen of this planet, to those Jews who died in Auschwitz, in no small measure because good Christian people like myself chose the way of silence. A self-respecting person can be a Christian only insofar as she or he understands well that Christian faith, like all religious faith, must serve first in the spirit of a Native American spirituality, the health and sacred happiness of the 'two-leggeds, four-leggeds, wingeds,' and the creatures whose bellies hug the earth.[14] We are not accountable finally to our institutional authorities but to God's world, and to helping make it just.

> *(Sing)*
> 'O God, our help in ages past,
> Our hope for years to come,
> Be Thou our Guide while life shall last
> And our Eternal Home.'[15]

In this Spirit, I am *delighted* to be a Christian, despite the disreputable name the Moral Majority has given us all. I am delighted to be a Christian because the Jesus story is a powerful source of memory for me. Not that Jesus is or was God; I do not believe that it is that simple. Not that Jesus is The Way, much less the only way, to God, because I do not believe it is that simple. Certainly not that Christianity has a leg to stand on when it comes to teaching truth or practicing virtue. I am a Christian because early on I hung on to the story of Jesus and his friends as having something to do with my life, my values, and my God. It is a story which can be, and is, read in many ways, some of them reprehensible. Thanks in no small part to my parents, and others responsible for my early religious education, the Jesus-story came through to me not as a story of obedience to authority. The Jesus-story was not a story of basically wicked people. It was not a story about right belief or conformity to commandments. The Jesus-story was not the story of a male god or a patriarchal Lord. Jesus was our brother. Jesus was our friend. I heard the Jesus-story as a love story, a tale about people taking people seriously, an image of life as we should live it together: a call to solidarity, our daily lives spilling over with concern for one another; advocacy for the poor, anger at hypocrisy and empty rituals and what I would later hear Adrienne Rich call the 'lies, secrets, and silence' which glue us together in societies dominated by unjust power-relations.[16] I heard the Jesus-story as one of compassion for those who are wounded. I heard the story as an invitation to marginalized people, outcasts, nonconformists, different sorts of people, all those sitting outside the gates of our public, consumer-oriented lives. By the time I was in elementary school it was clear to me that the Jesus-story stood in stark opposition to racism, specifically in the early 50's, to racial segregation of schools, bathrooms, stores, buses – and churches. That churches were segregated seemed to my young consciousness most extraordinary and entirely wrong.

All of which is to say that the church taught me something *in spite of* its own institutional sin and gave me a message which many of its leaders obviously did not mean for me to hear: that *Justice is another name for God*. The very God whom we call Love. Now I take this message very seriously, not that I live it very seriously or very well. I believe that Justice is God's name, and that there is no higher good than this, nothing more beautiful, nothing any truer than justice: right, mutual, reciprocal relation between and among all people; between people and other living creatures; between creatures and the wellspring of our passion for justice. I am delighted to imagine myself standing alongside all who struggle for and celebrate justice in great and small places of our lives, whether we are Christians, Jews, Muslims, Wicca Wimmin, Humanists, Feminists, Womanists, Atheists, Socialists, Communists, or simply good old secular Capitalist folk, who try to stand with the oppressed as best we can. I count myself among them. If our goal is really justice, our struggle is one, moved along by the power of the same Spirit. I am delighted to be a Christian and, as such, a person morally challenged to stand with those whose lives are broken by white supremacy, male-gender superiority, homophobia, anti-Semitism, economic exploitation, discrimination against the elderly, the young, the sick, the handicapped people in our society, imperialism in its many forms (national, religious, cultural, ethnic imperialism). I am delighted to be a Christian who, thanks to the *feminist* movement, has discovered her vocation as theologian, teacher, priest, preacher, writer, and lesbian activist on behalf of justice. Nothing has given me more pleasure than to come into a shared sense of purpose and vocation and power alongside many women and men of diverse racial/ethnic/religious backgrounds who are committed to doing what we can to help turn this society around (Latin American liberation theologians call it 'conversation') – so that all children, women and men will have access to food, shelter, education, work and leisure-time.

I am delighted to be a part of an institution where there are so many beautiful soul sisters, women struggling for life, for self-respect, for justice for all. I enjoy working alongside these women, our celebrations of woman-power, our resistance to evil. I take pleasure in being a priest of Christianity insofar as the religion we celebrate is becoming a justice-seeking, woman-affirming, earth-centered, sensual, body-celebrating faith – *which it is, insofar as we are shaping it so*. I cannot love a God of domination and control, a Deity who demands obedience, a body-denying, woman-hating, people-punishing projection of our least secure, most self-denying images. I lust after worship, to stand, to sing, to dance, to play in the source of compassion and justice, in the One who is the root of our revolutionary patience, who is the deep-flowing waters of our sexuality, the juice of our intimacy, the source of our love which is at once human and divine if it is one. Yet surely the Father still reigns in our sanctuary as in our nation and our world. For Christian feminists, the exclusive male-male bonding between father and son – as symbolized historically by the reified relationship between God and His Christ – will no longer do. We are beginning, in a fundamental way, to recreate the church. This is how I understand the roots of a Christian feminist spirituality for justice as well as the task of Christian feminist liberation theology.

Nothing is sacred if it serves to denigrate women, gays, Jews, Palestinians, blacks or others, or to secure the structures of oppression in the world and our religious institutions. Only a *radicalized* church will do, a church converted, a church turned round, a church denouncing much of its own history. This struggle will extend far beyond our lifetimes in this world. I stay because I was once there, a woman-child who heard the Jesus-story and got a message about God as justice. I stay because many sisters are still there. I stay because the church, at its best, is a sanctuary for refugees, an organizational base for feminists, an advocacy-agency for hungry people, cold people, abused women and children, gay men and lesbians, alcoholics, AIDS victims. I stay because to walk away right now would seem to be abandoning a burning house with loved ones still in it. As long as I have breath and strength and desire to struggle creatively in the church (and I may not always have those things), I will stay to help extinguish the flames of injustice. I am enough of a political hardhat to want to use whatever leverage we have as a Christian voice to turn this nation around. It seems to be both the most critical place I can be politically – for example, speaking and writing as a lesbian priest on behalf of gay and lesbian people – and also the best I can do pastorally among people of the world and church, for, as Gustavo Parajón, a Baptist pastor in Managua, asked some of us, 'What can be more pastoral than to be for justice and life?'[17]

Whether we are in any religious institution is of less consequence, finally, than whether we commit ourselves to acting on behalf of the oppressed. Not patronizingly, not charitably, but actually putting ourselves on the line with marginalized, trivialized, outcast people, standing with them, and if we *are* them, standing up to be counted ourselves. This is, I believe, the essence of any Christian spirituality which is rooted in justice.

To be silent in the face of lies – whether they are about others or about ourselves – what greater lie than this? To be passive in the face of injustice – what greater evil than this? History is littered with the bodies of those broken as the world watched. Whether we are religious or irreligious; whether we are steeped more in secular or sacred sensibilities; whether we are Jewish, Muslim, Christian, post-Christian, partly Christian, non-Christian, or anti-Christian, the question we must ask ourselves and one another is: What are *we doing* about the fact that the U.S. government is on the wrong side of every movement for justice, liberation, and self-respect in the world, both at home and abroad? I end with a couple of verses from an old hymn written by a former captain of a slave-ship. A white Christian man, who had been converted. I sing these few lines in honor of my father, Robert Clarence Heyward, another white Christian gentleman who was converted, more and more, to justice. He died last year and he loved this song. Please join me if you'd like to.

> Thru many dangers, toils and snares
> We have already come
> 'Tis grace that brought us safe this far
> And grace will lead us home.
>
> When we've been there ten thousand years
> Bright, shining as the sun
> We've no less days to sing God's praise
> Than when we first begun.[18]

Notes

1. From my book, *Our Passion for Justice: Images of Power, Sexuality, and Liberation* (Pilgrim, 1984), p. 151.
2. See Beverly W. Harrison, *Making the Connections: Essays in Feminist Social Ethics* (Beacon, 1985), for clarification of connections between women's well-being and other dimensions of justice.
3. Several helpful resources on the relation of economic exploitation to the overall texture of social injustice in the United States are Zillah Eisenstein, *The Radical Future of Liberal Feminism* (Longman, 1981); Angela Davis, *Women, Race and Class* (Random House, 1981); and Amy Swerdlow and Hanna Lessinger, eds., *Class, Race, and Sex: The Dynamics of Control* (G.K. Hall, 1983).
4. From Holly Near, 'No More Genocide,' *Hang In There!* Redwood Records, P.O. Box 40400, San Francisco, CA 94140, 1973.
5. From a sermon given at Union Theological Seminary, New York, NY, October 25, 1984, as quoted in the *Union News*, Jan., 1985, Issue No. 3, p. 2.
6. See Mary O'Brien, *The Politics of Reproduction* (Routledge and Kegan Paul, 1981), p. 5F, for use of term 'male-stream'; also Beverly W. Harrison, *Our Right to Choose: Toward a New Ethic of Abortion* (Beacon, 1983).
7. From Meg Christian, 'Mountain Song,' *Face the Music*, Olivia Records, Box 70237, Los Angeles, CA 90070, 1977.
8. See Angela Davis, *Women, Race, and Class*; also, Bell Hooks, *Ain't I Woman: Black Women and Feminism* (South End Press, 1981); Barbara Smith, ed., *Home Girls: A Black Feminist Anthology* (Kitchen Table: Women of Color Press, 1983); and Cherrie Moraga and Gloria Anyaldua, eds., *This Bridge Called My Back: Writings By Radical Women of Color* (Persephone Press, 1981).
9. Audre Lorde posed this question at a presentation sponsored by the Women's Theological Center, in Cambridge, Ma., Jan. 18, 1985.
10. Adaptation of 'God of Grace and God of Glory,' Harry Emerson Fosdick (1978, 1969) *Rejoice in the Lord: A Hymn Companion to the Scriptures* (Eerdmans, 1966).
11. See Valerie Saiving Goldstein's classic essay, 'The Human Situation: A Feminine View,' *Journal of Religion* (April, 1960), reprinted in *Womanspirit Rising: A Feminist Reader in Religion*, ed. by Carol P. Christ and Judith Plaskow (Harper and Row, 1979). Judith Plaskow has further expounded this theme in *Sex, Sin, and Grace: Women's Experience and the Theologies of Reinhold Niebuhr and Paul Tillich* (University Press of America, 1980).
12. This, of course, is a central thesis in Gustavo Gutierrez's *A Theology of Liberation: History, Politics and Salvation*, trans. by Caridad Inda and John Eagleson (Orbis, 1973), and in the many subsequent works in liberation theology.

13. Resources in feminist liberation theology include Rosemary R. Ruether, *Sexism and God-Talk – Toward a Feminist Theology* (Beacon, 1983); Elisabeth Schüssler Fiorenza, *In Memory of Her: A Feminist Theological Reconstruction of Christian Origins* (Crossroad, 1983); Sharon Welch, *Communities of Solidarity and Resistance: A Feminist Liberation Theology* (Orbis, 1985); Dorothee Sölle, with Shirley Cloyes, *To Work and to Love* (Fortress, 1984); and Carter Heyward, *The Redemption of God* (University Press of America).
14. I first heard the terms, 'two-leggeds, four-leggeds, and wingeds,' used by Mike Myers at the Theology in the Americas Conference in Detroit, 1980.
15. Verse of 'O God, Our Help in Ages Past,' based on Psalm 90, Isaac Watts (1674–1748), *The Hymnal 1940* (Episcopal Church Pension Fund, 1940).
16. See Adrienne Rich, *On Lies, Secrets, and Silence* (W.W. Norton, 1979).
17. Verses of 'Amazing Grace,' John Newton (1725–1807), *The Methodist Hymnal* (United Methodist Publishing House, 1966).

2.3 Men in Relationships: Redeeming Masculinity

J. Michael Hester

A few years ago a sales representative, whom I will name Dale, came alone for his first counseling session to tell me he had been involved in an affair with a woman at his church. He had confessed on Valentine's Day that he no longer loved his wife of twenty-two years. As a Christian and a father of teenage boys, he was in a bind. He was not committed to his wife and family. He was not committed to God. The more we talked the more I sensed how disconnected he was with life. His crisis at mid-life had caused him enough discomfort to call out for help. What kind of help did he need?

This man's dilemma represents a crisis I wish to address. Fortunately he and others have given permission for me to share parts of their stories. As Professor of Family Ministry and Director of the Gheens Center for Christian Family Ministry, I have committed my life to providing care for persons and families who experience relationship difficulties. The focus of the Gheens Center has been on the ministry of education, enrichment, and growth as well as counseling, treatment, and therapy. I use the term *family* to include all persons and their relationships. The relational dynamics of self, others, and God are central to my concern.

The Crisis of Intimacy

The crisis I witness in the counseling office is a crisis of intimacy. For twenty-two years Dale had not been able to achieve and maintain a satisfactory intimate relationship with his wife. Although he worked hard in the role of Protector/Provider, he was crippled when it came to matters of the heart. In the evenings he would spend time in his home office or watch television. He found it difficult to share any feelings about his day or to take an interest in his wife's world. Although he seemed to care for his sons, he did not invest much time or energy learning about their lives. Even in his affair he did not seem to experience much emotional closeness. His church and business worlds were also superficial. Often in his yearning for closeness he acted obnoxious and critical, which distanced others from him. He functioned as if he had a 'bubble' around him. The pain of his loneliness was often more intense for me to witness than for him to experience. He seemed to be starving for intimacy but did not know how to satisfy his hunger.

I have defined intimacy as a depthful sharing with another the joys and struggles of everyday living. It means much more than physical closeness or sexual activity. In their excellent book *The Art of Intimacy* the father-son psychiatrists and co-authors, Thomas and Patrick Malone, state,

> Intimacy is derived from the Latin *intima*, meaning 'inner' or 'inner-most.' Your inside being is the real you, the you that only you can know. The problem is that you can know it only when you are being intimate with something or someone outside yourself.... This sense of touching our innermost core is the essence of intimacy.[1]

Through relationships we experience the 'connectivity' or intimacy. In the second account of creation the Creator proclaims 'it is not good that man should be alone' (Gen. 2:18 RSV). God creates persons to be in community, to experience the good that comes from relationships. If alienation from ourselves, others, and God leads to emotional and spiritual dis-ease, then the experience of intimacy leads to whole person well-being. Intimacy provides sustenance for the journey. We experience intimacy as we trust another to share our innermost feelings and receive acceptance and affirmation of who we are. In contrast to Sigmund Freud's Will to Pleasure, Alfred Adler's Will to Power, and Viktor Frankl's Will to Meaning, Howard Clinebell claims the Will to Relate is the significant life force which meets our personal hungers for recognition, caring, esteem, dependency, and sexual satisfaction.[2]

Loneliness

Perhaps the opposite of intimacy is loneliness, a pervasive disease in America today. Gail Sheehy has suggested that loneliness is the natural offspring of twentieth-century democratization.[3] When individualism began to be valued more highly in the late nineteenth century, persons began to interpret their needs and their worlds for themselves. Such personal life interpretations led to growth and change. As people claimed their own needs and differences, fragmentation and alienation were often experienced in relationships. Although individuality led to personal well-being, it also sometimes led to anxiety, depression, and loneliness.

Loneliness, however, may be less a disease and more like hunger. In their study *In Search of Intimacy* Carin Rubinstein and Philip Shaver write,

> Just as hunger signals the body's need for nourishment, loneliness warns us that important psychological needs are going unmet. Loneliness is a healthy hunger for intimacy and community – a natural sign that we are lacking companionship, closeness and a meaningful place in the world.[4]

The changing relationship dynamics of this century make the search for intimacy more difficult. Changing expectations within marriage call for couples to meet intimacy needs in more meaningful ways. High divorce rates suggest that persons have been unable to meet the intimacy demands in marital relationships. New role definitions create confusion and cause uncertainty about appropriate ways for meeting intimacy needs. Economic forces and the demands to work reduce the available time for persons to care for their loneliness hunger. Different family shapes and sizes and our isolation from extended family make the search for intimacy more difficult. The fast pace of more demanding schedules results in fatigue and less opportunity for closeness. A more pluralistic society creates dramatic differences and conflict which also become barriers in relationships.

My professional and my personal experiences remind me again of the crisis of intimacy. Many simply do not have the necessary interpersonal competency skills. God has created humankind with characteristics to be relational and to experience bonding at a deep level; however, our history of relational sinfulness illustrates the difficulty we have with intimacy. We experience overwhelming alienation. The relationship with our inner self becomes disconnected. In our yearning for closeness with others, we neglect and damage relationships important to us. Ultimately, we long for a close relationship with God but find ourselves in spiritual loneliness as well.

Men and Intimacy

The primary focus of my concern in recent years has been on the intimacy difficulties of men. I have carefully observed how men relate with women, children, other men, and God. The purpose of this address is to deal specifically with the dynamics of male intimacy and to propose possibilities of redemption and growth for men in relationships. I must confess my anxiety about attempting such an analysis in a predominantly male institution. This may be the very place to begin, however.

My personal awareness has been helped significantly by my participation in a men's sharing group which we call the Brotherhood, not to be confused with a Southern Baptist organization! This faculty address is dedicated to my six 'brothers' who better be here today! By the way, the Brotherhood was actually a Christmas gift from my wife. She arranged the first meeting out of her awareness that I am easier to live with when I have a sharing group.

Why focus on men in relationships, especially in this day of women's awareness? When I went to the seminary bookstore to check on books about men, I found two shelves on women's studies. When I asked about the section on men's studies, the manager jokingly said the rest of the books in the store were men's books. The problem, however, is not a joke. Many wives and children bear the burden of men's difficulty with relationships often leaving them starving for attention. It is my conviction that men are also starving.

The Shell of Manliness

Perhaps the women's movement and their helpful efforts to raise consciousness can also be liberating for men. In his insightful book *The Male Predicament*, James Dittes asserts,

So this book is for those men for whom the shell of manliness is cracking or never did fit comfortably, for those men who are discovering that manhood is far richer than the charade of manliness. I try to give voice to the restlessness of yearnings long buried and muted, to the stress and weariness of bearing the heavy armor of manliness and of pretending to wear it nonchalantly and unimpeded.[5]

He goes on to tell the story of his childhood experience in the Christmas pageant playing Joseph, being instructed to stand strong and still and say nothing. By being the Good Scout he was to cover up all the feelings Joseph might be having at the time. Joseph, the patron saint for the modern working man, through his mute obedience and steadfast acquiescence, 'plays out energetically and unhesitatingly the script assigned to him, without pausing to question its suitability, thus, the male predicament.'[6]

Impact on Men's Health

Underneath the shell of manliness is a person who often lives in pain. Men are hurting several ways. In *The Intimate Connection*, a study of male sexuality and male spirituality, James Nelson suggests that the picture of men's health is not very good.[7] As infants our death rate is significantly higher, perhaps because we receive less nurture and touch. In childhood boys have a more difficult time establishing a secure gender identity under the pressure of avoiding 'effeminacy.' In adolescence our search for identity is often more dangerous and violent. The vast majority of murders are committed by men 18–24 years old. On average men die seven years sooner than women. Our incidences of suicide, chemical dependency, incarceration, and violent death are vastly higher. We postpone getting help for physical and emotional illnesses and then are hospitalized 15 percent longer. Our difficulty in expressing emotions is directly linked with higher incidence of major diseases. Nine of the ten leading causes of death in America are dominated by men. Once again men are the winners!

Fear

Men are afraid of close relationships. We need to be in control because competition is our mode of operation. If we disclose our innermost selves, someone might use it against us. Nelson suggests that most men relate through sexism, a style of taking charge, 'being on top.' Because we do not know our feelings very well, 'we live much of the time needing to prove ourselves through achievement and triumph. Since we relate competitively, especially with other men, we find vulnerability frightening.'[8] Men suffer from performance anxiety not only in sexual activity but in all aspects of life where we feel the pressure to be potent. Underneath, there is the abiding fear of failure and weakness.

Men have bought into the Myth of Manhood and have been left with an existential loneliness, a sense of separation from self and others. Someone suggested we live by the following Commandments of manhood written on our spirits:

1. Thou shalt not be weak, nor have weak gods before thee.
2. Thou shalt not fail thyself, nor 'fail' as thy father before thee.
3. Thou shalt not keep holy any day that denies thy work.
4. Thou shalt not love in ways that are intimate and sharing.
5. Thou shalt not cry, complain, or feel lonely.
6. Thou shalt not commit public anger.
7. Thou shalt not be uncertain or ambivalent.
8. Thou shalt not be dependent.
9. Thou shalt not acknowledge thy death or thy limitations.
10. Thou *shalt* do unto other men before they do unto you.[9]

At this point you may be having difficulty with descriptions which include all men. Certainly not all men are like this. Some women, especially of this generation, may even identify with the masculine role struggles. There are definite limitations to stereotyping, and not everyone would fit the characterization. For the sake of this presentation and our ministry with men in relationships, however, I believe we can profit from the recent research on men in America. Our understanding will equip us to be a part of the liberation from the bondage of manliness and the redemption of men for more meaningful living.

The Dynamics of Male Relationships

The research indicates that men tend to function in relationships as 'machines.' Herb Goldberg, a psychologist and male researcher, observes that traditional masculinity causes men to respond in certain ways which he calls complexes.[10] For instance, dependency and need are viewed as weakness, and men have difficulty asking for help. Our fear complex prompts us to overlook our real feelings and press on toward accomplishing the task. As a matter of fact, most male relationships tend to form around tasks. Our relationships are more 'shoulder-to-shoulder' than 'face-to-face.'[11] Men tend to be more active because passivity equals femininity. Our driven personalities, which often causes heart attacks and hypertension, push us to overstress without due recognition of fatigue. Our achievement anxiety makes it difficult for us to relax and just be. This works-righteousness syndrome creates a high degree of self-consciousness, self-judgment and fear of derision from others. While writing this paragraph, I received a call from a female business administrator of an agency Board of Directors on which I serve. After she apologized for calling me at home, interrupting my spring vacation, I quickly informed her that I was hard at work. As I hung up I laughed as I pondered my need to prove my worth so vigorously.

Emotional Exchange

The problems men have with emotions lead to many difficulties in the relational world. On the Myers-Briggs Type Indicator sixty percent of the American male population are Thinkers rather than Feelers.[12] Although cerebral functioning may help in the marketplace and academic setting, men's efforts to rationalize and intellectualize often cause breakdowns in relationships. Feelings are the currency for intimacy, and most men are inept with emotional exchange. Consequently, men are more adept in talking about their public worlds than their private and personal selves. Through extensive research *The McGill Report on Male Intimacy*[13] discovered that men talk about their tastes and interests, attitudes and opinions with their wives but are much less willing to share 'matters of the heart.' James Nelson believes men then rely on women to be their emotional expressers and interpreters of their feelings to themselves and others.[14] From my use of family systems theory in counseling, I frequently call on couples to process an experience or event emotionally. Most often men resent the exercise and feel helpless with such emotional processing.

As sexual beings, men tend to focus on sexual activity and the 'genitalization' of sexuality.[15] Since our genitals are external we are more controlled by visible, physical, and active sexuality. We separate sex from intimacy. Sexual pleasure is limited because we experience sex as an act, not as part of being close. Dale, my counselee, expected to have sex every evening after he had spent the entire day apart from his wife. No wonder she resented him and felt used. In another counseling relationship, the husband testified that he used sexual activity as a sleeping medication 'every night' for twenty years of marriage! He could not understand his wife's rage when she finally refused.

Fear of Being Feminine

Perhaps the most paralyzing complex for men is the fear of being feminine. Early on in our development we receive many messages about not being sissy, not crying, not playing with dolls, not wearing certain clothes, and not participating in certain activities for girls. We learn to avoid closeness because we might appear homosexual. This homophobia then influences our behavior the rest of our lives. In reaction we develop the 'macho man' image and get fixated on masculine symbols such as guns, cars, motorcycles, and football games. We do not allow ourselves to be penetrated, and we put up walls of false masculinity. Avoiding weakness and proving ourselves become the guiding forces for our behavior.

Relationships with Other Men

How do these dynamics influence men's relationships with one another? When discussing my faculty address with a colleague at another seminary, he shared a story about his family discussing the news that one of their male friends had recently been caught in an affair. His adolescent daughter responded, 'I wonder if men are more prone to have affairs because they don't have friends.' A provocative observation! My counseling experience with men who have affairs has indicated that most reach out to other women because they are lonely and searching for intimacy. Often they confess having someone with whom to talk is more important than sexual relationship.

Male friendships are 'buddies' who form around certain activities. As McGill's report testifies,

> One man in ten has a male friend with whom he discusses work, money, marriage; only one in more than twenty has a friendship where he discloses his feelings about himself or his sexual feelings.... The most common male friendship pattern is for a man to have many 'friends,' each of whom knows something of the man's public self and therefore little about him, but not one of whom knows more than a small piece of the whole.[16]

Men see friendships more as means to an end and not of value in and of themselves. In a Jungian analysis entitled *What Men Are Like* John Sanford observes that most male bonding takes place in our culture through sports. Many men say they have never been able to recreate the sense of companionship with other men that they had when they were involved in school athletics.[17] Men tend to talk about sports, sex, achievements, business, politics, or events. Their efforts at closeness often come through humor, banter, and insults. The 'put-down' is the male friendship trademark. A visit to our faculty lounge would verify this data!

Reasons for Relational Difficulties

How do men come to be the way they are? Such an analysis is a difficult task. Some might suggest that male characteristics are genetic while others would attribute them to environmental influences. Studies on androgyny, beginning with Alfred Adler, have helped us understand male-female dynamics with more clarity.

Male Socialization – Fathers and Other Men

One of the primary influences defining men's identity is male social-ization. We learn masculinity from the men who are important to us, especially in our family of origin. Edwin Friedman uses family systems theory to explain how relational characteristics are transmitted from 'generation to generation.'[18]

In one counseling relationship a married man in his late 20's was experiencing an identity crisis as a man and as a husband. I encour-aged him to identify men who had been important in his growing up. At the next session he returned with a diagram where he had arranged his four masculine models around the themes of Activity and Passivity, Power and Tenderness, Rational and Emotional. Since he was from the deep South, he described one of his primary modes as the 'Southern macho redneck' who was tough and controlling, often mean and insen-sitive. The other was the 'football coach' who was more relationally sophisticated but often intimidating and overpowering. My counselee was repelled by these two images. His main influence was his own father, who was the quiet, hardworking, intellectual type who did not get emotionally involved in relationships. Another significant influence was his pastor, who was tender and kind but seemed to be powerless and 'less than a man.' As he searched for a working masculine identity for himself, he attempted to combine the dynamics of power and sensi-tivity and discovered he could function more effectively with his wife, his boss, and his friends.

Last fall in a men's retreat I invited them to reflect on the men in their lives, an activity you may choose to do. Their small group conversation was alive with memories and stories, laughter and tears. One older participant recalled the last loving act from his father was the question just after his wedding. 'Do you need any money?' The next day his father died of a heart attack, never having said 'I love you.' Like many men one of the few ways this father could show love was providing for his child's financial needs. A new awareness came from sharing his story. My friend realized that his relational style, like his father's, was to provide for persons' physical needs more than share emotional presence.

War heroes, Great Depression survivors, and hardworking fathers have influenced my generation. As I talk with men today, I find them searching for different ways to be men. In a marriage counseling session, a powerful attorney confessed both anxiety and hope about trying to be a father to his own son. Growing up with an emotionally distant and upright father, he wanted to be a more available parent. The father-son relationship has lasting impact on the psychological and spiritual development of men. By paying special attention to his son's accomplishments, by appropriate and fun play, and by emotional open-ness, the father can help shape the son's masculinity into healthy mutual love and respect for persons. Throughout this research I have become much more aware of my relationships with my father and my son.

Mothers and Other Women

In addition to male influences, a boy's relationship with his mother seems to be critical in his identity formation. Many men I have seen in counseling have either experienced emotional fusion with or emotional distance from their mothers. The emotional connection between a small child and the mother and father is called bonding. John Sanford identifies both positive and negative mother complexes and their influence on men's relationships.[19] If there has been positive bonding, then the boy is likely to experience confidence in himself and an appreciation of the world of the feminine. At times, however, the positive complex may leave him unprepared to live in the larger world of difficult relationships, and he may have trouble maintaining lasting relationships with women, especially those dramatically unlike his mother.

Negative relationships with mothers often leave men an 'injured child' with a lasting distrust of women. My counselee, Dale, developed his bubble after his ego was attacked repeatedly by his mother, with whom he continued to have a negative and distant relationship. Like many men he vowed he would never open himself up to another woman.

The male sense of separation and disconnection from the world of relationships may in fact be linked to the radical separation he experiences from his mother. Nancy Chodorow in *The Reproduction of Mothering* has identified that growing girls

> come to define and experience themselves as continuous with others; their experience of self contains more flexible or permeable ego boundaries. Boys come to define themselves as more separate and distinct, with a greater sense of rigid ego boundaries and differentiation. The basic feminine sense of self is connected to the world, the basic masculine sense of self is separate.[20]

In establishing gender identity the male infant must define his identity through separation and individuation, whereas girls define theirs through attachment and identification.[21] Perhaps in the traumatic process of separation, the male learns to suppress emotional feelings and connectedness. This may be the reason for the male tendency to separate sex from intimacy. By being pushed away from the mother to find gender identity, boys begin a desperate and important search for clues about manhood from fathers. This search becomes more significant for masculine development when there are absent or ineffective fathers.[22]

Egocentricity

Sanford uses a Jungian perspective to make an assessment of masculine identity formation.[23] 'The awareness of being a separate person helps an adolescent begin the foremost task of adolescence: the building of ego identity.'[24] Adolescents typically go through a progression of identity states from confusion to insecure fixation, then through conscious searching and rebellion to the ultimate integration of the personality into a new identity. There is a natural time of self-preoccupation and egocentricity. Overcoming egocentricity is a vital part of psychological maturity, especially for men. Sanford defines egocentricity as 'a state in which a person is concerned only with his own defense and the fulfillment of his own ambitions, which ambitions, on close scrutiny turn out to be closely tied to his own defenses.'[25] Many men do not feel in possession of their manhood. They are confused about being passive and active and oscillate between weakness and brutality. Their bondage to the tyranny of egocentricity stands in the way of living life from the Real or authentic Self. They pay the price by living in anxiety, depression, and loneliness.

Redeeming Masculinity – The Possibilities for Growth

Whatever the causes of masculine identity formation, there are always possibilities for growth and change. Carl Jung has said, 'Seldom, or perhaps never, does a marriage develop smoothly and without crises; there is no coming to consciousness without pain.' Most men who wish to change their way of relating come to their awareness through much pain and personal crisis. It may be the pain of a broken marriage, a death of a child, the loss of a job, or the depression of loneliness. The crisis of mid-life often causes men to reexamine their intimacy needs and relationship skills. Frequently, they have devoted the first half of their adult lives to climbing the vocational and status ladder only to learn that meaning and purpose are not to be found at the top of the ladder. In response they often turn to relationships, sometimes with younger women or fast cars, to help them experience intimacy.

What does all of this have to do with the discipline of 'family' ministry? Today I am declaring a personal commitment and proposing a challenge to others to a new and redeemed masculinity. I believe we have the possibility to participate in changing manliness to more authentic, self-chosen modes of manhood. We can be liberated from roles that have often been restrictive and responsible for unsatisfying or even broken relationships. The time for growth and new possibilities is now.

We must begin by seeing and acknowledging the situation of manhood as it is. I hope this address has prompted you to examine and envision your own critique of men in relationships. I believe we are called to help men and women find liberation from the bondage of crippling roles. We must also explore relationship dynamics and increase our awareness of how our participation in the Myth of Manhood affects our lives and relationships. Beyond acknowledgement and new understanding, I believe we must experience intimacy beginning with our inner selves and move beyond to a more genuine intimacy with others. In recent months I have been invited by churches to lead men's retreats and assist them in examining their ministry with men through traditional men's groups as well as new possibilities for ministry.

My own Brotherhood which has been meeting monthly for three years has taught me the value of having a group for sharing and playing. At our gatherings we share a meal, tell stories, give an update on our life situations, and focus on the pressing concerns of one of the brothers. The most important agenda is to maintain connection, process events emotionally, and support each other.

Models for Redeemed Masculinity

Mark Gerzon in *A Choice of Heroes* offers possibilities for changing from traditional models of masculinity.[26] He suggests that the Frontiersman, the quick-fisted white male loner conquering the frontier through ravaging control, be replaced by the Healer, who cares for the environment and relationships. The Soldier, as defender and aggressor through repressing vulnerability and displaying violence, might be replaced by the Mediator, who is able to coexist peacefully. The Breadwinner, who finds meaning through work, success, and a paycheck, might become a Companion, who shares life and meaning with others. The Expert, who possesses knowledge to gain control, might be replaced by the Colleague, who shares power and leadership. Finally the Lord image, exhibited by the male who believes he is creator and sustainer of heaven and earth, would be replaced by the Nurturer, who invites others to join him in mutual empowerment. Men have become trapped by the traditional male models – Frontiersman, Soldier, Breadwinner, Expert, and Lord. Redeeming masculinity calls forth the Healer, Mediator, Companion, Colleague, Nurturer, providing a model not only for men but for humanity.

Beyond Androgyny

To become relational and experience intimacy, men do not have to become 'feminine' and take on characteristics which are foreign to their being. Androgyny, which integrates gender stereotypes into one being, has been helpful in overcoming the bondage of gender roles. James Nelson goes beyond androgyny, however, by declaring that true masculinity provides for vulnerability, relational power, and mutuality.[27] Men have the inherent ability to be open and receptive with others and to share power through interdependence. In addition to being all-powerful, men can also be soft and gentle. Instead of competition and constant measurement of self, men can live in community and collegiality, truly applauding the well-being of another.

Biblical Models – Jonathan and David

Perhaps the biblical story of Jonathan and David (1 & 2 Samuel) can provide for us a model of male friendship and intimacy. They were 'soul brothers' whose nurture for one another gave them strength for the journey. By relating 'heart to heart' they provided a gift of grace found through acceptance and openness. They were intentional about their relationship and carefully remained connected even in the midst of danger. My own experience with a Jonathan/David relationship over 26 years has given me special appreciation for soul brotherhood. Although we have lived apart, we have maintained monthly phone calls or visits. Instead of competing with one another, Jonathan and David were able to celebrate the gifts of the other. The value of their relationship was declared in their life-long commitment and covenant to each other. At Jonathan's death, David would write,

I am distressed for you, my brother Jonathan;
very pleasant you have been to me;
your love to me was wonderful, passing the love of
women. (2 Samuel 1:26 RSV)

New Testament

The New Testament provides many images of relational intimacy. The Greek *koinonia*, meaning fellowship or sharing something in common, was used to describe the early church and the fellowship of the Holy Spirit. It was also used in connection with Communion, the celebration meal of Christian community, when they experienced true intimacy with each other and God.[28] The Greek *agape* builds on the Hebrew *hesed*, meaning steadfast love for God and others. *Agape* refers to the love of God which enters into our world in Jesus Christ. Such Incarnational Love calls us to enter into the world of others, as well as to open our worlds for others to enter. Incarnational Love provides a model for redeeming masculinity and a renewal of intimacy with ourselves, others, and God.

Jesus Christ

Our ultimate model for male intimacy, therefore, is our brother, Jesus Christ. He provides for us the possibilities for manhood and personhood. He was able to balance power and vulnerability through relational love. He maintained achievement and productivity while being creative and sensitive. He balanced dominance and submission through collegiality and mutuality. He was able to combine his head and his heart in his life's vocation.

The relational paradigm found in Jesus Christ is his relationship with his Bethany family. As he entered into the worlds of Mary and Martha he allowed them to relate to him in ways most suited for each of them. Another intimate relationship, however, was with their brother and his friend, Lazarus, for whom he wept and literally laid down his life. By returning to raise Lazarus, Jesus risked his own life, and the Pharisees plotted to kill him (John 11).

Redeeming masculinity calls for us to break the bonds that enslave us. The images of false masculinity have to die. Without death there is no resurrection. In Jesus Christ there is the saving possibility for us all to experience new life. In Christ there is neither male or female (Gal. 3:28). The redemptive possibility is for shared humanity in which we experience community through our distinctiveness and our commonality. Redeeming masculinity from the bondage of manliness opens the way for nurturing and growth for all relationships.

For God so loved each one of us he related to us intimately through Jesus Christ that we may experience wholeness and a special quality of living and dying. Even as Jesus sacrificed his own vulnerability for his friend, we too are called to a new masculinity, yea, even a new humanity, by being intimate with our brothers and sisters through 'laying down our lives' (John 3:16 & 1 John 3:16, my paraphrase).

Through 'Amazing Grace' we are all redeemed!

This faculty address was delivered by Dr. J. Michael Hester on April 26, 1989.

Notes
1. Thomas Patrick Malone, M.D., and Patrick Thomas Malone, M.D., *The Art of Intimacy* (New York: Prentice Hall, 1987), p. 19.
2. Howard Clinebell, *The Intimate Marriage* (New York: Harper and Row, 1970), pp. 12–20.
3. Carin Rubinstein and Philip Shaver, *In Search of Intimacy* (New York: Delacorte, 1974), p. ix.
4. Ibid., p. 3.
5. James Dittes, *The Male Predicament* (San Francisco: Harper and Row, 1985), p. x.
6. Ibid., p. 3.
7. James Nelson, *The Intimate Connection* (Philadelphia: Westminster, 1988), pp. 12–13.
8. Ibid., p. 30.
9. Dick Vittitow, 'Changing Men and Their Movement Toward Intimacy,' in *Men in Difficult Times*, ed. Robert A. Lewis (Englewood Cliffs, N.J.: Prentice Hall, 1981), pp. 292–293.
10. Herb Goldberg, *The New Male Female Felationships* (New York: William Morrow, 1983), p. 28.
11. Nelson, *The Intimate Connection*, p. 57.
12. David Keirsey and Marilyn Bates, *Please Understand Me* (Del Mar, Cal.: Prometheus Nemesis, 1984), p. 20.
13. Michael McGill, *The McGill Report of Male Intimacy* (New York: Harper and Row, 1985), p. 39.
14. Nelson, *The Intimate Connection*, p. 42.
15. Ibid., p. 34.
16. McGill, *The McGill Report*, p. 157.
17. John A. Sanford and George Lough, *What Men Are Like* (New York: Paulist, 1988), p. 39.
18. Edwin Friedman, *Generation to Generation* (New York: Guilford, 1986), p. 41.
19. Sanford, *What Men Are Like*, pp. 22–23.

20. Nancy Chodorow, *The Reproduction of Mothering: Psychoanalysis and the Sociology of Gender* (Berkeley: University of California Press, 1978), p. 170.

21. Nelson, *The Intimate Connection*, p. 39.

22. Lillian Rubin, *Intimate Strangers* (New York: Harper and Row, 1983), pp. 38–64.

23. Sanford, *What Men Are Like*, p. 35.

24. Ibid., pp. 63–89.

25. Ibid., p. 67.

26. Mark Gerzon, *A Choice of Heroes: The Changing Faces of American Manhood* (Boston: Houghton Mifflin, 1982).

27. Nelson, *The Intimate Connection*, pp. 101–105.

28. Stephen Neill, John Goodwin, and Arthur Dowle, editors, *The Modern Reader's Dictionary of the Bible* (New York: Association, 1966).

2.4 Different Voices, Different Genes: 'Male and Female Created God *Them*'

James B. Ashbrook

This article explores the 'us-ness' of our shared humanity in terms of sex-gender differences, the richness of our diversity as male and female. Sex refers to our genetic predispositions while gender identifies the ways in which socialization shapes who we are. Mounting evidence suggests sex-specific and sex-related differences, especially in the ways we understand and engage reality.[1] In light of this I ask how these differences influence our individual experience, how they shape our professional colleagueship, and how they impact our work with clients, parishioners, and students.

Experience and Epistemology

Because our genetic conception is different we enter the world differently. Thus our cries for each other and our relationships with each other are different cries and different relationships. We develop different voices, to use the telling metaphor of psychologist Carol Gilligan,[2] because we inherit different genes and are shaped by different gender patterns.

Underneath ideologies about patriarchy, feminism, and exclusive versus inclusive language lies the issue of epistemology: 'how' do we 'know'; and based on that way of knowing, 'what' do we know? What we take to be knowledge comes from experience.

Differences in Experiencing. Historically, such differences center around the value placed on experience. Many men have expressed reservation about experience and so minimize 'women's intuition.' It is claimed that an experiential approach to knowledge easily falls into the trap of subjectivity. As a check, therefore, men approach issues as objectively as possible. The subjective is viewed with suspicion.

In contrast, many women prize experience.[3] Feminist thinkers criticize male-valued objectivity as being 'inherently distorting.'[4] Objectivity subverts some of life's 'real' regularities, such as menstruation. Without experiential involvement, we miss the emotional meaning of what is. Women thereby tend to view anything which is 'objective' with suspicion.

In an *Investigation of Brain Wave Symmetry: An EEG Imaging Study Based on the Wakeful Dreaming Process*, psychotherapist Charlotte Smith[5] found that topographic maps of brain electrical activity in a sample of 16 females and 16 males differed significantly and without exception. For males the highest amplitude appeared in the frontal cortex, indicating they processed the experience intentionally. For females the highest amplitude came in the central cortex, suggesting they processed the experience in a more sensory way. In addition, the data showed a lack of differential EEG desynchrony during the imaging task for females. These findings 'provided neuropsychological support for the hypothesis of greater bilateral flexibility in females during a self-generation imaging task.'[6]

Structural anthropologists have identified ways in which dichotomous symbols – contrasts rather than connections – tend to reflect and reinforce the power of those who are identified with what is taken as normative. This is especially true with the distinction between culture and nature and, by inference, between men and women. I submit that dichotomies, characteristic of the male dominant culture of objectivity, arise from the sharper division of labor between an analytic 2-dimensional left brain cognition, which uses the abstractions of words and numbers, and an integrative 3-dimensional right brain cognition, which draws upon the immediacy of the sensory and the symbolic.

That separation in cognition is more prevalent among men and, more especially late maturers in relation to language. A more even distribution of analytic and integrative processes across both hemispheres appears among women and, specifically, early maturers in relation to the development of language.[7] The more general style of knowing, female-related, is associated with a sense of continuity of experience, identification with others, and a participation in the ordinariness of the everyday.

Early maturers are more likely to be sensitive to the context in which they find themselves, to take in more of the interpersonal complexity of web of relationships, and to avoid setting people against each other. There is a closer connection with the sensory field at the affective level, as indicated by Smith's evidence of central processing in female imagers. The individual creates a holding environment – an emotional attunement – for others, an at-home reality in which one person's need and the other person's resource meet and fit. Psychiatrist Kenneth Wright links this pattern with the two-person communication of the infant and the mothering other.[8]

The specialized style of knowing, primarily male-related, leads to a certain independence, or distance, from the environment. One is selectively inattentive – or less sensitive – to what is going on in the immediate situation. The person becomes adept at extricating formal features from the environment. 'Entities' and 'objects' are isolated from their settings. These features are relevant to spatial organization and logical structure. Because of this the male person has more difficulty processing concrete data or certain other immediate presentations of 'reality.'

With Wright, I associate this objectifying distance with the presence of a third-person relationship from which the child is excluded, whether girl or boy. The other person sets the boundary, insists upon the limitation, and elicits another perspective. Out of that other perspective arises a sense of objectivity. In short, 'things' come into being. I-it interactions evolve.

Later maturers, when and if they are boys, are more likely to be insensitive to the context, to simplify its relationships, and to place its various aspects in sharper categories of 'right' and 'wrong,' 'good' and 'bad,' 'important' and 'unimportant,' thus dichotomizing reality. There is a distance from sensory immediacy by virtue of the representational symbolization of experience, as suggested by Smith's evidence of frontal processing in male imagers.

In brief, men attend to the physical world and its more abstract features, while women attend to the social world and its more tangible aspects.[9]

Differences in Object-Seeking Behavior. I speculate that these genetic predispositions about the nature of experience are reflected in the object-seeking activities of females and males. Women are more likely to interact with personal objects while men are more likely to respond to physical objects. Females are genetically predisposed to resonate with the maternal other,[10] while males are genetically predisposed to resonate with the paternal other. The implications of these biases toward the personal and the impersonal are subtle and pervasive, according to biopsychologist Jerre Levy.[11]

Feminine related qualities reflect more tolerance of ambiguity and mystery, while masculine related qualities focus on clear structures and definite decisions. The feminine exhibits more respect for nonrational contrasts, whereas the masculine demands logical reasons. The feminine trusts the intuitive, while the masculine depends more upon authority. The feminine deals more openly with feelings, while the masculine attends to analysis. The feminine exhibits a broad range of interests, whereas the masculine tends toward specialized interests.

When I combine such findings, I arrive at two related yet distinguishable speculations. One is that males tend to be oriented more to an abstract and compartmentalized environment; the other that females tend to be oriented more to an interpersonal and connected environment. In contrast to a simplified and thereby stabilized view of reality as perceived by men, women experience the real as more nuanced and thereby more alterable.[12]

We hear different voices because of different genes. Feminist thinkers rightly insist that in any generalization about experience we can only finally refer to male experience and female experience.[13] In saying this I would caution that we not negate the basic reality of our own unique individualities. Each of us is more than, and other than, either our gender or our sex.

Differences in Psychosocial Development. I believe these differences in experience based on brain organization underlie what we are learning about differences in psychosocial development.

Traditionally, Sigmund Freud focused upon the competition between the father and son for the wife/mother as the favored woman in their lives. In recent years, psychoanalyst Nancy Chodorow and psychologist Jean Baker Miller,[14] among many, reject that paradigm of competition for the more humane pattern of cooperation and 'women's growth in connection.'[15] Connection and cooperation arise from the bonding of mother and infant. Such cooperation, I suggest, reflects more evenly distributed cognitive processes while competition arises from contrasting – and potentially conflicting – specialization of hemisphere activity.

Further, Erik Erikson's theory of human development has identified a sequence of psychosocial features from trust through identity to intimacy, generativity, and integrity. The feminist criticism points out that girls develop in a different way. For them, identity and intimacy are simultaneous, not sequential. Autonomy is never separated from attachment. As Jean Baker Miller characterizes it, this second phase reflects more 'an enlarged "point of view" ... new configurations and new "understandings" *in the relationship*' than a separating and alienating distance from the other.[16]

The stages of growth, from this revised perspective of women's experience, blend self-and-others without giving priority to self-over-others or self-apart-from-others. Instead, we are always and ever self-in-relation-with-others, and others-in-relation-to-self. Again, I speculate that early maturation of language and bilaterality influence more of a sense of continuity in experience while later maturation of language and strong asymmetry contribute more to a sense of sequential experience.

Despite the widespread evidence of sex-gender differences, however, I remind myself as well as you of the qualifications which so easily come to mind about such generalizations.[17] Any two males or any two females can differ more than any particular male and any particular female. Further, left-handed males are more likely to exhibit a cognitive pattern similar to females than do strongly dominant right-handed males. Sex similarities are as prominent as are sex differences, especially in the large overlap on non-biological factors. Differences in hemisphere specialization are 'neither obvious nor consistent across all lateralized subsystems,' and may 'have more to do with sex-related differences in preferred strategies than with hard-wired differences.'[18]

The most predictive use of the gender variable requires us to put sex and gender in context. The question becomes, What specific conditions influence the display of sex-specific and gender-related behavior?[19]

Genetic Factors in Meaning-Making

Inner experience lacks objective reference. And the making of meaning, while initiated by the social realm, is always anchored in the inner realm. We must rely on metaphor and gesture and nuance to communicate what we experience. Further, under new, novel, or threatening experience we fall back upon our basic ways of experiencing reality, and these basic ways are neurognostically different. They are the nonconscious tacit aspects of our brain-mind which no word can ever adequately voice.

Genetic and Hormonal Differences. These neurosystem differences are found in hormonal and endocrine activity which initiate the differential patterns of female bilateral consciousness and male asymmetrical consciousness, each of which reflects elaborations of subsymbolic and nonconscious processing.

As early as the sixth week of pregnancy the crucial crystallization of sex difference begins.[20] Until that 'moment' the embryo is undifferentiated, neither female nor male; it is simply 'human potentiality.' Physician anthropologist Melvin Konner suggests that 'the basic plan of the mammalian organism is female and stays that way unless told to be otherwise by masculine hormones.'[21] Around the sixth week, fetal androgens begin 'organizing' the neuroanatomy of behavior for future reproductive activity. These androgens 'tune' certain cells to the hormones which will flood the body at puberty. Specifically, the androgen 'tuning' suppresses the capacity for monthly cycling in males.[22]

As birth approaches, the masculinizing hormones, primarily testosterone, have so affected the development of the brain that 'a trained observer, holding a microscope slide [of the hypothalamus] up to the light, can tell the sex of the brain with the naked eye.'[23] The importance of this prebirth difference can be sensed in the fact that the hypothalamus acts as 'an all-powerful liaison between brain and body,' a major center controlling feedback information about everything which happens to us. By monitoring this information, the hypothalamus maintains the balance and stability of our entire system, playing a primary role in such crucial activities as 'courtship, sex, maternal behavior, and violence.'[24]

Adolescent and adult differences are equally prevalent.[25] Being field sensitive and oriented toward interpersonal cooperation, females are more geared to sounds, faces, and emotion. They are more likely than males to agree with others, give them a chance to speak, and acknowledge what others have done. Basically, the 'enabling' interactive style of females acknowledges and supports others and keeps interaction going.

Being field independent and oriented toward competition, males are more geared to sights, objects, and abstractions. They are more likely to interrupt, use commands, and boast. Basically, the 'constricting or restrictive' style of males tends to derail interaction by inhibiting others and causing them to withdraw. Because they carry more emotional concern with 'turf and dominance,' they tend not to disclose their weakness and vulnerability.

I argue that these contrasts reflect differences in dendritic density, the aborization and connections of the neural networks of the brain.[26]

Females have many distributed connections, like bushes and branches, especially in the general sensory region and the back part of the corpus callosum. These densities contribute to their specialized skill in understanding the social world. They are better at perceptual speed and visual memory.[27] With left-handed males, they exhibit a higher rate of cerebral blood flow and greater percentage of fast-perfusing tissue, making them more adept in sensing and synthesizing, even as they use verbal strategies to solve nonverbal problems. I speculate that the reason they 'think longer' before deciding about something – whether food or clothes or evaluation of a workshop – is that they have more dendritic branches carrying information which must be consulted.

Males have many simpler dendritic connections, like trees and trunks, especially in the back part of the corpus callosum, and stronger connections in the right spatial areas. This combination makes them more specialized for understanding the physical world. Being better at perceptual closure and freeing visual patterns from complex arrays,[28] they are more adept in seeing and specifying, even as they use alternative strategies of logic or trial-and-error to engage problem-solving. I suggest that men tend to arrive at conclusions faster than women because they have fewer dendritic structures to take into account.

The sexes also exhibit different vulnerabilities.[29]

Male brains in general and the left hemisphere in particular are more likely to malfunction. A higher percentage of 'autism, schizophrenia, and psychopathy' appear in the male population, along with a tendency toward aggression. If a man suffers right side paralysis and loss of speech, the effects are more likely to be permanent.

Female brains present more right hemisphere malfunctions, especially mood disorders, along with a tendency toward affiliation. If a woman suffers right side paralysis and loss of speech, she is more likely to recover her ability to move and speak. Further, sex-related difficulties are overrepresented and underrepresented in such various areas as 'eating disorders; sexual/physical violence; incest; alcoholism; premenstrual syndrome; pregnancy and childbirth; body image; issues of power, entitlement, self-esteem; and decisions regarding career, lifestyle, and family.'[30]

Sex-gender differences make a difference that is a difference *because the cultural contrasts are derived from biological substrata!*

Differences in Use of Symbols and Spirituality

Cross-cultural evidence demonstrates consistent differences in ways women and men experience religious symbols and appropriate them.[31] Women's brains are predisposed to perceive life – and God – in terms of a pattern of connection and ordinariness and men to perceive life –

and God – in terms of a pattern of polarities and otherness. Whether influenced by genes and/or culture, women and men differ in how they symbolize their relation with God.

Pastoral theologian and psychologist J. David Pierce[32] sought to verify whether left and right brain processing patterns correlate with the way theologians view biblical material, an impressionistic suggestion I have been advancing for some time. He studied a sample of 104 students, 54 males and 50 females, from five seminaries, in terms of their perceptions of a selected scripture passage of Jesus with the disciples in a storm on the Sea of Galilee (Luke 8:22–25) and a photograph of Rembrandt's painting titled 'Storm on the Sea of Galilee.' By a highly technical statistical procedure he combined their responses and clustered them according to major themes.

Three distinct cognitive dimensions emerged. These accounted for 83% of the variance in the similarity of their judgments. Further, the average subject correlation coefficient of .91 indicated a highly reliable pattern. These dimensions were: Cost *versus* Blessing, such as a test of faith or ongoing presence; Relational *versus* Instrumental, such as peaceful light or attempting to stay in control; and Human Efforts *versus* Divine Power, such as crossing over or power of God.

In analyzing the data Pierce found that the sample of theologically liberal women used polar dimensions, such as 'human efforts' *vs* 'divine power' or 'instrumental' *vs* 'relational,' less than either the sample of men or the sample of theologically moderate or conservative women. We can infer from this sample that less liberal women have been socialized into the dominant male-oriented culture. The data give credence to the feminist criticism of a masculinized science and a masculinized theology. The average male – Pierce and myself included – tends to organize reality in terms of dichotomies. Other investigators of 'women's ways of knowing' are identifying a pattern of 'connected knowing' similar to Pierce's data.[33]

Caroline Walker Bynum, Stevan Harrell, and Paula Richman, in *Gender and Religion: On The Complexity of Symbols*[34] marshall cross-cultural evidence to demonstrate consistent differences in the ways women and men experience and appropriate symbols. Women use symbols to mute oppositions by means of paradox or synthesis. In contrast men emphasize opposition and contradiction. The presence or absence of dichotomies seems to be the distinguishing difference.

In a study of *Holy Feast and Holy Fast: The Religious Significance of Food to Medieval Women*,[35] Bynum shows that men construe much of reality 'in terms of either/or.' Thus, at the very core of male experience in the late Middle Ages we find dichotomies and reversals. Men construed the male/female dichotomy – the 'symbol of authority/ nurture, spirit/flesh, law/mercy, strong/weak' – in a broader way to express 'the contrast between God and soul, divinity and humanity, clergy and laity.' For them, the path of spirituality required a reversal of male dominance into a state of female-identification.

The female symbolized a 'dependence on God – both as a way of describing themselves as cared for by God and as a way of underlining their own renunciation of worldly power and prestige.'[36] Only thus could the contradiction between divinity and humanity be reconciled in the Incarnation: God-become-man (*sic*). Crisis of identity, conversion from sinful ways, reversal of role dominance, and the need to embrace the contradictions embedded in opposition and otherness characterized male experience.

Women's experience was one of 'continuity' with their social and biological realities. In their quest for God they became what they already symbolized; namely, 'the fleshly, the nurturing, the suffering, the human.' Instead of inverting what they were, they deepened what they were. Their symbols disclose less contradiction and more 'synthesis and paradox.'[37] Women gave the concept of 'human' a meaning beyond the dichotomy of male and female. Because of their sense of continuity with life, a concept of 'other' played little part.

Women, reflecting their origin in the two-person immediacy of mother-and-child, drew on symbolic aspects of life closer to their ordinary experience such as eating, suffering, and lactating. Women appropriated the dominant view of the cosmos in a way different from men and with different implications for both women and men. Because men were high and lifted up, they needed to be brought low, 'to renounce their dominance.' Women, however, deepened their ordinary experience 'when God impinged upon it.' Their bodies not only served as 'a symbol of the humanness of both genders but also a symbol of – and a means of approach to – the humanity of God.'[38]

For men the dominant symbols were of 'opposition' and 'otherness,' while for women the symbols were of 'continuity' and 'ordinariness.' Even when women used the same symbols and rituals as men, they invested these 'with different meanings and different ways of meaning.'

What was the case in the Late Middle Ages appears to be true today as well. Women's experience of God is more that of deepening their own humanity while men experience the longing to overcome their humanity. An awareness of these differences can enrich 'our understanding of both symbol and humanity,'[39] of both God and creation.

Implications for Pastoral Therapy

Two implications are unavoidable: first, power and status are embodied in every relationship and especially every relationship between a male and a female; and second, women tend to be more open to influence, yet feel at a disadvantage in mixed-sex interactions.[40] Although this generalization is an oversimplification, I would suggest that power reflects gender patterns while women being more open to influence reflects genetic predispositions.

Think of sex-gender differences as masculine power and tree trunks and feminine influence and bushes. Dendritic specificity and dendritic density. Women spin webs of meaning while men concentrate on a dialectical or either-or development of focal meaning. In light of these contrasts we can identify sex-gender-related survival interactions in our pastoral work.[41]

Experiences of dependency, uncertainty and ambiguity trigger the arousal of the sympathetic nervous system, leading to heightened vigilance and tension. But the survival behaviors of women and men differ.

Women tend to slow down, become cautious, hesitate and vacillate. Their survival seems to depend upon *not* acting, at least at the moment. A clue to that survival-via-hesitancy can be identified when we find ourselves becoming emotionally impatient: 'Stop beating around the bush.' 'What's holding you up?' 'Get the show on the road.' 'Come on, get a move on.' They are processing information at the general sensory and visceral levels prior to articulated consciousness.

In contrast, men tend to speed up, turn volatile, strike out or hang on. Their survival appears to depend upon *controlling* the situation, taking charge, at least at the moment. A clue to that survival-via-control can be discerned when we find ourselves getting angry or hostile: 'Who in hell do you think you are!' 'Stop beating on me.' 'You're not as smart as you think.' 'Take your problem and shove it.' They are processing information intentionally and consciously in the frontal regions.

A variation on hesitancy and control comes with the experience of the other looking to us for reassurance and answers. In such cases survival is associated with the relationship itself, moving closer and hanging on, at least at the moment. A clue to that survival-via-contact appears when we find ourselves feeling guilty about what is not happening: 'I'm sorry I didn't know what to do.' 'Forgive me for not being on top of that.' 'I should have known things would go this way.'

Impatience, hostility, guilt – each of these reflects a dance of survival between ourselves and those with whom we work. Our own reactions are clue to our colluding with others in avoiding the work of reality. Having said this, however, I add that these survival patterns tend to be sex-gender-related more than sex-gender-specific. Since we are all more simply human than otherwise, as Harry Stack Sullivan reminded us, we all carry these survival patterns of hesitancy, control, and closeness and their reciprocal reactions of impatience, anger, and guilt. They are embedded in our behavior, accessible only under heightened conditions of vigilance.

The flip side of survival is growth oriented interactions. Responsiveness, confidence, and intentionality activate adaptive patterns, the relaxed spontaneity of the parasympathetic nervous system. Again, we can identify sex-gender patterns. Women tend to emphasize partnership, a web of dendritic connectedness, the sharing of basic 'human alikeness.'[42] Men, in contrast, tend to emphasize capability and dependability, a focus of dendritic specificity. Partnership, capability, and dependability, however, are not qualities restricted to any one sex. These are fundamental human qualities. We differ only in the ways in which we manifest our commonality, our competence, and our reliability.

Conclusion

My point is this: the brains of men and women are organized differently. Specialization makes for opposites and covert hierarchy; bilaterality for continuity and cooperation. Some critics suggest these gender-related, but not gender-specific, differences could be construed as creating new stereotypes, another 'dichotomy.' That is not my intent.

Neither sex bears 'the image and likeness of God,' only the species does: 'male and female created God them' (Genesis 1:26–27).[43] For full knowing, the Godlike takes into account the experiences of both women and men. In studying the subtleties of male and female differences further brain research may eventually assist us in creating a model of behavior we can call fully 'human' and truly 'Godlike' – the male personality balancing the female in his being and the female balancing the male in her being – one image, of equal parts, becoming one humanity.

Different voices reflect different genes.

Notes

1. Sandra Harding and Merrill Hintikka (Eds.), *Discovering Reality: Feminist Perspectives on Epistemology, Metaphysics, Methodology, and Philosophy* (London: D. Reidel Publishing Company, 1983); Doreen Kimura, 'Male Brain, Female Brain: The Hidden Difference,' *Psychology Today*, 1985 (Nov.), pp. 50–58.
2. Carol Gilligan, *In a Different Voice: Psychological Theory and Women's Development* (Cambridge, MA: Harvard University Press, [1982] 1983).
3. Mary Field Belenky, Blythe McVicker Clinchy, Nancy Rule Goldberger, and Jill Mattuch Tarule, *Women's Ways of Knowing: The Development of Self, Voice, and Mind* (New York, NY: Basic Books, 1986).
4. Rosemary Radford Ruether, *Sexism and God-Talk: Toward a Feminist Theology* (Boston, MA: Beacon Press, 1983); Pamela Dickey Young, *Feminist Theology/Christian Theology: In Search of Method* (Minneapolis, MN: Fortress Press, 1990).
5. Charlotte Smith, *Investigation of Brain Wave Symmetry: An EEG Imaging Study Based on the Wakeful Dreaming Process* (Evanston, IL: Ph.D. dissertation Northwestern University, 1989).
6. Ibid. p. 127.
7. D.P. Waber, 'Sex differences in cognition: a Function of maturation rate?' *Science*, 1976, (May), pp. 572–573; Sally P. Springer and Georg Deutsch. *Left Brain, Right Brain*. Third Edition (New York, NY: W.H. Freeman and Company, [1981, 1985] 1989), pp. 183–184.
8. Kenneth Wright, *Vision and Separation: Between Mother and Baby* (Northvale, NJ: Jason Aronson Inc., 1991).
9. Jerre Levy, 'Varieties of Human Brain Organization and the Human Social System,' *Zygon: Journal of Religion and Science*, 1980, Vol. 15, No. 4, pp. 367–371.
10. Nancy Chodorow, *The Reproduction of Mothering: Psychoanalysis and the Sociology of Gender* (Berkeley, CA: University of California Press, [1978] 1979).
11. Levy, *op. cit.*
12. Ibid.
13. See, *e.g.*, Caroline Walker Bynum, Stevan Harrell, and Paul Richman (Eds.), *Gender and Religion: On the Complexity of Symbols* (Boston, MA: Beacon Press, 1986).
14. Chodorow, *op cit.*; Jean Baker Miller, *Toward A New Psychology of Women* (Boston, MA: Beacon Press, 1976).

15. Judith V. Jordan, Alexandra G. Kaplan, Jean Baker Miller, Irene P. Stiver, and Janet L. Surrey, *Women's Growth in Connection: Writings from the Stone Center* (New York, NY: The Guilford Press, 1991).

16. Jean Baker Miller, 'The Development of Women's Sense of Self,' in Judith V. Jordan, Alexandra G. Kaplan, Jean Baker Miller, Irene P. Stiver, and Janet L. Surrey, *Women's Growth in Connection: Writings from the Stone Center* (New York, NY: The Guilford Press, 1991), pp. 26–27.

17. Kathleen McCarthy, 'People Presume Women and Men Differ; Do They?' *APA Monitor*, 1990 (October), p. 33.

18. Joseph B. Hellige, 'Hemispheric Asymmetry,' in Mark R. Rosenzweig and Lyman W. Porter, (Eds.) *Annual Review of Psychology*: Vol. 41 (Palo Alto, CA: Annual Reviews, Inc., 1990), p. 74.

19. Kay Deaux and Brenda Major, 'Putting Gender into Context: An Interactive Model of Gender-Related Behavior,' *Psychological Review*, 1987, Vol. 94, No. 3, pp. 39–89.

20. Beryl Lieff Benderly, *The Myths of Two Minds: What Gender Means and Doesn't Mean* (New York, NT: Doubleday, 1987), p. 14.

21. Melvin Konner, *The Tangled Wing: Biological Constraints on the Human Spirit* (New York, NY: Harper Colophon, [1982] 1983), p. 122.

22. Benderly, *op. cit.*, pp. 17–18.

23. Konner, *op. cit.*, pp. 125–126, 115ff.

24. Ibid., p. 117.

25. Springer & Deutsch, *op. cit.*; Eleanor E. Maccoby, 'Gender and Relationships: A Developmental Account,' *American Psychologist*, 1990, Vol. 45, No. 4, pp. 513–20; Levy, *op. cit.*; Deborah Tannen, *You Just Don't Understand: Women and Men in Conversation* (New York, NY: William Morrow and Company, Inc., 1990).

26. Marian Cleeves Diamond, 'Age, Sex, and Environmental Influences on Anatomical Asymmetry in Rat Forebrain,' in N. Geschwind and A.M. Galaburda (Eds.) *Cerebral Dominance: The Biological Foundations*, (Cambridge, MA: Cambridge University Press 1984); Marian Cleeves Diamond, *Enriching Heredity, The Impact of the Environment on the Anatomy of the Brain* (New York, NY: The Free Press, 1988); Bryan Kolb and Ian Q. Wishaw, *Fundamentals of Human Neuropsychology*. Second edition (New York: W.H. Freeman and Company, [1980] 1985), pp. 363-372.

27. Kolb and Whishaw, *op. cit.*, p. 365.

28. Ibid.

29. Pierre Flor-Henry, *Cerebral Bases of Psychopathology* (Boston, MA: John Wright-PSE, Inc., 1983).

30. C.E. Schuler, 'Women, Psychology of,' in Rodney J. Hunter (Gen. ed.) *Dictionary of Pastoral Care and Counselling* (Nashville, TN: Abingdon Press, 1990), p. 1333; Rosalind C. Barnett, Lois Biener, and Grace K. Baruch, (Eds.), *Gender and Stress* (New York, NY: The Free Press, 1987); Marcie Kaplan, 'A Women's View of DSM-III,' *American Psychologist*, 1983 (July), pp. 786-798, 802ff.

31. Bynum, *et al., op. cit.*; Caroline Walker Bynum, *Holy Feast and Holy Fast: The Religious Significance of Food to Medieval Women* (Berkley, CA: University of California Press, 1987).

32. J. David Pierce, *A Multidimensional Scaling of the Cognitive Dimensions used by Seminary Students In Their Perception of Biblical Material* (Evanston, IL: Ph.D. dissertation Northwestern University, 1986); J. David Pierce, 'Styles of Believing Analytic and Imagistic,' in James B. Ashbrook (Ed.) *Faith and Ministry in Light of the Double Brain* (Bristol, IN: Wyndham Hall Press, 1989), pp. 243-61.

33. Belenky, *et al., op. cit.*

34. Bynum, *et al., op. cit.*

35. Bynum, *op. cit.*

36. Ibid., pp. 281–284.

37. Ibid., pp. 288–294.

38. Ibid., pp. 295–296.

39. Bynum. *et al., op. cit.*, pp. 14, 16.

40. Maccoby, *op. cit.*

41. The following patterns are adaptations of Heinz Kohut's transference patterns of mirroring, idealizing and twinship.

42. The phrase is from Heinz Kobut's definition of empathy. 'The Psychoanalyst in the Community of Scholars,' in P. Ornstein (Ed.) *The Search for the Self Selected Writings of Heinz Kobut*, Vol. 2 (New York, NY: International Universities Press, 1978), p. 713, quoted

by Judith V. Jordan, 'Empathy and Self Boundaries,' in Jordan *et al., op. cit.,* p. 79.

43. Phyllis Bird, 'Male and Female He Created Them:' Gen, 1:27b In 'The Context of the Priestly Account of Creation,' *Harvard Theological Review*, 1981, Vol. 74, pp. 2, 129–159.

2.5 Androgyny and Beyond

Roland Martinson

Are men different than women? Biological definitions of male and female divide almost all of humanity into nearly even halves. History presents men's experience to be different than women's. Women describe their experience to be disparate from men's. Men are not the same as women.

I. Differences and Likeness Between Women and Men

In what sense do men and women differ? Males and females differ genetically. Males have a Y chromosome; females have no Y chromosome, but one more X chromosome. Males and females differ anatomically. Their pelvic bones are shaped differently; they have different reproductive organs and genitalia; some of their glands and brain cells are different. Men and women differ physiologically. Their hormonal balances are not the same. Their metabolic functions and rhythms are different. Women menstruate during portions of their lives; men do not. There are also some general differences between men and women which are grounded in biology. Men are usually taller than women, although some women may be taller than some men. Men are more visually-oriented; women are more audio-oriented. Most women give birth. Many nurse children. Significant physical differences exist between men and women. However, after these physical differences have been accurately articulated, one discovers males and females are biologically more alike than different.

Are men's and women's differences merely biological? Historically, men have lived differently than women. Male and female power, income, roles, rights, temperaments, dress, interests and goals have been different, although not universally so in every civilization. Western civilization has been characterized by a dualism which presents men as more dominant, independent, active, rational, assertive, analytical, and combative; it presents women as more subordinate, dependent, passive, emotional, receptive, intuitive and tolerant. In North America, not all men and women are this way but most are expected to be this way. Men have studied predominantly male samples and cast their findings as representative of all human experience. Women disagree. They are naming their own experience and find it to be different than men's or what men say about women. In the United States, working women earn approximately 40 per cent less than working men. More women than men live in poverty. More women are single parents. More men than women are in the military and ordained ministry. Only men have been president of the United States. Significant societal differences exist between men and women. After these differences have been accurately articulated, one discovers males and females are culturally more different than alike.

Cultural studies of men and women reveal not only difference, but difference as the occasion for prejudice, oppression and abuse. Men are considered the norm; women the exception. Men are in charge; women are to follow. Men are fully enfranchised; women are not. Women have a lesser place in a man's world. Women are not the only ones to suffer. The stereotypical male roles and definitions of masculinity are major factors in diseases which kill men. The life span of the average male is seven years less than the average female in the United States.

How do these differences between men and women arise? Most of the differences between men and women have biological origins. Chromosomal, anatomical and hormonal differences are scientifically demonstrable. Their origins as well as their functions are known. There is general consensus on the source of these physical sexual differences. The origins of male and female societal differences are less clear and widely debated. Some social scientists claim biological roots for male and female differences in temperament, abilities and interests. Their arguments take one of three general lines of thought.

The first line of thought suggests societal differences between the sexes are due at least in part to differences between female and male nervous systems. As the male fetus develops in the womb, the testes secrete androgen which influences the growth of the brain. The female fetus does not produce this, nor an analogous hormone at this stage. Therefore, male and female brains differ and this difference is the basis for differences in behavior.[1] The second line of thought is psychoanalytical. It conceives of feminine or masculine behavior as response to body structure. In this view, one's experience of one's body or that of others is a major factor in producing sex-specific personality traits.[2] A third line of thought suggests a relationship between certain sexual hormones and behavior. One such view holds that testosterone is a major cause in male aggression.[3]

None of these lines of thought has been conclusively demonstrated. Each of them has been challenged by some social scientist. The psychoanalytical view has been particularly attacked by women. All these approaches, plus other viable hypotheses concerning the relationship between biology and societal sexual differences require more study. There is speculation, much bias, some plotted ground, but little solid knowledge.

How do the differences between men and women arise? Some differences have biological origins; other differences may. A great many of the differences in power, income, rights, roles, dress and goals are clearly social convention. Somehow combinations of thought and action resulted in beliefs, attitudes and social patterns greatly differentiating and subordinating women to men. In western civilization, a great many complex factors present themselves as possibly influencing this process: the need of males to have some meaningful and controlling connection to their offspring; the necessity in less technological cultures for women to be closely involved in the early stages of childrearing; the symbolic analogies from nature (particularly the animal kingdom in temperate climates); the role of brute strength in hunting-gathering, agricultural and industrial societies; the space to isolate oneself and one's group; the possibility of conquering another without destroying oneself; the philosophical legacy of Platonic dualism; and, the theological impact of the patriarchy of Scripture and the Christian church. These are but a few of the potential contributors. None has the power in and of itself to generate the great societal differences between men and women. All of these, together with the biological differences, create a powerful, shaping force. The social construction of reality needs more study. There is speculation, much bias, some plotted ground, but little solid knowledge.

How do the differences between men and women arise? Some differences definitely do have physical origins; other differences may arise from the physical. A great many seem to be social constructions. Much is unclear; many proposals are more a reflection of their author's bias than verifiable truth. More study is needed. However, an important corollary discovery has arisen from the inquiry. Human beings and human societies are extremely plastic and diverse. People can and do choose a great variety of vital lifestyles and values. Human beings and societies can participate in defining and determining significant dimensions of their sexual destiny.

Are the differences between men and women inevitable? Chromosomal, anatomical, hormonal and childbearing differences are biological. Does that mean they are inevitable? Maybe not. Usual, yes, but maybe not inevitable. Even these basic, biological realities are becoming malleable in a technological society. Chromosomal research, reconstructive surgery, drug therapy, and contraceptives are but a sample of the resources available for influencing these biological differences. From these basic female and male realities, the plasticity of human sexual differences increases as one moves toward cultural realities such as dress which changes in western civilizations nearly every year. Are the differences between men and women inevitable? Perhaps a few are; but in a sophisticated, technological society, a very few. Consequently, the studies of men and women in technological civilizations have raised a new and central issue.

Are the differences between men and women desirable? A cacophony of voices provide widely-divergent answers. Among the voices are those speaking a resounding, yes! 'Vive la difference,' some say. Preserve and foster the differences; these differences enrich life; they give it spice and variety. Other yea sayers use the Christian Scriptures or their religious tradition to prove that male and female differences are divinely mandated; some of these make it clear the differences are to include male domination of females. Other yea sayers shout: 'Different, yes and separate and enemies.' These people envision a battle between the sexes, at least until women have won their freedom and established justice for themselves. Among the cacophony of voices are those saying differences between men and women are not desirable or at least need to be greatly diminished. 'Unisex,' some say. Women must give up their second class ways and become like men to form a common brotherhood.[4] Although those who argue for unisex are few, there are many women who follow a male road toward what they believe to be liberation. Much more prevalent are those who present an androgynous vision for men, women and society.

II. The Androgynous Vision

Androgyny is not a new concept. Androgyny is a combination of the Greek words: andro, meaning male and gynos, meaning female. Strictly speaking, an androgynous person is one with both male and female natures and characteristics. In ancient Latin, androgynous equalled hermaphroditic. In ancient Greece, Dionysus was pictured as a being with both male and female natures. The search for the androgyne is a minor theme throughout western literature.[5]

Androgyny usually has a double, but limited meaning in contemporary usage.[6] An androgynous person has both so-called feminine and masculine characteristics; this person is independent and dependent; active and passive; rational and emotional; assertive and receptive; analytical and intuitive; combative and tolerant; etc. These traits and behaviors are expressed freely in response to different life situations. In general, contemporary usage, androgyny does not refer to anatomy or sexual orientation.

In its second contemporary usage, androgyny refers to a society in which both females and males and the so-called feminine and masculine traits and behaviors are equally valued and incorporated into the fabric of civilization. In this sense, androgyny is a symbol of societal equality, justice and freedom. Androgyny becomes a vision of individual and societal wholeness:

> The ideal of androgyny begins with the recognition that, out of the whole range of human potentialities, certain traits have been differentially assigned to men and to women, and that all such systems of arbitrary distinctions between the sexes are crippling to women and ultimately to everyone. Androgyny is a form of life in which every person will be enabled to become a whole human being.[7]

In this full blown form, androgyny envisions females and males who may possess different chromosomes, anatomy and hormones, but whose traits and behavior are similarly representative of the entire range of human existence. All roles, other than those most strictly anatomically determined, will be available to both sexes. Female children would not be socialized differently than male children. Both men and women will be fully enfranchised. Society will be informed by symbols and models of sexual equality, interdependence and completeness.

The androgynous vision is variously articulated and vigorously debated. There is much to commend it. The vast majority of so-called feminine and masculine traits and behaviors are clearly socially conditioned. Great energy goes into establishing and maintaining them. These sexual stereotypes create destructive facades, limit human potential and alienate people from themselves and one another.

> He is playing masculine. She is playing feminine. He is playing masculine because she is playing feminine. She is playing feminine because he is playing masculine. He is playing the kind of man that she thinks the kind of woman she is playing ought to admire. She is playing the kind of woman that he thinks the kind of man he is playing ought to desire.
>
> If he were not playing masculine, he might well be more feminine than she is – except when she is playing very feminist. If she were not playing feminine, she might well be more masculine than he is – except when he is playing very masculine....
>
> She is supposed to admire him for the masculinity in him that she fears in herself. He is supposed to desire her for the femininity in her that he despises in himself.
>
> He desires her for her femininity which is his femininity, but which he can never lay claim to. She admires him for his masculinity which is her masculinity, but which she can never lay claim to. Since he may only love his own femininity in her, he envies her her femininity. Since she may only love her own masculinity in him, she envies him his masculinity. The envy poisons their love.
>
> He, coveting her unattainable femininity, decides to punish her. She, coveting his unattainable masculinity, decides to punish him. He denigrates her femininity – which he is supposed to desire and which he really envies – and becomes more aggressively masculine. She feigns disgust at his masculinity – which she is supposed to admire and which she really envies – and becomes more fastidiously feminine. He is becoming less and less what he wants to be. She is becoming less and less what she wants to be. But now he is more manly than ever, and she is more womanly than ever.[8]

The androgynous vision would do away with these artificial and destructive conventions and replace them with socialization more in tune with personal uniqueness and societal health. Human energy could be freed for use in more creative pursuits. Individuals could be more true to themselves. Relationships between the sexes could become more genuine. Human abilities, particularly those of women, could be released and fostered in the marketplace, the church and the world as well as in friendships and families.

This androgynous vision enlarges to become a view of society. Sexual justice, equality and mutuality are its foundational building-blocks. They are seen to foster harmony, cooperation, security, human worth and interdependence. The vision sees women's as well as men's powers to be necessary for societal survival and development. It encourages tapping the full range of human potentialities to build a better world.

III. Beyond Androgyny

A society of justice, equality and mutuality between the sexes. Men and women encouraged to be genuine and fully themselves. All people, fully enfranchised, contributing to a vital, interdependent world. Is this not a desirable vision? The androgynous vision has weaknesses.

Androgynous persons are to possess both feminine and masculine traits and behaviors. Feminine and masculine labels are, in most cases, arbitrary. Where they are arbitrarily applied to human traits and behaviors, they need to go. They are not helpful; they perpetuate false images of men and women; they are infected by the assumptions androgyny is meant to overcome.

The difficulty goes deeper than labels. The androgynous vision would encourage both the so-called feminine and masculine traits and behaviors in individuals and society. The question arises: are all of these traits and behaviors desirable? Are either dominance or submission desirable goals for human behavior? What about manipulativeness, narcissism, and cunning? What common good can come from exploitation, ruthlessness and aggressiveness? The full range of traits and behaviors included in the so-called feminine and masculine needs to be scrutinized. Each trait or behavior can be weighed against its contribution to a just and humane society.

There is a more serious difficulty. The problem is not only with certain traits and behaviors that are undesirable, but with that view of reality which would split all traits and behaviors. Are independence and dependence, rationality and emotionality, analytical and intuitive, assertive and receptive or individuality and relatedness mutually exclusive? The dualism which informs most western understandings of reality would say so. Descartes speaks of the ideal individual as one who requires nothing but himself to exist. In this ideal an individual is to be independent, self-sufficient and autonomous. This dichotomous view of reality is artificial and destructive. It has not only separated men and women, but split history and nature, humankind from the earth, spirit from body and nation from nation. A new vision of reality is needed which takes androgynous concerns seriously, yet goes both behind and beyond androgyny.

Androgyny is susceptible to other dangers which need to be addressed in any vision of gender and relationship between the sexes. The androgynous vision could become a stereotype of the ideal person or society which is more oppressive than what it replaces. One could have a world in which an individual is not only free to develop the full range of constructive human traits and behaviors, but is under great compulsion to do so. In this world, everyone is to be everything. In this existence one finds autonomous definitions of persons and society not unlike those of Descartes. Finally, androgyny raises the question of who will participate in shaping the new vision of men and women and by what criteria. Certainly, much of it will just emerge from the dynamic forces already at work. But to the extent that humankind is able to consciously and deliberately influence the process, will only those presently enfranchised (men) shape the vision? Must not women as well as men, children as well as adults, past and future as well as the present and marginal as well as enfranchised participate? As they participate, they need to tap the constructive balances of the diversity and unity in the human situation.

A new vision of gender and sexual relationships is emerging. Ours is a pregnant moment for Christians to join in shaping changing sexual understandings. Our Christian faith has implications for gender issues; our biblical heritage provides perspectives; our traditions contain resources; our experience has much to offer.

A new vision of gender and sexual relationships might well consider the following:

1) The establishment of justice, equality and mutuality for females and males;
2) The enfranchisement of a broader range of constructive human traits and behaviors;
3) The reflection of genuine female and male differences in social construction;
4) The reflection of individual and societal particularities in social construction; and
5) The development of an interdependent vision of reality.

Although naive and flawed, the androgynous vision's call for sexual justice, equality and mutuality is fundamentally sound. There is strong support for these dimensions of the vision in the biblical message. Both men and women have been created by God in God's image. Both men and women receive God's blessing and charge to multiply and care for the earth. Both men and women are direct and full recipients of God's grace. Both men and women are called to be God's people and servants. Both men and women are heirs in God's future. These basic understandings of females and males suggest what men and women are to have: the freedom to discover who one is and what one wants to be; the right to share equally in making decisions which affect all humankind; the opportunity to develop all one's capacities, mental, physical and spiritual; the right to find satisfaction not only in nurturing and supporting others, but in being nurtured and supported; the right to be equipped emotionally, intellectually and materially; the right to stand on one's own two feet; the power to speak one's thoughts and to be heard by others; the opportunity to act and make one's actions effective. Whatever else the emerging vision of gender and sexual relationships is becoming, it must become a world of symbols, structures and dynamics which establish justice, equality and mutuality for both men and women. Symbols imaging opposing principles need to be challenged and reconceptualized. Structures fostering injustice, inequality and exclusivity need to be dismantled and reconstructed. Dynamics resulting in domination, isolation and exploitation need to be identified and redirected. Language, imagery, leadership, laws, institutions, roles, relationships, work and worship can reflect justice, equality and mutuality. Men and women of faith can explore and reconstitute each of these within the church and join other forces in doing the same throughout the world.

A new vision of gender might well enfranchise a broader range of constructive human potentialities. Certain human traits and behaviors have been linked to men and with men have been viewed as more powerful and desirable. Independence, activity, rationality, assertiveness, analysis, competition and individuality have been highly valued; dependence, passivity, emotionality, receptivity, intuition, cooperation and relatedness have been of lesser value or devalued. Androgyny would value all the so-called feminine and masculine characteristics in persons and society. A more discrete vision is needed. The biblical message presents humankind with a broad range of traits and behaviors; it does not present all human traits and behaviors as life-giving. Every human trait and behavior can be explored and evaluated as to its ability to promote life in individuals and society. Those which give life can be enfranchised and promoted. Those which do not, need to be carefully examined and reworked or rejected.

Who decides what gives life? Those representative of the society need to be involved. Persons of diverse racial, religious, socioeconomic, sexual, political and physical perspectives can be participants. Public conversation and persuasion is needed. The process itself can become a large part of the vision. The biblical view of reality is one wherein justice, equality and mutuality can break forth in symbols of God and human traits and behavior which promote truth, peace and well-being. Large dimensions of this work wait to be tackled by linguists, liturgists, prophets, politicians, biblical scholars, leadership developers, business leaders, social scientists, care-givers, etc.

Men and women are not as different as traditional stereotyping would have them be. Neither are men and women the same. God created humankind in God's image; female and male God created them. Almost all human beings are either man or woman or choose to become one or the other. The differences between females and males need be neither overworked nor unimportant. Different chromosomes, anatomy and hormones are not fully determinative of human destiny, but they affect human existence. Men don't give birth to children. Women don't produce sperm. There are separate women's and men's pro tennis circuits. Different histories, social conditioning and societal experiences are not fully determinative of human destiny, but they are realities men and women need to take seriously in their development. Men have dominated women. Women have been primary nurturers. In the United States, the average age of death is seven years earlier for men than women. Even though men and women are fundamentally much more alike than different, the differences are real, need to be taken seriously, and need not become the occasion for stereotyping nor exploitation. Female and male differences can be accurately discovered, articulated and validated. There need to be both female and male symbols of God. Motherhood and fatherhood share parenthood. But motherhood is not fatherhood. More women might well become jockeys; more men might well handle jackhammers. Men and women need to be thoroughly, if not evenly represented in decision-making structures which affect humanity. Women need to speak for women; men for men. Presently, women have different issues than men do in human liberation. Traditionally, sin may primarily exhibit itself as pride in men and timidity in women. Men's and women's realities are always contextual and need to be viewed in their concreteness. The emerging vision of gender and sexual relationships must be developed into a society in which the genuine differences between men and women are discovered and validated. Justice, equality and mutuality can be enhanced by particularity and diversity.

A new vision of gender and sexual relationships can provide symbols and models which open men and women to their uniqueness without creating a superhuman stereotype. What are the rich potentialities present in humanity? Which of them make for the good, right, and beautiful? How does one encourage the uniqueness in each man and woman? How does one foster the uniqueness of a particular civilization in a particular time and place? How does the freedom of a unique individual fit with the good of a particular society? Are there symbols and models which free and expand, rather than oppress and limit? Each of these questions needs to be asked separately and in relation to each other. One biblical view of reality suggests the importance of the uniqueness, worth and freedom of each person within the uniqueness, value and necessity of an integrated, interdependent world. Each person is a gift and has gifts for the community. Each individual has need of the community and can be enriched by the community's gifts. Each man, each woman can be free without having to be everything; each woman, each man can be free to work out their uniqueness in relationship to and enriched by the uniqueness of others in society. Friendships, marriages and families can take a variety of forms in providing for basic human needs. Partnerships between males and females can be mutually beneficial while infinitely different. Unique individuals can complement without dominating one another. Individuality and diversity can exist within relatedness and unity.

Most importantly, a new vision of gender and sexual relationships needs to be grounded in an interdependent view of reality. Plato can give way to the Yahwist; dualism can be reconstructed; and existence can be unified. Both stereotypical views of men and women and androgynous visions of persons emphasize a dichotomous view of reality. The first view splits both men and women and their character-istics; the second vision splits their characteristics and encourages persons to be autonomous. Neither position is adequate nor life-giving. The Old Testament view of reality is covenantal. God is the source and sustainer of all creation. The entire created order is organ-ically and volitionally connected to its source who has promised never to leave nor destroy it. Life within the existing creation is organic and volitional. It is based on interdependent patterns and promises. Both the patterns and promises are malleable and interconnected. The cultural and historical, which are the arenas of social construction, are to be based on covenants; that is, they are to be grounded in vows mutually agreed upon, respectful of all parties, open to renegotiation, inclusive of the full range of life and death issues and subject to inter-nal and external sanctions. In this view of reality females and males are unique, of equal value and mutually interdependent one of another, biologically and culturally. In this view of reality, individuality is not separated from, nor antithetical to, relatedness, but they are enabling dimensions of each other. One can only have individual existence out of one's relationships to others and the earth. One can only know relat-edness through individuation and maturation which creates the specificity from which to be an other. Existence is essentially connected and interdependent.

Valerie Saiving, a process theologian, borrowing heavily on the Whiteheadian concept of the 'rhythm of process'[9] holds a similar view of reality:

> Not only are individuality and relatedness compatible aspects of every actuality, these two principles require each other. And since they require each other, neither is more 'real,' important or valuable than the other. On the contrary, individuality and relatedness support and enhance one another. The more profound and complex an occasion's relationship to the world from which it arises, the greater its opportunity to achieve unique value for itself; the more unique its individual satisfaction, the more valuable its potential contribution to the world which supersedes it. What Whitehead calls the 'rhythm of process' at the heart of actuality is a rhythmic alternation between giving and receiving, between the appro-priation of others for the enrichment of oneself and the yielding up of oneself for the enrichment of others.[10]

Christian men and women can vigorously explore and present the covenantal view of reality; they can appropriate the compatible notions of process thought in pressing the case for an interdependent view of the world. Preachers, teachers, worship leaders and administrators might well proclaim, present, and organize within this conceptual framework. A theology born of foundational biblical concepts can reform our dualistically skewed tradition and provide a lodestar for men's and women's lives and a more just and lively world.

Notes
1. See John Money and Anke A. Ehrhardt, *Man and Woman, Boy and Girl* (Baltimore: John Hopkins Press, 1972).
2. See James Strachey, ed., *Sigmund Freud: Collected Papers* (New York: Basic Books, 1959).
3. See Steven Goldberg, *The Inevitability of Patriarchy* (New York: William Morrow, 1973).
4. See Simone de Beauvoir, *The Second Sex* (New York: Alfred Knopf, 1953). Although de Beauvoir is arguing for androgyny and makes many valuable observations, she pushes for a world in which women give up their evolutionary inferior traits and behaviors and become like men to form a 'brotherhood.'
5. See Elemire Zolla, *The Androgyne* (New York: Crossroads, 1981).
6. See Betty and Theodore Roszak, eds., *Masculine/Feminine* (New York: Harper and Row, 1969); and Dorothy Dinnerstein, *The Mermaid and the Minotaur* (New York: Harper and Row, 1976).
7. Valerie C. Saiving, 'Androgynous Life: A Feminist Appropriation of Process Thought,' in *Feminism and Process Thought*, ed. Sheila Greeve Davaney (New York: The Edwin Mellon Press, 1981) 15.
8. Betty and Theodore Roszak, vii and viii.
9. Alfred North Whitehead, *Modes of Thought* (New York: The Free Press, 1968) 88.
10. V. Saiving, 26.

3. Power and Relation

The operation of power within relationships has been a major concern of the feminist movement. In this section we reproduce three articles which explore this dynamic in very different ways but conclude that power within relationships is capable of being constructed and experienced not merely as domination. Daphne Hampson, in 'On Power and Gender', takes as her starting point for a discussion on power within the Christian tradition Carol Gilligan's analysis of the way men and women view themselves in relation to the world. Gilligan concluded that men tend to think of themselves as an isolated self in competition with others. They are threatened by relationships, by intimacy. They perceive ethics in terms of boundaries around individuals which others must not infringe. Women on the other hand see themselves in terms of connection with others. They are threatened by isolation and see ethics in terms of responsibilities to others. Men construct their world in terms of hierarchy, women in terms of webs. Hampson demonstrates the extent to which the Judaeo-Christian tradition has constructed its dominant model of God to mirror male self-perception. She also offers incisive criticism of those who wish to claim that God uses his power to intervene on the side of the suffering and oppressed, pointing out that it is not actually liberating for women to have men (whether human or divine) intervening on our behalf. The need is for men to step aside to allow women to work out their own future. The powerful male God is at the heart of the Christian tradition but so too is the model of powerlessness. On the cross God becomes powerless for us, breaking his self on our behalf. Hampson articulates the disquiet many women feel with this model, aware of the way it has been used to justify the marginalisation of women in the Christian tradition: 'Such a religion of self-sacrifice may indeed serve as the "opium" of women.' The virtue of the powerless is to claim power and pride, not sacrifice that which they have not even got. Women need to engage in an Exodus from those things which disempower them, to seek a new integrity, on the edge of patriarchy. So Hampson turns to empowerment, a concept which she believes has no place in the Judaeo-Christian tradition but which is lived out in women's groups where women hear one another into speech/being and in the process find a sense of self, a power locked inside. The virtue which is required for empowerment is friendship, relations of mutuality, justice, fidelity, respect and affection. In this process the self is found not lost, a person comes into their own. Hampson finds no Christian symbol or doctrine capable of empowering women and she herself, along with many women, is a spiritual person but not a Christian. The model of God needed for this paradigm is a God who is not separate from us nor above us, neither serving us nor sacrificing himself for us but one with us, enabling us to be ourselves and empowering us, not a separate self but the basis of all selves. Only with such a different image of God, and with the paradigm of empowerment at the heart of our ethic, is the possibility of a humanity based upon mutual empowerment possible.

Mary Grey in her article, 'Claiming Power-in-Relation: Exploring the Ethics of Connection', tests the view most famously articulated by the lesbian feminist theologian Carter Heyward that God is power-in-relation, and that the way to manifest God's presence in the world is through a recognition of and a building up of 'radical relatedness' and a sense of 'connectedness'. She first deals with the apparent failure of feminism to realise such radical relatedness within its own ranks and outlines some of the radical differences between women and the power dynamics in which they exist which have been ignored. She also notes that existing in a society which deprives women of a sense of self is bound to be damaging even to those women within the feminist network. Women must acknowledge that they too have colluded in oppression, of ourselves, of other women, and of nature. They too have become locked into the 'individualistic/ enclosed I'. These facts should not prompt us into dropping the dream of connectedness but propel us to work harder to develop a metaphysic and ethic of inter-relatedness. Drawing on women's experiences of 'epiphanies of connection', Grey argues that such experiences undermine the dualistic thinking that has done so much damage to our understandings of our selves and our relationships. In particular it demands that we see ourselves not as isolated selves but a self only in relation – 'I become only in relation to you. We are part of each other'. Grey also wants to claim interconnectedness as a new revelatory paradigm (for a fuller exploration of this see her book, *Wisdom of Fools? Seeking Revelation for Today*, SPCK, London, 1993). It is through interconnectedness that divine power-in-relation is mediated, power meaning the 'relational drive and energy' which empowers human beings and manifests God's presence between us. In the midst of a tragic world where webs of disconnection threaten to overwhelm us, it is important to be 'mutually messianic', redeeming each other through right relationship and giving each other the strength to sustain broken relationships.

Sandra Friedman and Alec Irwin, in 'Christian Feminism, Eros, and Power in Right Relation', explore the place of eros in constructing sexual theologies. The lesbian African-American poet Audre Lorde reclaimed the erotic as deep body knowledge, the life-force of all women, a power which lifts us beyond the dualisms of the tradition and which is operative in all our creative acts. It is deep joy. Carter Heyward was one of the first to reflect theologically on Lorde's reclamation of the erotic. She claimed eros is our deep desire for mutuality, the power that propels us towards others seeking right relationship. She believes that it is in the erotic that we have our fullest experience of the love of God. Under patriarchy the erotic has been made into the 'confused, the trivial, the psychotic, the plasticised sensation' (Lorde). Experience of real eros exposes this and further reveals the 'genderness of power'. It fills us with righteous rage, propelling those in touch with it to work for political change so that all human needs are met. Whilst all theologians who wish to reclaim the erotic want to emphasise that it is a power experienced in many different ways, not merely in the narrowly sexual, they would also want to say that the experience of the erotic in sexual pleasure has an important political dimension, for 'sexual union experienced under conditions of genuine mutuality empowers and galvanises the participants for effort in other areas'. There is no longer a barrier between the private and public, the bedroom and the political arena. Each is present in the other and inspired by it. Justice is at the heart of eros. Justice involves respect for others, respect for dignity, freedom, difference and honesty. It can also mean respecting someone enough to fight with them. Experience of eros gives us those essential brief foretastes of what is to come, it shows us that mutuality and justice are possibilities. The authors also deal with objections to theology grounded in eros, implicitly drawing attention to the difficulties of using the term in a societal context where its meaning is very specific and narrow. They also note the criticism made of erotic theology by some black and Asian women theologians, that the language used by those advocating an erotic theology could be interpreted as justifying pleasure-seeking as an alternative to political struggle. These same critics also point out that many women's experience of sex and its construction is so violent and so damaging that it is hard for them to believe that erotic theology could ever be liberating. Notions of sex and sexuality are not mediated to us pure and unspotted by societal values. There is not some pure essential experience of sexuality waiting to be uncovered. In patriarchal society sex is domination and submission. Many would argue that the way to redeem sexuality is to deal with the political reality of the gender dynamics of power.

Daphne Hampson is Lecturer in the Department of Divinity, University of St Andrews. Her article, 'On Power and Gender' was first published in *Modern Theology*, vol. 4, no. 3, April 1988, pp. 235–50.

Mary Grey is Professor of Contemporary Theology at the University of Southampton. Her article, 'Claiming Power in Relation: Exploring the Ethics of Connection' was first published in the *Journal of Feminist Studies in Religion*, vol. 7, Spring 1991, pp. 7–18.

Sandra Friedman and Alex Irwin's article, 'Christian Feminism, Eros, and Power in Right Relation' first appeared in *Cross Currents*, vol. 40, Fall 1990, pp. 387–405.

3.1 On Power and Gender

Daphne Hampson

In this paper I take three paradigms: powerfulness, powerlessness and empowerment. I suggest that the first two paradigms, powerfulness and powerlessness, particularly in the form of powerlessness through the abnegation of power, are major paradigms in the Judaeo-Christian tradition, and reflect a male structuring of reality. Feminists self-consciously, and I think women in general, have a paradigm of mutual empowerment. I suggest that that paradigm is not present in the tradition in any significant way. I then ask what a model of God would be like which was commensurate with women's practice of empowerment.

I turn first to powerfulness, power as dominant or exercised. That God is seen as powerful in the tradition is clear. I want rather to draw attention to the way in whch God is conceived as being powerful, what being powerful implies, and to suggest that it has certain features in common with the male structuring of reality. A good way to get at this is to look at Carol Gilligan's discussion of the way in which men and women structure reality in her book *In A Different Voice*.[1] Gilligan is a developmental psychologist at Harvard, and the book the result of much empirical research. Gilligan concludes tht the two sexes understand themselves in relation to the world and others very differently. Men think in terms of an isolated self. They see themselves as in competition with others. They are at the centre of their world, and they see the world in relation to themselves. What is threatening is that others should come too close. Men have problems with relationship. They see ethics in terms of individual rights and the delineation of boundaries so that people do not infringe the rights of others. By contrast women see themselves in relation to others. They are interested in connectedness and interdependence. What is threatening is that they should become isolated. Women have problems with differentiation of the self. They see ethics in terms of responsibilities to others and are disinterested in abstract rules. In experiments in which people are asked to write stories to go with pictures, men, to a significant degree, project violence into pictures which show people in close physical proximity. The study started through Susan Pollak's observation of what Gilligan calls the seemingly 'bizarre imagery of violence' in men's stories written in response to a picture of an apparently tranquil scene: a couple sitting on a bench by a river next to a low bridge. More than twenty-one per cent of the eighty-eight men set the task, wrote stories containing incidents of violence: homicide, suicide, stabbing, kidnapping or rape. None of the fifty women set the task projected violence into the scene. Women's stories overall contain less violence. Where women are inclined to see violence is in situations portraying what may be called impersonal achievement. Women most frequently projected violence into a picture showing a man at his desk in a high rise office block; the only picture showing a person on his own.

Gilligan concludes: 'Male ... identity is threatened by intimacy while female ... identity is threatened by separation.' Men think in terms of 'a self defined through separation', women 'a self delineated through connection'. The danger men describe in their stories of intimacy is a danger of entrapment, of being caught in a smothering relationship, or of humiliation. The danger women portray is the danger of isolation. Women see aggression to arise from 'the isolation of self and ... the hierarchical construction of human relationships'. They are concerned for 'activities through which relationships are woven and connection sustained'. Men, Gilligan concludes, think in terms of a model which may be called 'hierarchy', while women think in terms of 'web'. Men wish to be alone at the top and fear others will come too close. Women wish to be at the centre of connection and fear being too far out on the edge. I am amused that the only two men whom I have heard comment on Gilligan both took an instant dislike to the word web, saying it sounded like being trapped or a spider! But Gilligan did no more than pick up a word current in feminist discourse.

Turning now to the way in which God is conceived in the tradition. God's powerfulness is related to the fact that God is seen as separate, different and alone. God indeed is said to have aseity: he is entire unto himself and did not have to create anything else in order to be complete. He may be extremely arbitrary, but he does not thereby cease to be God to humans. In the light of what happens, Job questions God's goodness, but he does not revise his conception of God. Indeed, theodicy questions arise because people conceive of God as powerful and therefore able to intervene if he would. The language used for God reflects the conception. The highest powers people knew were kings, lords, judges and fathers: God was seen as being an extrapolation of what they were like.

The way in which God is seen in the tradition is part of a dyad and affects how human beings, the other pole, are seen. By contrast with God's greatness, humans know their smallness; by contrast with his goodness, their sinfulness. God is above, we below. Humanity is often seen as 'female' in relation to God (for Hosea, Israel is God's unfaithful wife; the church is the 'bride' of Christ and referred to as 'she') – a comment on the relationship pertaining between the two sexes. The words commonly used for God, king, lord, father all connote maleness. The language used for the relationship between God and humanity reflects the conception of that relationship. Christian prayers and hymns abound with words like command, honour, obedience, service, authority. A German student of mine wrote a paper analysing Karl Barth's vocabulary in volume II.1 of the *Church Dogmatics*. It was authoritarian. Of course God may be seen as a benevolent patriarch, but still a patriarch. In the Lord's prayer, which is central to how Christians conceive the relation to God, God is addressed as 'Father', the absolute head of the human family in the society in which the prayer arose; the same respect is paid to him as to an earthly ruler, 'hallowed be thy name'; it is prayed that 'his will' be done; and humans look to him directly for their daily bread, their life-sustenance, which comes from his bounty. One may add as a footnote that the great detractors of religion, Feuerbach, Marx and Freud, do not disagree as to what God would be like were there a God; which is why 'God' must be slain if humans are to come into their own. Such a conception of God, they contend, keeps mankind in childish dependence.

We may pause to consider what place women or the female play in this male world. For the female, as some kind of an abstract conception, there is some place. The female is the great other, the earth, and even humanity in relation to God. The active persons of the Trinity are both conceived as male, the Holy Spirit in its indefiniteness is sometimes conceived as female. The woman who symbolises the female for much of the tradition is Mary: she it is through whom the Son has birth, who stands silent at the foot of the cross, the Mary of the pietàs with the dead Christ across her knees holding all when the male world has gone wrong. Actual women, real live women, play no central role in the tradition; for the most part they go unnoticed. They are there in a subordinate and subsidiary capacity, basically servicing the male world. Sometimes they are respected for their work, or for their role as mothers, particularly as the mothers of sons. At other times they are scarcely more than property: 'thou shalt not covet thy neighbour's wife, ... nor his ox...'. For woman or the female as an active, independent agent, one looks in vain. There is no such representation in the Godhead. (Indeed 'the female' which is present in the tradition appears to correspond to a male projection of a lost side of themselves – their need for what is tender, loving, embracing and nurturative.) Women as the equals of men are notably absent.

There is of course in the tradition the theme of God in his powerfulness overturning the present order of society. Women are apparently included among those who will benefit. It is into the mouth of Mary of the Magnificat that the evangelist puts the words 'He hath put down the mighty from their seat and hath exalted the humble and meek.' Can women then come to make use of the theme of God's powerfulness? In a liberation theology God identifies himself with the oppressed. Thus some women see feminist theology as a liberation theology, parallel to, and holding much in common with, black and Latin American liberation theology. It seems to me that there are insuperable problems with this. Let me take my own experience in the struggle to get women ordained in the Anglican Church a few years back. For it is in situations of extremity that one's understandings are formed, or broken. I learned more about power and powerlessness, about male power and female powerlessness, in that situation than I have in any other. I shall not forget what it felt like to wear a T-shirt proclaiming 'Ordain Women Now', it having been forbidden by the police to carry banners, to be shoved behind barriers by the police to allow bishops to descend from their coaches, whom one was not impeding and some of whom were one's friends, and then to watch a procession in Westminster Abbey of hundreds upon hundreds of men, knowing that oneself and all other women were *a priori* excluded from being bishops because of our sex. What did it mean then, down on one's knees on the cold floor of Westminster Abbey to hear a woman's voice ring out with the words of the lesson: 'If God be for us, who can be against us?' I was in tears. So God was for us? But then there dawns on one the depth and extent of sexism, throughout all known human societies in all times and all countries. What then? Indeed what when one sees that the very notion of God which Christians have held serves to re-enforce that sexism? Then one can no longer keep goodness and God together. The only exit (other than atheism) is to change one's conception of God.

I am suggesting then in the first place that the theodicy problem is for women insuperable. I think it is worse than that for Jews, if it is not in bad taste to make such a comparison. For anti-semitism could perhaps plausibly be seen as an aberration, the work of humans in direct contradiction to the will of God. But sexism seems to be a flaw woven into the very fabric of human history. To say that the relation between men and women which has pertained is somehow that intended by the creator is, when one considers what the lot of women has been, to make God evil. The theodicy question on its own then, I would suggest, makes the paradigm of God as powerful unavailable to women. One might add to this the need at least to place a question mark against the notion that there is really any talk of the liberation of women or of their equality in the Bible.

I am not disputing here the analysis which says that the current structure of society needs to be overthrown. (I shall myself argue that it is incumbent on those who are powerless to claim power.) But why use a concept of God to back this up? It is not just that if this is God, then he is singularly ineffective; the theistic dimension is superfluous. The Chilean prisoners whom I support have put themselves on the line in the struggle to overthrow tyranny. But they do not (so far as I know) introduce a concept of God. If one does import God one gets into a tangle. God is an anthropomorphic being who is on the side of the righteous who are the oppressed, is he? But no, that is too sectarian. God must love one's enemies, and one must too. Then where is God?

Finally it must be said that the notion of God as powerful may appear to many feminist women unattractive. God is seen as displaying power in a way which is reminiscent of the power of males which they reject as immoral, even though exercising this power in their favour. Moreover it is not clear that a God, conceived after the traditional mould, is helpful. It is women themselves who are bringing about a change in their lives. There is a difference between a male human being who, from his position of power and out of the goodness of his heart, acts on behalf of women, and a man who steps aside, so allowing women to determine their own future and come into their own. A woman like me has come to resent a world of male activity *on behalf of* women. Why then should she want a powerful God to come and rescue her? My friend Arinda, confined for twenty years to a Chilean jail after the most brutal torture, writes asking for books on the struggle of women!

I come then to the second paradigm, that of powerlessness. Powerlessness is also clearly present in a major way in the tradition. However the form in which it is present is not without significance. It is present as powerlessness which has been reached through the abnegation of powerfulness. God through *kenosis*, self-emptying, divests power and comes as a humble man. Christ's death is often understood as an abandonment of power; the refusal to be the messiah whom the Jews awaited, the refusal to come down from the cross. It is in either case not simply a model of powerlessness, but of powerlessness voluntarily embraced when by right there could have been powerfulness. Indeed there is ambivalence! Post-pentecost the humble man of Galilee fast becomes Christ the Pantocrator, the ruler of creation, seated, in Christian art, on a throne like those of the rulers of this world. Nevertheless, the Christian tradition clearly has wanted to have as a central paradigm the divestment of power. An ecclesiastical procession has the mighty last. The pope is named the servant of the servants of God.

One aspect of this paradigm which I want to note is the way in which the powerlessness is connected with service of others. The incarnation takes place that God may be present for us. Indeed the powerlessness is often to the point of brokenness in order to be able to nourish others. The crucifixion is seen as God in Christ pouring out his life-blood for humanity. This is re-enacted in the eucharist; a celebration which consists in a breaking – a breaking through which others are fed. This is the dynamic of love. The supreme virtue of the Christian faith is *agape*; that love which does not count the cost, which, without regard for self, thinks only of another. Sin has often been seen as pride, as isolated self-sufficiency, the kind of model which I have discussed as powerfulness. Sin is self-centredness. Thus conversion becomes the breaking of the self so as to become present for God and for others in service. The Christian is crucified with Christ. Salvation consists in not being centred in self but centred on God.

It is as though men have known only too well their problem, and so have postulated a counter-model. The opposite from what was to be desired becomes what is virtuous. Instead of a model of the self which is isolated, self-sufficient, and independent in its power, we have a model of the self as broken for others, connected, and indeed not a 'self' existing in itself at all. It is a paradigm of sacrifice of self leading to nurture of others.

I want to suggest that this paradigm, which men may have found useful, is inappropriate for women. Feminist women seemingly reject it with unanimity. For a gospel of self-sacrifice, service and self-abnegation has been used to justify the position of women. Elizabeth Cady Stanton, the author of *The Woman's Bible*, wrote in 1895: 'Men think that self-sacrifice is the most charming of all the cardinal virtues for women. ... and in order to keep it in healthy working order they make opportunities for its illustration as often as possible.'[2] A view of woman as fulfilling herself through service has only too often been held up before her. The Virgin, represented as one who self-effacingly put herself at God's disposal, is the ideal woman. Motherhood in which a woman exists for her husband and children is another such model. Such a religion of self-sacrifice may indeed serve as the 'opium' of women, reinforcing the position to which a woman has already assigned herself, compounding her belief that 'one should not put oneself forward', and feeding a 'martyr' complex. Mary Daly writes in characteristic style:

> Patriarchal myth is refined in christianity so that Hag-ocracy will decline. Sugar-coating its necrophilic intent, it attempts to seduce Hags to resign our Selves and sign our own commitment papers to the institution of the Double Cross, doublethinking our Selves into total numbness and dumbness.[3]

The gospel of powerlessness has been appropriated by those to whom it should never have been directed.

Moreover if the doctrine of self-sacrifice and the paradigm of powerlessness are held up as exemplary before those who are struggling to change their lot, it may serve to undercut them. For resistance to injustice then comes to look un-Christ-like. At the time when I was destroying body and soul working for women to be ordained, deeply undermined in my humanity, a well-known prelate suggested to me that in my suffering I should look to Christ on the cross. But that is to suggest that someone should learn to put up with a basic denial of justice. To look to Christ in one's suffering could at the most serve as a palliative. Such advice does nothing to support that person in her struggle to overcome the injustice. It is one thing for a person to choose a path which may lead to suffering 'for Christ's sake'. It is quite another to suggest to someone who is powerless that her powerlessness should be her identity. The only possible response to being discriminated against, if one is to retain a sense of one's integrity, is to fight the discrimination with all one's might. Once one acquiesces in it one is lost: one comes to see oneself as a secondary person. For a privileged person who has himself been ordained to tell one who, on account of her sex, could not be, that she should look to Jesus, is to make Christianity into an ideology which reinforces sexism. Besides which the interpretation of Jesus' death which says that he chose powerlessness may well be open to question. It can equally well be said that it was his commitment to the struggle to empower those who were powerless which cost him his life.

The virtue required of those who are powerless may be the courage to claim power. 'No ... group', writes Rosemary Ruether, 'that seeks liberation from historic oppression is into the suffering servant myth.'[4] Judith Vaughan likewise, in her book *Sociality, Ethics and Social Change,* contends that love demands a different stance from those who are oppressed than from those who have power.

> The moral responsibility for those who are powerless and assigned to subordinate positions in society is to reclaim the power that is rightfully theirs by virtue of being human. It is to demand the power to define themselves in relationship to others and to co-determine what reality becomes.[5]

An equalisation of power is the prerequisite for the creation of a co-humanity. Women, writes Ruether, who have been taught that anger and pride are sinful, may have a peculiar difficulty in exercising the virtues of anger and pride – a pride not in the sense of a power which lords it over others, but of basic self-esteem. 'The whole male ideology of pride and humility' she writes 'has to be reevaluated by women.'[6]

I am therefore suggesting that the paradigm of the sacrifice of power, of powerlessness, is inappropriate for women. Women need to actualise themselves. But given that they need to empower themselves, is the model of new life through death that which is relevant to them? Is the passage of transition through which they need to move that of the breaking of an old self and the finding of a new? Is a 'twice-born' model useful? I think not. If women's problem has not been that of a self-enclosed self, a self which in its pride needed to be broken, but rather the opposite, lack of a sufficient sense of self – what Gilligan calls a problem of differentiation of the self – then a model which consists in breaking the self becomes singularly inappropriate. What women need is to come to themselves, to come to have an adequate sense of self. Thus feminist ethics may well not be the ethics of *agape*, of self-sacrificial love, nor may the theme of life-out-of-death be natural to women. There is some evidence that it is a theme which is found in cultures in which a male God predominates. Sheila Collins suggests that it arises out of the male experience: the little boy has to differentiate himself from the mother and be 'born again'. Male initiation rites typically involve 'rebirth' into a male community. The girl by contrast does not need to break from the mother. 'Where a mother-goddess predominated', she writes, 'life generating from life was the theme.'[7]

I have suggested that the two themes of powerfulness and of power-lessness through abnegation of power are present in the Judaeo-Christian tradition. I should look momentarily at Judaism. In the Jewish scriptures God's powerfulness is the major theme. An article by William Orbach, 'The Four Faces of God: Toward a Theology of Powerlessness', shows however that, beginning in the Middle Ages, Jews in their suffering came to see God as *powerless* as a way of solving the theodicy question as to why he did not act.[8] It is tempting to ask after the response of women to the pogroms *they* suffered during the same period. (Between the fifteenth and the seven-teenth centuries about a million women were burnt as witches.) Could it be that the theodicy question did not arise for them in the same way? One asks the theodicy question because one supposes one should be equal, so that it then comes as a shock when one suffers. Unlike the Jews who had a religion about a God who had rescued them and made them an elect people, women have never had an ideology which has told them that they should not be at the bottom of the heap. Did women in the Middle Ages, as do women in most countries of the world today, simply accept their lot?

Neither of the two models of powerfulness, power as self-aggrandise-ment, or power as powerlessness, power as self-loss, generally available in the symbolism of patriarchal religion are, I have concluded, useful to women in interpreting their reality.

Before turning to the third paradigm, that of power as empower-ment, I want to consider the theme of 'exodus': the exodus which women must make from being part of the male reality if they are to come into their own reality. Exodus is that movement from being subordinate within the male reality, to coming to stand on the edge of, and to some extent in contradiction to, the male reality.[9] I say that one stands 'on the edge' of something else, for the male reality is the norm in a patriarchal world. To some extent though women are coming to have their own reality; increasingly so as the number of feminists multiplies and feminist theory develops in all fields. Exodus may be an 'exterior' matter; I left the church. But feminists also discover that it is an interior journey on which they are embarked. Once commenced, however difficult, there is no way back. 'Sometimes I wish my eyes hadn't been opened' as a feminist song of the '70's went.[10] But when one has come 'to see', the place where one was appears as deception. One comes to have a new world-picture. Everything is affected.

Exodus therefore requires courage. It is a movement to being an outsider, but an outsider with a new integrity. The gain is the gain of oneself. The initial exodus, whether I from the church, or a woman from a home in which she was being battered to a women's refuge, may be saying something very positive about oneself; about one's will to survive, to recover, to gather up one's strength and start again. I decided on leaving the church on the way back from a hospital where I had been told that I should have an operation. Within weeks I was healing. For exodus is a coming to say something about who one is as a human being (made in God's image if one likes to put it theologically) and that one will no longer tolerate being undermined or treated as secondary. Men may react with hurt, surprise, or the statement that they meant nothing wrong. Exodus, whether from a sexist marriage or from sexist treatment at work, in the sense at least of coming to have a different understanding, is of course a prerequisite for the creation of a community of equals.

There is a fine discussion of what I have called exodus in Jean Baker Miller's best selling book *Toward a New Psychology of Women*.[11] Miller is a Boston psychoanalyst. She discusses the internal shift whch takes place as women heal. It involves coming to see that it is not 'all one's fault' but that the structures are oppressive; that far from blaming oneself, there is something to be angry about. Then one stops the process of inward destruction. Women's 'assertiveness training' (so-called) involves learning quietly and calmly to hold one's own, understanding the 'game' that is being played, and reflecting rather than taking on board the sexist presuppositions that are being directed at one. It is a slow process, with many bumps along the way, for it involves an overcoming of one's own self-definition as a subordinate person. The internal journey will involve a questioning of the most basic presuppositions about one's world and one's self. It may well be called an internal exodus for it is a dissociation from male structures and ways of thought; a coming to see them for what they are – *one* human possibility, not *the only* human possibility. The process of exodus is the process of empowerment. It is the coming to a new reality.

It is an interesting comment on the male perception of the male world as the norm for humanity, that women's exodus is often seen as deeply threatening. It is as though the male world-view, the male *Weltanschauung*, must contain all. Male security often seems to be pinned to the understanding of their reality as the only reality. Women's exodus is threatening because it suggests that it is not; it poses in concrete form the possibility of an alternative. Thus many men have been puzzled as women disappeared into women's groups, from which men are excluded, and which operated according to different principles from the way in which the 'normal' male world operates. The statement that one is religious, but not Christian, can cause bewilderment, as though the only way to be religious was to be Christian. I have noticed that people try to make me into something quite foreign in order to be 'rid' of me – I must be Jewish (because monotheistic), Buddhist, atheist – anything rather than post-Christian feminist. To be post-Christian feminist, implying as it does a criticism of Christianity, is too close for comfort. Or else one is 'really a Christian'; everything is to be *gleichgeschaltet*, incorporated, into the male reality. The extent of the reaction is extraordinary when one considers that the Christian church and religion are overwhelmingly the norm. It is the post-Christian feminist whom one would have supposed, if anyone, would feel 'threatened' as she stands alone, unable for example to join in Christian worship. Women, it is my experience, understand the situation much better; possibly not simply because they themselves only 'hang-in there' in the male reality by a thread, but because they are relative outsiders themselves within the male structure, being the opposite to what is the norm, and so do not to the same extent feel threatened by the idea that the male reality is not the only one.

I turn then to the paradigm of empowerment. Feminists have allowed to become self-conscious the way in which women in general empower one another. Theory has to be drawn out of praxis.[12] A suitable locus to which to pay attention, a place at which the practice operates, is the women's group. For the women's group has in recent years provided the crucible in which empowerment takes place, the matrix in which new insights are grasped. It is good to observe the group, for it is by looking at the group that one sees how people handle power, how they relate to one another. I am not speaking of a particular kind of group but of a practice. Often the group will be small, but it may be large, and its task may be anything from therapy to the discussion of philosophy. How should we delineate the practice? Through the very fact that the learning process is experiential, it is difficult to describe. People are open to one another, do not dominate one another, allow everyone to come to speech, comfort one another if need be, uphold one another, and allow people to be inarticulate as they feel their way to what it is they seek to express. The practice is chiefly marked by multi-levelled attentiveness and by the right timing. Claudine Hermann writes, in a piece collected in the anthology *New French Feminisms*:

> Physical or mental, man's space is a space of domination, hierarchy and conquest ... a *full* space. Woman, on the other hand, has long since learned to respect not only the physical and mental space of others, but space for its own sake, *empty* space.[13]

Not for nothing do women speak of 'hearing one another into being'. Empowerment means coming to new perceptions. A group of theology students may come to quite different understandings than those they learn at work. Empowerment means coming to find yourself. Women, say Sheila Ernst and Lucy Goodison, 'contact the power locked in ourselves'.[14] It means being surprised at yourself for what you dare say, be and do.

Women's experience of mixed groups seems to be only too often bad. The women who wrote *Piecing It Together: Feminism and Nonviolence* comment, of mixed peace groups:

> Some groups have hardly heard of 'women's lib', don't expect women to contribute much and are dominated by the chairman or a few vocal, confident members. More sophisticated groups waste hours on sectarian in-fighting, ego-tripping and internal political arguments.... It is a long,

slow process trying to carry over into mixed peace groups some of the lessons learned in the Women's Liberation Movement about the participation and validation of all members and all contributions, and it is all too easy for women's creativity and energy to be sapped by the struggle to communicate these lessons.[15]

Women who have become used to the feminist way of operating may find groups which operate in the other way inefficient. The whole apparatus of 'chairmen', minutes and procedural rules is apparently needed to control people and to keep the proceedings impersonal, abstract and objective. Meanwhile groups often fail to deal with the real issues. Sheila Collins writes of the mistaken male view that women who form a women's group do so in order to *reject* men:

> The truth of the matter is that women have found it impossible to discover their common humanity when males are present, or when women who think in masculine categories are present, because of the overwhelming tendency of the masculine-oriented world view to categorize, objectify, and subordinate an Other.[16]

It takes a strong group, used to women's way of operating, to control even a few people who do not want (or do not know how) to operate in that way, from being destructive of the group. The only mixed groups in which I have participated which operate successfully according to what I have described as women's way are Quaker groups; an observation I note Caroline Whitbeck also makes.

Behind this different practice there lies a different understanding of the human self in relation to others. Caroline Whitbeck, in her article 'A Different Reality: Feminist Ontology', contrasts the self-other *relation* of the feminist mode of operation, with the self-other *opposition* which characterises male interaction.[17] In a self-other *relation* one aims at mutual realisation. One sees the self as relational, not 'atomic'. Development takes place through listening and speaking with each other, instead of the male pattern of 'successive dualistic oppositions'. Differentiation of self and other does not depend on 'construing the other as opposite'. One is reminded of Gilligan's observation that women understand the self to have an essential relatedness, whereas men tend to have a self defined in opposition to others. Some feminists have put forward a theory to account for this difference. Nancy Chodorow, drawing on British psychoanalytic object relations theory, suggests that during the first few years of life the boy child has to differentiate himself from his mother, and so suppresses his early relatedness (which was a relatedness to her); identity becomes a power contest. The girl, by contrast, does not have to suppress relatedness in order to be herself, for she is of like sex. The solution, she suggests, lies in fathers being as emotionally available as mothers, so that the boy can identify in a feeling, nurturative way with a parent who, like him, is male.[18]

Whether or not this theory is correct, it is certainly the case that men in subordinate positions do not appear to possess women's skills in relating. Indeed they often conform to male type in exaggerated manner. Women will frequently be the victims of this, as the only people over whom such men do have power; and whom they therefore dominate in order to try to gain a status which society has not afforded them. It is said that the raping and battering of women owes to men's sense of powerlessness. Judging by their literature, black women have been brutally oppressed not only as blacks but in the first instance by their menfolk. It was the custom among Russian serfs for a whip to be placed above the marital bed as a symbol of male authority, the whip traditionally being presented to the groom by the father-in-law. Paulo Freire comments, in *Pedagogy of the Oppressed*, that what the oppressed man seeks, is himself to become the oppressor.

Before leaving the discussion of empowerment, I want to draw attention to the location of the practice of this paradigm. That location is on the edge. This relates to what was said of exodus. The paradigm is precisely an alternative to what is the norm; the world at large is male. The location is 'on the edge' when women hive off into women's groups, or when women's groups in church or university operate according to a mode which stands in contrast to that of the body within which they are set. It is true also of the Society of Friends which has been on the sidelines of the mainline church, representing in its mode of operation an alternative. And it has always been the case that this paradigm was practised as women talked outside their front doors, reared their children, and lived in an extended network of mothers and aunts on the edge of the male world of work. What is new is that women are posing this alternative in the midst of the male world, and challenging the presupposition that male should be the norm.

What then is that virtue which is required for the paradigm which I have called empowerment? In an excellent article 'What is Feminist Ethics?' Eleanor Humes Haney suggests that 'the good' be defined as that which nurtures us all. Contrasting this with the Christian ethic of *agape* (self-giving), Haney points to the practice of 'friendship'. She writes:

> To make friendship central is both to transform the power relations that most often hold between individuals, groups, and people and the earth, and to be a participant in that transformation. Friendship is a relation of mutuality, respect, fidelity, confidence, and affection. It is impossible in, and therefore a rejection of, most competitive patterns, adversarial patterns, exploitive patterns, authoritarian patterns, and paternalistic patterns of relating. To begin to make friendship a reality is to begin acting as a friend. That is, to demonstrate in one's speech and behavior that one is not superior or inferior and that one will no longer countenance being related to in those ways.[19]

Friendship, says Haney, involves a 'centering'; 'a finding and a living out of the still point, the axis, the center of one's own life'. Centering is both a critique of, and a contradiction to, the self-sacrifice and being centred on God characteristic of Christian ethics. It is a becoming whole. It is the experience of living freely – graciously and gracefully, of being at-home-in-the-universe and so moving through one's life and the world with ease and authority. We may say that whereas powerfulness means self-aggrandisement, and abnegation of power means self-loss, power as empowerment means coming 'to' oneself. Indeed it may well be said that it has been men's inability, generally speaking, to come 'to' themselves which has caused such havoc in our world. For only those who come 'to' themselves feel no need either to dominate others, or to go in for a self-abasement which is equally destructive of community. A person who has come 'to' her or himself can partake in a friendship in which, in a relation of mutuality, each becomes more fully that which they have it in them to become. Empowerment implies a different understanding of the self from either the self-enclosed self which dominates others, or the destroyed self which lives outside itself in a mistaken service of others.

Can the paradigm of empowerment be found in the Judaeo - Christian tradition? One possible candidate might be the Trinity. I shall suggest however that it fails on a number of counts as a reflection of that of which women are speaking. It is not clearly a model of equality, but contains also an element of hierarchy. The Father and the Son are said to be alike in all save *in their mutual relation*; which is indeed symbolised by the use of the words 'Father' and 'Son', implying as they do hierarchy. The Son has a relationship of *dependence* on the Father. Moreover, the love between Father and Son is said to be that of *agape*, total self-giving, rather than, for example, *philia*. I have suggested that the feminist virtue is not best characterised as *agape*. Last, but not least, the Trinity is scarcely a model which feminists can take to heart as symbolising a mutuality between two poles, one of which is characterised as female and the other male! The Christian religion does not have, as its central symbol, equality between man and woman.

It may be said that Jesus empowered others. This is certainly true. Women may well want to look to his life, and his relationships, rather than to his death. But it is not a model of mutual empowerment. Do we have any evidence that anyone else, let alone a woman, enabled Jesus to develop his self-understanding? The statement sometimes made that 'Jesus was a feminist' can I think certainly not be allowed to stand. There is no evidence that the equality of women was even an issue in the society in which he lived. We do not find him challenging the secondary role which women played in Jewish religion, he accepted male roles and female roles as defined by his society – to which his parables witness, and he without qualms referred to God as 'Father'. We know that, perhaps against the custom of his time, he allowed a woman to sit at his feet. We have no picture of Jesus sitting at a woman's feet, learning from her. To say that Jesus (and I think St Paul) were ahead of their time, and that they were personally kind to women, may well be the case. That is not to say that they were feminists.[20]

Is God however seen as empowering human beings? In wanting to conceive of God as one who empowers us, I am aware that there are strands in the tradition which correspond to what I wish to say. God may be seen as the basis of ourselves, that through which we come into being. To this I shall return. Nevertheless it must be said that Christian and biblical theology has primarily conceived God quasi-anthropomorphically – hence the language commonly used for God. With such a conception of God, as separate from us and in some way like us, it is not possible (if God is to be God) to speak of mutual empowerment. Thus I would certainly want to maintain that within the main stream of the tradition – in which God is conceived in sufficiently anthropomorphic terms that the conception which is held of God acts as an ideology which affects human relations, and in which Jesus is seen as God or as symbolic of God so that his relationships become normative or authoritative for human behaviour – I do not see depicted a theme of mutual empowerment. I must conclude that the tradition significantly lacks an understanding of empowerment which corresponds to the feminist paradigm. It notably does not contain symbols which signify equality between women and men.

I turn finally to the question as to what understanding of God would be commensurate with the paradigm of empowerment. Is the concept of God available to one who lives within this paradigm? For a God who is not commensurate with one's ideals quickly becomes dispensable. How can a concept of God be held in conjunction with feminist thinking about the self, and the self-other relation? What understanding is commensurate with feminist ethics? Let us rehearse what it is that has been found wanting in the paradigms of powerfulness and of the abnegation of power. Women who are coming into their own will be through with any notion of a God who is an 'other' who overrules them, in relation to whom they should be asked to act heteronomously, according to a will not their own. Such a God is in the worst image of the human male. But equally, I have suggested, women may have no use for a God who condescends to be with them in their weakness. Paternalism fits ill with feminism. Besides which feminists no longer want to identify themselves as weak. Women are discovering the sense of wholeness which comes from being self-directed, free, effective, and inter-dependent with others. How can the concept of God be related to this?

The model surely which fits, is that in which God is seen as not separate from us, not in apposition to us, not over-riding our will, and non-dominative. Equally, in which God is not seen as serving us, nor as sacrificing God's self for us, nor asking us to lose ourselves. That is to say God must be seen as one with us, as enabling us to be ourselves, as empowering us. God must be seen to give us strength and insight not as one gives who gives a donation, but in working through us. To revert to our earlier vocabulary, we may say that God is involved in the web. No, more than that. For were God but one member in the web, God would not be God. God sustains the web itself.

For God is not a self like we are, but the basis of all selves. If we are to have a religious understanding of the self, then God must be seen as integral to the self, not something other than the self, to which we subsequently relate. We need a model of the self as being related in its very being to God; a relation more fundamental than, and different from, the I-Thou inter-relations we have with other people. This of course is something which has found expression in Catholic theology. In Protestant theology it is present most clearly in the thought of Friedrich Schleiermacher. Schleiermacher conceives God precisely not as an other in apposition to ourselves, but as the ground of our selves; God is our sense of being derived, of having an absolute dependence. With this understanding of the self's relation to God, it is possible to be religious without one's concept of God being such that God could undermine human autonomy and integrity. God is not one who stands over-against us, who could potentially dominate us, or who could suggest an action which to carry out would be for us to act heteronomously. God is conceived as building up our self-integrity, differentiating us, and involved in the relations between us. God enables us to become what we have it in us to be.[21]

Perhaps we may entertain a vision of a new humanity, a co-humanity in which there is mutual empowerment. A world in which power is not exercised, in which the few do not coerce the many, or one sex dominate the other. A world in which service and self-giving which are unproductive for the one who serves and gives is reduced to a minimum. A world in which, in mutuality, people feel in charge of their destiny. This should be our model of utopia, the proximate norm on which we should set our sights. Nor can it be allowed to remain simply a vision if we are to save our world. It must become an actuality, and that fast. Feminism and the new awakening of women are the greatest hope for our world; perhaps the last hope. The question is whether feminist practice can be brought into play in any significant way. Well may we ask with the French feminist Marguerite Duras: 'Can men forget everything and join women?'[22]

This paper was given at the conference of the Society for the Study of Christian Ethics, September 1985.

Notes
1.   Harvard University Press, 1982. Quotations pages 39, 8, 35, 45, 43.
2.   Quoted by Barbara Hilkert Andolsen 'Agape in Feminist Ethics', *Journal of Religious Ethics*, 9 (1981), p. 75.
3.   *Gyn/Ecology* (The Women's Press, 1979), p. 75.
4.   'The Suffering Servant Myth', *Worldview* 17 (March 1974), p. 45.
5.   p. 152.
6.   *Sexism and God-Talk* (Beacon Press, 1983), p. 186.

7.   *A Different Heaven and Earth* (Judson Press, 1974), p. 204.
8.   *Judaism*, 32, no. 2 (1983), pp. 236–47.
9.   The term 'exodus' is associated within feminist thought with Mary Daly. In 1972, preaching in one of the most prestigious churches in the United States, Memorial Church in Harvard Yard, Daly concluded her remarks by inviting the women in the congregation to follow her out of the church, symbolising women's exodus from the male church, and then proceeded to walk down from the pulpit and out into Harvard Yard, followed by many women. Daly has subsequently made use of the metaphor in her writing. I use it here for that interior exodus which women undertake from being part of the male reality.
10. Carole Echler.
11. Beacon Press, 1976.
12. I am not of course suggesting that only in feminist thought are theory and praxis closely related, though feminists have made it a methodological principle that this should be the case. The presupposition of this article is that male religion has reflected relations pertaining within patriarchy.
13. 'Les coordonnées féminines: espace et temps' [Women in space and time] in *Les voleuses de langue* [The tongue snatchers] (des femmes, 1976), reprinted in ed. Elaine Marks and Isabelle de Courtivron, *New French Feminisms: An Anthology* (University of Massachusetts Press, 1980), p. 169.
14. *In Our Own Hands* (The Women's Press, 1981), p. 4.
15. The Feminism and Nonviolence Study Group, 1983 (ISBN 0 9508602 0 4), p. 44, 45.
16. Collins *op. cit.* p. 206.
17. Ed. Carol C. Gould, *Beyond Domination: New Perspectives on Women and Philosophy* (Rowman and Allanheld, 1984). Quotations pages 76, 81.
18. *The Reproduction of Mothering: Psychoanalysis and the Sociology of Gender* (University of California Press, 1978).
19. 'What is Feminist Ethics? A Proposal for Continuing Discussion', *Journal of Religious Ethics* (8/1 1980), pp. 115–124. Quotation pages 118–19.
20. In relation to Jesus see for example Ben Witherington, *Women in the Ministry of Jesus* (C.U.P., 1984). Witherington argues that, in contrast to much of the surrounding society, Jesus was not overtly sexist: 'we do not find negative remarks about the nature, abilities and religious potential of women in comparison to men on the lips of Jesus...'. (p. 125). But he is also clear that Jesus did not challenge the patriarchal nature of his society: 'Jesus was attempting to reform, not reject, the patriarchal framework of His culture...'. (p. 129). John Wijngaards (in a booklet which advocates the ordination of women) expresses the situation with clarity: 'Jesus did, of course, have a new kind of relationship with women.... The question here is whether in these relationships with women he 'deliberately and courageously broke' with the social customs of his time. The answer is clearly: No. It is true, in one or two cases Jesus went beyond the limits which a Jewish rabbi would impose on his dealings with women ... this can be explained as compassion.... There is, however, no question of a direct attack against discrimination. Jesus did not fight for the emancipation of women in the same way that he made a stand for the poor. He has frequent clashes with the pharisees about the sabbath and other traditional observances. Not once is he recorded as having a dispute to remedy the oppression woman was under. The question of emancipation simply never arose. It could not arise. The social climate was not ripe for it.' (*Did Christ Rule Out Women Priests?* (1977), p. 36).
21. I would however think it to be the case that some people, and other people at some times, need to conceive of God as in apposition to themselves in their prayer. But this does not necessarily mean that it is the case that God actually is in apposition to us: that we conceive of God in this way may owe to how we are as persons, since in human relations another is by the nature of the case a 'thou' in relation to our 'I'. It may also be that a person has a sense of being 'led' or 'directed', as though by another, by God. Again this does not mean that God is in fact such an other. These are questions which I should much like to see explored further.
22. From an interview by Susan Husserl-Kapit, *Signs*, Winter 1975, reprinted in Marks and de Courtivron *op. cit.* p. 174. '*Men*' underlined in original.

3.2 Claiming Power-in-Relation: Exploring the Ethics of Connection

Mary Grey

Introduction

A basic insight of feminist studies is that women often describe their experience using the terms relatedness and interconnection. Mutuality and solidarity are preferred ways of operating for the feminist movement. Feminist theologian Carter Heyward – in some ways a pioneer of relational theology – based her understanding of God on the idea of 'power-in-relation.' Claiming power-in-relation is making God present in the world, she wrote.[1] Where there is no relation, God is not. What is more, 'connectedness' and 'radical relatedness' are more illuminating images by whch to understand our way of being in the world and our experience of Divine presence than a philosophy based on individualism and separation.

In this paper, I will test this idea as a basis for feminist ethics. That is, does using an image like power-in-relation, or, as I prefer to call it, a 'metaphysic of connection',[2] or interconnectedness, present a liberating ethic for women or trap us further into destructive, oppressive patterns of relating? My first question is how the experience of bonding and solidarity has actually worked in feminist networks: if it has not worked, what obstacles have been encountered? Second, I present an alternative model to that of individualism – a metaphysic of connectedness. Third, I explore this as both *revelatory paradigm and moral imperative.* The conclusion develops practical ways in which this model might offer new hope in conflictual situations.

The 'Honeymoon' Days of Sisterhood

The early stages of the women's movement were the halcyon days of solidarity: 'sisterhood is powerful' and the 'cosmic covenant of women' (Mary Daly) were frequent inspiration for bonding. As Judith Plaskow put it in a recent paper:

> The dream we had in the heady, early days of the feminist movement, that the bonds of sisterhood would annul or eradicate traditional divisions of religion, race and class, and that we could formulate an analysis of women's situation and a program for action that would embrace *all* women was based not on engagement with the particularity of women's

experience, but on a wave of a magic wand that made difference invisible.[3]

Although bonding-in-solidarity was felt to be the way towards eradicating structural oppression – the declared feminist agenda – this very bonding seemed to disguise divisiveness at many levels. Despite utopic visions of freedom and of a nonviolent world in harmony with the environment, despite the recovery of women's stories, lost from history, there is an apparent loss of faith, a disillusionment, in the actual effectiveness of bonding. Even the recovery of the stories has in some ways added to this. I see the following as key areas of difficulty:

- Poor women are separated from middle- and upper-class women by structures of poverty and class.
- Jewish women find it painful or even impossible to dialogue with Christians where it is not acknowledged that Christian theology developed at the cost of blaming the Jewish faith for the death of Christ, and, in the feminist case, for the death of the Goddess and the rise of God the Father.
- Black women find it almost impossible to dialogue with white women because of the history of white women's collusion in their oppression. This collusion has a history but also modern expressions.[4]
- Differences in sexual orientation impede dialogue. Heterosexual women barely grasp the contempt and the marginalization from which lesbian women suffer – and in which heterosexual women may collude. But lesbian women may fail to appreciate the lack of freedom and the degree of manipulation in which heterosexual women are often trapped. Marriage can often prevent genuine women's friendship.
- Single women and elderly women are marginalized by suffocating 'coupledom' or exclusive focus on youth.

All these obstacles are connected to some degree with the way women have been socialized to understand our own selves. Because women have internalized an ethic of self-denial and have been socialized into (frequently) demeaning forms of dependency and service, the range and nature of the bonding groups essential for the liberating or therapeutic process has been unappreciated. Many different forms of internalizing the 'victim' or 'self-denying' ethic exist, but because the oppressive social norms that cause these remain largely unchanged – especially in Church circles, there being no equal opportunities commission for the Church! – simply identifying this dynamic does not change it. A woman's sense of self can be so negative that, despite the bonding of the women's movement, loss of self-esteem can reoccur at different phases and crises of the life cycle.(Anita Spencer's book *Seasons* is very helpful for charting the tasks and pitfalls a woman faces at different developmental stages.)[5]

The problem is that our bonding occurs in a society whose very structures of consciousness are damaged. That the man/woman relationship suffers from damaged mutuality is clear. But there are wider chasms than this. The long exploitation of the planet which recurs in different insidious forms – the *Recurring Silent Spring*, as a recent book put it[6] – shows that the misuse of nature follows from seeing her through the prism of a machine to be manipulated, controlled, dominated as inert matter, separate from us. The fact that women have shared in similar exploitation tends to hide the fact that women, too, have colluded in the exploitation of nature. This in turn has destroyed a sense of community between Western women and women living in communities still respecting nature's rhythms.

A final factor must be added to this dismal catalogue of obstacles to bonding. When I encounter the courage of Third World women in the face of oppression, I confront a suffering whose extent I can barely fathom. In the face of the vibrant faith springing from such a situation, how can I speak of dialogue? What forms of connection are appropriate here?

But if feminist theology is about a spiritual *vision* – which I believe to be a united factor – we are engaged in a journey or process toward a more authentic dialogue. This first phase has revealed the many pitfalls. Seeing ourselves as an integral part of oppressive structures we must acknowledge the truth that Rosemary Ruether has offered: 'Women are not the great innocents of history!' This is the truth Martha Quest stumbled on at the end of a long journey to self-affirmation. In *The Four-Gated City*, the final volume of Doris Lessing's five-volume saga *The Children of Violence*, Martha was hit by the revelation 'I *am* what the human race is. I am "The Germans are the mirror and catalyst of Europe"; also "The dirty Hun, filthy Nazi." '[7]

We all participate in the basic energy or thrust of the world for positive or destructive ends. So, in seeking the vision that can ground women's solidarity more effectively we must reckon with the extent to which the very structures and processes of knowing, perceiving and feeling are wounded by ethics of domination and cultural superiority, by the language of binary oppositions, and by the way all structures of our human interaction have become locked into the absolutizing of the 'individualistic I,' the 'enclosed I' for whom full mutuality is impossible. But the very fact that our differences and tensions have now been thrown into such sharp relief does not detract from the original insights of sisterhood and solidarity. Far from it: it is this tireless digging away for the root causes of oppression which has exposed these painful conflicts. I argue not that connectedness is a futile dream but that the contemporary ethical model which encourages the development of the individual, motivated by self-interest, success-seeking, achievement-oriented, seeking mastery without counting the cost, must be replaced by an ethics of connection, interdependence and the interrelatedness of all things.

A Metaphysic of Connection

The term *the connected self* was first used by Catherine Keller.[8] In an article on the ethics of inseparability Keller repeats the discovery of the woman Shug, a character from Alice Walker's *The Color Purple:*

> She say, My first step from the old white man was trees. Then air. Then birds. Then other people. But one day when I was sitting quiet and feeling like a motherless child, which I was, it come to me: the feeling of being part of everything, not separate at all. I knew that if I cut a tree, my arm would bleed.[9]

Women experience many such 'epiphanies of connection.' The history of women's spiritualities is discovering the many ways in which connectedness has been a strength.

In a 'metaphysic of connection,' the interdependence and interconnection of all things are seen on the widest possible scale. It is not simply that all *people* interconnect but that all living things are organically interconnected. This presents *personal* relations from being romantically idealized and sees the basic energy, movement and becoming of every organism in the world to be relational.

This way of seeing things derives in part from what is known as process thought, which views God and world as mutually involved in a process of becoming. Process thought deals not in macro- but in micro-units, tiny pulsations of being, or units of becoming. So it is easier to see how each pulsation organically influences something else – in the way that an explosion reverberates across a valley, influencing every living organism in that valley. On a small scale, think of a single shot in a film sequence: what appears to be a single shot is actually composed of a series of photographs – separate, but organically cohering in the whole. On a large scale, think of the nuclear experiments on the Pacific islands: air, water, soil were all affected. Pregnant women gave birth to deformed babies. And the whole tragedy interrelates with the weapons industry and the power-balance of East-West politics.

To think organically affects how we see interrelational dependencies and also affects our self-understanding. Not only do we *not* separate body/soul/mind/heart/erotic feeling from a holistic self-image, but we do not define ourselves as persons over against other persons. Organic, nondualist thinking demands that much as starting point. The self can be seen as a nondualist process of *many selves*, of becoming a self-in-relation, a connected self. I become in relation to you. We are part of each other. What is more, our mutual becoming happens in and through environmental influences, our situatedness in crowded cities or green fields, being limited by space-time dimensions which either encourage or block our growth. There is a mutual vulnerability between ourselves and that part of the cosmos in which *we* happen to be situated. Thus *interconnectedness* is both a new revelatory paradigm and a moral imperative.

Two objections will have already sprung to mind. I have just described how relatedness appears to have caused insoluble problems for the feminist movement. And, secondly, hasn't contemporary psychology of women clearly told us that women are primed developmentally to relate, and that this is proving to be our undoing? Because we hold relationship so dear, because we define ourselves almost totally in relational terms, and invest so much of ourselves in relationship, we submit to unjust and demeaning forms both at home and at work. Despite the significant achievements of *some* women in *some* situations, the secretary is still forced into the mold of the boss's wife or mistress, mothers still define themselves in relation to husband and children, and women are twice as likely as men to suffer from depressive illnesses or even commit suicide as a result of negatively experiencing relational involvements.[10] Furthermore, this depression caused by a loss of sense of self and sense of life's meaning can be experienced at *all* stages of the life cycle. Nor does it help to assume that *in itself* the pattern of heterosexual relating is the cause. Lesbian relationships too can break up through violence, leaving a woman devastated, where woman-identified relationship was assumed to be mutually self-affirming to the two involved.[11]

This seems to suggest that epiphanies of connection or interconnectedness spell utter disaster. In their recent psychological and sociological research, Jean Baker Miller, Nancy Chodorow and Carol Gilligan have all pointed out the dangers to women of the development of empathic and relating skills. Jean Baker Miller warns of the danger of 'fluid ego boundaries' and of a mediated sense of self.[12] Nancy Chodorow shows how the relational situation develops very differently for the young boy and girl. From the boy's great need for *differentiation* from his mother comes the male need to be *separate*.[13] Thus separation/connection becomes the male/female polarity. The male need to preserve individualization and identity through distance from the female world succeeds because women acquiesce in placing their relational/empathic skills in the service of male achievement. In serving masculine needs women live out relationality in dependent forms. The capitalist world added to this the stereotype of the travelling hero: pirate, explorer, absentee marketing executive, dependent on the stable woman tending the hearth. Odysseus wanders while Penelope weaves. Men's absence from the home has been socially sanctioned – women's has had to be justified. How, then, can interconnection be a revelatory paradigm?

Connectedness as Revelatory Paradigm

My argument is that connectedness and interdependence are deeper realities than separation and 'the enclosed I.' The problem is to understand and *enable* differentiation, pluralism and diversity – whether religious, racial or sexual – in such a way that the experience of one ethnic or faith group does not hold an exclusive position. If it is possible to establish that all human desire as well as the yearning of the whole of creation is for deep, meaningful and just relation, insofar as epiphanies of connection can be discerned, I argue that these point to a profounder explanation of the 'truth of the universe.'

Facing the philosophical challenge here, one must ask whether there ever could be a discernible 'truth of the universe'? Immanuel Kant argued that ultimacy will always escape us. We content ourselves with artificially structuring what we 'see' as 'real.' We can never penetrate the model we use to reality itself. What guarantee could there be that the model of connectedness or just relating, 'the power that drives to justice and makes it' as Carter Heyward put it, has any claim to ultimacy as the fundamental energy of the universe?

Here I think a solution is offered in Carol Gilligan's call to discern the 'different voice.'[14] Gilligan refers here to an ethics of care which issues from women's experience, which she contrasts with an ethics based on rights and fairness, developed by her late colleague, Lawrence Kohlberg. Ethics of care, attention or responsibility spring from the experience of *trying to be faithful to relation or connection*, where this is known to be the bedrock of existence. It issues from touching a wellspring where tenderness, a passionate caring for the entirety of the relational nexus presents itself as ultimate. This is the experience of many groups in society who struggle to articulate a profundity of meaning which always eludes articulation and categorization. This profundity of meaning highlights something more significant than a reactionary, essentialist identification of women as society's nurturers and caregivers.

Cassandra, prophet and princess of Troy, 'saw' another truth but was condemned by Apollo never to be believed when articulating what she saw. We normally encounter Cassandra through the patriarchal interpretation of Aeschylus; but more recently, feminist rewriting of the myth has appeared.[15] Christa Wolf, in her novel *Cassandra*, shows Cassandra reflecting, 'Why did I want the gift of prophecy, come what may? To speak with *my voice: the ultimate.* I did not want anything different.'[16] Dare I suggest that, with the paradigm of interrelatedness, we approach a degree of ultimacy, and that the reason it eludes articulation and conceptualization is that relational truth – like all truth – is forced to express itself through the inadequate, distorted vehicle of language? That is, one can speak in 'another voice,' but *never* totally authentically, because the language does not exist. The language of relationality – like the language of grace – is the most vulnerable one of all. It is defined by a double dynamic: giving/receiving, feeling/thinking. But – and here is the pitfall – it wants to maintain itself even in the absence of response. As Janet Morley so beautifully put it in her book of psalms:

> And though there is no one to hold me
> Yet I will hold my heart open.[17]

To return once more to Christa Wolf's Cassandra: as she nears death her visual powers increase but her ability to express herself decreases. Words leave her and only images are left: 'The last thing in my life will be a picture, not a word. Words die before pictures.'[18] To speak relational truth, is to speak as Cassandra did, with angst, to struggle against falling back into the use of the conventional 'we,' which is not the 'we' of pure relation. Christa Wolf calls this an 'addiction to agreement' (*ubereinstimmungsucht*): this means losing an authentic voice in order to win facile approval, in order to avoid 'rocking the boat.'

Secondly, interconnectedness can claim to be a revelatory paradigm because this is the means, above all, through which Divine power-in-relation is mediated. *Power* in this context means the relational drive and energy which *both* empowers human becoming and ecological growth and is the locus of Divine presence in the universe. *Divine presence* is used here both in the sense of ultimacy, the Sacredness of Being, and the process of coming to know and experience this (the drive to connect). Seeking to co-create in forming more just patterns of relating, new forms of mutuality, is both actively making God incarnate, and becoming not *passive* but *receptive* to the ways in which God is already active as energizing presence.

This does not necessitate returning to an Aristotelian/Kantian split between underlying reality and outward manifestations. Nor does it mean trying to prove the case simply by reiterating – without reasoned analysis – the power of the image of connectedness (which was a recent, unjustified, criticism of *Weaving the Visions*, Carol P. Christ and Judith Plaskow's recent collection of articles developing the significance of mutuality and relatedness for feminist religious thought).[19]

From many angles it can be seen that 'connection' is no abstract principle, but an energizing way of living and experiencing. A metaphysic of connection is a historical process. It is both a personal and communal process. As Keller, following Whitehead wrote, 'My process of "being myself" is my origination from my possession of the world.'[20] *Selving* means becoming a self; the word is taken from Gerard Manley Hopkins's poem 'As Kingfishers Catch Fire':

> Each mortal thing does one thing and the same:
> Deals out that being indoors each one dwells;
> *Selves* – goes itself; *myself* it speaks and spells
> Crying What I do is me; for that I came.[21]

Just as I gather the world into me, so I too am gathered into world-becoming, with my whole relational nexus. Thus it is possible to discern moments in history when men and women, through the language, imagery and ethics of interconnectedness, worked with the relational grain of existence in a positive way. But what cannot be ignored are the appalling tragedies that occur when 'right relation' is trampled on, militarily, from the massacres of the Chinese warlords to the Holocaust, and socially, when the respected institution of the family masks incest, child abuse and violence against women. In these instances human agency grasps fundamental energy for destructive purposes. Historical decisions that transform the relational scene (like the creation of apartheid in South Africa) mean that certain possibilities are lost or destroyed. Certain aspects of God have died.

This is where memory as a tool is relevant. Each culture and religion has symbols in which its history is remembered and made creatively present. For Christianity the Cross is the symbol of God's participation in the historical process of building just relation. It is also the symbol of the impaling of women – and other subjugated groups – on the cross of patriarchy. Could it also be the guarantee that the cumulative loss, the pain, the death of each small child is held as part of the process of building right relation *now*? What is remembered must be *re-membered* (Mary Daly's emphasis), integrated into the process of claiming relational power now and into the future. Hence the stress on 'empowering memory.'

But whereas memory reclaims strengths of lost foremothers and sisters, it also opens up festering wounds, as the present predicament acquires a history and an almost fated inevitability – like the long history of slavery, viewed globally. It is not what is remembered, but what cannot be forgotten, that causes anguish. The particularities of suffering threaten to overwhelm the overall commitment to relation. For Cassandra to preserve her authentic voice, Achilles must always be the 'raging beast,' Hecuba the colluding woman, the Greeks are always the alien others. How, then, is the metaphysic of connection as paradigm of ultimacy to be reconciled with a moral imperative to maximize connectedness?

Maximizing Connectedness – Connection as Moral Imperative

Maximizing connectedness is a multilevel endeavor. It begins with redefining the self. If we see ourselves, not as the absolute 'I' over against the world, but as connected, in relation, the first thing that happens is a sense of freedom. We are set free from the burden of the past by our refusal to accept domination, poverty and discrimination as our only options. If what I name as 'myself' is in fact a fluid unity of many self-moments, there are many more creative possibilities and choices for future becoming. I can choose direction. I can learn and unlearn from entrapped moments of my life without denying or undervaluing the historical roots of a particular oppression. I do not play out a prearranged script. Being connected does not spell death to the self's free determination and creativity, but is the framework for making these concrete. Although becoming freer means being able to choose for maximal relational potential, it also means understanding realistically that choice and power to change are heavily dependent on economic circumstance. Even in the worst circumstances women's relational strengths have potential. A friend, a British criminologist, interviewing women in prison tells me of the strengths female bonding can provide for female prisoners whose self-esteem is low. Yet these very strengths are found threatening by prison authorities, who seek to undermine them.

The second task is to reassess the attachment/separation dynamic in one's life. Not *all* attachment is connection in the sense I use it. Not *all* separation is destructive. Many women entering middle adulthood experience a 'connected aloneness' which is comparable with religious contemplation and even to the mystical experience. (It could even be said that in a *spirituality of connectedness* lies the contemplative vocation.) But do we have the right to walk out of unhealthy dependency relationships? This cannot mean abandoning the elderly, infants or handicapped – even when this burden of care is yet another obstacle to women's autonomous agency. To me the only answer is that we have to become what Heyward calls 'mutually messianic,' redeemers of each other, with the ability to sustain broken relation – even our own – on personal and political levels. Yet care and connection as moral imperatives should not dictate the sacrifice of one sector of the populace for another.

The next two tasks reveal a more hopeful dimension. For the third task is that of self-development within the context of the environment's process towards healing. Within a life-style where all things are connected it will be illogical to use health remedies, beauty techniques, food, clothes or household aids which improve our sense of well-being at the expense of the environment. We are embarked on a common journey. With this in mind, the natural world itself can be experienced as 'redeeming strength' (a theme which I explore elsewhere).[22] The healing strength of nature is one of the dimensions to be reclaimed from women's history.

Finally, claiming relational energy as moral imperative invites women to use hitherto hidden strengths as redemptive tools. 'Embodied theology' really does mean acting boldly, but in a holistic and not a manipulative manner. Both Carter Heyward and Rita Brock have shown how claiming erotic bodily energy as sacred power can mean reverencing each other, touching each other – our selves, our lives, our political priorities – in liberating ways.[23] Struggling to break the dualistic split between rationality and emotion means daring to articulate the discoveries of feeling-knowing, the strength of a knowledge rooted in bodily experience. Only thus will the long exploitation of women's bodies and the body-denying ascetic spiritualities of many faiths begin to be overcome.

Conclusion

How then does the moral imperative to 'maximize connectedness' move us beyond the impasses described at the beginning of this paper? To whom and with whom are we in relation? First and foremost, a metaphysic of connection means discovering our own authentic voices. This happens *in relation* to the group in which I am historically and culturally rooted. This means that women of privilege – for whom it has not been a great problem to discover a voice – have the responsibility to empower other groups of women, with whom we are as a political group *in relation*, to discover, own, celebrate and mourn a story in all its particularity. *Differentiation* not *assimilation* must ground right relation. What this connectedness may mean for a privileged group of women is that the only form of relation possible is to listen, to learn and to begin a journey of conversion as response to the lessons of history. The joy of a spiritual vision is the faith in its power to heal wounds. But this vision must be rooted in respect for the context of a group's experience (for example, the experience of Muslim women in Britain since the publication of Salman Rushdie's book); it must be attuned to the possibilities of the moment. The time may not be ripe for forgiveness. Authentic dialogue may not be an option. But a metaphysic of connection seeks always to discover *deeper sources of connection:* in our being human, in our being women, in our shared responsibility for the planet. Even in recognizing the sin of broken relation and assuming its burden we bring the energy for just relation into the political scene.

IN THE BEGINNING IS THE RELATION
IN THE END – THE HEALING
BUT IN THE PRESENT – THE ENERGIZING OF CREATION FOR JUSTICE

Notes

1.   Carter Heyward, *The Redemption of God: A Theology of Mutual Relation* (Washington, D.C.: University Press of America, 1982).

2.   This phrase was first used – to my knowledge – by Catherine Keller, in *From a Broken Web: Separation, Sexism and Self* (Boston: Beacon Press, 1986).

3.   Judith Plaskow, 'Feminist Anti-Judaism and the Christian God' (Paper delivered at the conference of European Women in Theological Research, Frankfurt, September 1989), 2.

4.   See, for example, Rhoda Reddock's work on slavery in the Caribbean. Reddock shows that white slaveowners prevented slaves from marrying and having children; it was 'more profitable to get a good price' for the slave than to spend money on rearing slaves' children. Reddock's work is cited by Catherine Halkes, ... *En Alles Zal Herschapen Worden* (And All Shall be re-created: Thoughts over the wholeness of Creation, in the tension between nature and culture) (Baarn; Ten Have, 1989; English translation, London: SPCK, 1991), 57. For contemporary corollaries see the autobiographical work by Maya Angelou, *I Know Why the Caged Bird Sings* (London, Virago, 1984). In her essay 'Beyond the Peacock: The Reconstruction of Flannery O'Connor' (in *In Search of Our Mother's Gardens* [London: The Women's Press, 1982]), Alice Walker explores the differences that define the lives of two women writers from the same region, one white, one black.

5.   Anita Spencer, *Seasons: Women's Search for Self through Life's Stages* (Paramus, N.J.: Paulist Press, 1982).

6.   H. Patricia Hynes, *The Recurring Silent Spring* (New York: Pergamon Press, Athene series, 1989).

7.   Doris Lessing, *The Children of Violence: Martha Quest, A Proper Marriage, A Ripple in the Storm, Landlocked, The Four-Gated City.* All published by Collins, Grafton paperbacks. Quote from *The Four-Gated City*, 539. See also Carol P. Christ, 'Explorations wth Doris Lessing in Quest of the Four-Gated City,' in *Women and Religion*, ed. Judith Plaskow and Joan Arnold Romero (Missoula, Montana: American Academy of Religion and Scholars Press, 1974), 153ff.

8.   Catherine Keller, *From a Broken Web*. See also 'Feminism and the Ethic of Inseparability'

in *Women's Consciousness, Women's Conscience*, ed. Barbara Andolsen, Christine E. Gudorf and Mary D. Pellauer (San Francisco: Harper and Row, 1985), 251-64.

9.   Shug, in *The Color Purple* by Alice Walker, quoted by Keller, 'Feminism and the Ethic of Inseparability,' 251.

10.   For documentation on the incidence of depression in women, see the papers of the Stone Center for Developmental Studies, Wellesley College; the research of Marcia Guttentag quoted in Maggie Scarf, 'The More Sorrowful Sex,' *Psychology Today* 12, no. 11 (1979).

11.   See Lynn Segal, 'The Beast in Man,' *New Statesman and Society*, 8 September 1989.

12.   Jean Baker Miller, *Toward a New Psychology of Women* (Boston: Beacon, 1978).

13.   Nancy Chodorow, *The Reproduction of Mothering' Psychoanalysis and the Psychology of Gender* (Berkeley: University of California Press, 1978).

14.   Carol Gilligan, *In A Different Voice* (Cambridge: Harvard University Press, 1982).

15.   See, for example, Marion Zimmer Bradley, *The Firebrand* (London: Michael Joseph, 1988).

16.   Christa Wolf, *Cassandra*, trans. Jan Van Heurck (London: Virago, 1984), 4. For a reflection on Wolf's Cassandra, see Petra Von Morstein, 'A Message from Cassandra – Experience and Knowledge: Dichotomy and Unity,' in *Feminist Perspectives: Philosophical Essays on Method and Morals*, ed. Lorraine Code, Sheila Mullett, Christine Overall (Toronto: University of Toronto Press, 1988), 46-63.

17.   Janet Morley, *All Desires Known* (London: MOW and WIT, 1988), 51.

18.   Wolf, *Cassandra*, 21.

19.   Carol P. Christ and Judith Plaskow, eds., *Weaving the Visions: New Patterns in Feminist Spirituality* (San Francisco: Harper and Row, 1989). For a review, see Carol LeMasters, 'Unhealthy Pluriformity,' *The Woman's Review of Books* 7:1 (October 1989), 15-16.

20.   Alfred North Whitehead, *Process and Reality: An Essay in Cosmology*, corrected edition, ed. Griffin and Sherburne (New York: Macmillan, 1978), 22.

21.   Gerard Manley Hopkins, *Poems* (New York: Oxford University Press, 1948), 98.

22.   Mary Grey, *Redeeming the Dream: Feminism, Redemption and Christianity* (London: SPCK, 1989; Mystic, Conn.: Twenty-third Publications, 1990). See ch. 3, 'Women and Nature: A Redeeming Connectedness.'

23.   Carter Heyward, 'Touching our Strength: The Erotic as Power and the Love of God' (Paper delivered at the Groningen University Congress, *Vrouwen over Grenzen*, Groningen, April 1989); Rita Nakashima Brock, *Journeys by Heart: A Christology of Erotic Power* (New York: Crossroad, 1988).

3.3 Christian Feminism, Eros, and Power in Right Relation

Sandra Friedman, Alexander Irwin

What Michel Foucault terms the irrepressible proliferation of discourse on sexuality has, over the last ten or fifteen years, received unexpected confirmation from Christian theologians determined to outbid each other in their zeal to 'extract the truth from sex.'[1] Christian feminists and womanists[2] have shaped the most original and challenging religious discourse on sex, gender and relationality. Among its conspicuous characteristics is a heavy reliance on the concept of eros, which includes but reaches far beyond the domain usually designated by 'sexuality.' A significant number of feminists and womanists have claimed importance for the eros principle not only in personal relationships, but also in the areas of social ethics and of politics.

Since classical times, a fertile ambiguity has been attached to the erotic. In Plato's *Symposium*, the prophetess Diotima identifies Eros as the child of Plenty and Poverty, a 'great *daimon*,' intermediary between the divine and the human realms. Destined to play an ever shifting role – neither fair nor foul, neither rich nor poor, neither bad nor good – Eros is always 'in a mean between the two.' The spurring force in sexual attraction, he is at the same time the principle which animates all intellectual and spiritual endeavors; he evokes hunger after beauty, goodness and wisdom (201d–212a).

Although the concept of eros is found in Christian thought from Augustine and the Pseudo-Dionysius through the writings of such modern figures as Paul Tillich,[3] womanists and feminists employ it in a variety of contexts, both theological and secular, expanding the sphere of the erotic in unexpected ways.

Lesbian experience and concerns have been central to the elaboration of new understandings or eros. Audre Lorde and Carter Heyward have made notable contributions to this effort, arguing that one primary benefit of adopting an eros vocabulary is precisely that such a vocabulary signals a firm rejection of reductive patriarchal understandings of sexuality. Lesbian experience breaks with the 'natural' paradigm of heterosexual genital intercourse structured by the dialectic of (male) domination and (female) submission. It has been argued (though in this case not by an author who takes an explicitly lesbian stance) that by 'reformulating issues of sexuality in terms of eros,' feminist theory can 'escape the traps laid by the specifically masculine definition of sexuality that is so widespread in our culture,' and move toward developing 'a cultural construction of sexuality that does not depend on hostility for its fundamental dynamic' (Hartstock, 166).

It is easier to describe feminist/womanist eros negatively than to define it positively. The work of African-American poet Audre Lorde has served as a touchstone for almost all womanist and feminist writing on the erotic. Exquisite erotic passages are woven into her poetry (see: 'Bridge Through My Window,' 'On a Night of the Full Moon,' 'The Winds of Orisha,' 'Progress Report,' and 'Love Poem,' in *Chosen Poems*). In her brief but seminal essay, 'The ·Uses of the Erotic: The Erotic as Power' (1978), Lorde portrays eros as a fundamental expression of the 'lifeforce of women,' an empowering creative energy of decisive importance in all areas of life. Rooted 'in a deeply female and spiritual plane,' the erotic is 'the nurturer or nursemaid of all our deepest knowledge,' transcending the traditional oppositions between rational knowledge and intuitive feeling, spiritual insight and physical pleasure. The erotic embraces a spectrum of experience from sex to 'building a bookcase, writing a poem, examining an idea' (53–57).

For Haunani-Kay Trask, too, the 'new eros' is a life-force which reconciles dualistic oppositions and 'integrates the sensual and the rational, the spiritual and the political.' It points toward 'a release and refashioning of the life instincts from the vantage point of women's essential experiences. The emphasis is on physical and emotional gratifications that connect 'life' and 'work' (92–93, xi). Susan Griffin characterizes eros in similar terms as experience in which 'meaning is never separate from feeling,' and in which there is at the same time 'no feeling which does not ring through our bodies and our souls all at once.' The 'whole range' of human creative capacities is potentially embraced under this heading (254).

Feminist psychoanalyst Jessica Benjamin employs a different, and seemingly more conventional, approach to the language of eros. She uses it primarily to refer to sexual activity between adults. Yet Benjamin detects vital erotic components in the bond between mother and infant, and more broadly in all genuinely intersubjective relationships where communion is allied with acknowledgement of and respect for the irreducible autonomy of the other. Like the fundamental relationship between mother and child which prefigures it, erotic union constitutes a paradigm of the situation of mutual recognition in which intersubjective tension is maintained, allowing 'both partners to lose themselves in each other without loss of self' (29).

Still another side of the erotic is illuminated by theologian Elga Sorge. She describes 'all-transforming, creative eros' as a genuinely cosmic power, indeed as 'the strongest force that exists.' Feminist theology is concerned with developing 'religion based on unfragmented love and healing eros.' Viewing creative eros as a sacred force offers a standpoint for 'discerning and transforming' those Christian symbols and beliefs which have heretofore been allowed to function in repressive and life-denying ways (38). Pursuing a similar understanding of eros, Rita Nakashima Brock has sought to shape a life-affirming 'christology of erotic power.' Brock argues for the rejection of the image of Jesus as a lonely religious hero, and prefers to speak not of the Christ, but of a 'Christa/Community' shaped by the unifying force of eros.

The image of Christa, the female Christ figure, is an important symbol for authors attempting to introduce new understandings of the erotic into theological discourse. Brock writes:

> As I recall, the first use of the term Christa was in reference to the crucifix in the Cathedral of Saint John the Divine in New York City. The Christ on the crucifix, labeled Christa, was female. In using Christa instead of Christ, I am using a term that points away from the sole identification of Christ with Jesus.... Using the term Christa/Community affirms my conviction about the sacredness of community. (113–14 [ch. 3, endnote 2])

'The Crista/Community of erotic power is the connectedness among the members of the community who live with heart,' in a relational matrix created and maintained by eros (70).

To date the most thorough and challenging discussion of eros in the Christian feminist/womanist literature is that found in Carter Heyward's *Touching our Strength: The Erotic as Power and the Love of God*, a milestone in the development of Christian theological reflection on the subject. Drawing on the work of Lorde, Dorothee Sölle, Brock and other spiritually oriented authors – as well as on the writings of such secular theorists as Zillah Eisenstein – Heyward constructs a vision of the erotic which synthesizes perspectives developed in many different areas of womanist and feminist thought.

Heyward's approach to defining eros comprehends its breadth and complexity. She identifies the erotic as a desire: a yearning which urges us 'to taste and smell and see and hear and touch one another,' shaping forms of pleasure and communication which celebrate our embodiment. Erotic longing is not simply sexual desire. Rather, it is 'our yearning to be involved' in each other's bodies, feelings, lives. The essence of eros is, Heyward insists, a relational movement: 'the movement of our sensuality,' which, as an energy of the whole body-self – of the sensual/intellectual/emotional/moral person – flows 'transpersonally among us' at the same time that it 'draws us more fully into ourselves' (*Touching*, 187; cf. 93; 113–14). Eros is the urge toward mutuality, toward rightness in relation.[4] It is 'the source of our capacity for transcendence,' not in the sense of a spiritual flight from the world, but rather of a ' "crossing over" among ourselves, making connections among ourselves' (*Touching*, 99).

Nor does Heyward hesitate to connect the erotic with the divine. Through eros we have 'our most fully embodied experience of the love of God.' The erotic is 'the divine Spirit's yearning, through our body-selves, toward mutually empowering relation' (*Touching*, 99). Christa, symbol of the need for healing power in connectedness, can be seen as 'a Christian name for eros' (*Touching*, 116).

The multivalence, the 'thickness' of eros in feminist and womanist writings is one of its most valuable attributes. We can begin to gain a clearer understanding of the possible significance of the new eros for theology and for liberatory political work by delineating the principal elements in the works we have reviewed. Four common themes emerge, reflecting the principal areas in which womanists and femi-nists have assigned a crucial role to eros:

- *Eros is pleasure.* The individual experiences eros, Audre Lorde affirms, as 'the open and fearless underlining of [her] capacity for joy.' The erotic 'is an internal sense of satisfaction to which, once we have experienced it, we know we can aspire' ('The Erotic,' 56, 54).

The immediate catalysts of erotic pleasure are diverse. Sex, art, poetry, intellectual activity, communion with nature, constructive work – all can yield access to deep and nourishing joy. Lorde claims that, once the empowering pleasure of eros is recognized, 'every level upon which I sense opens to the erotically satisfying experience.' Eros 'flows through and colors my life with a kind of energy that heightens and sensitizes and strengthens all my experience' ('The Erotic,' 56–57). By showing the ecstatic pleasure they are capable of experi-encing, the erotic teaches individuals to demand the most from themselves, their relationships, their work. 'For having experienced the fullness of this depth of feeling and recognized its power, in honor and self-respect we can require no less of ourselves,' measure our lives by no standard lower than the 'deep and irreplaceable knowledge of [our] capacity for joy' ('The Erotic,' 54, 57).

Alice Walker identifies an openness to passion and pleasure – '*regardless*' – as one of the basic attitudes of the womanist. Although she does not use the word eros, Walker describes an approach to life very close to what Lorde speaks of as living 'in touch with the erotic.' A womanist: 'Loves music. Loves dance. *Loves* the spirit. Loves love and food and roundness. Loves struggle. *Loves* the folk. Loves herself. *Regardless*' (*In Search of Our Mothers' Gardens*, xii).

- *Eros is relational.* Though it touches and transforms individu-als in their deepest and most intimate dimensions, eros is not a private experience. It is shaped by and in movement toward another person, being, object, idea. The erotic awakens and opens us to the other. It is fundamentally and essentially an energy of relation, of connection-making. Eros, Rita Nakashima Brock suggests, is a life-process 'constantly flowing and growing in relationships.' Erotic power 'is the fundamental power of existence-as-a-relational-process' (53;41). The erotic calls us beyond the boundaries of our selves at the same time that it deepens our sense of self.

In *The Color Purple*, Alice Walker describes the 'feeling of being part of everything, not separate at all' (203) which reveals our profound relational connection to nature, to other people, and to God. This deeply erotic feeling includes a strong element of physical pleasure, yet it flows out toward things and persons with which or with whom 'normal' sexual relationships would be excluded: trees, air, birds, friends of the same gender, the divine itself. It awakens Walker's heroines to a sense of the intimate interconnectedness of all life.

- **Eros is a cosmic force.** As a cosmic force of creativity and love, eros can be imaged in non-theistic ways. In the work of secular poets and theorists, eros is often described as 'life-force,' a suprapersonal, empowering energy on which individuals can draw, in pleasure and in struggle (see Lorde, 'The Erotic,' 55; Trask, *Eros and Power*, 92f). As Audre Lorde points out, this life-force manifests itself in a variety of different contexts and under many different forms, all of which deserve to be honored for their ability to deepen and enrich our feeling, our wisdom and our capacity for action ('The Erotic,' 56–57).

The cosmic power of eros can also be conceived theistically. Heyward identifies God as 'our power in mutual relation,' and argues that, since we come to know the divine in our experience of human relationality, there is clearly an important sense in which 'God is erotic power,' a truly Christic – liberating, healing, transformative – energy (*Touching*, 188;91). The value of the Christa symbol may be to 'help us envision and embody the sacred/erotic power, which is really our Christic (fully human, fully divine, fully creaturely, fully creative) power' (*Touching*, 117). In similar terms, Dorothee Sölle has claimed that 'God is our capacity to love,' revealing herself in the matrix of our human relationships. In this relational context, the traditional theological distinction between human eros and divine agape must give way to a unified understanding of love as divine/human power embracing 'sexual love, charity and love in the social and political realm' (*The Strength of the Weak*, 138).

Brock uses images that strive to bridge the gap between traditional theistic conceptions and a more pantheistic/animistic understanding of eros as a 'life-giving force' present in all things. 'The presence and revelation of erotic power is the divine dimension of human existence,' she writes. 'In the beginning is the divine Eros, embodied in all being. As the incarnate, life-giving power of the universe, divine erotic power is the Heart of the Universe' (46).

- **Eros is political.** For Lorde and other womanists and feminists, eros connects deep feeling, wisdom and responsible action. It plays a central role in deciding how (and whether) the individual will act politically. This rather surprising claim merits extended examination.

The idea of assigning to the erotic a central place in the theory and the practice of politics may at first seem surprising, although the notion is not, of course, entirely novel (see: Marcuse, *Eros and Civilization*; Reich, *Sex-Pol*). The idea that 'the personal (including the sexual) is the political' has been something of a stock phrase in feminist circles for a number of years. Some Christian feminist and womanist theorists, however, have gone beyond the vagueness of the formula to make precise and challenging assertions about the political 'uses of the erotic,' and about the nature of the connection between personal erotic experience and effective political engagement.

Generally speaking, these discussions of the political dimension of eros have been organized around three central principles: eros as an analytic concept, as an energy of revolt, and as a catalyst of creative empowerment and positive political values.

Eros and Sexuality as Analytic Concepts

Along with their secular counterparts, Christian feminist and womanist authors have insisted that the concept of eros provides an important intellectual/analytic tool for decoding social power relationships, even those relationships which are (or appear to be) situated outside the domain of the sexual. Elaborating on the feminist insight that the systematic oppression of women by men underlies all forms of social, economic, political and cultural praxis within patriarchal society, feminists have developed the principle that eros provides a tool for understanding the basic human needs and relational structures on which social and political institutions are founded. Using the criterion of eros as a life-giving creative energy, they critique those social structures in which the erotic impulses are thwarted and essential human needs consequently left unmet. In secular scholarship, Nancy Hartsock has most convincingly defended this use of eros as an analytic category. A broadly defined eros concept is, she claims, vital for exploring 'the sexual meanings of issues and institutions which are not explicitly genitally focused.' Grounding analysis of social and political forces in an understanding of the erotic can highlight 'the genderedness of power,' and 'the relation of sexuality to issues of power and community' (166–68).

Such Christian feminists as Dorothee Sölle and Shirley Cloyes have also analyzed the oppression of women by men as a crucial aspect of the commodification of human relationships in capitalist society. In a social order structured by class exploitation and frantic consumption, gender roles and the sexual act itself are used as tools of oppression. Alienated sex negates the 'eternal eros' which seeks to build authentic, life-enhancing relations among persons. A concept of healthy and nurturing erotic relations can help to reveal the points at which our human needs are frustrated by the socio-economic order. It can measure the depth of alienation and point to areas in which fundamental political change must be effected (*To Work and to Love*, 115ff).

Carter Heyward emphasizes the need to utilize categories related to eros in order to create a social history capable of elucidating 'the connections between the control of women's bodies for procreation; the suppression of homosexuality; the economic system of a particular place and time.' Citing the analyses of sexuality and power relationships by Foucault and Jeffrey Weeks, Heyward argues for a 'historical understanding of sexuality' that breaks free of essentialist categories and looks at the complex interaction between sexuality, religion, and economic and social institutions (*Touching*, 38ff.).

Eros as an Energy of Revolt

The use of eros as a tool in the analysis of social and political relationships is the least unconventional among Christian feminists' applications of the erotic to the political and moral spheres. The other two such applications that we wish to discuss involve claims about the impact, not of the idea, but of the experience of eros in politics and ethics.

Christian feminists and womanists have seen in eros an immediate source of the energy of revolt necessary for struggle against oppressive political and social power structures. Lorde, Harrison, and Heyward, though they emphasize the positive, nurturing aspects of the erotic, also describe its combative dimension. The experience of the erotic and the feelings it awakens sustain the anger which energizes the fight against oppression. There is an organic and necessary connection between the 'work of love' and the 'power of anger,' both on the level of personal ethics and in political action.

Audre Lorde insists that eros represents the 'bridge which connects' the spiritual and the political. The erotic, by the very pleasure that it affords, empowers and impels us to refuse and combat sex-, race-, and class-based exploitation – to reject the humiliation, institutionalized mediocrity, and cheap compromises meted out by partriarchal authorities. 'In touch with the power of the erotic within ourselves ... we begin to give up, of necessity, being satisfied with suffering and self-negation.' Charged with the anger at injustice which belongs to the deepest nature of eros, 'our acts against oppression become integral with self, motivated and empowered from within' ('The Erotic,' 56, 58).

Beverly Harrison has focused on the critical and transformative role of love, including the erotic, in ethics and sociopolitical struggle. She stresses the integral connection between the experience of love and the 'power of anger' which expresses itself in political struggle for justice. Where anger rises, 'there the energy to act is present. In anger, one's body-self is engaged, and the signal comes that something is amiss.' Anger alerts us to the need for change. We must not allow ourselves to 'lose sight of the fact that all serious human moral activity, especially action for social change, takes its bearings from the rising power of human anger.' In order to maintain its politically potent character, the anger of which Harrison writes must be intertwined with and rooted in our experience of connection through love. Yet at the same time, honest and authentic love relations depend upon the recognition of anger as a positive transforming force: 'Where anger is hidden or goes unattended, masking itself, there the power of love, the power to act, to deepen relation, atrophies and dies' (14–15).

In these analyses, lesbian experience and the discourses fashioned from it move into the center of the picture. Carter Heyward maintains that lesbians and gay men find themselves in an ironically privileged position when it comes to understanding the radical dimension of love in which eros becomes revolt. She prefers the term 'rage' to that of 'anger,' underlining with her choice of words the passion and urgency which inform erotic rebellion. Born and nurtured in the face of institutionalized suspicion or outright hostility, lesbian/gay eros will have a thread of rage woven into its very fabric. 'Our passion as lovers' fuels 'our rage at injustice.' Far from being mutually exclusive, rage and compassion, eros and political resistance 'belong together' (*Our Passion for Justice*, 87).

'To say that I am a lesbian,' Heyward asserts, 'is to make a statement at once personal and political.' What homosexuals are 'perceived to be about (and what some of us are about intentionally) is not simply the right to lead our own private lives, but rather an overhauling of the social structures of our time,' a revolutionary transformation of the 'economic, religious, educational, business and other structures' which characterize late-twentieth-century capitalist society (*Passion*, 90–91); experiencing the erotic as power becomes in Heyward's work both the final goal of liberatory struggle on the part of the sexually oppressed, and the source of the combative energy necessary to carry on the fight.

Power in Right Relation

Transformed by creative eros, political struggle becomes not merely struggle against, but struggle *for*: for the broadest possible application of the principles of justice and mutuality to which our erotic experience introduces us. In other words, eros teaches persons to rebel against oppressive structures and life-denying values; at the same time, it helps them discover new values and modes of relationship to replace the old. Some Christian feminist authors see a close connection between our experience of erotic relatedness and the effectiveness, indeed the very existence, of our engagement in the struggle to realize justice. Our experience of eros is not the only determinant of our involvement (or lack thereof) in politics. It is, however, these authors claim, an important source of the emotional and spiritual empowerment, of the wisdom, and of the will which we must bring to political struggle if our engagement is to be effective.

Eros – including the sexual dimension of the erotic – liberates energies for the physical, emotional and spiritual effort involved in justice work. Carter Heyward insists that the aspect of eros which we know through sexual pleasure is not irrelevant to political thought and action. Sexual union experienced under conditions of genuine mutuality empowers and galvanizes the participants for effort in other areas: 'Sexual orgasm can be literally a high point, a climax in our capacity to know, ecstatically for a moment, the coming together of self and other, sexuality and other dimensions of our lives,' including the political (*Touching*, 33). Furthermore, through pleasure in shared effort, the tasks involved in political work can themselves become 'eroticized,' at least in part. The immediate experience of the erotic changes the 'color,' the emotional tone, of the work undertaken, helping us to find pleasure in the effort connected with the pursuit of political change (Lorde, 'The Erotic,' 57–59).

Yet eros does more than offer a wellspring of vital energy that can be tapped for the purposes of political struggle. The erotic as the experience of both the fulfilment and the endless reawakening of yearning for mutuality in relationship teaches us in an immediate and personal way that right relation between human beings is in fact possible, and that such forms of just relatedness can transform human existence. Rightness in relation – mutually sustaining and empowering attunement – is, we learn, a goal toward which human beings can work, and which, together, they can achieve.

Lorde, Heyward, Sölle, Brock and other feminist and womanist authors insist that the significance of the apprenticeship to eros should not be underestimated. Sharing erotic joy, we learn how ecstatically beautiful life can be in its highest moments. And we perceive what it is that makes such moments possible. These privileged experiences of fulfilment are born in situations in which justice – dynamic, erotic mutuality – has been called into being among us. There are no oppressors and no victims, only human beings who have come together in what Brock terms the non-hierarchical 'play space' of mutual recognition, cocreation, healing (36–37). In this erotic space, we taste the joy and the creative energy that justice produces in human life.

That space is neither saccharine nor uncritical. Audre Lorde is grateful for her erotic connections to 'those sisters with whom I have danced hard, played, or even fought' ('The Erotic,' 59). Unqualified affirmation is not a necessary ingredient of erotic connection. What does belong to the nature of eros is justice. This means respect for the other, acknowledgement of her dignity and freedom, above all in those areas in which she differs from ourselves. It also means honesty: respecting the other enough to share our convictions with her, and if need be to fight with her, when we believe she is wrong.

Through the connections woven by eros, womanist and feminist authors have argued, justice ceases to hover as a vague abstraction and takes on tangible and cogent meaning *for us*. In the give-and-take of our erotic lives-in-relation, the abstract idea becomes a sustaining value. In this sense, Carter Heyward writes, our values are 'never simply our own private opinions.' Our understanding of justice grows in a situation of erotic 'relation to those whose lives we trust' (*Touching*, 95). Justice as an aim of political effort can become most powerfully credible for us, Heyward believes, through the personal experience of erotic justice, the mutuality which is our 'shared experience of power in relation.' Through mutuality, 'we are called forth more fully into becoming who we are – whole persons with integrity, together. Our shared power is sacred power, and it is erotic' (*Touching*, 99).

The Christian feminists Heyward, Sölle, and Shirley Cloyes have formulated an even more radical hypothesis concerning the connection between erotic experience and justice-making in the political sphere. They believe that the joy and pleasurable attunement experienced through authentic eros express themselves directly and spontaneously as a political impulse: the will to strive for the creation of social and political conditions under which equally intense erotic – that is, sensual and creative, as well as sexual – satisfactions would be available to all members of the society. Sölle and Cloyes assert that: 'Genuine erotic love opens the hearts and minds of lovers to other people.' To love deeply is to gain knowledge 'not only of our partner,' but also of the full community of human beings. 'Because we grow into wholeness through love,' they claim 'we yearn for reconciliation with the disenfranchised of the earth. In other words, the more I make love, the more I want to make the revolution' (*To Work and to Love*, 150–52).

It would be a mistake to minimize the psychological and philosophical radicality of this position. These Christian feminists claim to be identifying a type of committed and effective engagement in the political sphere which springs directly out of what is usually thought of as the intensely private experience of erotic communion. This account involves a fundamental and bold assertion about the relationship between the two spheres: the public/political and the intimate/erotic Sölle, Cloyes and Heyward deny the existence of a purely 'private' erotic sphere. Sexuality is deeply impacted by practices of social construction, and is as such inescapably political. Going beyond this fundamental insight, these authors see eros not simply as passively shaped by political and social forces, but as actively shaping ethical and political values that affirm life and generate power for effective justice struggle.

The eros feminists and womanists describe is not an esoteric experience linked to obscure and specialized practices. Rather, it is an unfolding of the fundamental and potentially universal human joy in competent creative activity and in communicative interaction with others. Eros signifies more than an enhancement of personal pleasure. It expresses possibilities for wider cooperation and transformation at the social level. Having tasted – perhaps fleetingly and fragmentarily – the joy that eros brings, we can learn to work toward shaping situations of erotic fulfilment in our own lives; working for our own realization as erotic beings demands our working for the liberation of others' erotic-creative potential.

This claim enables us to understand more clearly what Sölle, Heyward, and other authors mean by authentic, mutual or non-alienated eros, as opposed to dehumanizing sex which is the norm in our culture. (See *To Work and to Love*, 150–55; *Touching*, ch. 3, 6; *Journeys*, 'Introduction' and ch. 2.) The erotic in its authentic, liberating form is moral in its essence. Such eros seeks by its very nature to engender the conditions of social justice that would permit its own widest dissemination. Erotic pleasure of this sort demands, like good news, like the tidings of a birth, to be shared. It creates in the person who experiences it a moral need to see it propagated.

This intuition is decisive for much Christian womanist and feminist thought on community-building and political struggle. Authentic erotic joy does not isolate the partners in a closed world of private satisfactions; it demands instead to be shared as widely and as generously as possible. Such joy requires and initiates its own translation into the communal-political sphere. This does not occur as an afterthought, but belongs to the essence of the phenomenon of erotic connection as Christian feminist authors have described it. To have experienced true joy means to want that joy for others, as well as for oneself. For Sölle, 'Love is not separable from justice. The drive to make love and to make justice should be one.' (*To Work and to Love*, 152). Carter Heyward asserts that there is direct continuity between authentic erotic passion and our 'passion for justice': 'To love you is to sing with you, cry with you, pray with you, to act with you to recreate the world. To say "I love you" means – *Let the revolution begin!*' (*Passion*, 93).

Objections to Eros Theology

Many will raise questions about the empirical justification for affirming the existence of a direct and empowering connection between the experience of eros and radical political engagement. In our society, it might well be claimed, the erotic is omnipresent, yet progressive political commitment and solidarity are in short supply, indeed. To this objection, however, feminists and womanists supportive of the eros principle will answer that the experience of authentic interpersonal eros in our culture is not only not universal, but that such experience, even among persons who consider themselves sexually liberated, has been and continues to be exceedingly rare. It is not simply that the alienating, pornographic sex celebrated in our society as the only legitimate paradigm of human erotic interaction does not entirely correspond to the understanding of the erotic developed by feminist and womanist authors. Rather, this common understanding of sexuality

– rooted in sado-masochistic fantasies of domination and control – represents the antithesis, the radical negation, of the relational eros described in feminist/womanist discourse.

In fact, the scarcity of genuine erotic mutuality in our culture accounts for the difficulty in tracing the empirical effects of eros on the current political situation. Violent and depersonalizing sex is indeed ubiquitous; eros as the sharing of power and pleasure in right relation is only beginning to be recognized as a possibility. We suggest that as authentic eros experience becomes available to more and more persons, there will in fact be more testimonies like that of a lesbian student quoted by Carter Heyward: 'My love for and commitment with women in relation has come to call me to an ever more radical justice praxis' (*Touching*, 119).

A more serious objection to the emerging discourses on eros is connected with the problem of race and class relations. It is clear that even what feminists and womanists wish to regard as 'authentic' erotic joy runs, like other forms of pleasure in a racist and capitalist society, the risk of being denatured and appropriated as a supplementary 'lifestyle enhancement' by those belonging to the already-dominant racial and class groups.

Feminist theorists' shaping of a new vocabulary based on the experience of erotic joy and empowering mutuality might well look, to women who are the direct victims of racial and class oppression, suspiciously like an attempt on the part of affluent white women to avoid the harsh and often decidedly unjoyful realities of concrete political struggle. On the subject of such struggle, bell hooks notes with terse irony that it is in fact 'rarely safe or pleasurable' (28). Certain members of privileged groups will clearly be only too willing to seize on elements of feminist/womanist eros-discourse as an authorization for pleasure-seeking under the guise of political activism. Such discourse will undoubtedly in some cases reinforce the cherished belief (aggressively criticized by hooks and others) that by 'feeling better about ourselves' and our intimate relationships, we are *already* involved in a significant type of political praxis (hooks, *Margin to Center*, 27f, 43–65).

The risk that authentic eros might, in a caricatured form, become another expression of race/class privilege, another sophisticated species of pleasure reserved for those with the leisure to devote themselves to its cultivation, is real. However, the decisive role played by such African- and Asian-American women as Audre Lorde, Alice Walker, Haunani-Kay Trask and Rita Nakashina Brock in shaping new discourses on the erotic suggests that the risk can be avoided. Neither poetry nor eros, according to Audre Lorde, should under any circumstances be thought of as a luxury reserved for the leisure class. Both are vital tools for the oppressed in their struggle to free themselves from mental, emotional, and linguistic traps into which they have been forced. Lorde's observation on poetic language in general is particularly apt as a characterization of the emerging discourse on the erotic: it 'lays the foundation for a future of change'; it functions as 'a bridge across our fears of what has never been before' ('Poetry is Not a Luxury,' 38).

Eros, then, is both a description of experiences and structures already proven and in place, and a calling into being of 'what has never been before.' Authors such as Andrea Dworkin are skeptical about the power of liberal ideas and warm words to combat the institutionalized sexual and economic exploitation which characterizes our society (see her essays 'Violence Against Women,' 'The ACLU: Bait and Switch,' 'Why So-Called Radical Men Love and Need Pornography,' and 'Feminism Now'). Though there is little empirical evidence of the political impact of the new eros, it would be wrong to conclude either that eros as described by some womanists and feminists does not exist, or else that it will never be politically significant. Drawing such conclusions would be failing to grasp the extent to which the new language of eros can catalyze the empowering erotic connections which Lorde, Heyward and others have discussed. It would, as well, leave unacknowledged the transformative power which many of us have felt in moments of erotic communion.

Toward Universality

Through eros, through the sharing of creative power in a just relationship, we receive an experience of joy which will not leave our lives unchanged. Like Celie in Walker's *The Color Purple*, as the unimagined force and depth of authentic erotic connection begin to reveal themselves to us, we find our attitudes toward all areas of our lives transformed. We learn that joy shared and multiplied in mutuality is not a possibility reserved for another world; we are capable of experiencing it here and now. And in this assurance we find the power to 'talk back' to those who have tried to deny us joy. Such erotic power is not available only to a select group, or dependent upon a knowledge of abstract theories. It is rooted in nothing more obscure than the simple willingness to take seriously basic human experiences of creative pleasure, mutual care and connectedness, and to acknowledge that it is these experiences which give meaning to our existence.

Such experiences are potentially available to all persons. The sight of others' suffering becomes an irresistible demand for action when we perceive those others not as broken objects, faceless entities made and shattered by economic forces, but as potential bearers of the same creative eros which has brought a new depth of fulfilment to our lives. Eyes opened to the possibility of erotic joy cannot close themselves again conveniently before the daily spectacle of joy mutilated. Having tasted the power of human creative potential implicit in the erotic makes each encounter with a human life twisted by poverty and injustice a call which forces us into action. The pain we feel is a demand for change not out of respect for an abstract concept of justice, but out of passionate desire to share the eros which gives, strengthens and transforms life. Anger of the kind that Lorde, Harrison, and Heyward describe wells up hot against the devastation of erotic possibilities – others' possibilities, and our own.

Over time, we believe, the feminist and womanist discourse on eros as an empowering experience of mutuality will create a conceptual and affective framework within which eros can be thought about, discussed and experienced in a new way. In its personal dimension and its political consequences, the new eros will become available to increasing numbers of women and men who were previously unable to name, and consequently unable to know it.

Of course, in a context in which sexual violence and abuse pervade all levels of our social existence, it would be foolish to suppose that eros could immediately be accepted as an unambiguous value. In particular for those persons who have themselves been victims of sexual abuse, the idea of a healing eros is deeply problematic, if not positively offensive. However, womanists' and feminists' understanding of eros as an energy of embodied relation which is not limited to – or even necessarily connected with – genital sexuality opens perspectives for healing connections among persons whose lives have been damaged by sexual violence.

Freeing ourselves from the depersonalizing dynamic of violence and exploitation which has governed understandings and experiences of sexuality in patriarchal society means, womanists and feminists claim, inventing a new vocabulary in which to describe and give shape to new forms of sexual/erotic relatedness. Authors like Lorde, Heyward, Brock and Sölle have taken up this task. Their eros discourse possesses that poetic power to 'give name to those ideas which are ... nameless and formless, about to be birthed, but already felt' (Lorde, 'Poetry is Not a Luxury,' 36).

Especially in the realm of Christian thought – so visibly dominated by a tradition of hostility toward women, human embodiment, sexuality and the material world in general – creating a new language of eros has radical implications. Carter Heyward does not exaggerate when she suggests that eros as she understands the term demands a transvaluation equivalent to a genuine revolution in Christian moral and theological thinking (*Touching*, 47, 114–118). It is time, she writes, 'to speak the truths of our lives insofar as we can, with one another's presence and help,' while 'cultivat[ing] carefully together those truths we cannot yet speak, truths that may still be very unformed and young.' For in cultivating a new language of the erotic, 'We are shaping history with our words' (*Touching*, 47).

Notes

1.   The plethora of books connecting Christian theology with questions of gender and sexuality or presenting discussions of sex in a theological perspective includes an astonishingly wide

spectrum of theological points of view. A sample: Mary Daly, *Beyond God the Father* (Boston: Beacon, 1973); Philip Sherrard, *Christianity and Eros: Essays on the Theme of Sexual Love* (London: SPCK, 1976); Margaret Miles, *Fullness of Life: Historical Foundations for a New Asceticism* (Philadelphia: Westminster, 1981); James B. Nelson, *Between Two Gardens: Reflections on Sexuality and Religious Experience* (New York: Pilgrim, 1983); Rosemary Radford Ruether, *Sexism and God-Talk: Toward a Feminist Theology* (Boston: Beacon, 1983); Paula M. Cooey, Sharon A. Farmer and Mary Ellen Ross, eds., *Embodied Love: Sexuality and Relationship as Feminist Values* (San Francisco: Harper & Row, 1987); James G. Wolf, ed., *Gay Priests* (San Francisco: Harper & Row, 1989); Greg Speck, *Sex: It's Worth Waiting For* (Chicago; Moody Press, 1989).

2.   The term *womanist* was coined by Alice Walker in *In Search of Our Mothers' Gardens* (xi–xii). The word has been used to draw attention to the specific contributions of women who 'affirm themselves as *black* while simultaneously owning their connection with feminism' (Delores Williams). See Williams' 'Womanist Theology: Black Women's Voices,' in Judith Plaskow and Carol Christ, eds., *Weaving the Visions: New Patterns in Feminist Spirituality* (San Francisco: Harper & Row, 1989), 179–186.

3.   For a historical account of the influence of eros on Christian thought and piety, see the classic study by Anders Nygren, *Agape and Eros*, translated by Philip Watson (Philadelphia: Westminster, 1953). Nygren views eros as the 'born rival' of the authentically Christian concept of love as *agape*. For more positive readings of eros from recent male theologians, see for ex. Paul Tillich, *Love, Power, and Justice* (New York: Oxford, 1954), and Daniel Day Williams, *The Spirit and the Forms of Love* (New York: Harper & Row, 1968).

4.   Heyward explicitly refuses an understanding of 'mutuality' as a simple synonym for 'reciprocity.' She condemns the widespread liberal view of just relationships as founded on a strict economic model of 'fair exchange.' Mutuality, in her definition, is not a static attribute, but rather a 'relational movement.' Mutuality means, '*sharing power in such a way that each participant in the relationship is called forth more fully into becoming who she is – a whole person.*' *Touching*, 191; italics in original.

5.   This theme was discussed in several sessions of Beverly Harrison's seminar on 'Sexuality and Social Order in the Ethical Perspective,' Union Theological Seminary, New York City, Sept.-Nov. 1989. We are grateful for the experiences, questions and criticisms shared by members of the seminar, especially those who are themselves survivors of sexual abuse.

References

Benjamin, Jessica. *The Bonds of Love: Psychoanalysis, Feminism, and the Problem of Domination*. New York: Pantheon, 1988.

Brock, Rita Nakashima. *Journeys by Heart: A Christology of Erotic Power*. New York: Crossroad, 1988.

Dworkin, Andrea. *Letters From a War Zone*. London: Secker and Warburg, 1988.

Griffin, Susan. *Pornography and Silence: Culture's Revenge Against Nature*. New York: Harper & Row, 1981.

Harrison, Beverly Wildung, with Carol Robb. 'The Power of Anger in the Work of Love.' In *Making the Connections: Essays in Feminist Ethics*. Boston: Beacon, 1985.

Hartsock, Nancy, *Money, Sex, and Power*. Boston: Northeastern University Press, 1985.

Heyward, Carter. *Our Passion for Justice: Images of Power, Sexuality, and Liberation*. New York: Pilgrim, 1984.

—*Touching Our Strength: The Erotic as Power and the Love of God*. San Francisco: Harper & Row, 1989.

hooks, bell. *Feminist Theory: From Margin to Center*. Boston: South End, 1985.

Lorde, Audre, *Chosen Poems Old and New*. New York: Norton, 1982.

— 'Poetry is Not a Luxury.' In *Sister Outsider*. Trumansburg, NY: The Crossing Press, 1984, 36–39.

—'Uses of the Erotic: The Erotic as Power.' In *Sister Outsider*, 53–59.

Marcuse, Herbert. *Eros and Civilization*. Boston: Beacon, 1966.

Plato. *The Symposium*. In *The Dialogues of Plato*. Translated by B. Jowett. Oxford: Clarendon, 1953.

Reich, Wilhelm. *Sex-Pol: Essays, 1929–1934*. Edited by Lee Baxandall. New York: Vintage, 1972.

Sölle, Dorothee. *The Strength of the Weak*. Philadelphia: Westminster, 1984.

Sölle, Dorothee, with Shirley Cloyes. *To Work and to Love*. Philadelphia: Fortress, 1984.

Sorge, Elga. *Religion und Frau: weibliche Spiritualität im Christentum*. Stuttgart: Kohlhammer, 1985.

Trask, Haunani-Kay. *Eros and Power: The Promise of Feminist Theory*. Philadelphia: University of Pennsylvania Press, 1986.

Walker, Alice. *The Color Purple*. New York: Simon & Schuster, 1982.

-*In Search of Our Mothers' Gardens: Womanist Prose*. San Diego/New York: Harcourt, Brace, Jovanovich, 1983.

4. Sexuality and Marriage

The topic of Christian marriage, its interconnection with related topics like the family and divorce, its identification within Christianity as the sole context for sexual intercourse, the criticisms of patriarchy and inequality brought against it, and the range of responses to these criticisms, deserve a whole book. The selection which follows engages only with a small number of issues meriting attention. The extracts chosen vary in length and depth. The chapter as a whole combines simple theological insights with more detailed theological analysis and criticism. It draws on North American and African experience and on Protestant, Roman Catholic and Greek Orthodox traditions of theology.

William Willimon, Stanley Hauerwas and Allen Verhey argue that the love which is at the heart of marriage is not the romantic attachment which leads to the decision to marry, but the commitment which is acquired through the process of living and growing together. We do not choose our parents and children. Although we to some extent (and in some societies) choose our partners, we cannot choose how our partners will change. But we can still learn to love them. Hauerwas and Verhey address pre-married people, warning them that they must move beyond both Christian apologetic and secular propaganda which are alike influenced either by a 'romanticism' which fantasises about perfect relationships or a realism which accepts sexual activity is a fact of (early) life and seeks to minimise harmful consequences. The Christian alternative is to view marriage as a covenant where there is a shift of meaning away from intensity and towards *continuity*. Genital activity before or outside the covenant of marriage becomes a different issue, viz. 'whether the narrative we provide for ourselves sexually forms a character ready to sustain the common history God may call us to develop with another.'

German Martinez' essay, 'Marriage as Worship: A Theological Analogy' seeks to make available the resources of catholic and orthodox spirituality to married partners striving to attain that growth in love of which Willimon, and Hauerwas and

Verhey speak. He outlines a 'conjugal spirituality' or 'spirituality of stability'. Its components are 'agape-love, donation, communication and faith sharing'. Partners minister to each other in the name of Christ because their marriage, like worship 'is the total validation of the other in the devotion and service, celebration and mystery of a relationship'. Christ is the lover and husband of all humanity. He is our covenant-maker. While western theology largely abandoned contracts for covenants in its theology of marriage, the eastern church continued to present 'a balance between a highly positive view of conjugal life – an earthly type of spirituality – and a mystical, liturgical theology'. In Christian marriage, enriched by its foundation in divine love, 'self-bestowal in the spirit of agape is the common source in which the spouses meet the Holy ... The God-agape is present in both the exceptional and the common experiences of the spouses, whether in the care of a family meal, or the involvement of a psychological and sexual intimacy, or the entering into the self-offering of Christ.'

None of the essays so far in this chapter has raised the question whether 'covenant continuity' or 'conjugal spirituality', while theologically desirable, is socially possible. Emmanuel Martey's essay, 'Church and Marriage in African Society' provides a grim reminder that relations of power between men and women, institutionalised by marriage, may oppress women and require them to remain in marriages where they remain, to say the least, subordinate. While patriarchal marriage is not confined to Africa, Martey shows how African women 'have been subjected to a combination of patriarchal structures from both Africa's own and the invading cultures'. The Bible has been used by a male priesthood and ministry to reinforce patriarchy and male chauvinism. The imposition of absolute monogamy has humiliated women locked into polygamous marriages and reinforced 'the husband's right over his wife's or wives' labour'. Female circumcision and polygyny remain great evils, yet the church has done little to oppose them. Martey calls for a depatriarchalized church in Africa, a new revitalised church which is the agent of liberation, justice and peace.

William Willimon's essay 'The People We're Stuck With' first appeared in *The Christian Century*, 107, Oct 17 1990, pp. 924-5. Stanley Hauerwas and Alan Verhey's essay 'From Conduct to Character – A Guide to Sexual Adventure' first appeared in *The Reformed Journal*, 36, 11, No. 1986, pp. 12-16. German Martinez is priest in residence at St. Mary's parish, Greenwich, Connecticut, and Professor at Fordham University, New York, U.S.A. His essay 'Marriage as Worship: A Theological Analogy' first appeared in *Worship*, 62, July 1988, pp. 332–353. Emmanuel Martey's essay 'Church and Marriage in African Society: A Theological Appraisal' first appeared in *African Theological Journal*, 20, 2, 1991, pp. 136–147.

4.1 The People We're Stuck With

William H. Willimon

One reason that Mother's Day is so cherished by our parishioners, even though not by many of us pastors, is that our parents remind us of our indebtedness to others for almost everything important: our lives, our looks, our values. I wish, however, that Mother's or Father's Day fell upon All Saints' Day. Saints are also reminders of our indebtedness. We believe only because someone – Samson, David, Sarah, Ruth – lived the faith before us, told us the story in a manner that was worthy of our imitation. Saints are our great-great-grandparents, and we are their children in the faith. No believer is self-made.

People who actually know something about the Bible may be less than pleased to have a Samson or a Sarah as a grandparent. They may look saintly in stained-glass windows, but in their day few called them saints. People seem more saintly after they've been dead 1,000 years. But if you had to live with them or stare at them across the breakfast table rather than across a Gothic-style church, you might question why they are our saints. Of course, we don't choose saints. They are given by the tradition of the synagogue and the church.

And that pinpoints a major difference between us and the world of the Bible. Today, when we speak of family, parents or children, we're apt to speak sentimentally, unrealistically, if not downright deceitfully of our 'happy family': Ozzie, Harriet, June, Ward, Wally, the Beaver, George and Barbara. When the Bible speaks about parents and children in faith, it speaks honestly: Sarah, Samson, David, Bathsheba.

Our dishonesty is surprising, considering the state of the American family. Never has the divorce rate been higher, never have we had more problems with spouse, child and elder abuse. What did presidential candidates talk about before they discovered that American families (though apparently not their own families) are in a mess? I doubt that politicians know what to do about parents and children in our families, not because they don't care, but because, when it comes to understanding what it's like to be a parent or a child today, our politicians don't know how to think about family any more than we do.

In the name of freedom, we Americans created something called 'the individual.' Nothing is more important to Americans of the political right or left than maintaining the sovereignty of the individual and his or her options, freedom and independence. As a result, relations between husbands and wives become a contract between two individuals who jealously guard rights and prerogatives. Relations in the family come to resemble the rest of our society – a conglomeration of friendly strangers. We've created a world where privacy is sought more than community, where no one is asked to suffer for anybody else and where we want both to be intimate and still able to shake hands and say goodbye with no bad feelings. Such thinking makes relations between parents and children incomprehensible.

What makes being a child or a parent so unusual is this: you didn't choose your parents and they didn't choose you. You don't choose relatives; they are given. Even if you adopt a child, that child will grow to be so unlike the baby whom you brought home from the adoption agency that you will continually know that this child is someone who has been *given* rather than selected. As parents and children in a modern world that worships individual rights and freedom, nothing is odder than learning to love someone whom we didn't choose.

To a surprising degree, this lack of choice extends even to the person we marry. Most people think that the toughest part of marriage is deciding whom we ought to marry, making the right choice. We say we are deciding whether or not we are in love with this person, whether we are emotionally attached. The church traditionally has cared less about our emotional attachments. The church cares about whether or not we are people who are capable of sustaining the kind of commitment that makes love possible. The pastor leading a marriage ceremony does not ask, 'John, do you love Susan?' The pastor asks, 'John, *will* you love Susan?' Love is defined here as something we promise to do, a future activity, the result of marriage rather than its cause. That sounds odd to those of us devoted to the idea of choosing the 'right' person. Yet for most of the church's history, marriage occurred among couples who hardly knew each other before the wedding.

Most of us are grateful that, at least in our society, arranged marriages are passé. Still, one reason parents send their children to prestigious universities is so that they can meet prestigious members of the opposite sex. We all know that it's helpful to marry someone with a similar social, economic and religious background. Through piano lessons, summer camp and a B.A. degree, parents give their children the illusion that the choice of someone to marry is not being arranged. I'm not being cynical here. Cultures that still practice arranged marriages (and are up-front about it) have much lower divorce rates than ours. ('Who should be entrusted with such important matters?' asks a friend from India. 'Someone who has actually been married and has 50 years of life experience, or someone who has never been married and has had no experience except school?' I didn't have a ready answer.)

I think we should be more open about the arranged, unchosen aspects of our marriages because it enables us to think clearly about the peculiar ethical demands placed upon us in families as husbands, wives, parents and children. We are conditioned to think that only what we decide for ourselves is right for us. The trouble with such a view is that marriage, like parenting, requires that we make sense out of being stuck with certain people for no good reason or justification. Most of us learn to make the best of it. Right there is a glimpse of us at our best. For right there is where we learn to be faithful, to love strangers even though we did not choose them as someone we might have liked to love.

Stanley Hauerwas has argued that we always marry the wrong person. That is, we never marry the one we thought we were marrying – because marriage changes us. So you wake up one day and realize that the person next to you is not the person you committed your life to five years ago. Of course, you are not the same person either. What do you do? If marriage is the correct choice of the right person to whom you are emotionally attached, you are in big trouble. The person has changed; so have your emotions. Nobody ever chose to marry a person who is addicted to alcohol, or who develops a terminal illness. But sometimes you wake up in a marriage and that is the person you've got.

Being a parent is like that too. Parents never get the children they thought they were giving birth to. That's why I'm unhappy with the term 'planned parenthood,' as if it's only desirable to have children if you have planned or chosen them. Who plans to have a severely retarded child, or a rebellious child, or a child who plays the drums in a rock band? Sometimes we get such a child. And what then? You can choose an automobile, but you can't choose a child. You must *receive* a child. The Bible says a child is a gift, not a possession or a project.

Nobody knows what he or she is getting into as a husband or wife, a parent or a child. Don't get me wrong: I'm all for marriage preparation, and we ought to do more of it. But the trick is preparing for a lifetime of commitment to someone who is always changing. You can't prepare for how annoying another person can be. You can't prepare for all the ways a child will challenge you, disappoint you and, worst of all, come to look just like you, only to desert you for college. And because you can't, what you need is some means of being part of an adventure which you can't control, the end result of which you do not fully understand. Morally, we move into the future on the basis of the commitments which we made without knowing what we were getting into.

What we need, when we marry or have a child, is some means of turning our fate into our destiny. As Christians, our faith provides us the means to live together as parents, children, husbands and wives. Just as we didn't choose Samson or Sarah to be our grandparents in faith, so we didn't choose Jesus to be our savior. He came to us, not the other way around. John's Gospel makes this explicit: Jesus says to his disciples, 'You did not choose me. I chose you so that you might bear fruit' (John 15:16). And because God has chosen us and continues to care for us, we are free to risk being faithful, even to those whom we didn't choose.

4.2 From Conduct to Character – A Guide to Sexual Adventure

Stanley Hauerwas and Allen Verhey

It is commonplace to observe that our culture's sexual mores have been changing. Christians generally, and Christian ethicists in particular, seem unsure about what to say or how to respond. It is not accidental that many young people turn to their doctors for advice rather than to their pastors. We regret that situation – and not just because we want to protect some professional turf but because we think the Christian community ought to be able to give some good advice to young people, and to give it well. We don't blame doctors or young people; we blame people like us, Christian ethicists, preachers, and professors, who really are confused about what to say and how to say it.

That may itself seem a strange thing to say, for it is generally thought that for all our confusion about whether a particular war is just or whether a particular life must be preserved, Christian morality is quite clear about sex. The church's position is clear: No, you may not commit adultery, and No, you may not have sexual intercourse before marriage. What could be clearer than these prohbitions?

But those prohibitions are one source of the confusion. Notice that we did not say the prohibitions are wrong, only that they are one source of the confusion. We remember sermons when we were young which were full of prohibitions and warnings in an effort, we always thought, to get young people to behave themselves. We also rememer how exciting and adventuresome such sermons made unchastity sound and how boring 'righteousness' seemed by contrast. Young people love the lure of an adventure, including a sexual adventure.

That's one problem, then, a problem identified by Augustine long ago: our 'fascination with the forbidden,' the lure of the prohibited. But there is another problem. In the attempt to say *why* these prohibitions exist, Christians have generally done what seems to us the right thing: they have celebrated sexuality. Christian ethicists have usually fallen over each other in their attempts to say good things about sex. God created us sexual beings, they say. Adam needed Eve to be whole, they say. They were 'one flesh,' they say. That's the way God intended it, they say. 'The reason God prohibits it to young people is that it is such a wonderful thing,' they say. And that, we suggest, is a little confusing to young people. Again notice that we didn't say it is wrong. We said only that it begins to be confusing. We are not saying that such claims are incoherent as a justification for the prohibitions, only that the coherence is not exactly obvious to a young person who has some real affection for another person and that it may be disturbing to a young person who has yet no 'fulfillment' in another sexual being.

Perhaps the church's simultaneous prohibitions of certain sorts of sexual behavior and celebrations of sexuality could be coherent in another time and culture, but it is more difficult (and more important) for the church to be understood on the subject of sexuality in our culture. We wish to note two features of our culture, one ordinarily commented on and the other ordinarily ignored: the media and the political tradition.

The media take one of two approaches: either realism or romanticism. Romanticism's basic assumption is that love is a necessary (and sufficient) condition for sex and marriage. Love may be defined in various ways, but it usually comes down to the quality of the interpersonal relationship between two people. Television examples are almost endless – boy has chance to score with the young flirt; upset parents rely on maturity and morality of boy; boy doesn't score; parents congratulate and console him with assurance that one day Ms Right will come along and their sex will be part of a meaningful relationship.

Now, again, notice that we did not say this was wrong – how can we when a good deal of Christian literature focuses on the 'depth' of commitment between two people as an index of permissible sexual involvement? James Nelson (*Embodiment*, p. 127), for example, says, 'The physical expression of one's sexuality with another person ought to be appropriate to the level of loving commitment present in that relationship.'

All of that may be true, but it's a lot for young people to remember in the back seat of a Buick. And even if they remember it, alone in the dark with passions stirring, the 'level of loving commitment' is hard to test without self-deception. There may be good questions to ask at such a time: Is our loving commitment honest if we need to do it secretly? Is our relationship genuine if we're unwilling to make it legally binding? Is the level of our commitment deep enough if we still have separate checking accounts? If we are called from singleness to marriage, will we happily tell our own children about this evening some day? Those are good questions, but they point away from the romanticism of much of the media and much Christian literature on sexuality.

The other approach of the media – and of some Christian ethicists – is pragmatic realism. Realism says, 'Look; young people today *are* sexually active. Forget about the glory or evil of sexuality; just try to keep people from getting hurt.' The realist starts by acknowledging sexual activity and tries to 'demystify' it. Sexual activity is one human activity among others. It can be a profound gesture of human commitment or just plain fun; but people, including young people, are going to 'do it' – so try to keep the damage down. Should we permit doors to be shut during dorm visitations? The realist says, 'It may at least prevent some grass stains.' Or, better, perhaps: 'As long as students are responsible – i.e., informed about and disposed to utilize contraceptives.' Or, best of all, perhaps: 'As long as they know what the sexually experienced know, that it's hard to keep sex just plain fun.' The realist thinks it important to talk candidly, not mystifyingly, about sex.

Now, notice, again, we don't say this is wrong. Indeed, we think candor about sex is something the church has to learn, but realism is only an admission that we have little advice to give about sexuality itself and less capacity to give that bit of advice well. Realism assumes that the way things are is the way they ought to be – or at least that the way things ought to be has very little relevance to the way things are. Moreover, it is ready to assume that sexual morality is really a matter of what each individual thinks is good for him or her, as long as somebody else does not get hurt.

That brings us to the political tradition, for the assumption of the liberal political tradition is that individuals are the best judge of what is good for them. The glory of the liberal political tradition is its guarantee to each one of the liberty to pursue the good life as he or she sees it as long as it is compatible with the equal right of all others to a similar pursuit. Again, we are not saying this is wrong, but it does and can provide only a minimal account of sexual morality – sexual relations are permitted only between consenting adults. This is true enough, but if its minimalism is not acknowledged, it can distort the moral life and the sexual life. It fails to call attention to what people *should* want. It tends to silence rather than nurture public discourse about what the good sexual life is and requires. Claims about the good sexual life may be – indeed, must be – tolerated as private visions of the good, but they are trivialized precisely as *private* visions. And it becomes increasingly difficult for the church to talk about sex in public – but for different reasons now than that we think it somehow dirty and obscene. It may be clean – or even good clean fun – but it's a private matter and a matter of the individual conscience.

If there is a public morality beside the political principle of equal freedom, it is the utilitarian injunction to do that act whose consequences will be pleasant rather than harmful. Now moralists can make some little headway with warnings about failed contraceptives, pregnancy, the self-inflicted violence of abortion, venereal disease, and so forth. But when Christians celebrate sex as much as they do, the pleasure and human fulfillment it seems to promise plausibly outweigh even such horrifying risks. Moreover, sex begins to be considered in terms of its utility – as a means to an end and, by small steps, as a *technique* to achieve human fulfillment. If it doesn't deliver on its promises, our technique must be blamed, our clumsiness or inexperience with erogenous zones, rather than our expectations reevaluated.

We have forced the reader to be very patient with these complaints about sexual morality. You deserve better than a list of complaints about the mess sexual ethics is in. But we will try your patience by listing them again before risking an acount of sexual morality.

1. Sexual ethics relies too much on negative prohibitions.
2. Sexual ethics, in its effort to justify its prohibitions, celebrates our sexuality without sufficient reservations.
3. Sexual ethics is too romantic; it focuses too much on the quality of the relationship as an index for the level of sexual involvement.
4. When sexual ethics tries to be realistic, it fails to say anything about what the good sexual life should be like.
5. Sexual ethics has been too influenced by the liberal political tradition which makes sexual morality a private and personal matter and, as long as the sex is between consenting adults, nobody else's business.
6. Sexual ethics has been too influenced by the utilitarian moral tradition which balances pleasure and pain and finally renders sex a technique to get happiness and human fulfillment.

Now, then, a student comes and says: 'What's wrong with a little fooling around?' What would we say? And how can we bring Scripture to bear on such a question?

The first thing we might say is that sex is not a bowl of buttons. It sounds a curious and unpromising place to begin, but many Sunday afternoons ago, there was a boy who would play with the bowl of buttons his mother kept in her sewing and mending cabinet. He would dump the buttons out and try to flip them like tiddlywinks back into the bowl. Sunday afternoons were boring in his house, and it was sort of fun. The fun was the technique, and the importance for his young hands was skill and dexterity. Now sex is not like that; it is not a bowl of buttons. It is not simply a technique for getting some pleasure in the middle of a boring afternoon or semester. It is not simply a matter of technique and dexterity, a matter of skill, to secure some small (or large) pleasure. Sex has meaning beyond the quality of its performance. Yet sex as skill, as performance, as dexterity, as a bowl of buttons, is the vision of sexuality one frequently sees in our sex-saturated society. The proper technique and presto: fulfillment. Sex becomes a happiness technology. The rule is simple enough for bumper stickers, 'If it feels good, do it.'

The point is that the young person who has to make a decision about whether to fool around also has to make a decision about how to construe sex. Is it part of a technology of pleasure? or part of a covenant? It is not enough, however, to say how sex should not be seen. We must be prepared to offer another understanding of sex to young people. Something like this has biblical warrant:

Persons *have* skills, but they *are* sexual, and there is something as mysterious about sex as there is about persons – and about temples.

No matter how much we know about technique, human sexuality remains a mystery. This is the mystery: that two persons become one flesh (Gen. 2:24; 1 Cor. 6:15–20). Sexual relations always involve us as *whole* persons, as embodied spirits or in-spirited bodies, with our capacity to make and keep covenant. In making a choice about how to understand sex when confronted with sexual decision, we also confront choices about the sort of *persons* we want to be and to become. We can live our sexual lives as technical experts or as whole (and vulnerable) persons, as pleasure seekers or covenant makers and covenant keepers (to use Lewis Smedes' nice phrases). It is not quite a matter of *making* sex one thing or another. There remains in every act of coitus, and perhaps in the vulnerability of nakedness and any clumsy gesture toward lovemaking, a sign of God's intention with sex, for there remains an implicit exchange of entrusting and commitments. To ask during the intimacies of making love, 'But will you love me tomorrow?' is to impugn the *committal* of the act. Note that one may ask about the depth of one's affection, the intensity of one's affection, but not about the *continuity*. 'How much do you love me?' does not insult the act. 'How long will you love me?' does. Maybe it is *not* this way naturally – maybe that is just the way we have come to see sex in the Christian community informed by Scripture. But even the realist knows 'It's hard to keep sex just plain fun.' At any rate, of this we are sure: that our confrontation with our own sexuality calls us to make important decisions not only about whether to fool around some, but about both the meaning of sex – whether it is a technology of pleasure or a mystery of commitment – and about ourselves – whether we are pleasure-seekers or covenant-makers (and covenant-keepers).

Sex is a mystery. We may – and we should – delight in this mystery. Witness the Song of Solomon. And we should – and we may – be sober about this mystery. Witness Proverbs 7. The sexual act celebrates the mystery of one whole and exclusive relationship covenanted of two persons who are committed not only to each other but to the cause of the one who creates and keeps covenant and renews all things – including them. The sexual act celebrates not the act itself, not technique, not even the intensity (or 'depth') of attraction two people can feel for each other or the fulfillment of desire one person can find in another. It celebrates a covenant, begun in vows, carried out in fidelity, and given to a future of Christ's righteousness, Christ's service, also and especially toward each other. Such is the delight and sobriety – and adventure – of the mystery of sex.

This adventure is not romanticism. The index for sexual relations has shifted from the depth or intensity of the interpersonal relationship to *continuity*. The romantic hero or heroine sets out on an adventure in quest of intensity – not continuity. Fidelity is not important – and may be an impediment. The sexual hero or heroine in the Christian account sets out on an adventure in quest of continuity – and fidelity is crucial. Extramarital sex may provide new romantic intensity when married life and married sex have become routine, but it is ruled out by the heroic quest for continuity. Premarital sex may promise romantic excitement and a relationship deeper and more intense than anything a young person has known before – but for a moment – and that moment must be ordered toward and governed by the heroic quest for continuity.

The anti-romantic character of this adventure is captured in 'Hauerwas's law': 'You always marry the wrong person.' The one thought to be Mr Right turns out not to be. Ms Right tends to show up after marriage. But the adventure of marriage is learning to love the person to whom you are married. You do not fall in love and then get married. You get married and learn what love requires. Love does not create a marriage; marriage teaches us what a costly adventure love is. Of course, the quest for continuity will involve nurturing the quality, the depth, even the intensity of the relationship, but not as the object of the quest; it is rather a part of what a sexual covenant, what continuity, requires.

The delight in this adventure is kept from celebration of sex itself or technique by being joined to sobriety and mystery. And the sobriety of this adventure is kept from the sort of realism that refuses to consider what good sex is by being tied to delight and mystery.

We may delight in sexuality, but sobriety will keep us from expecting too much from it. Human fulfillment is not found in sexuality. It is found in Christ. Extravagant expectations can be idolatrous, and the church has not been sober enough about sexuality. The church does not – but should – call attention to I Corinthians 7 – to the gift and vocation of singleness as a sign of the fulfillment of the ages and of human fulfillment. In Christ sexual relations are neither a necessary nor sufficient condition for human fulfillment. Short of theological and biblical claims, we need simply to say in candor that sex is as frequently messy and boring as it is spiritually fulfilling. If we said that more plainly, extravagant expectations could be lowered, the possibility and plausibility of saying 'no' could be nurtured as well as commanded, and the harm of unfulfilled expectations lowered.

We may have sober expectations of sexual activity – and we should still delight in it. Sobriety is not prudishness. Indeed, our readiness to delight in sexuality will not condemn technique or pleasure or the fulfillment of the desire of each in the other, but subordinate it to the mystery and to the heroic quest of continuity in an act of covenant-making and covenant-keeping. Technique, after all, may enhance the *intensity* of delight for a moment, but technique alone quickly becomes boring (witness the bowl of buttons), and sexual relations reduced to technique or delight or romance quickly move from one technique to other more exotic ones in the quest for pleasure or intensity. Commitment and covenant provide less intensity, to be sure, but more continuity and sexual relations within covenant can slowly advance to the consummate pleasure of holding hands in memory and promise.

Well, all of this may be a lot for young people to remember in the back seat of a Buick, too. Yes, it is. So, we're back to the prohibitions, the things it's quite easy to remember. We suppose that what we have said will ground prohibitions against premarital and extramarital sex, but we also think that this advice – if it is good advice – cannot be said well in the form of prohibitions. The focus has shifted from conduct to character, from what acts we are ready to permit to what sort of people we would be and become, from rules to virtues.

Chastity, after all, is not a state – like virginity – it's a virtue, a habit formed of conviction and perspective, and it's not lost necessarily if in a moment of passion one's virginity is lost. Chastity is a form of fidelity to one's sexual identity where singleness is honored and the heroic quest of marriage is for continuity.

The issue is not whether genital activity is permitted after one month or two years or after marriage. The issue is whether the narrative we provide for ourselves sexually forms a character ready to sustain the common history God may call us to develop with another. If we own a vision of sex as a technology of pleasure, we establish certain habits. If we own a vision of sexuality as mystery demanding delight and sobriety, we establish certain habits. If we own an identity as pleasure-seeker or romantic hero in quest of intense relations, we establish our character. If we own an identity of covenant-maker and covenant-keeper, of a sexual heroine in quest of continuity, we establish a different character. That's why they're important. But rules and prohibitions can leave us just as unchaste and lustful as ever, even if we never violate them. 'You have heard it said from of old...,' Jesus said.

What young people need most is the lure of an adventure where conquest means more than the sexual possession of another, and a community capable of nurturing and sustaining a character for such an adventure. Singleness and marriage are, we think, great adventures. Merely repeating the rules may succeed only in making chastity and fidelity seem boring.

To the question 'How far can we go?' the response is, 'What sort of story do you want to tell of yourself and of your sexuality? What sort of character do you want to own as your own?' Or, 'If you are called from singleness to marriage, will you happily tell your spouse and your children about what you did? Will the story nurture continuity in your marriage and sustain your calling to nurture the Christian integrity of your own children?'

The last word may well be that it's *still* a lot to remember in the back seat of a Buick. But a good character, a virtuous character, can usually do the right thing without having to think about it very much and is able to do the right thing even when the available arguments seem weak or indeed to point to a different act, when the adventure is demanding (as, of course, adventures tend to be).

4.3 Marriage as Worship: A Theological Analogy

German Martinez

Marriage and worship are both primary and universal human realities where manifold dimensions converge: body and spirit, earthly elements and symbolic actions, natural phenomena and divine mystery. Though historical by their nature and always historically related, they essentially transcend the realities they embody. The pledge of the old Anglican wedding ritual, 'with my body I thee worship,' speaks profoundly of this central meaning. Like worship, which etymologically means 'ascribing worth to another being,' marriage is the total validation of the other in the devotion and service, celebration and mystery of a relationship.[1]

Worship, therefore, can be applied to marriage analogously. This analogy suggests theological concepts which are most relevant in articulating the core of a much needed conjugal spirituality. Marriage and worship are, in fact, a typical case of coherence, even at the strictly anthropological level, from at least three major perspectives: symbolic action, depth of meaning, and self-transcendency.[2]

Symbolic actions are the language people use to express the experience of both shared beliefs through worship or the shared love of a marital relationship. The nature, the inner reality, of a marital relationship is to be rooted in love, as the nature of worship is to be grounded in faith. Without belief worship is meaningless; without love marriage is empty. In both cases there is a symbolic and existential relationship. Worship embodies an inner life, a belief through rituals, since the ritual is the cradle of religious belief. It has the proper language and external gesture of inner realities – as does a marital partnership. Its verbal or bodily expressions, its quality and reality of intimacy, its celebrations and struggles, in summary, the whole interaction of self-giving and self-serving relationship of a man and a woman in marriage stems from an inner reality of that love. These are – or are not – embodied in love. Spirituality depends on the truthfulness of that relationship whether in marriage or in worship, and that truthfulness will be apparent in the symbolic and existential language of the relationship.

The depth of meaning is envisioned in the many possible orders of reality to which marriage and worship can refer. That is precisely why symbolic actions and language come into the picture. The ordinary experience of a community of love, or a community of faith, provides the metaphors people use to express their value, and the prophetic revelation describes the covenant of God to his people. Marriage and worship are, in fact, so complex and rich that they are very difficult to define. We all have experienced love – the primary end of marriage – and we all participate in ritual actions, but we take pains to share with others those kinds of experiences. In this aspect the complexity of love and of religious ritual is very clear. This fact bespeaks their intrinsic link and mutual support in various levels of meaning. 'Love,' says L. Mitchell, 'whether of God or of the girl next door, is all but impossible to express except through outward symbolic action, that is, through ritual acts.'[3]

Finally, self-transcendency intrinsically defines worship as it does marriage. Any definition of worship, even from the point of view of many anthropologists, centers around this essential dimension, as expressed in Evelyn Underhill's classical definition, 'the response of the creature to the Eternal.'[4] Similarly, the total reality of a community of marital life and love cannot be understood without the vertical dimension of that created love, the beyond experienced within the encounter between I and Thou. This intimate encounter by its dynamism is enclosed by, and moves toward the ultimate mystery, God himself. God becomes the basis of the encounter, as Martin Buber's interpersonal principle of the external Thou demonstrates.[5] Charles Davis, in his classic study of the nature of religious experience and feeling, reaches the same conclusion from a different perspective. 'Human feelings,' he says, 'by their dynamism, point beyond themselves; they are an expression of self-transcendence.'[6] The self-giving marital love, as a symbol of divine love, straining toward God, reveals and celebrates the mystery of God; this is worship. True marriage, like true worship, is rooted primarily, therefore, in self-transcendent love. They both relate to something in the foundations of human consciousness and point beyond their reality. God is thus made present.

This analogical relationship between marriage and worship, which, as stated above, includes symbolic action, depth of meaning and self-transcendency, underlies the biblical understanding of marriage. Conjugal spirituality can only be properly understood against this background. It is against this background of an eminently human love that the biblical perspective of God's covenant reveals its full depth of meaning.

God's nuptial relationship with his people in the Old Testament becomes the paradigm of the most intimate human relationship. The human experience of love parallels that relationship of fidelity and becomes the most telling metaphor of Israel's covenant. 'Marriage, then, is the grammar that God uses to express his love and faithfulness.'[7] Similarly, in the New Testament perspective, Christ, the lover and husband of humanity,[8] renews the covenant by his sacrifice and becomes the paradigm of Christian marriage. The nuptial reality between Christ and his church is the actual foundation and source of the Christian spirituality of marriage. The Spirit of the risen Lord inspires the daily living of the spouses in a personal and faithful self-donation.[9]

Worship, more accurately spiritual worship, exemplifies the ideals of the covenant and consequently of marriage. Israel is called to offer a spiritual worship of obedience to the word and to maintain God's covenant, because this covenant is established after Israel's liberation and passage to faith in Yahweh's love and faithfulness. The 'chosen and priestly people' acknowledge this covenant with a life and service of spiritual worship.[10] The prophets and the psalmists use this same language of worship and marital relationship to dramatize that love between Yahweh and Israel.[11]

Christ renews the liturgical conception of the prophets 'in spirit and in truth.' He dies to establish a new covenant. Very often the liturgical symbolism of the New Testament is rooted in the prophets. The reality of the covenant, definitively concluded in Jesus Christ, is evoked by Paul in Ephesians to establish a parallel between marriage and the union of Christ with his church. The reference here to baptism and the eucharist in the context of the mystery of Christ's cross exemplifies once more the spiritual foundation of marriage as spiritual sacrifice. In fact, Christians are called to be themselves a proclamation of praise of God's love, in the image of Christ, who offered himself up through the Holy Spirit, as the only fitting worship to God.[12]

This application of a biblical-liturgical theology to marriage fills the writings of the early church, which, in turn, inspired the Roman sacramentaries (5th–8th cent.). The later Roman ritual of marriage, however, beginning in the eleventh century makes only sporadic reference to this biblical theology and spirituality of marriage. In its place a contractual mentality arose.[13] In patristic theology, on the contrary, any aspect of marriage as a contract is notoriously absent. The spiritual perspective of marriage centers around the idea of the mystery of marriage seen in the nuptial and sacrificial relationship of Christ and the church. This relationship constitutes the source and foundation of the theology of marriage in the fathers' tradition.[14]

The Eastern Churches are a telling example of a profound and compelling theological spirituality of marriage along the biblical lines of the covenantal relationship of spiritual sacrifice. They have focused on the agape-sacrifice spirituality of marriage, which constitutes the mystical and sacramental reality of marriage. Man and woman's partnership of love is represented poetically as an icon of a mystery of praise. They are ministers in their priestly vocation of an offering of life and love to each other.[15]

In his classic research on marriage in the East, Cardinal Raes has shown the foundation of this biblical and liturgical spirituality. The splendid Eastern rituals present a balance between a highly positive view of conjugal life – an earthly type of spirituality – and a mystical, liturgical theology. Both horizontal and vertical dimensions are rooted in biblical symbolism. It is against the background of the human reality that the church's nuptial offering by Christ at the wedding banquet of the cross is conceived as the foundation of a conjugal spirituality: 'Christ-husband, who had married the holy and faithful Church, and had given to her at the cenacle his body and blood ... raise your right hand and bless husband and wife.'[16]

This priestly ministry of Christ has nothing to do with sacred objects. By the same token, marriage as worship goes beyond the boundaries of created sacralization. The 'one flesh' is holy from its roots only by the created act of God-agape. In this regard, Catholic theology has long ago acknowledged the impact of desacralization in the New Testament, which sees human values observed from the eschatological reality of Christ. 'For his is the peace between us ... and has broken down the barrier ... destroying in his own person the hostility caused by the rules and decrees of the law' (Eph 2:14–15).[17]

Worship is, therefore, analogously applied to marriage only under this assumption. In its broad sense it embraces all the secular values, the day-to-day experience and the totality of the challenges of becoming one, if lived as a symbol and reality of the transcendent presence of God-agape. The mystery of life embodied in the mystery of Christ is the background and source of an inclusive spirituality of marriage which demands to be celebrated in the mystery of worship.

This divine dimension of the secular sphere of marriage is neither mythical sacralization, nor mystical idealization. E. Schillebeeckx rightly states that 'faith in Yahweh in effect "desacralized," or secularized, marriage – took it out of a purely religious sphere and set it squarely in the human, secular sphere.'[18] Since marriage is foremost secular value, Christian spirituality rejects the false dichotomy between sacred and profane and views the presence of the holy in that secular value. Worship, with its secular character, provides the prism of a larger supernatural context.

Mystical idealization, on the other hand, whether concerned with worship or marriage, devalues the goodness and beauty of the order of creation. True religion is rooted in human experience and feeling which are very important channels in the encountering of the mystery of the Holy. Davis accurately puts the question in this way: 'How is it, then, that religion, mystical religion particularly, has – with reason – been seen as the enemy of the body and the affections?'[19] As people establish communication in worship with the absolute through symbols, so the partners are drawn into the inner life of God through the mutuality of their bodily and spiritual selves, the total being.

These misinterpretations are at the bottom of the ruinous cleavage between faith and life, and are the cause of alienation of many people from the church in the vital sphere of marriage. Furthermore, they run counter to a theology which presents marriage as the natural sign and milieu of God's saving and healing love.

The lifelong process of initiation in an intimate communion of marital life should thus be seen within the perspective of worship; a praise of the God-agape. This worship perspective rightly generates a vital spirituality which is essential to a vital marriage, because spirituality is the totality of the personal experiences celebrated as a gift of God and in the intimacy with God which is the very meaning of worship. The spouses, in acknowledging God's intimate presence in each other, accept each other as his permanent gift and perfect each other in their own path of spirituality. This intimacy with God empowers them to a life of holiness, in liturgical terms, to be the 'memory' of the Lord.

This theological analogy of worship which sacramentally subsumes all human experiences and from which true spirituality unfolds provides a fundamental orientation and unity of conjugal spirituality. It is not a comprehensive panorama of the complex challenges of marriage and family living, but it integrates four vital realities into a whole: agape-love, donation, communication, and faith sharing.

Agape of Intimacy, Meal and Eucharist

Agape defines the fundamental quality of love and has been applied to the eucharistic meal of intimate fellowship of early Christianity, celebrated at home. This new analogy of worship, based on the spiritually profound, symbolic and transcendent concept of agape, offers fruitful insights to understanding the core of marriage spirituality.

In fact, the sharing of self and the sharing of a meal in married life are not strictly utilitarian bodily functions only because of agape. Body and bread sharing in this respect are gift and communion, that is, agape. It is an intimate sharing which possesses a symbolic quality of donation and devotion, of reverence and care. The Christian eucharist, as agape-meal and agape-offering of the glorious Christ, builds upon the natural significance of that sharing of a fellowship meal. Consequently, mutual intimacy of body and bread are integral to the daily experience of conjugal spirituality, if lived in the spirit of agape as being 'in the Lord' (1 Cor 7:39) and celebrated in the source and center of every Christian spirituality, the eucharist.[20]

A cleavage between faith and life in this most important reality of family life on which human growth and fulfillment depend has borne tragic consequences, especially in a world of great change and challenge. This is so because this cleavage cripples conjugal spirituality in its core: the life-giving and life-uniting reality of agape-love of which God himself is the ultimate reality and source, but which has to be lived in the concrete and the human. On one hand, this kind of love is an irreplaceable gift of being, understood and accepted in the deepest self in rejection of the collective depersonalization of modern society. On the other hand, this self-bestowal in the spirit of agape is the common source in which the spouses meet the Holy and their spirituality unfolds in the day-to-day experiences of life. The God-agape is present in both the exceptional and the common experiences of the spouses, whether in the care of a family meal, or the involvement of a psychological and sexual intimacy, or the entering into the self-offering of Christ. These are only three privileged moments from which an all-embracing home spirituality can be enriched.[21]

The importance of this line of thought stems from the clarifying nature of agape in regard to the ambiguities of love in our present culture. Serious psychological analysis provides the background for a solid understanding of the complex reality of love in answering the question: What is agape?

Agape means a way of being; it is a creative process; it never fails because it is unconditional, self-giving and self-sacrificing. This productive activity of loving is not a goddess, says Erich Fromm, because the worshipper of the goddess of love becomes passive and loses his power. In fact, no one can *have* love because it only exists in the *act of loving*, as Fromm rightly describes it.[22] The mode of 'having,' so pervasive in contemporary human relations, can be deadening and suffocating. The crisis of intimacy with all its human counterfeits and psychological barriers depends on such an existential structure in human relations.

The presence of God makes possible the experience of transcendence through love. The New Testament presents this transcendence as a dynamic relationship with which a person is empowered by the mystery of the divine love. The biblical God is a God of intimacy and passion. In fact, God is simply love (1 Jn 4:8, 16).

Marriage, especially in the theology of John (Jn 2, 1-12) and Paul (Eph 5:25, 32), is a total and all-embracing communion after the image of the nuptial sacrifice of Christ, who gives up his nuptial body.[23] The philosophical and psychological analysis often misses this transcendent perspective, but corroborates the teaching of Scriptures on the same basic human realities of agape. Thus they are essential characteristics of a spirituality of marriage: unconditional, sacrificial, caring and self-renewing love. Thus 'love never ends' (1 Cor 13) because it tells the other person that he or she will never die.[24]

Stressing the importance of the spiritual nature of agape-love, the reality of eros-love is reaffirmed because that transcendent agape would be meaningless without the sexual desire of eros. The exaggerated fear of 'keeping perverse desire within its proper bounds'[25] divorced for centuries, at least in theory, sexual passion, tenderness and intimacy on one hand, and marriage spirituality on the other. J. Ratzinger draws, in this respect, a cogent biblical analogy: 'As the covenant without creation would be empty, so agape without eros is inhuman.'[26] Persons are embodied spirits relating symbolically through the language of their body. Profound personal relations demand real personal intimacy in the integrity of a community of love.

A false dichotomy between spirit and flesh has undermined the truth of creation of male and female in the image of God. Furthermore, it has emasculated human sexuality, the capacity to love and procreate, in its physical and spiritual being and doing. The dialogic structure of sexual intimacy, in fact, complements and broadens the being of man and woman,[27] and at the same time, as a saving mystery in faith, symbolizes and causes union with God. Therefore, marital spirituality and sexual intimacy are not enemies but friends, because the author of life and love is present in their sacramental sexual experience. They are called to holiness in intimacy with the divine love through their celebration of the total commitment in a body, soul and spirit intercourse – 'nakedness without shame.'[28]

Intimacy expresses the interpersonal capacity of a total life-sharing, not only through the eros of passion, warmth and mature sexual encounter, but also through the agape of commitment, acceptance and self-disclosure. Intimacy cannot be reduced to tactility or even sexuality. It is a way of being and relating in closeness to the other in the life-process of creating a community. What Erik Erikson and other social scientists state concerning the conditions for interpersonal intimacy has to be taken seriously in the theological underpinning of conjugal spirituality.[29] The spirituality of marriage takes into account what human scientists have to say because of the secular nature of marriage. They present the real and fertile ground in which spouses meet the Holy. Those human conditions, like the attitude of reverence and devotion, the ideal of unselfish love and spiritual nakedness, the spontaneity of freedom and authenticity, all become true hallmarks of conjugal spirituality. By the same token, competition and stagnation, angelism and repression are rejected. To live humanly in the authentic faith of the passionate and committed God of the covenant is the highest form of intimacy.

In fact, no one has better captured this shared intimacy of God as a lover with a passion for truth and life than the prophets, the Song of Songs, the psalmists, or the Christian wisdom of the mystics like Teresa of Avila and John of the Cross.[30] A correlation exists between God's touching us deeply and wholly and the experience of human intimacy. To discover this correlation is to discover the key to marital spirituality.

Existential intimacy is, therefore, absolutely necessary for human life. Paradoxically, many people have lost the capacity to share intimacy because of a highly competitive individualism, and this speaks to us of the need to stress it in reference to family life. It calls for total sexual intimacy in marriage, but touches the larger mutuality of the partners' interaction, especially around the family table.

Meals are especially privileged moments of the intimate presence because of the reality of caring and sharing they entail. Their intimate presence is irreplaceable in a society of high mobility in order for the spouses to remain 'in touch' and to keep fondness alive. The agape of sharing a meal, as described before, is an integral part of being together. The 'I-Thou' character of sharing strengthens a love commitment. It is like a 'natural sacrament'[31] of love and life which supports family communication and points in faith to the agape of the eucharist. The intimacy of a meal, like the intimacy of the body, rejects idolization as much as it rejects utilitarianism. Body and food are gifts from God which have to be cherished and treated with reverence. The eucharist, which celebrates the Lord's Supper, brings about a healing of human ambiguities and a deeper celebration of the agape of committed love.

Daily Dying and Rising

Living and dying is the basic pattern of all life. Christian faith paradoxically reverses this natural pattern into a mystery of death into life through the transsignification of human life by worship. This mystery of dying to death itself, an act of transcendental worship, thus belongs to the core of spirituality. Ideally, this spirituality means a radically new manner of relating to others, based on inner personal freedom and the passion of love.

This applies specifically to marriage because of its interpersonal reality; a dependability and independence, where the other spouse in his/her interior space is never fully known or validated. That new lifestyle cannot exist without the couple's experience of a free oblatory love. Modern society, with its greater mobility and its greater expectations from personal relationships, its competition and rejection of the idea of self-sacrifice – among other factors – has created a culture where relationships marked by depth of concern and the devotion of faithfulness are the exceptions.

True love is the sign of true freedom, but true freedom in marriage does not exist without a human response to the intimate longing of the other person, and without the coherence of creative fidelity. 'There can be no true freedom without our first having emptied ourselves of self, so that we might open ourselves to the only reality capable of fully satisfying our powers of love and knowledge,' says Rene Laturelle.[32] The couple encounters that 'only reality' in the infinite God through a relationship 'in depth' that is characterized by self-control, dependability and commitment. In the Christian perspective it is a matter of faith and love, because through these gifts Christians have been called to freedom in dying and rising each day. The gift of self (love) results in a possession of self (freedom) and establishes the most intimate and most challenging of all human relationships.

This relationship of marriage is influenced throughout life by internal and external factors which affect each partner and, at the same time, by the different stages of development throughout the family's lifetime. Couples experience the ebb and flow, the ups and downs, the fervor and dryness of life itself. 'Marriage,' in the words of Mary G. Durkin, 'is not a smooth curve drawn on the chart of life. It is, rather, a series of cycles, of deaths and rebirth, of old endings and new beginnings, of falling in love again.'[33] The 'happily ever after' mentality of a perpetual ecstasy not only builds up false expectations and leads to disillusionment, it denies the paradoxical reality of the life-giving oblative love and forgiveness, the healing and freeing discipline of self-control, and the redemptive idea of purification necessary for any dynamic and creative love relationship.

In today's society it is more than ever apparent that a marital life span consists of various stages or passages which every couple will experience in the course of their relationship. This developmental reality must be seen as the necessary starting point of any understanding of the process of marital relationship. Through the years of change and growth the two become many different people with different needs and expectations. Can marital unity and fulfillment still be maintained in this being and becoming? Certain social scientists insist that it is possible through a 'creative marriage' which nurtures the basic values of caring, empathy, mutual respect, equality, trust and commitment.[34] These basic values are without a doubt the human thread of a covenantal partnership. The pressure of a career, the challenges of parenthood, the disagreements and tensions of the everchanging modes of modern living, cannot but affect the aliveness of a relationship. A couple hears the call to holiness in this very web of the unending seasons and changing faces of their marital journey.

A spirituality of stability is needed today. It means a spirituality of 'staying in love,' which embodies, on one hand, the courage to be a partnership[35] – the existentially strengthening effect of self-donations – and, on the other hand, in Christian terms, the wisdom of the cross – the nuptial journey of Jesus through the total donation and service. The former provides a healthy and dynamic tension against the senescence of time; the latter is a rock of stability against external and internal fragmentive dependencies.

Any attempt to grow and endure based solely on endless analysis, or even developmental ideas of a relationship is bound to fail because the growth of two people is never an automatic process and is always unpredictable and complex. Besides the realistic expectations and lifestyle of each couple, there is a spiritual element which motivates and makes self-knowledge and self-revelation possible. Only authentic faith is transforming and life-giving – no magical effects or external miracles are needed. Nevertheless, since the paradox of the cross, the hallmark of faith, stresses the idea of self-sacrifice and donation, it shows the futility of human self-fulfillment, which actually leads to failure. Religion is not meant to be a guarantee of success, but an unrelenting call to faithfulness. Both the human, which is transient, and the divine, which has an ultimate value, actualize human plenitude.

Dying and rising in marriage reveal the depth of meaning in a spirituality of donation and service. It is the sharing of the paschal mystery. Husband and wife realize that every act of faithfulness is the actualization of the incompleteness of the paschal mystery in them. They marry each other many times in many different ways, always rising to a deeper life. Their living out, in hope, the ideal in the midst of human weakness always brings about growth because of the presence of the cross in their lives, which is their eucharist. The perspective of worship broadens that meaning again, since both eucharistic worship and marriage are covenant signs and actualization of God's love.[36]

From the altar of their everyday experience through which they build an irreplaceable community of love and minister to each other in the domestic church, the spouses offer the concrete unfolding of their spiritual sacrifice to God.[37] The specific applications of this realistic spirituality are numerous. The playful, caring, earthly and meaning-bestowing atmosphere of the house provides the ideal milieu to live authentic worship, but it needs the ritual celebration which can trans-figure and heal the fragility of human relations through the force of the celebrated divine life.

Gift-Given Communication

Communication is the lifeblood of the interpersonal communion of the partners. The quality of their relationship has many different degrees of actualization because it rises and falls as the couple's sharing does. It is either an authentic encounter or the failure of encounter. This interpersonal communion is a great challenge because it reveals, on the one hand, the uniqueness of each individual and appears, on the other hand, as a self-gift, which has to be acknowledged as such by either spouse. Created by an inviolable interiority, which constitutes my freedom and my human dignity, I am gifted with words and love to validate the existence of the other. I surrender freely what I freely received – my very self – in the encounter with another person.

Theological reflection is not yet implied, at this anthropological level of one's need for relating to another. A totally new dimension of the spirituality of the spouses in striving for effective communication in giving and sharing is opened up in the light of the mystery of God's self-communication. Analogies which provide a model for a life-generating communication can be drawn from a theology of divine revelation.

Revelation is a happening of God's unconditional love, expressed in mysterious ways, in deeds and words to humankind all throughout history. This happening of God's initiative leads to an encounter with his people, and lets the people know how much he can do for them. In the sharing of the living reality of God himself people participate in the eternal truth resulting in the development of their full potential for being. This participation is actualized in the mystery of worship, since worship is revelation and gift-given communication. And so is marriage.

The forms of communication in the historical revelation of Scripture, as in the marital relationship are inexhaustible. The analo-gies of both cases, however, lead to the same conclusive characteristics of essential communication: dialogue, communion, presence and power.

Dialogue through empathy and freedom is vital to human relations. The importance of dialogue as a keystone of effective communication stems from the dialogic structure of human existence. In his existential visions of human reality, Buber not only stressed the intersubjectivity of human communication, but saw this interpersonal reality linked intrinsically to God's reality and the way to him. God is mysteriously mirrored in the relationship with the other. This interpersonal and transcendent vision has been blurred in a modern consumeristic society.[38]

If the sacredness of personhood is the basis of any meaningful dialogue, the well-being of the other is the goal of marital dialogue. Quality dialogue based on sincere devotion to human dignity and radical acceptance of mutuality leads to effective communication. Couples who develop the right attitudes of creative communication (which is an art, not an information technique), speak in open and honest language, conveying ideas and emotions, listening and sharing, affirming and encouraging.

These are the central aspects of loving-giving communication. The different systems of decision-making, the skills and methods emphasized by modern psychology, and many other helpful suggestions and insights adapted to the variables of a marital relationship are important. On the other hand, the humanistic view will insist on the qualities of a mature and liberated person and on developmental concepts of marital interaction. Nevertheless, these will never work without a conversion of heart and spiritual growth.

A dialogic spirituality in the light of the biblical word makes possible that conversion and growth. Spouses turn to each other and to God. In fact, God takes the initiative in calling husband and wife to dialogue, since both the spouses and God speak the same language of lovers.[39] Like worship, where God and his people engage in dialogue, the spouses 'gift' one another in an oblative dialogue.

Depth of communion is the result of meaningful dialogue. The fire of communion in living and loving is maintained through the vehicles of communication: those of mind and body. To establish a relationship marked by the depth of communion of intimacy is a great challenge because it demands total freedom and spiritual nakedness. Furthermore, external pressures and internal ambiguities might compromise that experience of personal freedom. A possibility opens up through God's grace which calls us to true freedom. As Augustine said, 'We are not free within ourselves, nor free from ourselves until we have encountered him who causes us to be born ourselves.'[40]

Again, the narrative of God's activity, revelation, provides a model for dialogue of communion. Revelation, in fact, is personal communion in which God recreates the freedom and value of the person and makes possible the encounter with others and with God himself. The barriers of self-centeredness are overcome and communion becomes an ongoing reality. God is the ultimate possibility of communion for the couple who stand as the most telling metaphor of God's self-donation to his people.

Communication as communion occurs, therefore, only when the partners' relationship is characterized by an ongoing, free and intimate relationship. The permanent call to communion breaks the emotional and mental restrictions of mutually alienating attitudes. The partners are free and open, and they give life to one another in the give and take of marriage. Finally, they create an interpersonal intimate living in which their lives are moved by one another. As real and intimate encounter, this type of communication as communion is worship.

Presence is a kind of personal communication in itself. To be together, even without much talk strengthens a love relationship which, in turn, generates an atmosphere of communication. It can even nurture deep emotions because the body language is the most original and basic human language.

Partners are eminently present to each other through their bond of love and commitment. On one hand, their being present to each other in their daily interaction and human experiences is the essential part of their communication with the complex and rich variety of nonverbal communication. On the other hand, this presence is validated with words which speak their world vision, their desires and frustrations, dreams and joys.

That presence is salvific because the partners through their commitment participate in the concrete, loving intimacy of God himself. Ths is at the core of marital spirituality.

The analogy to the mysterious presence of God's self-communication further deepens our understanding of this spirituality. The living dialogue with God in the everpresent revelation, and the marital love relationship, are both alive through the awareness of presence. Both realities are foremost a happening, but they are confirmed with words.

Present to each other, husband and wife encounter their lives in a healing and supportive way, and they experience the challenges and demands of their journeying together. Enclosed mysteriously within the presence of God, marriage is actually the fertile ground of the true worship of self-sacrificing love and, therefore, of a true and unique spirituality.

Finally, communication is power because it is always a dynamic force, an ongoing reality which reveals and, at the same time, affects the person. 'One of the greatest gifts God has given to spouses,' says John G. Quesnell, 'is the power to give life to one another. Through the medium of speech, spouses can communicate or destroy life in one another.'[41]

Since this power is love generating through an intimate mutual understanding, especially through the quality of listening, it is the closest reality to total communication. But total communication, like complete knowledge of the other, is a lifetime task, never an actual reality. Hence, the challenge of this most powerful human interaction.

The mystery of the inviolable interior space of the other already reveals a divine parenthood.[42] From the beginning God pronounces a word of life to establish a community of love. This word of life is not only creative from the beginning, but it permanently validates human existence as an ineffable power of salvation.

Translated into the art of communication, this theology of revelation creates a most important area of conjugal spirituality: communication as creative power toward perfection. So as the word of God demands faith and trust, communication in marriage is only possible in empathy and love. The spouses empower each other with deep and constant dialogue, as does the God of revelation whom they image in faithfulness. Their commitment to their union and to their fellow humans, if lived out in faith as self-gift of genuine communication, becomes a living sacrifice which worship celebrates.

Faith Sharing in the Domestic Church

Vatican II, referring to marriage and the family as a 'domestic church,' regained a rich bibilical and patristic theology of the priestly dignity of the Christian couple.[43] This priestly dignity stems, not from the exercise of any sacred function, but from the natural sacramental character of their union, lived in the all-embracing nuptial mystery of Christ symbolized by the Christian couple. They meet the Holy through their human core and are empowered by the Holy through their covenant.

Another important vision which derives from that priestly dignity is the ministerial function of the laity as partners in the service of the church and as community builders. This vision, which is being gradually recovered, demonstrates the importance of the theological concept of the domestic church. From this perspective, not only does the couple learn its call to minister to their own concrete existence in the image of the church, but the ecclesial community develops the attitude of respect and mutuality of the family partnership from the model of the domestic church. In fact, the partnership of the family, which 'is a living image and historical representation of the mystery of the Church,'[44] stands today as a most compelling metaphor of the church.

This new communal and sacramental perspective will enrich a theology of marriage and the family today especially in the context of the contemporary crisis of traditional Christian values. The present, in fact, more than ever before, is strong in experiences, but weak in faith. From this perspective of the growth of the family as a living reality of the family of families (that is, the church), two different dimensions of the conjugal spirituality emerge: the inward family living within itself, and the outward faith witnessing beyond itself.

The inward family living in the 'sanctuary of the Church in the home'[45] is spiritual if experienced as God's permanent free gift through the different inner components of its reality: a place where love, the law of family living, is experienced in its full and rich meaning; where humanization, identity, and the integration of human sexuality develops; where faith through the word is nurtured and shared, and, consequently, Christ is present; where prayer and contemplation are a reality; and where responsible parenthood and education lead into the integral reality of being human.

The outward faith witnessing depends on the same concept of the family as a living cell of a living organism. As such, the couple manifests the mystery of Christ which is present in its life and love. They make their actual experience visible, and so they become an extension of the church. As a community of hospitality, as a community which witnesses to its faith in the concrete experience, and as a community which takes part in the building up of the church. The fostering of justice and peace, the humanization of culture, and especially the evangelization of society in the sphere of politics, economy and science are essential tasks of the lay ministry.

The life of this small community of worship 'receives a kind of consecration' which reaches and transforms all of its conjugal existence because it is called to be a presence and testimony to Christ's ministry which transforms all human reality. The spouses' profoundly humane and historical spirituality becomes a credible sign and instrument of salvation, as they 'manifest to all people the Savior's living presence in the world, and the genuine nature of the Church.'[46]

The theological analogy between church and family is not simply a useful pious comparison, but is deeply rooted in Christian tradition, both biblical and historical.

The New Testament tradition of the 'domestic church'[47] is abundantly testified to in numerous references and centers around the essential meaning of Christian marriage which describes and actualizes symbolically the transcendent mystery of Christ and his church (Eph 5:21–33). This central Pauline affirmation created a conjugal spirituality in the early church which viewed marriage as spiritual worship, donation and service of the partners.

The early literature of the fathers of the church also has abundant references to the same analogy, especially John Crysostom. His main point of departure is the idea of Christ's privileged presence in 'the house of God' (the family), of which the Canaan wedding is a telling example in the light of the theology of John's Gospel. John Chrysostom sees the mystery of Christ and the church in the perspective of marriage as a 'substantial image' and 'a mysterious icon of the Church.'[48] In Paul Evdokimov's words, 'The grace of the priestly ministry of the husband and the grace of the priestly maternity of the wife form and shape the conjugal existence in the image of the Church.'[49]

The historical tradition goes back to the very dawn of the Christian community and its worship, for at the beginning of Christianity 'the Church meets in the house of' a Christian family.[50] Houses were not only literally churches (like Dura-Europos), but households gave birth to communities. The worshiping community, as distinct from the sacred temple gathering, originated in the bosom of the family, around the table, and under the couple's hospitality. They became a prophetic instrument of evangelization. The cases of Lydia and Cornelius are only two telling examples of decisive developments of the nascent Christianity: the former represents the beginning of the expansion of the total church to Europe (Acts 16:14–15) and the latter is the first official acceptance of the Gentile world (Acts 10:1–23).

The theology of the domestic church constitutes, certainly, a sound vision of marriage and family spirituality, especially from the perspective of spiritual worship. As a metaphor of the total church, it struggles to live an analogous reality of caring and hospitality, of celebration and forgiveness, of prayer and peace, and of an unbroken unity in the midst of a broken society. In this family church, 'where all the different aspects of the entire Church should be found,'[51] marriage is a concrete experience of Christian life in 'faith working through love' (Gal 5:6).

The theological understanding of the intimate faith sharing at home, like the understanding of the other important realities of agape-love, donation and communication, provide the basis for the assertion of the existential and intrinsic relationship of marriage and worship at the core, not only of life, but of the Christian mystery itself. In specific Christian terms, the self-bestowal of the marital embrace and the sharing of one eucharistic cup and bread intersect in the mystery of the cross, the paradigm of Christian worship. Marriage can only be a vital and fulfilling reality of love when lived as a profoundly human and spiritually transcendent experience of spiritual worship in bed and board, children and society.

Notes

German Martinez O.S.B. teaches in the graduate school of religious studies at Fordham University.

1. James F. White, *Introduction to Christian Worship* (Nashville: Abingdon 1981), 25.
2. For a discussion of the importance of the analogical method and its application to theology and worship, see David Tracy, *The Analogical Imagination* (New York: Crossroad 1981), 405–21.
3. L.L. Mitchell, *The Meaning of Ritual* (New York: Paulist 1970), xii.
4. 'For worship is an acknowledgement of Transcendence,' she says in her classic study *Worship* (New York: Crossroad 1936), 3.
5. In his existential vision he insists on the dialogical structure of a human being which is the path to the absolute, and which links human beings necessarily to God. Marriage only radicalizes this human interpersonal reality and its transcendency. M. Buber, *I and Thou* (New York: Ch. Scribner's Sons 1970).
6. Ch. Davis, *Body as Spirit: The Nature of Religious Feeling* (New York: Seabury 1976), 16.
7. W. Kasper, *Theology of Christian Marriage* (New York: Seabury 1980), 27. God's plan in Genesis is conceived in the light of Exodus: the mystery of man and woman in love is the symbol of God's covenant of grace, especially dramatized in the prophetic revelation (Hos 1, 3; Jer 2, 3, 31; Ez 16:1–14; Is 54:62).
8. Cf. Ti 2:11; 1 Jn 4:9.
9. Especially in Paul's vision in the light of Exodus and Genesis, of Christ's bridal relationship to the church (Eph 5:21–33).
10. Ex 12:25, 26; 13:5; 19:5; Dt 10:12.
11. Jer 7:22–23; Hos 6:6; Dan 3:39–41; Ps 39:7–9; Ps 49.

12. Cf. Eph 1:4–6; Phil 3:3; Heb 9:14.
13. *Sacramentarium Veronense*, nos. 1105–10, ed. L. C. Mohlberg, RED 1 (Rome 1956), 139–40; *Le sactramentaire gregorien*, ed. J. Deshusses, Spicilegium Friburgense 16 (Fribourg 1971), no. 838ff.
14. Cf. G. Martinez, 'Marriage: Historical Developments and Future Alternatives,' *The American Benedictine Review* 37 (1086), 376–82.
15. John Crysostom (4th–5th century) is the best example of this theology, for instance, in Homily 9 on 1 Timothy (PG 62:546ff).
16. R.P.A. Raes, *Le Mariage: Sa Célébration et sa spiritualité dans les Eglises d'Orient* (Belgium: Editions de Chevetogne 1958), 12. Cf. E. Schillebeeckx, *Marriage: Human Reality and Saving Mystery* (New York: Sheed and Ward 1965), 344–56.
17. Says Y. Congar in his thorough study of the sacred in the Bible, especially in reference to Ephesians 2:14–15: 'Jesus abolished definitely the separation between the sacred and the profane regarding people, places and times' ('Situation du 'sacré' en regime chrétien,' in *La liturgie aprés Vatican II* (Paris 1967), 385–403).
18. *Marriage*, 12.
19. *Body as Spirit*, 34.
20. Cf. *Eucharisticum Mysterium* 3 and 6, *Documents on the Liturgy* (1963–1979): Conciliar, Papal and Curial Texts (Collegeville: The Liturgical Press 1982), 395.
21. Cf. K. Rahner, *Foundations of Christian Faith* (New York: Seabury 1978), 116–33; Jon Nilson, 'Theological Bases for a Marital Spirituality,' *Studies in Formative Spirituality* 2 (1981), 401–13.
22. Erich Fromm, *To Have or To Be* (New York: Harper et Row 1976), 44–47.
23. For the notion of the nuptial sacrifice of Christ, the author is dependent on P. Evdokimov, *The Sacrament of Love: The Nuptial Mystery in the Light of the Orthodox Tradition* (New York: St Vladimir's Seminary Press 1985), 122–23.
24. Loving another person means telling him or her: You will not die, according to the French philosopher Gabriel Marcel, quoted by Walter Kasper, *Theology of Christian Marriage* (New York: Seabury 1980), 22.
25. St Augustine, *De Genesi ad litteram* 9:7, 2, CSEL 28/1 pp. 275–76.
26. 'Zur Theologie der Ehe,' in *Theologie der Ehe* (1969), 102.
27. We are 'sexed being,' says Maurice Merleau-Ponty, *The Phenomenology of Perception* (New York: Humanities Press 1962), 154–71.
28. Pope John Paul II, 'The Nuptial Meaning of the Body,' *Origins* 10 (1980), 303, quoted by Ch. A. Gallagher and others, *Embodied in Love: Sacramental Spirituality and Sexual Intimacy* (New York: Crossroad 1984).
29. Cf. Erik Erikson, *Insight and Responsibility* (New York: Norton 1964), 127–29.
30. Besides the biblical quotations in footnotes 10 and 11, see Ex 10 (Yahweh is a passionate, committed lover), Psalm 139 (Intimacy with God) and Song of Songs: 2:5–9; 3:2–5; 4:12–16; 6:3, 8; 8:6–10; Teresa of Avila, *Interior Castle* and John of the Cross, *The Living Flame of Love*.
31. 'Centuries of secularism have failed to transform eating into something strictly utilitarian. Food is still treated with reverence. A meal is still a rite – the last "natural sacrament" of family and friendship' (Alexander Schmemann, *For the Life of the World: Sacraments and Orthodoxy* [New York: St Vladimir's Seminary Press 1973], 16).
32. *Man and his Problems in the Light of Jesus Christ* (New York: Alba House 1983), 243.
33. A.M. Greeley and M.G. Durkin, *How to Save the Catholic Church* (New York: King Penguin 1984), 126.
34. Such as M. Krantzier who speaks of 'marriages within a marriage' when he identifies six natural 'passages' corresponding to first years, career, parents, middle and mature years of marriage (*Creative Marriage* [New York: McGraw Hill 1981], 37). These change-patterns have to be taken seriously as 'the signs of life' to be read in order to understand a proper spirituality of the family.
35. The author borrows this concept from P. Tillich and applies it to marriage. 'Every act of courage is a manifestation of the ground of being' (*The Courage to Be* [New York: Harper and Row 1958], 181).
36. David M. Thomas, in one of the best syntheses of theology and secular values of marriage, warns against overemphasizing developmental concepts and undervaluing the need of a radical acceptance. See *Christian Marriage* (Wilmington: Michael Glazier 1983), 119–20.
37. Cf. Rom 12:1–3 and 1 Pet 2:5.
38. M. Buber, *I and Thou*, 123–68: 'Extended, the lines of relationships intersect in the eternal You' (123).

39. See footnotes 10, 11 and 30.
40. St Augustine, *Confessions* 10:27, 38. Paul and John's theology stress Christian call to freedom in Christ (Gal 5:1, 13; 4:26, 31; 1 Cor 7:22; 2 Cor 3:17; Jn 8:32, 36).
41. J. Quesnell, *Marriage: A Discovery Together* (Notre Dame: Fides/Claretian 1974), 88.
42. M. Buber, *I and Thou*, 123-68.
43. *Lumen gentium*, no. 11, ed. W.M. Abbott, *The Documents of Vatican II* (1963-1965), 29. Cf also *Gaudium et spes*, nos. 47-52; 248-58; *Apostolicam actuositatem*, nos. 2-10, 489-501, especially *Familiaris Consortio (On the Family)* of John Paul II, nos. 13, 55-58 ('Spouses are therefore the permanent reminder to the Church of what happened on the cross.' 'Of this salvation event marriage, like every sacrament, is a memorial, actuation and prophecy,' no 13), *Origins* 11 (1981), 437-66.
44. 'In communion and co-responsibility for mission' are the words used to define relationships between ordained and nonordained ministries, which should prevent 'continuous wavering between "clericalism" and "false democracy"' ('Vocation and Mission of the Laity Working Paper for the 1987 Synod of Bishops,' 33-57, *Origins*, no. 17 [1987], 11-14).
45. *Apostolicam actuositatem*, no 11, Abbott, 502-03.
46. *Gaudium et spes* 48, 252.
47. Cf. Rom 16:5; 1 Cor 16:19; Philem 2; Col 4:15, among many other references.
48. *In epistulam ad Colossenses*, PG 62:387; quoted by P. Evdokimov, *The Sacrament of Love* 139.
49. *Evdokimov*, 139.
50. *He kat'oikon ekklésia* to designate house communities, or faithful gathering in a household, different from 'the whole of the Christian movement,' or 'the household of God.' Cf. E. Schillebeeckx, *The Church with a Human Face* (New York: Crossroad 1985), 46-48; N. Provencher, 'Vers une théologie de la famille: l'Eglise domestique,' *Eglise et Théologie* 12 (1981), 9-34.
51. Paul VI, *Evangelii nuntiandi*, 71, *Origins* 5 (1976), 459.

4.4 Church and Marriage in African Society: A Theological Appraisal

Emmanuel Martey

'Indeed, if the books of the bible can be said to agree on any one issue with respect to women, it is that the woman suffers her greatest humiliation and subjection to the man in the institution of marriage.'[1]

This unequivocal statement by Teresa Okure of Nigeria shows that, to an African woman theologian, it is not only the traditional biblical interpretation that is patriarchal and discriminatory against women, but also the biblical text itself can be humiliating and oppressive. It cannot therefore be gainsaid, if her statement is indeed true, that, with regard to the issue of women, there are texts in the Bible which could be rightly described as 'texts of terror'.[2]

If it is imperative that any theology which calls itself *Christian* must appeal to the Bible, which feminist theologians have characterized as an androcentric text, written by men in a patriarchal context and which has long been used and interpreted to protect the patriarchal status quo, then to embark on doing feminist theology in the African *Christian* Church is an onerous task indeed. The African woman theologian faces the dilemma of trying to find a place for African women in the bible which is not subordinate, while at the same time acknowledging the patriarchal nature of 'the books of the Bible' and their subsequent historical interpretation. Such is precisely the dilemma which confronts Okure as she sets out to talk about 'women in the Bible'. It is therefore not at all surprising to see that she concluded from her analysis of Scripture that the Bible has both a liberative thread and an oppressive thread running through it, as far as the issue of women is concerned.[3] She is also able to stress the fact that feminist hermeneutics provide not only a critique of past patriarchal paradigms, but also a new interpretative framework of the place of women in the biblical text, as well as in religious institutions and pastoral life.[4]

While on the one hand Okure sees the Bible as 'the embodiment of the revealed will of God' which 'plays a decisive role for Christians in their approach to the issue of women today'[5]; on the other hand, it is also 'a patriarchal book not only because it was written by men (and for the most part for men), but because over the centuries it has been interpreted almost exclusively by men.'[6] The truth of the matter therefore is that, with respect to women, 'the Bible and its interpretation embody both a divine and a human element'. The liberative elements originate from the divine, the oppressive elements stem from the human; while the one stresses the egalitarian relationship between the woman and man who are both seen as created in God's image, the other, which is socioculturally conditioned, is sinful and portrays women's inferiority.[7]

From the liberative perspective, women are seen in the Bible as co-workers with God and agents of life as, for instance, is exemplified in Rebekah and Mary. Teresa Okure sees two main areas where the oppressive elements are most operative, namely; 'the institution of marriage and the concern for ritual purity'.[8] For her, what makes the Bible a patriarchal book is its stress on the husband's 'absolute authority over the wife'. The subjection of the women is indeed the tradition of Scripture as a whole, and cannot be limited only to Genesis 3:16. Both in the Old Testament (cf. Deut. 22:13–21) and in the New (cf. 1 Cor. 11:2ff; 1 Tim. 2: 11f; Tit. 2:2f; Col. 3:18; Eph. 5:22), the humiliation of women is present and also in the Wisdom Literature (cf. Sir. 42:14). This phenomenon of the plight of women, Okure concludes, is not only found among the Jewish community but it is universal and therefore deserves a meticulous study. In the African Church, the way the Bible has been used to justify and to sanctify women's subordination has been a major concern, especially of African women theologians.

Marriage And The African Church

Since the advent of Christianity to Africa there has been the tendency to claim that the Judaeo-Christian tradition has really valued women in the Church – a claim which neither studies in formative Judaism nor earlier Christian writings would support. For instance, the Apostle Paul stated quite clearly: 'Let a woman learn in silence with all submissiveness. I permit no woman to teach or to have authority over men; she is to keep silent' (1 Tim. 2:11). From the same Paul, wives are to be subject to their husbands (Eph. 5:22). With reference to Genesis 3:16, Josephus wrote: 'The woman, says the Law, is in all things inferior to the man. Let her accordingly be submissive ... for the authority has been given by God to the man'.[9] In his analysis of the status of women in formative Judaism, Leonard Swidler came to the conclusion that:

> In the formative period of Judaism the status of women was not one of equality with men, but rather, severe inferiority, and that even intense misogynism was not infrequently present. Since the sacred and the secular spheres of that society were so intertwined, the inferiority and subordination of women was consequently present in both religious and civil areas of Jewish life.[10]

With such evidence as cited above it is difficult indeed to accept any claim that the Judaeo-Christian tradition really valued women especially since the subordination/domineering interpretation of Scripture, which became normative for Jewish society, was carried over into the Christian era. Consequently both patristic and medieval theologians, as well as the missionaries who brought Christianity to Africa, were incapable of opposing male-domination, and frequently projected their androcentric suppositions onto the texts of Scripture. Louise Tappa of Cameroon is therefore right in her suggestion that the classic text of Genesis 3:16 which has been used for centuries to justify and sanctify male domination, shows that 'patriarchy is the oldest form of human domination' and did not start with the Christian Faith; it is thus to 'be read as descriptive of a situation arising out of the order of sin. It is not God's prescription.'[11]

Moreover, with the coming of Christianity in a foreign garb, the women of Africa have been subjected to a combination of patriarchal structures from both Africa's own and the invading cultures. From the outset, Western missionaries 'placed emphasis on the institution of Christian marriage citing it as both the cornerstone of the faith and the key to the christianization of Africa.'[12] This was done with the belief that a new morality would emerge if Christian marriage took the place of traditional marriage. Consequently, absolute monogamy was enforced upon African people and the wives of polygamous men were denied full membership of the Church. Even today, when the leadership of most mission churches has passed on to Africans, there are still some churches which deny baptism to the wives of polygamous men. Those who are baptized but who 'backslide' into polygamy are then considered as adherents and are refused Holy Communion. Thus the Eucharist is used as a means of punishment instead of a means of grace.

The African Church, as an offspring of the missionary movement, has had a long history incorporating the patriarchal interpretation of Scripture and practice. During a long period of interpretation, instead of a more egalitarian view of Scripture being reached, patriarchy has rather been reinforced and is now treated as an absolute, unalterable truth which provides authority and justification for the continued subordination of women in the churches. For instance, with Christian marriage in the Church, the African woman loses her name because she has to take the name of her husband.[13] Reflecting on the African Church's attitude to Scripture and the plight of African women in marriage, Bette Ekeya of Kenya laments:

> Always there is the underlying view that it is the woman's lot to suffer in marriage because the Bible says so (1 Tim. 2:14; Gen. 3:16). Was it not the woman, who after all, brought evil and disorder in the world by her sin? She should therefore take what life metes out to her and accept it as part of her atonement for causing man to sin....

But then she adds;

... Often this interpretation of the story of the Fall is taken literally, with complete disregard of the historical and cultural setting of the story. The revolutionary interpretation to it which Jesus gave by his own example is quite ignored.[14]

Ekeya mentions two other oppressive elements which add up to the suffering of the African woman apart from the cultural norms and taboos that hold her in subjection. These are 'the loaded interpretation of certain biblical passages and the predominantly male Church ministries and institutions.'[15]

For the African woman theologian therefore, the Bible is not just an androcentric/patriarchal book which evolved out of a male-dominated Jewish environment, but even, in its historical interpretation, androcentric prioritization of values has been systematically at work and male chauvinistic values and attitudes have still prevailed. These attitudes still prevail in the African Church today. Among others, Ekeya has demonstrated how the African Church's teaching and interpretation of some biblical passages 'hurt a certain percentage of African women' as these passages place them 'outside the salvation community'.[16] For instance, the Church's teachings on certain scriptural passages have created problems and contributed to women's humiliation and subjection. One such teaching is on the issue of polygamy. The way the Church interprets Matthew 19:4-6 prevents African men from becoming Christians as they are told 'to send away their wives and choose only one with whom they could contract the sacrament of matrimony'.[17] Besides, the Church fails to recognize traditional (or customary) marriages and regards such relationships as premarital cohabitation; thus, women who marry in the traditional way are considered not as wives but concubines, and their offspring as illegitimate children.

Another teaching that perpetuates women's subjection is the Church's interpretation of Colossians 3:18 and Ephesians 5:22 in which is emphasized the woman's subjection to the man in marriage rather than complementarity and mutuality. On this issue, Ekeya wrote:

> The Church's emphasis on the subjection of the wife to her husband in marriage has given many men an excuse of being tyrannical to their wives, even to the extent of physically assaulting them.... In marriage, as the Church presented it to our people, woman is the subject who can and often must be ... disciplined.[18]

It becomes obvious from what we have discussed so far concerning the African Church, the Bible and the African woman on the issue of marriage, that the theological voices of African women need to be heard. There are two reasons why the theological voice of the African woman can no longer be ignored. First, women must be heard if 'the imbalance and impoverishment of Scripture' caused by the one-sided interpretation of men are to be corrected and women's 'distinctive way of perceiving reality' is also brought into the biblical interpretation.[19] This feminist insight would no doubt challenge both past biblical interpretations which assigned women to a secondary position, and present attempts to sustain that subordination within the African Church and its hierarchy. Second, women's voices must be heard if the Church in Africa is not just to survive but, more importantly, to pass the test for the commitment to its liberating heritage. But what is even more challenging to the African Church is the case which marriage in traditional society provides for African liberation theology. To the subject of marriage in traditional Africa we thus turn.

Marriage In African Traditional Society

The position of African women in traditional marriage can best be analyzed and well understood in terms of the system of production which forms the base of all social relations. Therefore to gain an insight into how marriage in traditional society makes the African woman suffer humiliation and subjection, we must first grasp the productive relations that exist between the male and female genders.

In traditional Africa the social organization of production is closely associated with the family and therefore, kinship plays a crucial role in the economic infrastructure. Familial and kinship structures express production relations. For instance, marriage in traditional society places the husband's right over his wife's or wives' labour.[20] Thus in such societies social control of production takes place through kinship relations and the woman naturally stands at the centre of the whole system since she produces the labour force, and as the 'producer of producers', she constitutes 'the most powerful prospective means of production'.[21] Apparently under such circumstances, where women remain central and occupy a supremely important position in the productive system, controlling them means controlling the reproduction of the production unit. Such a control has tremendous political implications in social relations, especially in marriage. One analyst has perceptively pointed out that

> In political terms, control over access to women legitimizes social hierarchy, namely, the authority of the old over the young, of the dominant over the dominated lineages, of one caste over another and so on.[22]

But these political implications of the subordination of women have had effects not only on traditional societies but also on the politics and economics of modern African states, as they emerged out of the colonial era. What is even more devastating is that modern African leaders have not realized that the root of most of the continent's problems has come from the domination of women. Cutrufelli is by no means the only writer who has perceived the root-cause of Africa's multifaceted problems in terms of female subordination. Jennifer Seymour

Whittaker has succinctly and forcefully stated in her book with the thought-provoking title, '*How Can Africa Survive*?' that 'conditions in Africa will never get better until the lot of women is improved.'[23] How should the African Church and its theology relate or respond to such a revealing fact? Of course, one could not help agreeing with Whittaker that if Africa 'is to survive', then, women's conditions must be ameliorated. African rulers in neocolonial states, as well as leaders of the Churches, are yet to appropriate the prophetically sagacious saying of Aggrey of Ghana that 'if you educate a man you educate an individual, but if you educate a woman, you educate a whole nation'.

Unlike in developed countries where the instruments of production are machines and where sophisticated tools are used, in traditional Africa goods are produced mainly by human beings. Because of this, much attention is placed on marriage and childbearing. Marriage is therefore looked upon as 'a sacred duty which every normal person must perform' and failure to do so under normal circumstances becomes 'a major offence in the eyes of society' and people will be against anyone who refuses to marry.[24] But marriage is only a means to an end and not an end in itself. Mbiti brings this out more clearly when he notes that 'marriage fulfills the obligation, the duty and the custom that every normal woman should ... bear children'. He sums it up well:

> The supreme purpose of marriage according to African peoples is to bear children, to build up a family, to extend life, and to hand down the living torch of human existence. For that reason, a marriage becomes fully so only when one or more children have been born. It is a tragic thing when no children come out of a marriage. The people do not consider it to be truly a marriage, and other arrangements are made to obtain children in the family.[25]

It is indeed 'tragic' for a woman in traditional African society to be childless; a barren woman is regarded as a curse for the whole society and becomes a nuisance to the husband and his family. A woman is easily divorced if she is unable to have her own children.[26] The worth of a woman in such a society, one might conclude, is in her ability to reproduce. Cutrufelli is thus right in cogently stating the issue of the feminine question in terms of 'work/motherhood and production/reproduction'.[27]

What is even more revealing is the fact that most (if not all) of the exploitative and oppressive elements against women in traditional social customs have to do with reproduction and production in one way or another: whether one talks of early betrothal; forced marriages or the lack of choice in marriage partners; few or no divorce rights for women; menstrual taboos or long rites of passage which place young women in seclusion for years.[28] In fact, the list could go on, but for the lack of space, we would like to discuss only two of the traditional customs in marriage which deal with reproduction and in which

African women suffer the most humiliating experiences. They are as well some aspects of African culture which pose a tremendous challenge to the Christian Church in Africa. These are (i) polygamy or more precisely, polygyny; and (ii) clitoridectomy or female circumcision.

Polygyny

As we have shown the traditional understanding of the meaning of marriage is to bear children. It also dictates the pattern the institution of marriage should take. It is therefore not surprising that most African societies favour polygamous marriage which always means polygyny and not polyandry. Such a marriage thus becomes 'a mechanism which facilitates the fulfillment of male aspirations'.[29] A writer has demonstrated how a patrilineal society, where children belong by right to the paternal clan, favours polygyny more than a matrilineal society. As this author communicates to us an essential message on the issue under discussion, we quote her *in extenso*:

> Polygamy is an almost universal institution in Africa.... The (paternal) clan will be more willing to make the necessary sacrifices for the acquisition of other wives if it feels sure about the legal possession of the children. The matrilocal systems view polygamy much less favourably. It would be difficult for a polygamous husband to exert effective control over wives scattered in various villages, or to fulfill his conjugal and paternal obligations. Also, the matrilocal system is frequently characterized by the husband's status of relative dependence on his wife's family and consequently on his wife herself. Thus, among the matrilocal people of South Kantanga, if a man decides to take a second wife, he must have the consent of the first one; this, at least in principle, is never required among the patrilineal peoples.[30]

Although less favoured by some traditional societies however, polygamy exists in almost every African society. And whatever advantages or benefits its advocates enumerate, polygamy ends up in reproduction and production, increase in the reproduction of the labour force (children) and increase in the reproduction forces (wives and children). In all of these, the woman becomes more of a tool than a human being. She becomes merely a tool by means of which goods are produced.

Polygyny creates untold hardships and serious problems for the African woman. For instance, there are certain days a wife cannot see or talk to the husband, even on important issues, because these are not 'her days', as the days are shared among the wives. Any persistence to see the man may incur the resentment of the other wife – her rival. Polygyny ushers the women into a world of jealousies and uncertainties. Usually, the relationship between co-wives is terrible and sometimes dangerous. For example, in order to win the husband's favour rivalry and accusations against each other may ensue. It is even reported that 'magic drugs' are used to 'prevent a man having an erection with any woman except for the one who has administered them to him'.[31] No doubt the African proverb which says, 'A man with five wives has five tongues' illustrates how deceitful polygyny is to the African woman.

Female Circumcision

Clitoridectomy or female circumcision is one of the traumatic ways by which female reproduction of the labour force is controlled and guarded. It involves the mutilation of a portion of the female organ, the clitoris, and in certain traditional societies it is 'regarded as the *conditio sine qua non* of the whole teaching of tribal law, religion and morality.'[32] Although one may argue that both sexes undergo this circumcision process, there is a great difference and indeed consequence between clitoridectomy and male circumcision. Whereas in the latter the sexual pleasure is not affected, in the former it is, because the reason for this rite is not only to preserve virginity but also to suppress the woman's sexual feelings. Women who go through this traumatic experience are thus deprived even of the pleasure in the act which makes them reproduce the labour force. For this reason, some writers have rightly argued that the trauma of clitoridectomy is 'a way of rendering women sexually subordinate'.[33]

Certainly African women theologians are justified in their lament that 'the demands of tradition are applied more to women than to men. Yet, African women are expected to bear all this without protest.'[34] There is no gainsaying that polygyny and clitoridectomy are only two examples in which

> African traditions still blatantly display distortions due to male orientation of societal values. (And) no matter the cogency of arguments by male and female traditionalists for persisting with any of the discriminatory practices, there can be no denying that the roles played by women have not received fair recognition and have therefore not been optimally incorporated in the process of development.[35]

Because of the central role that African women play in reproduction, in African literature they are mainly portrayed as wives and mothers, thus focusing on the sexual aspect of their lives. Put differently, 'male bias' in anthropological writings concentrates mainly on African women's sex roles, while other aspects of their lives, such as political, social and economic roles, are not meticulously explored. Predominantly, this is how African women have entered into academic studies, and most academic literature analyzes them, not as actors, but rather as objects, neglecting their activities beyond childbearing, child-caring and house maintenance. In fact only men's activities in society 'have often been defined as those worth investigating.... Thus women enter scholarly studies predominantly in the realm of marriage and the family.'[36]

Conclusion

We conclude with the inescapable question, What does this insight into the humiliating experiences of African women in the institution of marriage mean for the African Church and its theological reflection and biblical hermeneutics?

It is our opinion that any insight gained from the foregoing analysis of the African scene regarding marriage must be set within a theological context to remind the Church of the oppressive and humiliating situation in which one 'mode of humanity', the feminine, lives; and thereby find a lasting solution to the issue of women on the continent. Hitherto the African Church with the parochialism of its male-oriented theology has failed to analyze the male-dominated institution of marriage and has rather adhered to the patriarchal interpretation of Scripture.

The emergence of women's voices in theological reflection therefore poses a tremendous challenge to the Church which often attaches itself to the oppressive status quo and calls for its transformation. For the African woman, what the male-dominated Church on the continent needs is a complete 'metamorphosis' and not just 'improvement'. Dorothy Ramodibe of South Africa has therefore made a distinction between what she calls the 'old oppressive Church' and a 'new liberating Church'. For her, women and men cannot build the African Church together as long as the men continue to dominate, exploit and oppress the women. She writes:

> It is impossible to correct, develop, or improve the Church, within the same old system to accommodate women. Women want to *change* the Church and not simply 'improve' it. Women want *liberation* of the Church from men.[37]

The Church in Africa can therefore be liberated only if it *is depatriarchalized*. Ramodibe thus calls not for the 'rebuilding' of the existing male-dominated Church, but for the 're-creation' of a new Church in Africa which will be 'a source and agent of liberation, justice and peace in all aspects'.[38] What Ramodibe sees as the major task for such a new liberating church is not merely the examination of its theology, history and traditions but above all, the Bible itself. It is therefore 'important that women reread the Bible, because the Bible we have now has been edited with the influence of male domination. It is men who composed it and it used male symbols.'[39] Certainly, the *rereading* of Scripture which the feminine question calls for, is not the task of African women alone; it is for African men too.

Notes
1.   Teresa Okure, 'Women in the Bible' in Virginia Faibella and Mercy Oduyoye (eds), *With Passion and Compassion: Third World Women Doing Theology* (Maryknoll, New York, Orbis Books, 1988), 54.

2. See Phyllis Trible's book with the same title, *Texts of Terror: Literary-Feminist Readings of Biblical Narratives* (Philadelphia, Fortress Press, 1984).
3. Okure, 'Women in the Bible', 52.
4. Ibid., 55–57.
5. Ibid., 47.
6. Ibid., 56 cf. 54.
7. Ibid., 52.
8. Ibid., 54, For our purpose, we concentrate on the former.
9. Josephus, *Apion* II, 201.
10. Leonard Swidler, *Women in Judaism: The Status of Women in Formative Judaism* (Metuchen, New Jersey, Scarecrow Press, 1976), 167. For details on 'Marriage Women' see 139ff, and for 'Women as sex objects', 126ff.
11. Louise Tappa, 'God in Man's Image' in J.S. Pobee and B. von Wartenberg-Potter (eds), *New Eyes for Reading: Biblical and Theological Reflection By Women From the Third World* (Geneva, WCC, 1986), 101.
12. Terri A. Castaneda, 'African Women and Christianity' in *International Christian Digest*, Vol. 3 No. 6 July/August, 1989, 21.
13. See for example, Mercy Oduyoye, 'Be a Woman, and Africa Will Be Strong' in Letty Russell, Kwok Pui-lan, Ada Maria Isasi-Diaz, and Katie Cannon (eds), *Inheriting Our Mothers' Gardens: Feminist Theology in Third World Perspective* (Philadelphia, Westminster, 1988), 39, where she talks about how African women are today, resisting against this patriarchal practice.
14. Bette Ekeya, 'Woman, For How Long Not?' in Pobee and Wartenberg-Potter, *New Eyes for Reading...*, 64.
15. Ibid., 59.
16. Ibid., 62.
17. Ibid., 63.
18. Ibid., 63–64.
19. Okure, 'Women in the Bible', 56.
20. See Maria Rosa Cutrufelli, *Women of Africa: Roots of Oppression* (London, Zed Press, 1983), 43.
21. Ibid., 41.
22. Ibid., 41.
23. Cited by Margaret Shank, 'Unequal Partners' in *West Africa* No. 3720 (London), November 28 December, 1988, 2232.
24. John Mbiti, *Introduction to African Religion* (London, Heineman, 1975), 98. Mbiti adds that 'in all African societies, everything possible is done to prepare for marriage and to make them think in terms of marriage'.
25. Ibid., 104–5.
26. In most cases, the fault of childlessness is placed at the door of the woman and not the man. It is only when the man has married other woman (or women) and still no child is born or, when the divorced woman conceived with another husband that society begins to question the man's potency.
27. Cutrufelli, *op. cit.*, 2.
28. See James L. Brain: 'Less Than Second-Class: Women in Rural Settlement Scheme in Tanzania' in Nanct Hafkin and Edna Bay (eds), *Women in Africa: Studies in Social and Economic Change* (Stanford, Stanford University Press, 1976), 267. Brain describes how the women among the Luguru and the Kutu in Tanzania are 'curbed at puberty by one of the longest rites of passage in the world' with the period of seclusion lasting 'as long as six years' but 'more recently it has been reduced to two or three.'
29. Remi Clignet, *Many Wives Many Powers* (Evanston, 1970), 357. Cited by Hafkin and Bay, *op. cit.*, 1.
30. Cutrufelli, *Women of Africa*, 53.
31. *Ibid.*, 54.
32. Jomo Kenyatta, *Facing Mount Kenya* (London, Secker & Warburg, 1938), 133; cf. Mbiti, *Introduction to African Religion*, 10.
33. Hafkin and Bay, *Women in Africa*, 19.
34. Rosemary Edet and Bette Ekeya, 'Church Women in Africa: A Theological Community' in Fabella and Oduyoye (eds), *With Passion and Compassion*, 6.
35. The 'Editorial', *West Africa* No. 3683 (London), 21 March 1988, 487.
36. Hafkin and Bay, *Women in Africa*, 1.
37. Dorothy Ramobide, 'Women and Men Building Together the Church in Africa', in

Fabella and Oduyoye (eds), *With Passion and Compassion*, 15.
38. Ibid., 17–18.
39. Ibid., 19.

5. Sexuality and Spirituality

The connection between sexuality and spirituality in Christian thought has been almost completely severed by a pervasive (and unbiblical) body/soul dualism. The difficulties encountered in reintegrating sexuality and spirituality provide the key to understanding the extent of the lasting influence of dualistic thought on Christian theology generally.

The two authors in this short chapter both carry forward the work of integration. James Nelson in his essay 'Reuniting Sexuality and Spirituality' argues that what is often referred to as the 'sexual revolution' is part of a wider movement, marked in the words of Paul Ricoeur, 'by a desire to reunite sexuality with the experience of the sacred'. Nelson finds 'seven signs' of a 'paradigmatic shift in the religious perception of human sexuality', and suggests that together they comprise a renewed understanding of sexuality and spirituality which is more far-reaching than even that renewed emphasis on loving companionship among Protestants in the 17th century.

Marvin Ellison traces two contrasting connections between sexuality and spirituality in his 'Sexuality and Spirituality: An Intimate – and Intimidating – Connection'. The *intimidating* connection is provided by an 'other worldly' spirituality' (exemplified by Kierkegaard) which sets human love against divine love, and sometimes turns out to be in the grip of sexism, heterosexism and fear. The *intimate* connection is a 'this-worldly' spirituality which is incarnational and therefore 'looks to the material, the mundane, the corporeal as the primary locus for disclosing both human and divine power'. Ellison encourages his readers to practise 'this-worldly' spirituality by, among other things, working for gender and sexual equality and the overcoming of patriarchy. This, he says, is a 'higher, more demanding sexual ethic'.

James B. Nelson is Professor of Christian Ethics at United Theological Seminary of the Twin Cities, New Brighton, Minnesota, U.S.A. His essay 'Reuniting Sexuality and Spirituality' first appeared in *The Christian Century*, 104, pp. 187–190, Feb. 25, 1987. The Rev. Dr. Marvin Ellison Jr. is Bass

Professor of Christian Ethics at Bangor Theological Seminary, Bangor, ME, U.S.A. His essay 'Sexuality and Spirituality: An Intimate – and Intimidating – Connection' first appeared in *Church and Society*, 80, pp. 26–34, Nov/Dec 1989.

5.1 Reuniting Sexuality and Spirituality

James B. Nelson

Tht title of this Christian Century series, *After the Revolution: The Church and Sexual Ethics*, suggests two things: that there has been a sexual revolution, and that the revolution is over. Though in some ways both claims are true, in other ways the revolution has just begun. Clearly the past quarter-century has witnessed significant changes in the cultural and religious understandings of sex roles, sex outside marriage, homosexuality, single-parent families, the explicit portrayal and discussion of sexual matters and so on. These shifts were spurred by a new American affluence, by the Pill, by the flood of women into the work force, by the destabilization of traditional values during the war in Vietnam, and by a new societal emphasis on self-fulfillment. None of these changes was total and none occurred without consider-able resistance; yet it is evident that something of major importance happened.

Then, in the Orwellian year 1984, no less an authority than *Time* magazine declared that 'The Revolution Is Over' (April 9). Veterans of the sexual revolution, said *Time*, are both bored and wounded. The one-night stand has lost its sheen, we were told. 'Commitment' and 'intimacy' are in (helped by the scourges of herpes and AIDS), and celibacy is again a respectable option. The 'me generation' is giving way to the 'we generation.' Religious and political reaction has followed the rise of feminism, gay/lesbian activism and the plurality of family forms.

All this is true enough. But it is not that simple – particularly not in regard to religious attitudes. Some years ago Paul Ricoeur observed that there have been three major stages in the Western understanding of the relation of sexuality to religion (cf 'Wonder, Eroticism and Enigma,' in *Sexuality and Identity*, edited by Hendrik Ruitenbeek [Dell, 1970], pp. 13 ff.). The earliest stage closely identified the two forces, incorporating sexuality into religious myth and ritual. In the second stage, accompanying the rise of the great world religions, the two spheres were separated: the sacred became increasingly transcendent while sexuality was demythologized and confined to a small part of the earthly order (procreation within institutionalized marriage). Sexuality's power was feared, restrained and disciplined.

Ricoeur notes that there now seems to be emerging a third period, marked by the desire to reunite sexuality with the experience of the sacred. This desire is prompted by a more wholistic understanding of the person and of the ways in which sexuality is present in all of human experience. If sexual expression is still seen as needing ordering and discipline, as it was in the second period, there is also, as there was in the first period, a sense of its spiritual power.

I, too, believe that we are edging into that third period – however unevenly. Of course, the sexual revolution of the '60s and '70s was itself uneven: some of the constructive power of sexuality was released, and gains were made in sexual justice and equality, but at the same time some sexual experience was trivialized. Nevertheless, that revolution did create an important opening to the third period.

Perhaps never before in the history of the church has there been so much open ferment as there is now about issues of sexuality. The outpouring of treatises, debates, studies, pronouncements and movements bent on reforming religious-sexual attitudes (or protecting them from unwanted change) has been unprecedented. In all of these developments there are signs that a paradigmatic shift in the religious perceptions of human sexuality is under way. There are seven signs of this shift that I find particularly striking.

1. *There has been a shift from theologies of sexuality to sexual theologies.* Before the past two decades, the vast preponderance of christian writers on sexuality assumed that the question before them was simply: What does Christianity (the Bible, the tradition, ecclesiastical authority, etc.) say about sexuality? Now we are also asking: What does our experience of human sexuality say about our perceptions of faith – our experience of God, our interpretations of Scripture and tradition, our ways of living out the gospel?

This shift derives in part from a recovery of 19th-century liberal theology's emphasis on experience as important theological data – an emphasis now embraced by various forms of liberation theology. It derives, too, from the feminist and lesbian/gay movements, both of which have claimed that it is their consciousness of sexual oppression that has afforded them crucial insights about the ways of God in human relationships. The term 'sexual theology,' like the term 'liberation theology,' suggests this dialogical, two-directional investigation.

The two-way conversation model reminds us that theology cannot presume to look down upon human sexuality from some unaffected, Olympian vantage point. It reminds us that every theological perception contains some elements and perceptions conditioned by sexual experience, and every sexual experience is perceived and interpreted through religious lenses of some kind. The difference between a unidirectional and a dialogical method is the difference between a theology of sexuality and a sexual theology.

2. *There has been a shift from understanding sexuality as either incidental to or detrimental to the experience of God toward understanding sexuality as intrinsic to the divine-human experience.* Sexual dualism has marked much of the Christian tradition. In this dualism, spirit is opposed to body, with spirit assumed to be higher and supe-

rior and the body lower and inferior. The companion of this dualism has been sexism or patriarchy: men identify themselves essentially with the spirit (mind), while men identify women with the body (matter), and assume that the higher needs to control the lower.

Implicit in sexual dualism has been the notion of divine impassivity – the *apathy* of God. If the body is marked by passion and if spirit is passionless, then bodily hunger (*eros*) has no connection with the divine. God is without hunger, and the human hungers (of which sexuality, with its drive to connection and intimacy, is one of the most basic) seem to have no connection with our experience of God.

While the recent sexual revolution often seemed more intent on self-fulfillment through unfettered pleasure than on the quest for intimacy, it did prompt new theological reflection on the spiritual significance of sexual hunger. If some of our Protestant forebears of three centuries ago were right in believing that companionship, not procreation, is central in God's design for sexuality, then the human hunger for physical and emotional intimacy is of enormous spiritual significance. It ought not to be denigrated as unbecoming to the spiritual life. Thus theology has been giving new attention to the insight that sexuality is crucial to God's design that creatures do not dwell in isolation and loneliness but in communion and community.

Accompanying the attack on dualism has been the reclaiming of incarnational theology. This theology emphasizes that the most decisive experience of God is not in doctrine, creed or ideas but in the Word made flesh – and in the Word still becoming flesh. Here has been another opening to the possibility that sexuality is intrinsic to the experience of God. Such experience has been described by Nikos Kazantzakis: 'Within me even the most metaphysical problem takes on a warm physical body which smells of sea, soil, and human sweat. The Word, in order to touch me, must become warm flesh. Only then do I understand – when I can smell, see, and touch' (*Report to Greco* [Cassirer, 1965], p. 43).

3. *There has been a shift from understanding sexual sin as a matter of wrong sexual acts to understanding sexual sin as alienation from our intended sexuality.* The Christian tradition has had a pronounced tendency to define sexual sin as specific acts. This approach gained momentum during the early Middle Ages when penitential manuals were first written detailing the nature of specific sins and their proper penances. Those manuals paid the greatest attention to sexual matters. Indeed, in our heritage, 'sin' and 'morality' have had a markedly sexual focus (a 'morals charge' never refers to an economic injustice!). Sexual sins thus became physiologically definable and capable of neat categorization. They were those particular acts either prohibited by scriptural texts or contrary to natural law – acts done with the wrong person, in the wrong way or for the wrong purpose.

Actually, Christian theology at its best has recognized that sin is not fundamentally an act but rather the condition of alienation or estrangement out of which harmful acts may arise. However, it has taken a long time for theology to acknowledge that sexual sin is fundamentally alienation from our divinely intended sexuality. To put it overly simply but I hope accurately: sexual sin lies not in being too sexual, but in being not sexual enough – in the way God has intended us to be. Such alienation, indeed, usually leads to harmful acts, but the sin is rooted in the prior condition.

Sexual sin lies in the dualistic alienation by which the body becomes an object, either to be constrained out of fear (the Victorian approach) or to be treated as a pleasure machine (the *Playboy* philosophy). It lies in the dualistic alienation by which females are kept from claiming their assertiveness and males kept from claiming their vulnerability. It lies in the alienation which finds expression in sexual violence, in Rambo-like militarism, in racism, in ecological abuse. The uncompleted sexual revolution began to recognize some of this. While in its superficial and exploitative moments it wanted to wipe away the category of sexual sin ('If it feels good, do it'), in its better moments it helped us see that sexual sin is really something different from, and more than, particular acts which can be neatly defined.

4. *There has been a shift from understanding salvation as antisexual to knowing that there is 'sexual salvation.'* Because spiritualistic dualism has conditioned so much of the Christian tradition, Christians have inherited a disembodied notion of salvation: salvation means release from the lower (fleshly) into the higher (spiritual) life. Accordingly, popular piety has typically viewed the saints as asexual beings, without sexual needs and desires and sometimes even without genitalia.

The sexual revolution helped convince many Christians that an incarnationalist faith embraces the redemption of alienated sexuality as well as other estranged dimensions of our lives. *Justification by grace* signifies God's unconditional, unmerited, radical acceptance of the whole person: God, the Cosmic Lover, graciously embraces not just a person's disembodied spirit but the whole fleshly self – the meanings of which theology is only beginning to explore.

Sanctification means growth in holiness (or wholeness and health – the root word is the same). Many have begun to realize that God intends increasing sexual wholeness to be part of our redemption. Like any other good belief, this view can be perverted, but it need not be. Sexual sanctification can mean growth in bodily self-acceptance, in the capacity for sensuousness, in the capacity for play, in the diffusion of the erotic throughout the body (rather than in its genitalization) and in the embrace of the androgynous possibility.

5. *There has been a shift from an act-centered sexual ethics to a relational sexual ethics.* For all of its oversimplifications, Joseph Fletcher's *Situation Ethics* (1966) prompted a good deal of ethical rethinking. More sophisticated approaches to contextual-relational ethics and an ethics of response/responsibility, differently expressed by

such thinkers as H. Richard Niebuhr and Paul Lehmann, had a major impact on ethical thought in the '60s.

Act-oriented sexual ethics had dominated most of the Christian tradition, bearing the assumption that the rightness or wrongness of a particular sexual expression could be ascertained by the intrinsic value or disvalue of the action itself, without serious consideration of the relational context. The alternative seemed normlessness and subjectivism, particularly dangerous in sexuality issues, where passions run high. A relational sexual ethics has appeared to many as a way of avoiding legalism on the one hand and normless subjectivism on the other.

Roman Catholic sexual ethics, with its strong natural law tradition and clearly defined ecclesiastical teaching authority, has been more inclined toward objective sexual norms than has Protestant ethics with its heavy scriptural orientation. Both, however, have been more objectivistic and act-focused in sexual issues than in any other moral sphere. In recent years, however, numerous persons in both traditions have moved toward a new and creative sexual ethics.

Act-oriented ethics has appeared inadequate not only in cases with unique contexts and meanings, but in light of a growing recognition that Christian sexual ethics has been inadequately integrated into a wholistic spirituality. If sexuality is the physiological and psychological grounding of our capacities to love, if our destiny after the image of the Cosmic Lover is to be lovers in the richest, fullest sense of that good word, then how does sexual ethics figure into our spiritual destiny? What are our creative and fitting sexual responses to the divine loving? What are the appropriate sexual meanings that will embody the meanings of Word becoming flesh?

These are the questions that seem increasingly appropriate to many. For example, in a promising and controversial book published ten years ago, a group of Roman Catholic scholars proposed that Catholic sexual ethics stop centering on procreation, natural law and the physical contours of sexual acts and focus instead on the creative growth toward personal integration. Such growth and integration, they suggested, would be promoted by sexual expressions that are self-liberating, other-enriching, honest, faithful, socially responsible, life-serving and joyous. These, the authors proposed, are marks of a gospel ethic of love (Anthony Kosnick *et al.*, *Human Sexuality: New Directions in American Catholic Thought* [Paulist/Newman, 1977]). Rome's clear retreat from such Vatican II directions as these is evidence that the paradigm shift is still very uneven. But countless members of the Catholic Church know that a significant change is under way.

6. *There has been a shift from understanding the church as asexual to understanding it as a sexual community.* Through most of the church's history it has viewed sexuality as either incidental or inimical to its life. But the sexual revolution resulted in a growing self-

consciousness and empowerment on the part of the sexually oppressed. Religious feminism articulated the ways in which the church has always been a sexual community – the ways it has incorporated patriarchy into its language, worship, theological imagery, leadership patterns and ethics. A rising gay/lesbian consciousness performed a similar function in regard to the church's heterosexism. Gradually, other groups – singles (including the widowed and divorced), the aging, those with handicapping conditions, the ill – have begun to recognize how churchly assumptions and practices have sexually disenfranchised them.

Another impetus for claiming and reforming the church as a sexual community has come from the increasing desire to reunite sexuality and spirituality. The realization that Protestant worship has been marked by a masculinist focus on the spoken word and by a suspicion of bodily feelings suggested the need to explore and touch the varied senses more inclusively. The recognition that most theology has given only lip service to the incarnation, failing to take ongoing incarnationalism seriously in both method and content, inspired the effort to explore the doing and meaning of body theology. The fact that Christian education has seriously ignored sex education prompted the attempt to address sexual meanings as part of faith's journey, for young and old. Much of the recent ferment in theology, ethics, worship, leadership, pastoral care and education has been a direct result of this effort to recognize and reform the church as a sexual community.

7. *There has been a shift from understanding sexuality as a private issue to understanding it as a personal and public one.* Sexual issues will always be deeply personal, but personal does not mean private. One mark of Victorian sexuality was its privatization. Not only was sexuality not to be talked about, it was to be confined to a small portion of one's private life. But this, quite literally, was idiocy (the Greek root for *idiot* refers to the person who attempts to live the private life, ignorant of the public domain).

One of the church's recent discoveries is the public dimension of sexuality issues. On the social-action agenda of mainline denominations today are sexual-justice issues regarding gender and sexual orientation. No longer foreign to church concern are issues of abortion, family planning and population control, sexual abuse and violence, pornography, prostitution, reproductive technologies, varied family forms, sexually transmitted diseases, teen-age pregnancy and the reassessment of men's identity. All these issues are obviously sexual, and all are public.

Even newer than this development is the nascent discovery of sexual dimensions in issues that previously had not appeared to have sexual connections, such as social violence. Violence, whether in the form of crime in the streets, the arms race, or economic or foreign policy, has important sexual aspects. To be sure, the sources and manifestations of violence are complex. But what do we make of competitiveness, the cult of winning, the armoring of emotions, the tendency to dichotomize reality, the abstraction from bodily concreteness and the exaggerated fear of death that is manifested in a morbid fascination with it? These phenomena feed social violence, and all are deeply related to distortions of sexuality, particularly of male sexuality.

Years ago James Weldon Johnson observed that sexuality is deeply implicated in race problems as well. Historically, white males' categorization of women ('either virgins or whores') proceeded along racial lines: white women were symbols of delicacy and purity, whereas black women symbolized an animality which could be sexually and economically exploited. White male guilt was projected onto the black male, who was imagined as a dark, supersexual beast who must be punished and from whom white women must be protected. Black mothers nurtured their sons to be docile, hoping to protect them from white male wrath. That upbringing in turn complicated black marriages and led to certain destructive attempts to recover black 'manliness.' We are the heirs of a distorted racial history in which sexual dynamics have been a major force.

Sexual dynamics are also pervasive and significant when we examine economic exploitation and ecological abuse. Two decades ago, Peirce Teilhard de Chardin observed: 'The prevailing view has been that the body ... is a *fragment* of the Universe, a piece completely detached from the rest and handed over to a spirit that informs it. In the future we shall have to say that the Body is the very Universality of things.... *My matter* is not a *part* of the Universe that I possess *totaliter*: it is the *totality* of the Universe possessed by me *partialiter*' (*Science and Christ* [Harper & Row, 1968], pp. 12 f). Theology has been slowly recognizing this fact.

The sexual revolution of the '60s and '70s is mostly over, and some of its superficial and exploitative forms of freedom have proved to be just that. Hurt, boredom and disease have sobered more than a few – and the forces of religious and political reaction rejoice. But this revolution was a harbinger of a much more significant change that Ricoeur foresaw. The change is just beginning. It is uneven, misunderstood and resisted, as well as eagerly welcomed and hoped-for. Nevertheless, in my view a paradigmatic shift is indeed under way.

This will not be the first time in Christian history that a major shift has taken place in the perception of sexuality. In the 17th century some Protestants – especially Puritans, Anglicans and Quakers – began to affirm that loving companionship, not procreation, is the central meaning of sexuality. This cultural-religious revolution is still unfinished. I take heart from the fact that even more far-reaching change is taking place as we investigate how sexuality and spirituality are part and parcel of each other, and as we affirm that the Word continues to become flesh and dwell among us. *This* revolution has just begun.

5.2 Sexuality and Spirituality: An Intimate – and Intimidating – Connection

Marvin M. Ellison

First, the Confession

While I am grateful for moments of grace in which I have been able to 'hold things together' and affirm myself both as a sexual person and as a person of faith, my spiritual pilgrimage is also full of pain, doubts, confusion, anger, betrayals, and silences about the connection between sexuality and spirituality. I am sure that some of the tensions and conflict experience are generated by my own misunderstandings and inadequacies, but I am also persuaded that my faith tradition and church have not provided good modeling on how to be a self-respecting person who is simultaneously sexual and spiritual.

My conviction is that unless we can experience and speak of God's grace in and through our bodies, in and through our sensuous connectedness to all reality, we do not know God's presence and power. Salvation is necessarily concrete and of the flesh. I yearn for the kind of *en-fleshing* of Christian spirituality that encourages me to *embrace more radically the life of the flesh.* Nor is that yearning mine alone.

Genuine Christian spirituality encourages this embrace rather than turning us away from our embodied sensuality and passions as if to find holiness/wholeness elsewhere. The 14th-century nun Dame Julian of Norwich affirmed that 'Our sensuality is grounded in nature, in compassion, and in grace. In our sensuality, God is.'[1] And that is where we need to be, as well. Unless we falsely spiritualize what Christian love means, we can also say, 'Where there is embodied love, God is.'

Two readings have helped me to name the tensions between two conflicting Christian spiritualities that view this 'life in the flesh' very differently. I suggest that we carefully analyze the significance of these contradictory spiritualities for our personal well-being and for social justice advocacy.

The first perspective, exemplified in the life and thought of Søren Kierkegaard, the 19th-century Danish theologian, proposes an irreconcilable tension between human and divine love with an elevation of love-of-God as 'higher than' and superior to love between persons. Kierkegaard had hoped to marry a young woman named Regina Olsen, but when she finally accepted his proposal for marriage, he broke off the engagement because he feared that his love for this woman would jeopardize his ability to love God unreservedly. Kierkegaard believed that true devotion to God required that he deny himself 'earthly delights' in order to be open to and fully concentrate on 'higher things': God's love, which transcends all other loves. His love for another person was in conflict with and a distraction from loving God.

The choice Kierkegaard made reflects the powerful and persistent influence of otherworldly spirituality on Christian piety and practice, in which the believer turns to God only by turning away from the world, from this life and from concrete, everyday realities and concerns. Such dualistic theologies and worldviews diminish the integrity of human existence by denying the importance of where we choose to invest our passions and attach our loyalties in the face of human suffering and rampant injustice. Moreover, as Martin Buber explains, to sever love of God from love of this world, of others, and of ourselves, is 'sublimely to misunderstand God.'

> Creation is not a hurdle on the road to God, it is the road itself. We are created along with one another and directed to a life with one another. Creatures are placed in my way so that I, their fellow-creature, by means of them and with them, find the way to God. A God reached by their exclusion would not be the God of all lives in whom all life is fulfilled.... God wants us to come to God by means of the Reginas [and Rogers] God has created, and not by renunciation of them.[2]

A this-worldly spirituality fully honors the unity of human personhood as a spirit/body whole and also celebrates that the presence and power of divine love is mediated in and through our human relationships and flesh. As Robert McAfee Brown writes, 'This suggests that spirituality and sexuality, rather than being understood as opposites, should be understood as intimately and inextricably bound together, two expressions of a single basic reality rather than two different realities.'[3]

In her novel *Beloved*, Toni Morrison evokes this concrete, sensuous, and passionate spirituality as she describes the remarkable healing power of a holy woman, Baby Suggs, who preached to black slaves a powerful message of redemption:

> She told them that the only grace they could have was the grace they could imagine. That if they could not see it, they would not have it.
> 'Here,' she said, 'in this here place, we flesh; flesh that weeps, laughs; flesh that dances on bare feet in grass. Love it. Love it hard. Yonder they do not love your flesh. They despise it.... *You* got to love it. This is flesh I'm talking about here. Flesh that needs to be loved.... Love your neck; put a hand on it, grace it, stroke it and hold it up.'[4]

A this-worldly spirituality rejects the notion that salvation involves escape from the body or a turning away from the embodied goodness around us. Rather, authentic faithfulness looks to the material, the mundane, the corporeal as the primary locus for disclosing both human and divine power; it regards physical touch as a privileged mode for communicating deep caring and mutual pleasure in company with others.

Christian ministry is sharing power, and naming and aligning ourselves with that sacred and awesome power that flows in and through us to bring wholeness, well-being, integrity, and at-one-ness of human life in relation to others and the created order. Sexuality and spirituality are intimately and unavoidably connected because they deal with that kind of power-in-relation we believe to be genuinely sacred and life-giving. Sexuality, our embodied sensuous connectedness to all reality, is our human capacity and longing for intimacy and communion with others and with God. Sexual desire lures us toward connecting with others and helps us gain strength in our vulnerability to receive as well as give affirmation and care.

Otherworldly Christian spirituality has a noticeable fear of, as well as fixation with, the power of sex. The pervasive discomfort with the body and dis-ease about sex show the ongoing power of a spirit/body dualism and the related male/female dualism that are so characteristic of Western Christianity. The depth of body-alienation and, therefore, self-alienation in this culture is clearly evident. Erotic passion is continually disparaged as corrupting and as an evil power at war with positive spiritual energy. Therefore, to trust that eroticism is essential to our human well-being and to our God-relation requires courage. Courageous, too, are those who affirm that erotic power is a moral good, that is, the source of creative personal power seeking mutual relations with others and grounded in care, self-respect, and other-regard.

I am convinced that a spirituality *without* erotic passion becomes lifeless and cold. God becomes an abstraction, an idea rather than a living presence in our lives. I am searching for a Christian spirituality that acknowledges that the human calling is to make passionate love in this world, in our beds and in our institutions. To love well means to share the gift of life with zeal and great generosity and to seek right relations with all others, relations of genuine equality and mutuality, of shared power and respect.

The pervasive fear of sex and of strong passion which the church has encouraged is coming perilously close to killing off our love of life in the flesh and our passion for justice in the church and in the world. As I understand Christian faithfulness, the passionate doing of justice – of righting distorted power dynamics and breaking every pattern of domination and subordination – is at the heart of *any* spirituality worth having. Owning the goodness of our sexuality and of our erotic desire for wholeness and connectedness is, therefore, not inherently selfish or self-indulgent, but rather the indispensable grounding for engaging joyfully in working to create justice for ourselves and others.

An incarnational faith skittish about the goodness of the body and about sensuous pleasure may well bore itself to death. In order to reclaim its spiritual integrity, the church must stop discouraging sensuous touch and communication between consenting adults and redirect its attention toward encouraging – and celebrating – responsible, loving, empowering mutual sexual relationships wherever they occur, among the married and the not-married, among gays and lesbians, among heterosexual persons. The church must also overcome its preoccupation with questions of sexual orientation and cease its endless harangues about the dangers and illegitimacy of sexual diversity. It is high time for the church to 'come of age' about sex and sexual pluralism in the church and in the society.

Ecclesial maturity about matters of sexual intimacy also requires us to acknowledge candidly that our conventional categories for naming normal and abnormal sexuality distort rather than disclose what is most important and valuable about our sexuality. What matters ethically, humanly, is not the sameness – or difference – of the gender of persons in relation, but rather the quality and character of their relationship. Not *who* we are, but *how* we are with each other is ethically significant.

Simply put, the fundamental debate within the church is not over the rules of who sleeps with whom but rather a conflict over the normative character of our sexual and social relationships. What is at issue are our values and commitments to an inclusive and egalitarian 'ethic of common decency.' We need to be teaching – and struggling to embody – a higher, more demanding sexual ethic than one that passes judgment exclusively on the basis of patriarchal sexual categories.

The Contemporary Crisis of Sexuality

At the heart of this crisis of sexuality is the ongoing struggle to overcome male gender superiority throughout the social order, including in the pulpit and the bedroom. The church will not offer much constructive counsel on human sexuality unless we deal forthrightly with how sexism and heterosexism distort all dynamics of gender relations and human intimacy patterns.

To analyze the contemporary crisis of sexuality, we need to understand that human sexuality is not predetermined naturally or dictated by biological mandates but rather is intensely malleable, constantly reshaped by social and cultural dynamics. Sexuality is socially constructed in myriad, intricate ways. Far from being a fixed 'essence' or transcultural constant, human sexuality forever is renegotiated and redefined among contending social forces and, therefore, also is subject to greater humanization or dehumanization.

Human sexuality is always culturally encoded, ascribed with certain meanings and shaped according to certain values and societal purposes. 'Reading' a particular sexual code requires an acknowledgement that every society makes arrangements for the organization of erotic life. Our society – and our churches – are not unusual in this regard. Moreover, it is important to recognize that the nature of sex has to do not only with sex (as an exchange of erotic energy) but also with what it means to be male and female and with the proper ordering of gender relations. Critical questions about any sexual code include asking about who is and who is not empowered to name themselves and be listened to, in the valuing of their lives in relation to others.

In our patriarchal culture an elaborate and historically complex structuring of sexuality has been built on the assumption of fundamental differences and inequality between men and women, and upon the moral rightness of male dominance and control of women's lives and their bodies. Men are socialized to exercise power over others and to stay in control of their feelings by remaining 'logical,' 'rational,' 'cool.' Women, on the other hand, are socialized into social dependency and encouraged to accept their powerlessness 'for their own good.'

By the logic of sexist dualisms, if men are strong, physical, rational, and in control, women must be weak, spiritual, intuitive and emotional, and dependent, under someone else's control. In sum, men and women are thought to be complementary beings, each a half-personality. In the sex act, the two are brought together to become one whole and move under *his* control.

This perspective also suggests that erotic desire is sparked by opposites attracting. Patriarchal eroticism makes inequality of power and status sexy and desirable. Sex is often experienced as a dynamic of conquest and surrender, a matter of exercising power and control over another or of being controlled and under someone else's power and direction. As feminist analyses of the pornography industry rightly show, male domination over women and children is eroticized and, through powerful visual imagery, reinforced as both natural and right.

Sexism declares that male gender superiority and power over women is morally good, and also beneficial to women. Heterosexism[5] extends the logic of sexism by insisting that 'real' men dominate women sexually and socially and that ·'normal' women are sexually submissive and socially compliant, ready to make their lives available for the service of others. Heterosexism (or compulsory heterosexuality) stigmatizes gay men and lesbians as sexual deviants, but pressures all persons to play their 'proper' sex-stereotyped roles and conform to dominant/subordinate power dynamics. Heterosexism insists that all men are more powerful than women, and that some men are more powerful than others.

Men who do not properly perform their dominant role vis-à-vis women are treated as failed men and often perceived to be homosexual, whether accurately or not, and 'like women,' that is, without power and status. Any strong, self-assertive, and independent woman will likely be labelled lesbian, a 'man-hater,' because she does not keep to her place of socially constructed inferiority. Heterosexism and homophobia, by stigmatizing sexual non-conformity, reinforce compliance to sexist social roles and relations. External enforcements, including violence, teach all of us that penalties will be meted out to those who do not stay within prescribed roles of gender inequality.

The contemporary crisis of sexuality is fundamentally a crisis in *heterosexuality*, in the dominant cultural pattern for male/female social and sexual relations. In a society in which sexism and heterosexism are pervasive, the preoccupation with the gender of sexual partners is not surprising. *With whom* we have sex, the *gender* of the person to whom we are erotically attracted, is given enormous weight and has become the standard to determine whether persons are 'normal' or 'abnormal,' 'deviant' or not. Our dominant sexual code insists that only heterosexuality is good but more importantly, that only a *sexist* ordering of social relations – male dominance and female submission – is legitimate and proper.

Christian spirituality is deeply implicated in this unjust system of alienated power relations insofar as the church continues to equate what is moral with what is sexist and unjust, namely, that 'good sex' and proper sexual and social relations require men to stay on top and in control of 'their' women, and for women passively to accept the inevitability of such arrangements. As long as the problem of sexuality continues to be misnamed in the church as 'the problem of homosexuality' rather than sexism and heterosexism, we will castigate those individuals who deviate from the patriarchal norm and fail to challenge the institutionalized injustice which blocks the Spirit's movement in our midst for renewal and transformation. 'The basic issue,' as James Nelson puts the matter, 'is really not about "them," but about all of us. How can we live less fearfully and more securely in the grace of God?'[6]

Resources for Reconstructing Christian Theology and Ministry with Respect to Sexuality

What is shaking the foundations in the church and society is the open call, especially by feminist women and gay men, to struggle for a *nonsexist moral order* in the bedroom no less than in the boardroom, the pulpit, and the seminary classroom.

We need to be very candid about this struggle. We work, play, make love, raise children, and pray in the midst of a life-rending ideological battle between a patriarchal and a feminist liberation paradigm of human social and sexual relations. This conflict is not something to bemoan but rather accept and work through, as we acknowledge that each and every theological and moral claim we make is ideological, through and through, in either supporting or challenging existing social arrangements and norms. Not conflict but the *evasion* of conflict signals the loss of genuine spiritual power and 'aliveness.'

The reasons for so much fear of feminism and gay liberation in the church is that these movements no longer grant moral legitimacy and authority to the patriarchal order of things. Quite openly, they aim to topple the *patriarchal* family structure, the anchor for the public moral ordering of all other social relations. The fear among defenders of male gender privilege is that this seditious sentiment may, indeed, be catching! Recruitment to new loyalties, especially strong commitment to struggle for genuine gender and sexual equality, is very fearsome.

Resistance to feminism and gay liberation is best viewed as resistance to adopting a radical ethic of justice and mutuality in matters of sexual intimacy *and* social relations. Resistance stems, in part, from the fear of many men that if 'full, consensual sexuality were to become the standard for acceptable sexual relations, they would be deprived of many, perhaps most, of the sexual acts they now enjoy.'[7] That is the conclusion of the authors of a study on rape, subtitled 'The Price of Coercive Sexuality.'

There is much truth in that observation. I also believe that religious persons and institutions, as well as our thinking and perceptions, are deformed by participation in dynamics of oppression. Similarly, persons and institutions are *transformed* by genuine resistance to injustice.[8] A liberating Christian spirituality embraces the movement toward equalizing both gender and all other social relations as a gift of new life. In that struggle is found hope and joy, and also allies. Joining with others is especially important because spirituality concerns not what we do in solitude or isolation but rather in community. Since few of us were adequately educated by church or family to live as genuine equals with others, our best resource to learn mutuality before God and with others may well be the sexual outcasts among us, those marginalized as outsiders and non-conformists to the patriarchal family – especially feminist women and gay men who are struggling to reorder human sexuality in more loving and just directions.

What makes the telling difference, in our sexual ethic and in our sexual theologies, is not our biology, sexual orientation, or 'lifestyle.' Rather, Christian spirituality is shaped primarily by our engagement – or by our refusal to participate in the work of justice.

I suggest the church ponder the difference and unavoidable conflict between a patriarchal Christian spirituality, on the one hand, and an egalitarian, justice-centered Christian spirituality, on the other. This division marks the great divide in our church today.

Notes

1. Quoted in James B. Nelson, *The Intimate Connection: Male Sexuality, Masculine Spirituality* (Philadelphia: Westminster Press, 1988), p. 24.
2. Quoted in Robert McAfee Brown, *Spirituality and Liberation: Overcoming the Great Fallacy* (Philadelphia: Westminster Press, 1988), pp. 104–105. I am indebted to Brown for this illustration of the need for new theological and ethical perspectives on sexuality and spirituality. See his chapter-length study, 'A Case Study: Spirituality and Sexuality,' pp. 97–108.
3. Brown, p. 100.
4. Toni Morrison, *Beloved: A Novel* (New York: Alfred A. Knopf, 1987), p. 88.
5. This analysis of heterosexism is dependent on the insights of two lesbian/feminist activists and theorists: Carter Heyward, 'Heterosexism: Enforcing Male Supremacy,' *The Witness* 69

(April 1985), pp. 18-20, and Suzanne Pharr, *Homophobia: Weapon of Sexism* (Inverness, CA: Chardon Press, 1988).

6.   James B. Nelson, *Embodiment: An Approach to Sexuality and Christian Theology* (Minneapolis: Augsburg Publishing House, 1978), p. 210.

7.   Lorenne Clark and Debra Lewis, *Rape: The Price of Coercive Sexuality*, quoted by Marie Fortune and Denise Hormann, 'Sexual Violence,' *JSAC Grapevine* 11:3 (September 1979), p. 5.

8.   On theological reflection as an integral component of liberation struggles, see Beverly Wildung Harrison, *Making the Connections: Essays in Feminist Social Ethics*, ed. Carol S. Robb (Boston: Beacon Press, 1985), esp. pp. 259 ff.

6. Sexuality and Love

Love is clearly at the heart of Christian faith, yet the problems posed by it are immense. Historical understandings of sexual love have, in the west, been influenced by the rise of courtly and later romantic ideals, yet the extent to which either is able to contribute to a *theological* understanding of love, human and divine, is contentious. 20th Century Protestant theology has been impoverished by exaggerations of the distance between divine self-giving love (*agape*) and human self-interested love (*eros*). Feminist theologians have responded by exposing the androcentric assumptions behind these contrasts, and by drawing attention to the oppressive power of an ideology of self-giving interpreted and administered by men.

The first two essays in this chapter contribute substantially to a necessary revisioning of Christian love, both of them using women's experience as a source of theological reflection. Sally Purvis, in 'Mothers, Neighbors and Strangers – Another Look at Agape', sets out the experience of mother-love as 'an excellent model for the content of *agape*'. She rejects the 'disinterested' approach to *agape* exemplified by Kierkegaard, replacing it with the intensely interested and other-regarding love which is found in the experience of mothering. This love is inclusive, other-regarding and unconditional. Theologically it is much closer than disinterested *agape* to the love displayed in the parable of the good Samaritan where the Samaritan behaves, not like a neighbour, but 'like a lover'. Whereas the self presupposed by mainstream agapic love is said to shun the particularities of deep involvements, the kind of self which expresses mother-love is 'present, connected, involved, intensely caring'. Purvis' resounding conclusion, 'based upon both exegetical and experiential evidence', is that 'indifferent universality is eclipsed by caring intensity as the ethical focus of agape.'

Jennifer Rike in her essay 'The Lion and the Unicorn: Feminist Perspectives on Christian Love as Care' is equally critical of the isolated self for whom relations with particular others is problematic. Following Valerie Saiving's analysis, she notes that while men have been historically prone to the sins of pride and arrogance, women have been prone to the sins 'which result from the relative inability to assert or develop the self'. Faced with this legacy women do not need or want to hear that they must devote themselves to self-sacrificial love. The historical question about the proper place of self-love in the Christian life assumes a new importance in this context, but Rike wisely and boldly warns us against attempting to answer it. This is because the 'operative conception of selfhood' which the question assumes is an androcentric product, writing an essential separateness between individuals into its foundations. A better way forward is a relational concept of the self, and a new 'model of feminist Christian love as care'.

Rike sees the opposition of *agape* and *eros* in the work of Nygren as the climax of the older and broader Protestant tendency to polarise divine self-giving love and human self-love. The Roman Catholic M.C. D'Arcy retained the two basic loves ('*eros* which is symbolized by the proud and powerful lion, and *agape* which is symbolized by the humble, fanciful unicorn') but he depicted them as in competition with each other; he expressed them within a wider philosophical and sexist dualism; and he ignored relationality as a fundamental category. Rike thus concludes that 'the *agape* and *caritas* models are beyond saving.' Following the work of Nell Noddings, 'the revised conception of human selfhood as connective or relational' is introduced. Not only is this a more adequate model of the self, it renders redundant accounts of love based on the model of the self which it replaces.

Feminist Christian love as care aims at 'enhancing the life and well-being of others, and through others, of the self'. It is concerned 'to promote genuine mutuality and open receptivity to the other, and through the response of the other, to the self'. This caring may well be sacrificial but will also take due account of our limited capacities and make us realise 'we are creatures of God, finite and dependent upon God for the power to do the good'. Such care avoids the extreme self-sacrifice that leads to self-destruction and the extreme idealism which in its desire to feed starving millions ignores unemployed neighbours. Rather 'God commands that we honor and serve God, not by tithing and sacrifices, but through tender and merciful caring for one another'.

While these two analyses of love have profound consequences for sexual experience, Karen Lebacqz and Deborah Blake relate Christian understandings of love directly to it. Their essay 'Safe

Sex and Lost Love' warns that sexual activity can be safe yet cruel. Safe sex can be motivated by fear; defined by genital activity and associated with blame. While there is an important place for safe sex in public discourse, 'morality and safety are not the same'. Christian sexual morality is rooted and inspired, not by fear, but by 'love and concern for the partner, mutuality and vulnerability, truthfulness, and trust'.

Sally B. Purvis's essay 'Mothers, Neighbors and Strangers – Another Look at Agape' was first published in *Journal of Feminist Studies in Religion*, 7, pp. 19–34, Spring, 1991. Jennifer L. Rike teaches at the University of Detroit Mercy, PO Box 19900 Detroit, MI 48219-0900. Her essay 'The Lion and the Unicorn: Feminist Perspectives on Christian Love as Care' was first published in *Encounter*, 51, pp. 247–255, 1990. Karen Lebacqz and Deborah Blake's essay, 'Safe Sex and Lost Love' was first published in *Religious Education*, 83, pp. 201–210, Spring, 1988.

6.1 Mothers, Neighbors and Strangers – Another Look at Agape

Sally B. Purvis

It may be a biographic accident that my richest and most powerful experience of agape, of unqualified, unconditional love for another, has come with my experience of being a mother. The two experiences are not identical; there is much in my mothering that is not agapic, and my experience of intensely other-regarding attitudes and activities is not confined to my relationships to my children. While there may be mothers who experience agape more fully with their spouses or friends, the most sustained and trustworthy embodiment of agape in my life is my experience of being a mother to my two sons.

There is dissonance, even contradiction, between the traditional characterization of agape as 'disinterested love' and my experience of agape as intensely interested. The tradition has articulated a deep suspicion of the role of 'special relations' for agape;[1] my experience suggests that the 'special relation' of being a mother can serve as a model for agape. As a Christian feminist ethicist, I claim the priority of women's experience, including my own, over a tradition that has excluded women's accounts of their own experience.[2] Furthermore, I share with other feminists the suspicion of 'disinterest' as a normative feature of human relationships in general and love in particular. Writing within the 'tradition' of Christian feminist ethics, I will use my experience of being a mother as an evaluative tool to critique the tradition and as a creative tool to revise it.[3]

As a starting point for my critique of the traditional interpretation of agape as 'disinterested love,' and as a counterpoint to the model I will offer, I will briefly investigate Søren Kierkegaard's discussion of agape in *Works of Love*[4] and will submit it to a general critical inquiry. I will then describe the contours of mother-love as I have experienced it, noting its constitutive features. I will consult a scriptural account of agape, Luke's parable of the good Samaritan, to demonstrate that exegetical evidence supports an interpretation of agape as 'intensely interested.' Finally, I will note some of the strengths and weaknesses of mother-love as a model for agape and suggest some normative implications for Christian ethics' stance toward the well being of women.

The Problem in Extremis

In his influential analytical survey of Christian interpretations of agape, Gene Outka writes,

> The normative content most often ascribed [to agape] I have called equal regard, involving in Barth's words, 'identification with his [sic] interests in utter independence of the question of his [sic] attractiveness.'[5]

On this account, agape is other-regarding, impartial, nonexclusive.[6] Self-interest is, if not absent, at least minimal and peripheral.[7] Agape is responsive to generic rather than to idiosyncratic characteristics of persons.[8] In other words, persons are recipients of agape not based on who they are but only on the fact that they are. Søren Kierkegaard is an influential representative of the traditional interpretation of agape as disinterested love. In *Works of Love* Kierkegaard writes:

> Therefore, among the works of [agapic] love, let us not forget this, let us not forget to consider THE WORK OF LOVE IN REMEMBERING ONE WHO IS DEAD ... The work of love in remembering one who is dead is thus a work of the most disinterested, the freest, the most faithful love. Therefore go out and practice it; remember one dead and learn in just this way to love the living disinterestedly, freely, faithfully. In the relationship to one dead you have the criterion whereby you can test yourself [as a Christian lover].[9]

Kierkegaard claims that in order to purify love of all of the complications that ordinarily surround it, to eliminate the dizzying diversity of life in which love is found,[10] we focus on the practice of 'remembering one who is dead' as a model for Christian agape. His exemplification of agape captures in an extreme form the traditional interpretation of agape as equal regard. Is this the richest source of understanding of agape?

Within the traditional definition of agape, Kierkegaard's claim is plausible. He characterizes this 'work of love' as the most disinterested, the freest, and the most faithful example available in human experience. First, there is no possibility that the love will be reciprocated because the dead one is utterly inaccessible to the person who is alive. The lover can expect no return on her or his love, no repayment of any sort. This love is utterly disinterested. Second, there is nothing in the beloved that calls forth our love. In Kierkegaard's terms, there can be no 'compulsion' to love because the 'dead has no rights in life.'[11] Time will work to make the memory fade; remembering is an act of free choice with no influence from the reality of the beloved. The object of the love has effectively disappeared; in his or her absence the love is perfectly unconstrained by anything outside the lover. Third, this love is the most faithful. The dead do not change, or at least not in any way that affects the relationship. Therefore if change occurs, it must occur in the living. Thus remembering one who is dead

becomes a perfectly controlled laboratory for measuring the fidelity of
the living. It seems that Kierkegaard has captured some essential
features of agape as equal regard. If pushed to its logical limits, agape
as 'equal regard,' the love that emphasizes 'generic characteristics' in
impartial and totally other-regarding attitudes and activity, the love
that makes no distinction and accepts no reward and that eliminates as
illegitimate the lovableness of the object, may be perfectly experienced
only when the object of the love is utterly inaccessible and thus func-
tionally irrelevant.

Kierkegaard's analysis suggests serious discontinuities between at
least some features of traditional interpretations of agape on the one
hand and persons' intuitions about and experiences of love on the
other. It is surely the case that the love command is unconditional and
that agape cannot depend for its obligating power upon the vicissitudes
of the individual preference of the agent or the charm of the recipient.
However, agape as the tradition described by Outka has interpreted it
ends by erasing the persons that are supposed to be beloved. Radical
impartiality mustered in service of radical equality may, and in
Kierkegaard's thought does, render invisible and even irrelevant the
life that agape is presumably supposed to celebrate and support.

What are some of the philosophical and psychological assumptions
of the tradition? Space limitations preclude my doing more than indicating them, but they are widely discussed and have been developed in
more detail elsewhere. First, as Outka notes, there is deep suspicion
on the part of the traditional agapist of the extent and effects of self-
interest. Underlying that suspicion is an understanding of the human
person as essentially separate from and in some fundamental way in
competition with other persons.[12] Each person's 'interests' are understood and described in metaphors of conflict; the picture that emerges
is the now familiar Western liberal individualistic anthropology.

Whence this characterization? It may be suggestive at this point to
note the substantial overlap between the depiction of agape as equal
regard and the Kantian principle of respect for persons which is one
articulation of Kant's emphasis on autonomy as the distinctively moral
feature of human being.[13] The traditional agapist whose shadow can be
discerned through his impartiality and detached magnanimity is
brother to if not identical with the 'liberal man' of John Rawls or
Alisdair MacIntyre's liberal tradition.[14] As with Kant and his descen-
dants in the Western liberal political tradition, the emphasis on
autonomy and detachment from specific features of specific lives
brings with it a concomitant deemphasis on relationality and particularity. While acknowledging that there is indeed material overlap
between the content of agape and the Kantian principle of respect for
persons, we must still question the effect of the Kantian ontology on
normative formulations of agape.[15]

The second range of questions raised by Kierkegaard's analysis has
to do with the appropriateness of detachment as the fundamental atti-

tude for loving. Kierkegaard's position is extreme, but by its very exaggeration it alerts us to the issue of the dissonance between our experience of love on the one hand and the traditional features of and obligations entailed by agape on the other. Between any ordinary human experience of loving and the nature and demands of agape lies a thicket of complex theological issues; I claim no necessarily direct access from the one to the other. What I am suggesting is that the traditional interpretation of agape as detached and disinterested raises questions about what can loosely be called moral psychology. As Gene Outka articulates so well, one of the tasks of any presentation of normative agape is to hold together impartiality and uniqueness, or in other words, to uphold the fundamental value and dignity of every concrete human life. That fundamental value and dignity are prior to any judgments we may make regarding the content of that life, and they make demands and place constraints upon our attitudes and actions toward every human person. Yet the shape and occasion of our responding in Christian love are always dependent upon a context, always embedded in the messy, rich, deeply invested moments of human experience. Given the inevitable conjunction of immediate reality with its immediate obligation to love and the potentially universal scope of that obligation, it may be the case that a better description than detachment can be found to characterize the attitude that agape enjoins and that is better able to facilitate persons responding with Christian love. Jumping ahead of the argument, the nursery might better replace the graveyard as agape's school room.

The agapic normative tradition represented by Outka and exemplified in the extreme by Kierkegaard is very uneasy about special relations. In Outka's words,

> ... obligations pertaining to [special relations] may become the effective center of gravity, so urgent and really ultimate that they swamp universal human dignity as such.[16]

He goes on to say that the agapist's suspicion of human nature and special relations lead 'him' to 'begin at the other end, with the negative restraints and positive injunctions applicable in any human relation.'[17]

These suspicions are persuasive. They appeal to our experience of the difficulty humans have in loving anyone well, never mind the towering obstacles to loving everyone well. One could multiply ad nauseam examples of and reasons for love's inadequacy to perform or produce what love has promised. Furthermore, when love fails us, our own or another's, the traditional agapist correctly points out that we tend to pull back, shorten our reach, become more defensive and less responsive to neighbors as well as to strangers. We *are* self-referential creatures, and the other regard that agape enjoins is indeed difficult.

These are not so much philosophical claims as they are insights of moral psychology. Their persuasive power develops at the level of human experience, at its best and at its worst, one can share the traditional agapist's suspicion of the human ability to love truly and well and be equally suspicious of the picture of the lover to which the agapist would have us refer. That is, we need not hold an elevated opinion of human nature or the possibilities of human love in order to question and even to reject the exegetical and experiential adequacy of the traditional agapist's picture of the agapic lover.

It is to experience that we all must appeal for the persuasive power of our claims about what is humanly possible. If we reflect on different experiences, we shall develop different notions of and models for agape. This fundamental insight of feminist methodology applies to Kierkegaard and other traditional interpretations of agape as it does to contemporary feminists.

In the love command itself there is reference to human experience: 'as you love yourself.' Outka's study offers an excellent summary and analysis of the ways in which various Christian thinkers have interpreted the role of self-love in relation to agape.[18] I will not engage that conversation but will offer instead another experience of human love that can function as an experiential model and foundation for agape: a mother's love for her children.[19]

Mother-love as a Model for Agape

Prior to describing some of the features of mother-love that are helpful in identifying an alternative to Kierkegaard's model for agapic love, some qualifications are in order. First, I am aware of the danger to *mothers* of romanticizing them, us, and it is not my intention to do so. I am convinced of the value of the distinction between the implacable ideal of 'motherhood,' which all too often bludgeons real mothers with their shortcomings, and the difficult, challenging and often confusing work of mothering.[20]

I need, however, to make a further distinction, that between 'mothering' and 'mother-love.' Borrowing a term from classical ethical theory, 'mothering' as discussed by Adrienne Rich, Nancy Chodorow, Sara Ruddick and others[21] is a 'practice,' a rich assortment of attitudes and behaviors that coalesce around intrinsic goals and values.[22] The concrete experience of 'mothering' covers a much broader spectrum of attitudes and behaviors than I will address in my discussion of mother-love; in other words, 'mothering' involves a lot more than loving. There is much in my experience of mothering that is more informative about the nature of resentment, or boredom, or the panic of being trapped, than about love. The mix is beautifully captured by this entry from Adrienne Rich's journal:

> To be caught up in waves of love and hate, jealousy even of the child's childhood; hope and fear for its maturity; longing to be free of responsibility, tied by every fibre of one's being.[23]

To speak of mother-love is not to encompass the experience of mothering. However, if I am to avoid the danger of courting the very romanticism about mothers that I formally reject, I must place mother-love in the broader context of mothering with its panoply of feelings and attitudes. It is not the experience of *mothering* per se that offers a model for agape but only the mother-love which in my case undergirds the practice and explodes with intensity and clarity only sporadically in the midst of so much else. The mother-love that I will describe is a love experienced to a greater or lesser degree, and my experience offers glimpses of a love that I often fail to embody and enact. It is not, then a romantic impulse that generates my discussion of mother-love as a model for agape. Rather it is the fragmentary and awkwardly expressed but nonetheless powerful experience of that love that impels my analysis.

Is it legitimate to isolate mother-love, even analytically, from the rest of what mothers do and to use that love as a model for agape? I can answer affirmatively because it is my experience that mother-love announces itself with a voice that is not drowned out by the inevitable chorus that surrounds it, a chorus composed of other feelings, immense distractions, deadening trivia. The voice is not always audible, certainly, but the occasions when I hear it, when I am speaking with it, are full of energy and clarity. Love never happens apart from the lively chaos that is the tangle of a busy day, but it cannot be reduced to that tangle. Mother-love is not all there is in my relationship with my children, but it is there, and it is distinctive and recognizable.[24]

With the above qualifications in mind, let us explore the possibility that mother-love can function as a model for agape. What are the common features of a mother's love for her children that are relevant to agape? First, mother-love is inclusive. It is dependent upon the mother-child relationship but is independent of the specific characteristics of the child. There is a disposition on the mother's part to devote herself to the well-being of the child from birth and for its lifetime without knowing the particular talents or future achievements of that small person. The mother is prepared to and in fact does love that child whoever she or he turns out to be. Her regard for the child is both predicated upon the child's uniqueness and unmediated by the specific qualities of that child. Furthermore, mothers with more than one child often love them all 'the same' even though they are quite different and may not be equally appealing by any number of 'objective' standards. The inclusivity of mother-love must be juxtaposed to the preference that many mothers feel for one of their children over another. I do not always *like* my children equally, but my fundamental commitment to their well-being does not depend upon the appeal of their personalities at any given time.[25]

Second, the love is both intensely involved and other-regarding. At times there is no clear line between the needs of the lover and the needs of the beloved. The needs of the child as expressed in cries of different volume and tone are experienced by the mother as in some sense internal to her own being. Her child's hunger is as demanding of her response as her own, or more so. While the needs of the child may conflict with the needs of the mother, and often do, there are instances when the interests of the child and the interests of the mother coincide. That is, the *mother's need* may be to feed the child, comfort her, rock him, etc. There is no inevitably competitive structure between the mother and child, though competition can and does arise. The relationship is basically cooperative. Furthermore, the mother's actions with regard to the child are primarily and fundamentally responsive to the child's needs, though she may initiate activities. She is acting largely on behalf of the other in response to the other's signals of need. As a corollary to the intense and other-regarding nature of mother-love, it is important to note that the acts of love must change constantly and rather dramatically, at least in the childhood years, in response to the rapidly changing nature of the child, and that this change is accommodated nicely by the constancy of the love itself.[26]

Modern psychology in many forms envisions the process of human maturation as one of 'separation' from one's parents and particularly from one's mother. That conceptualization might suggest that the intensity of mother-love would diminish as the child grows and that in its mature state, agape would be transformed from intensity into detachment. My experience suggests that while the needs of the child change, and thus the deeds of love change, the sense of connectedness, the commitment to the well-being of the child (of whatever age), and the intensity of the love do not diminish. My children are now teenagers, so I cannot speak personally about the experience of being mother to an adult. I do know that thus far their needs shape my response, including their need for freedom. I experience both the joy of their growing competence to manage their own lives and the anguish of watching their failures, stifling my urge to rescue them (or trying to) on behalf of their need to learn that they can survive failure and remain intact. Their growing independence does not engender my detachment.

Third, mother-love is unconditional. It is not dependent upon nor can it be cancelled by the behavior of the child. A mother can experience intense pain as a result of her child's activities. She can and does suffer with a suffering child. She can and does attempt to correct attitudes and behaviors that do not accord with her values, or her understanding of what her child's well being entails. Even if all her efforts fail, and when her child fails, she continues to love no matter how far her child departs from her interests and her plans for her or his life. The interest that the mother has in her child's 'success' on her own terms does not destroy her love for the child, though it certainly causes pain and probably strained relations. It may be that her love leads her to understand and accept the projects of her child, or conflict may continue. In any case, the difference does not destroy the love. Furthermore, the love is not 'located in the agent' as Kierkegaard's account would have it; it remains intensely other oriented. It is *that* child with all the joy and the pain that is the focus of the love.

It may be important to reiterate at this point that mothers do not manage in any sustained way what I am describing as mother-love. Under the best circumstances, mother-love is only one feature of mothering, a complex of feelings and attitudes and behaviors and relationships many of which have origins very different from love in any form. Furthermore, rarely is mothering done 'under the best circumstances.' Perhaps nowhere is the conjunction of the personal and the political experienced more powerfully than in the practice of mothering. The distortions, the evils, of racism, classism, sexism, heterosexism, poverty, isolation, drugs, disease, powerlessness that often characterize the context of mothering in our culture can, I would argue, be so powerful as to eradicate mother-love. The love is not magical. Yet there are moments, even whole stages of life in many less than ideal lives, where the other-directed, intensely caring mother-love is experienced by mother and the experience has heuristic value in relation to agape.

Both the traditional interpretation of agape as disinterested equal regard and my model of mother-love claim to be expositions of Christian love, love whose narrative roots are in Scripture. Which description of agape better accounts for the features of Christian love?

Agape in Scripture

What *do* the Scriptures tell us about the normative content of agape? Specifically what can we learn about the relationship between love for specific, concrete persons who may have special claims on us and the other-regarding 'love in general' that is abstracted from and independent from anyone in particular?[27]

In contemporary discussions, 'love command' may refer to one, or more, of three new Testament formulations: love your neighbor, love your enemies, and do to others what you would have them do to you. These three agapic commands are related, but it is important not to conflate them. They are not identical, and the most important formulation in our dialogue with the ethical agapic tradition is 'love your neighbor.'

The prominent formulation upon which discussions of neighbor-love are based is found in all three synoptic Gospels. Here is Mark's version, closely paralleled in Matthew and Luke:

> And one of the scribes came up and heard them disputing with one another, and seeing that he answered them well, asked him, 'Which commandment is the first of all?' Jesus answered, 'The first is, 'Hear O Israel: The Lord our God, the Lord is one; and you shall love the Lord your God with all your heart, and with all your soul, and with all your

mind, and with all your strength.' The second is this, 'You shall love your neighbor as yourself.' There is no other commandment greater than these.' (Mark 12:28–31)[28]

The command to love the neighbor is strongly tied to the command to love God, though the contours of the connection remain unclear.[29] I will avoid the complexities of the relationship between love for God and love for neighbor; however it will be necessary to note, though not to explore, the theological context of the command to love our neighbors.

How should we interpret the command to love our neighbor? Fortunately Scripture offers an answer, or at least a response to that question, in the famous story of the good Samaritan found in Luke 10:29–37.

The story is prompted by the question of a lawyer, 'seeking to justify himself,' presumably seeking to establish the conditions under which it could be said that he had obeyed the dual love command. 'And who is my neighbor?' he asked, questioning the scope of the command. Jesus, as is so often the case, answers a slightly different question from the one he is asked. It has been widely noted that while the lawyer's question is posed in terms of the recipient of agape, Jesus answers in terms of the agent.[30] There is another shift as well. With his description of the *indifference* of the priest and the Levite, Jesus dismantles any expectation that 'neighbor' can be defined on ethnic or religious grounds. On the other hand, it is important to notice that Jesus assumes that the listener understands 'neighbor' as a social category, and based upon that understanding s/he brings certain expectations to the story upon which Jesus can then play. Jesus had to assume an understanding that he could then subvert; the commonsense understanding is logically prior to its revision.

Jesus then introduces the Samaritan, an unexpected examplar for neighborliness to his Hebrew audience. The Samaritan goes on to illustrate the *behavior* that constitutes the definition of a neighbor. It turns out that 'neighbor' as a social category has been replaced in this story by 'neighbor' as a behavioral category, and Jesus', or Luke's choice of a Samaritan to exemplify the behavior underscores the transition. Furthermore, the behavior that becomes the content of the category 'neighbor' also becomes normative, at least for the lawyer; at the end of the story Jesus says to him, 'Go and do likewise.'

We know that Jesus' revision of the commonsense understanding of 'neighbor' begins by claiming that 'neighbor' is not a social category but a behavioral one. That is, a neighbor is someone who acts like a neighbor. Did, then, the Samaritan fulfill the behavioral expectations for a neighbor? He begins that way, with compassion and attention to the stricken man's immediate needs. He binds his wounds and delivers him to an inn where he could be cared for. But then the story goes on to say that he stayed overnight at the inn with him, gave the innkeeper money to cover what had already been spent, and promised to pay whatever additional expenses the wounded man incurred, *without limit*.

The second part of the story mirrors and intensifies the first. Just as the expectations for identifying a neighbor based upon social categories are broken by the priest and the Levite, so the expectations for identifying a neighbor based upon a commonsense understanding of neighborly behavior are broken by the Samaritan, not by unfulfillment but by overfulfillment. The Samaritan was not behaving like a neighbor in incurring unlimited liability for the expenses and needs of the wounded man; he was behaving like a lover.

Notice again what has happened to the lawyer's original question about *whom* he should love as a neighbor. It has been augmented with a response to the question of *how* he is to love his neighbor, and the response goes well beyond anything he would normally expect a neighbor to do. This parable exhibits a feature common to all of Jesus' parables: extravagance. Jesus has begun with everyday, ordinary expectations about who people are and how they are to behave and has undermined those expectations in the direction of extravagant, compassionate, dedicated care based not upon specific 'idiosyncratic' features of the wounded man but only on his need.

Where would Jesus' listeners have encountered such care, either as agents or as recipients? They would know of this love in their most intimate, loving relationships, with family members, friends, lovers – the 'special relations' about which the agapic tradition that Kierkegaard exemplifies is so suspicious. Just as people feel shock when priests and compatriots are callous and uncaring, so there is shock value in seeing neighbors act like lovers. And that shock depends upon knowing the difference between neighbors and lovers.

Far from positing an inevitable conflict between the content and scope of agape on the one hand and that of 'special relations' on the other, Jesus' parable reports the closest connection. Far from indifference to the particularity of the recipient of agape, the injured man's needs provided the pattern for the Samaritan's care. One point of the parable is that there was nothing about the identity of the wounded man that obligated in particular the attitude and behavior of the Samaritan. This is the point that the agape tradition has chosen to emphasize. However, there is at least one other point to the story: the neighbor is to behave like a lover. Rather than suggesting that special relations are in substantive conflict with the demands of agape, this parable sugests that the one is the model for the other.[31]

Mother-love Revisited

Luke's parable is not describing mother-love, but it is possible to draw some significant parallels between it and the love shown by the Samaritan. Like the Samaritan, a mother responds in love to whatever children she may have regardless of their individual characteristics. Like the Samaritan, her acts of love are primarily responsive to the needs of her children; they are other-regarding in nature even when responding to the child's needs interferes with some agenda of her own.[32] Like the Samaritan she is a lover when she can be, unconcerned about what legal requirements there may be with regard to her behavior but rather focused on the immediacy of the demands that she attempts to meet. Like the Samaritan, her attitude toward those she cares for is not one of detachment but of intense involvement. Detachment might fail to reveal what it is she needs to see in order to respond in love.

At this point we may begin to hear echoes of Outka's concern that the demands of special relations 'may become the effective center of gravity, so urgent and really ultimate that they swamp universal human dignity as such.'[33] Is it not odd to recommend as a model for agape a form of love that can be as consuming, physically, emotionally, psychologically, even morally as mother-love? Does not mother-love so eclipse concerns for others that there is in fact a conflict betwen mothers' love for their children and considerations of the needs, even rights of others? Is not mother-love the *narrowest* rather than the broadest scope love could have?

The objections would be fatal were I equating mother-love and agape. That is not my position. Rather I am suggesting that mother-love can provide an excellent model for the content of agape. I am suggesting that agape fully experienced would be similar to mother-love extended to the whole of humanity. Put another way, I am suggesting that the second part of the love command could fruitfully be restated as, 'Love your neighbor as a mother loves her children,' with the caveat that the mother-love be healthy and unimpeded by social discrimination of any number of kinds. I will return to this point.

The problems of scope that the mother-love model highlights can be related to the problems that Jesus responded to in his parable of the good Samaritan. The type of activities that mothers engage in on behalf of their children go as far beyond our ordinary expectations of neighborly behavior as did the actions of the Samaritan. If the person lying wounded in the road were her child, we would expect that the mother would respond with whatever care the child required that it was in her power to provide. But if it were not her child? Then the requirements of agape would tell her that she was obligated to respond, and her experiences of mother-love would provide the information she would need about what the response would entail. She may learn from her love for her children how she is to respond to the stranger.

If the 'self' that the mainstream agapic tradition has described as the model for agape is remote, distant, detached, the self that expresses mother-love is present, connected, involved, intensely caring. The problems that the former model has in expressing the *content* of agape in any experientially meaningful way are paralleled by the problems the latter model has in moving agape beyond her small circle to encompass all the persons she meets or could ever meet.[34]

It is appropriate at this point to invoke skepticism about the possibility of responding to all persons whose needs we encounter with the love with which we respond to our children when we respond to them in love. It is one of the strengths of the mother-love model that it confronts us with the real life difficulty we do in fact experience as we attempt to live out the love command. The challenge of agape as a normative claim is not to empty our consciouness of the particularities of persons around us nor to devise some way to love persons generically. The challenge is to be fully mindful of the concrete realities of persons and to respond in love.

There are legitimate limits based on human finitude that the traditional understanding of agape has allowed. Those limits would apply to mother-love as a model for agape and would in fact be taken with great seriousness as part of the emphasis upon the concrete realities of concrete persons. Nonetheless, loving everyone as we love our children is a hard command; that formulation focuses on exactly the difficulties that the story of the good Samaritan exemplifies. Thus, the mother-love model for agape is in fundamental agreement with the tradition outlined and represented by Outka in identifying the problem of self-absorbed persons trying to live out the command to love our neighbors. However, the analysis of the problem and the proposed solution are different. Rather than rejecting special relations as hopelessly contaminated by self-interest, the mother-love model offers an experiential instance of intense and very special love that nonetheless has heuristic value for agape. No perfect examples are experientially available, but the fragments are sufficient to sculpt the agapic model.[35]

Does mother-love have heuristic value for those who have not been mothers? Probably not. I am not claiming that mother-love functions well as a model for nonmothers. It may be that persons who have received mother-love, however imperfectly, can form the moral consciousness engendered in the experience of mothering, but perhaps not. It is my experience as a mother that has given birth to this model. In any case, I am not arguing that mother-love is the *only* agapic model in human experience; it is not even the only model in my experience, though it is the most powerful. Rather it is one rich example of a special relation that is a partner, rather than a threat, to agape. Mother-love is embedded in the practice of mothering; the practice of mothering is embedded in the institution of motherhood. If mother-love is one window to agape, as I have argued, then Christian ethics is required by the centrality of agape to dismantle the institution and to reform the practice so that mother-love can be nurtured, not stifled or assassinated by the oppressive context in which it is lived out.[36] There is no inherent contradiction between mother-love and agape; in fact, there are significant and informative parallels, both conceptual and experiential. Christian ethics need not continue to gaze with a suspicious stare on the 'special relation' between mother and child but rather needs to be engaged in eliminating the distortions, the evils, that make the ongoing experiences of mother-love seem miraculous.[37] Mother-love requires from Christian ethics neither control nor tempering; it demands the simple step of nurturing, with justice as well as love, women who are mothers, which requires, of course, nurturing all women. Unfortunately, the tradition often seems not to understand the connection between the well-being of all women and the well-being of mothers and thus nurtures neither, in spite of its centuries of preoccupation with agape.

In this essay I have sought to clarify the content of the obligation to love the neighbor, not to render a verdict on its power or possibility. My arguments are in concert with those of feminists who have challenged the interpretations of agape that would characterize it as exclusively or predominantly self-sacrificial and who have stressed instead its mutuality based upon women's experience of loving. Likewise mother-love presents itself as a more fruitful model for agape than 'the work of love in remembering one who is dead.' Based upon both exegetical and experiential evidence, indifferent universality is eclipsed by caring intensity as the ethical focus of agape.

Notes

1. From Augustine to Garth Hallett's recent study (*Christian Neighbor-Love; An Assessment of Six Rival Versions* [Washington: Georgetown University Press, 1989]) the tradition has focused on the relationship between love for God, love for self, and love for others. Whether, as in Augustine's case, special relations are easily accommodated in the *ordo amoris* (*Christian Doctrine*, trans. J. Shaw in *Nicene and Post-Nicene Fathers*, vol. 2), or as with Gene Outka (*Agape: An Ethical Analysis* [New Haven: Yale University Press, 1972]) and Søren Kierkegaard (*Works of Love: Some Christian Reflections in the Form of Discourses*, trans. Howard and Edna Hong [New York: Harper Torchbooks, 1962]) they are viewed with suspicion, to my knowledge there has been no articulation of a specifically *positive* role for special relationships in the understanding of agape.

2. Feminist methodology exposes the standpoint-dependent nature of all knowledge and explicitly develops the centrality of women's experience for our reflections. The literature that articulates this methodology is vast; I will note some central texts in theology and ethics. For two classic treatments, see *Womanspirit Rising: A Feminist Reader in Religion*, ed. Carol P. Christ and Judith Plaskow (San Francisco: Harper and Row, 1979), especially section I, and Rosemary Radford Ruether, *Sexism and God-Talk: Toward a Feminist Theology* (Boston: Beacon Press, 1983), especially chapter 1. See also Sallie McFague, *Models of God: Theology for an Ecological, Nuclear Age* (Philadelphia: Fortress Press, 1987), Beverly Harrison, *Our Right to Choose: Toward a New Ethic of Abortion* (Boston: Beacon Press, 1983), bell hooks, *Feminist Theory: From Margin to Center* (Boston: South End Press, 1984).

3. For other critiques of 'radical disinterest' as a model for human relationships, see Christine Gudorf, 'Parenting, Mutual Love, and Sacrifice,' Ruth Smith, 'Feminism and the Moral Subject,' and Catherine Keller, 'Feminism and the Ethic of Inseparability' in *Women's Consciousness, Women's Conscience: A Reader in Feminist Ethics*, ed. Barbara Hilkert Andolsen, Christine E. Gudorf, and Mary D. Pellauer (Minneapolis: Winston Press, 1985). Also see Caroline Whitbeck, 'A Different Reality: Feminist Ontology' in *Beyond Domination: New Perspectives on Women and Philosophy*, ed. Carol C. Gould (Totowa, N.J.: Roman and Allanheld, 1983), Carol Gilligan, *In A Different Voice: Psychological Theory and Women's Development* (Cambridge: Harvard University Press, 1982), and Jean Baker Miller, *Toward a New Psychology of Women* (Boston: Beacon Press, 1978).

4. See note 1.

5. Outka, 260.

6. Ibid., 9.

7. Ibid., 55–74.
8. Ibid., 12.
9. Kierkegaard, 328. Caps in the original.
10. Ibid., 317.
11. Ibid., 323.
12. See works cited in note 3 for a critique of this conception of the human person.
13. Outka notes numerous times the resemblance between Kant and his own understanding of agape, but he does not articulate the ontological or anthropological commitments a Kantian position entails.
14. The masculine language is intentional. The 'liberal man' is not a generic concept. See Whitbeck's article cited in note 3.
15. Whitbeck, 67.
16. Outka, 272.
17. Ibid., 273.
18. Ibid., 55–74.
19. I am not arguing that mother-love ought to *replace* 'love of self' as the experiential referent for the love command, only that it can offer another experience of human love that is a valuable source of information about agape. How one characterizes the relationship between self-love and mother-love will largely depend, of course, on how one interprets the nature of self-love and its role in agapic love for others.
20. The distinction was made by Adrienne Rich, *Of Woman Born: Motherhood as Experience and Institution* (New York: W.W. Norton, 1976), see especially chapter 10, pp, 256–80 and by Sara Ruddick, *Maternal Thinking: Toward a Politics of Peace* (Boston: Beacon Press, 1989), 28–57.
21. Rich, *Of Woman Born*, Nancy Chodorow, *The Reproduction of Mothering* (Berkeley: University of California Press, 1978).
22. As cited in Allen Verhey, 'The Doctor's Oath – And a Christian Swearing It,' in *On Moral Medicine: Theological Perspectives in Medical Ethics*, ed. Stephen Lammers and Allen Verhey (Grand Rapids, Mich.: W.G. Eerdman's Publishing Company, 1987), 74.
23. Rich, 22.
24. A further qualification may be indirectly relevant regarding my claims. In the Christian tradition, the command to love one's neighbor is embedded in a thoroughly theological context: the context for agapic love for neighbor is total love for God, 'with all your heart and with all your soul and with all your mind and with all your strength.' The undoubtedly complex relationship between the two parts of the dual love command is not specified by the command itself. What we can establish is that love for one's neighbor is normatively fashioned as inexorably tied to love for God. Thus, on the experiential level, claims about agape are confined to those who love God. Agapic lovers are not, of course, exclusively Christian. They are, however, theocentric. Thus the perspective becomes definitive. From the perspective of God-lovers, no one is exempt from the command to love God, and thus the population of those who are required to love the neighbor encompasses everyone. On the other hand, if one does not love God, then the requirement to love the neighbor will not be experienced as an obligation, though neighbor-regarding obligations may be established on philosophical grounds.
25. See Adrienne Rich's discussion of the particular difficulty feminists in this culture may face in liking their sons (pp. 205–217).
26. For an expanded discussion of the role of change in mothering, see Ruddick, 89–93.
27. Agape was not invented by Christians. The love command as articulated by Jesus has its origins in the Old Testament. (I am aware of the problems associated with the terminology of 'old' and 'new' testaments, but I have found no satisfactory replacement.) The first part of the love command, the command to love God, is found in Deuteronomy 6:4–6. The second part, the command to love one's neighbor as oneself, is in Leviticus 19:18. While one could argue that the entire Hebrew Scriptures are a statement and an explication of the first part of the love command and an attempt to work out its relationship to and implications for the second, the commands are explicitly stated only these two times, and never together. It is interesting to speculate whether Jesus was the first to combine them. The noun *agape* and forms of the verb *agapeo* together appear over two hundred fifty times in the New Testament; the importance of the concept is suggested if not demonstrated by its frequency.
28. Luke's version (10:25–28) does not use the 'first ... second' language, but it does include the much fuller specification of commitment to God found in Mark's and Matthew's formulations; Matthew's text follows Mark in using the 'first ... second' distinction. All scriptural

quotes are from the RSV.

29. The command to love the neighbor is found once in the New Testament apart from the command to love God, Matthew 19:19, in a context reminiscent of its setting in Leviticus.That is, it appears in a short list of negative and positive obligations to other persons. All of the other injunctions in Matthew's list are from the Ten Commandments.

30. See, for example, Eduard Schweizer, *The Good News According to Luke*, trans. David E. Green (Atlanta: John Knox Press, 1984), 169.

31. Of course it is the case that the demands of a special relation will conflict with the demands of agape in terms of finitude. The Samaritan would have neither the time nor presumably the money to treat every mugging victim in first century Palestine the way he treated the man in the story. The Scripture simply does not deal with that issue.

32. The problem that mothers have balancing their own needs and the needs of their children, particularly small children, has not received the professional attention I hope it will. We know of it largely through the 'child care crisis,' a phrase that masks much anguish and a litany of lived tragedies, large and small.

33. Outka, 272.

34. It is an unjustifiable exaggeration to extend the demands of the love command to 'all persons,' though it does apply to all the persons with whom I come into contact. What could 'love' in that case possibly mean? On the other hand, in this shrinking world in which the actions of persons especially in developed nations have such impact on persons in other nations, the demands of agape can be extended to include all those who could be affected by my actions.

35. Questions about the extent to which persons can, do and will actually fulfill the demands of the dual love command can only be partly addressed in the realm of moral psychology or ordinary human experience. Those questions return us to the theological context in which the command is given, and heard. Does the neighbor see the neighbor differently so that the neighbor is easier to love? Is the lover of God somehow enabled by the practice of loving God to love the neighbour? Does the lover of God experience God's love in ways that ease or even impel love for the neighbour? This tangle of questions and others that could be raised are beyond the scope of this convention.

36. See the last chapter of Rich's *Of Woman Born* (cited above) for one case study of the institutional annihilation of mother-love.

37. It would be interesting to investigate the relationship between the Christian tradition's suspicion of sexuality in general and its homophobia in particular as they relate to traditional interpretations of agape, but I am unable to pursue the issue here.

6.2 The Lion and the Unicorn: Feminist Perspectives on Christian Love as Care

Jennifer L. Rike

Theology has undergone a Galilean revolution in the past two centuries as the impact of the Kantian critique upon metaphysical knowledge has reverberated throughout its disciplined reflections. Recognition of the limits placed upon human knowing by its inherent structures has not, however, simply shattered prior pretentions to absolute knowledge of God; it has also served to clarify the nature of the theological task. This task is now understood to be an essentially hermeneutical one: theology is the interpretation of the Christian fact or mythos[1] in light of an interpretation of contemporary human experience. The theological viewpoint expressed is always relative to the particular perspective upon experience invoked in the interpretation. Consequently, no absolute viewpoint upon the whole is possible, only moving viewpoints fully conscious of the conditions upon which they stand.

In the past thirty years, women have become increasingly concerned that the interpretations of human experience employed historically in the Christian traditions reflect the gender of their interpreters. Up until this time, most Christian theologians (or at least, those theologians trained for the academy and influential in defining orthodoxy) have been male, white and Western; consequently, their understandings not only of experience but of the Christian tradition have been at best one-sided portrayals, at worst systematic distortions of the human condition which ultimately serve to exploit and oppress women and minorities. Convinced that continuing to understand self, God and world in established traditional fashions would threaten the very survival of the world, many women have joined other groups in attempting to reinterpret their faith in accordance with more inclusive interpretations of human experience.

This commitment to making women's experience a source for theological reflection has coincided with an upsurge of research in a number of disciplines into the distinctiveness of women's experience. Feminist theologians have turned to literature, history, sociology and developmental psychology, in addition to other cultural and religious perspectives, to determine what experiences might be distinctive to women in order to gain renewed insight into what it means to be human.* Since love in the Christian tradition is the power of God present and active in existence to heal, reconcile and reunite humanity with itself and with its divine ground, reflection upon the proper expression of that power through human agency has occurred in tandem with reflection upon the nature of being human. Recognizing sexist distortions in the traditional accounts of the human, some women have criticized the related, traditional views of love for being androcentric and so oppressive to women and minorities, and a few have attempted reformulations of the traditional views in terms freed from sexist bias.

Unfortunately, most of the feminist critiques rendered thus far have failed to follow through with constructive proposals grounded in more adequate interpretations of human experience and of the Christian traditions. Usually they suggest a couple of criteria or attributes which a more adequate conception of love must possess to make up for the inadequacies of the androcentric versions. While all offer valuable insights into the nature of love, none has attempted to develop a complete and systematic account of it from a self-consciously feminist perspective. Indeed, the scope and complexity of such a project is fairly daunting, and cannot be attempted here either.

Still, I propose to undertake the first step in that direction by identifying the dilemma central to androcentric conceptions of Christian love by analyzing the main Christian traditions on love in light of some feminist critiques of them. That dilemma depends upon an inadequate conception of the nature of humanity, one distorted by a typically male perception of experience. It can be resolved only by recourse to a revised conception of humanity informed by insights into the human condition suggested by distinctively female experience. Garnering the insights of my sister theologians, I will demonstrate how a reformulated conception of Christian love as care is grounded in a revised conception of humanity and in different strands in the Christian tradition than those to which the traditions typically appeal. What follows exemplifies feminist theological method as well as the heart of the reformist, feminist vision of Christian existence; an existence in which both genders and all races live in an egalitarian and holistically structured world.

The Critique:
The Lion and the Unicorn Fighting 'Round the Town

In her now classic article, 'The Human Situation: A Feminine View,'[2] Valerie Saiving launched the feminist critique of Christian (most especially, neo-orthodox) doctrines of sin and grace by arguing that Christian theologians had systematically distorted them by developing them through reflection upon their own, distinctively male experience. Although her approach has been criticized for suggesting a kind of biological determinism, her main points have been accepted and further developed by others.[3] Drawing upon the insights of developmental psychologists, anthropologists and historians throughout her article, Saiving argues that the developmental processes of little girls and little boys are distinctively different in ways which decisively influence their character structures and their perceptions of reality. Both little girls and little boys identify with their mothers as infants, but when their psycho-sexual identities begin to develop, their ways part.

Girls learn that they need only wait for their femininity to emerge for their sexual identity to be secure: virtually without any effort on their part, their most distinctively feminine trait, their child-bearing capacity, will slowly mature. They need only to continue to act in accordance with their initial identification with their mothers and to fulfill the prevailing social expectations that they become wives and mothers to corroborate further their identities as women. As a result, women tend to develop essentially passive character structures, passive ways of dealing with and responding to reality.

In contrast to little girls, however, boys learn very early on that to be male, to be a *man*, means to be not like a mummy but like daddy. To be a man means they must break with their initial identification with their mothers, leave the private safety of the home, and develop some sort of athletic, occupational or professional expertise which will ensure their place and status in the public world. Moreover, unlike women who have the indisputable evidence of their femininity in the children they mother, fatherhood is a far less permanent and secure proof of masculinity. Young men learn that they must prove themselves to be masculine again and again, every time anew, in sexual relation-ships. As a result, men tend to develop active character structures, assertive ways of dealing with and responding to reality.

These differences in character structure, Saiving argues, make men and women prone to different types of sin. The active character struc-ture renders men more prone to the sins of pride and arrogance, of being not just assertive but aggressive and ruthlessly competitive, manipulating persons as objects for selfish ends rather than respecting them as persons in their own right. On the other hand, women's rela-tively passive character structures have rendered them prone to what Saiving terms 'feminine forms of sin,' the sins which result from the relative inability to assert or develop the self – triviality, lack of an organizing center, over-dependence on others for a sense of self, and so on.[4]

Until recently, male theologians have presumed to speak for all of humanity when formulating what saves humanity from sin in diametri-cally opposed terms: if self-interested exploitation of others, pride and egotism are sinful, then perfectly self-sacrificial love saves us from sin. But women who already tend to be self-effacing and -sacrificial do not *need* to hear that to have pride is sinful, while to humble them-selves in self-sacrificial service to others is the only saving way. Needless to say, this emphasis upon the self-sacrificial character of Christian love, especially in Protestant understandings of Christian love as *agape*, has all too often led women down the paths not just of triviality but of self-destruction.[5]

Now it has frequently been believed that the Christian moral tradition's emphasis upon the self-sacrificial character of love distinguishes it from all others.[6] Certainly, Jesus did insist that the first commandment is to love God with all of our mind, heart and soul, and our neighbors as ourselves ... but how *did* he understand that prepositional 'as'? Typically, neighbor-love has been modeled after the kind of total self-surrender suggested by Jesus' sayings concerning the sacrifices required by discipleship[7] and his own act of obedient self-surrender on the cross to yield this emphasis upon self-sacrifice.

Feminists wishing to remain Christian but protesting such an exclusive emphasis upon self-sacrifice have appealed, if only implicitly, to two criteria of what is genuinely redemptive or revelatory of an authentic relation to the divine from a feminist perspective.[8] The first criterion for what is genuinely revelatory in feminist theology is that it must promote the full humanity of women. This in itself is nothing new: the Roman Catholic tradition has long insisted that grace fulfills nature, and does not negate it. But Catholicism's perception of human nature also suffered from androcentric bias, and so *de facto* excluded the second criterion of revelation from a feminist perspective, namely, that it must draw upon the distinctive experiences and insights of women as sources for theological reflection. From such a feminist perspective, the Christian doctrine of love as self-sacrificial other-regard must either be susceptible to radical reformulation or the Christian tradition must be deemed hopelessly patriarchal, sexist, and beyond redemption.

How can the Christian conception of love be reformulated to meet these criteria without forsaking the distinctive character of the Christian faith? The most obvious solution is to include a dimension of self-love and self-affirmation within a more comprehensive emphasis on self-sacrifice. Such a move highlights the mutuality which emerges in a genuinely self- and other-affirming relationship.[9]

One sign that this might be the right track is that discussions of self-love and mutuality have aroused no little confusion, controversy and conflict in the Christian tradition. Protestants have frequently opposed self-love to Christian *agape*, and been suspicious of any mutuality in neighbor-love for fear that it is a reward sought by the truly selfish.[10] Roman Catholic views of Christian love as *caritas* usually include properly ordered self-love as a dimension of true Christian love, but such understandings are typically found within dualistic and hierarchical visions of reality in which spirit is considered superior to matter, reason superior to emotion and sensuality. Within this type of perspective, affective, emotional and sexual needs must be subordinated to the 'higher' loves of God and of spiritual and intellectual endeavor. Moreover, within this perspective, women tend to be associated with the subordinate poles of the dualisms (with matter and the animal appetites, not with spirit and its goals); hence, the distinctive experiences and modes of behavior of women are often overlooked and underrated; often, idealized in a way which also ultimately denigrates the real thing.[11] All too often, a justifiable self-love is mentioned in passing and then forgotten. In brief, the controversy and confusion surrounding self-love in the Christian tradition has been fueled, on the one hand, by an androcentric suspicion of self-love as necessarily sinfully self-interested, and on the other, by dualistic, hierarchical and, in the final analysis, sexist modes of thought.

These dynamics reached their climactic self-expression in the twentieth century *agape-eros* controversy surrounding the book of that title by Anders Nygren.[12] So fearful was Nygren that selfishness and pride might sully God's pure gift of Godself in grace, that in his view *agape* or true Christian love, on the one hand, and self-love or *eros*, on the other, are purely antithetical. Humanity is only a funnel through which God sends God's love to the neighbor, and *caritas* is a hybrid monster of *agape* and *eros* which has nothing to do with Christian faith at all.[13]

Responding critically to this Lutheran Protestant perspective[14] from a more typically Roman Catholic one, in his book *The Mind and Heart of Love*[15] M.C. D'Arcy draws upon a wealth of historical, mythical and psychological data to argue that there are two loves, *eros* which is symbolized by the proud and powerful lion, and *agape* which is symbolized by the humble, fanciful unicorn. Far from being antithetical, these two loves must co-exist in equilibrium for the health and salvation of the person. The self-transcending and -surrendering centrifugal drive of *agape* must be counterbalanced by the self-assertive and -perfecting force of *eros*. If either type of love predominates, the results are equally destructive: too much *eros* engenders ruthless and aggressive egotism; too much *agape*, irrationalism and self-immolation.[16]

D'Arcy's analysis is distinguished by its unabashedly dualistic characterization of each love: *eros* or self-regarding love is rational, possessive, and assertive in its struggle for self-perfection; *agape* or other-regarding love is emotional, and giving to the point of being self-denying. While both types of love operate within both sexes (as anima and animus are present in every psyche),[17] the wealth of D'Arcy's analysis emphasizes how the female of every species willingly surrenders herself to her offspring for the sake of the continuation of the species; with regard to human beings, he continually valorizes mother-love.[18]

To his credit, D'Arcy highlights the necessity for elaborating the anthropological foundations of Christian love, and for attempting to specify the precise dynamics of *eros* and *agape*. But his simplistic opposition of reason to emotion and imagination, of taking to giving, and of self-assertion to self-sacrifice remains in the final analysis androcentric. He persistently distinguishes two competing loves, which must be unified and balanced in the individual, instead of considering them to be two dimensions of the dialectical dynamics of one love. This accentuates their presumably antithetical character, and reinforces the stereotypes of women as naturally self-sacrificial and of men as self-possessed and perfecting. From this perspective, *agape* and *eros* will always be, as Lewis Carroll writes, 'fighting 'round the town.' We might well note the appropriateness of D'Arcy's appeal to Carroll's account: the indefatigable Unicorn wins the skirmish, but the Lion, bone-weary but boisterous, refuses to admit defeat and ends up with twice as much cake as the rest.[19]

The Reconciliation of Lion and Unicorn: Feminist Christian Love as Care

Is it possible to reconcile the lion and the unicorn? *Eros* with *agape*? The self-regarding with the other-regarding dimensions of love? On first glance it would appear that it is not: to take something for oneself would seem to diminish what one has to give the other. If that is true, then someone is always the loser, and the best to be hoped for is that the loser is not always the same person, group or sex. But that way of formulating the dynamics of love is already distorted by androcentrism in the operative conception of selfhood, while the solution to this apparent dilemma lies within the insights into selfhood offered by distinctively feminine experience.

Consider D'Arcy's conception of the love which fulfills humankind: it achieves a balance between the out-going, centrifugal forces of self-transcendent agapic love, and the in-turning, centripetal forces of self-affirming, erotic love. But the image fails to inform precisely at the most crucial point: it suggests the image of a tornado – notoriously unstable, even evanescent entity – when an image for a balanced, centered and evolving entity is needed. Clearly, to understand the reality which heals and redeems in terms of two loves in precarious balance with one another is no solution. Again we are led to question the underlying assumption that taking for oneself diminishes what one has to give to the other. That assumption applies within a vision in which human beings are understood to be autonomous, self-motivating and -supporting agents. It is precisely this conception of selfhood that feminists challenge. Drawing upon a wealth of clinical data and their own experiences, they argue convincingly that to be a self is to be a self in relation – a self in multifarious modes of connection to other selves, a self constituted in and through these connections.[20]

Catherine Keller has drawn from a variety of disciplines to develop three models of selfhood – as separative, soluble and connective – which serve to highlight our point. She argues that the Western religious and philosophical traditions have tended to depict selfhood androcentrically in terms of the masculine mythic ideal of the solitary, wandering and conquering hero, Odysseus. This ideal has promoted a notion of separative selfhood, a self fulfilled in denying and severing affective ties by remaining distant and autonomous in seeking that elusive holy grail of personal fulfillment. Such an ideal suggests that to be influenced by others, much less to be tied down to them by bonds of commitment, is to diminish the self; only by denying the influence of others upon them, and by projecting the other outward where it can be easily possessed and controlled, does the separative self feel secure. Within this context, each self has all it needs to continue to fulfill its potentialities. To be a self is to separate oneself off from and in opposition to the other.[21]

The adequacy of this portrayal of the nature of selfhood is cast into doubt by the experiences of women who are required to provide for men at their own expense, the creative and sustaining connections which enable men to maintain their illusion of solitary independence. Separative selfhood requires a counterpart in 'soluble' selfhood, in women who spend their lives waiting patiently and impassively as Penelope did, weaving at her loom during the day and pulling apart her day's work in the night, for it is achieved only at the expense of the sacrifices of others, most especially, of women whose soluble selves can melt into their 'others' because they have no real self to lose. For these women, the unilateral direction of responsivity in such relationships has drained their energies, and become so absorbing as to swallow them.[22]

The growing testimony of developmental psychology has supported a notion of connective selfhood, or in its own terms, of self-in-relation. While one stream of tradition developed in response to Freud did recognize the importance of the relations of the infant to its primary caretakers by developing 'object-relation' theory, they have remained bound by a conception of selfhood as essentially separative: development toward maturity is understood to be toward greater separation, individuation, and autonomy.[23] In contrast, feminist psychologists have responded wth 'subject-in-relation theory,' in which development toward maturity is marked by greater relationship and differentiation. Moreover, the role of mutual empathy in relationship, a state in which each person in the relationship is openly receptive to (not manipulative of) the other as well as the self, is highlighted as integral to the ongoing construction and development of the self.[24]

This view of selfhood is not new; it is further confirmed by process philosophy and theology, and Keller combines the insights of all three disciplines to develop her notion of connective selfhood which, for our purposes, highlights the root fallacy in the assumption that self-regarding and other-regarding love need be in opposition to one another. If the self is not a hard, enclosed sphere, but rather a reality with permeable boundaries which *experiences* the other as other and yet as an internal, constitutive influence upon the self, then to give to the other is to enhance not only the other but the self. Attempting to describe the nature of the relational, connective self, Keller writes:

> I become who I am in and through and beyond the particular activity of connection. Connectivity lets the world in before the subject comes to

be; and the subject lets go the moment it has become. I am empowered by the energies of the others as my own past selves, or as the others of my world; I may exercise powerful influence upon the course of the supervening world; but my self is a structure of spontaneity, lacking the sort of solidity that controls self or other. It consolidates – becomes solid *with* its world – but it does not solidify as something apart. It may channel, inspire, tug, coalesce or plan ... [but not control or manipulate].[25]

What model of loving might we develop on the basis of this insight into selfhood as created and sustained by connections to other? In my estimation, the *agape* and *caritas* models are beyond saving. They are so loaded with connotations regarding the need for self-sacrifice and for the repression of affective, emotional and erotic dimensions of the self that any attempt to modify them will be overwhelmed by the weight of the traditions that surround them. Some feminists, wishing to emphasize the empowerment afforded by affective, reciprocal relationships, have chosen to reconstruct the conception of *philia*, friendship in the western traditions.[26] Friendship does highlight the value of relationships between women in a society which ignores and denigrates such relationships, and emphasizes the transformative power of horizontal relationships in a faith which emphasizes the value of the vertical. (It is no coincidence that the divine *agape* descends unilaterally from on high in the theological visions of most of the neo-orthodox theologians.) Still, the term suggests relationships selected out of a number of possible other relationships, and so does not readily include the dynamics of all relationships in historical and cosmic process.

I propose a model of feminist Christian love as care. This term shares with the other models the obvious advantage of having historical roots within the Christian traditions, but because it is grounded in the revised conception of human selfhood as connective or relational, it circumvents the dilemma faced by the androcentric models of love.

Many current feminist reflections upon love appeal, more or less explicitly, to this revised conception of selfhood, and through it, to a conception of love as care. This is readily evident in Beverly Wildung Harrison's eloquent arguments that love is the power to 'act-each-other-into-well-being,' a power women have always actively exercised through their procreative powers and developed further through fulfilling their social roles as wives and mothers.[27] Women are the primary providers of nurturance and care in a private world excluded in large measure from the realms of public power. But such care is tremendously powerful, for it creates persons and communities in and through the enlivening effects of mutuality in connectivity. Anger is a work of love most especially when it is directed against those forces which would destroy life by sundering the very web of relations which makes possible the personal and communal reality distinctive to human life. It is an emotional signal that something is amiss in the quality of a relationship in which we are immersed. To accept and act out of that anger in ways which enhance self and other as well as the bonds of community between them, rather than to bow to social pressure to repress it, is itself a profound act of caring.[28]

But how, more exactly, does understanding Christian love as caring circumvent the problem of balancing self- and other-regard intrinsic to traditional models of love? Among a number of recent publications on caring,[29] the work of moral philosopher Nell Noddings[30] is most helpful. Noddings' model of caring develops in greater detail the implications for moral theory of the revised model of humanity as relational. This state of relationality requires that persons be responsive to the needs of others in ways which do not violate the needs of the self responding. From her perspective, the use of rules and principles to determine personal obligations is but another evasive tactic by those who wish to deny their connections to others and, *ipso facto*, the range of their responsibility to them.[31] Reliance on rules and principles promotes a detachment from the other, and suppresses the sensibility which calls forth genuine caring.

Noddings defines caring succinctly as the 'genuine response to the perceived needs of others,'[32] and then traces its dynamics in terms of two ideas: engrossment and motivational displacement. Engrossment is the burdened, empathic state of mind and emotions which arises when we are concerned about another's well-being. It signifies the way in which one person, the one-caring, is present or actively receptive to another, the cared-for, in a number of ways: listening attentively in conversation, considering the special needs of the other in the circumstances at hand before acting to meet them, and so on.[33]

When this receptive state of engrossment occurs, so does a motivational shift: the one-caring allows herself to be motivated by the needs of the one cared-for, and puts herself into the service of the other. She feels compelled to act on behalf of the one cared-for as though it were for herself. This motivational displacement requires commitment to act in behalf of the one cared-for, a commitment which requires renewal over time.[34]

To care about another to the extent that we intently, intensely attend to the other's needs suggests that such other-regarding care entails self-sacrifice. Noddings realistically notes the dread we all feel when we anticipate being asked for more than we can readily give, and the conflicts which arise when our commitments pull us in different, mutually exclusive directions. Still, to respond to the imperative to care is to enhance the self:

> when I am as I need the other to be toward me, I am the way I want to be
> – that is, I am closest to goodness when I accept and affirm the internal
> 'I must.'[35]

The caring which connects the self to others reconnects the self to itself through the other. Caring for and being cared for empowers the self to care for herself. Nourishing a sense of our ideal as one-caring sustains the self when caring falters, either when the self loses her desire to care or when the other fails to respond to the care given. If the self is constituted in relation, then to serve and enhance the well-being of the other is to serve and enhance her own well-being.[36] Indeed, this implication of Nodding's account points out the inadequacy of her phrase 'motivational displacement' to describe the substitution of concern for the well-being of another for concern for one's own. If relations to others are constitutive of one's personal selfhood, then the boundaries between one's own self and its good, on the one hand, and the other-self and his or her good, on the other, are dissolved into the community of selves inexorably bonded to one another. From this perspective there is no real 'displacement' of motivation from concern for self to concern for other because there is no real distinction between them. This, however, is obviously not the case. Even though human selfhood is constituted in and through relations to other, singular selves still exist as distinct individuals, each with his or her unique personal history, and physical, psychic and spiritual make-up. The uniqueness of the individual is not completely subsumed by the uniqueness of the sets of relationships operative in each self's constitution (past and present); each person remains, to some extent, a being distinct from other beings, a being who experiences concern for self to be on occasion in conflict with concern for the other.

Noddings implicitly recognizes this difficulty, both in her choice of the phrase 'motivational displacement,' which suggests that the boundary between other and self remains to the extent that the focus of one's caring must be shifted, and in her awareness of the problems which arise for the one-caring. She notes the concern women share with men that the ties that bind not engulf or constrict the care-giver by insisting that the *impulse* to care must be protected in the one-caring. The natural impulse to care must be the firm foundation for an ethic in which caring becomes an ideal requiring commitment beyond what is supported by such an impulse. We need not justify the self-concern essential to maintaining not only ourselves as the ones-caring, but the *impulse* to care within us.[37] Noddings suggests that motivational displacement with someone repulsive to the self on a long-term basis is neither really possible nor desirable. The limits of the one-caring must be respected in the relationship. To accept our passions and hatreds enables us to use them as conditions for the expression of care. Acceptance of our affections enables us to care most effectively and efficiently.

In this way, a model of love as care, based upon an understanding of selfhood as connective or relational, avoids the double jeopardy of traditional doctrines of love: it supports no act of caring for the other which does not also, in some way, enhance the self, and it supports harnessing the powers of human affective and emotional response in pursuing the ethical ideal of caring for others.

Christine Gudorf poignantly illustrates the fallacy in assuming that all true self-sacrifice must be totally disinterested in her personal account of raising two adopted handicapped boys. The sacrifices she and her husband made on the behalf of these boys were intensely self-interested: the more the boys became able to care for themselves and to participate in normal societal arrangements, the more the parents benefited – not simply in being freed from mundane caretaking functions but in being freed to experience their spiritual strength and resourcefulness, and to follow through with the interests parenting these special children gave them. In this way, their relationship with their sons not only enabled their children to become persons; it constituted them themselves in their personal, social and historical realities. While countless sacrifices were made, the goal was always greater mutuality among members of the family and the communities in which they took part.[38]

As a concern and activity aimed at enhancing the life and well-being of others, and through others, of the self; as a concern to promote genuine mutuality and open receptivity to the other, and through the response of the other, to the self, such caring is feminist. Indeed, feminist theologians agree in this with the mainstream Christian tradition: love is precisely that power which creates and sustains relations between individuals, and so creates persons and community. It differs from the tradition in its perception of how that is done: not through the passivity of total self-sacrifice, but in the active receptivity which creates genuine mutuality, and through that mutuality, loves the self in loving the other. The power of God/ess is personally appropriated as a power expressed through and transformative of personal moral agency.

Traditionalists will surely challenge that understanding Christian love in terms of this model of caring sacrifices its distinctively Christian character. Jesus did not enjoin us to love just those persons whom we find it easy, pleasant or convenient to care for, but to respond to all who appear before us in need. Certainly Noddings recognizes that certain sacrifices must be made in every caring relationship, but assumed pragmatically that in actuality, we can only truly care for a few. Trying to care for everyone in need is simply an impossible ideal, so we should rest content with doing what we can. Indeed, even our initially limited aspirations tend to expand precipitously to demand more of us than we ever accomplish, so why torture ourselves with guilt over our inability to be responsive to everyone? Attempting to care for those persons repulsive to the self on a continual, long-term basis, while perhaps desirable when the need is great and immediate, will in the long run only drain the one-caring of the ability and motivation to care, rendering attempts to care ineffective and perhaps self-destructive. Too often the ideal of caring self-sacrificially, that is, without regard for the self's own feelings and needs is sought by hopeless idealists who would far rather 'sacrifice' to feed starving millions half-way around the globe than help the unemployed neighbor down the street.

For the Christian justifiably wary of making the needs and limits of the self a factor in determining what love woud have us be and do, it is worth noting two possible grounds for doing so from the perspective of Christian doctine. First, to the extent that her account of caring honors a person's feelings, it accepts that God works through our needs in letting us know what God would have *us* be and do in working God's own will in the world. Second, to the extent that her view takes into consideration human finitude, it recognizes that we are creatures of God, finite and dependent upon God for the power to do the good. So while Noddings' counsel to accept one's limits comes from a considered pragmatic acceptance of the realities of human existence, there are theological grounds to support her view.

Still, Noddings has her own idealistic strain, one particularly unhelpful in dealing with this very issue. When we are under pressure from the demands caring make upon us, she relies upon some 'natural' impulse to care to take over and afford us the necessary power to continue, and when natural feelings fail, she appeals to the ideal of caring to strengthen our determination. While she occasionally admits the frailty of the impulse to care within the self, she still insists that women's innate ability to care will suffice. We need only call up our memories of caring and being cared-for to know what to do.[39]

Such optimism in a feminist is hard to fathom. As the dualist, separatist, patriarchal powers of this world deny their responsibility for caring for its people and its elements, as we reside nervously one push-button away from total annihilation; as we poison the air we breathe, the water we drink, the soil we grow our food in; as we store millions of tons of grain until they rot while the poor and the homeless go hungry, Noddings blithely overlooks the impulse within us to *refuse* to care.

From a Reformed Christian perspective, the depravity of humanity necessitates our appealing to the source of all power to love to sustain us in our commitments to care, and to illuminate our choices in carrying out those commitments. To do so is not to project all power onto a transcendent being, somehow above and beyond our humanity; it is to recognize our dependence upon a power greater than ourselves but also continuous with ourselves, a power in and through which we actualize in history our humanity to the greater glory of that power. Moreover, our personal memories of caring will not suffice for those who experienced a dearth of care in their lives. Better the venerable collective memories told in Scriptures, story and song. Can the feminist who would remain Christian find in the Scriptural testimony regarding Jesus of Nazareth support for a model of love as caring? I believe so.

When Jesus, after reciting the love commandment, was asked who is the neighbor, he said nothing of self-sacrifice, but told the parable of the Good Samaritan who so carefully attended to the needs of the man beaten by bandits (Lk. 10:27–37). His insights into what love commands were not restrained by rules: when challenged for healing and for allowing his hungry disciples to pluck heads of grain when passing through a field on the Sabbath, Jesus did not back down (Lk. 6:1–10). God commands that we honor and serve God not by tithing and sacrifices, but through tender and merciful caring for one another. Refusing to be bound to the letter of the law, Jesus appealed to a deeper sense of God's will to insist that we forgive sins against us not seven but seventy times seven times, to not cast out a spouse in disgrace, to sin no more in intention than in deed. As he enjoined would-be disciples to let the dead bury the dead while they pursued the Kingdom of God, he promised great rewards to those who faithfully gave to others in God's name. Indeed, what term better encapsulates Jesus' attitude and actions toward the rich and poor alike than 'caring'? We no longer expect the Kingdom in apocalyptic fashion, but the joyful life which genuine caring brings forth is surely a foretaste of whatever future Kingdom might be forthcoming. While self-sacrifice is at times required by love faithful to God and neighbor, it is only a dimension of truly responsive loving care.

Now I realize that sorting out what Jesus, as opposed to the Gospel writers, actually thought and said about what it means to love is a notoriously problematic project. We might justify appealing to these passages, rather than on the ones teaching self-sacrifice exclusively, on the grounds that the latter were directed toward Jesus' immediate disciples, but most Christians understand being faithful in terms of discipleship. From a feminist theological perspective, Jesus may indeed manifest what it means to care in a definitive fashion, but he is not the only person to have done so, nor is the New Testament the only text to which women can turn for disclosure of the meaning of care. Moreover, the New Testament accounts themselves are decisively influenced by the androcentrism and patriarchalism of the time. If the criterion of true revelation is that it promote the fulfillment of the full humanity of women, then the feminist canon need not be restricted to the Christian scriptures.

In fact, the attempt to make Scripture serve purposes far beyond those intended by the authors has been the source of immeasurable grief and suffering in Western civilization. Feminists who would be Christian might well hearken to Monique Wittig's enjoinder to remember a time when women were not oppressed: 'Make an effort to remember. Or, failing that, invent.'[40] Women must imaginatively reconstruct the androcentric texts of their fathers, write their own stories of liberation from the compulsion to immolate themselves for others, write (as Christine Gudorf has) their own stories of caring and being cared for. Such stories express the power of God/ess at work in our lives, not through obedience and submission, but through the power of anger, resistance to oppression, and the joy born of genuine care.

Notes
1. The terms 'fact' or 'mythos' are those terms selected by David Tracy and Theodore Jennings respectively to refer to the persons, events, rituals, scriptures and traditions which constitute Christianity. The ambiguity of their terms helps make our point – there is no reality uninterpreted by the religious imagination to which we can appeal for the meaning of the Christian faith, as the pluralism of the New Testament witnesses to the historical Jesus readily testifies. David Tracy, *Blessed Rage for Order* (New York: Seabury Press, 1975), p. 43. Theodore W. Jennings, Jr., *Introduction to Theology: An Invitation to Reflection on the Christian Mythos* (Philadelphia: Fortress Press, 1976), pp. 53–54.
2. 'The Human Situation: A Feminine View,' originally in the *Journal of Religion*, 1970; reprinted in *Womanspirit Rising: A Feminist Reader in Religion*, ed. Carol P. Christ and Judith Plaskow (San Francisco: Harper & Row, 1979), pp. 24–42.
3. Saiving has been criticized for espousing an essentialist position of biological determinism while underplaying the role of social conditioning in creating differences between the sexes. I believe her attention to evidence garnered by anthropologists such as Margaret Mead and Ruth Benedict partially redeems her from this critique. In any case, attempts to broaden the model of women's experience she develops have not contradicted her conclusions but further supported and built upon them. See, for instance, theologian Judith Plaskow's *Sex, Sin and Grace: Women's Experience and the Theologies of Reinhold Niebuhr and Paul Tillich* (Washington, DC: University Press of America, 1980); and psychologist Nancy Chodorow's 'Family Structure and Feminine Personality,' *Woman, Culture and Society*, ed. by Michelle Zimbalist Rosaldo and Louise Lamphere (Stanford, CA: Stanford University Press, 1974), pp. 67–88, and *The Reproduction of Mothering: Psychoanalysis and the Sociology of Gender* (Berkeley, CA: University of California Press, 1978).
4. Saiving, 'The Human Situation,' p. 37.
5. Valerie Saiving was not the first to recognize the problematics of self-sacrificial love for women. The suffragettes Elizabeth Cady Stanton and Anne Howard Shaw, a Methodist minister, also recognized its detrimental effect upon them. (See Barbara Hilkert Andolsen, 'Agape in Feminist Ethics,' *Journal of Religious Ethics* 9 [1981]: 74–75.) Saiving was, however, the first to demonstrate the connection between the distinctiveness of women's developmental experiences and character structure, on the one hand, and the ambiguity of the self-sacrificial ideal for women, on the other.
6. For some contemporary exponents of this view, see James Gustafson, *Can Ethics Be Christian?* (Chicago: University of Chicago Press, 1975), especially pp. 65–81; and Gene Outka, *Agape: An Ethical Analysis* (New Haven: Yale University Press, 1972).
7. Some of these sayings are: 'Leave the dead to bury their own dead.' (Luke 9:60a); 'If anyone strikes you on the right cheek, turn to him the other also and if anyone would sue you and take your coat, let him have your cloak as well; and if anyone forces you to go one mile, go with him two miles.' (Matthew 5:39b–41).
8. Most notably, Judith Plaskow follows through on Saiving's ground-breaking analysis, and evaluates the theologies of Paul Tillich and Reinhold Niebuhr to see to what extent they have attended to dimensions of women's experience (Supra, n. 3). Other examples are Andolsen, Cady and Gudorf, in notes 9, 28, and 38 respectively, below.
9. Plaskow's analysis of the doctrines of grace of Tillich and Reinhold Niebuhr repeatedly points up the necessity for highlighting the role or self-love, but she herself attempts no constructive proposals (Supra, notes 3 and 8). In contrast, Andolsen does follow through on Saiving's charges to argue that self-sacrifice should be subordinated to the mutuality borne of the affirmation of self as well as of other as the primary characteristic of agapic love. 'Agape in Feminist Ethics,' pp. 76–77. Her review of the twentieth century discussion of *agape* is also helpful.

    Margaret Farley has also argued that mutuality is not antithetical to true Christian love. Since the relationships between neighbors inspired by Christian love should be patterned after the relationship between nature and grace as envisioned by Roman Catholic theology, human nature should be not passively receptive (as pure self-sacrifice demands) but *actively* receptive to the other. This active receptivity is marked by equal regard between the persons involved, and the mutuality which such active receptivity equally engaged in engenders, as well as the yielding at the center of true self-giving. 'New Patterns of Relationships: Beginnings of a Moral Revolution,' *Woman: New Dimensions*, ed. Walter Burkhardt (New York; Paulist Press, 1977), pp. 51–70.
10. Søren Kierkegaard's understanding of Christian love exemplifies this fear well. *Works of Love: Some Christian Reflections in the Form of Discourses*, trans. Howard and Edna Hong (New York: Harper & Row, 1962), especially pp. 247–260.

11. Farley notes that historically the Roman Catholic tradition has managed to continue its deni-gration of women and feminine forms of experience in its views of love: first, by its theological interpretations of women as passive (most especially, because of false under-standings of their procreative role), and so its identification of agapic love as also passive; second, by assuming that since women were lesser beings than men, they merited less regard and sacrifice on the part of others. 'New Patterns of Relationship,' pp. 56–60.

12. *Agape and Eros*, trans. Philip S. Watson (Chicago: University of Chicago Press, 1982). This book was first published in England by the S.P.C.K. House: part 1, in 1932; part 2, vol. 1, in 1938; part 2, vol. 2, in 1939; revised, in part retranslated, and published in one volume in 1953.

13. Ibid., pp. 476–558.

14. The distortions of Nygren's interpretation of Luther's views of Christian love must not be overlooked. For an excellent discussion, see Carter Lindberg, 'Martin Luther: Copernican Revolution or Ecumenical Bridge?' *Una Sancta* 24 (1): 31–38.

15. *The Mind and Heart of Love: Lion and Unicorn: A Study in Eros and Agape* (New York: Henry Holt & Company, 1947).

16. Ibid., pp. 14–15, 226, 228, 234, 255.

17. Ibid., pp. 174–193, 217, 259.

18. Ibid., p. 220.

19. Lewis Carroll, *Through the Looking Glass* in *The Complete Works of Lewis Carroll*, intro. Alexander Woolcott (New York: The Modern Library, n.d.), pp. 221–232.

20. The work being done by Jean Baker Miller, Judith V. Jordan, Janet L. Surrey, Alexandra Kaplan, Irene P. Stiver, Blythe Clinchy and others at the Stone Center for Developmental Services and Studies, Wellesley College, Wellesley, Massachusetts, is especially significant for the understanding of the distinctiveness of women's and men's development. See Judith V. Jordan *et al.*, *Women's Growth in Connection: Writings from the Stone Center* (New York: Guilford Press, 1991).

21. In her recent book *From a Broken Web: Separation, Sexism and Self* (Boston: Beacon Press, 1986), pp. 22–46.

22. Ibid., pp. 1–18, idem.

23. D.W. Winnicot, Heinz Kohut, Otto Kernberg, and Harry Guntrip were the most renowned of this group.

24. See supra, n. 21. Also Janet L. Surrey, 'Self-in-Relation: A Theory of Women's Development,' in *Women's Growth in Connection*, pp. 51–66; Margaret Edith Craddock Huff, 'Women in the Image of God: Toward a prototype for Feminist Pastoral Counseling,' unpublished Ph.D. dissertation, Boston University, 1987, pp. 70–86; Nancy Chodorow, *The Reproduction of Mothering: Psychoanalysis and the Sociology and Gender* (Berkeley, CA: University of California Press, 1978).

25. Keller, *From a Broken Web*, p. 200.

26. Janice G. Raymond, *A Passion for Friends: Towards a Philosophy of Female Affection* (Boston: Beacon Press, 1986); Mary E. Hunt, 'Lovingly Lesbian: Toward a Feminist Theology of Friendship,' *A Challenge to Love: Gay and Lesbian Catholics in the Church*, ed. Robert Nugent (New York: Crossroads, 1983), pp. 135–155.

27. Beverly Wildung Harrison, 'The Power of Anger in the Work of Love: Christian Ethics for Women and Other Strangers,' *Union Seminary Quarterly Review* 36, Supplement (1981), p. 47.

28. Ibid., p. 49. See also Linell E. Cady, 'Relational Love: A Feminist Christian Vision,' *Embodied Love: Sensuality and Relationship as Feminist Values*, ed. Paul M. Cooey, Sharon A. Farmer, and Mary Ellen Ross (San Francisco: Harper & Row, 1987), pp. 135–150, for a supporting view.

29. The recent work of Carol Gilligan has inspired much current reflection, especially among moral philosophers, about the meaning of care. Gilligan argues that women's perceptions of morality are markedly different than those of men, perceptions entirely congruous with the work of the psychologists and theologians we have cited above. Men's self-understandings as agents of action *separate* from others engenders a notion of morality in which set rules determine the meaning of fairness and the forms of reciprocity between separate selves, and in which relationships are constituted by the roles from which duties come. In contrast, women's understanding of themselves as *connected* to others engenders their understanding morality in terms of how it enhances connection with others: morality is determined by the adequacy of their responsivity to and care for others, and their relationships are grounded in that fundamental state of interdependence. *In a Different Voice: Psychological Theory and Women's Development* (Cambridge, MA: Harvard University Press, 1982). 'Two

Perspectives: On Self, Relationships, and Morality,' *Harvard Educational Review* 53 (2), pp. 125–145.

30. Nell Noddings, *Caring: A Feminine Approach to Ethics and Moral Education* (Berkeley, CA: University of California Press, 1984).
31. Ibid., pp. 5, 40, 47, 87.
32. Ibid., p. 53.
33. Ibid., pp. 17–20, 30, 33–34, 40, 60–61, 66, 64, 78, 150, 160, 169–170, 176, 180.
34. Ibid., pp. 16, 18, 26, 53, 69–70, idem.
35. Ibid., p. 49.
36. Ibid., pp. 49–50, 99.
37. Ibid., p. 100.
38. Christine E. Gudorf, 'Parenting, Mutual Love, and Sacrifice,' *Women's Consciousness: Women's Conscience*, ed. Barbara Hilkert Andolsen, Christine E. Gudorf, Mary D. Pellauer (San Francisco: Harper & Row, 1985), pp. 175–192.
39. Noddings, *Caring*, pp. 97–99.
40. *Les Giullilers*, trans. David DeVay (New York: Avon Books, 1971), p. 89.

* Feminists in recent years have come to realize that it is notoriously difficult to determine what characteristics distinguish women from men; indeed, many argue that the whole project is misguided. Currently, feminists in academia divide roughly into two main camps: cultural feminists who tend to espouse an historically naive essentialism, attributing certain characteristics to all women, and post-structuralist feminists who argue that gender differences are completely socially constructed and the terms 'woman' or 'feminine' totally meaningless. Both of these methodologies are seriously flawed. In particular, neither offers us realistic ways of understanding and transforming society in nonsexist, egalitarian and holistic directions. I proceed on the thesis that, however difficult it is to determine the differences between men and women without succumbing to sexist distortions and oppressive universalizing claims, these differences do exist and are significant. Moreover, women's insights into their distinctive experiences (even those caused by sexist distortions and exploitation) offer invaluable insight into the nature of the human condition. I espouse the positionalist methodology suggested by Linda Alcoff, which proposes that we explore the 'complex of habits, dispositions, associations, and perceptions which engenders one as female'. Linda Alcoff, 'Cultural Feminism Versus Post-Structuralism: The Identity Crisis in Feminist Theory,' *Signs: Journal of Women in Culture and Society* 13 (3) 405–36, at 424. See my defense and exercise of this method in 'The Cycle of Violence and Feminist Reconstructions of Selfhood,' *Contagion: Journal of Violence, Mimesis and Culture* (1995).

.

6.3 Safe Sex and Lost Love

Karen Lebacqz and Deborah Blake

AIDS, 'Intercourse,' and Sexual Ethics

It is probably no mistake that we use the term 'intercourse' to refer both to conversation and to one of the most intimate of sexual acts. How we talk and how we conduct ourselves sexually both say a great deal about us.[1] In this essay, our concern is how the conversation about AIDS in our society affects the possibilities of a Christian sexual ethic. How is the AIDS crisis influencing and directing our discourse about sex and sexuality? What impact does our understanding of AIDS have on sexual ethics?

'Safe sex' has become the contemporary catchword. Advertisements urge it, pamphlets tell us how to practice it, and safe sex clubs have emerged in sections of large cities.[2] But what is 'safe sex?' And what is the talk about safe sex doing to the way we think about our sexuality and our community?

The participants needed for this discourse are many. We speak here as Christian ethicists, one Protestant and one Roman Catholic. We believe that there is an important place for the concern about safe sex, but we also contend that the concept may endanger a genuinely Christian sexual ethics. Indeed, we hold that lines delineating proper roles in the discourse have become blurred, with the result that Christians may mistakenly adopt a safe sex standard as adequate for Christian sexual ethics. We will argue that safe sex is a legitimate public health concern but that it is not the same as a Christian sexual ethic.

Public Health Discourse: 'Safe Sex'

The role of public health officials is to maintain the health of the community through surveillance, research, prevention, and treatment of disease. In the case of AIDS, initial surveillance and research identified and characterized the disease. The human immunodeficiency virus (HIV) was found to be the causative agent. Patterns of transmission have been identified: The virus is transmitted by entry into one's bloodstream of bodily fluids – specifically blood and semen – which have a transmissible concentration of HIV. People at risk are intravenous drug users sharing needles; fetuses of infected mothers; recipients of contaminated blood products (e.g. hemophiliacs); and those practicing anal intercourse, vaginal intercourse, and possibly oral/genital intercourse with an infected partner.

Direct treatment of AIDS and ARC have been unavailable to date. Since AIDS is a deadly disease, this leaves prevention as the remaining – and urgent – public health action. Screening of blood supplies, avoidance of contaminated needles, and avoidance of high risk gential activity are the major public health strategies to prevent spread of the disease. In particular, 'safe sex' education and changes in sexual behavior have been found to be a significant means for reducing the risk of transmission of the AIDS virus.

Thus, 'safe sex' has captured the mind of the American public. Safe sex has a decided role to play in protecting the public health by preventing the spread of the disease in populations at risk. It is a worthy and important step in the protection of people's health and lives.

But safe sex, which was intended as a public health measure to prevent disease transmission, has crossed over into the realm of sexual ethics. And it is a sexual ethics characterized by the elements that held Christian sexual ethics in bondage for centuries. We suggest that a proper public health concern for self-protection in the face of the AIDS crisis has become an improper total response to sex and sexuality. There is a place for 'safe sex,' but only a place. 'Safe sex' does not provide an adequate Christian sexual ethic.

Public Discourse: Fear, Physicality, and Blame

The flip side of concern for safety is fear. The undercurrent of the public health discourse that has captured the American imagination is one of defensiveness, self-preservation, and fear. The 'sex-can-kill-you' message of the safe sex campaign places an aura of evil around sex and sexuality. It also begins to return our attention solely to the physical: Sex becomes a matter of what 'acts' one does and whether the physical parts of our bodies are sufficiently protected (e.g., whether condoms are used). Thus, in the wake of the safe sex campaign, there is a danger that we will return to an earlier era of thinking of sex as basically evil and dangerous and of focusing exclusively on the physical dimensions of it.

Our past tradition of teaching about sexual ethics was built upon a similar basis of fear and focused on the physical act and its consequences. Joseph Fletcher characterized this ethic in a delightful limerick:

> There was a young lady named Wilde
> Who kept herself quite undefiled
> by thinking of Jesus
> and social diseases
> And the fear of having a child.[3]

This is the 'safe sex' of a previous age. It was sexual ethics based on fear. Sex was 'defiling,' and the way to remain pure was to avoid sexual contact by keeping alive the fears attached to it – fear of pregnancy and fear of sexually transmitted disease.

The safe sex of the present age is not so different. Fear of pregnancy, syphillis, and gonorrhea is replaced by fear of AIDS, but the dominance of fear remains the same. Thus, the contemporary parallel to Fletcher's clever limerick might look like this:

> If safe sex is what you would find,
> To the danger of AIDS don't be blind;
> use condoms with care,
> stay in just one pair,
> Monogamy is not a bind!

'Safe sex' can be variously interpreted to include the use of condoms and non-intrusive sexual play or to mean monogamous long-term sex with a 'clean' partner. As Alice Kahn parodies, sex is in danger of becoming so 'safe' that we'll never want it again.[4]

Some are glad for the 'safe sex' age, feeling that it will reaffirm some traditional values of family, monogamy, and carefulness with one's body. One gay spokesperson declares, 'Now that the sex has been taken away, the freewheeling sex, I'm left with the family and it's not so bad to exist with that.'[5] In the wake of fear, some traditional values may reemerge. But fear is not an acceptable justification for these values.

Fear brings with it an uglier side. Fear and blame are often companions. So it is in the case of AIDS. A recent survey showed that while people in the U.S. claim to feel a great deal of compassion for AIDS sufferers (78 percent), less than half (48 percent) thought that AIDS victims should be allowed to live normally in the community. Most significantly, nearly half (45 percent) thought that most people with AIDS have only themselves to blame, and 42 percent thought that the disease was a punishment for a decline in moral standards.[6] These poll results coincide with reports of a suspicious fire that gutted the house of a Florida family whose three sons, all hemophiliacs, are infected with the HIV virus, though they do not yet exhibit signs of AIDS. The advent of AIDS has sparked public hysteria and fear-based responses to sexuality.[7]

Moreover, in the mind of the American public, it would seem, AIDS is linked inextricably to the gay community.[8] AIDS is a serious problem among intravenous drug users, but it is the transmission of AIDS through sexual contact – particularly homosexual contact – that has captured the American imagination. The fact that AIDS is *not* a 'gay' phenomenon elsewhere in the world has had seemingly little impact on the American perception.

This linking of AIDS and gay sexuality in the popular mind is important. It affects and even determines the way we respond to the AIDS epidemic. Because we have seen AIDS as a 'gay' issue, we have seen it as a gay problem and responsibility rather than as a health problem and public responsibility. Our health resources have been slow to respond.[9] Families of victims have been afraid to seek assistance for fear of stigmatization.[10] Harrassment of gay men has increased since public awareness of AIDS.[11] Curt Clinkscales, head of the National Alliance of Senior Citizens and a self-characterized conservative Republican and Reagan supporter, nonetheless criticizes Reagan's newly-appointed panel on AIDS for trying to turn AIDS into an issue of homosexual lifestyle: 'All the Commission will be is a sounding board for people who look at AIDS as a curse of God.'[12]

In short, along with fear of AIDS and the campaign for 'safe sex' comes blame: blame of the victims of AIDS for their own plight and blame of the gay community for promulgating a disease on society. AIDS is the 'price' anyone pays for being sexually active, and those who have sex with their own kind are accused of deliberately putting everyone at risk.

Thus, we might add a second verse to our contemporary limerick:

> There was a young man named Rex
> Who with his own kind enjoyed sex.
> The price that he paid
> was that he got AIDS,
> Thus 'proving' that he was a hex.

When sex is discussed under the rubric of safety, the gay community is blamed for making the rest of the world not 'safe,' and the individual AIDS patient is blamed for not having practiced safe sex. 'God "AIDS" the gays' reads one church sign.[13] American sympathies may go out to those who contracted AIDS through blood transfusions or other 'faultless' means but not to those whose disease is considered the result of – indeed, the divine punishment for – their 'lifestyle.' 'Fear of the disease has become a facade for the expression of latent hatred for and oppression of homosexual people.'[14]

We may not have totally reverted to the days when sex was 'defiling,' but we are not far from thinking that sex is dirty or wrong because it is so inextricably linked to disease and death. Safe sex may be important as a public health measure, but it has brought with it a public discourse in which fear dominates, coupled with a return to physicality in the sexual arena. Fear fosters a rise of blaming responses in the social arena.

The Discourse of Christian Sexual Ethics

Our past tradition of teaching about sexual ethics was built upon a similar basis of fear and focused on the physical while also denigrating the body. Sexuality was understood to be basically evil. This ethics grew out of and was sustained by the Gnostic, Greek, Jansennist, and Puritan influence on the developing church.

In recent years, however, there has been a significant development in Christian approaches to sexual ethics.[15] Working from Scripture, church tradition, the empirical sciences, philosophy, and the experience of church communities, a changed view of sexuality has emerged.

This view sees human sexuality in broad terms: 'Human sexuality ... is our way of being in the world as female or male persons.'[16] It is profoundly good. It involves the person at all levels of existence – personal and social, psychological, biological, and spiritual:

> The mystery of sexuality is the mystery of the human need to reach out for the physical and spiritual embrace of others. Sexuality thus expresses God's intention that people find authentic humanness not in isolation but in relationship. In sum, sexuality involves more than what we do with our genitals. More fundamentally, it is who we are as body-selves who experience the emotional, cognitive, physical, and spiritual need for intimate communion, both creaturely and divine.[17]

In short, human sexuality in contemporary Christian ethics is seen as primarily relational, spiritual, and integral to our very humanness.

A Christian sexual ethic, then, is not confined to concerns for 'safe sex,' nor is it a code of sexual behavior.[18] It is built upon an anthropology of human wholeness and affirms the goodness of sexuality and its essential relationality.

Discourse in the Gay Community

It is the gay community that has been most profoundly devastated by the AIDS epidemic in America. And it is this community that reveals some of the most helpful insights about the meaning of sexuality in the face of a deadly epidemic. Frankness in the discussion of 'safe sex' is bringing discourse about sex and sexuality out of its shroud of secrecy. As those who have AIDS speak of their disease and of their lives, the closet of homosexuality is being opened, the secrecy and myths are being dispelled.

'Bob,' for example, entered gay life after a divorce, having never had a relationship with a man before. 'He is a man of moderation, integrity, goals, and ability.'[19] After learning that he had ARC, Bob stopped being genitally active. Bob reflects on his sexuality in language reminiscent of that used by Christian ethicist James Nelson: ' "Homosexuality ... is not what one does sexually. It is an emotional desire. It's still love." ' Bob argues that ' "everything that can exist in heterosexual relationships can exist in homosexual relationships" ' and concludes that ' "if God approves of one, then God must approve of the other." '[20]

At the other end of the spectrum is 'Alan.' Alan went through two profound changes in his sexual life. Originally, he thought of sexual intercourse as a 'special, consummate act.' But when he first entered gay life 'he had no role models.' He therefore went to bars seven nights a week, thinking that this was what gay men did. Sex was reinterpreted for him in the gay bar scene, where he participated in 'fast and easy sex.'[21] Then, when he was diagnosed with ARC in 1983, he changed his lifestyle again.

'In retrospect,' claim the editors of this volume, 'Alan regrets that his self-esteem was so low that he felt his only avenue of affirmation was in settings conducive to dangerous conduct.'[22] In short, Alan participated in fast and easy sex because it was his way of being affirmed as a gay man in the face of the 'double life' that he was forced to live, pretending to be heterosexual for the benefit of his family and peers. 'If his home and social environment had been more acceptant of homosexuality, perhaps...what he and others risked would not have been necessary.'[23]

What Have We Learned?

From Christian ethics and from the gay community several lessons may be learned for the development of a Christian sexual ethic in the face of AIDS.

First, an accurate view of the gay community is necessary. Not all gay sex is 'fast and easy.' Indeed, of the stories of gay men told in *AIDS: Personal Stories in Pastoral Perspective*, almost none fit the stereotype of gay sex as 'fast lane' living. Many are stories of long-term, deep, abiding love.

Second, the AIDS crisis should reaffirm our need to reconceptualize sexuality. Armistead Maupin suggests that because some direct modes of sexual contact are not available to those trying to be safe in the AIDS era, sexuality is being re-eroticized and re-romanticized, and the fullness of sexuality is being recaptured.[24] Sexuality is not just what we do with our genitals: it is love and commitment and desire and a total way of being. Christian sexual ethics should be based on a perception of the fullness of sexuality in human life and of its deep connection to intimacy and communion.

Third, many gay men seek loving, committed, careful ways of being sexual in the world. When those ways are denied by the larger society, these men may find alternative expressions of sexuality. The discrimination and prejudice gay men encounter can make them retreat to a separate world of baths, bars, and casual sex: 'Our society makes us hide this important part of ourselves and denies us access to more conventional ego strokes. So we take to the sheets.'[25] Those who would condemn a presumed gay 'lifestyle' must ask what they have done to contribute to it.

Fourth, in the face of ARC and AIDS, the gay community has responded well to the cry for 'safe sex.' Individuals have been very careful to avoid infecting others, and group practices such as 'safe sex' clubs have arisen.

But is safe sex necessarily moral sex? Morality and safety are not the same. At the root of moral sex is love and concern for the partner, mutuality and vulnerability, truthfulness, and trust. Sex can be 'safe' without exhibiting any of these characteristics.[26] Sex can be safe and still be wrong because it is 'coercive, debasing, harmful, or cruel to another.'[27] Just as the fact that sex is monogamous does not necessarily make it right, so the fact that it is safe does not necessarily make it right.

Moreover, while the safety of one's *partner* should certainly be a concern for anyone practicing Christian sexual morality, self-sacrificial love is a human possibility. Safety of *oneself* has always been understood in Christian tradition as less than the fullness of love.[28]

Safe sex, then, is not necessarily moral sex. This is partly because safe sex is linked to fear and self-protectiveness. Fear is non-Christian, even anti-Christian. To reestablish a sexual ethic based on fear is to permit Christian values to be submerged into cultural values that are at root antithetical to the Christian message.

What Do We Teach?

Two elements are needed for a valid Christian sexual ethic in the face of the AIDS epidemic. One is an adequate understanding of the virus that transmits susceptibility to AIDS and of the communities at risk for AIDS. As with the transmission of any virus, AIDS raises public health issues and a concern for safety.

The more central element necessary for a Christian sexual ethic in the face of the AIDS epidemic is an appropriation of Christian values. A Christian ethic does not – indeed, cannot – consist in a list of 'do's' and 'don't's' intended to protect ourselves and make sex safe. Concern for the practice of safe sex is legitimate and has its place in a Christian ethic. But an exclusive focus on safe sex is not an adequate Christian sexual ethic. The concern for safety brings fear. Fear is easily turned into blame and scapegoating.

Fear and scapegoating are not Christian approaches to our neighbor. It is, therefore, fundamentally a theological issue, argues Nelson, when those seeking after security do so through the 'false' mechanism of rejecting all who appear to embody their insecurities. He proposes a response 'from the heart of the Christian gospel.' 'To those whose insecurity is so painful that they must find scapegoats on whom to lay blame for all anxieties and evil,' suggests Nelson, 'there is that One who demonstrates the triumph of grace announcing that all are free to live as those who are accepted.'[29]

Love and acceptance are fundamental to the Christian gospel. In our desire for 'safe sex,' we must be sure that we have not lost the heart of the gospel, which is love.

Notes
1. Indeed, in *The Sexual Language* (Ottawa: The U. of Ottawa Press, 1977), Andre Guindon proposes that sexuality is best understood as a form of communication.
2. Armistead Maupin, well-known author of *Tales of the City* about gay life in San Francisco, interviewed in *The Berkeley Monthly*, September 1987.

3.   Joseph Fletcher, *Moral Responsibility: Situation Ethics at Work* (Westminster, 1967), p. 88.
4.   Alice Kahn, 'Sex So Safe You'll Never Want It Again,' *San Francisco Examiner*, Sunday Punch section, Agent 23, 1987, p. 5.
5.   Maupin, *The Berkeley Monthly*, p. 19.
6.   George Gallup, Jr., 'ID Cards Favored for AIDS Sufferers,' San Francisco Chromicle, vol. 123, no. 194, August 31, 1987, p. 7.
7.   James Nelson notes that fear is the dynamic underlying the vindictive and punitive attitudes of the religious right. The fear is fed by a pervasive dualism that has both political and sexual manifestations: politically, it divides the world into 'good' capitalists and 'bad' communists; sexually, it divides the sexes into a hierarchical ordering and divides the 'good' soul from the 'bad' body. In short, the world can be divided into 'good' and 'bad' people, those who are 'saved' and those who are 'damned.' Among the 'damned' are all those who do not fit the traditional narrowly-drawn sex role stereotypes and sexual behavior patterns. *Between Two Gardens* (NY: Pilgrim Press, 1983), chaper 9.
8.   Dennis Altman, *AIDS in the Mind of America: The Social, Political, and Psychological Impact of a New Epidemic* (Garden City, N.Y.: Doubleday, 1986).
9.   For a discussion, see Altman, *AIDS in the Mind of America*, pp. 40–57.
10. See Earl E. Shelp, Ronald H. Sunderland, and Peter W.A. Mansell, eds., *AIDS: Personal Stories in Pastoral Perspective* (N.Y.: Pilgrim, 1986), p. 108: 'With few exceptions these families had decided to withhold information from pastors and congregations.... They did not wish to expose themselves and their families to the stigma that they were painfully aware most people applied to the illness and its victims.'
11. Craig Wilson, 'Gay Harassment in Jerusalem,' *USA Today*, July 14, 1989, p.10
12. Quoted by Elizabeth Fernandez in *The San Francisco Examiner*, Sunday August 23, 1987, p. 1. Fernandez charges that the panel 'is largely composed of conservatives who conform to an ideology espoused by the Reagan administration but rejected by mainstream medical authorities.'
13. Shelp *et al.*, *AIDS: Personal Stories*, p. 107.
14. Shelp *et al.*, *AIDS: Personal Stories*, p. 75.
15. A helpful overview is provided in James P. Hanigan, *What Are They Saying About Sexual Morality?* (N.Y.: Paulist Press, 1982). See also Lisa Sowle Cahill, *Between the Sexes: Foundations for a Christian Ethics of Sexuality* (Philadelphia: Fortress, 1985); Philip S. Keane, *Sexual Morality: A Catholic Perspective* (N.Y.: Paulist, 1977); James B. Nelson, *Embodiment: An Approach to Sexuality and Christian Theology* (Minneapolis: Augsburg, 1978); Anthony Kosnik *et. al.*, *Human Sexuality: New Directions in Catholic Moral Thought* (N.Y.: Paulist, 1977); The United Church of Christ, *Human Sexuality: A Preliminary Study* (N.Y.: United Church Press, 1977).
16. James Nelson, *Between Two Gardens*, p. 5.
17. James Nelson, *Between Two Gardens*, p. 6.
18. This essay is written in response to a position statement that asks, 'Is it possible to develop, within a religious framework, a sexual moral code which will protect individuals from sexually transmitted disease and, possibly, death?' We take exception to this framing of the question. To begin with the assumption that we should develop a *protective* sexual ethic is already to presume the very question that should be under consideration: What are the grounds for a *Christian* sexual ethic?
19. Shelp *et al.*, *AIDS: Personal Stories*, p. 56.
20. Ibid., p. 59.
21. Ibid., p. 62.
22. Ibid., p. 63.
23. Ibid.
24. Armistead Maupin, interviewed in *The Berkeley Monthly*.
25. 'John,' quoted by Shelp *et al.*, *AIDS: Personal Stories*, p. 94
26. After noting that 100 gay men gather in safe sex clubs to 'jerk off' together, Armistead Maupin declares that their behavior is 'perfectly safe and perfectly moral.' It may be perfectly safe; but is it perfectly moral?
27. The United Church of Christ, *Human Sexuality: A Preliminary Study* (N.Y.: United Church Press, 1977), p. 104.
28. Some gay men wittingly risk their own health by making love to their infected partners, choosing to affirm love over death.
29. Nelson, *Between Two Gardens*, p. 152.

7. Lesbian and Gay Sexuality

Homosexuality has been a major preoccupation of almost every Christian denomination in the western world for the past thirty years. Homosexuality has raised issues of authority and the nature of sexuality and its purpose for the Churches. The debates have been long and hard and largely reached a stalemate because they have tended to focus on the nature of biblical authority, which as Stephen Barton points out earlier in this book, is a difficult and ultimately abortive place to start. Lesbian, gay and bisexual people frustrated by the Churches' refusal to start from their own experience, have begun to do theology for themselves and to suggest ways in which they might inform a wider Christian theology of sexuality. In this section two men and two women offer some models for a Christian theology of relationship based upon lesbian and gay experience. Alison Webster, in 'Revolutionising Christian Sexual Ethics: A Feminist Perspective', drawing upon her own experiences (which mirror those of many women) exposes and analyses the poverty of the sexual values promoted by Christianity which (along with secular society) has idolised heterosexuality and failed to provide men and women with a theological language in which to describe and make sense of other intimate relationships. Love between women, often the most important love in a woman's life, has been trivialised and dismissed or associated with freakish lesbianism. She argues the importance of accepting that sexuality and gender are socially constructed and recognising that 'compulsory heterosexuality' (to quote Adrienne Rich) is a political institution designed to keep women in a certain place. The Church legitimates this institution with arguments about complementarity which have little meaning for those women who find complementarity, 'otherness', in other women rather than men. Webster argues that a new sexual ethic based upon the experiences of women and gay people will recognise the political dimension of sexuality. It will also look to lesbian and gay relationships as carrying with them the possibility of equality, a possibility lacking in heterosexual relationships in a patriarchal context. Sexuality will no longer simply be reduced to genital activity but recognised as an essential element of our whole persons, operative in all relationships.

Robert J. Williams, in 'Towards a Theology for Lesbian and Gay Marriage', makes a persuasive case for inclusion of lesbian and gay committed relationships within the institution of marriage. Williams tackles all the arguments against such a move – he reminds those who would argue that marriage is essentially a relationship between a man and a woman that a similar argument was used against the ordination of women. He tackles those who maintain that lesbian and gay people are incapable of forming a lifelong union. Writing as an Episcopalian he argues the Church's ranking of companionship over procreation in the purposes of marriage opens it up to lesbian and gay couples. He demonstrates that lesbian and gay people may be more practised in the art of mutuality than heterosexual couples because 'society has not defined role expectations for our relationships'. Legality is not an obstacle either as there is historical precedent for the Church recognising marriages unrecognised by the state. If the Church believes that one of the purposes of marriage is the 'safeguarding and benefit of society', and it also believes that one of the ways to do this is to encourage people into committed covenanted relationships, then a liturgical celebration of same-sex unions is important. Williams draws attention to the lack of a substantial theology of marriage. He believes this is because the marriage liturgy's primary historical purpose has been the sanctification of a legal contract, with the result that the Church has not asked questions about the nature of marriage. Williams suggests the necessary construction of a theology of marriage must be grounded in companionship and mutuality. It is a sacrament of redemption i.e. it frees us to become lovers, a sacrament of justice and a sacrament of incarnation which committed lesbian and gay people already participate in by virtue of the quality of their relationships. The time has come, Williams believes, for the Church to recognise this fact.

Elizabeth Stuart in 'Lesbian and Gay Relationships: A Lesbian Feminist Perspective' offers an alternative vision to that of Williams and other gay male theologians. Writing as a lesbian feminist she cannot accept that marriage is an institution to which lesbian and gay people should aspire. She accuses the Church of idolising marriage to a destructive degree particularly for women. She offers an alternative model for committed relationships drawn from lesbian and gay experience and grounded in an alternative tradition within Scripture and Christian history

– covenanted friendship. She argues that only by making friendship the heart and soul of Christian sexual ethics can we develop an ethic which will be inclusive of heterosexuals, lesbian and gay people, celibate people and single people. They need to learn to be just, good friends.

Daniel A. Helminiak in 'The Trinitarian Vocation of the Gay Community' seeks to answer a question posed by the Catholic theologian John McNeill, 'For what purpose? Why does God create homosexual people?', by suggesting that certain facets of life within the lesbian and gay community may mirror the life of the Trinity, the qualities of which are inviolable individuality, equality, interdependent relations, unconstrained by gender specifications. Within the lesbian and gay community friendships between men and women flourish, equality exists within relationships, people defy society's gender constructions and affirm uniqueness and difference – all qualities represented in the doctrine of the Trinity. 'Thus, the gay community has the possibility and so the vocation of offering our world a model of ideal Christian life in practice.'

Alison Webster is the Programme Coordinator for the Institute for the Study of Christianity and Sexuality. Her article, 'Revolutionising Christian Sexual Ethics: A Feminist Perspective', first appeared in *Contact,* vol. 197, no. 1, 1992, pp. 25–9.

Robert Williams' article, 'Towards a Theology for Lesbian and Gay Marriage', first appeared in the *Anglican Theological Review*, vol. 72, 1990, pp. 134–57.

Elizabeth Stuart is Senior Lecturer in Theology at the University of Glamorgan. Her article, 'Lesbian and Gay Relationships: A Lesbian Feminist Perspective', appears here for the first time.

Daniel A. Helminiak's article, 'The Trinitarian Vocation of the Gay Community', first appeared in *Pastoral Psychology*, vol. 36 (2), winter, 1987, pp. 100–11.

7.1 Revolutionising Christian Sexual Ethics: A Feminist Perspective

Alison Webster

If there's one thing Christian teaching shares with secular society, it's the emphasis placed on the necessity of (heterosexual) coupledom and marriage. The most vivid memory of my teenage years is of the constant, merciless and tiresome pressure to find a boyfriend, and ultimately to marry him. The Christian youth club was a place where girls went to meet boys; Christian Societies at College were places where students met their future spouses. At church, adults watched each other's and their own offspring with jealousy and anxiety respectively, as they attracted, or didn't, a member of the opposite sex. In the secular sphere, teenage magazines – a million miles away from church in other ways, bombarded me with the same message: starve, shave and paint yourself – anything to get a man. Indeed, the pressure from the adult world to get ahead in the 'courting game' was so relentless that I sometimes wondered what was in it for them.

The difference between the sacred and secular values I imbibed was, of course, what you did with a man once you'd got one. The time was when church and society were united in prohibiting sex before marriage. Now, while secular society takes it for granted that sex will be part of any committed intimate relationship, the church officially retains its taboo on 'sexual intercourse outside the marriage bond'.

My personal experience of Christian sexual values was therefore bitter-sweet. Before I made the grade and found a boyfriend I felt anxious, under stress, inadequate and guilty. Once I'd got one, there was the sweet relief of being welcomed into the fold of adulthood – the comfort of normality. As my relationship developed, the mystique which adults had carefully constructed around 'having sex' (by which they meant the penetrative heterosexual kind) seemed to evaporate. Developing physical intimacy made that traditional line between acceptable and non-acceptable sexual behaviour anomalous and irrelevant. The line that had been drawn for me seemed to have no rationale, other than avoiding pregnancy, and there were other ways of doing that. So when I made love, it was a tinge of guilt that I was betraying my childhood religion, but a guilt which was easily assuaged by the comfort of knowing that I was doing what the rest of society expected of normal, healthy young people.

Underlying this bitter-sweet experience was a feeling of frustration with the banality and superficiality of the sexual values I had inherited from the church and society. For it felt to me that intimate personal relationships – overtly sexual or not – were about more than one's marriage prospects. The powerful feelings of attraction I had for a couple of older women who were my guides and mentors, and the warmth and loyalty of my friends could not be adequately expressed by my inherited relationship-language. Instinctively I felt these to be more important than any sexual relationship I would ever have had with a man, but I had no vocabulary to express that feeling. I still find the language of Christian ethics deficient in this respect, and it is feminism that has made good that deficiency.

The pressure upon young Christian women to find a husband, and to a lesser extent on young men to find a wife has, of course, a lofty theological explanation. From a mixture of biblical and non-biblical sources, the church has developed a world order founded upon the inherent complementarity of male and female. It is God's intention, theological orthodoxy states, that a woman should find her self-fulfilment in the 'otherness' that is man. Men find a different kind of fulfilment in the 'otherness' that is woman – more of an optional extra. Theologians and church people talk of 'God's intention for the world' consisting in a system of western style nuclear families, at the centre of which is heterosexual marriage.

It is this notion of the structure of the cosmos which feminists, Christian and secular, call into question. At the heart of the challenge are three affirmations. First, that it is good for women to be alone. The aim of feminism has been to empower women, encouraging a sense of autonomy and self worth outside the orbit of man. As Daphne Hampson puts it:

> Feminism, both in theory and praxis has been concerned for women to come into their own. Only too often have women been unable to sufficiently value themselves ... To advocate – within a feminist context – that persons should come into their own, is not once more to understand the self as the atomic entity of which feminists are so critical. For women conceive of selfhood to be achieved in and through 'relationship'. One may say that there needs to be a creative tension between autonomy (which in the past has been denied women) and relationality.[1]

Traditionally, women's identities have consisted in their relationship to a man. A woman is someone's wife, daughter, mother or lover. Women who have lived alone have been the objects of derision and social censure. The Victorian stereotype of the 'spinster': the old maid, prey to complexes and neuroses, the pitiful creature who failed in the marriage market is still a powerful image inducing many women to marry. In contrast, the feminist redefinition of 'spinster' is:

> one who has chosen her Self, who defines her Self by choice neither in relation to children nor to men; one who is Self-identified; a whirling dervish, Spiraling in New Time/Space.[2]

The second important affirmation is that *it is good for women to love women*. Scholars Janice Raymond[3] and Lillian Faderman,[4] and theologian Mary Hunt[5] have demonstrated how the concept of women loving women, as friends and lovers, has been expunged from history, and how the strength and power of that love has been, and still is, devalued and trivialised. But the truth is that for most women, other women are an extremely important focus for their lives despite this lack of affirmation. Mary Daly has pointed out that, ironically, women find more authentic 'otherness' in other women. Our sameness as women provides a shared experience that allows the particularity of each one, the real 'otherness' unmediated by patriarchal baggage, to emerge.[6]

Significantly, passionate friendships between women which were a crucial and accepted part of the lives of middle class women in the eighteenth and nineteenth century and earlier, changed significantly in the late nineteenth century when women gained the possibility of economic independence, and such love became threatening to the social order.

Sexologists then transformed love between women into freakishness, creating a stereotype of the lesbian, who was considered to be a member of an intermediate sex, neither female nor male.

The third important feminist insight is that *sexuality and gender are socially constructed*. The Christian idea of 'natural' roles for women and men, and the consequent inevitability of heterosexuality are challenged by this. In her essay, 'Compulsory Heterosexuality and Lesbian Existence', Adrienne Rich analyses the forces employed to conscript women into heterosexuality. Among the more obvious she lists, 'the chastity belt, child marriage, erasure of lesbian existence (except as erotic or perverse) in art, literature, film; idealisation of heterosexual romance and marriage.'[7] These forces combine to provide the means of assuring the male right of physical, economical and emotional access to women. She concludes that, for women, heterosexuality may not be a 'preference' at all, but something that has to be imposed, managed, organised, propagandised, and maintained by force. Janice Raymond adds that women and men are constructed so as to necessitate heterosexual union. Sex roles must be created so that no human being of either gender is fully capable of independent functioning and heterosexual coupling then seems natural and inevitable.[8]

According to this lesbian feminist analysis, heterosexuality is a political institution, which is founded upon the ideology of 'difference'. In so far as Christian teaching promotes a narrow and restrictive telos for male and female through its emphasis on 'complementarity' it both reflects and contributes to this political system, and deserves to be challenged. Anne Borrowdale points out:

> Writings for Christian men often stress the importance of male headship, and writings for Christian women emphasise the importance of submis-

sion. Teachings about submission are picked up by women in violent situations. One battered woman was counselled by her pastor: "Each time your husband hits you just think of it as an opportunity to be a little closer to Jesus and the angels."[9]

In addition, images of God as exclusively male contributed to the denigration of women that has characterised Christian history, as does the all-male priesthood which still predominates in the Christian church. There is a need for a revolution in Christian sexual ethics, informed by the insights of feminism.

What will the new ethic look like? In the first place, sexuality will no longer be seen as merely an individual moral issue, but also as a deeply political one. Sexuality is not merely about what people do in the privacy of their bedrooms. As sexual beings we are all profoundly influenced by society outside of the bedroom, so the 'public' and the 'private' cannot easily be separated. This does not rule out an appropriate level of privacy which should, of course, accompany our intimate relationships. But the trouble with Christianity is that it has often kept the wrong things private. Rape and sexual harassment of women and the abuse of children, for instance, have been considered to be issues of private morality, treatment of them lacking a realistic analysis of gender and power in relationships. Such issues have a political aspect because they are perpetrated in a society which has constructed a male sexuality which is aggressive, violent and uncontrollable, and judges men on the assumption that their behaviour is inevitable and therefore excusable. Female sexuality is a derivative of this: passive, submissive, and meaningless in isolation. That which is 'sexy' in our society involves dominance of men over women – an inequality maintained by violence, or the threat of it. The challenge which faces Christianity is to make equality and mutuality 'sexy' in a sexist society where such a concept is anathema.

With that end in mind, the Christian churches could do much worse than to look at lesbian and gay relationships as a possible model for the future. Given the construction of gender in our society, there is a structural inequality between men and women, which makes all heterosexual relationships necessarily unequal. When men marry women, they carry into the relationship considerable social and political power. The organisations of state will back their power through religion, the courts and the social services. However hard an individual couple may strive to be equal, the social reality cannot be denied. In contrast, lesbian and gay relationships at least hold the possibility of equality. Obviously, there are plenty of other factors which will work against the equality of partners in a same-sex relationship: age, economic means, class, race etc., but the major inequality of gender is missing. In striving to create a new sexual future, Christianity must recognise that it has much to learn from lesbians and gay men.

How will the new sexual future come into being? Traditionally,

Christian sexual ethics have been formed by those in power in the churches on behalf of everyone else. The rules and guidelines which currently exist are therefore experienced as at best irrelevant, and at worst oppressive to a large number of Christians: women in particular. In so far as feminism has encouraged empowerment, autonomy and recognition of our interrelatedness as human beings, the new ethic must be self-defined and self-imposed. These self-defined guidelines will not be individualistic, neither will they promote the much-feared 'free for all'. Rather, in line with what has already been expressed above, the overall purpose of any ethical guideline informed by feminism will always be to protect those with less power from those who have more.

Finally, in line with the 'holistic' character of feminism, the discussion process by which sexual ethics will be formed and reformed will be one in which sexuality is always contextualised within relationships. Sexuality is not a discrete area of life characterised by genital activity. It is an integral part of who we are as total personalities. There is therefore no human being alive for whom sexuality is irrelevant, because all human beings, by definition, exist within a complex web of relationships. Only some of these, if any, will be overtly sexual, but all of them involve sexual, embodied beings.

Notes

1. Daphne Hampson, 'Luther on the Self: A Feminist Critique,' in *Feminist Theology: A Reader, Anne Loades* (ed), SPCK 1990, pp. 220 and 222.
2. Mary Daly, *Webster's First New Intergalactic Wickedary of the English Language*, The Women's Press, 1987, p.167.
3. Janice Raymond, *A Passion for Friends*, The Women's Press, 1986.
4. Lillian Faderman, *Surpassing the Love of Men*, The Women's Press, 1981.
5. Mary E. Hunt, *Fierce Tenderness: A Feminist Theology of Friendship*, Crossroad, 1991.
6. Mary Daly, quoted by Mary E. Hunt, ibid, p.69.
7. Adrienne Rich, *Compulsory Heterosexuality and Lesbian Existence*, Only Women Press, 1981, p. 12.
8. Quoted by Sheila Jeffreys, *Anticlimax: A Feminist Perspective on the Sexual Revolution*, The Women's Press, 1990, p. 298.
9. Anne Borrowdale, *Christianity and Pornography*, A write up of her lecture delivered at an ISCS conference, April 1991, printed in the ISCS Bulletin 4, Summer 1991.

7.2 Toward A Theology for Lesbian and Gay Marriage

Robert Williams

Increasingly, the issue of the appropriateness of a liturgical blessing of same-sex committed relationships is becoming an agenda item for church conventions at the parish, diocesan, and national levels in the Episcopal Church in the United States, as well as in other provinces of the Anglican communion and other denominations. These discussions are typically quite heated, and to avoid confrontation, discussion is often cut short by parliamentary action – some form of 'tabling' the debate. In a good many cases, the discussion is cut short because, it is alleged, we do not have a clear theological framework for understanding such blessings. The 'Blue Book Report' of the Commission on Health and Human Affairs prepared for General Convention 1988 took this approach:

> The Commission is not ready to take a position on the blessing of same sex couples. This question does raise a myriad of other questions, such as the meaning of marriage, the meaning of blessings, the origin of homosexual orientation, etc.[1]

I happen to believe that the concern about a 'theological framework' in these debates is almost always a smokescreen, a parliamentary action to curtail a debate that threatens to get out of hand. The fact that we have no clear 'theological framework' does not seem to deter us, after all, from performing any of a number of other liturgies (such as heterosexual marriage). We haven't had a clear theology of confirmation for centuries, yet we keep on confirming, over the protests of a number of theologians and liturgical scholars who would like to see the practice of confirmation, as distinct from baptism, ended. It is doubtful whether one could claim the Anglican communion has a clear or unified theology of the Eucharist, for that matter.

Even if the concern about the lack of a theological foundation is simply a smokescreen, it is an effective one. With our excessive fear of conflict within the church, important and necessary discussion is brought to a premature end. In an attempt to prevent the curtailing of future debates on this topic, I would like, then, to offer one possible approach to a theology of same-sex unions.[2]

A Rose By Any Other Name

Most discussions about the appropriateness of a liturgical blessing of same-sex unions – including the testimonies of those who argue for as well as *against* the idea – begin with the statement that a homosexual union is not a marriage.[3] Many supporters of the idea feel the very word 'marriage' is so emotionally charged that it is better to diffuse that emotion by avoiding the use of the word.

The title of this article, 'Toward a Theology of Lesbian and Gay Marriage', was deliberately chosen. 'Gay Marriage' is a term most people find startling, but, I believe, for reasons that are more emotional than rational. Not many years ago, the term 'woman priest' had a similarly disturbing effect. Our visceral reactions to such terms are instructive: They tell us more about our actual, 'operational theology,' than the rational statements we make. The thesis of this article is that a covenanted relationship between two women or two men is just as much a Christian *marriage* as that between a man and a woman; and the only way to overcome this visceral reaction to the term 'gay marriage' is to make a point of using it frequently.

Sometimes, in fact, objections to the word *marriage* for same-sex unions imply that what is being proposed is something *better than* marriage: 'Marriage in our society is such an archaic, patriarchal institution. Why should gay men and lesbians want to buy into something that is so in need of reform?' While I wholeheartedly agree that the institution of marriage (and the liturgy) are in desperate need of reform, I must ask why, then, we continue to consign heterosexual couples to it. Any argument that can be made against homosexual marriage on this basis is also an argument against heterosexual marriage.

Others, on both sides of the issue, seem to accept the circular logic that a homosexual union is not a marriage because marriage is, by definition, a transaction between a man and a woman. Bishop William Swing of California appointed a commission (as a result of some flurry at a diocesan convention) to study the issue of blessing same-sex unions; then rejected the committee's work, objecting particularly to the proposed liturgy they drafted. Subsequently, Bishop Swing published a liturgy he has authorized for use in the diocese. Called 'The Affirmation of a Relationship,' it is to be used between the Prayers of the People and the Peace in the Sunday Eucharist, and it is carefully designed *not* to resemble a marriage. (An angry gay priest in the Diocese of California recently told me he has recently refused to perform heterosexual marriages. 'I'll affirm your relationship at a Sunday liturgy,' he tells heterosexual couples, 'but I won't do straight weddings until I can do gay weddings.')

In a newsletter to his diocese explaining his rejection of the liturgy originally proposed by the commission, Bishop Swing wrote, 'Thus far, everything I've seen appears to resemble a second class or derivative marriage. It appears to me that "blessing a same-sex union" is only a euphemism for "marriage".'[4] That the liturgy that was proposed by the California liturgical commission does resemble the marriage rite is clear enough; but why would Bishop Swing consider it a 'second class' marriage – unless he defines a 'first-class' marriage as being a *heterosexual* marriage?

In their concern to affirm the goodness of marriage ('despite its obvious failures'), the Standing Commission on Human Affairs and Health (of which Bishop Swing is a member) has used the same circular logic, and in so doing has committed its gravest error. The report states:

> The Commission affirms marriage as the standard, the norm, the primary relationship in which the gift of human sexuality is to be shared. There was no debate among us on this issue.[5]

In the context, the Commission makes it clear the 'marriage' they are affirming as the 'norm' is *heterosexual* marriage. In another part of the report, the Commission decries the fact that an assumption that homosexuality is a sickness, an evil, or a perversion prevents meaningful conversation between heterosexuals and homosexuals at 'the fully human level,'[6] and yet their undebated assumption of heterosexual marriage as 'the standard, the norm' relegates not only lesbians and gay men in committed relationships, but also all single people – heterosexual as well as homosexual – to the realm of 'substandard' or 'abnormal'. It is important to realize that the Church can affirm and strengthen heterosexual marriages without making that affirmation dependent upon contrasting them with alternative relationships or with the state of being single. The declaration of marriage as the 'norm' is a significant barrier to an objective evaluation of other ways of being sexual.

The definition of marriage given by the Constitution and Canons of the Episcopal Church,[7] and the definition a man and woman must subscribe to in order to be married in the Episcopal Church do in fact define a marriage as a transaction between a man and a woman; but the type of reasoning expressed by Bishop Swing above sounds suspiciously like one of the objections we heard to the ordination of women: that a woman cannot be ordained because ordination is, by definition, something that is conferred on a man. If this is the case, we simply need to recast this canon in more inclusive language. We can adopt a position akin to that taken on the ordination canons in 1985, 'This Canon shall be interpreted in its plain and literal sense, except that words of male gender shall also imply the female gender.'[8]

Expanding the definition of marriage to include same-sex couples as well as opposite sex couples is a far better solution than creating a separate entity for the blessing of gay-lesbian relationships. Then we would still have *marriage* for some people, and something else for others. The implication is that the 'something else' is something *less*. When the issue is one of social justice – and, given the Church's key role historically in promoting homophobia, any issue dealing with lesbian/gay issues in the Christian church is a social justice issue – we should be reminded of a lesson we hopefully learned in the black civil rights struggles of the sixties: the notion of 'separate but equal' inevitably creates *unequal* institutions.

Such a definition is not, of course, a *theology*; but it is a necessary starting point for constructing a theology. My contention is that we now have a legalistic *definition* of what constitutes acceptable conditions for a marriage, rather than a *theology* of marriage, because we have been slow to affirm the sacramentality of marriage. Instead, marriage has been one of the most blatant instances of the Church acting in service to the state, blessing what is essentially a legal contract, more concerned with property than with grace. Yet since the definition is in place, and we are accustomed to judging marriages not by how much grace they seem to exhibit, but by how well they meet the requirements of our legal definition, the definition must be dealt with first. My method here is, first, to examine the definition of what constitutes an appropriate marriage in the Episcopal church, and to consider whether a marriage between two women or two men can meet these criteria; and then to propose a more positive theological approach to marriage that, I believe, is appropriate for all marriages – homosexual as well as heterosexual.

A Working Definition

Beginning with the definition of marriage in the canons of the Episcopal Church, and expanding its inclusivity so that it can describe same-sex as well as opposite-sex unions, I propose the following definition of Christian marriage:

> Marriage is a lifelong union of two persons in heart, body, and mind, as set forth in liturgical forms authorized by this Church, for the purpose of mutual joy, for the help and comfort given one another in prosperity and adversity; sometimes also for the procreation and/or rearing of children, and their physical and spiritual nurture.

A Lifelong Union

Among the stereotypes of gay men in our society is that we[9] are more 'promiscuous' than heterosexuals, and that we cannot form lasting unions. Neither stereotype has much basis in truth. Sociologists David P. McWhirter and Andrew M. Mattison, in their book *The Male Couple: How Relationships Develop*,[10] a study of 156 male couples over a five-year period, found an almost even distribution in their random sample among couples who had been together 1–5 years, 5–10 years, and over 10 years. Of their 156 couples, 95 had been together more than five years; 20 couples had been together more than 20 years. These statistics parallel or are slightly higher than the statistics of a random sampling of heterosexual couples, which, McWhirter and Mattison comment, is remarkable in light of the fact that the male couples have 'none of the obvious binding ingredients' shared by heterosexual couples, whose relationships are encouraged by society.[11] McWhirter and Mattison's data was collected over ten years ago, before the AIDS crisis had changed sexual attitudes, and today most male couples are more committed than ever to forming lasting partnerships. Lesbian couples tend to be considerably more stable than either male couples or heterosexual couples, largely because women in our society are socialized to be monogamous.[12]

'Promiscuity' is an imprecise word. If the word is taken to mean simply engaging in any sexual activity outside of a legally recognized marriage, then certainly all gay men and lesbians, with the exception of a handful of celibates, are, by definition, promiscuous. If, however, 'promiscuity' is defined to mean engaging in brief sexual encounters with a large number of sexual partners, the empirical data again indicates that the statistics are about the same for homosexuals as for heterosexuals. In fact, Michael Schofield, in his study, *Promiscuity*,[13] concluded those who are 'promiscuous' are largely those who are *able* to be. Single people, heterosexual and homosexual, who live alone or have access to a private space, are the most likely to have a large number of brief sexual encounters. Schofield writes,

> This enquiry ... reveals that there is no such thing as a promiscuous type. It is more useful to regard promiscuity as an activity which thousands of quite different people take part in at some period of their lives.[14]

My experience in pastoral ministry with the lesbian and gay community, including extensive work with male couples, leads me to believe the goal of a 'lifelong union' is one most lesbians and gay men desire. Virtually all gay and lesbian couples I have met intend their relationship to be lifelong; and the vast majority of single lesbians and gay men I have known are actively seeking a partner with whom to establish a lifelong union. I would have the same objections to blessing the marriage of a gay couple who did not intend permanence that I would to blessing the marriage of a heterosexual couple under similar conditions; but I find the majority of same-sex couples are quite ready to 'solemnly declare' they 'hold marriage to be a lifelong union.' At the same time, we must take care that in the move to affirm same-sex marriages, we do not further marginalize gay, lesbian and straight single people. Most talk about 'promiscuity' tends to do so, particularly when it is contrasted with the 'norm' of marriage.

The Purposes of Marriage

An important change was made in the canonical declaration of intent from the 1985[15] to the 1988 version of the canons. Until 1988, the language of the declaration the couple must sign as a prerequisite to marriage, as specified by canon, used somewhat different language than the opening exhortation in the liturgy for the Celebration and

Blessing of a Marriage in the Book of Common Prayer. The wording has been changed, so that the declaration required by the 1988 canons does use the same language as the Prayer Book definition. Both the documents now assert:

> The union of husband and wife in heart, body, and mind intended by God for their mutual joy; for the help and comfort given one another in prosperity and adversity.[16]

Earl H. Brill, in his discussion of marriage in *The Christian Moral Vision*, Book 6 in The Church's Teachings Series,[17] extracts for his discussion two themes from this list – 'fellowship' (the word formerly used in the canonical declaration in place of 'joy) and 'mutuality.' His categories seem useful here, although I find *companionship* a more precise word than *fellowship* – certainly a more inclusive word.

Companionship

The greater emphasis on the *companionship* aspect of marriage has characterized Anglican thought since the Reformation. Martin Bucer argued in 1551 that 'mutual society, help, and comfort' should be listed before procreation in the exhortation, for it is the primary purpose of marriage:

> three causes for matrimony are enumerated, that is children, a remedy, and mutual help, and I should prefer that what is placed third among the causes for marriage might be in the first place, because it is first. For a true marriage can take place between people who seek neither for children nor for a remedy against fornication ...[18]

Jeremy Taylor also spoke of companionship as the primary purpose of marriage:

> The preservation of a family, the production of children, the avoiding of fornication, the refreshment of our sorrows by the comforts of society; all these are fair ends of marriage and hallow the entrance: but in these there is a special order; society was the first designed, 'It is not good for men to be alone' ...[19]

The liturgical reform for which both Bucer and Taylor argued was instituted, but not for over 400 years. The first American Prayer Book, and all subsequent books until 1979 dropped the entire discussion of the purposes of marriage from the opening exhortation, although essentially the same information was included in the canonical declaration of consent (the wording of which was very much like the current form, except that 'lifelong' was not included), which began to be required in 1949. Both the 1979 American Prayer Book and the English Alternative Services Book (1980) have finally heeded Bucer's advice, listing the companionship aspect before the procreation aspect (which is now in conditional language in the American Prayer Book).

James B. Nelson, in his analysis of sexuality in Protestant traditions, sees the ranking of companionship over procreation as one of the 'commonalities' of all mainstream Protestant approaches to sexual ethics:

> Protestantism rather early abandoned procreation as the primary purpose of marriage and sexual expression. Instead of procreation, the fundamental aim became the expression of faithful love.[20]

This aspect of companionship, variously referred to by other words such as society, mutual help, mutual joy, comfort, etc. is the beginning point for any theology of marriage, heterosexual or homosexual. It is rooted in the biblical tradition that God, seeing it was not good for the first human to be alone, created a companion for Adam.[21] Marriage, then, is seen as the gift of a loving creator, as a remedy for human loneliness.

The desire to love and be loved, to be a lover and the beloved, is so central to human nature that when it does not exist in an individual, it is a remarkable exception. Those who seem to have the 'gift' of celibacy, for instance, may be exceptions to the general human need for a lover; but they must meet their companionship needs in alternative ways, such as intensive community living arrangements. For the vast majority of people, however, this innate need for deep companionship is normally met through one 'primary relationship.'

The Genesis creation myth affirms our need for companionship is not a flaw or a shortcoming, but a component part of our created nature. An earlier myth, a version of which is found in Plato's *Symposium*, speaks of the universal human quest for one's 'other half'. Plato's story, like the Genesis story, attributes the human condition to a fall from grace occasioned by hubris, by trying to be 'like gods.' Human beings, Plato's Aristophanes claims, were once double – four arms, four legs, two heads – and when they became arrogant, the gods split them in half, which 'left each half with a desperate longing for the other.'[22] Plato, writing in a society that held homosexuality in considerably higher esteem than ours, suggested what we would today call 'sexual orientation' depended upon the gender of one's 'other half' – some of the original, double human beings were male/male, some female/female, some male/female.

Plato's assessment of the human condition is, in many ways, more accurate and certainly more humane than most Christian theologies have been. With the Genesis account, it simply affirms that it is part of being human to experience a 'desperate longing' for a lover; but unlike Genesis, it affirms some people will seek a lover of the opposite sex, others of the same sex.

It should be obvious that gay and lesbian persons suffer as much from loneliness as do heterosexuals – perhaps even more so, due to our marginalized position in society. In fact, homophobia and heterosexism elicit such strong emotional responses that lesbians and gay men are often estranged from their natal families, and thus deprived of what is, for most other marginalized groups, a primary source of care and nurture. A theology of same-sex relationship images God saying to gay men and lesbians, as well as to their heterosexual counterparts, 'It is not good for you to be alone,' and providing, through a profound relationship with a companion (most commonly called a 'lover' in the gay community) for their 'mutual comfort and joy.' In a gay or lesbian relationship, as well as in a heterosexual relationship, 'each may be to the other a strength in need, a counselor in perplexity, a comfort in sorrow, and a companion in joy.'[23] For a parish community to celebrate and bless such a relationship is simply to say to the couple, 'We share your joy, and we see your love as a gift from a loving Creator.'

Mutuality

Brill's analysis of marriage in The Church's Teachings Series, while acknowledging it 'is a rather late development in Christian history,' states *mutuality* is one of the 'presumptions' for marriage in the current understanding of the Episcopal Church.[24] He gives specific examples of mutuality, such as the division of labor in household chores, and the equal consideration of each party's career decisions. Brill suggests many men have found it difficult to put such mutuality into practice. 'Many men still expect their wives to wait on them, pick up their socks, cater to their whims, and make them the center of their lives,' he writes.[25]

Ironically, if mutuality is indeed one of the 'presumptions' for marriage in the Episcopal Church, it is a condition most lesbian or gay couples would find easier to meet than some of their heterosexual peers. McWhirter and Mattison speak of the process of 'equalizing of partnership' of the male couples in their study during their first year together:

> Tasks are assumed individually, usually because each person enjoys his partner's ability to show what he, uniquely, can bring to the relationship. There are no set 'husband' and 'wife' roles. Each man usually can perform all necessary tasks at some level of competence. Men together learn early that it is equally blessed to give and to receive, even when the temptation is to prove love by giving more.[26]

Lesbian poet Judy Grahn writes of her social function as a 'visible lesbian' living in a white, working-class neighborhood as including a certain modeling of mutuality for heterosexual couples:

> Firstly, by my clothes and bearing I model a certain freedom for women. Secondly, as two women living together, my lover and I strengthen the position of every married woman on the block, whether she knows and appreciates it or not. (Her husband probably does.)[27]

Of course, many heterosexual couples can and do achieve truly mutual relationships, too. Brill's assertion is that *all* Christian couples have a moral obligation to do so. Yet it is, as Brill points out, often difficult for heterosexual couples – heterosexual *men*, particularly – to overcome their societal gender-role conditioning in order to achieve real mutuality. Gay and lesbian couples, on the other hand, have little choice. Society has not defined role expectations for our relationships, and we must create our own systems for decision-making and divisions of labor. The result is that many gay and lesbian couples have achieved an expertise in mutuality of relationship. If homosexual and heterosexual couples had a forum for interaction (such as a parish couples' group) it just might be that heterosexual couples would find they can learn much from lesbian and gay couples.

Children

A significantly large number of gay men and lesbians are parents. Some have children from previous heterosexual marriages. Others are choosing to become parents, through such means as adoption or acting as foster parents. Increasingly large numbers of lesbians, particularly, are making use of alternative reproductive technologies (i.e., in vitro fertilization with donor sperm) in order to give birth to children.[28] Many gay men, too, are choosing to be parents through alternative reproductive technologies – often a lesbian choosing to become pregnant will choose a gay male friend as the donor, for instance; and a variety of shared parenting arrangements are made in such cases.

The fact that many lesbians and gay men are choosing to become parents, coupled with the fact that many heterosexual couples choose not to have children, has significantly changed the relationship between marriage and parenting. The empirical data showing that children raised in gay or lesbian households, or in single-parent households, are just as 'normal' and 'well-adjusted' (and just as likely to be heterosexual) as children raised in traditional, nuclear families relegates the concern for 'the welfare of the children' to the realm of nostalgia or hysteria.[29] In fact, some of the most serious problems that do significantly affect the welfare of children, such as incest and child abuse, are found almost entirely in 'traditional' mother-father households, almost never in single-parent or gay or lesbian households. One might just as well argue that children raised by lesbian parents stand a better chance of being 'well-adjusted.' The experience of growing up in a non-traditional household does appear to give children some advantages. Black lesbian feminist Audre Lorde asked her 14-year old son, Jonathan, what he felt were the positive and negative aspects of having grown up with lesbian parents:

> He said the strongest benefit he felt that he had gained was that he knew a lot more about people than most other kids his age that he knew, and that he did not have a lot of the hang-ups that some other boys did about men and women.

And the most negative aspect he felt. Jonathan said, was the ridicule he got from some kids with straight parents.

'You mean, from your peers?' I said.

'Oh no,' he answered promptly. 'My peers know better. I mean other kids.'[30]

Since 1979, the marriage liturgy for heterosexuals in the Episcopal Church has made it possible for a couple who never intend to have children to participate in the liturgy with integrity. Most of the liturgy speaks of the companionship aspect of the marriage. The prayer for children,

> Bestow on them, if it is your will, the gift and heritage of children, and the grace to bring them up to know you, to love you, and to serve you.[31]

is marked so that it may be omitted from the prayers. The only holdout is the phrase in the opening exhortation on the purpose of marriage, and it is couched in conditional language:

> and, when it is God's will, for the procreation of children and their nurture in the knowledge and love of the Lord.[32]

This clause, too, should be made optional – one of the needed reforms in the marriage liturgy. Consider a marriage between a man and a woman who are both over 70; or a marriage between a man who has had a vasectomy and a woman who has had a hysterectomy. While such couples could say they are willing to procreate children if 'it is God's will,' is it not a little ridiculous to ask them to make such a statement? (In fact, with such a casuistic approach, a gay male couple could just as well promise to procreate children together if 'it is God's will!')

Since the advent of greatly improved birth control methods, it is now possible to separate sex and reproduction; and the Episcopal Church has, for at least ten years, officially blessed the marriages of hetero-sexual couples who intend to be sexual but not to reproduce. If we define marriage as being necessarily a transaction between a man and a woman simply because of the possibility of procreation, then, it is time to change the definition to match the reality.

Legality

Another objection that is sometimes raised to same-sex marriage, that is not included in the liturgical or canonical definitions of marriage discussed above, is Title I, Canon 18, Sec. 2(a):

> No minister of this Church shall solemnize any marriage unless the following conditions are complied with:

(a). He [sic] shall have ascertained the right of the parties to contract a marriage according to the laws of the State.

The argument is that, since no state currently recognizes gay or lesbian marriages, no one ordained in the Episcopal Church can officiate at one without violating the above canon.

This canon is, among other things, a direct violation of the principle of separation of church and state, a giving up of the church's authority to the state. This entire topic of the relative roles of church and state in the institution of marriage is a troublesome one. Dan Stevick, in his handbook on canon law, states flatly, 'The priest, in officiating at a marriage, acts as an officer of the community or state as well as of the Church.'[33] A number of Episcopal priests already are very uncomfortable with the knowledge that in performing a marriage, they act as agents of the state. Many are calling for a clearer separation of the civil contract of marriage from the blessing and celebration of that marriage by the church.

Canon I.18.2(a) was originally passed by General Convention 1904 (the present wording in 1973)[34] in order to codify a long list of prohibited marriages. Simply requiring the marriage to be according to the laws of the state was an easy way to carry out these prohibitions without having to spell out in canon law exactly what relationships were not acceptable for marriage. The more appropriate solution, of course, is for the church to carefully delineate its own guidelines about whose marriages can be blessed, and not allow civil governments to make those decisions for us.

There is historical precedent for the church recognizing marriages the state does not recognize. In the Roman empire, a marriage between a slave and a free citizen was not legally binding, but the *Apostolic Tradition of Hippolytus* indicates a female concubine could be accepted as a catechumen. Although not 'legally' married, she was not considered to be living an immoral life, for – provided she treated her situation as a marriage – the church recognized it as such.[35] In the American colonial church, although slaves could not legally contract marriages, Anglican clergy often officiated at the marriage of two slaves.[36] And finally, inter-racial marriages were not legally recognized by some states until very recently.[37]

Similarly, the fact that the marriage of two men or two women is not yet recognized by any civil government in the United States[38] should not be a barrier for such marriages being blessed by the Episcopal Church. In fact, as gay activists continue to struggle for legislative rights, it is a very real possibility that states may begin to accord legal status to gay and lesbian marriages, and the Episcopal Church may once again find itself in the embarrassing position of having to charge its outmoded canons in order to catch up with the state. It seems preferable that the Church take a more positive, prophetic role – setting an example for the civil government to follow, rather than vice versa.

Safeguarding Society

Another church-state issue is the curious clause in the canonical declaration of intent, up until 1988, that one purpose of marriage is 'the safeguarding and benefit of society.'[39] Although the statement has been removed from our current canons, the influence of the idea lingers. It is unclear exactly what is the intention of this statement, but it seems to be derived from the quaint phrase that used to be in the exhortation in the liturgy itself, listing as one of the purposes of marriage 'the avoidance of fornication.' The 1552 Prayer Book added for those who 'haue not the gift of continencie.'[40] Ironically, although the Episcopal Church has (thankfully) seen fit to remove 'the avoidance of fornication' from the reasons for heterosexual marriage – at least in the public statement in the liturgy – we seem to be witnessing a return to the mentality of 'avoidance of fornication' in the discussions of same-sex unions.

Unquestionably, the AIDS crisis has contributed to the sense of urgency with which the church is now viewing issues of human sexuality in general, and the blessing of same-sex unions in particular. It is perhaps reasonable to expect the widespread use of a liturgy for the celebration and blessing of a gay union could encourage committed coupling and, in the long run, have some effect on the incidence of AIDS cases. That effect, however, would probably be minimal, and a desire to control AIDS is a poor reason for blessing same-sex marriages. If the Church is to institute a liturgical blessing for lesbian and gay couples, it should be because the Church wants to celebrate and bless the life of that couple in the life of the Church – not in order to get them to make some sort of public promise to be monogamous, in the hopes that will somehow curtail the spread of AIDS. An indication of such an attitude is the comment of Bishop Swing of California, in his diocesan newsletter following his rejection of the work of the Bishop's Theology committee analyzing a liturgy for same-sex blessings, 'I am much more concerned about promiscuity than homosexuality.'[41]

That a marriage should, ideally, be a sexually exclusive relationship, and that the Church has the right to refuse to bless the marriage of a couple that does not intend such exclusivity, is not in question; but if the Church is not to make a mockery of the word *blessing*, we must be very careful that what we are saying to the gay couple standing before us is, 'We celebrate your love for each other;' not, 'This is the lesser of two evils – certainly better than being single and promiscuous.' We must hope the Church does not do the right thing for the wrong reason.

If, on the other hand, the Church is concerned to encourage as many people as possible to live in committed relationships, a liturgical celebration of a same-sex covenant would certainly help do so. In the Episcopal Diocese of Rochester, New York, where same-sex blessings have been performed with official diocesan sanction for over 17 years, diocesan statistics show that those same-sex couples who have had a liturgical blessing of their union and the pre-ceremonial counseling that is a prerequisite not only have a higher 'success rate' than same-sex couples who did not have the ceremony, but also a higher rate than married *heterosexual* couples.[42]

There is another possible meaning embedded in the concept of 'the safeguarding and benefit of society' that is equally problematic. That is simply the expectation that marriage somehow 'stabilizes' society, and that the more people who are safely contained in monogamous marriages, the more stable the society will be. Actually, given the appallingly high incidence of domestic violence,[43] it could as well be argued that marriage *contributes* to the instability of society.

The notion that it is the business of the Church to be concerned with 'the safeguarding and benefit of society' should be questioned. St Augustine refuted this concept several centuries ago in his opus magnum *City of God*. The view of the Church as the guardian of society seems to be a legacy of the Anglican past tradition of being the state church. In a nation in which the monarch is given the title 'Defender of the Faith,' the Church is certainly charged with the task of stabilizing the society. The question is whether in so doing the Church loses its primary identity. In a more pluralistic culture, we have rediscovered the importance of the Church as a critic and conscience of society. At times, the Church, to be true to its prophetic tradition, must challenge and goad society; and at such times it will be perceived as not safeguarding but *threatening* the 'stability' of the society.

The fact that the Church has acted primarily as the 'agent of the state' in performing marriages is perhaps why we have not developed a satisfactory theology of marriage. The Christian marriage liturgy has been primarily a religious sanction added to a civil, legal contract – a contract more concerned with property than spirituality. We have not examined our theology of marriage because we have not had to. The heart of the institution of marriage has been the civil contract. The current question of blessing lesbian and gay marriages raises the issue that has long been ignored: Apart from the legal property contract, what *is* a marriage? It is not so much that we do not have a theology of *gay and lesbian* marriage as that we do not have a clearly articulated theology of *marriage*. A sound theology of marriage would be equally applicable to heterosexual or homosexual couples.

Constructing a Theology of Marriage

A Christian theology of marriage would, first of all, be rooted in the concepts of *companionship* and *mutuality* mentioned above. It would begin with the biblical affirmation of Genesis 2: That it 'is not good' to be alone, and that our loving God has provided means for us not to be alone, one of the most important of which is a committed, lifelong, ever-deepening union in 'heart, body and mind'[44] with a spouse. The very possibility that a relationship such as that we celebrate and bless in marriage can exist is a sign of the love God has for us. The condition of mutuality helps us affirm human dignity and autonomy, and avoid distorting our view of God from loving creator into a fearsome divine tyrant.

I believe the process conceptuality, with its insistence upon God as divine 'Love-in-Act,' is helpful here. From a process perspective, since the world is made up not of static entities, but of actions, God is not simply *love* as an abstract noun, but the divine *Lover*, who actively seeks us out and offers loving relationship to us, and encourages us to form loving relationships with other people as reflections and icons of God's divine love.

Marriage as Sacrament

Traditionally, the Church has taught marriage is a sacrament. It is not, in the Anglican tradition, one of the 'two great sacraments' that are 'necessary for all persons,'[45] but is a sacrament, and thus defined as an 'outward and visible sign of inward and spiritual grace.'[46] Of what, then, is marriage a sacrament? What is the 'inward and spiritual grace' of which marriage is the 'outward and visible sign'?

The Catechism itself is distressingly vague, and seems to suggest the very fact a couple can stay married is itself the sign of the grace of marriage:

> Holy Matrimony is Christian marriage, in which the woman and man [sic] enter into a life-long union, make their vows before God and the Church, and receive the grace and blessing of God to help them fulfil their vows.[47]

I wish to suggest, building upon the Episcopal Church definition of marriage, at least three ways we can see marriage in sacramental terms – as a sacrament of *redemption*, as a sacrament of *justice*, and as a sacrament of *incarnation*.

A Sacrament of Redemption

In its aspect of companionship, Christian marriage is an outward and visible sign of our redemption. A recent writing by process theologian Norman Pittenger, *Freed to Love: A Process Interpretation of Redemption*,[48] attempts to interpret the traditional Christian concepts of sin and redemption in a way that can be both 'appropriate to the Christian tradition as a whole,' and also 'intelligible: understandable in the light of our present knowledge and relevant to the situations in which men and women actually find themselves.'[49]

Briefly, Pittenger proposes, as an interpretation of *sin*, 'the alienated and estranged condition (from self, from others, eventually from God).' Pittenger further describes the condition of sin as our feeling of 'unacceptability,' which in turn renders us incapable of loving others.[50] *Redemption*, then, is God's self giving (in Christ) as Love-in-Act, which, when properly understood and accepted, replaces our alienated and estranged condition with a loving relationship; and restores our ability to love others 'in Christ.' Hence the book's title, *Freed to Love*.

In his exposition of sin and redemption, Pittenger is, as he acknowledges, very close to the thought of Paul Tillich, who described *sin* (our inevitable state of existence) as separation, among individuals, from oneself, and from God;[51] and *grace* as reconciliation. The process concept of God as Love-in-Act, to use Pittenger's favorite phrase, provides a very different nuance than does Tillich's concept of God as 'Being itself.' Tillich's understanding of grace seems to emphasize the individualistic and internal aspects, while Pittenger's view of redemption is more interpersonal and corporate. Redemption, for Pittenger, has a personal, internal aspect – indeed, it *begins* as an individual experience – but it is necessarily manifest in loving relationships with others, primarily in the Christian community.

If Pittenger's interpretations of sin and redemption are valid, then to be 'redeemed,' as Pittenger so dramatically phrases it, is to be 'freed to love.' To be redeemed is to *become a lover*. Marriage, then, the union between two human lovers in 'heart, body, and mind'[52] is a sacrament of our redemption.

Yet a sacrament, according to the classical definition, is more than a *sign* of grace; it is also a *means* of grace.[53] Marriage also fulfils this definition of a sacrament. The Christian Church is often spoken of as a 'school for love.' Marriage, and specifically Christian marriage, is another 'school for love.' Establishing loving relationships with other human beings is not an easy task. We have all been so wounded in our previous attempts to love and be loved, to be accepted and accepting, that we find loving difficult. This is precisely the condition of 'original sin' that both Tillich and Pittenger describe as the inability to love. The point of Pittenger's reinterpretation of redemption is that realizing we are loved and accepted by God is the starting point for becoming freed to love others; but still, we have to start cautiously. For the vast majority of people in the world, the relative security found in a committed relationship with one 'significant other' offers us a safe haven in which to practice love. (The security that can be developed in such a relationship is why sexual exclusivity is important – not as a limitation, but as a positive strengthening and building up of that one relationship, by reserving sex, one of the most intensive and most vulnerable acts of love, for that relationship alone.)

In some sense, we must affirm the experience of the parish community as central in the Christian life; for it is the concrete experience of Christian love expected, as the Catechism teaches, of all Christians, through the 'two great sacraments' of baptism and eucharist, while marriage is a sacrament 'not necessary for all persons.'[54] Yet whether or not marriage is 'necessary for all persons,' it is clearly *desired* by most persons. Most of us are so constituted that we need and want to build an intense love with one other person, 'a haven of blessing and peace,'[55] from which we 'may reach out in love and concern for others.'[56]

St Aelred of Rievaulx, a 14th-century Cistercian abbot (who, it seems appropriate to point out in the context of this discussion, was homosexual[57]) developed a rather unique mystical theology of companionship that recognized just this fact – through a profound, committed relationship with one other person, whether spouse or 'special friend,' we actually increase our capacity to love, so that we are gradually able to offer Christian love to a wider and wider circle of others – but always with varying degrees of intimacy: 'I take it for granted we cannot all enjoy each other,' Aelred wrote. 'Our true enjoyment is bound to be restricted to a small number.'[58]

Aelred spoke of such a primary relationship, which he encouraged each of his monks to develop with another monk, as a necessary retreat from which to draw strength for the more general expressions of love:

> It is in fact a great consolation in this life to have someone to whom you can be united in the intimate embrace of the most sacred love; in whom your spirit can rest; to whom you can pour out your soul ... through whose spiritual kisses – as by some medicine – you are cured of the sickness of care and worry ... whom you draw by the fetters of love into that inner room of your soul, so that though the body is absent, the spirit is there, and you can confer all alone ... with whom you can rest, just the two of you, in the sleep of peace away from the noise of the world, in the embrace of love, in the kiss of unity, with the sweetness of the Holy Spirit flowing over you; to whom you so join and unite yourself that you mix soul with soul, and two become one. We can enjoy this in the present with those whom we love not merely with our minds but with our hearts; for some are joined to us more intimately and passionately than others in the lovely bond of spiritual friendship.[59]

Aelred saw scriptural precedent for such a relationship in the Johannine account of Jesus and 'the beloved disciple,' whose companionship he described as a 'heavenly marriage':

> Although all the disciples were blessed with the sweetness of the greatest love of the most holy master, nonetheless he conceded as a privilege to one alone this symbol of a more intimate love, that he should be called 'the disciple whom Jesus loved.'[60]

The current marriage liturgy implies this notion of the growth of Christian love, from the particular to the general, in one of the prayers over the couple:

Give them such fulfillment of their mutual affection that they may reach out in love and concern for others.[61]

Parenting, then, is one – but only one – expression of this 'overflow' of love, this reaching out from the security of the spousal relationship into a love for others.

A Sacrament of Justice

It is the relatively recent teaching that mutuality must be an aspect of Christian marriage that makes marriage a sacrament of justice. As noted by Brill above, for the Church to bless a marriage today, it must be a mutual relationship, not a dominant/subservient relationship; and gay and lesbian couples particularly are in a position to make such admittedly difficult mutuality a reality. In fact, lesbian and gay couples have much to teach the Church about how two adults who respect each other as equal partners can build a relationship of mutual love that is based on cooperation rather than competition.

I do not mean to suggest all gay and lesbian marriages are ideal. Men in our society are conditioned to compete, and so a male couple, particularly, finds it very difficult to overcome their conditioning in order to not view each other, at some visceral level, as competitors. Even the attempt to establish equality can become competitive, 'like boys who count marbles to make sure each has an equal number.'[62] McWhirter and Mattison similarly suggest the fact men are taught to be 'providers' is threatening to a male couple's relationship, as each partner will tend to want to 'take care of' the other.'[63] Establishing mutuality is a task, requiring a significant investment of energy; but lesbian or gay couples have two significant motivators to assist them: first, the fact that they are the same sex, and do not have culturally-defined roles to play in the marriage; and also the fact that, as marginalized people, lesbians and gay men are likely to be more sensitive to issues of dominance and control, and to consciously work to avoid them in their relationships.

The insistence upon mutuality as a criterion of the validity of a Christian marriage does not imply the partners must make identical contributions to the marriage. Specific roles will emerge in an equal relationship, but they will be based upon individual preference and a natural 'division of labor.' Two individuals with widely diverse financial situations can establish a mutual relationship in which the partners contribute, not '50-50,' but each according to his or her ability, recognizing that the partner who may have less money or less earning ability contributes to the relationship in other ways. Similarly, the partners need not be mirror images of each other in order to have a mutual marriage. There is some evidence, for instance, that among same-sex couples, an age discrepancy of a few years can be a strengthening factor.[64]

If marriage is a 'school for love,' it is also a school for justice. The experience of living intimately with another human being, whose needs, wishes, and preferences daily confront and conflict with my own gives me practical experience in dealing with other decisions and conflicts on a larger scale – and so marriage not only is an icon of justice, it is also a *means* of justice. The mere fact of working out an equitable partnership between two adults with different needs, wants, abilities and gifts brings to the home level the communal (and Christian) principle: from each, according to ability; to each according to need (which is, after all, a paraphrase of Acts 4:34–36).

It is the unfortunate western Christian association of marriage with legal contract, above all else, that works against developing mutuality in marriage. A contract, which is worded 'if you do A, then I'll do B; and if you fail to do A, I am not obligated to do B,' is not a valid foundation for a Christian marriage. The ultimate contract is the 'pre-nuptial agreement,' which many have recognized as violating the intent of Christian marriage, for it suggests conditions that take precedence over the marriage vows themselves, conditions that would release one partner from the marriage upon the failure of the other partner to perform according to the agreement – but a pre-nuptial agreement differs from a standard marriage contract only in intensity, not in type. A more appropriate foundation for a Christian marriage is a *covenant*, which, in contrast to a contract, says, 'I will do A and you will do B,' and the two clauses are not dependent on each other. If you do not do A, I am not released from my obligation, under the covenant, to do B.

Most marriages in scripture, of course, were not based on covenants. Since, throughout most of biblical history, a woman was treated as a form of property, marriage was primarily a contract between a man and his wife's father, concerned more with exchange of property (including the woman) than mutuality. There are, however, examples of two friendship covenants of mutuality and justice between two people of equal status. It is inevitable, but still deliciously ironic, that they are both between people of the same sex – David and Jonathan and Ruth and Naomi.[65]

As Metropolitan Community Church minister Larry J. Uhrig has pointed out, it is particularly ironic that the words of Ruth's covenant with Naomi have been quoted (or set to music) often by heterosexual couples at their marriage ceremonies, 'while ignoring their context.'[66] The words are a beautiful expression of the type of lifelong, mutual covenant upon which Christian marriage should be based, but they were said, in the scriptural account, not by a husband to a wife, but by a younger woman to an older woman, a couple who decided to stay together even though the men to whom they had been attached had died, therefore dissolving the legal ties between them:

Entreat me not to leave you or to return from following you; for where you go I will go, and where you lodge I will lodge; your people shall be my people, and your God my God; where you die I will die and there will I be buried. May the Lord do so to me and more also if even death parts me from you.[67]

A Sacrament of Incarnation

One of the chief characteristics that distinguishes a marriage from other forms of intimate friendship is that it is expected and asssumed to be a sexual relationship, as indicated by defining marriage as a 'union ... in heart, *body*, and mind.'[68] It is in this sexual aspect that marriage is a sacrament of incarnation.

The central doctrine of the incarnation of Christ is perhaps the most unique doctrine of Christianity, that which sets it apart from other world religions. Very early in Christian history it was realized the doctrine of the incarnation of Christ had important implications for the treatment of the human body. Margaret Miles, for instance, has asserted the early Christians 'cared for living bodies and dead bodies because they understood that the Incarnation of Christ had once and for all settled the issue of the value of the human body.'[69] Anglican reformation theologian Richard Hooker wrote, 'The honor which our flesh hath by beinge the flesh of the Sonne of God is in manie respectes greate.'[70] James B. Nelson has argued a Christian theology and ethic of sexuality should be based upon the principle of incarnation or 'embodiment.'[71]

Mystics for centuries have made the connection between the longing for union with God and the longing for union with another person that is the sexual urge. In fact, our embodied sexual longings – the intense and inevitably frustrated desire to transcend the boundaries of our skin and be truly at one with another person – can be seen as an icon, even as a manifestation of, our desire to experience union with God. We do not ever achieve this union, either with another person or with God, in any lasting way in our present existence; yet we can occasionally catch glimpses of the eschatalogical promise of such union. A primary occasion for such foretastes of the Realm of God is the fleeting sense of union we can feel during sexual activity, and particularly during a shared orgasm. Beverly Harrison has observed orgasm is a 'powerful metaphor for spiritual blessing and healing.'[72] This orgasmic blessing, both its brief and occasional realization and its implied promise of eternal blessing, makes sex within marriage a sacrament within a sacrament – a rich sacrament of incarnation.

Conclusion

While from the point of view of the larger society, marriage is primarily a contract involving property, distinctively *Christian* marriage, a covenant relationship between two equals, is appropriately called a sacrament, for it is potentially a sacramental manifestation of God's redemption, God's justice, and God's incarnation. When freed from the unfortunate associations marriage has acquired, such as an overemphasis on procreation and on legal contract, Christian marriage is equally valid for heterosexual or homosexual couples, available to both as a sign of grace and a means of grace. When marriage is properly understood – as Martin Bucer argued over four centuries ago – as being primarily for companionship, not for procreation or parenting or 'the avoidance of fornication,' then its grace is operative equally for all couples who wish to enter into a covenanted relationship, whether they are a man and a woman, two women, or two men.

Notes

1. Episcopal Church Commission on Health and Human Affairs Report, Final Draft, 1–25–88, p. 22.

2. It is not within the scope of this paper to debate whether homosexuality *per se* is a valid Christian lifestyle. As a gay Christian, I assume that it is. For those who seek more information on the topic of homosexuality, I recommend John S. Spong, *Living in Sin? A Bishop Rethinks Human Sexuality* (New York: Harper & Row, 1988); and on the etiology of homosexuality, James D. Weinrich, *Sexual Landscapes: Why We Are Who We Are, Why We Love Whom We Love* (New York: Scribners, 1987).

3. The Metropolitan Community Church, a primarily lesbian and gay denomination with evangelical roots, has performed blessings of same-sex couples for several years. As a matter of policy, they insist upon using the term 'Holy Union' for such blessings, to distinguish the church ceremony from the legal entity of marriage. Occasionally, MCC ministers do perform heterosexual marriages, for which they have legal authority, and they do call these 'marriages.'

4. The Bishop's Newsletter, The Episcopal Church in the Diocese of California, VI:15, November 21, 1986. The Diocese of California has recently approved a liturgy called 'The Affirmation of a Relationship' for use in the Sunday liturgy. It is very carefully designed so that it does *not* resemble a marriage in any way.

5. H&HA report final draft, p. 11. Emphasis in the original. It might be pointed out that if the Commission had 'no debate' on this issue, it was probably not a sufficiently inclusive group to represent the variety of church opinion – a criticism made when a resolution was presented to General Convention 1988 requesting that an openly-gay person be added to the Commission. The resolution failed.

6. H&HA report final draft, p. 20.

7. Title I, Canon 18, Sec. 2(b) and Sec. 3(d).

8. 1985 Constitution and Canons, Title III, Canon 5, Sec. 1.

9. I take quite seriously the insight from various revisionist theologies that the notion of an 'objective' viewpoint is a fiction, and that it is more honest to declare one's biases openly. I write as a gay man who lives in a gay Christian marriage. The issue of the recognition of gay and lesbian marriages is not an issue about which I can speak dispassionately. Whatever customs and canons of scholarship may be violated in the process, it seems much more honest to me to use first person pronouns when discussing gay people. – RW

10. Prentice-Hall, 1984.

11. Ibid., p. 206

12. See Betty Berzon, *Permanent Partners: Building Gay and Lesbian Relationships that Last* (New York: E.P. Dutton, 1988), p. 160.

13. London: Gollancz, 1976

14. Ibid, p. 69.

15. 1985 Canons, Title I, Canon 18, section 3(d).

16. BCP, p.423; Canons 1988 Title I, Canon 18, Section 3(d).

17. Seabury, 1979.

18. *Censura*, 'The Order of Service for the Consecration of Matrimony'; 'the first reason for matrimony,' tr. E.C. Whitaker, *Martin Bucer and the Book of Common Prayer*, Alcuin Club Collections No. 55, 1974.

19. Jeremy Taylor, 'The Marriage Ring,' Sermon XVII in *A Course of Sermons for All the*

Sundays in the Year, Vol IV in Reginald Heber and Charles Page Eden, eds., *The Whole Works of the Right Rev. Jeremy Taylor, D.D.*

20. James B. Nelson, *Between Two Gardens*, p. 66.
21. Genesis 2:18–24.
22. *Symposium* 191a, p. 543.
23. BCP, p. 429.
24. Brill, ibid., p. 99–100
25. Ibid., p. 100
26. McWhirter and Mattison, ibid, p. 31.
27. Judy Grahn, 'Flaming Without Burning: Some of the Roles of Gay People in Society,' in Mark Thompson, ed. *Gay Spirit: Myth and Meaning* (New York: Stonewall Editions/St. Martins Press, 1987), p. 7.
28. The Commission on Health and Human Affairs is perhaps more uncomfortable with alternative reproductive technologies than with homosexuality. It is intriguing that the two issues are so closely related – so many of the women choosing artificial insemination are lesbians that the lesbian and gay community often speak of the 'lesbian baby boom.'
29. See, for instance, Joy Schulenberg, *Gay Parenting: A Complete Guide for Gay Men and Lesbians with Children* (New York: Anchor Press/Doubleday, 1985); or Cheri Pies, *Considering Parenthood: A Workbook for Lesbians* (San Francisco: Spinsters Ink, 1985).
30. Audre Lorde, 'Man Child: A Black Lesbian Feminist's Response,' in *Sister Outsider: Essays and Speeches by Audre Lorde* (New York: Crossing Press, 1984), p. 80.
31. BCP, p. 429.
32. BCP, p. 423.
33. Dan Stevick, *Canon Law: A Handbook* (Seabury, 1965), p.150.
34. Standing Commission on Constitution and Canons of the General Convention, *Annotated Constitution and Canons for the Government of the Protestant Episcopal Church in the United States of America, Otherwise Known as the Episcopal Church, Adopted in General Conventions 1789-1979*, Volume I – better known as 'White & Dykeman' (New York: Seabury, 1982), p. 403-414.
35. Apostolic Tradition 16; see commentary by Gregory Dix, *The Treatise on the Apostolic Tradition of St. Hippolytus of Rome* (London: SPCK, second edition, revised Henry Chadwick, 1968), p. viii.
36. See, for instance, chapter 3 of Pauli Murray, *Proud Shoes: The Story of an American Family* (New York: Harper & Row, 1978).
37. I am not aware of statistics, but I would hope the Episcopal Church would have been willing to bless the marriage of an inter-racial couple even if it were not recognized as valid by the state.
38. Same-sex partnerships have recently been accorded full legal status in Denmark, and several American cities, including New York and San Francisco, have extended 'domestic partnership' rights to municipal employees in same-sex relationships.
39. 1985 Canons I, 18, 4(d).
40. Book of Common Prayer 1552, published as *The First and Second Prayer Books of Edward VI* (New York: Dutton/Everyman's Library, 1968).
41. Swing, 'Bishop's Newsletter,' ibid.
42. Walter Lee-Szymanski, and Horace Lethbridge, 'The Blessing of Same-Gender Couples: A Rochester, N.Y. Experience,' published (photocopy) by the Episcopal Diocese of Rochester Commission on Homophile Ministry, c/o The Rev. Walter Lee-Szymanski, Calvary St. Andrews, 68 Ashland Street, Rochester, NY 14620.
43. For instance, statistics show one is at greater risk for assault, physical injury, and murder in one's own home than in any other setting. Rita-Lou Clarke, *Pastoral Care of Battered Women* (Westminster Press, 1968) p. 28.
44. BCP, p. 423.
45. BCP, Catechism, pp. 858, 860.
46. Ibid., p. 857.
47. BCP, Catechism, p. 861.
48. Morehouse-Barlow, 1987.
49. Ibid., p.2.
50. Ibid., p. 41–46.
51. Paul Tillich, 'You Are Accepted,' in *The Shaking of the Foundations* (Scribners, 1948), p. 154.
52. BCP, p. 423.
53. BCP, Catechism, p. 857.

54. BCP, p. 860.
55. BCP, p. 431.
56. BCP, p. 429.
57. This was the controversial but well supported claim John Boswell made in *Christianity, Social Tolerance, and Homosexuality: Gay People in Western Europe from the Beginning of the Christian Era to the Fourteenth Century* (Chicago: University of Chicago Press, 1980), p. 222; and the evidence does seem rather overwhelming. The House of Bishops agreed: When adding Aelred to the Episcopal church calendar, his homosexuality was a part of the discussion.
58. Aelred, *On Spiritual Friendship* 3.35, p. 138.
59. *Mirror of Charity* 3.109–110; tr. in Boswell, ibid., p. 225–226; interestingly omitted from Walker and Webb's translation, *op cit*.
60. Ibid. The translation is Boswell, p. 226. This passage, too, is omitted from the Walker and Webb translation.
61. BCP, p. 429.
62. McWhirter and Mattison, ibid., p. 33–34.
63. Ibid., p. 32.
64. Ibid., p. 35.
65. I am indebted to Larry Uhrig, cited below, for pointing this out.
66. Larry J. Uhrig, *Sex Positive: A Gay Contribution to Sexual and Spiritual Union* (Boston: Aylson Press, 1986), pp. 18, 60–62.
67. Ruth 1:16–17.
68. Title I, Canon 18, Section 3(d); BCP, p. 423; emphasis added.
69. Margaret R. Miles, 'The Incarnation and its Meaning for Human Embodiment,' Matriculation Address, September 1985, Episcopal Divinity School, Cambridge (unpublished manuscript).
70. Richard Hooker, *Laws of Ecclesiastical Polity* 54.4.32.
71. The concept is most concisely expressed in Nelson's *Embodiment*, cited above; more developed in his *Between Two Gardens*, also cited above. Nelson also explores specifically *male* sexuality and theology in *The Intimate Connection: Male Sexuality, Masculine Spirituality* (Philadelphia: Westminster Press, 1988).
72. Beverly Wildung Harrison, 'Misogny and Homophobia: The Unexplored Connections,' in Carol S. Robb, ed., *Making the Connections: Essays in Feminist Social Ethics* (Boston: Beacon Press, 1985), p. 149.

7.3 Lesbian and Gay Relationships: A Lesbian Feminist Perspective

Elizabeth Stuart

In his book *Body Theology* James Nelson distinguishes between a 'theology of sexuality' and a 'sexual theology',

> A theology of (or about) sexuality tends to argue in a one-directional way: What do scripture and tradition say about our sexuality and how ought it to be expressed? What does the church say, what do the rabbis say, what does the pope say? ... [A sexual theology asks] What does our experience as human sexual beings tell us about how we read the scripture, interpret the tradition, and attempt to live out the meanings of the gospel?[1]

A lesbian feminist reflection upon lesbian and gay relationships will usually be done in the context of sexual theology rather than a theology of sexuality. This is because Christian feminists interact with scripture, tradition and Church with a hermeneutic of suspicion. We have slowly come to the realisation that the ideology of patriarchy underpins most, if not all, of the scriptures and tradition. We can no longer accept anything on trust as God's word or revelation, everything is tested to determine who benefits or suffers from a particular belief or ethic, what power relations are in play. For a lesbian feminist the Bible is not a sacred text in the usual sense of that term – it is not beyond criticism or partial rejection. How can it be when it has been used to oppress, marginalise and disempower all kinds of people for centuries? If we cannot turn to scripture or tradition as authoritative starting points for reflection on lesbian and gay relationships, then where do lesbian feminists locate authority? Where do they look for divine revelation?

The Authority of Experience

No longer able to rely on any external authority, women have had to learn to trust their own experience and it is from this basis that lesbian feminists do theology. From our own experience we know that truth does not drop down onto us from somewhere 'up there' but emerges in and through our relationships. It is in relationships that disclosure and meaning emerge, in the betweenness of persons. Therefore we should seek God not in eternal truths passed down to us in books or through ecclesiastical power-structures but in the webs spun between people, in what Mary Grey calls a 'new awareness' or 'dawning consciousness'.[2] The lesbian feminist theologian Carter Heyward points out that the word 'authority' comes from the Latin verb *augere*, which means to cause to grow, to augment that which already is. It is not a possession but a dynamic power, the power of God's presence that causes justice, mutuality and compassion to grow between persons.[3] Like the disciples gathered together after the resurrection we find Christ 'in the middle' or 'between us' (Luke 24:36). This 'new awareness' or 'dawning consciousness' then becomes a measure with which to judge scripture and tradition and all Church teaching.

Christian lesbian feminists then have no hesitation or embarrassment in simply rejecting the biblical and traditional prescriptions on homosexuality as wrong and non-authoritative, because in the experience of lesbian women these precepts, if taken seriously, create brokenness rather than wholeness, inequality rather than mutuality, injustice rather than justice. They form part of the patriarchal, body-hating teaching which has oppressed women for centuries. On the other hand, their experience teaches them that loving lesbian or gay relationships create and manifest the qualities that reveal the presence of God. Carter Heyward, writing of the experience of lesbian love, puts it like this,

> With you I begin to realise that the sun can rise again, the rivers can flow again, the fires can burn again. With you, I begin to see that the hungry can eat again, the children can play again, the women can rage and stand again. It is not a matter of what ought to be. It is a power that drives to justice and makes it. Makes the sun blaze, the rivers roar, the fires rage. And the revolution is won again. And you and I are pushed by a power both terrifying and comforting. And 'I love you' means 'Let the revolution begin.'[4]

So lesbian feminist theologians reach the same conclusions as many other theologians on the acceptance of lesbian and gay relationships but by a very different route. I should emphasise that the lesbian feminist method of doing theology is not as subjective or individualist as it may appear to be. Personal experience must always be tested against experience of others, which is why all feminists place such importance upon the sharing of experience in story-telling. I alone cannot determine whether my way of being in the world and the relationships I make are suffused with the power of the divine. I have to be prepared to open myself to be assessed and judged and called into greater mutuality, justice and compassion by others, both present and past, and that judgement process includes scripture and tradition. Christian feminist theologians do not simply jettison the scriptures as irredeemably patriarchal, for scripture and tradition have shaped and formed us. But we refuse to make idols of them, we refuse to lock God into them, we do them the honour of entering into a relationship with them. The gay theologian Gary David Comstock describes the dynamics of this relationship in relation to the Bible,

Instead of making the Bible into a parental authority, I have begun to engage it as I would a friend – as one to whom I have made a commitment and in whom I have invested dearly, but with whom I insist on a mutual exchange of critique, encouragement, support, and challenge ... Although its homophobic statements sting and condemn me, I counter that those statements are themselves condemned by its own Exodus and Jesus events. Just as I have said to my friends, 'How can you express love and be a justice-seeking person and not work to overcome the oppression of lesbians and gay men?' in my dialogue with the Bible I ask, 'How can you be based on two events that are about transforming pain, suffering, and death into life, liberation, and healing, and yet call for the misery and death of lesbians and gay men?'[5]

Revelation can occur in the interaction between persons and scripture as it does between persons, for when we read the scriptures we are simply interacting with our ancestors in the faith. The Bible is above all else a collection of works which testify to different groups' experience of God over a very long time-scale. There are parts which we will struggle with and ultimately reject and parts we will welcome. The same holds true for tradition. The important point to grasp is that for a feminist theologian, as for any theologian in the Catholic tradition, revelation has not ceased but continues at this very hour in the interaction between persons, because that is where God is. Many Christian feminist theologians take the central doctrine of Christianity – the incarnation – very seriously indeed and take it to its radical conclusion, a conclusion that only the Death of God theologians got anywhere near. In the person of Jesus of Nazareth we encounter the truth that God is not 'up there' or 'out there' but in our midst. If you like, God collapses himself into the person of Jesus, so that 'in Jesus we see a person rooted in God as source and resource of relational energy, wanting to draw his friends into this relational matrix (John 17:20–26)'.[6] God is embodied in Jesus and his relationships. The resurrection assures us that, despite Jesus' death, God continues to be embodied – but where? The answer is 'in us'. This is the meaning of the story of the Spirit coming upon Jesus' followers. God is now incarnate in relationships between persons who strive for what we might call 'kingdom values': justice, mutuality, compassion, peace, *shalom*. We are reminded of this at Church every time we participate in the eucharist. We hear the words 'This is my body ... This is my blood' and we eat and drink; they become part of us, part of our bodies. Any relationship, gay or straight, will be judged according to the degree to which it manifests those 'kingdom values'. There are some classes of relationship in which it is impossible to discern those values, e.g. sexual relationships between adults and children which are, by their nature, based upon unequal power relations, but both heterosexual and homosexual relations as classes of relationship are capable of manifesting 'kingdom values'. This criterion for judging relationships will stand lesbian feminist theologians in good stead when the Church begins to wrestle, as it surely must, with a debate that has been going on for decades in the academic field of lesbian and gay studies. This is the debate between essentialism and social constructionism. Essentialists believe that our sexuality is an intrinsic part of our nature which is largely unaffected by society: if I had been born two thousand years ago I would have been a lesbian, not in name, but in every real sense that I am now. Social constructionists argue that the concept of a homosexual nature was not invented until the nineteenth century. Before that there were people who engaged in same-sex sexual acts but this said nothing about their essential nature. So if I had been born one thousand years ago I may have had sex with women but I would not have understood myself to have a different sexual nature to someone who did not. Many gay people run away from this debate and grasp at scientific and medical evidence of 'gay genes', aware that if the social constructionist view triumphs we will no longer be able to demand toleration or rights on the basis that our homosexuality is an essential part of our nature and that we cannot help being what we are. But many lesbian feminists know from personal experience that sexuality can be extremely fluid and one's 'sexual orientation' can change. They would argue that accepting a social constructionist understanding of sexuality would set us free from what one writer has called 'the tyranny of the natural' because this concept is revealed to be a social construct. We can take some responsibility at least for who we are, what we are to become, how we act and how we shape others. The emphasis would shift from *who* we are to *how* we are, which seems to me to have strong biblical echoes. In Matthew 25: 31–46 the separation into 'sheep' and 'goats' is not made on the basis of any status but of how well they have loved. The social constructionists have shown how sexual acts are virtually empty of meaning and only acquire meaning in context. So a man and woman engaging in penetrative sex may be enjoying a beautiful expression of their love, or may be in the act of rape. A kiss from the woman bearing ointment is a different experience from a kiss from Judas for Jesus. Bisexuality and transsexuality are not taken seriously by the Church or by society at large, nor indeed by the lesbian and gay community, because they undermine the cut and dried classification of sexuality and sex with which society operates and throw too many spanners in the works. A social constructionist view of sexuality undoubtedly leaves lesbians and gay men more exposed to abuse and oppression by a society that does not operate according to 'kingdom values'. However, I believe this view is ultimately liberating because it releases everyone from a strait-jacket of fixed natures and removes so many barriers to relating; we become people open to change through relationships, open to the disturbing, transforming presence of God in the betweenness of persons in relationship.

Ideals and Idols

As Christians how are we to understand lesbian and gay relationships and what qualities do we expect to see manifest in them? There are theologians who argue that lesbian and gay relationships are of equivalent status to[7] or are marriages.[8] They argue this on the basis that homosexual unions can fulfil most of the purposes of marriage as set down by the Church. For example the Alternative Service Book of the Church of England defines marriage as being given

> that husband and wife may comfort and help each other, living faithfully together in need and in plenty, in sorrow and joy. It is given, that with delight and tenderness they may know each other in love, and through the joy of their bodily union, may strengthen the union of their hearts and lives. It is given that they may have children and be blessed in caring for them and bringing them up in accordance with God's will, to his praise and glory.

Same-sex couples may be unable to fulfil the third purpose of marriage but this puts them in the same position as heterosexual couples unable to have children for whatever reason. I think it is no accident that those who argue along these lines, whether homosexual or heterosexual, are usually men. Lesbian feminists tend to be highly suspicious of arguments which try and define their relationships in terms of marriage or try and argue that our relationships can exhibit the characteristics of marriage. A few quotations from a variety of feminists speaking about marriage will indicate why:

> [It] is a labour relationship ... The marriage ceremony parallels with the signing of indentures, or even more with the selling of oneself into personal, domestic slavery when one can see no other way to support oneself adequately.[9]

> [It] is not a union of souls or a partnership of equals. It is not a highly developed form of relationship but the most degraded.[10]

> [It] is an institution which robs a woman of her individuality and reduces her to the level of a prostitute.[11]

> Chief vehicle for the perpetuation of the oppression of women.[12]

> Someone coming from another planet and looking at a marriage contract and the semi-slavery it entails for the woman would think it insane that she should enter into it voluntarily.[13]

Few would or could deny that, historically speaking, marriage has not been an ideal relationship for women and even today, despite lip-service being paid to equality, it is a lucky woman who finds it in marriage. Overall, the mental health of women deteriorates significantly when they get married[14] and we are all surely aware of the scale of violence and abuse that can take place in marriage. The purposes of marriage as set out in the ASB are not being fulfilled for a large number of people. As a headline in a national newspaper put it 'Lovely idea – shame about the reality'. In our country one in three marriages ends in divorce, the average span of what is supposedly a life-long relationship is nine years. And yet politicians, Church and society still push marriage as the ideal relationship: if anything goes wrong it is not the institution's fault but human frailty and sin. Marriage itself seems to be above criticism. It has become an idol. We are all supposed to offer ourselves up to it and those who will not or cannot (like lesbian and gay people) are expected to remain celibate and/or acknowledge that our relationships could never live up to the ideal. Feminists are highly suspicious of ideals of any sort, since they can be used as a weapon to disempower and subjugate, the ideals of woman-hood embodied in the Virgin Mary and the page three girl being obvious examples.

Part of the problem is that we have burdened marriage with too much. We have taken an institution which began as an economic contract, a union of two sets of assets in a male-dominated society, in which love had little or no place, and in the space of but a few hundred years we have redefined it so that now we see it, in our culture at least, as a life-long commitment of love where the people involved motivated by romantic love are supposed to fulfil the other's emotional needs.[15] A feminist would want to ask: can an institution which was conceived on the premiss of unequal power relations ever fulfil the purposes of marriage outlined in the ASB and therefore should lesbian and gay people be looking to marriage as a model for structuring and under-standing their relationships? And many lesbian feminists would answer a resounding 'no' to both those questions. However, it would be foolish and dishonest to ignore the fact that many heterosexual marriages do work and do fulfil the purposes of marriage as set down in the ASB. Commitment, hard work, and a great deal of struggle can produce relationships which obviously manifest the presence of God within them. Now, a lesbian feminist would want to ask, if marriage as an institution does not automatically guarantee this kind of relationship and if lesbian and gay couples can also manifest these values in their relationships, is there another model of relationship shared by both gay and straight couples upon which their relationships are grounded? I believe the answer will be 'yes, friendship'.

Just Good Friends?

Surveys of lesbian and gay couples have revealed that most lesbians and gay men in stable partnerships do not think of themselves as married but define their relationships in terms of friendship.[16] Heterosexual couples enjoying a happy marriage are also likely to attribute the success of their relationship to being best friends first and foremost. The particular qualities of friendship are that it is a relationship based upon equality, mutual affirmation and acceptance, justice and interdependence. It is not an inward, privatised relationship based upon concepts of ownership but an outward looking, over-flowing relationship. As Mary Hunt, the lesbian feminist theologian, has put it,

> I mean by friendship those voluntary human relationships that are entered into by people who intend one another's well-being and who intend that their love relationship is part of a justice-seeking community.[17]

And several hundred years ago St Aelred of Rievaulx wrote movingly about the nature of friendship,

> He is entirely alone who is without a friend. But what happiness, what security, what joy to have someone to whom you dare to speak on terms of equality as to another self, one to whom you can unblushingly make known what progress you have made in the spiritual life; one to whom you can entrust all the secrets of your heart ... what, therefore, is more pleasant than so to unite to oneself the spirit of another and of two to form one ... whoever abides in friendship abides in God, and God in them ... God is friendship.[18]

Indeed, if we are looking for models of relationship in the scriptures then we will find friendship held up and celebrated as being of God much more than marriage. It is surely highly significant that in the Hebrew scriptures those with whom God enters into formal covenants (agreements) are thereafter referred to as God's friends (Exodus 33:11; Isaiah 41:8). Covenants were usually made between conquerors and the vanquished and served to structure unequal power relations. The friendships of David and Jonathan and Ruth and Naomi are held up as examples of covenanted love. In the story of Jesus we do not know whether he was married or not, but we do know that his ministry consisted of making friends with the friendless, loving people into wholeness through friendship. In John's Gospel he talks explicitly about this,

> I do not call you servants any longer, because the servant does not know what the master is doing; but I have called you friends, because I have made known to you everything that I have heard from my Father. (John 17:15)

Before we pursue this model of relationship further it is important to deal with arguments against it – many lesbian and gay couples may understand their relationships in terms of friendship but are they right to do so? Jeffrey John raised some objections to my theology of friendship that I first outlined in *Daring to Speak Love's Name*.[19] I quote him at length because it is important to identify and deal with the arguments against this model:

But in Christian doctrine a marriage, even considered apart from procreation, is far more than friendship, and the term friendship is wholly inadequate to cover what marriage and sexual commitment imply theologically. There is no warrant at all in scripture or tradition for making friendship the theological model for a sexual relationship ... God is a faithful, covenanting God; and our sexuality is meant to express faithful, covenanted commitment to one partner ... Friendship in any normal use of the word does not imply sexual activity, still less does it in any theological use, and it is an abuse to try and force it to do so. Stuart calls on Aelred of Rievaulx in her support, but Aelred is perfectly clear that, though limited physical demonstrations of affection between monastic friends could be counternanced, sex could not. It is equally misleading to cite Ruth and Naomi, David and Jonathan, Jesus and the Beloved Disciple, because there is no reason to suppose that any of these friendships, deep as they were, were sexually expressed. Friendship and a relationship of sexual commitment are qualitatively different. One may have many friends; one may not, within any moral framework which remotely links with Christian teaching, have many sexual partners.[20]

Dr John's response to my theology of friendship exposes very clearly the different theological approaches distinguished by James Nelson.[21] He begins with scripture and tradition and endeavours to construct a theology of lesbian and gay relationship from that basis. I begin from lesbian and gay experience and bring scripture and tradition into dialogue with it. We go by different routes but our destinations are in sight of each other.

My first response to John's criticism would be to pick up on some of the language he uses. He talks of marriage being 'more' than friendship, of the term friendship not implying any sexual activity. From a lesbian feminist standpoint, one of the most disastrous things that ever happened in Christian thought was the absorption of a dualistic understanding of human nature which dissected human beings into bodies, thought to be inherently weak and evil, and souls, which were the parts that belonged to God and longed to be released from matter and returned to God. Sexuality was associated with the body and hence had to be repressed or else strictly controlled within the bonds of marriage. Along with the dissection of human nature came the dissection of human love: *agape* and *philia* (friendship) were pure, spiritual loves involving no bodily desires whereas *eros* and *epthymia* were the lowest forms of love associated with bodily desire. Non-sexual friendship became the ideal relationship, usually located in monastic communities. However, at the Reformation another shift took place which, whilst still emphasising that friendship had little or nothing to do with passion or the body, replaced the ideal of celibacy with the ideal of marriage. So that friendship was regarded as being of much less importance than marriage. Both these attitudes to friendship still have some currency in our society as Dr John demonstrates but they certainly have no basis in scripture at all and women, in particular, are claiming that they have no basis in our experience either. We are embodied beings and our bodies and sexuality are involved in every relationship we enter into, for our sexuality

> is the desire for intimacy and communion, both emotionally and physically. It is the physiological and psychological grounding of our capacity to love. At its undistorted best, our sexuality is that basic *eros* of our humanness – urging, pulling, luring, driving us out of loneliness into communion, out of stagnation into creativity.[22]

So it makes no sense to say that the friendships between Ruth and Naomi, David and Jonathan and Jesus and the Beloved Disciple were not sexually expressed, for without their bodies (and hence their sexuality) there would not be any relationship between them. It is the attempt to confine sexuality and its expression to marriage that has caused the marginalisation of lesbians and gay men and an emotional overload in marriage which many marriages cannot bear. Friendship is a sexual relationship, because it is a bodily relationship which expresses love. The passion that existed between David and Jonathan is obvious testimony to that fact, although I, no more than Dr John, would not dare to presume they made love. The line between what Dr John would describe as sexual and non-sexual relationships is not as clear as we have been brought up to believe and is even fainter in our close friendships. This might be deeply disturbing to some who have been brought up to believe, as we all have, that friendship is a 'pure' love unsullied by sexuality. However, lesbian feminists who believe that the drive of our sexuality is the drive to connect with others in justice and mutuality and therefore the experience of God welcome and celebrate the sexual dimension to friendships.

Friendship is a sexual relationship: does that mean, as Dr John seems to presume it must, that it is perfectly acceptable to engage in intimate sexual acts with more than one or with all of our friends? Lesbian feminists have turned suspicious eyes on monogamy and have come to the conclusion that monogamy has been a useful tool of patriarchy and capitalism. Friedrich Engels exposed the power dynamics behind monogamy in his analysis of class antagonism.

> The first class antagonism which appears in history coincides with the development of the antagonism between man and woman in monogamous marriage, and the first class oppression with that of the female sex by the male. Monogamy was a great historical advance, but at the same time it inaugurated, along with slavery and private wealth, that epoch, lasting until today, in which every advance is likewise a relative regression, in which the well-being and development of one group are attained by the misery and repression of the other.[23]

The recognition of the part played by monogamy in the oppression of women has led some Christian lesbian feminists to reject it as an essential ingredient of lesbian and gay relationships. Among these women is Carter Heyward,

> To be nonmonogamous is not necessarily to be, in the pejorative sense, 'promiscuous' – wanton and nondiscriminatory – in our sexual practices and choices of sexual partners. It may be rather a way of participating in the embodied fullness of different special relationships ... Fidelity to our primary relational commitments does not require monogamy. But learning to value sexual pleasure as a moral good requires that we be faithful to our commitments. This is always an obligation that involves a willingness to work with our sexual partner, or partners, in creating mutual senses of assurance that our relationships are being cared for. Thus we are obligated to be honest – real – with each other and to honour rather than abuse each other's feelings.[24]

However, I find myself forced to disagree with Heyward about monogamy. There *is* a difference between most of our friendships and those that are expressed in complete mutual body self-giving in sexual intercourse and this is to do with vulnerability. We yearn for relationships based upon mutuality, justice, compassion and complete affirming acceptance. All our friendships are an expression of that yearning but for that yearning to be fulfilled, complete and utter vulnerability, radical vulnerability, must exist between the friends. We long to 'jump about stark naked', to use a phrase of Kirkegaard's, to be completely ourselves with another person and for them to be so with us. Our desire to give ourselves and receive another in complete sexual self-surrender is an expression of that yearning and also a powerful symbol of it. The problem is that various forces in our society conspire to keep us apart from each other, to assume masks and play roles. In such an environment any kind of vulnerability carries risks of rejection and deep hurt; radical vulnerability in which we open ourselves completely to another, to reveal the 'ground of our being', carries the risk of destruction. We are human and therefore we are prone to sin, to give into those forces which conspire against mutuality and justice. Every friendship we make is a triumph over the forces of sin. A relationship of radical vulnerability is not only a triumph over the forces of disconnection but an experience of what life could and should be about, it is an acted parable of 'the kingdom'. Because radical vulnerability is a process, not a moment, achieved above all through a journey into deeper and deeper trust based upon deeper and deeper exposure of ourselves, we need some assurance that the other person will be there tomorrow to reaffirm us as we are and will struggle through the inevitable problems and tensions that arise in relationships. In many respects all friendships are based upon such implicit assurances, as Gareth Moore has noted,[25] but in a relationship of radical vulnerability implicit assurances are not enough, for the safety of both people explicit commitment, a covenant, is necessary. This covenant need not be pledged with great ceremony and certainly does not depend for its validity on the willingness of the Church to approve and bless it. The Church has long taught that as far as marriage is concerned it is the couple themselves who perform the sacrament of marriage, the Church simply blesses it and even when the Church has no part in it, for example, when a couple get married in a registry office, it is still regarded as valid. The whole point of a relationship of radical vulnerability is the exchange that takes place within it: I pledge myself to you as I am and give myself to you and you do the same. We want to grow into radical vulnerability together. We are on the way to becoming not just two individuals but part of each other, a community, as Jesus said, 'one flesh'. We have said to each other 'This is my body ... This is my blood'. Making love is both the sign and sacrament of what is and what is to come. The exquisite pleasure arises out of the mutual self-opening, acceptance and affirmation, the ability to let go, to be safely out of control. A commitment to monogamy seems to me to be a vital part of this process for we have to feel safe and secure with our partner – jealousy and insecurity are feelings antithetical to radical vulnerability, they actually prevent it or destroy it. Relationships of radical vulnerability are by nature fragile, they need attention and concentration if they are to survive. It is quite understandable why feminists want to react against the concept of ownership that has for so long been at the heart of marriage and instead put the emphasis on freedom in relationships. But the great advantage of being a lesbian or gay man is that our primary relationships are made outside the male-female dynamic of inequality. Even today men and women are conditioned to expect and accept relationships based upon unequal power relations and ownership. Two women or two men may find themselves struggling with other differences that involve issues of power and justice, e.g. race or class or financial inequality, but not that. This allows them more freedom to build their own relationships on the basis of equality, justice and compassion, despite external oppression. They do not need to feel owned or swallowed up, they have the opportunity to create something new that does not rely on old models of relating.

We are people in process, in a constant state of change, and because of this all our relationships are vulnerable to disconnection and to the forces of entropy. It is of the essence of a relationship of radical vulnerability entered into with freedom and between equals that the parties involved will be deeply committed to it. Their covenant must be taken very seriously. But changes around us or on us can cause the sustaining power of the relationship to diminish or cease and God to be experienced as absent. Some theologians argue that it is essential for the Church to emphasise the ideal of a life-long monogamous relationship even for lesbian and gay people because it will serve to make couples on the brink of separation think twice about going through with it. The problem with ideals, from a lesbian feminist perspective, is that they can often prevent theology from being rooted in reality. So that when people find they 'fall short' of an ideal they have no theological resources for dealing with the pain and confusion and guilt. Many women have been trapped in destructive relationships to serve the ideal/idol of life-long marriage or have found themselves margin-alised after making the decision to end an impoverishing soul-destroying relationship. From a lesbian feminist perspective it is more helpful to emphasise the freedom of the parties involved to with-draw from a relationship if they feel no longer able to fulfil the terms of their covenant or that it has been broken beyond redemption. It is essential that women (and men) have and feel they have autonomy and freedom in their relationships within the context of justice and mutual-ity, otherwise the covenant is not real.

It is, of course, perfectly possible to make love outside a context of radical vulnerability and anyone with any knowledge of the lesbian and gay community (or indeed the heterosexual community) knows that this is a common phenomenon. For some men and women what might be labelled 'promiscuous' behaviour may be a sincere search for radical vulnerability. We live in a society of instant gratification and commodification. If we cannot get what we want immediately we can shop elsewhere, if we get fed up with one brand we can try another. This attitude has even permeated into the way we look at religion so we should not be surprised if it has soaked into our way of relating. Clubs, bars and magazines make a mint out of such attitudes and as for many such places are the only source of contact with other gay and lesbian people it is easy to get swallowed up by the culture. Those who have experienced pain, hurt and rejection in a committed relationship may be so wounded that they dare not search for the like again. In a homophobic culture it is actually in many ways safer to avoid commit-ted relationships because commitment may increase visibility and therefore expose the persons concerned to attack, discrimination and so on. What is clear is that a lesbian feminist cannot argue that God stands outside such encounters demanding that people live up to an ideal, because God is not encountered 'out' there or in abstract ideals but in relationships. But we can say that God is there in the midst of their lives in the drive towards others and that the desire for connection with others, however superficial, is a call, a summons into something deeper, a faint vision of what could be, an invitation into something more radical.

I refuse to talk about relationships of covenanted radical vulnerabil-ity as 'marriages' or as being 'more than friendships' because to do so is to take them out of the webs of friendship and place them on a different plane. This is what has happened with marriage: the implicit assumption is that when two people get married they now 'own' each other. The experience of a relationship of radical vulnerability (which is not possible to achieve where concepts of ownership are involved) is an experience of radical connection with another person, a solidarity which is profoundly empowering and which makes those involved aware of (a) the lack of interconnectedness in the rest of the world and (b) the fact that right relations between people are possible. By empha-sising the fact that covenanted relationships of vulnerability are friendships first and foremost the couple are not disconnected from the rest of their friends. They remain part of a constellation of friends, a community into which their love can flow generating justice and mutuality and from which they can draw support for their covenant and types of friendship which they cannot give to each other. The doctrine of the Trinity could be understood as a powerful symbol of the fact that we seek community, not simply coupledom, and that although our profoundest experience of connectedness may be in a committed relationship of radical vulnerability, one person cannot nor should not be expected to meet all our emotional needs. The same sexuality that fuels our yearning for a relationship of covenanted radical vulnerability drives us out to make and sustain other friendships. Of course, acknowledging that all our friendships are sexual relationships and being aware that the boundaries between most of our friendships are blurred could be said to create a great deal of danger and threat to the relationship of radical vulnerability. No doubt this is true but the solution is to take responsibility for ensuring that justice is done to all friends according to the nature of covenants made between them. Sometimes painful choices have to be made which will lead to the loss of one friend for the sake of another but flight from responsibility by, for example, withdrawing from all friendships except the one of radical vulnerability is to treat those other friends as 'its' rather than 'thous' and is to abandon the project of 'kingdom' building. It is the passion, joy and delight we experience in *all* friendships that inspires and encourages us to transform the world. We see that it can be possible to relate to many people justly. To sacrifice that for the sake of our own insecurity is sinful for it is to give in to the powers of injustice and entropy.

Friendship is an inclusive relationship, everybody is capable of experiencing it, by emphasising the friendship that is at the heart of a covenanted relationship we do not separate off the couples involved but affirm that they are involved in the same project as the rest of us. Some because of circumstance or choice do not enter into relationships of radical vulnerability; such people are still sexual beings and still offer themselves bodily to others in other ways. These people have more time and energy to invest in a greater number of friends than those involved in a relationship of covenanted vulnerability. We are all guilty of buying into what Sally Clines calls the 'genital myth', the myth that sexual activity, in terms of going to bed with someone, is an essential ingredient of a happy life.[26] Celibates remind us that this is not so, that the essential ingredient for a happy life is friendship. By defining all our possible relationships in terms of friendship we discover a greater sense of connection with each other. This emphasis should also allow us to see that having children is not the only or most important expression of love. We are all aware from our non-covenanted friendships that friendships generate much that is good and beautiful and creative which nourishes and enriches our world.

Historically, however, the generation of children has been held up by the Church and society as the only acceptable outcome of marriage. Heterosexual couples who do not have children are often referred to as 'selfish' and those who cannot have their own children often go through enormous pain and distress. Many lesbian and gay couples long to have their own children and some do through artificial insemination or surrogacy. I wonder how much of that longing is an internalisation of society's expectations, a desire to prove to ourselves and to others that we are a 'proper' couple. In a grossly over-populated world, where millions of children are abandoned or orphaned, some rethinking needs to be done for the sake of justice for future generations, the non-human species and our planet, all of which demand our friendship. By defining covenanted relationships in terms of friendship we could steer the emphasis away from having children and on to a variety of forms of generativity which may include the adoption or fostering of children (at present not usually an option open to gay and lesbian couples) but will also include the building up of community, supporting the elderly and sick, teaching, writing, making music and art, in other words all those things which contribute towards the building up of *shalom*.

Dr John maintains that 'there is no warrant at all in scripture or tradition for making friendship the theological model of a sexual relationship'. He believes that the only model offered is that of marriage. I disagree with this on several levels. First, remember that I believe that all friendships are sexual relationships and I believe that the friendship manifested by friends in the scriptures, e.g. between David and Jonathan or Jesus and his disciples, is passionate, deep and bodily. But if we are referring to friendships of radical vulnerability then I would argue that when marriage is offered as a model of a sexual relationship it is usually lacking in that radical vulnerability. For example, Hosea's famous description of God the husband pursing his faithless wife is not based upon the model of two people giving themselves to each other in radical vulnerability. It is based upon a relationship in which the husband has all the power, and forces his wife to return to him by depriving her of the things she needs to exist and shaming her (Hosea 1–3). Similarly St Paul's instruction to husbands and wives in Ephesians 5 presumes unequal power relationships. Most often relationships of radical vulnerability are portrayed in the context of friendships in which sexual intercourse presumably did not take place, e.g. in Jesus' relationship with his disciples, Ruth and Naomi, David and Jonathan. The exception is the Song of Songs, a collection of disparate poems where 'the mutuality and fidelity between lovers, the sensuousness of their relationship, their devotion to each other, clearly emerge'.[27] We should not expect to find many models for sexually expressed relationships of radical vulnerability in the scriptures, or in traditions which grew out of societies where sexual activity was confined to and part of relationships based on unequal power relations.

What we find in the story and person of Jesus is a call into world-transforming friendship. Significantly, he makes his covenant of friendship by offering his body to us on the cross and in bread and wine. It is our task to integrate sexual activity into that new model of relating, trusting in the revelation of God in and through our own experience. As St Paul said, we have to work out our own salvation with fear and trembling, 'for it is God who is at work in you, enabling you both to will and to work for his good pleasure' (Philippians 1:13).

Conclusion

Debbie Alicen has pointed out that the word 'friend',

> derives from a word meaning 'free'. We generally consider a lover to be more important than a friend ... The fathers provided us with the phrase 'just friends' to indicate that it is 'someone I don't *have* (possess) sex with,' and the absence of overt sexual behaviour in a relationship makes it deficient and worth less than being 'lovers' ... A friend is someone who allows us the space and freedom to be, while relationships with lovers often feel binding.[28]

A lesbian feminist theological approach to relationships takes the concept of freedom at the heart of friendship and integrates it into the committed relationships of radical vulnerability that we all long for. In doing so we end with a model of committed relationship very similar to the definition of marriage provided by the ASB, but we believe that historically and structurally marriage has worked against friendship and served to divide up different classes of relationship, disconnecting people from each other. So we do not want our committed overtly sexual relationships associated with marriage, we want them associated with friendship. Like Stevie Smith, we know that never nearer shall we move 'to love than a friend's love'. We believe that friendship is the world-transforming, kingdom-building relationship revealed to us by God through Jesus and our own experience, and our embodied sexual selves are intimately involved in that. It is mistaken and false to try and isolate our sexuality and sexual expression to sexual intercourse in the context of a committed relationship because not only does this risk over-burdening that relationship, it deprives our friendships of the driving force needed to sustain them and through them change the world. Perhaps only women could develop or relate to a theology along these lines, because although I am very reluctant to make generalisations, it does seem that many men's experience of friendship is different to that of women. James Nelson argues that most men do not have real friends because they are afraid of self-disclosure,[29] afraid of handing power over themselves to another person, whereas women have seldom had power over themselves and have had to look to the affirmation of other women to gain any sense of self-worth or empowerment. Perhaps women's friendships and particularly lesbian friendships can reveal to men who have yet to experience real friendship just how meaningful, pleasurable and transforming friendships can be. If we could be 'just friends' in all our relationships then the kingdom of God would be at hand.

Notes

1. James Nelson, *Body Theology*, Westminster/John Knox Press, Louisville, Kentucky, 1992, p. 21.
2. Mary Grey, *The Wisdom of Fools? Seeking Revelation for Today*, SPCK, 1992.
3. Carter Heyward, *Touching Our Strength: The Erotic as Power and the Love of God*, Harper and Row, San Francisco, 1989, pp. 72–86.
4. Carter Heyward, *The Redemption of God: A Theology of Mutual Relation*, University Press of America, Washington DC, 1982, p. 162.
5. Gary David Comstock, *Gay Theology without Apology*, Pilgrim Press, Cleveland, Ohio, 1993, pp. ll–12.
6. Mary Grey, *Redeeming the Dream: Feminism, Redemption and Christian Tradition*, SPCK, London, 1989, p. 97.
7. Jeffrey John, *'Permanent, Stable, Faithful'*: Christian Same-Sex Partnerships, Affirming Catholicism, London, 1993.
8. Adrian Thatcher, *Liberating Sex: A Christian Sexual Theology*, SPCK, London, 1993, pp. 144–159.
9. Diana Leonard, *Sex and Generation: A Study of Courtship and Weddings*, Tavistock, London, 1982, p. 261.
10. Charlotte Perkins Gilman, *Women and Economics: The Economic Factor Between Men and Women as a Factor in Social Revolution*, Small Manyard, Boston, Massachusetts, 1899, p. 5
11. Mrs Flora Macdonald Denison in 1914 cited in Carol Lee Bacchi, *Liberation Deferred? The Ideas of the English-Canadian Suffragists 1877–1918*, University of Toronto Press, Toronto, 1983, p. 31.
12. Marlene Dixon cited in Midge Lennert and Norma Wilson, *A Woman's New World Dictionary*, 51% Publications, Lomita, California, 1973, p. 7.
13. Sue Bruley, 'Women Awake: The Experience of Consciousness-Raising, in Feminist Anthology Collective, *No Turning Back: Writings from the Women's Liberation Movement 1975–1980*, The Women's Press, 1976 London, p. 64.
14. Julian Hafner, *The End of Marriage*, Century, London 1993.
15. Susan Dowell, *They Two Shall be One: Monogamy in History and Religion*, Collins Flame, London 1990.
16. M.R. Loner, 'Permanent Partner Priorities: Gay Relationships', in J.P. DeCecco, *Gay Relationships*, Harrington Park, New York, 1988. Peter M. Nardi, 'That's What Friends are For: Friends as Family in the Gay and Lesbian Community', in Ken Plummer, *Modern Homosexualities: Fragments of Lesbian and Gay Experience*, Routledge, London, 1992, pp. 108–120.
17. Mary Hunt, *Fierce Tenderness: A Feminist Theology of Friendship*, Crossroad, New York, 1991, p. 29.
18. Aelred of Rievaulx, *On Spiritual Friendship*, Cistercian Publications, Washington DC, 1974.
19. Hamish Hamilton, London, 1992.
20. John, *op. cit.*, p. 18.
21. See note 1 above.
22. Nelson, *op. cit.*, p. 26.
23. Friedrich Engels, 'The Origin and History of the Family, Private Property and the State' in Karl Marx and Friedrich Engels, *Selected Works*, vol. 3, Progress Publishers, Moscow, 1970, p. 233.
24. Heyward, *Touching Our Strength*, pp. 136–137.
25. Gareth Moore, *The Body in Context: Sex and Catholicism*, SCM, London 1992, pp. ll3–ll4.
26. Sally Clines, *Women, Celibacy and Passion*, Andre Deutsch, London, 1993.
27. Roland E. Murphy in *The New Jerome Biblical Commentary*, Geoffrey Chapman, 1991, p. 463.

28. Debbie Alicen, 'Intertextuality: The Language of Lesbian Relationships', *Trivia*, 3, Fall, 1983, pp. 6–26.
29. James Nelson, *The Intimate Connection: Male Sexuality, Masculine Spirituality*, SPCK, 1992, pp. 47–66.

7.4 The Trinitarian Vocation of the Gay Community

Daniel A. Helminiak

John McNeill has repeatedly raised the question about homosexuality,
For what purpose? Why does God create homosexual people?[1]
McNeill and others have begun the slow process of developing a spirituality for gay people.[2] This essay makes another contribution to that
project and so helps to unfold the positive possibilities in the homosexual experience. This essay develops a trinitarian facet of the answer
to McNeill's question by portraying the possibility for Christian living
within the gay and lesbian community as an earthly parallel to the
inner-trinitarian life of God.

That the Trinity is a profound mystery does not mean that the Trinity
cannot be understood. Rather, it means that the Trinity offers a surplus
of meaning. Its mystery cannot be exhausted. Within this wealth of
meaning, one thing is certain: the Trinity is a mystery of the unity of
three individual Subjects in relationship, 'three Persons in one God.'

Already caution is required. As Thomas Aquinas insists repeatedly,[3]
we know *that* God is but we do not know *what* God is. We understand
God only analogously.[4] But especially talk of 'Persons' in God calls
for caution. In trinitarian theology 'person' is a technical term. It indicates the distinctness of three *Subjects* in one nature: divinity, or, in
the case of Christ, the unicity of one *Subject* in two natures: divinity
and humanity.[5] In contemporary usage, both popular and philosophical, the term 'person' means something else.[6] In contrast to medieval
ontological concerns, according to contemporary psychological
concerns the term 'person' indicates *what kind* the subject in question
is. So today 'person' implies what would classically be named 'nature'
and points to the intelligence, self-determination, dignity, and feelings
of the human subjects. Those who have such qualities are 'personal'
beings, 'persons.' Despite these differences and without further technical elaboration, meditation on the Trinity can still be relevant to the
ordinary Christian community and can provide accurate insight and
useful inspiration.

The Trinity is a perfect community of love.[7] In God Three distinct
Subjects share one life, one mind, one will, one being. They share that
so perfectly that they have everything in common except their individual identities. Moreover, their individual identities are determined
precisely by their sharing divine life. They are constituted by their
relations to one another. The Son proceeds *from* the Father, and the
Holy Spirit proceeds *from* the Father and (or through) the Son. So
there is only one God, but there are Three who are that God.[8]

Granted such Christian belief, four issues become the focus of this paper: 1) inviolable individuality, 2) among equals who are, 3) dependent on interpersonal relations, but 4) unconstrained by gender specifications. This paper first elaborates these issues as found in the gay community, then draws parallels with the Trinity, and finally indicates some pastoral implications of this comparison.

Human Relationships Within the Gay Community

Friendships beyond gender limitation.   Well known and prized within the gay community are female-male friendships that are free of all genital interest.[9] Such friendships exist not only between couples who are themselves both homosexual but also between couples, one of whom is homo- and the other heterosexual.

In contrast, in society at large men as well as women lament the difficulty of maintaining real friendships with one another. Erotic interest almost inevitably intervenes to complicate or destroy their relationships. This is apparently so because they are sexual beings with heterosexual interests. However, in light of the deep non-genital male-male and female-female friendships that also exist in the gay community, this explanation alone must be too simple. Rather, it seems, culturally based and societally reinforced sex-role expectations provide another explanation. In a heterosexual culture – one that acknowledges the validity only of heterosexuality – men and women tend to be cast vis-a-vis one another as sex partners. Deep male-female friendships do not feature large in such a culture. So the frequent actuality of precisely such friendships within the gay community represents a new hope for society at large. This contribution is significant.

Equality in relationships.   Part and parcel of true female-male friendships is the acknowledgement of both friends as somehow equal. In contrast, typically our society still treats women as second-class citizens. Further elaboration need not be made. The point here is simply that in the gay community an alternative is emerging. In the frequency of its female-male friendships, the gay community grants the dignity, individuality, and worth of both men and women – alone and in relationships with one another. This dynamism points to the equality of all persons.

This statement of equality within the gay community holds true across the board – not only when comparing men with women but also when comparing men with other men or women with other women. At the present time, the stigma attached to homosexuality is so strong that it acts as a leveling agent. Compared with one's homosexuality, one's social status, wealth, education, and renown pale in significance. Unfortunately race – though to a lesser degree than in the straight community – physical beauty, and youth remain important criteria for evaluating people in the gay community, as in the straight community.

Yet, beyond these, the gay subculture tends to see through most other externals sacred to the broader culture and to accept people on their personal worth. All persons are equal.

Personal growth through interrelationship.   By definition homosexuality implies intense, feeling-filled same-sex relationships. Far beyond what the broader culture allows, the gay community permits affection and its expression between two men or two women. Especially two men's free expression of affection strikes at the heart of the standard patriarchal culture. But the issue here is not the negative gay challenge to a patriarchal system; it is rather the positive gay contribution to the dissolution of sex-role stereotypes.

Our culture raises little boys and little girls to fit the expected models. Girls are to be soft and delicate. They may freely express their own feelings and are to be sensitive to others' feelings. Their role is to serve, to accommodate others. To the boys they are to be attractive, even seductive. And they are to be passive; their role is more to be supportive than initiating. They gain their influence through their men; they are the supposed proverbial 'good woman behind every good man.' On the other hand, boys are to be rugged and aggressive. Boys learn to control their feelings. They are rational, not emotional; and this sometimes means they are unfeeling, insensitive. They are the leaders, the go-getters. They cannot afford too much sympathy and they may not cry. For girls, the boys are the prize, the assurance of security and protection, the coveted husband-guardian. For the boys, the girls are a comfort, a support, a plaything, a toy, an ever willing respite from the battle of life.

Much can be said for or against these stereotypes. Many will object that the above paragraph is a caricature or that the times are changing or have already changed. Others, hopelessly ignorant of history and anthropology on all fronts,[10] will insist that men and women have always been as just described and by divine decree are to remain that way. In any case, society forms girls and boys to complement one another. The strengths of the ones tend to be the weaknesses of the others. Then, working together, a man and a woman may easily achieve success, according to the same culture's prescription for success.

Complementarity of sex roles benefits society at large. But what of the individuals? Are they to be sacrificed to society's goals? Unfortunately, the answer is Yes. That such 'sacrifice' occurs is necessary and even right. It is part of the human process of socialization. Wariness is needed only when socialization becomes dehumanization. But this danger is always real, and the stakes are always high.

Precisely because it touches these cultural issues at the core of social structure, the gay liberation movement elicits strong emotional reactions. This movement is saying that stereotypical mores are demanding too much, debilitating men and women in general and completely squelching the affectional life of lesbian and gay people in particular. Personal relationships, as the gay community envisages them, demand that people stretch beyond the standard sex-role stereo-types and move toward what has been called androgynous wholeness. At its best, the gay movement calls people to a fuller and richer human life. Gay awareness insists on the wholeness of each person, the value of every one, and the equality of all as people. The expected result is the emergence of a more humane world.

Obviously, the main issue here is interpersonal relationships and personal growth. The issue is the same one that emerges from other contemporary movements, especially the feminist movement and its younger brother, the 'men's group' movement. And lying behind all these is the twentieth-century breakthrough in psychological aware-ness.[11] By contrast, the main issue is not genital activity, homosexual or heterosexual.[12] Unfortunately, this point needs to be made explicit since many think only of genital activity when homosexuality is in question. The main issue here is not that.

Preservation of personal uniqueness. Neither is the goal some 1984-like homogenization of all individuals into androgynous bland-ness. If from one point of view relationships within the gay community transcend gender, from another point of view they do not. After all, at the very core of the gay contribution is the insistence that men may love men and women may love women with deeply felt affection. Precisely this insistence was the contribution of the gay St Aelred of Rievaulx in his classics on Christian love, *The Mirror of Charity* and *On Spiritual Friendship*.[13] So it is important that it is really a man or really a woman that one is loving. In the contemporary gay community a man does not particularly want to relate to an effeminate man on the pretext that the relationship is then somehow heterosexual, and the parallel holds in the case of lesbians. Likewise, though all have a basic equality in the gay community, personal identity is not lost. On the contrary, the personal uniqueness of each is highlighted and valued. The gay community is noted – perhaps even notorious – for its support of colorful, creative, lively, self-expressive individuality. The very word 'gay' bears this connotation. One implication of androgyny is precisely the validity of one's being one's full and unique self.

The above four points summarize the possible contribution of the gay community toward a richer understanding of the human as male or female. First, the basis of human relationships is beyond gender. All relate to all, men and women alike, in the full breadth of human capac-ity. Second, all are basically equal; in friendship there are no subordinates. Men relate in profound friendship with women, women relate with other women, and men with other men. The reign of patri-archy is overthrown. Third, all nonetheless retain their individuality. Men are men, women are women, and each is an individual, unique, gifted, and valuable as such. Fourth and finally, personal relationships are understood as growth-producing. People become who they are through commitment to one another. For this reason relationships in all their possible configurations are valued.

The Gay Community as Trinitarian

A comparison between inner-trinitarian life and the ideal of relationships developing within the gay community can now be made. As with all comparisons between the human and the divine, the statements will be analogous, the parallels only suggestive. Yet the basic mutual relevance of these two topics will be clear.

First, there is the issue of gender. We call the First Person in God 'Father' because that was Jesus' usage. Historical-critical studies make us well aware that Jesus' usage was conditioned by the patriarchal culture in which he lived. Even Jesus, Eternal 'Son' Incarnate, precisely because he was truly human, was limited in his human understanding and expression even about God.[14] Subsequent Christian doctrine and trinitarian theology make it clear that the essential relationship between the 'Father' and the 'Son' is not one of male camaraderie but one of generation. The 'Son' is *born* of the 'Father.' The 'Father' *begets* the 'Son.'

That essential issue, once clarified, can be expressed in terms other than those in which it was originally made known. In fact, in a different cultural situation this issue needs to be expressed differently if the original meaning is to be retained. Making its point, the Council of Toledo in 675 spoke of the Son's being born 'of the womb of the Father.' This is undeniably a feminine image. So one must be able to express the Christian truth about the Trinity correctly by speaking of the First Person also as Mother.[15] This term preserves the essential relationship, generation. The term 'Eternal Parent' would be equally correct, as would also be the term 'Mother-Father.' This last term has the distinct advantage of being strange, so its very usage reminds us that God is not like us or like anything else that we know. God is neither male nor female. And God is neither mother nor father, but God is both and more than both. On the other hand, the term 'Creator' is not an adequate substitute for 'Father.' God, Three in One, is Creator of the Universe, and all Three in God, in their respective ways, are Creator.[16] Styling the Eternal Parent merely as 'Creator' obscures the essential constituent of the Trinity, the inner-trinitarian relations of generation.

Saving that essential, non-sexist alternative terms for the Second Person in God are also possible: Only-Begotten, Begotten of God, Eternal Offspring, Eternal Child of God. Finally, the term 'Holy Spirit,' free of gender connotations, may stand. Well meaning but uninformed attempts to insert femininity into the Trinity in the person of the Holy Spirit merely exacerbate the problem by granting real gender to Those in God. An even worse usage, calling the Holy Spirit 'Mother Spirit' as a complement to the 'Father' in God, completely muddles trinitarian theology. This usage suggests that the Holy Spirit is a source of generation in God, whereas the Spirit is the terminus of all processions in God. And this usage might suggest that the Begotten of God is born of the 'Father' and the 'Mother' (the Holy Spirit), whereas the Holy Spirit proceeds from those other Two.

Though we may have difficulty developing a non-sexist trinitarian terminology, in the perfect community of love that is the Trinity, gender is simply not an issue. The relationship of distinct Subjects open to each other in complete self-giving is all that matters.

Here is a parallel with the personalist thrust operative within the gay community at its best. There not gender but true concern for other people is the accepted criterion of human relationship.

Second, the Three in God are who they are by relationship to one another. The processions of the Only-Begotten from the Eternal Parent and of the Holy Spirit from the Eternal Parent and the Only-Begotten set the distinctions among the Three. These relationships of origin and only these determine the distinct divine Subjects in their individuality.

That state of affairs parallels the personalist thrust within the gay community. There people are encouraged to be who they are and to become who they are through their relationships with others. The individuality of each one is not thought to be predetermined or fixed prior to interaction with others. Rather, each discovers personal possibilities and so becomes him- or herself in relationship with others. Limits are broadly drawn. One is what one is willing to risk in relating to another. In some way, then, the human situation is like the divine situation.[17] Interrelationship is at the heart of one's being who one is.

Third, the Three in the Trinity are equal; all are God. The perfect self-giving of the Mother-Father results in the Begotten of God, perfectly equal to the Father-Mother in all things except a distinct identity, 'bornness' of the Eternal Parent. Likewise, the perfect self-giving of the Eternal Parent and of the Eternally Begotten results in the Holy Spirit, also perfectly and equally God as they are. The Trinity is a community of equals sharing one life, one being, in harmony and perfect unity.

That equality in God parallels the ideal equality among people open to one another in honest and loving relationship. As humans relate with one another in truth and love and learn to share more and more in common, *what* they are – but not *who* they are – overlaps. They become one.[18] The gay community provides an environment that can foster such relationship. Transcending the limits determined by social sex-role stereotyping, women and men relate to one another in the gay community as friends, as equals. Likewise, stretching their personalities to androgynous wholeness, men with men and women with women relate in affection and love. They relate, as they must, not as half-persons – man or woman, formed by socialization to complement their opposite – and not, then, out of personal inadequacy or societal expectation, but out of the fulness of their personhood. The opposites expand, overlap one another, and find equality. All share the same – now not male or female but simply authentically human – qualities. Again, this human situation of equality somehow mirrors that in the Trinity.

Finally, Eternal Parent, Only-Begotten, and Holy Spirit retain their distinct identities despite their absolute unity as God. Those whose very identities are determined by the generative relations with one another, identical though they be in all else, must be distinct Subjects. They are not lost in non-differentiation because they are all equally one God. Similarly, people in the gay community remain who they are, man or woman, this one and not that one, despite the fact that all are equal and all are equally open to relating to all others. The ideals of the gay movement do not entail dissolving the differences between the sexes or between individual people. On the contrary, being gay forces one to find oneself and to be oneself. At the present time, at least, being gay entails a quest for self that straight people need never consider.[19] Precisely by means of unifying relationships, unique to the people involved, the gay community fosters and preserves personal individuality. Again, the Trinity provides the model.

The Vocation of Gay Christians

On those four points and with varying degrees of strictness, divine life within the Trinity shows a parallel with an ideal fostered within the gay community. Viewed with an optimistic eye and accepted with a Christian mindset, that ideal points to the vision of perfected Christian life announced in John 17:21–23: 'May they all be one. Father, may they be one in us, as you are in me and I am in you ... With me in them and you in me, may they be so completely one that the world will realize that it was you who sent me ...'[20]

The essence of Christian belief is that authentic human growth on earth is ultimately the result of God's own love, the Holy Spirit, poured out among us,[21] so in Christ humans become like God; they are divinized.[22] Loving one another as co-equal, co-determined, yet inviolably distinct people beyond gender limitations, humans grow into trinitarian life. Precisely because of distinctive aspects of the lesbian and gay community, life on earth for people within that community is a growing participation in God's own life, the completion of Christ's work among us, and the result of the Holy Spirit's mission to us. Thus, the Christian gay community has the possibility and so the vocation of offering our world a model of ideal Christian life in practice.

Some may be surprised by these conclusions about the Christian potential of the gay liberation movement. This would be true especially for those who 'know' the gay community only through the prevalent and predominantly pejorative stereotypes and are unfamiliar with the deeply religious and Christian segments of that community, or whose depth of theological insight is limited by a biblical or doctrinal fundamentalism. Nonetheless, it appears that members of the gay community who live deliberately in Christ *must* be destined for sharing the inner-trinitarian life to which all are called in Christ. If so, then they must grow in that life precisely by living their human lives on this earth. And since they are lesbian and gay, they must grow in their life in Christ precisely as gay and lesbian. There is no other possibility. Then, since they are indeed growing in trinitarian life, it is completely appropriate that aspects of their particular situation be highlighted and held up to the rest of the Christian community as indications of how God's life among humankind may grow. This is especially true when certain values in their life, in contrast to the culture at large, may significantly foster that divine life – as in the present case.

The possible surprise at these conclusions is merely that which always results from concrete application of the Christian message and especially from application to a particularly misunderstood and generally hated segment of the human race. The scandal is merely the scandal of God's love for us as revealed in Christ. It is the scandal of the good Samaritan or the woman at the well or the call of Matthew or the favor shown to Zacchaeus or the Sabbath cure of the paralytic. It is the scandal of the human life and bloody death of God's Only-Begotten. When God decides to become intimately involved with humankind, the result is seldom what humans would expect.

Of course, this potential for growth in God's life is no exclusive property of the gay community. What is true here of the gay community must also be said of all Christians. All are called to love all others, male or female, gay or straight, as equals, respectful of individuality, growing in both human and divine life by means of interrelationship. 'There are no more distinctions between Jew and Greek, slave and free, male and female ...'[23] These themes are not unique to the gay community. The real issue is not sex acts or sexual orientation but humanity and its potential for love in Christ.

Nonetheless, these themes highlight the core of the possibility for social transformation for the good arising in a unique way within the gay community. Like everyone else, if they are to love at all, lesbians and gay men must love where they are able, in gay and lesbian relationships. But unlike others, in order to love effectively, lesbians and gay men simply *must* expand their psycho-sexual self-images and develop relationships beyond those conceptualized in current sex-role stereotypes. Otherwise their relationships will be hopelessly superficial and will never survive, for there is virtually no institutional support for those relationships. They have no alternative: lesbian and gay people simply must love deeply and truly. So, for those who know it, the Christian gay community is an obvious example of these Christian themes in actualization.

Or again, what is described here as part of the gay liberation movement is really part of a broader cultural movement. Today's concern for restructuring sex-roles and deepening personal relationships goes well beyond the gay community. The question is a human one, not a gay or straight one. But gay and lesbian people have a greater stake in this general movement than do others. If the movement fails, others stand to lose a possibly higher quality of human relationship and personal fulfilment. Gay and lesbian people stand to lose the possibility of love relationships altogether – as well as their jobs, their homes, their family ties, and even their lives: homophobic prejudice runs deep. So it is no wonder that renewed expressions of human love and relationship, now available to all, flourish especially in the gay community.

Not exclusively, then, but with a certain priority, gay and lesbian people are able – and so are called – to contribute to the fulfilment of a central aspect of Christ's work, to reproduce on earth the inner-trinitarian life of God in heaven. Theirs is to further love among all people – co-equal, growing by interpersonal relationship, respectful of individuality, and beyond the stereotypical limitations of gender. Aware of this vocation, those who minister to lesbian and gay people in various contexts may foster commitment to it. The culmination, of course, is nothing other than participation for all in divine fullness, the answer to Christ's prayer, 'Father, may they all be one – as you are in me and I am in you. May they be one in us.'

Notes

1. John J. McNeill, *The Church and the Homosexual*, (Kansas City: Sheed Andrews & McMeel, Inc., 1976); 'Homosexuality, Lesbianism, and the Future: The Creative Role of the Gay Community in Building a More Humane Society,' in *A Challenge to Love: Gay and Lesbian Catholics in the Church*, ed. Robert Nugent (New York: Crossroad, 1983), 52–54.
2. John E. Fortunato, *Embracing the Exile: Healing Journeys of Gay Christians* (New York: The Seabury Press, 1982); Jeannine Gramick, ed., *Homosexuality and the Catholic Church* (Chicago, Illinois: The Thomas More Press, 1983); Brian McNaught, *A Disturbed Peace: Selected Writings of an Irish Catholic Homosexual* (Washington DC.: Dignity, Inc., 1981); Richard Woods, *Another Kind of Love: Homosexuality and Spirituality* (Garden City, New York: Doubeday and Co., Inc., Image Books, 1978); Harry Britt, 'From Pulpit to Politics,' *Journey* (Easteride, 1986): 3–4, 23; Steve Pieters, 'AIDS: A Gay Man's Health Experience,' *Journey* (Pentecost, 1986): 13–14.
3. Thomas Aquinas, *Summa Theologica*, I q. 2, a. 4, ad 2; q. 12, a. 12, ad 1, a. 13, ad 1.
4. Daniel A. Helminiak, *Spiritual Development: An Interdisciplinary Study* (Chicago: Loyola University Press, 1987), Chapters 5 and 9.
5. Daniel A. Helminiak, *The Same Jesus: A Contemporary Christology* (Chicago: Loyola University Press, 1986), 129–145.
6. Bernard J.F. Lonergan, *De Deo Trino, II. Pars Systematica* (Rome: Gregorian University Press, 1964), 153–161; 'Christ as Subject: A Reply,' *Collection: Papers by Bernard Lonergan, S.J.,* ed. Frederick E. Crowe (Montreal: Palm Publishers, 1967), 164–197.
7. Daniel A. Helminiak, 'Yes, There is a Perfect Love,' *Religion Teacher's Journal 16:7* (Jan., 1983), 4–6.
8. Bertrand de Margerie, *The Christian Trinity in History*, trans. Edmund J. Fortman (Still River, Massachusetts: St. Bede's Press, 1982); William J. Hill, *The Three-Personed God: The Trinity as a Mystery of Salvation* (Washington DC: The Catholic University of America Press, 1982); Walter Kasper, *The God of Jesus Christ*, trans. Matthew J. O'Connell (New York: Crossroad, 1984); Lonergan, *De Deo Trino*; Karl Rahner, *The Trinity*, trans. Joseph Donceel (New York: Herder & Herder, 1970).
   Contemporary one-sided emphasis on God's active presence among humankind, conceived in terms of an obscurely defined 'economic Trinity,' evacuates the Christian doctrine of the Trinity of all real meaning. Only words, three different names for God, remain, E.g., Catherine Mowry LaCugna, 'Making the Most of Trinity Sunday,' *Worship*, 60 (1986), 210–224, esp. n. 19. Such a modalist understanding of Trinity cannot support the present – or any! – pastoral application. Where there is one God but not Three distinct Subjects in God, all talk of community in God or of human participation in divinity is groundless.
9. The myth that gay men abhor women and lesbians abhor men is simply absurd.

10. Maxine E. Margolis, *Mothers and Such: Views of American Women and Why They Changed* (Berkeley: University of California Press, 1984).
11. Cf. Sylvia Chavez-Garcia & Daniel A. Helminiak, 'Sexuality and Spirituality: Friends, Not Foes,' *The Journals of Pastoral Care* 33 (1985), 151-163; Fred S. Keller, *The Definition of Psychology* (Englewood Cliffs, New Jersey: Prentice-Hall, Inc., 1973 [1937]); Katinka Matson, *The Psychology Today Omnibook of Personal Development* (New York: William Morrow & Co., Inc., 1977).
12. Francis Mugavero, 'The Gift of Sexuality,' *Origins* 5, 37 (1976), 581, 583-586.
13. John Boswell, *Christianity, Social Tolerance, and Homosexuality: Gay People in Western Europe from the Beginning of the Christian Era to the Fourteenth Century* (Chicago and London: The University of Chicago Press, 1980), 221-226; Aelred Squire, *Asking the Fathers: The Art of Meditation and Prayer* (London, SPCK, 1973; New York: Paulist Press, 1976), 78.
14. Helminiak, *The Same Jesus.*
15. Daniel A. Helminiak, 'How to Talk About God,' *Religion Teacher's Journal* 15:5 (Sept., 1981), 24-26; *Spritual Development,* Chapter 8.
16. De Margerie, *The Christian Trinity in History,* 186-192.
17. For a precise statement of the difference between the self-constituting relationships among the divine Subjects and among human subjects, cf. Daniel A. Helminiak, 'One in Christ: An Exercise in Systematic Theology,' Unpublished doctoral dissertation, Boston College and Andover Newton Theological School, 1979, 356-358.
18. Cf. Helminiak, 'One in Christ.'
19. Cf. David Davidson, 'The Spiritual Dimension of the Gay Experience,' *Christopher Street,* Issue 106-9, 10 (Dec., 1986), 29-33.
20. For a systematic account of this Christian mystery, see Helminiak, 'One in Christ,' and *Spiritual Development,* Chapters 7 and 8.
21. Rom. 5:5.
22. Tad Dunne, *Lonergan and Spirituality: Towards a Spiritual Integration* (Chicago: Loyola University Press, 1985); Daniel A. Helminiak, 'Four Viewpoints on the Human: A Conceptual Schema for Interdisciplinary Studies,' *The Heythrop Journal,* 27 (1986), 420-437, 28 (1987), 1-15; *Spiritual Development.*
23. Gal. 3:28.

8. Sexuality and the Body

It is one of the mysteries of Church history, never adequately explained, as to how a religion which focused so strongly on the belief that God created the material world 'and it was good', and proclaimed that God had become human flesh, could become so suspicious of the body, so frightened of sexual pleasure. If anybody was under the impression that either Christianity or society as a whole had transcended this discomfort with the sexual, then reactions to the AIDS crisis proved them wrong. In this section there are three articles which examine not only the destructive implications of Christianity's fear of the body but also make pleas for Christianity to recover delight in sexual pleasure as a central part of reclaiming a God who is at work in and through the universe.

William R. Stayton, in 'A Theology of Sexual Pleasure', reflects on contemporary scientific surveys of bodily response to sexual pleasure. He offers his own model for understanding sexual arousal and pleasure – Stayton's Paneroticism – which acknowledges that virtually anything can have erotic value. Sometimes this is appropriate, where it is positive, nurturing and just; sometimes it is inappropriate, where it involves the exploitation or hurting of another person. He highlights the importance of self-pleasuring in teaching people to relate to and love their own bodies. He also draws attention to the sexual dimension of many forms of spirituality. Stayton believes that these must start from the principle that sexual desire and activity is good, it only becomes sinful when it involves hurt or exploitation. He discusses various barriers that exist in western culture which prevent a full appreciation of sexual pleasure: women and men are sexually traumatised, bombarded constantly with images of unjust sexual activity; they value sexual ignorance; sex is presented as a great mystery which it is inappropriate to talk about; the Church has not valued sexual pleasure. Still clasping a sometimes well-disguised procreation ethic, the Church focuses on sexual acts not relationships. Stayton argues that sexuality and spirituality are intimately related. It is God's intention that we are sexual persons and that our sexuality is a vital part of our quest to love.

William D. Lindsey, in 'The AIDS Crisis and the Church: A Time to Heal', analyses the Roman Catholic Church's approach to people living with HIV and AIDS, through the process of unmasking the Vatican discourse on homosexuality. He argues that the distinction made between sexual orientation and practice (by no means confined to the Roman Catholic tradition) prevents the Church from embracing the full personhood of a gay man living with HIV and therefore prevents the Church from offering healing to him, i.e. a safe social space in which his dignity is respected. He also draws attention to the way in which Church teaching gives license to homophobic violence whilst at the same time explicitly condemning it. Lindsey argues the need for Catholic theology to 'turn to the subject' in dealing with homosexuality, replacing nature at the centre of the discourse with social construction. This will enable theologians to recognise the social dimension of the discourses about homosexuality, the connections between homophobia and misogynism and so on. The Church must 'unmask the hidden significance of the term "homosexual"' as the first step in constructing a sexual ethic. Such an approach will force the Church to recognise that anything less than overt support for gay and lesbian rights will implicate it in homophobic violence. This in turn should lead it to adopt a liberationist hermeneutic of the tradition.

Barbara P. Payne, in 'Sex and the Elderly: No Laughing Matter in Religion', deals with one of the last taboos surrounding sexuality – sex in old age. Our disgust and/or embarrassment with this topic reveals our deep rooted fear of our bodies and sexual desires. Many people still believe that sex is something they should grow out of. The fact that older people are expected to love one another but not have an active sex life reveals the dualisms which still clutch at our hearts and minds. Payne's study looks at the connection between sex and religion (an approved pastime for our senior citizens). She notes that as religious congregations age the Churches will have to deal with the fact of sexual activity among the elderly and respond to the experience of men and women endeavouring to live out their vocation to be sexual beings into old age. This will mean dealing with a large number of single people – divorced, widowed and never married – and the decisions made by elderly people to engage in sexual relations without marriage, thereby maintaining their independence whilst enjoying the love and support of a companion. Homosexuality among the elderly is also becoming increasingly visible. As Payne points out, the Bible is much more honest and positive in its attitude towards sex among the elderly than the twentieth-century Church. It may well be the experience of the elderly which ultimately forces Christianity to repent of its body-hating past and accept the goodness of God's gift of life-time sexuality.

William R. Stayton's article, 'A Theology of Sexual Pleasure', was first published in the *American Baptist Quarterly*, vol. 8, June 1989, pp. 94–108.

William D. Lindsey is a theologian living in Belmont, North Carolina, USA. His article, 'The AIDS Crisis and the Church: A Time to Heal', was first published in *Theology and Sexuality*, vol. 2, March 1995, pp. 11–37.

Barbara Payne has retired from academic life. She is a geron-tological consultant in Bogart, Georgia, USA. Her article, 'Sex and the Elderly: No Laughing Matter in Religion', was first published in the *Journal of Religion and Ageing*, vol. 3, Fall-Winter 1986, pp. 141–52.

8.1 A Theology of Sexual Pleasure

William R. Stayton

A comment which I hear very often is 'What is a Baptist minister doing in the field of human sexuality? It seems incongruous!' What a sad commentary on the perceived relationship between religion (especially that of Baptists) and sexuality! The perception most often offered is of a 'Jerry Falwell' type, denouncing such forms of sexuality as persons with a homosexual orientation. Actually, the fact is that being a minister in a local congregation led me to this new form of ministry as a sex educator and sex therapist. My story undergirds my belief that we are born both spiritual and sexual. One of the tasks of life is integrating into wholeness these two aspects of our being.

Early in 1965, while I was serving the First Baptist Church of Gloucester, Massachusetts, my high school youth group asked me if I would offer some sessions on sex education. My feelings were mixed. I felt excited, challenged, scared, and perplexed. Excited because they were asking for something I did not have the courage to ask for when I was their age; challenged because sexuality is an ethical and moral issue and the church was certainly the proper arena for sex education; scared because I had no idea how the congregation would view such a venture; and perplexed about what I should tell them. What do they need to know? Where would I get my information? Could I be honest, truthful and open with them? What if there was conflict over my answers to their questions? Could I lose my job? I turned to two other clergy in the community and together we decided we would support each other and together offer a four-session course. Among our congregations we had about 60 young people. We asked them to bring signed notes from their parents saying they could take our course. The night the course opened, we had several hundred young people show up – all with signed notes from their parents. We had to go to the sanctuary of the largest of the three congregations. There we were in a sanctuary, under the cross, talking about sex. I must admit it did throw me at first.

The kids were great! I learned more from them during that four weeks than they learned from me. How eager they were to learn! How incredibly incisive were their questions! How sensitive they were to my discomfort! The course was a hit. In fact, within six weeks, the Board of Education of Gloucester asked us if we would offer a course for Junior Highs and hold it in the high school facilities. For that course, we recruited all of the local clergy who would participate and offered a concurrent course for parents. Again, we had a large turnout and a tremendous success. Then other churches and councils of churches heard about our program and asked me to run similar programs for them. Soon I was traveling all over New England setting up sex education programs. It became very apparent to me how hungry our people are to know about their sexuality and how closely our sexuality is bound to our spirituality. Eventually I ended up in this ministry full time. It constantly amazes me how many ordained clergy are in the sexology field. Their stories are not much different than mine.

In this paper, I would like to share a theology about sexual pleasure that has evolved as a result of study, my own thoughts, and experiences in this ministry. I am going to offer some biblical, scientific, and cultural contributions which I believe are important to developing a theology of sexual pleasure.

The Bible and Sexual Pleasure

Contrary to the belief of many Christians, the Bible is not a sex book: that is, the writers of the Bible were not as concerned about the acts of sex as they were about human relationships and the motives and consequences of sexual acts. There is no question that writers were well aware of the forces of passion and love as one reads, for example the beautiful love song of the Song of Songs, with its powerful climax:

> Love is as powerful as death; passion is as strong as death itself. It bursts into flames and burns like a raging fire. Water cannot put it out; no flood can drown it (8:6–7).

It is tragic that so many within the Christian faith have dwelt on a few scriptural references and force-fit them into their own concepts of sexual morality. It is hard to understand the Christian mind that can be so flexible and non-literal regarding such topics as semen and menstruation (Lev 15: 16–30), treatment of a disobedient son (Deut 21:18–21), women in church (1 Cor 14: 34–35), submission of wives (Eph 5:6), slavery (Eph 6:5), and the proper dress and behaviour of women (1 Tim 2: 9–15), but when it comes to topics like masturbation (Gen 38: 6–10), homosexual practices (Gen 19: 1–28; Lev 18:22; 20:13; Rom 1:26–27; 1 Cor 6:9–10; 1 Tim 1:9–10), transsexualism and transvestism (Deut 22:5), and sex and the unmarried, there is rigid inflexibility and a claim of absolute literal interpretation of the Bible.

Regarding the passages above about masturbation and homosexuality, I would make the following comments. First, it is a gross misinterpretation to associate Genesis 38:6–10 with masturbation. This passage is about the sin of Onan, which occurred when Onan refused to fulfil his obligation under the Levirate law to impregnate his dead brother's wife, Tamar. Not having our current scientific knowledge regarding coitus interruptus as a poor and unreliable method of birth control, Onan used this practice to keep from inseminating Tamar.

Second, since the topic of homosexuality, which is such an important issue in the church today, is going to be covered elsewhere in this journal, I will limit my comments. Most helpful to me in understanding the biblical references to homosexuality have been Derrick Sherwin Bailey, *Homosexuality and the Western Christian Tradition*,[1] John J. McNeill, S.J., *The Church and the Homosexual*,[2] and James B. Nelson, *Embodiment*.[3] From these writers, it seems apparent that the Bible does not speak about homosexuality as a sexual orientation. Furthermore there is some question as to whether biblical authors, especially Paul, are talking about homosexuality at all. Some scholars now believe that Paul is referring to pederasty, a practice common in his time. If homosexual acts are what Paul is talking about, then it seems that he is discussing these acts as if they were being engaged in by heterosexual persons (see Rom 1:26–27).

Truly, if Jesus Christ is the central figure in history for Christians and the focus of God's humanizing action, then it is an important fact that he never refers to any of the sexual practices described above. Using Jesus Christ as our norm, all practices and biblical texts should be judged in light of his person and teachings. When he was asked: 'Teacher ... what is the greatest commandment in Law?' Jesus answered by quoting from Leviticus and Deuteronomy. '"Love the Lord your God with all your heart, with all your soul, with all your mind." This is the greatest and the most important commandment. The second most important commandment is like it: "Love your neighbor as you love yourself." The whole Law of Moses and the teachings of the prophets depend on these two commandments' (Matt 22: 36–40; also Mark 12: 28–34 and Luke 10: 25–28). Jesus himself makes love the central core of his message and ministry. Nowhere does he, even in his teachings of self denial, condemn sexual pleasure. His concern always seems to be the wholeness, the spiritual well-being, and loving relationships of persons.

Science and Sexual Pleasure

In the last twenty-five years, there have been many great contributions to our understanding of sexual pleasure coming out of the medical and behavioral science. There are three major contributions which to me are foundation stones for understanding the natural function of sexual pleasure and its theological significance.

Masters and Johnson. William Masters, M.D., and Virginia Johnson of St Louis can be credited with beginning the movement towards understanding the physiology and chemistry of human sexual functioning. As a result of their groundbreaking work in *Human Sexual Response*[4] they were also instrumental in describing the dysfunctions that occur when the physiological and/or chemical system is blocked from functioning. They describe the dysfunctions, their etiology and treatment, in their second book on *Human Sexual Inadequacy*.[5]

Masters and Johnson divide the sexual response cycle into four phases: excitement (or arousal), plateau, orgasm, and resolution. Masters and Johnson described in detail each of these phases in both the female and male.

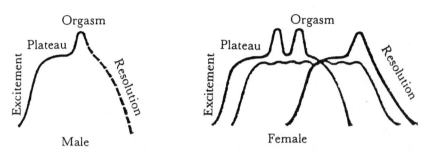

Masters and Johnson, 4 Phases of Sexual Response

As a result of their work, we discovered that males and females are born sexual and that sexual responses occur from before birth until death. While still in utero, females vaginally lubricate and males have erections. This phenomenon occurs while males and females are asleep, every 40–80 minutes, until death unless interrupted by disease or chemical interventions. If human beings respond sexually from before birth until death, then this has important implications for our understanding of our creation as sexual beings with the potential for sexual pleasure as a natural part of our life.

The fact that sexual response is pleasurable has theological significance. It could be said that the Creator intends sexual pleasure for the human creature. For example, females have an organ, the clitoris, which has no other function than sexual pleasure. While it has an analog in the penis, the penis has other functions such as urination and as a way of transmitting sperm. Pleasure is intricately woven into human sexual response. If sexual pleasure was intended only for procreational purposes within the marriage bond, then God has played a terrible joke on the multitudes throughout history who never married or could not have children or who theoretically could have had over 30 children during their child-bearing years! Must not our theology take into account the fact that we have the capacity to experience sexual pleasure at birth and that sexual pleasure can be experienced until death?

Helen Singer Kaplan.   In the late 1970s, Dr Helen Singer Kaplan of Cornell University proposed an important fifth stage to the sexual response cycle, which precedes the original four. She called this the desire phase. She found that people could be blocked from sexual pleasure and response before excitement or arousal could take place. Such people have an aversion to sex and to sexual pleasure. So Dr Kaplan did a study of the components of sexual desire. She wrote this up in a very helpful book, *Disorders of Sexual Desire*.[6] Among the causes of a lack of desire were such factors as childhood sexual trauma, child sexual abuse, rape, negative attitudes towards sex, low self-esteem, and religious orthodoxy that repressed sexual expression. It is amazing to me how many people I see suffering from a lack of sexual desire who blame their dysfunction on their religious upbringing. To me this is an indictment of Christian theologies that have failed to take into account a theology of sexual pleasure or even a theological affirmation of sexual expression other than for procreative purposes.

David M. Reed. An important contribution to our understanding the psychological nature of sexual response was proposed by Dr David M. Reed of Jefferson Medical College in Philadelphia. His theory has yet to be published, but in my judgement is crucial to understand the importance of sexual pleasure. He calls his theory ESP, or the theory of the Erotic Stimulus Pathway. He describes ESP in four phases.

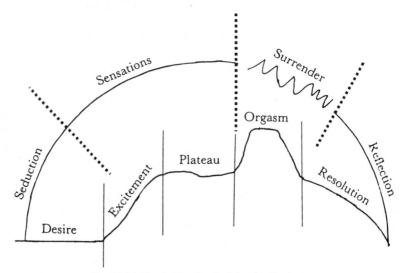

David M. Reed, *The Erotic Stimulus Pathway*

Dr. Reed's model is based upon a theory of psychosexual development. When young people begin to date, they are experiencing the first stage of ESP, the Seduction phase. This important stage has two components: first, seducing oneself into being interested in another person and second, learning how to seduce the other person into being interested in you. For young people this stage is enough in itself.

For example, I will never forget my first date. I can remember how excited I was when my 7th grade classmates told me that Julie liked me. I can remember how that relationship progressed during the 7th grade. We used to send notes to each other, then we started talking on the telephone to each other, and finally she invited me to the end-of-the-year dance. It was a formal dance. The time I spent picking out my clothes, taking a long bath, getting ready, combing my hair even amazed my parents. Then, even though I was only 12 years old, I went to the medicine cabinet in our bathroom and splashed a lot of my father's Old Spice aftershave lotion on my face. My father drove us to the dance and picked me up. It was a wonderful evening – in fact it was perfect! There was no sex – I am not sure that I really even knew much about sex then, but it was a very important learning experience. I was developing the art of seduction, which later would play a vital part in sexual pleasure. I still think of that wonderful date whenever I wear Old Spice.

The next phase of ESP is the Sensations phase. Our senses are nature's aphrodisiacs. They are all that a person needs to gain and maintain sexual arousal and pleasure. The importance of touch, vision, hearing, smell, and taste can not be overstated. Touch is a chief means of healing and pleasure, but all too often, touch becomes a way of controlling and punishing. Then it becomes abusive and a person so abused will have great difficulty in deriving pleasure from this very important sense. Seeing and hearing one's beloved and the sight and sound of sex can be very stimulating unless one is taught that the body is gross and the sounds of sex are frightening. The smell and taste of sex also stimulate, unless one has been told the smell is bad and to taste sex is wrong because the sexual organs are dirty. As a sex therapist I have learned how important the senses are to helping a couple with a dysfunction. The fewer senses the couple uses the more difficult it will be to help them become functional. Sexual function depends on sexual pleasure and that pleasure is based on our sensations. Yet how do we educate our children with this knowledge?

The third phase in ESP is called the Surrender phase. For orgasm to take place as a pleasurable experience, one needs to let go and give control over to the experience. If one has been taught to be overcontrolled or there are power struggles in the relationship, then the psychophysiologic response will be affected.

The fourth and final phase, the Reflection phase, is most important. How a person feels immediately after the sexual experience will act as feedback to future sexual experiences with that person. If the immediate reflection is positive; that is, warm, loving, pleasurable, then the desire will be stimulated for the next time. If, on the other hand, the reflection is negative; that is, the person did not like the way he/she experienced his/her response, or is negative about the partner or the situation, then the feedback will act to lower desire for the next time.

A common problem in long term relationships is that couples forget the importance of the seduction phase and go right for the sensations or orgasm phase. An example is the couple who lets sex go until the last experience of an already busy day just before going to sleep. Typical is the couple who has a 'quickie' at 11:20 p.m., between sports and Nightline (or Johnny Carson), during the weather report. When this occurs over time, then even the sensations begin to lose their power. It is interesting that in working with couples involved in extramarital affairs, one of the major experiences that makes the extra-marital affair exciting is that the Seduction phase is reintroduced into a relationship. Keeping seduction alive in a long term relationship is vitally important and should be taught as part of a person's preparation for marriage.

Again, it is impressive how important sexual pleasure is in human relationships and sexual function. Yet how often do we prepare our children or help adults within the context of the church to experience the fulness of God's intention for sexual pleasure? Where is a theology for this important aspect of life?

Sexual Orientation and Sexual Pleasure

In recent years, there have developed a number of theories regarding erotic responses and sexual orientation. Alfred Kinsey and his associates[7] saw sexual orientation on a bisexual continuum from exclusively heterosexual to exclusively homosexual, based on experiences and fantasies with other persons. He offered a seven point continuum from 0–6, as follows:

Exclusive heterosex-uality	Predom-inant heterosex-uality with incidental homosex-uality	Predom-inant hetero-sexuality with more than incidental homosex-uality	Ambisexuality	Predom-inant homosex-uality with more than incidental hetero-sexuality	Predom-inant homosex-uality with incidental hetero-sexuality	Exclusive homo-sexuality
0	1	2	3	4	5	6

Source: McCary, J.L. *Human Sexuality* 3rd ed. (New York: Basic Books 1971), p. 339.

Kinsey Sexuality Scale

Kinsey believed that a 0, or exclusively heterosexual person, would be one who never had any type of genital homosexual experience, desire or fantasy. A 6, or exclusively homosexual person, would be one who never had any type of genital heterosexual experience, desire or fantasy. In between these two extremes would be gradations of homo-sexual and heterosexual experiences, desires or fantasies. Almost any textbook on Human Sexuality has information on the results of Kinsey's study on sexual orientation based on 5300 men and 5900 women.

Interestingly, cross-cultural research indicates that the majority of societies that have existed are non-repressive regarding sexuality, unlike the United States which is one of the more repressive cultures to have existed. Ford and Beach[8] and Marshall and Suggs[9] indicate that in non-sexually repressive societies, the majority of people are in the 2 (predominantely heterosexual with more than incidental homosexuality) category.

Significant in the research is the indication that people are born with bisexual potential. Most of the well-known researchers in the field, from Freud to Kinsey to Masters and Johnson, agree about the bisexual potential of the majority of people. In fact, there is no research to indicate that humans are born to be zero on the Kinsey scale. To the contrary, evidence indicates that humans are born sexually neutral, or Kinsey three, and have the potential of developing in either or both directions between homosexuality and heterosexuality. Further, only in sexually repressive cultures, such as our own, do we find such a high value on exclusivity at either the 0 or 6 end of the scale. One needs to remember that we are talking about erotic potential, not necessarily lifestyle or life experience. In my judgment, this information has profound implications regarding theology, as will be discussed later in this article.

Another researcher, Fred Klein,[10] deepened Kinsey's concepts further by creating a grid for describing sexual orientation and its complexity. Klein identifies issues of sexual attraction, sexual behavior, sexual fantasies, emotional preference, social preference, lifestyle, and self-identification, using the Kinsey Rating Scale to get a profile. This multi-dimensional grid has been very helpful to the therapist in working with persons who feel confused about their sexual orientation.

In my experience as a sex educator and sex therapist, I have not been fully satisfied by either the Kinsey or Klein models, because I find that people are sexually aroused by more than other people of the same or opposite sex. In my 25 years as a psychotherapist, I have found that sexual orientation is a very complex phenomenon. In 1980, I was asked to be an issue editor on the subject of human sexuality for a nursing journal, *Topics in Clinical Nursing*,[11] where I presented an expanded model for looking at sexual orientation. In Francoeur,[12] this model was named Stayton's Paneroticism.

The thesis of my model is that potentially anything in the universe can have erotic value for someone. Sometimes this can be very appropriate, at other times, inappropriate. For example, being turned on erotically by the beauty of nature or good music is totally appropriate in this model, while being turned on by hurting oneself, someone else, or acting out sexually with children is totally inappropriate. As I listen to people in my practice discussing their sexuality, I am convinced that there is nothing in this universe that someone does not turn on to. As a theologian and as a psychologist, I am concerned about all the dimensions of a person's relationships, sexual and non-sexual, whether with the self, the things in their life, or with whatever is ultimate in their life. I have tried to reflect this concept in the following diagram.

I

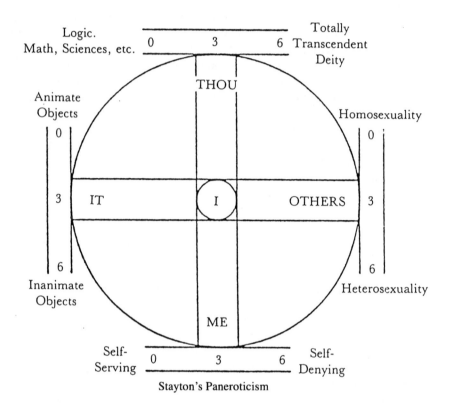

Stayton's Paneroticism

In considering this model, it is my premise that besides responding erotically to another person or persons, humans can also find sexual pleasure in relating to their own bodies. In working with an individual, it is very important to assess the relationship with the self. If we introduce a Kinsey-type rating scale, we would find at one end of the continuum a person who is totally self absorbed. Pathologically, we call this narcissism. At the other end of the continuum is a person who would deny him or herself any pleasure. We would diagnose this person as having a martyr-complex syndrome. The ideal of health would be someone in the 3 range, who holds in creative tension the ability both to serve self or deny self when either would be appropriate. this would also be true sexually. Self pleasuring in the context of a healthy self-image can be very helpful in developing one's sexual response cycle. An almost unanimous perspective in the field of sexuality today is that autoeroticism is healthy, desirable and important to adult sexual adjustment. Masturbation is a lifelong and enjoyable practice for many people in our culture. In cases of dysfunction, it is common to recommend masturbation as a part of the treatment plan (if it is within the person's value system). Does this not have implications for Christian education? Young people should be given an understanding of masturbation and its health-giving benefits throughout the life cycle. We emphasize the importance of healthy self-esteem, yet, almost all Christian sexuality education curriculum either presents masturbation as negative or ignores it as if it did not exist.[13] The church, too often, instills guilt rather than affirmation for this practice, thus causing one to be cut off from an important part of the relationship to the self.

Another dimension of a person's relationship is to objects. Again, if we introduce a Kinsey-type scale, we would find at one end of the continuum inanimate objects; at the other end, the animate world. In relation to inanimate objects, erotic responses and sexual pleasure occurs with almost any object. The more common responses reported to the therapist are clothes, art, rubber, vehicles of transportation, nature, explicit erotic material, money, and parts of the body. This list can be supplemented with literally thousands of other possibilities.

In sex therapy it is not unusual to hear people report being sexually aroused by art, music, particular foods or drink, a particular setting such as the seashore, a stream, a mountain lake, vacations, or strenuous activities like sports. Particular clothes, parts of the body, certain smells, or good communication are also often listed as important to a person's ability to experience erotic feelings. I consider these healthy and positive aspects of a person's sexual orientation. There are also unusual, but harmless, objects or activities, such as rubber artifacts, dressing in clothes of the opposite sex, or particular articles of clothing which are needed for erotic arousal. Finally, there are the unusual, but harmful 'turn ons,' such as being aroused by weapons, infliction of pain or inappropriate acting out sexually that is against the public morality.

On the other end of this continuum are those who find they are aroused erotically by animate objects, such as a favorite pet or a particular type of animal. It is a fact that many people, especially in our culture, get their touching needs met through their houshold pets. While this does not usually lead to sexually acting out, the pet can still become the object of the person's preference for an emotional outlet. The vast majority of these experiences do not result in childhood, adolescent or adult pathology unless the person is discovered in the act of having sex with the animal and made to feel shame or alienation from family or friends. It is in the process of being discovered and the reaction of the discoverer that psychological damage can occur. Of course if animals are the only recipients of a person's sexual feelings, then it is appropriate to refer the person for therapy.

Because sexual orientation is set very early in life, probably by 5 or 6 and not later than 7 years of age, it is very difficult, if even possible, to change a person's orientation through therapy later in life. Through therapy the person can explore other possible erotic alternatives and learn to control the need for harmful erotic behavior. In some cases, such as pedophilia (adults who are sexually attracted to children), the medical profession can now help the person control the impulse to sexually molest children through the use of medication, combined with psychotherapy.

Probably the most controversial dimension in my model is the one in relationship to the Thou in one's life. In the years that I have been presenting this model, I have talked with scores of deeply spiritual persons who have experienced sexual pleasure and response during periods of meditation, prayer and communion. While this may sound blasphemous or pathological to some, it seems to make perfect sense to others who have experienced the sensuality of spiritual feelings. Indeed, the Bible frequently pictures humanity's relationship to God with the language of marriage. The Bible talks about the bride and the bridegroom, the marriage of God and Israel, of Christ and the Church, and of our oneness with Christ, so that it does not seem out of context to see a whole relationship with our Creator God as having an erotic component.

As a young person, one of my favorite events was the occasional Sunday night 'Singspiration' at our church. Some of the gospel tunes that we sang were very sensual indeed. I especially remember 'I come to the garden alone, while the dew is still on the roses. And he walks with me and he talks with me and tells me I am his own.' What sensual feelings that tune used to evoke in me. As Francoeur[14] states in response to this transcendent dimension:

> A few artists and poets, like the Pre-Raphaelite Dante Gabriel Rossetti (1828–1882) and the Romantic William Blake (1757–1827), England's greatest visionary poet, have captured the transcendental dimension, human sensuality, and eroticism. The mystical writings of two medieval Spanish saints, Teresa of Avila and John of the Cross, contain many examples of transcendental erotic expressions in poetry and meditations. In more recent times, the work of anthropologist Loren Eiseley and the astronomer–poet Carl Sagan have touched on the domain of transcendental cosmic sensuality. The Tantric Buddhist tradition of sexuality with its symbolic lingam/yon (the male and female principles) and the temple sculpture of Hinduism express the transcendental/erotic dimension in the Eastern cultures.

If 'nature's intention' is to create persons who are fully sexual in every sense of the word and every dimension of their relationships, then how do we present this aspect of our creation in a theological framework? What pleasures are appropriate and what are not appropriate? This is the challenge for the theologian of today.

Culture and Sexual Pleasure

Our culture has developed several barriers which hinder the development of a creative theology for sexual pleasure. The first barrier is that our culture is sexually traumatized. We are bombarded daily by a type of unnatural sexuality which is highly commercialized, exploitive, and presents women as sex objects. This view is found in our advertisements and in the visual, spoken, and written media. We are led to believe that the only highly sexual person is the person with the perfect body, bodily dimensions and weight, and who is young, and not religious. Rather than presenting another, healthier view, the church is seen as anti-sexual, except for procreational sex within marriage. Many people in our society grow up with a model of a celibate marriage, because they cannot imagine their parents having a meaningful, highly eroticized sexual relationship. If children grow up to believe that, at best, they should be suspicious of their sexuality and, at worst, to hate their sexuality, then they do not have a good foundation on which to build a healthy attitude toward experiencing sexual pleasure.

The second barrier to a theology of sexual pleasure is that our culture values sexual ignorance. While valuing knowledge and education generally, when it comes to sexual self-knowledge the value is reversed and we go on the premise that it is better not to know. Most parents dread the day their child becomes sexually aware or inquisitive. The most common scenario is that the child asks some questions about sex; the mother turns the answering of the question to the father (if the boy asks), and the father becomes tongue-tied and stammers through some evasive and incoherent jumble of words. If the daughter asks, the mother gives her a booklet put out by the Kotex Company. If we give our children anything, it is usually the basics of sexual plumbing and some anatomy, but usually nothing about what will make for being a good lover. Somehow there is a fear that if children are given a good knowledge and understanding of sexual response and pleasure, they will immediately go out and 'get into trouble.' The fact is that most childhood and early adolescent sexual acting out is a form of experimentation based on sexual ignorance.

The third barrier to a theology of sexual pleasure is that our culture is sexually secretive. Sex is presented as the great mystery and the more mysterious it is, the more healthy and pleasurable it will be when marriage occurs. Sex is presented as so personal, so intimate, that it is inappropriate to share one's deepest fantasies and sexual thoughts with anyone. Strong judgements are often made on the person who has erotic fantasies that do not coincide with 'normal' heterosexual, monogamous, and married sexual intercourse. Lustful thoughts and sexual passion are not to be admitted to by the Christian, so that such thoughts are kept down in the recesses of the most secret place within.

The fourth barrier is that the church has not valued sexual pleasure, nor included sexual pleasure as a value in Christian education curriculum. Basically there are two opposing sexual value systems within the church.[15] Both are just as ancient as the other and each has prominent spokespersons throughout history. The first sexual value system is the one most identified with the church. It is based on a procreational ethic, which sees male sperm as the bottom line because the sperm is the 'seed of new life.' Women are seen in this value system as having the role of nurturer and supporter. Like the child who asked his/her parent where he/she came from, and the reply was: 'Well Daddy planted his seed in Mommy and that seed grew up and became you!' In this unscientific explanation, there is no concept of the egg carrying life, just as the sperm does. In this view, procreation requires intercourse with another person of the opposite sex, within marriage, and in a manner which promotes pregnancy. For the purist in this value system, birth control, abortion, masturbation, homosexuality, premarital sex, alternative sexual lifestyles, and erotic sexual behaviors other than intercourse would be prohibited. The focus of concern for this value system is entirely on the 'acts' of sex carrying the moral value.

The second sexual value is based on the nature of relationships, rather than various 'acts.' This view holds that the Bible and Christianity are about human relationships. The bottom line of this value is Jesus' statement, cited earlier in this paper, on loving God, one's neighbor and one's self. Various sexual 'acts' and lifestyles are measured against the norm of what are the motives and consequences of the 'acts' and how do they enhance relationships with self, others, and God. This view holds that there is nothing inherently sick or sinful about the 'acts' of sex that are done mutually, without coercion, without harm to any of the participants, and out of sight and sound of unwilling observers.

These two sexual value systems are not compatible. The first does not value sexual pleasure, but emphasizes the procreational nature of sexuality. The second values sexual pleasure as enhancing the quality and intimacy of loving relationships. If we are to develop a theology for sexual pleasure, it will have to come out of a value system that emphasizes the dimensions of a persons relationship – with self, others, the 'its' in life, and the Thou.

Defining a Sexual Theology Based Upon a Pleasure Principle

It is my thesis that love, spirituality, and sexuality are inextricably bound together. As I have tried to point out in this paper, nature's (and God's) intention seems to be to create persons who are sexual in the fullest sense of the word, with a sexual system that responds to sexual pleasuring. 'And God saw that the Creation was GOOD' (Gen 1:31). How then do we take all the information above and work it into a theology of sexual pleasure that is relevant for daily Christian living? *The New Britannica-Webster Dictionary and Reference Guide* (1986) defines theology as follows:

> the study and interpretation of religious faith, practice, and experience, esp., thought about God and his relation to the world.

If we take the last part of this definition, that is, God and God's relation to the world, then it is important to ask 'What is in the mind of God regarding our creation?' There are several ways of exploring the mind of God.

One of those ways is through the Bible. A powerful description of God in the New Testament is that God is Love (1 John 4:8–9). Jesus certainly presented a God of love in his ministry and he affirmed this when he responded to the Pharisees with 'the great commandment' to love God, oneself and others. John affirms love as central when he states that '... God loved the world so much that he gave his only Son' (John 3:16). Love seems to be a central reality in the mind of God and is not abstract or static, but dynamic and active. The love described above also defines God's relationship to the world and how God wants humans to relate to each other.

Another way to sort out the mind of God is through the findings of scientific research. If all of creation is from God, then the more we can learn about creation, the more in touch we will be with the mind of God. In the works that I have cited above of Masters and Johnson, Kaplan, Reed, and many others not cited, we have learned much about human sexual function. I am in awe at our creation as sexual beings. Our capacity for love, for relationship, and our ability to respond to intimate relationships with such deep and meaningful sexual pleasure is a humbling experience. To restrict sexual pleasuring to the procreational function, and to validate sexual pleasure only when it occurs in heterosexual relationships, diminishes the creative capacities God gave humans for expressing love.

Finally, the mind of God can be discerned whenever humans seek wholeness, that is, to integrate mind, body and spirit. The quest for wholeness and spiritual oneness with God and with each other is experienced in every period of history and among all peoples. When the integration of love, sexuality and spirituality are experienced, God's intention is born anew in the world. Sexual pleasuring does not hinder either spiritual growth or service to humanity. The current focus on sexual meaning in our time is a reaction of humans striving to understand the nature of their sexuality. Many are fearful of implications. Maybe one of those implications will be the rediscovery that the entire universe is our potential sexual orientation and that we can find sexual pleasure in all the dimensions of our life. That will happen when we join our sexual self with our spiritual self and seek appropriate ways of expressing that pleasure in all our relationships.

> And we ourselves know and believe the love which God has for us. God is love, and whoever lives in love lives in union with God and God lives in union with him.

Notes

1. Derrick Sherwin Bailey, *Homosexuality and the Western Christian Tradition* (London: Longmans Green, 1955).
2. John J. McNeill, S.J., *The Church and the Homosexual* (Kansas City: Sheed Andrews and McMeel, 1976).
3. James B. Nelson, *Embodiment* (Minneapolis, MN: Augsburg Publishing House, 1978).
4. William Masters and Virginia Johnson, *Human Sexual Response* (Boston: Little, Brown, 1966).
5. William Masters and Virginia Johnson, *Human Sexual Inadequacy* (Boston: Little, Brown, 1970).

6. Helen Singer Kaplan, *Disorders of Sexual Desire* (New York: Simon and Schuster, 1979).
7. A.C. Kinsey, W.B. Pomeroy, C.E. Martin, *Sexual Behavior in the Human Male* (Philadelphia: Saunders, 1948); A.C. Kinsey, W.B. Pomeroy, C.E. Martin, and P.H. Gebhard, *Sexual Behavior in the Human Female* (Philadelphia: Saunders, 1953).
8. C.S. Ford and F.A. Beach, *Patterns of Sexual Behavior* (New York: Harper and Row, 1951).
9. D. Marshall and R. Suggs, eds., *Human Sexual Behavior* (Englewood Cliffs, NJ: Prentice-Hall, 1972).
10. F. Klein, *The Bisexual Option* (New York: Arbor House, 1978).
11. William R. Stayton, 'A Theory of Sexual Orientation: The Universe as a Turn On,' *Topics in Nursing*, Vol. 1, No. 4 (1980), pp. 1–8.
12. Robert T. Francoeur, *Becoming a Sexual Person* (New York: John Wiley & Sons, 1982).
13. William R. Stayton, 'Religion and Adolescent Sexuality,' *Adolescent Sexuality and Pregnancy*, ed. Donald Greydanus (New York: Thieme-Stratton, Inc., 1985).
14. Robert T. Francoeur, *Becoming a Sexual Person*.
15. William R. Stayton, 'Alternative Lifestyles: Marital Options,' *Contemporary Marriage: Special Issues in Couples Therapy*, Daniel C. Goldberg, ed. (Homewood, IL: Dorsey, 1985).

8.2 The AIDS Crisis and the Church: A Time to Heal

William D. Lindsey

> 'Good people – *very* good people – I doubt not, there are among the Romanists, but the system is not one which should have such sympathy as *yours*. Look at Popery taking off the mask in Naples!' (Charlotte Brontë, Letter of 6 August 1851, in Elizabeth Gaskell, *The Life of Charlotte Brontë*).

> 'Renters, Americans believe, are by nature morally deficient, unstable, and dangerous' (Constance Perin, *Belonging in America*).

Masks have a curious double effect: they simultaneously enable and impede discourse. The *persona* of Graeco-Roman theater was both the means by which an actor addressed the audience – literally, the *persona*, the transmitter of sound – and a mask concealing the actor's identity. Because of this double effect, discourse that is either consciously or unconsciously masked poses a profound hermeneutical challenge for interpreters. They must engage this discourse at its 'literal' level and at the same time subvert literal sense to unmask what is non 'literal.' 'Literal' sense can so set the stage that the act of disclosing non-literal significance becomes mere repetition of the 'literal', or, if it moves beyond this level, can seem so incidental to what is literally said as to appear to be non-sense.

Contemporary literary theory suggests a way around this bottleneck between interpretation as paraphrase and as parallel, that of alternate or tangential discourse. Emily Dickinson in a remarkable poem enjoins us to 'tell all the Truth but tell it slant – success in Circuit lies.' The ability to tell the truth Dickinson-style, slant and circuitously, and to persuade us that this telling is itself truer than what we had previously considered true, is for Frank Kermode the mark of a powerful critic, one who is able 'to make the work under consideration look different, to alter its internal balances, to attend to what had been thought marginal as if it must be brought closer to the center, even at the cost of losing what had hitherto seemed manifestly central' (p. 36).[1] Successful unmasking occurs when one finds a way to speak about what is being unmasked that is *not* predetermined by the literal, but that so persuasively follows an unexpected track of thought within the literal that it opens up hidden significance in what is being interpreted. As Thomas Kuhn's work on specific paradigm-shifts, *The Structure of Scientific Revolutions*, suggests, compelling paradigms do not so much achieve linguistic 'replication' of what is observed, or convincingly refute what has been said previously, as they spin persuasive novel discourses about what *might be the case*, if an unexpected mode of seeing is allowed to frame the discussion (see also Toulmin, pp. 98–125; Masterman, pp. 59–89; Küng and Tracy; and Tracy, pp. 17–19).

Unmasking of old and adoption of new paradigms commonly occurs when the explanatory ability of the old wanes and new, more engaging, hermeneutics proffer themselves. Times of crisis often precipitate cultural paradigm-shifts. Crises call upon cultures and institutions to look more closely at those presuppositions that have dominated discourse about central cultural problematics in the past, and to refashion these given in light of new information and new perspectives arising out of crisis. In what follows, I propose that the AIDS crisis is such a time for the church – a crossroads, a dark *kairos* – in which the church must look anew at some of its most fundamental presuppositions about homosexuality. This crisis calls the church to face more adequately the ways in which its sexual ethic with regard to gay persons functions as a mask for intents and effects that may not be deliberate, but that nevertheless flow from that teaching and prevent gay people from hearing the gospel proclaimed by the church as the good news of God's salvific love for all humanity.

The AIDS Crisis and Healing

In responding to the AIDS crisis with remarkable alacrity, setting up hospices and other ministries, the church faithfully enacts one of its central evangelical vocations, that of healing (Schüssler-Fiorenza, pp. 229–30). However, though the church displays exemplary fidelity to the gospel by providing healing ministry to persons with AIDS, this ministry is not without significant irony. The relationship of the church to the gay community is vexed by unresolved tensions which drive to the heart of the church's outreach to AIDS patients – theological presuppositions impede and distort this ministry in quite fundamental ways. Though one ought not to assume that all AIDS patients are gay men – indeed, such an assumption contributes to the stigmatization of those who have AIDS and disguises the growing number of other social groups affected by the disease – in the view of many gay AIDS patients, the central irony in the church's ministerial initiative is this: the same church that extends healing concern maintains that a homosexual orientation is intrinsically disordered. Or, if it grants the moral neutrality of the orientation, the church teaches that genital sexual activity on the basis of that orientation is objectively sinful. For many gay persons with AIDS, these theological convictions assure that the church's healing concern appears ultimately to be directed to *someone other* than the patients themselves. By divorcing the sexuality of gay people from their humanity, by treating sexual orientation or activity as accidental to that humanity, the church gives the impression of ministering not to actual persons who are suffering *qua* persons, but to bodies separated from psyches. If Stanley Hauerwas (*Suffering Presence*) is correct when he maintains that healing is entering the circle of another's existence to affirm the essential humanity of the sufferer, when suffering threatens to isolate him from the human community, then in the final analysis, one must ask whether ministry premised on such negative assumptions about gay sexuality can affirm the integral humanity of those to whom it is offered, and so be fully healing.

As its etymology indicates, the word 'healing' implies intent concern for the *wholeness* of the one being healed. Medical science increasingly recognizes that what we naively call 'body' and 'mind' function as a continuum in the human person. Contemporary medicine has become convinced that any effective process of healing must be directed to the whole person, a person who is both *psyche* and *soma*. 'Physical' healing commonly requires that the person's psychic integrity be respected, fostered, and assured. Healing ministry is, then, more than ministry to an ailing body. It is ministering to a person: healing desires the wholeness of the person being healed.

This analysis of the process of healing has several crucial implications for the church's response to the AIDS crisis, and for its sexual ethics. The first implication is this: as long as the church approaches the phenomenon of homosexuality with the assumption that one can cleave the sexuality of gay people from their personhood, it cannot effectively heal gay persons with AIDS.[2] Something so integral to a person's psychic constitution as sexual orientation (or responsible and loving sexual activity expressing that orientation) cannot be detached from the body while ministry to that body takes place. Yet this *soma-psyche* detachment is precisely what the church envisages, when it assumes that it can offer healing to gay AIDS patients while denying the integrality of gay sexuality to the person being healed.

As numerous theologians have noted, an insupportable dualism vitiates the church's traditional understanding of human sexuality. This dualism is nowhere more apparent than in the teaching of the church regarding homosexuality. In much traditional Christian teaching about sexuality, sexual acts are considered in isolation from the human agents and intents lying behind them, as though sexual acts in particular and sexuality in general are adjuncts of or accidental to human personhood. The inference to be drawn from traditional teaching is that sexuality is something that can be set apart from the person and 'used' or 'channelled' at will. The pernicious effects of this dualistic approach to human sexuality are too well known to be catalogued here (see Heyward). For the purposes of my argument, I want merely to highlight how this dualism fosters a destructive mind-body, person-sexual orientation split in church ministry to gay AIDS patients. Healing demands respect for the human integrity of the patient. If the church cannot minister effectively to gay persons with AIDS because its dualistic theology of human sexuality prevents it from embracing their personhood, then perhaps the AIDS crisis is not so much an occasion for the church to be *healer*, as to be *healed*. A church that is *itself* emphatically split by mind-body, personhood-sexuality distinctions (one thinks, for instance, of the myriad ramifications of such distinctions in clerical-lay relationships)[3] is unable to image the body of Christ to a broken world, unable to function effectively as a channel of healing grace to that world.

A holistic understanding of healing has a second important implication for the church's response to the AIDS crisis. This is that healing requires concern not only for the whole person, but for the *social space* of the sick person. As the sociology of knowledge demonstrates, societies construct human beings in manifold ways (see Mannheim; Berger and Luckmann). And as liberation theology passionately maintains, most societies construct some people as non-persons, as marginal characters in the drama of social existence. If we move beyond the privatized notion of health that dominates what Christopher Lasch, Philip Rieff, and T. Jackson Lears call our 'therapeutic culture', we begin to see that disease always raises *structural* questions, questions about how the structures of society impact different people differently, and about those metaphoric understandings of disease that are latent within the structures of society. Why, for example, do the illnesses of marginal persons receive less attention than those of the powerful or 'normal'? And why does the social mainstream sometimes view the illnesses of stigmatized groups as just punishment for their imagined moral shortcomings? As Susan Sontag has pointed out (*Illness as Metaphor; AIDS and Its Metaphors*), far from being a univocal category referring merely to diagnostic classifications of disease, 'illness' is a social construction by which society assigns either positive or negative valuation – reward or punishment – to the sick.

Clearly, the AIDS 'crisis' is from this standpoint a powerful social construct, one that allows homophobic societies first to identify a particular illness *as* a crisis, and then to classify this illness as a predictable consequence of homosexual behavior. The word 'plague', with its rich biblical resonances, hovers always in the background of much social rhetoric about AIDS. When one considers that the identification of AIDS as a gay plague persists in many people's minds in spite of statistics showing that, at a global level, AIDS afflicts heterosexual Africans in larger numbers than it does gay men, and that the rate of HIV infection is rising in the United States among women and various other minority groups while declining among gay men, one can see the extent to which AIDS and the AIDS crisis are social constructions.

A social-construction reading of healing challenges privatized understandings of the church's ministry to gay people with AIDS. As a provocative passage in Ernst Bloch's *The Principle of Hope* argues, like illness, health is primarily a social category, not merely a private one:

> Health is by no means solely a medical notion, but predominantly a societal one. Restoring to health again means in reality bringing the sick man to that kind of health which is respectively acknowledged in each respective society, and which was in fact first formed in that society itself (2.465).

At its most fundamental level, such an understanding of healing implies that a healing church must seek to create a *healing social space* in a society that often allows no such space for gay persons or for AIDS patients. Since both gay people and AIDS patients are stigmatized in many societies, a church that desires the healing of gay AIDS patients must clearly and unreservedly place itself on the side of those who combat such stigmatization. Quite simply, the church cannot hope to heal gay AIDS patients unless it heals the social space of gay people.[4]

In this respect, too, the dark *kairos* of the AIDS crisis calls for the church to be healed, to seek its own wholeness before it can function effectively as a channel of God's healing love. In order for the church to respond adequately to the call to combat stigmatization of gay people, it must first acknowledge its own complicity in such stigmatization. That such stigmatization is implicit even in ecclesial documents which ostensibly reject homophobic violence became clear to me several years ago in a class I was teaching, an introductory course in Christian ethics at a small Catholic university. As a supplement to a text dealing with the morality of homosexuality, I had students read the 1986 Congregation for the Doctrine of the Faith 'Letter to the Bishops of the Catholic Church on the Pastoral Care of Homosexual Persons', which argues that homosexual persons are intrinsically disordered, and that every homosexual genital act is objectively gravely immoral because it contravenes the natural intent of human sexuality.

In one of our class discussions of the Vatican document, a thoughtful student made a surprisingly insightful critical observation. I knew this student rather well, because she had taken a course with me previously and we often chatted after class. She was an excellent student from a staunchly Catholic and rather conservative family – not a background that would predispose her to approach the Vatican document hypercritically. Her comment had to do with the section of the pastoral letter decrying violence against gay people. When we discussed this passage, the student stated, 'I find it hard to believe that the letter really *means* what it says here. How can it oppose violence against gays when everything else in the letter is an expression of violence against gay people?' This critical observation suggests that the church teachings sometimes function on two levels, the level of what is 'literally' said, and the level of subtext, of signals texts give that go beyond the literal, and that may not be intentional within the text. One does not have to impute wilful duplicity to official church teaching about homosexuality to recognize that, when one weighs its denunciation of violence towards gay people against its excessively negative assessment of gay sexuality, what comes across to many people is *not* sympathy and compassion, but scorn and condemnation. We church-goers must not delude ourselves: our unnuanced and asituational consideration of homosexuality clearly gives go-ahead signals to those who perpetrate homophobic violence in our societies, however much we ourselves politely demur from such violence.

Sexual Ethics: The Turn to the Social Subject

Underlying all that I have just said has been a strong assumption that it is impossible for ethicists to assess the phenomenon of homosexuality in the contemporary world without recourse to tools of social analysis. In the rest of this essay, I want to make this assumption central to my case, to flesh it out, defend it, and provide concrete examples of ways in which the turn to the social subject in sexual ethics radically (and constructively) revises how moral theologians view homosexual orientation and behavior. My bottom line is this: the AIDS crisis is revelatory for the church in that it shows the time is at hand for a paradigmatic shift in sexual ethics, a turn to the social subject. In urging that healing is always the healing of the entire person, and that the person cannot be satisfactorily comprehended apart from the societal matrix that gives shape to her personhood (so that healing is also healing of the social space of persons), I have laid a foundation for this argument.

Now I want to build on this foundation by maintaining that the AIDS crisis demonstrates more acutely than ever that sexual ethics demands social ethics. For too long, the two fields of discourse have been completely separate and closed to each other. For sexual ethics in particular, the consequences have been disastrous. Even up to the present, theologians in this field (notably Catholic theologians) continue to speak of 'nature' or 'human sexuality' as if social ethics has not substantially reframed our consideration of these categories of analysis. But failure to ask social ethical questions about homosexuality in light of the AIDS crisis quite simply forecloses some of the most important, unsettling, and provocative questions that the crisis yields for Christian sexual ethics. As I hope to establish, one cannot thoroughly examine the morality of homosexuality today if one assumes that social ethical questions are peripheral, rather than central, to this issue.

The phrase 'the turn to the subject' has become a bellwether phrase for twentieth-century Catholic theology, one that functions as a virtual summary of its agenda. After the Kantian turn to the knowing subject as the center of philosophical inquiry and Maurice Blondel's appropriation of this philosophical move for Catholic theology, thinkers from Rahner to Lonergan and beyond have built their systems on the Blondelian insight that, if God-talk is to have any meaning for real people in the world in which we live, the theologian must find some point of insertion for the divine in human existence. The theological enterprise now so commonly conceives itself in this anti-extrinsicist way, especially after Vatican II, that for theologians to think otherwise about their fundamental objective would be hardly possible.

If my line of inquiry up till now has made any sense, some important reasons for the hegemony of this phrase in modern Catholic theology will be immediately apparent. It points a way to the formulation of profound paradigmatic shifts in how we think about the theological task in the modern world. To use the analytical terms I employed earlier: the phrase gives theologians a means of talking about what they do that is tangential to but grounded in previous paradigms (in particular that of neo-Thomism), that addresses issues central to this theology (e.g. how human beings appropriate proffered grace) without replicating what the previous theology said or speaking so parallel to it that they appear to have shut off conversation with the previous paradigm. The phrase 'turn to the subject' tells the truth, but tells it slant; it moves to the center what had previously seemed marginal, so that we are now compelled to grant that our former manner of seeing the relationship between God and humanity was not the only possible way to see, and that other ways of perceiving might yield equally interesting theological systems.

In order to illustrate concretely what a turn to the *social* subject in sexual ethics would entail, I need to focus on a position that, while being a promising point of departure from the traditional Catholic moral assessment of homosexuality, is not *sufficiently* revisionary, precisely because it allows magisterial teaching, with its preponderant emphasis on nature, to determine the terms of the debate, and does not allow social ethical insights enough room. This position is that held by Charles Curran, Lisa Sowle Cahill, and Richard McCormick. It may be characterized thus: given that some persons appear to be constitutionally homosexual from birth or early in their psychological development, and given that this orientation is itself morally neutral, committed monogamous homosexual relationships may be a defensible moral choice in some situations; yet heterosexual marital love remains the norm for Christian sexuality, and, even when expressed in a monogamous relationship, homosexual love falls short of the ideal for Christians and betokens the 'brokenness' of postlapsarian creation (Curran, *Catholic Moral*, pp. 184–219; *Transition and Tradition*, pp. 59–80; McCormick, *Notes, 1965–1980*, pp. 393–97; *Notes, 1981–1984*, pp. 11–12; Cahill, pp. 171–87).

This position, one motivated by pastoral concern for gay people, represents a praiseworthy attempt to move beyond the physicalist natural law ethic of magisterial teaching on human sexuality. It carefully engages the traditional arguments from the weight of Christian tradition (in which one finds a rather consistent negative evaluation of homosexual acts, albeit an evaluation that John Boswell's work [*Christianity, Social Tolerance, and Homosexuality*] shows us may not have been nearly so uniform and omnipresent as we have assumed), and from the weight of scriptural evidence, which, as Cahill argues, appears to support the normativity of marital heterosexual love. It also shows a fine sensitivity to the situationality of all moral analysis, an emphasis that has been central to classic Catholic moral theologies, and that needs to be kept to the fore in a period in which conservative moral theologians so overemphasize the universality of norms that they threaten to flatten ethical discourse far more than the tradition itself has customarily done.

However, in the final analysis, the position of Curran, McCormick, and Cahill is what might be called a *half-way* ethic, one that falls somewhere between the magisterial teaching represented by the 1986 Vatican document, and teachings that assess the morality of homosexual love at a decisive tangent to the traditional natural law approach. It does not break radically with the discourse field of the traditional teaching; it allows that discourse field, with its emphasis on nature construed in narrowly physicalist terms, to predetermine what it may say about the morality of homosexuality.[5] This is not by any means to suggest that the theologians above accept the physicalist interpretation of natural law; each has emphatically challenged this understanding. What demands attention, nevertheless, is how the tradition's very concern with nature places the debate about homosexual orientation or acts on a footing that causes one to view homosexuality as that which has to be defended, to read scripture with a hermeneutic privileging heterosexual marital love, and to ignore the social consequences of all that one says about gay sexuality, as if they are inconsequential to the discussion of the morality of homosexuality.

But what if one engages the tradition in a very different way, decisively displacing nature from the center of discourse and asking whether the growing consensus of psychologists that homosexual orientation is established early in life, if not at birth, allows us to prescind from the nature question, and frees us to look more closely and critically at how social structures construct the lives of those persons who are by nature homosexual? This displacement of the center of our discourse from nature to social ethics would then move along a path opened by Michel Foucault's thought-provoking observation that 'sexuality must not be thought of as a kind of natural given which power tries to hold in check, or as an obscure domain which knowledge tries gradually to uncover. It is the name that can be given to a historical construct' (p. 105; see also Bloch, 1.68). If the aphorism that sexuality is a historical construct points the way our tangential journey to investigate the morality of homosexuality will take, we will emphasize aspects of the tradition or biblical revelation (e.g. norms having to do with justice) quite different than those emphasized either in the present magisterial teaching or its liberal transformation at the hands of Curran, McCormick, and Cahill. Most importantly, we will employ a hermeneutic that allows us to speak more openly and honestly about the *social effect* of both traditional and contemporary Christian teachings regarding homosexuality on the lives of gay people. In the final analysis, a turn to the social permits us to speak about the morality of gay people as if we are speaking about the *actual, lived, embodied existences* of real people, and not, as the tradition has so often done, as if we are speaking *alongside* people, offering healing to people whose full humanity we have difficulty affirming.[6]

If we turn to the social subject and tell the truth about the morality of homosexuality from the slant and circuitous route, we might discover something like the following. In what societies and churches say about homosexuality, *something more* is almost always at stake than we commonly recognize or admit. The primary value of doing sexual ethics with an eye to the social is that it permits us to isolate this something more, to explain why it is there in our sexual ethics, and how it functions, even quasi-independently of what we actually postulate when we formulate our propositions about homosexuality.

In her astonishing anthropological studies of American suburban life and *mores* entitled *Belonging in America* and *Everything in Its Place*, anthropologist Constance Perin demonstrates that, behind our discourse about people such as renters, African-Americans, handi-capped persons, and homosexuals, an 'infrastructure of symbols and myths' operates (*Belonging*, p. 104; *Everything*, p. 124-5). In Perin's analysis, the choice of many suburbs to exclude those construed as threateningly different has little to do with any *real* threat the different pose to suburban society, and much to do with such irrational and deeply held beliefs as that the different are contaminating or are trick-sters. Thus when suburbanites interviewed by Perin reported that 'renters ... are by nature morally deficient, unstable, and dangerous' (*Belonging*, p. 99), they spoke not on the basis of rational analysis or empirical research, but on the basis of what 'everybody already knows', i.e., on the basis of those myths that bind a particular social group together, and appear essential to its continued existence as a group. Perin's conclusion: when suburbanites speak about renters, *something more* than flat assertion is enfolded in their rhetoric; if one wishes to challenge unjustifiable practices of economic or social exclu-sion in any given social structure, one must do so not by combating what people *say* about the stigmatized different, but what they *mean* when they speak. That is, one must ask questions of hermeneutical suspicion to expose those sub-rational beliefs – the something more – that hover within speech and institutions, and to show how these beliefs yield social practices that are unjust (*Everything*, pp. 124-25).

As an anthropologist, Perin approaches her subject with the following questions of hermeneutical suspicion: why do societies create categories to classify the different as the ominous; why do they even choose in the first place to differentiate in demonizing ways, when the threat of the different is not immediately apparent? These questions parallel Cornel West's (*Prophesy Deliverance!*) insightful analysis of the 'normative gaze' of a society. West asks why any given society establishes a 'normative gaze' that compels those living in it to determine that *this* difference (e.g., skin pigmentation) and not *that* (e.g., foot size) is worth noticing, and to classify the difference in a way that creates categories of normality and abnormality. He also notes that, once set in place, a normative gaze becomes what is taken for granted by a society, as if in noticing difference and classifying some differences according to the rubric of normality, we are simply reading nature in a value-free way (see also Lorde, pp. 114–23). In Perin's view, societies make such choices because social categories that covertly institutionalize a particular irrational myth such as that the different contaminate become handy conduits of other negative attitudes of the society. Once developed, such categories take on a life of their own, so that it becomes easy to move from seeing the renter as different, to regarding him as lazy and morally deficient. Perin concludes that social categories such as 'renter' or 'homosexual' are not self-evidently problematic: they are *made* to be problematic by certain societies (*Everything*, pp. 124–25).

Echoing the pioneering insights of anthropologist Mary Douglas in her work *Purity and Danger*, Perin addresses the issue of homosexuality directly by noting that many societies see the 'interstitial' as threatening: people or phenomena that stubbornly refuse to fall neatly into one social category or another, one social group or another, pose a threat to the very structures that underlie the society (ibid.). They do so by having the potential to demonstrate that social categories are not natural givens, but are constructed by human choice to serve human ends. The interstitial is precisely the 'monstrous', a word that, in its etymological roots, has primarily to do with revelation/de-monstration; 'monsters' show us to ourselves, our societies to themselves, in ways that can reveal disquieting truths. This is why societies create negative social categories into which to place menacing interstitial persons.

If Perin is correct, buried within many social discourses about gay people are a number of suspicions that have little to do with the ostensible reasons for which societies discriminate against gay people (Gramick, pp. 11–12). The prevalent myth that gay people wilfully transgress secure gender lines causes them to be seen, quite literally, as people in the interstices of society. And that is to say that they are also people with the ability to disclose the disquieting truth that these lines and the roles they engender are socially constructed. Such revelatory difference threatens to demonstrate truths so unsettling that we must find ways of controlling and disarming it. In the final analysis, societal decisions to exclude and discriminate against gay people may have little to do with what empirical studies prove to be the case regarding gay sexuality (e.g., that gay men are not women trapped in men's bodies, or lesbians men in women's bodies), and much to do with the fear of the revelatorily different. The very term we use to denote gay people scientifically, that protean and infelicitous neologism 'homosexual', carries this fear deep within itself, and scholars and theologians who have recourse to the term need constantly to be suspicious of its potential to function as a lightning-rod for such fears.

Continuing on its slant, circuitous course, a sexual ethic making the turn to the social might journey into the past to note that, when societies wish to suppress the revelatorily different, they sometimes employ a principle that the historian H.R. Trevor-Roper calls the 'interchangeability of victims.' In his history of the European witch-craze of the sixteenth and seventeenth centuries, Trevor-Roper finds a persistent and troubling tendency of those conducting the witch-trials to conflate various demonized groups (pp. 34–5). In court notes, witches were commonly equated with or identified as Jews, even when all evidence suggests that the person being charged was not Jewish; and witches were not uncommonly put to death in robes bearing the star of David. Clearly, *something more* than the desire to extirpate a discrete socially reprehensible group of persons is at work in phenomena such as the witch-trials or the Holocaust (p. 105).[7] When societies need to suppress the different, and even (as in the witch craze or Nazi Germany) to develop quasi-scientific discourses to justify that suppression, the specific nature or crime of the victim may not be so important as the fact that the victim *is* a victim, one who represents a convenient socially stigmatized category. Is it any accident that most of those charged with witchcraft were women?[8]

A sexual ethic that turns to the social would also move to the present to examine striking ways in which the social category 'homosexual' provides a conduit for social attitudes that, on the face of it, are not closely related to homosexuality itself.[9] As feminist theologians have noted (Harrison, pp. 135–51; Ruether, p. 21), there is an evident connection between misogynism and homophobia, a connection African-American playwright Lorraine Hansberry delineates sharply in her observation that 'homosexual persecution and condemnation has as its roots not only social ignorance but ... anti-feminist dogma.'[10] A hermeneutic seeking to unmask the hidden significance of the term 'homosexual' in American culture today must conclude that the manifold forms of violence our society practises against gay people presuppose that nexus of social structures and attitudes feminist thinkers identify as patriarchy. A primary task of theologians concerned to seek justice for gay people is clearly to show what hides within much anti-gay rhetoric, to show that such rhetoric is often not really about sexuality so much as it is about maintaining patriarchy and those readings of the Bible that privilege patriarchy.

In light of this insight, our hermeneutic of suspicion will ask why such societies often stigmatize male homosexuality more strongly than they do lesbianism (though the heinous violence lesbians encounter in patriarchal societies ought not to be ignored). When most people who oppose softening societal restrictions against gay people talk about what they fear, it becomes clear that they have in mind male homosexuality and not female: is this because gay women are thought to be climbing out of the inferior female role into the desirable male one, whereas gay men, who have fallen to the despised level of women, more perceptibly threaten to subvert the central symbol of power and order in their societies, that of the strong male?

If one follows the turn to the social subject in sexual ethics to its ultimate destination, one arrives at the conclusion that Christian moral theologians cannot continue to talk about the morality of homosexuality as if something more is not present in all that church and society say about homosexuality. That something more inhabits the bodies and social spaces of gay people as violence, unjust discrimination, exclusion from community, internalized self-hatred, etc. And that something more is not merely homophobia: it is also misogyny, a haughty disdain for *anything* perceived by patriarchy as feminine, including the natural world itself.[11] To the extent that official church teaching or theological inquiry continues to speak about homosexuality as if this discourse is not about the real lives of real people who experience violence and injustice, and as if ecclesial-theological rhetoric about homosexuality is not susceptible to a hermeneutic of suspicion that would expose the patriarchal misogyny hiding within it, to that extent all that we say about homosexuality will simply, sadly, be beside the point.

Perhaps at some moment in the past, church teaching and theology could have carried on as if the term 'homosexual' *were* univocal, unproblematic, not inhabited by meaning behind the mask. But as more gay persons claim the right to have a voice in academic or ecclesial discussions of homosexuality, and as social analysis becomes commonplace in every area of Christian ethics, it is impossible for us to go on talking as though the mask has not been penetrated. When churches and theologians continue to define homosexuality without admitting to their discussions the voices of gay persons, or without recourse to social analysis that unravels the cultural meanings of the terms they use so blithely, one must begin to ask whether some other agenda, one that transcends that of careful ethical analysis of homosexuality, is not actually at work in church and academy. In a penetrating investigation of the beginnings of the fundamentalist movement in the United States, Betty DeBerg (*Ungodly Women*) finds such an agenda operative behind fundamentalism's insistence on biblical inerrance. She shows that, from the movement's inception, a patriarchal concern to control women and canonize the Victorian middle-class Christian model of the family strongly impelled fundamentalism, and this impulse informs much that it asserts about biblical texts.

DeBerg's findings are not without pertinence for the contemporary American Catholic discussion of homosexuality, since her research has also discovered a constant tendency of the American Catholic church to ally itself with the gender politics of fundamentalism, from the beginnings of the movement to the present. As she notes, in this alliance both fundamentalists and the American Catholic church have continuously resisted gay rights (pp. 70–71, pp. 152–53). Those concerned to carry on dialogue today about issues of sexual ethics within American Catholicism must ask an important critical question about this union. Is it felicitous? Can the American Catholic church ally itself with American fundamentalism without appearing to endorse aspects of the agenda of the Christian right that are entirely alien to traditional Catholic notions of the good society (e.g., universal health coverage), and without allowing itself to channel some of the least honorable impulses of Western Christianity today? With regard to the issue of homosexuality, about which American Catholic bishops have made some enlightened and morally challenging statements, can the church play politics with fundamentalists without giving gay people signals that contravene episcopal teaching?

These questions need to be asked particularly in the aftermath of the recent CDF document entitled 'Some Considerations Concerning the Response to Legislative Proposals on the Non-Discrimination of Homosexual Persons.' If, as some insider reports have maintained, the document was commissioned primarily by North American advisors to the CDF, then its issuance in July 1992 raises extremely disquieting questions about the Vatican's willingness to ally itself with the Christian right at a moment when this group was seeking to play a decisive role in the 1992 presidential election, since the issue of gay rights was central to campaign discussion. If this is true, then the Catholic who wishes to promote *all* aspects of Catholic social teaching cannot help being bewildered, since hardly anything in the social and economic views of the American fundamentalist movement reflects the outlook of Catholic social teaching.

Critical questions about the coalescence of conservative Catholic and fundamentalist politics in the United States today need to be asked all the more in the era in which we live, in which violence against gay people appears to be rising precipitously. As Rosemary Radford Ruether notes (p. 21), homosexuality is likely to be *the* scare issue of the 1990s; both in the political arena and in American church discussions of the topic, it is becoming increasingly evident that the term is charged with negative significances, that vastly transcends anything the term represents in reality. In those mainline Protestant churches that have recently thrashed out sexual ethical problems in official church forums, for example, one sees a highly exercised reaction against attempts to revise traditional teaching about homosexuality – a reaction that suggests the extent to which churches can be culturally driven, even as they proclaim a gospel critical of culture. As the much publicized discussions of the matter in the Presbyterian church shows, the sticking point for many people is precisely *not* the problem of revising the traditional sexual ethics of the church. Most mainline Protestant churches have implicitly done this, through benign acceptance of divorced and remarried people, heterosexual people living together without benefit of marriage, heterosexual activity outside marriage, etc. The sticking point is quite clearly homosexuality, and the efforts theological advisory boards have made to demonstrate that the very ethical principles that have permitted churches to revise their sexual ethic with regard to heterosexual people ought in justice to apply equally to homosexual people have not convinced large numbers of mainline Protestants to change their minds about the issue. Clearly, *something more* is at work in the attitudes of American Christians about gay people and gay sexuality, something beyond the rational.[12]

In such a cultural climate, the American Catholic church needs to ask itself whether the half-way ethic of its best moral theologians *is* the best it has to offer gay people. Viewed from the standpoint of the tradition, this ethic is admirably sensitive to the situations of gay Catholics. But viewed from other standpoints, specifically that of an ethic more strongly informed by social justice concerns and more acutely and concretely aware of the homophobic tendencies of American culture, the ethic is hardly sufficient. Not only does it have the appearance of an ethic sympathetic outsiders have constructed for gay people without recourse to the voices of gays themselves, it identifies gay persons as signs of the brokenness of creation and as those failing to attain the ideal standard of Christian morality – as if *all* human existence after the Fall is not broken, and as if the perceived 'sinfulness' of gay people carries a symbolic import far in excess of that carried by signs of brokenness, such as our culture's rapacious greed and willingness to ravish the earth to support our 'standard of living'![13] Furthermore, the half-way ethic gives the appearance of having stopped half-way in its critique of the natural law basis of magisterial teaching about sexuality, and of having used that critique inconsistently to the exclusive advantage of heterosexual married persons, and not to the advantage of gay persons.

In a now classic essay on sexual ethics entitled 'Abortion: An Ecumenical Dilemma', Gregory Baum calls for a revision of the traditional Catholic natural law ethic regarding sexuality. He maintains that when the Catholic church officially recognized the ecclesial reality of other churches at Vatican II, it granted that it could learn from the Spirit-led historical experiences of these churches. In particular, he urges the Catholic church to learn from the wisdom of those Protestant traditions that see the architectonic sexual principle as faithful stewardship of the divine gift of sexuality, rather than fidelity to nature as biologically given. I call Baum's essay classic not merely because it has been often reprinted, but because it so succinctly formulates an insight that runs through much post-Vatican II discussion of sexuality.

However, what is notable in the work of many theologians dealing with matters sexual is that critique of the natural-law basis of Catholic sexual morality is applied more or less exclusively to issues having to do with heterosexual marriage, such as that of artificial contraception, and not at all to the issue of homosexuality.

Whatever one may wish to say otherwise in criticism of the traditional magisterial sexual ethic, one must at least grant it the virtue of consistency. Its physicalist interpretation of natural law applies across the board to all forms of sexual behavior, including masturbation, (hetero)sexual activity outside marriage, adultery, and homosexuality. One notes, of course, that it applies this norm *exclusively* to matters sexual; as a number of theologians including Baum have pointed out, in the realm of social ethics, the magisterium dispensed with the natural law foundation some time ago and adopted a biblical stewardship norm. The half-way ethic of Curran, McCormick, and Cahill, on the other hand, appears to have no clear criterion for having decided to accept the critique of natural law with regard to heterosexual marital sexuality, while excluding gay sexuality from that critique, as if the natural law ethic is still compelling in this discrete area.

I note this exclusion not to make pedantic distinctions, but because this inconsistency seems to me to have everything to do with the argument I have pressed throughout this essay. For while I applaud those courageous theologians who have shaped the half-way ethic to move Catholic sexual ethics in new directions, I see within the ethic a very serious shortcoming. Because it fails to ask sharp social ethical questions, including suspicious questions about its own tendency to treat homosexuality as a case apart in sexual ethics, it leaves wide room for the theological discussion to absorb cultural biases. In the final analysis, the half-way ethic is a *liberal* ethic, one that shares the shortcomings of all liberal theologies: it has too little distrust of modern liberal, scientific culture; and it is not sufficiently aware of the norms that ultimately determine its conclusions, particularly when the norms are those of the surrounding culture and not the church, which is *always* susceptible to critique in liberal theology. Ultimately, for those who wish to formulate a justice-centred ethic for gay sexuality, it may ironically be *more* problematic than traditional church teaching is, because it lacks a strong and clear ethic over against culture, in a culture that offers little hope to gay people.

In contrast (and in conclusion), I wish to propose that a viable Christian sexual ethic regarding homosexuality must foreground social justice. I have two modest proposals for how the contemporary church can pursue an ethic of justice-love regarding homosexuality. First, in a culture in which discussions of homosexuality are fraught with pernicious significance that greatly exceeds what is ostensibly discussed, and in which practically anything the church says that stops short of open avowal of gay rights can be perceived as complicity in this cultural violence, the traditional principle of non-maleficence demands that the church should speak about homosexuality cautiously, tentatively, less assuredly and authoritatively, and more as if the real lives of real people subject to violence are at stake in the discussion. Given that there are compelling reasons to think that homosexual persons do not choose their orientation, and strong reasons to question the tenability of the traditional view that homosexual persons are disordered or that every act of homosexual genital activity is always objectively gravely sinful, the church has an abundantly clear moral obligation to adopt this listening and pastoral approach to homosexual people, and to leave behind in the dustbin of history the fulminating, dogmatic approach of the 1986 CDF pastoral letter, or the more recent CDF document regarding legislative proposals about gay rights. Perhaps now is the time for the church to listen for a while, and not to speak!

Second, as the church reads the scriptures to discover what they 'say' on the topic of human sexuality, it needs to adopt a liberationist ethic. I have suggested that a primary shortcoming of the half-way ethic is that it does not have a clear, critical hermeneutic for reading the scriptures, and this lack of a hermeneutical avowal or commitment leaves its reading of the bible open to unreflective cultural biases. One can of course read the scriptures to yield the conclusion that heterosexual marital love is normative for the Judaeo-Christian tradition, as Cahill does. But one can, as supporters of slavery did throughout Christian history up to the nineteenth century, also use the bible to argue that *slavery* is normative for Judaeo-Christian culture. Slavery is as *prevalent* – and as culturally acceptable – in the culture in which the biblical text was composed as heterosexual marriage. But does the mere uncritiqued *prevalence* of a practice throughout the biblical text automatically establish its ethical normativity for the tradition? One must ask this particularly in the presence of texts that (both in the case of human sexuality and of slavery) run against what one perceives as the 'norm.' Despite the impression that prevails among American middle-class Christians, the New Testament is in some respects more *anti*-family than otherwise: Jesus enjoins those of his followers who choose celibacy for the sake of the kingdom to do so; Paul says that the unmarried ought to stay unmarried if they can manage to do so; the gospels set family member against family member.[14]

The point is, one must adopt some hermeneutical norm to enable one to determine *which* texts – in a complex, multi-textured, multivalent set of books – ought to be 'picked up' by the tradition; and that norm must be explicit, to enable the theologian to exclude those unacknowledged cultural biases that threaten to skew her reading of the scriptures.[15] If this norm is the liberationist norm of justice-love, then those employing it will, in Walter Benjamin's much-cited phrase (p. 256), 'brush history against the grain' to discover that the scriptures may ground an ethic for gay persons very different from either that of traditional Catholic teaching or the half-way ethic, an ethic that will perhaps follow a line of thought found in Dorothee Sölle and Gustavo Gutíerrez's appeal to the church to concretize and historicize love today. Sölle argues that 'love is indivisible, that it cannot be broken down into sexual love, charity, and love in the social and political realm' (p. 138). In saying this, she wishes to combat a particular application of the traditional Christian distinction between divine charity and human erotic love, one that would deny to gay people the right to express erotic love on the grounds that such an expression contravenes charity. In Sölle's view, 'we know ... that those who condemn the power of sexual love make other people incapable of the love that we call charity and mercy' (ibid.).

Similarly, Gutíerrez attacks those 'fleshless' notions of charity that have sometimes dominated the thinking and practice of Christians, in which one assumes that one can prescind from the real, concrete humanity of the 'object' of one's charity – that one can love a person while loving 'beside' him or her. In Gutíerrez's view, such charity is foreign to human love, and therefore nonexistent. All that the scriptures say about the neighbor as our avenue to God militates against dehumanizing instrumentalization of the neighbor, against the assumption that in loving the neighbor, we can separate from her essential humanity those aspects that we consider unworthy of Christian charity, for

> the neighbor is not an occasion, an instrument, for becoming closer to God. We are dealing with a real love of persons for their own sake and not 'for the love of God', as the well-intended but ambiguous and ill-used cliché would have it – ambiguous and ill-used because many seem to interpret it in a sense which forgets that the love for God is expressed in a true love for persons themselves (pp. 114–6).

If we read the scriptures via a liberationist hermeneutic, we shall discover that the love of God is always a love of kenotic solidarity that seeks the level of the other, that so loves that it cannot do other than enflesh itself in the real humanity of the other. Because God's love is solidarity rather than condescending charity, 'God and love are inseparable. It is not possible – and this is probably the gravest error of all conservative theologies – to tear God and love apart and to say that God is primary and permanent while love is some secondary, derivative thing' (Sölle, p. 136).[16] 'Look at Popery taking off the mask': in the final analysis, behind the mask that society places on gay persons are human beings who pose no more threat to social order than did Roman Catholics in nineteenth-century England. How many years Englishmen and women lived with misplaced fears of papal political designs on their island, how many social energies having little to do with these particular fears were expended via that scapegoat, before people realized that the pope has, indeed, no divisions. As Stalin's famous question about how many divisions the pope has suggests, fear of the papacy's political power was an empty vehicle for other prejudices and fears. In the AIDS crisis, when mask after mask appears ready for removal, when the church's gospel of God's universal salvific love demands to be embodied in the lives of gay people, the church stands at a *kairos* moment that calls to mind other moments in the past (the conquest of the Americas, the slave trade, Nazi Germany's holocaust of the Jews) when it had the opportunity to proclaim that gospel to societies that refused to see the essential humanity of victims. In these past moments, some Christians courageously proclaimed the gospel of God's universal salvific love, and particular love for the marginal. Sadly, the church itself, as an institutional structure and power, often moved less courageously and hesitated to adopt a critical stance towards exploitation of the native peoples of the Americas, slavery, and the Holocaust, even after critical sectors of secular society had done so. Whether the AIDS crisis will be such an event for the church, one in which it fails to respond to the *kairos* as many of its most prophetic members are doing so, by challenging society to see human beings where it has previously seen only masks, remains to be seen.

Notes

1. Russian theorist Mikhail Bakhtin speaks similarly of 'carnivalization', the free play of many discourses in a given text, in rebellion against a hegemonic discourse that seeks to establish unitary power over all others: see *Dialogic Imagination*, pp. 58–61, 72, 77; *Speech Genres*, p. 135; and Lodge, p. 22.

2. On the damage incurred by those who must 'live split' between a publicly accepted *persona* and a part of themselves that they perceive as essential, creative, and powerful, yet also as unacceptable or even monstrous, see Rich, p. 175.

3. For an illuminating analysis of the roots of the lay-clerical dualism, as it emerged in Catholic magisterial teaching about human sexuality in the patristic period, see Laeuchli. Laeuchli argues that the church of Vatican II has refused to entertain the possibility that traditional Catholic teaching about sexuality can be revised, because buried within this traditional discourse are power arrangements that foster clerical domination of the laity.

4. On the hidden wound of racism in American society, and how it is protected by linguistic structures that create stigmatized social space for African Americans, while insulating white Americans from having to confront their prejudices, see Berry. Berry emphasizes that wounds such as racism harm not merely the stigmatized, but those who inflict the wounds.

5. In critiquing the narrow physicalism of the magisterium's understanding of natural law, I do not wish to imply that one cannot discover in other interpretations of natural law grounds for a more positive ethic of homosexual love – see e.g. Aquinas' insistence in the *Summa Theologiae* (Prima secundae, quaestio 94) that human beings know what is natural via their desires. Even more suggestive is Aquinas' observation (Prima, quaestio 47, art. 1) that the diversity of life forms created by God is necessary for us to appreciate the grandeur and infinite nature of God – what one form of life lacks, another has, in order to reflect the myriad and complex nature of the divine. This doctrine of the fecundity of creation has enormous implications for sexual ethics; one can argue from it for the divine intent that some people be created gay in order to mirror aspects of the creator that non-gay persons cannot mirror.

6. On the tendency of repressive societies to deny the bodily for the sake of manipulative power over the bodies of some people, see Scarry, p. 57.

7. On the witch craze as demonstrating how human communities can act in accord with beliefs that, once unknown, come to be taken for granted, and exhibiting 'the power of the human imagination to build up a stereotype and its reluctance to question the validity of a stereotype once it is generally accepted', see Cohn, p. 255.

8. For a recent overview of the complex problem of determining who were in fact the victims of the European witch craze, which concludes that over 80–85% of those charged with witchcraft in Europe and the British Isles were women, see Barstow, esp. pp. 23–29.

9. On sexuality as one of the elements in societies' ordering of power that is 'endowed with the greatest instrumentality: useful for the greatest number of maneuvers and capable of serving as a point of support, as a linchpin, for the most varied strategies', see Foucault, *History*, 1.103.

10. Cited without attribution of source in Patricia Yollin, 'Lesbians Come of Age', *San Francisco Examiner*, June 6, 1989, p. 18. See also Isay, p. 128.

11. In linking homophobia to misogyny, I do not by any means wish to deny that gay men are capable of adopting misogynistic positions. One must ask, for example, if resistance to women's aspirations to justice within the structures of some churches (as in the women's ordination movement) is fueled by a misogyny that receives the support of gay priests.

12. For an incisive analysis of the subtext of press representation of the Presbyterian taskforce report on human sexuality, by an author of the report, see Janet Forsythe Fishburn, 'The Presbyterian Sexuality Report: A Case Study in the Language of Moral Discourse' (unpub., 1992, Conference on Public Discourse about Religion in America, Center for the Study of Religion and American Culture).

13. On the 'profound symbolism' of any arrangement made by any dominant group for the less powerful as a central problem to be addressed by any ethic grounded in justice, see Rich, p. 10.

14. The paucity of texts (themselves complicated by hermeneutic and translation problems) in the scriptures purporting to forbid homosexual activity might also be noted; evidently, 'homosexuality' was not for the biblical writers the crucial moral issue modern moralists have made it out to be. When one compares the few biblical texts that appear to deal with homosexuality with the wealth of texts forbidding practices we might now call capitalistic, one wonders even more at our contemporary allocation of weight to the 'homosexual' texts, and our elision of the others.

15. On the need for *all* readings of scripture and tradition to have a 'gospel directionality' towards justice for the disempowered, see Coleman, p. 255; for an enlightening differentiation between biblical notions of justice and typical notions found in mainstream American culture, see McCormick, *Health and Medicine*, pp. 77-78.

16. Sölle, *Strength*, p. 136.

References

Bakhtin, Mikhail. *The Dialogic Imagination*. Ed. Michael Holquist and trans. Caryl Emerson. Austin: Univ. of Texas, 1981.

— *Speech Genres and Other Late Essays*. Ed. Caryl Emerson and Michael Holquist. Trans. Vern McGee. Austin: Univ. of Texas, 1986.

Barstow, Anne Llewellyn. *Witchcraze: A New History of the European Witch Hunts*. New York: Harper Collins, 1994.

Baum, Gregory. 'Abortion: An Ecumenical Dilemma.' *Commonweal* 99 (1973), pp. 231-35.

Benjamin, Walter. *Illuminations*. Trans. Harry Zohn, ed. Hannah Arendt. New York: Schocken, 1969.

Berger, Peter and Thomas Luckmann. *The Social Construction of Reality*. Garden City: Doubleday, 1967.

Berry, Wendell. *The Hidden Wound*. Boston: Houghton Mifflin, 1970.

Bloch, Ernst. *The Principle of Hope*. Trans. Neville Plaice, Stephen Plaice, and Paul Knight. Cambridge: MIT Press, 1986.

Boswell, John. *Christianity, Social Tolerance, and Homosexuality*. Chicago: UP of Chicago, 1980.

Cahill, Lisa Sowle. 'Moral Methodology: A Case Study.' *Chicago Studies* 19 (1980), pp. 171-87.

Cohn, Norman. *Europe's Inner Demons: An Enquiry Inspired by the Great Witch Hunts*. New York: Basic, 1975.

Coleman, John. *An American Strategic Theology*. New York: Paulist, 1982.

Curran, Charles. *Catholic Moral Theology in Dialogue*. Notre Dame: UP of Notre Dame, 1976.

— *Transition and Tradition in Moral Theology*. Notre Dame: UP of Dame, 1979.

DeBerg, Betty A. *Ungodly Women: Gender and the First Wave of American Fundamentalism*. Minneapolis: Fortress, 1990.

Douglas, Mary. *Purity and Danger*. London: Routledge and Kegan Paul, 1966.

Foucault, Michel. *The History of Sexuality; I, An Introduction*. Trans. Robert Hurley. New York: Vintage, 1980.

Gramick, Jeannine, ed. *Homosexuality in the Priesthood and the Religious Life*. New York: Crossroad, 1989.

— 'Prejudice, Religion, and Homosexual People.' In Nugent. pp. 3-19.

Gutíerrez, Gustavo. *A Theology of Liberation*. Trans. and ed. Caridad Inda and John Eagleson. Maryknoll, New York: Orbis Book, 1988.

Harrison, Beverly Wildung. *Making the Connections: Essays in Feminist Social Ethics*. Ed. Carol Robb. Boston: Beacon, 1985.

Hauerwas, Stanley. *Suffering Presence: Theological Reflections on Medicine, the Mentally Handicapped, and the Church*. Notre Dame: Univ. of Notre Dame, 1986.

Heyward, Carter. *Touching Our Strength: The Erotic as Power and the Love of God*. New York: Harper & Row, 1989.

Isay, Richard. *Being Homosexual: Gay Men and Their Development*. New York: Avon/Farrar, Straus and Giroux, 1989.

Kermode, Frank. *Forms of Attention*. Chicago: University of Chicago, 1985.

Kuhn, Thomas S. *The Structure of Scientific Revolutions*. Chicago: Univ. of Chicago, 1962.

Küng, Hans and David Tracy, ed. *Paradigm Change in Theology*. New York: Crossroad, 1989.

Laeuchli, Samuel. *Power and Sexuality: The Emergence of Canon Law at the Synod of Elvira*. Philadelphia: Temple UP, 1972.

Lasch, Christopher, *The Culture of Narcissism*. New York: W.W. Norton, 1979.

— *The Minimal Self*. New York: W.W. Norton, 1984.

Lears, T. Jackson. *No Place of Grace: Antimodernism and the Transformation of American Culture, 1880–1920*. New York: Pantheon, 1981.

Lodge, David. *After Bakhtin*. London: Routledge, 1972.

Lorde, Audre. *Sister Outsider*, Freedom, CA: Crossing, 1984.

Mannheim, Karl. *Ideology and Utopia: An Introduction to the Sociology of Knowledge*. Trans. and ed. Louis Wirth and Edward Shils. New York: Harcourt, Brace, 1936.

Masterman, Margaret. 'The Nature of a Paradigm.' In *Criticism and the Growth of Knowledge*. Ed. Imre Lakatos and A. Musgrave. Cambridge: Cambridge UP, 1970. pp. 59–89.

McCormick, Richard A. *Health and Medicine in the Catholic Tradition*. New York: Crossroad, 1987.

— *Notes on Moral Theology, 1965 through 1980*. Lanham, MD: UP of America, 1981.

— *Notes on Moral Theology, 1981–1984*. Lanham, MD: UP of America, 1984.

Nugent, Robert, ed. *A Challenge to Love: Gay and Lesbian Catholics in the Church*. New York: Crossroad, 1983.

Perin, Constance. *Belonging in America: Reading between the Lines*. Madison: Univ. of Wisconsin, 1988.

— *Everything in Its Place*. Princeton: Princeton UP, 1977.

Rich, Adrienne. *On Lies, Secrets, and Silence*. New York: W.W. Norton, 1979.

Rieff, Philip. *The Triumph of the Therapeutic*. New York: Harper & Row, 1966.

Ruether, Rosemary Radford. 'Homophobia, Heterosexism, and Pastoral Practice.' In Gramick, *Homosexuality in Priesthood and Religious Life*, ed.

Scarry, Elaine. *The Body in Pain: The Making and Unmaking of the World*. New York: Oxford, 1985.

Schüssler-Fiorenza, Francis. *Foundational Theology: Jesus and the Church*. New York: Crossroad, 1984.

Sölle, Dorothee. *The Strength of the Weak*. Philadelphia: Westminster, 1984.

Sontag, Susan. *AIDS and Its Metaphors*. New York: Farrar, Straus and Giroux, 1988.

— *Illness as Metaphor*. New York: Farrar, Straus and Giroux, 1978.

Toulmin, Stephen. *Human Understanding*, I: *The Collective Use and Evolution of Concepts*. Princeton: Princeton UP, 1972.

Tracy, David. *The Analogical Imagination*. New York: Crossroad, 1981.

Trevor-Roper, H.R. *The European Witch-Craze of the 16th and 17th Centuries*. Harmondsworth, Eng.: Penguin, 1969.

West, Cornel. *Prophesy Deliverance!* Philadelphia: Westminster, 1982.

8.3 Sex and the Elderly: No Laughing Matter in Religion

Barbara P. Payne

When Abraham, a man of 100 years, and Sarah, a woman of 90 years, were told they would have a son, they both laughed – not because of Abraham's age, but because of Sarah's age.[1] In the Old Testament, it is not considered unusual for a man to father a child after he is 100 years of age. It was the limits of the child-bearing age for the female that made the possibility of mothering a child at the age of 90 a laughing matter.[2] Perhaps this ancient biblical account is the first recorded incidence of sex differences in ageing and the sexual activity of older persons being viewed as a laughing matter.

Given the biblical bases for longevity and continued sexual activity, it seems strange that in 1986 sociologists' research confirming that older people fall in love in the same way that young people do would appear in *Psychology Today* and a syndicated Associated Press article,[3] and that birthday cards, cartoons and jokes would continue to make the sex life of older adults a laughing matter.

Even more difficult to understand is the omission of references to the sexual interests and needs for intimacy of older adults in denominational literature. Although the denominations have responded with programmatic books, they have given little or no attention to sexuality or sex differences in the age structure of their membership. An exception is Beecher's guide for clergy and congregations in ministry with older persons. He includes a short but excellent section on 'the masculine-feminine polarity.'[4]

While the Bible, science fiction writers and gerontologists treat the sexuality of older persons more positively than do religious writers and denominational leaders, gerontologists have given little attention to the role of religion and participation among the elderly.[5] As a consequence, the two most persistent myths about aging are that sex is for the young and religion is for the old. Contrary to these popular beliefs, adults do not necessarily turn to religion as they age,[6] nor do they lose sexual interest or cease to be sexually active. However, religious sanctions and beliefs about sexual behavior and negative social attitudes about the sexual needs of older persons do affect the way older people respond to their sexuality.

The sexuality and religiosity of older persons are usually addressed separately. We propose to examine sex differences in aging, sex roles and behavior of older adults in relation to religious beliefs and participation. We have identified for this purpose five megatrends to serve as a framework for the analysis of sex and aging and their implications for the church/synagogue in the future.

In everyday usage, sex and religion are used to describe a range of characteristics and behaviors. Sex is used interchangeably to refer to all sexual characteristics, identity, gender roles and behavior. For most social scientists, sex refers to the two mutually exclusive biological and physiological characteristics of the male and female; gender designates the behavior associated with enacting roles ascribed by society to males and females along with an individual's own sexual identity, i.e., feminine or masculine; and, sexuality refers to the emotional and physical responses to sexual stimuli.

Religion is the popular term that refers to personal religiosity, religious practice, and organizational participation. The social scientist studying religion and aging usually differentiates between religiousness, personal faith or non-institutional religious responses and religious participation in formal religious organizations. The social scientist's usage of sex and religion will enable a more discrete identification of the trends which will impact the church/synagogue.

From Youth to Adult Congregations: The Demographic Imperative

In less than 20 years we have moved from a youth society to an aging society. In 1986, the acceleration of this age shift gained public attention. As Baby Boomers (born between 1945–1960) began to turn 40, headlines in the business section of the Atlanta Constitution announced that 'The World Is Not Just For The Young; Atlanta's Median Age is 31.1.'[7] For the first time in US history there were as many people over as under 30 years of age. The trend that the Baby Boomers will set is projected to raise the median age nationally to 36 by the year 2000 and to age 42 by the year 2050.[8] Equally as dramatic is the report that the fastest growing segment in the population is over 85 years of age and that this demographic trend is expected to continue.[9] Traditionally, churches/synagogues have been youth and couple oriented. Even though churches have been graying at a greater rate than the US population, the shift to an adult or an intergenerational orientation is occurring at a slower pace within congregations than in the public and business sectors.

The membership for Protestant denominations is estimated to range from 37–47 per cent over the age of 55. Furthermore, most major denominations can expect an unprecedented high rate of clergy retirement in the next ten years.[10] Consequently, as the congregations age the active clergy will be younger. This trend will make it essential for seminary education to include gerontological content and an emphasis on intergenerational relationships.

Most of the Judeo-Christian national organizations are awakening to the age shift in their membership. However, the responses seem to be focused mostly on social service needs and age specific programs. The time has come to address the continued need for intimacy and affirmation of sexual identity and activity throughout adult life – into the biblical over 100 years of age. Adult members, especially the Baby Boomers, who have experienced the sexual revolution will provide the impetus for more education within the context of their religious faith on human sexuality in the mid-to-late life.

Although the Baby Boomers have been the more sexually liberated as young adults, they are unlikely to be prepared for or to understand the age changes in sexual performance and opportunities. Many will believe that sex after sixty is a laughing matter – when it refers to their parents. When they are over sixty it will be a serious matter. As the Baby Boomers experience the age changes, they will seek reliable information about life stage intimacy needs and performance. They will be the leaders of an aging sexual revolution in which continued sexual activity will be a normal expectation, not the subject for jokes.

Gerontologists have known for some time that most older people are sexually active. While age has been identified as the most important factor affecting frequency and the form of sexual activity, there is no physiological basis for predicting inevitable sexual dysfunction accompanying aging. On the contrary, the Duke Longitudinal Research study found that, for some older persons, sexual interest and activity actually increase with age.[11] These gerontological research findings need to be utilized by the clergy in their counselling and religious interpretations.

Support for local clergy to address the sexual needs of older members was given in 1974 when the National Council of Churches, the Synagogue Council of America and the United States Catholic Conference issued an interfaith statement on sex education affirming that:

> human sexuality is a gift of God to be accepted with reverence and joy; ... It is more than a mechanical instinct. Its many dimensions are intertwined with the total personality and character of the individual. Sex is a dynamic urge or power, arising from one's basic maleness or femaleness, and having complex physical, psychological, and sexual dimensions. These dimensions, we affirm, must be shaped and guided by spiritual and moral considerations which derive from our Judeo-Christian heritage. Sex education is not however, only for the young, but is a life-long task whose aim is to help individuals develop their sexuality in a manner suited to their life stage.[12]

Implications for the church/synagogue

As the age of the church/synagogue shifts from youth to an adult membership, sex after sixty will no longer be a laughing matter but the reason for life-span sex education and social programs to provide opportunities for heterosexual interaction.

The influence of the sheer numbers of the Baby Boomers and their sexual life styles will shape the future direction of these changes. The shift to an older adult membership will make it imperative to rely on retired members to fill the functional lay leader roles in the congregations. This age group, with the most discretionary time and income, will be a major source for recruitment and training for diaconal ministry. The youth-to-adult to older-adult congregations will require a trained lay older adult leadership to carry out the goals and programs for all age members.

From Male to Female Congregations

For fifty years the Gallup report on Religion in America has shown church/synagogue membership to be highest among women.[13] However, being in the majority did not constitute a female-orientated congregation. The women's movement and the increase in the number of older women have caused a shift from male-dominated (and not majority) church/synagogue to one in which women are not only increasing in membership but also filling traditionally male lay and professional roles.

Longevity is not experienced equally by males and females. In 1984, life expectancy at birth for the male was 71.1 and for the female it was 78.3 years. For those reaching the age of 65, females had a life expectancy of 18.7 more years and men had an additional 14.5 years. This difference in life expectancy at birth and at age 65 results in a ratio of males to females which varies dramatically with age. Until the age of 24, there is only a slight difference in the numbers of males and females. After age 25, their sex ratio begins to change until by age 65 women outnumber men three to two. Among those over the age of 85 in 1984, there were 40 men for every 100 women or four women for every man.[14]

These sex differences in life expectancy result partly from sex differences in the cause of death. Women have benefited from medical advances in treating infectious diseases, pre-natal care and birth control. Men are more likely than women to die of degenerative diseases such as cancer and heart disease. Although there has been progress in treating the diseases, it has not been as great as for infectious diseases.[15] There is some speculation, supported by the slight increase in life expectancy for the male and decline for the female, that the mass entry of women, especially the Baby Boomers, into the work force may make women more vulnerable to the degenerative diseases that have contributed to the shorter life expectancy of the male. Others speculate that as the male is relieved of the financial stress as the sole financial support for the family he will be less vulnerable to degenerative diseases. This could narrow the life expectancy differential significantly by the year 2000.

The implication of this trend is that the sex-ratio disparity can be expected to be greater in the church/synagogues than in the general population. The sex ratio differential among the older age groups and the age differential between youth and adults will impact program emphases and leadership. These age-sex trends could result in: (1) a more intergenerational organizational structure or a polarity and conflict between the young and older adults; (2) either a high dropout rate among older men who are uncomfortable with the increased disproportionate number of men to women or their increased involvement in the church/synagogue because they have more discretionary time; and (3) the Baby Boomer women filling more lay and professional leadership roles in the church/synagogue.

Regardless of which of these alternatives are taken, the sex ratio disparity among older members will force some programmatic and leadership changes in the congregations.

From Married to Single

Congregations have not only been youth and male oriented, but couple and family oriented. Congregations have been characterized by a 'Noah's ark' syndrome in which all are expected to enter two by two. This Noah's ark syndrome is a sex-negativism that places primacy on sexual activity as procreation. Important as this aspect of sexuality is, it is age specific for women and does not represent the total experience of human sexuality.

The disparity of males to females among older adults means that there are fewer married couples. In 1984, 40 per cent of adults age 65 and over were married. Twice as many older men (78%) were likely to be married than older women (40%). There were five times (7.8 million) widows as widowers (1.5 million) and the disparity increases at older ages.[16] In 1985, 68% of women 75 and older were widowed compared to less than 23% of men over age 75. This gender disparity is a consequence of age-specific death rates for adult men and their tendency to marry younger women.[17]

Divorce among older people has increased faster than the older population as a whole in the past 20 years. Four per cent of all older persons were divorced – more older women than older men. Furthermore, elderly widowed men have remarriage rates about seven times higher than widows. Among the future elderly (men and women) approximately one-half of the men and women will have been divorced at least once by the time they reach the age of 75.[18] This may seem like a dismal projection, but on the positive side, they (men and women) will know how to enter and exit a single lifestyle. For women, this may be the best preparation for the eight to ten years most of them over the age of 65 can expect to be widowed or divorced.

A small number (less than 8%) of older persons never marry. Since many young adults are delaying or rejecting marriage, the number of never married older persons may be expected to increase.[19] Studies on marital status and life satisfaction are in general agreement that married persons are happier, healthier and longer-lived than the never-married, widowed or divorced.[20] Marriage minimizes the negative impact of retirement, reduced income and declining health. This life satisfaction difference may be attributed to the major functions that marriage performs for couples: intimacy, interdependence, a sense of belonging, a shared life history, and continuity of life style.[21]

Marital satisfaction varies among older couples, but most of the studies reported that older wives and husbands appreciate each other and are highly satisfied, whether it is a long- or short-term marriage. Given the personal investment of time, energy and themselves in the marriage and the alternative of living alone in late life, most dissatisfied older marrieds choose to continue the relationship.[22]

The church/synagogue is challenged to respond to never-married, widowed and divorced older members who also have the need to minimize the negative impact of retirement, reduced income and declining health.

Implications for the church/synagogue

Gender differences in marital status are much greater among older age groups and can be expected to continue. Responses to this marital heterogeneity by the church/synagogue will include: (1) older singles groups to provide social support and activities that increase morale and life satisfaction; (2) support groups for those experiencing loss of a spouse by divorce or death; (3) marital counseling and adaptation of the marriage ritual for late-life remarriages; (4) couple groups for the older newlyweds; and (5) marriage revitalization and enrichment groups for long-lived intact-survivor marriages.

All of these groups will need leaders, counselors and clergy who are knowledgeable about normal physiological aging and gender changes in sexual functionality.

From Either/or to Multiple Choice

Marriage continues to be the most valued state for most Americans. At least 95% marry at least once and most who divorce before they are sixty tend to marry again. Although death and divorce reduce the numbers of older marriages, approximately half of the 26 million older Americans are married. Of course, this means that approximately half of these older Americans are not married and that the sex ratio disparity reduces the chances for remarriage, especially for women.

The opportunity for heterosexual activity on the part of the older female, unlike that of the older male or young female, is still more apt to be determined by the availability of a husband and his sexual capability. Unmarried older men maintain sexual activity and interest levels similar to that of married men. Women do not because they lack available and appropriate sexual partners.

The sexual revolution of the past two decades has widened the choices for adults of all ages. The trend has been away from sexual intimacy within marriage or to multiple choices. Although marriage continues to be highly valued by older persons and a life style experienced by most, it can no longer be the only alternative.

The choices other than marriage include: (1) companionship and dating; (2) co-habitation; (3) homosexuality; (4) affairs with married persons; (5) polygamy; and (6) no sexual partner.

Marriage and dating may be the only choices sanctioned by the church/synagogue. However, the sex ratio disparity among older persons can be expected to influence these limited sanctions in the future. Certainly, the Judeo-Christian faith has an Old Testament precedent for multiple partners. Courtship and dating may lead to marriage or to a 'steady' relationship. Dating behavior among older persons is reported to be more varied and the pace of the relationship tends to be accelerated. Bulcroft and O'Conner-Roden report that sexual involvement is an important part of the dating relationships for most of the older persons in their study. While sexuality for these dating couples included intercourse, the stronger emphasis was on the nuances of sexual behavior, such as hugging, kissing and touching. This physical closeness helped fulfill the intimacy needs of older people, needs that were especially important to those living alone and whose sole source of human touch was often the dating partner. Sex also contributed to self-esteem by making people feel desired and needed. As could be expected, older persons choosing to have a sexual relationship outside of marriage violated the religious values that they have followed. Consequently, older people frequently hide the intimate aspects of a relationship.[23]

Some older persons elect to openly live together. For some this may lead to marriage. Many older people reject marriage as a solution to their need for a sexual relationship because they are not willing to give up their independence, the possibility of deteriorating health and the financial complexities of a legal relationship. Brubaker observes that although the number of people over the age of 65 cohabitating has decreased slightly, cohabitation is increasing in most age groups.[24] This leads us to expect the trend toward cohabitation to gradually increase. The choice of dating with intimacy and cohabitation raises the religious question about the reason for marriage. Do older people have the same reason for marriage as young people? Is the delay in marriage by young adults based on the same rationale that older people use to reject marriage, i.e., the view that marriage is for procreation? This ambiguity about marriage by both young and older adults may stimulate the church/synagogues to formulate sanctions and rituals that address age-related sexual expressions and relationships.

Another form of cohabitation is homosexual. The visiblity of homosexuality among younger adults may lead older adults, especially older women, to choose this life style to meet their needs for intimacy.

Unanswered is the effect of AIDS on the *number* of homosexuals in the future. However, it is most likely that a homosexual cohabitation will continue to be the choice of a small proportion of older persons.

Over forty years ago a medical doctor, Victor Kassells, recommended a limited polygamy after the age of 60. He pointed out that this would be a return to a practice that at one time was considered proper in the Judeo-Christian ethic. He argued that:

> marriage enables the unmarried older woman to find a partner. ... Most women have an increase in libido after the menopause simply because they lose the fear of pregnancy. A polygynous marriage enables them to express this desire, instead of remaining repressed through a continent widowhood.[25]

As for men, Kassells observed that many sexologists claim the male is polygamous by nature. Furthermore, there is no established age of a male climacteric. Male impotence, not related to disease or medication, may be due to boredom, or an uninterested partner. Polygamous marriage might be a solution to a number of sexual problems of the aged. Kassells may have a good solution, but the strength of the Christian belief in a monogamous relationship, at least serially within and outside the marriage, makes it unlikely that this choice will be sanctioned in the future.

More likely to increase are affairs outside the marriage. As partners within a long-term marriage experience changes in health, interests and compatibility, discrete affairs that protect the marriage partners may be a choice for some older persons.

Always open as choice is no sexual partner. Many widowed persons find a new freedom without sexual relationships. They focus their energy and interests on other activities and relationships. The importance that Americans of all ages place on sex suggests that this will not be the voluntary choice of most older adults in the future.

Implications for the church/synagogue

The need and requests for counseling related to these choices can be expected to increase. Consequently, the professional training for clergy and other counselors will include not only the sexual needs, choices, sociopsychological problems unique to older persons, but also the religious conflict and dilemma older persons experience.

Church/synagogue rituals related to marriage and sexual practice will need to be adapted to the non-procreative stage of life so that the joy of intimacy, experiencing one's sexuality and identity on human sexuality will be extended to older members.

From Exclusion to Inclusion

This fifth trend is a logical consequence of the other trends discussed above. For the never married, widowed and divorced older adult, the congregation has the opportunity to provide the many opportunities for forms of sexual expression, such as caring, touching, hugging, kissing and dating. Congregations may also serve as a surrogate extended family. The exclusion of the unique problems of older married couples for marital counseling training will give way to an inclusion which views marriage within a life stage model. Younger and older persons will benefit from such inclusion.

The single older persons will be included in the singles ministry of the church/synagogue.

Sex education and premarital counseling will include age changes in sexual needs and interest and age appropriate counseling. Theological statements and rituals will be included and adapted at the congregational level to increase the human sexuality of older persons.

The inclusion of older persons in all religious matters related to sex, sex roles and sexuality will destroy the bases for making sex and the elderly a laughing matter.

Notes

1. 'Genesis,' Chapter 17:17; 18:12–13. *The Holy Bible*, revised standard version (New York: Thomas Nelson and Sons, 1953), pp. 10–12.
2. Stagg, Frank. *The Bible Speaks on Aging* (Nashville, TN: Broadman Press, 1981).
3. Bulcroft, Kris & Margaret O'Conner-Roden. 'Never Too Late,' *Psychology Today*. June 1986, pp. 66–69; 'Old Folks Who Fall in Love Still Teenagers at Heart,' The Atlanta Journal/Constitution, May 29, 1986.
4. Beckner, Arthur H. *Ministry With Older Persons: A Guide for Clergy and Congregations* (Minneapolis: Augsberge Publishing House, 1986).
5. Payne, Barbara. 'Religiosity.' In Mangen, David J. & Warren A. Peterson (eds.), *Social Roles and Social Participation*, Vol. 2 (Minneapolis: University of Minnesota Press, 1983), pp. 343–388: Kechnet, Vincent. *Religion and Aging: An Annotated Bibliography* (San Antonio, Texas, 1982).
6. Alston, Jon R. & Wingrove, Ray (eds.). 'Cohort Analysis of Church Attendance, 1936–69.' In *Social Forces*, 1949, September, pp. 57–17.
7. 'The World is Not Just for the Young: Atlanta's Median Age is 31.1,' The Atlanta Journal/Constitution, June, 1986.
8. *Aging America: Trends and Projections* (1985–86 edition) (Washington US Senate Special Committee on Aging), The American Association of Retired Persons, The Federal Council on Aging & The Administration on Aging, 1986.
9. Thoason, James, A. & Horacek, Bruce S. 'Self Esteem, Value, and Identity: Who are the Elderly Really?' *Journal of Religion and Aging*, 3(1/2): pp. 5–15.
10. Payne, Barbara. 'Protestants.' In Erdman Palmore (ed.), *Handbook on the Aged in the United States* (Westport, Connecticut, 1984) pp. 181–198.
11. Palmore, Erdman. 'Sexual Behavior.' In *Social Patterns in Normal Aging: Findings from the Duke Longitudinal Study* (Durham, North Carolina: Duke University Press, 1981); Butler, Robert & Lewis, Myra, *Sex After Sixty* (New York: Harper & Row, 1976; Peterson, James A. & Payne, Barbara. *Love in the Later Years* (Association Press, 1975).
12. 'Interfaith Statement on Sex Education' (National Council of Churches, Synagogue Council of American, United States Catholic Council). In Gordon, S. & Libby, R. *Sexuality Today and Tomorrow* (North Setuate, Mass: Duxbury Press, 1975), pp. 154–156.
13. Gallup, Jr., George. *Religion in America, 50 years: 1935–1985* (Princeton, NJ: Gallup Report, N0236, May 1985).
14. *Aging America: Trends and Projections* (1985–86 edition). (Washington DC: US Senate Committee on Aging, The American Association of Retired Persons, The Federal Council on Aging and The Administration on Aging, 1986.
15. Ward, Russell A. *The Aging Experience* (Second ed.), (New York: Harper & Row, Publishers; 1984), pp. 207–209.

16. Glick, Paul C. 'Marriage, Divorce and Living Arrangements of the Elderly: Prospective Changes,' *Journal of Family Issues* 5:7–26, 1984.
17. 'Developments in Aging: 1985,' Volume 3 (Washington, DC: Special Committee on Aging, United States Senate, 1986).
18. Brubaker, Timothy. *Later Life Families* (Beverly Hills, California: Sage, 1985).
19. *Psychology Today* (see footnote 3)
20. Ward, Russell A. 'The Never Married In Later Life,' *Journal of Gerontology* 34:861–869, 1979. Gubrium, Jay F. 'Being Single in Old Age,' *International Journal of Aging and Human Development* 6:29–41, 1975; Longino, Jr., Charles F. & Lipman Aaron. 'The Married, The Formerly Married and The Never Married: Support System Differentials of Older Women in Planned Retirement Communities,' 1982; Norvel, Glenn. 'The Contribution of Marriage to the Psychological Well-being of Males and Females,' *Journal of Marriage and the Family* 37(3):594–601; Brubaker, 113–116 (see footnote 18); Uhlenberg, P. & Myers, M. 'Divorce and The Elderly,' *Gerontologist* 21(3), 276–82, 1981.
21. Atchley, Robert. *Social Forces and Aging* (4th ed.), (Belmont, California: Wadsworth, 1985).
22. Gilford, Rosalie. 'Marriages in Later Life,' *Generations* X(4):17–21, 1986; Skolink, A. 'Married Lives: Longitudinal Perspectives on Marriage.' In Eichorn, David et al. (eds.) *Present and Past in Middle Life* (New York: Academic Press, 1981).
23. Bulcroft, Kris, and O'Conner-Roden, Margaret (see footnote 3).
24. Brubaker, Timothy (see footnote 18).
25. Kassels, Victor. 'Polygamy After 60,' *Geriatrics* 21, No. 4, April 1966.

9. Sexuality and Violence

Feminist and womanist writers have long argued that we live in a cultural context which structures our relationship in terms of domination and submission. We have only recently begun to become aware of the scale of domestic violence, rape and sexual abuse. And the Churches have been surprised to find themselves not immune from the disease of violence. Indeed many have argued that the Christian tradition and the way it is interpreted today plays an important part in forming the mindset that sanctions abuse. In this section three theologians tackle this difficult but vitally important issue. Marjorie Procter-Smith, in '"Reorganising Victimisation": The Intersection between Liturgy and Domestic Violence', asks some interesting questions about the relationship between Christian liturgy and domestic violence. She argues that the fact that violence goes on in the homes of church-going Christians should lead us to ask what it is that they are hearing, seeing and doing in liturgy that allows that violence to go on. Liturgy both expresses what we believe and shapes our identity; it therefore has a power in our lives which we may not be conscious of. Procter-Smith draws attention to the use of the Bible in Christian worship. It is treated as the word of God, proclaimed as truth beyond disagreement or debate. The patriarchal and misogynistic nature of many biblical texts are proclaimed in Church as truth. This does seem to have some effect on abusers – some claim divine right to punish women and women often interpret their abuse as divinely sanctioned – Genesis 1 and 2 and the household codes of the New Testament feature highly in these interpretations. Procter-Smith also exposes the way readings about or concerning women are often married together in lectionaries to reinforce notions of women's inferiority to and dependency upon men. She notes that lectionaries often omit positive, affirming passages on women altogether. Use of androcentric language in liturgy renders women invisible and sustains the presumption that the male is normative. The use of exclusively male images of God – particularly the overuse of the image of God as father – identifies God with the husband or father abuser. Sin is associated with rebellion in liturgy, not with abuse of power of exploitation of the vulnerable. The predominance of males as liturgical leaders and bowing and kneeling before clergy serve to reinforce the identification between dominant masculinity and God. Procter-Smith argues that the Church must give the liturgy back to the people and therefore back to women whose experiences must take a central place. Every element of the liturgy must be reworked to rid the liturgy of its overarching structure of domination and submission and to name the sins of violence.

A very different approach is taken by James Poling, in 'Child Sex Abuse: A Rich Context for Thinking About God, Community and Ministry'. He explores some wide ranging issues raised by the phenomenon of child abuse. He believes that evil in the human self results from a failure to engage in empathetic bonding with others, and that the result is a 'lack of a cohesive self of power and meaning'. Poling suggests that the whole community must take some responsibility for those individuals who fail to develop a cohesive self and who in some cases go on to abuse children. They fail the children when they do not provide adequate protection but they also fail the abuser by failing to address his injured self. Poling uses the image of an interconnected web. We are all involved in that web and we can only hope to break cycles of violence and abuse if we recognise the potential in all of us to abuse. If we can follow Jesus in accepting good and evil in ourselves without losing integrity we may have found an important key to ending abuse. Poling suggests that we see in God a God who has struggled with destructive aggression and so can be compassionate towards others in their struggle. This could be an important model for the Church as it struggles with its own violence and abusive behaviour. 'Is God one who has agonised over destructive power and thus can set limits on me with firmness and compassion?' Feminists would want to draw attention to Poling's failure to acknowledge and reflect upon the gender dimensions of abuse and the part the Church plays in reinforcing female powerlessness. They would want Poling to recognise explicitly that, whereas we may all have destructive instincts, we do not all sexually abuse people, even if we are survivors of abuse ourselves. Some would argue that Poling's focus on the abuser rather than the abused and his reclamation of a destructive God just reinforces the impression that the Christian tradition is always on the side of the abuser not the abused.

Loren Broadus, in 'Sex and Violence in the Family and

Church', offers a vivid picture of domestic violence drawn from his experience as a pastor and some theological reflections upon that experience. His recognition is that one of the main reasons men abuse women is simply because 'it works'. He demonstrates an awareness of the gender dynamics of power often missing from clergymen's attempts to wrestle with this issue. His analysis of abuse by clergy is useful and timely. His practical advice should help the thousands of congregations in all denominations struggling with this issue which has been so badly handled by Church authorities over the years.

Marjorie Procter-Smith's article '"Reorganising Victimisation": The Intersection between Liturgy and Domestic Violence', also appears in *Violence Against Women and Children: A Christian Theological Sourcebook* (Continuum, November, 1995).

James Poling is Professor of Pastoral Theology and Counselling, Colgate Rochester Divinity School, New York, U.S.A. His article, 'Child Sex Abuse: A Rich Context for Thinking About God, Community and Ministry', was first published in *The Journal of Pastoral Care* vol. 42, no. 1, Spring 1988, pp. 58–61.

Loren Broadus's article, 'Sex and Violence in the Family and Church', was first published in *Lexington Theological Quarterly*, vol. 26, January 1991, pp. 13–23.

9.1 'Reorganizing Victimization': The Intersection between Liturgy and Domestic Violence

Marjorie Procter-Smith

> I can never romanticize language again
> never deny its power for disguise for mystification
> but the same could be said for music
> or any form created
> painted ceilings beaten gold worm-worn Pietàs
> reorganizing victimization frescoes translating
> violence into patterns so powerful and pure
> we continually fail to ask are they true for us.
> –from 'The Images' in *A Wild Patience Has Taken Me This Far*,
> Adrienne Rich[1]

What do domestic violence and the liturgy have to do with one another? Certainly the relationship is not immediately manifest. The church's liturgy, after all, is public; domestic violence is domestic: that is, it takes place in what is regarded in our society as a private domain, the home.

But perhaps the distinction between 'public' liturgy and 'private' violence is too sharp. The Christian liturgy has its roots deep in the domestic liturgies of Judaism, especially the table blessings and the Passover meal. Until the Peace of Constantine and the development of Imperial Christianity, all of the church's liturgies were necessarily both domestic and private, with the church itself being understood as the new 'family': the household of God. The fact that domestic violence occurs in the homes of 'church-going' Christians, including the homes of Christian clergy, ought to make us wonder what is being heard, seen, said, and done in our Christian assemblies that allows the violence to continue.[2] How have we failed to make it clear that the physical, emotional, and sexual abuse of women, children, the elderly is an offense also against God and the Christian community? How can we do better? These two questions will guide this exploration of possible connections between the liturgy and domestic violence.

First, the perpetuation of domestic violence is a sin. The typical victims of domestic violence are those members of a family or household who are smaller, weaker or in some way dependent (i.e., financially) on the abuser. The presence of violence (whether physical, sexual, or psychological) violates the relationship of trust which is necessary for a healthy functioning of any family, community, or relationship. The use of violence or abuse eliminates the possibility of equality, mutuality, or cooperation. Alongside the casual, taken-for-granted attitude toward wife-battering must be set the society-wide silence about the reality and extent of the problem.[3] That silence and acceptance has been and continues to be terribly costly for the victims of violence and abuse. To name this violence as sin is to challenge both the silence and the acceptance, and to make it the concern of the whole church.

Second, domestic violence is a sympton of the more extensive social sin of sexism (and often, its companion, racism). Women stand a much greater chance of being victims of abuse than men (some estimate one out of two women are victims of physical, sexual, or psychological abuse; girl children are more likely to be sexually abused than boys [between one in five and one in three girls, and one in eleven boys, it is estimated, are sexually abused before age 18]), and their abuser is most likely to be a family member, primarily the father (94% of all incest cases reported are father-daughter incest).[4] The abuse of children and the elderly may be regarded in some sense as a corollary to the abuse of women, since they occupy a status comparable to that of women in our society in their marginality and enforced dependence on adult males. The hard reality of domestic abuse puts a face on those often rather vague concepts of sexism, patriarchy, and androcentrism. It may help us to recognize how deeply sexism is imbedded in our culture to recall that the origin of the expression 'rule of thumb' was the English common law that a man may beat his wife with a stick no thicker than his thumb.

The liturgy is fundamentally the 'work of the people,' and therefore the primary business of all Christian people, including women, the young, and the old. 'Liturgy,' *leitourgia*, has its origins in the civil-political arena, as does the term *ekklesia*, 'chuch.' The *ekklesia* is 'the actual assembly of free citizens gathering for deciding their own spiritual-political affairs.'[5] The *leitourgia* is the public work done by them and, on their behalf, by their public servants.[6] At the same time, the tradition in which the liturgy has come to us is androcentric and patricarchal; it is a product of cultures which, however much they may have varied, have agreed in regarding women and children as marginal or invisible. By 'patriarchal' is meant the social structure in which the basic social unit is the male-headed household and the male head of such a household is the only full member of the political state. Thus the term 'patriarchal' does not mean simply male rule of women, but a structure of interlocking patterns of dominance and submission in which not only gender but also age, class, race, and status become important factors.[7] Because women and children (together with the elderly, who in our present culture are also marginal or invisible) are the primary victims of domestic abuse, it is important to attend to elements of the liturgy which reflect androcentric or patriarchal assumptions. Second, the liturgy is the worship of God; it is not therapy, education, or social work. Any or all of these (and much more besides) may be needed in order to prevent domestic violence, but the liturgy can not do them. To admit ulterior motives, however well-intentioned, into our worship, will inevitably result in the failure of both our inappropriate intentions and our worship. To put it another way: this paper is concerned with the point at which domestic violence as a social reality and the church's liturgy intersect. Neither the root source nor the ultimate solution to the problem of domestic violence lies in our liturgy.[8]

Nevertheless, the liturgy is much like language. On the one hand it expresses what we believe and who we believe we are, in word and song and gesture. At the same time, it shapes our identity and self understanding in relation to God and to the world, both by what is said and done, and by what is omitted. Because liturgy not only expresses what we believe but tells us what we ought to believe, and how we ought to act, it is a powerful shaper of human consciousness.

Christian liturgy, like any other 'form created,' can disguise and mystify domestic violence and its roots, making the abuse seem not only acceptable, but even divinely sanctioned. And because liturgy (again, like language) shapes us gradually and in tiny increments, words and gestures which are used regularly and repeatedly, although appearing small, have a powerful effect. The intersection between liturgy and the occurrence of domestic violence therefore, will be explored by examining the use of the Bible in liturgy, the implications of androcentric liturgical language, the church's marriage rites, and the non-verbal elements of the liturgy. Finally we will examine specific possibilities for change.

The Word of God

The central verbal element in most Christian liturgy is the Word: the proclamation of and exposition on the Scriptures of the Old and New Testaments. In this liturgical context, moreover, the reading of Scriptures is not presented, as it might be in a Bible study group or a class, as a text to be studied, discussed, and evaluated, but as the 'Word of God.'[9] Non-verbal gestures of deference to the Bible, the reader, or to the reading itself intensify this assumption. Since it is presented as the 'Word of God,' it is not a matter for debate or dispute; instead, the congregation is expected to sit (or stand) and listen passively, to 'hear with joy what (God) say(s) to us today.' It is presumed, then, that the texts read are not only undebatable, but also that they have a present authoritative claim on us.

Therefore, the use of the Bible in liturgical proclamation immediately raises problems. The patriarchal and, in many cases, misogynist nature of the Bible has been thoroughly examined of late by such Biblical scholars as Phyllis Trible, Phyllis Bird, and Elisabeth Schüssler Fiorenza. Schüssler Fiorenza sums up the findings of such research succinctly:

Not only is scripture interpreted by a long line of men and proclaimed in patriarchal churches, it is also authored by men, written in androcentric language, reflective of religious male experience, selected and transmitted by male religious leadership. Without question, the Bible is a male book.[10]

Therefore, she wryly proposes that all Biblical texts should carry a warning label addressed to women: 'Caution! Could be dangerous to your health and survival.'

People who work with battered women note the frequency with which abused women interpret their abuse as divinely ordained, and cite scriptural support for their interpretation. One woman said, 'God punished women more,' and cited Genesis 3:16. Another, who complained to her husband that she had sustained injuries after one of his attacks, was told by him: 'your bones are my bones – just like it says in the Bible.' Another, regularly beaten and raped by her husband, interpreted this abuse as God's correction of her tendency to rebel against her husband's authority.[11] In general, battered women who were strongly religious tended to interpret their experiences of abuse according to the Genesis stories of the creation and the fall; the New Testament 'household code' admonitions to wives to be subject to their husbands; the saying of Jesus about divorce; and assorted other Gospel texts which urge meekness, self-abnegation, suffering and sacrifice as marks of the Christian life. Based on her own experience of conducting Bible study groups for battered women, Thistlethwaite concludes that 'the religious sanction in the household codes for the submission of women is a primary legitimation of wife abuse and must be challenged by women.'[12] Schüssler Fiorenza's proposal is even more sweeping: 'Patriarchal texts should not be allowed to remain in the lectionary but should be replaced by texts affirming the discipleship of equals.'[13] Decisions about which texts justify the oppression of women and others in general and the abuse of women in particular, and which texts challenge or correct such abuse cannot be made without careful attention to the function and uses of Scripture in contemporary society.

An examination of current lectionaries, however, reveals that the two most frequently cited texts in the justification of violence against women – Genesis 1–2 and the household codes – are part of the three-year Sunday cycle:

Episcopal, Lutheran, CCT: Gen 2:4b–9, 15–17, 3:1–7
(the second creation story and the fall, with the creation of woman omitted): 1st Sunday of Lent, Year A.
Episcopal, Lutheran, CCT: Gen 2:18–24
(the creation of woman from the rib of the man):
Episcopal: Proper 22, Year B; Lutheran: 20th Sunday after Pentecost, Year B
Episcopal, CCT: Ephesians 5:21–33

(the first element of the three-part household code; Lutheran has Eph. 5:21–31): Proper 16, Year B (Lutheran 14th Sun. after Pentecost, Year B)

Including these texts in these lectionaries endows them with ecclesiastical authority. Furthermore, their relationship to the other texts for the day offers a particular interpretation of them. Thus, the text from Genesis 2 recounting the creation of woman is coupled in all three lectionaries with Mark 10:2–9, Jesus' saying on divorce, which concludes, 'What God has joined together let not man (sic) put asunder,' a text which has been frequently used to keep women in an abusive or life-threatening marriage. By joining it to the creation of woman text the lectionary implies that there is a direct relationship between woman's created nature and the indissolubility of marriage. A listener might very well conclude not only that the marriage bond is forged by God, but also that to be married is part of woman's nature, rather than a state which she may choose or reject. If the psalm appointed for that Sunday is used, the picture is complete. Psalm 128 recounts the blessings a God-fearing man may expect, including:

> Your wife will be like a fruitful vine within your house;
> Your children will be like olive shoots around your table.
> Lo, thus shall the man be blessed who fears the Lord. (vv. 3–4)

Preaching, the application of the Biblical 'Word of God' to a specific community, is more difficult to analyze. It is of necessity localized and particularized, and defies generalities. Nevertheless, the importance and power of the sermon must never be underestimated. Sermons which speak without nuance of the virtue of 'submitting to the will of God,' for example, or of the way in which 'God sends us suffering to test our faith' may have critical or even fatal consequences when heard and believed by a woman who may be considering leaving an abusive husband. Preachers tend to fail to recognize that people often take their sermons very seriously, perhaps more seriously than the preacher. They also sometimes fail to recognize that women may hear a sermon's message differently from men listeners. A sermon on 'forgiveness' will resonate differently to an abusive husband than to his victimized wife. In spite of the fact that women are the majority in most church pews, sermons are almost always addressed to men.

The lectionary also proclaims by what it omits. Susan Thistlethwaite notes that 'the text with which many abused women find the most identification is John 7:53–8:11' – the story of Jesus' defense of the woman taken in adultery. To these women, the powerful impact of the text comes from their recognition that Jesus defends a woman who is about to be physically battered.[14] The text is not in any of the three lectionaries under consideration. Also absent from the lectionary is Jesus' healing of the woman bent over (Luke 13:10–17), in which

Jesus violates the Sabbath laws on the woman's behalf and defends her healing against the objections of religious leaders.

The Words of the Liturgy

While Biblical texts form a significant and particularly authoritative verbal element of liturgy, there are also other words. The language of prayers, blessings, hymns, acclamations also carries its weight. Of concern here is the language about the human community and the church, language about God and language which implies dominant-submissive relationships.

The problems of the use of androcentric language to speak of people in general have been thoroughly examined and assessed.[15] It may be sufficient here simply to note the two factors in the use of androcentric language which have bearing on our subject. First, androcentric language is bound to the androcentric and patriarchal social structures it both reflects and helps to sustain. Violence against women and children within the patriarchal family is subtly sustained by the use of language which presupposes that the male human being is the norm. Second, androcentric language renders women invisible, which not only makes it difficult for women to recognize their own needs for health and safety as legitimate, but also makes such recognition difficult for the entire community. Clearly the use of androcentric language carries these (and other) liabilities in all manner of discourse. But its significance is deepened when used in a liturgical context, as, for example, when a minister, presumably addressing the congregation in the name of God, calls them 'brothers'.

Language about God is certainly one of the most pressing theological issues facing the church in this day. The exclusively male language which is still predominant in most traditions and in most liturgies has been vigorously attacked and just as vigorously defended. We may ask, however, what significance this male image of God has for the perpetuation of domestic violence. It has often been assumed that for those whose experiences with their own fathers have been negative, as in an abusive relationship, the image of God as Father can have no positive value. Others, recognizing that religious symbols are more complex and operate far more subtly than this, have argued the opposite: that those who have been abused or abandoned by their fathers have a greater need for a heavenly Father. But this correlation would seem to be too simple too. As Mary Pellauer notes, women who have been abused by men, particularly over a period of years, tend to generalize their fear and distrust from the abuser (or abusers) to all men. They become 'simply unable to trust men any longer.'[16] Women with religious convictions may extend this generalization yet further, and conclude that because God is male, 'he,' too, cannot be trusted, and feel that they have been abandoned by God.[17]

There is a still deeper problem with male God-langauge which has bearing on the perpetuation of domestic violence: the mirroring of patriarchal family/social structures and patriarchal father-God religion. Paul Tillich recognized this (without recognizing its implications) when he wrote, 'If God is symbolized as "Father", he (sic) is brought down to the human relationship of father and child. But at the same time this human relationship is consecrated into a pattern of the divine-human relationship.'[18] Mary Daly, in *Beyond God the Father*, recognizes the implication of this for women: 'If God in "his" heaven is a father ruling his people, then it is the "nature" of things and according to divine plan and the order of the universe that society be male dominated. Within this context, a mystification of roles takes place: The husband dominating his wife represents God "himself".'[19] One hundred years before Mary Daly, Antoinette Doolittle, a Shaker theologian, had put the same point even more succinctly: 'As long as we have all male Gods in the heavens we shall have all male rulers on the earth.'[20]

Thus women who are subject to all manner of life-threatening abuse by their husbands often interpret that abuse as punishment by a Father-God who is readily identifiable with the husband, or at least working through him. Those who work with abused women report the difficulty such women have in accepting the idea that their abuse is neither deserved nor divinely sanctioned. To challenge such abuse is to challenge God. The effect of Father-God language, then, given our patriarchal social and familial structures, is to legitimate male dominance and violence and to inhibit women's legitimate anger and protest against such treatment.

Other forms of language which imply relationships of dominance and submission carry the same liabilities as Father-God language. Titles such as 'Master' and 'Lord' ('King,' 'Ruler,' 'Sovereign', etc.) presuppose that there are also servants and subjects. While it may be argued that the application of such titles to God implicitly subverts all earthly or human authority, it is also readily apparent from our everyday experience that the servants and subjects in our society are overwhelmingly women and children, primarily the women and children of color. Language of dominance and submission goes beyond titles for God to include expressions of the sort reflected in the prayer of confession in the United Methodist 'Alternate Text,' which is not only addressed to the 'Eternal Father,' but identifies sin with willful rebellion and repentance with obedience:

> When we gather together to praise God, we remember that we are his people *who have preferred our wills to his. Accepting his power* to become new persons in Christ, let us confess our sin before God and one another. Eternal Father, we confess that often *we have failed to be an obedient church*:
>
> > we have not *done your will*,
> > we have *broken your law*.

we have *rebelled against your love*,
we have not loved our neighbors,
we have not heard the cry of the needy. Forgive us, we pray.
Free us for *joyful obedience*,
through Jesus Christ our Lord. Amen.[21]

The identification of sin with rebellion and repentance with obedience narrows our understanding of the meaning and manifestations of sin in our midst. It precludes or at least does not mention the possibility that sin might also be manifested in abuse of power, exploitation of the vulnerable, or patterns of oppression which violate the unity and health of the body of Christ. When such language is linked with Scriptural and hymn texts which image the Church as the obedient bride of Christ, a powerful chain is forged which prevents the abused woman from being able to break out of the cycle of violence in which she lives, without committing sin.

Marriage Rites

Do contemporary Christian marriage rites reinforce these patterns which inhibit the ability of women to reject violence against themselves? Unquestionably the 'traditional' rites, which include the 'giving away of the bride,' the asymmetrical marriage vows which demand obedience of the wife only, and the use of legal language from English common law for the transfer of property in the vows, provide powerful reinforcement for the assumption that the husband has 'divine right' to rule over his wife. The newer reformed rites in the current Episcopalian, Lutheran, United-Methodist, and Roman Catholic liturgies have taken some steps to eliminate these liabilities. For example, the giving away of the bride is absent from all of the new rites.[22] The asymmetry in the vows has been eliminated by dropping references to obedience. The legal language remains intact in the Episcopal and United Methodist revisions, but is much modified in the Lutheran rite.[23] Some elements openly affirm the equality and mutuality of Christian marriage, as in the opening address of the minister in the UM rite ('The Apostle Paul announced that where Christ is present there is surely equality as well as unity'),[24] and in the prayers following the marriage vows in the BCP ('Give them grace, when they hurt each other, to recognize and acknowledge their fault, and to seek each other's forgiveness and yours.' p. 429).

Given these relatively hopeful signs, it is discouraging to examine the proposed scripture readings for the new rites. In the Episcopalian, Lutheran, and United Methodist rites, the proposals include Genesis 2:18–24; Ephesians 5:21–33; and Mark 10:6–9 (or the Matthean parallel, Mt. 19:4–6), the significance of which for the perpetuation of domestic violence has already been discussed. The Episcopal and United Methodist rites also suggest Ephesians 3:14–19 ('the Father from whom every family in heaven and on earth is named'). The

United Methodist rite's suggestions include the following texts:

> Isaiah 54:5–8: 'For your Maker is your husband, the Lord of Hosts is his name ... For the Lord has called you like a wife forsaken and grieved in spirit ...' Jeremiah 31:31–34: '... I was their husband, says the Lord.'
>
> 1 Peter 3:1–9: 'Likewise you wives, be submissive to your own husbands ... So once the holy women who hoped in God used to adorn themselves and were submissive to their husbands, as Sarah obeyed Abraham, calling him Lord ...'

In addition, the suggested readings in all of the rites under consideration include texts such as 1 Corinthians 13, Colossians 3:12–17, and Romans 12:9–18, which enjoin such virtues as meekness, forbearance, and forgiveness. The intent of these latter texts may have been to foster mutuality and cooperation (and of course none of these texts are writing of the marriage relationship but of relationships within the Christian community). But as both Schüssler Fiorenza and Thistlethwaite point out, such texts are often interpreted as applying more specifically to women than to men, as the 1 Peter text does. The sermon may make this implicit cultural assumption explicit, as may other elements in the rite, such as the nuptial blessing in the Roman Wedding Mass, which is addressed to the woman only or predominantly. Rite B prays, 'Give your blessings to N., your daughter, so that she may be a good wife (and mother), caring for the home, faithful in love for her husband, generous and kind.'[25] The Lutheran, Episcopal, and United Methodist rites all follow the announcement of the marriage by the minister with the words from Mt. 19:6: 'Those whom God has joined together let no one put asunder.'[26]

At the heart of all Western Christian marriage rites is a simple legal transaction expressed in the exchange of vows between the two contracting parties. Recent rites acknowledge, implicitly at least, the equality of the two parties by the symmetrical wording of the vows exchanged. Although the contract is entered into 'until death,' the violation of the terms (i.e., 'to love and to cherish') by one party, which violence surely is, must be considered a breach of contract.

Unfortunately, the equality and freedom of the two contracting parties is obscured in these rites by an emphasis on the indissolubility of the bond (which is, after all only *one* term in the contract) and by the use of language and scripture which identifies the husband with God or Christ.

Non-verbal Language

Liturgy is more than words. It also includes a non-verbal element which is both powerfully influential and enormously difficult to analyze and assess. The non-verbal language of gesture, posture, vesture, and physical environment has been generally ignored or treated as a secondary matter of 'ceremonial,' detachable from liturgical texts and less significant than the texts themselves. It has taken anthropologists and social scientists to remind us that our liturgies communicate in more than words.[27] Because the application of this perspective to liturgy is so new, we can only suggest possible connections and relationships between non-verbal elements of liturgy and domestic violence.

The predominant presences of males as liturgical leaders has a definite connection with the use of androcentric and patriarchal language. It reinforces the implicit assumptions in such language, namely that adult males are simultaneously representative human beings and adequate representatives of God. The argument of the 1976 Vatican Declaration on the Admission of Women to the Ministerial Priesthood depends upon what might seem to be an extreme expression of this view: 'The Christian priesthood is therefore of a sacramental nature: the priest is a sign ... when Christ's role in the Eucharist is to be expressed sacramentally, there would not be this "natural resemblance" which must exist between Christ and his minister if the role of Christ were not taken by a man. In such a case it would be difficult to see in the minister the image of Christ.'[28] While most Protestants probably would reject this *form* of the argument against women as liturgical ministers, they nevertheless are content to assume that men are more adequate representatives of God than women.[29] The reluctance of abused women to turn to male pastors for help, and conversely their relative readiness to confide in a woman minister may be construed, in part, at least, as evidence of both the complexity and significance of this representative function. The male liturgical minister, speaking words in an androcentric language shaped by patriarchal presuppositions, is a powerful combination of verbal and non-verbal elements which may continue to legitimate male authority by identifying it with divine authority.

Bodily attitudes and postures may do the same. A clergywoman whose husband is also ordained once told me, 'I never take communion from my husband. I refuse to kneel before him.' Certainly postures such as standing when the clergy enter the church, bowing one's head to them, or kneeling before them are not only signs of respect but also express relative social status.[30] Even when such signs are of respect for or reverence toward God, the Bible, or the presence of Christ in the Eucharist, when the human mediators are invariably or predominantly males, the same mystification process we observed in the case of language takes place. Actions may indeed speak louder than words.

Even in churches which do not employ many changes in posture it is often easy to observe the expression of relative social status. In these cases it is relative movement and posture which is eloquent. When one person (or a small group of persons) does virtually all of the speaking and moving, the power lies with the speaker and mover. The pastor who stands for most of the service and does most of the speaking makes the congregation into passive spectators and hearers. When the leaders are usually male and the passive, seated congregation mostly female, expressions about relative power and status are combined with gender identity to encourage female passivity and acceptance. For the woman who is or has been abused, such encouragement is dangerous and destructive.

Making a Free Place on Which to Land

I curse you, I say.
    What that mean? he say.
    I say, Until you do right by me, everything you touch will crumble.
    He laugh. Who you think you is? he say. You can't curse nobody. Look at you. You black, you pore, you ugly, you a woman. Goddam, he say, you nothing at all.
    Until you do right by me, I say, everything you even dream about will fail. I give it to him straight, just like it come to me. And it seem to come to me from the trees.
    Whoever heard of such a thing, say Mr. –. I probably didn't whup you ass enough.
    Every lick you hit me you will suffer twice, I say. Then I say, You better stop talking because all I'm telling you ain't coming just from me. Look like when I open my mouth the air rush in and shape words ...
    A dust devil flew on the porch between us, fill my mouth with dirt. The dirt say, Anything you do to me already done to you. ...
    I'm pore, I'm black, I may be ugly and can't cook, a voice say to everything listening. But I'm here.
    Amen, say Shug. Amen, amen.

> –*The Color Purple*,
> by Alice Walker[31]

Alice Walker's Celie, the heroine of *The Color Purple*, suffers years of abuse first at the hands of her stepfather and then from her husband, whom she cannot bring herself to name in her letters to God and to her long-lost sister Nettie. The moment in the novel when she is at last able to draw on her own strength and on a strength that comes from beyond her and to curse her husband is the turning point for Celie and for her abusive husband. We have considered some of the ways in which the church has, in its liturgy, bound women to abusive relationships and restrained them from protesting against their own abuse. How might the church, in its liturgy, reverse the cycle of violence, loose the bonds, and enable women to reject relationships and environments which are dangerous to their health and well-being?

On the level of a general principle, we must work toward a recovery of the notion of the liturgy as 'the work of the people.' As long as liturgy is regarded as the proper domain only of (predominantly male) clergy, church bureaucrats and academic theologians, it will never be the work of the people. On the contrary, liturgy as the people's work must recognize that the majority of the people in the pews in every tradition and denomination is women. Therefore the experiences of women and their struggles for survival and dignity must take a central place as the locus out of which the primary theology which is the liturgy grows. Elisabeth Schüssler Fiorenza has named this idea 'womanchurch.'[32] Similarly, Aidan Kavanagh has argued that 'Mrs. Murphy and her pastor' are the primary theologians of the church, whose theology is expressed not in 'concepts and propositions,' but in the daily working out of faith.[33] The chances are good, statistically speaking, that Mrs. Murphy is or has been a victim of domestic violence or abuse. Thus, the way in which she has struggled with and survived that experience is of primary significance to the church and to its worship, as is the prevention of the continuation of that abuse in the lives of her daughters.

The liturgy as 'work of the people' also means that the liturgy as event must be restored to the gathered community. It can no longer remain the performance of the clergy, making the community mere passive observers. The restoration of elements such as the prayers of the people and the kiss of peace in which the people of God exercise their priestly ministry is vitally necessary. Physical restraints, such as pews, and barriers, such as altar rails, must be removed in order to free the community to be active.

The relocation of the matrix of liturgical theology in the struggle of women for survival and dignity in the context of their own faith has implications for the doing of liturgy. If we take seriously the theological significance of the presence of domestic violence suffered by women, children, and the elderly, we must begin to do differently the elements in our liturgies which have permitted or perpetuated this suffering.

The interpretation of the Bible and the use of the Bible in liturgy must undergo a significant shift. The 'intersection of the Bible with contemporary culture, politics and society' must become more important.[34] Preaching would have to be done out of the matrix of the struggles of women and others for justice and dignity. The lectionary needs to be reconstructed in such a way that oppressive texts which demand submission or devalue persons are excluded. At the same time, texts which contain painful stories of women's suffering, texts which Phyllis Trible calls 'Texts of Terror,' need to be included, so that the reality of such suffering will not be forgotten.[35]

The 'household of God,' unlike the patriarchal household of our culture, is characterized by cooperation, mutuality, and equality. It is a household without 'fathers' (Mark 10:29–30), and without relationships based on dominance and submission. Relationships of dominance and submission reflected in verbal and non-verbal transactions must be eliminated, and transactions which reflect mutual respect, cooperation, and equality encouraged. Non-reciprocal actions, such as standing when the clergy enter, or receiving a blessing from clergy, for example, reinforce relationships based on patterns of dominance and submission, whether lay-clergy, male-female, or adult-child.[36] On the other hand, the liturgy already has within it seeds of reciprocal actions, such as, for example, the bow exchanged between presider and people, the kiss of peace (as long as it is not 'clericalized' by being passed first among the clergy), and (verbally) the dialogue between presider and congregation at the beginning of the Eucharist prayer. A reciprocal absolution after confession is now part of the official United Methodist Sunday service and the Lutheran daily office.

Social sins of sexism such as domestic violence must not continue, as they do now, protected by silence. The recognition, confession, and repentance of and restitution for such offenses is not a 'private matter,' but a concern of the whole household of God. Language of prayer, especially prayers of confession and intercession, must recognize and confront this form of sin as well as others. Prayers of confession should name complicity in the perpetuation of domestic violence, by failing to speak or act, as one of the sins to which we are prone. Prayers of intercession ought always to mention the victims and the perpetrators of violence in the home among the petitions for those in need or trouble.

The proclamation in the liturgy of the justice of God can not be allowed to remain vague and unspecific. The implicit critique of unjust social structures (both within and without the church) needs to be made explicit. The church needs to learn to say not only 'Yes, Amen' to God's righteousness, but also 'No, this must not be' to injustice. Although the use of curses (such as the 'commination' of the 1552 BCP) is unfamiliar and alien to most of our present practices, curses can provide the opportunity for repentance and conversion.[37] In *The Color Purple*, Celie's prophecies about Mr. – are accomplished. He does suffer all of the ills which she promises. But Celie's curse also becomes the means by which he is able finally to repent and be transformed. A litany might be modeled either on the 'Communications,' taken chiefly from Deuteronomy 27 and focusing on offenses against the community, especially the vulnerable, or on the 'Reproaches' of the Good Friday liturgy, focusing on offenses against God. Either type could be an opportunity for repentance and conversion.

The women who have been victims of violence must recognize their own need to gather for their own purposes to heal, to find support, to express anger at God, to curse. Such gatherings will require their own unique liturgies and rituals, born out of the suffering and the struggles of the women. Curses, blessings, healings (such as laying on of hands and anointing), and rites of purification may be needed.[38] It is important for the church to recognize and legitimate these gatherings (although women ought not wait on such recognition). It is even more important for the church not to use such gatherings as an excuse to fail to deal with the issue of domestic violence in its mixed assemblies, or to marginalize the subject as a 'woman's issue.'

Exploring the intersection of liturgy and domestic violence is painful, wrenching, and costly. It is painful to acknowledge the depth of the social sin of sexism which expresses itself in violence against women, and the extent to which the church in its liturgy has abetted that violence, the dreadful price in distorted and destroyed lives paid by the Christian community. It is wrenching to contemplate the changes that are called for. The changes will be costly. The process of identifying domestic violence as a social ill, providing shelter and care for victims and help for abusers, doing the essential research and study of the roots and resolutions of such a disease has already begun, and will continue unless hindered by New Right political forces. Providing the necessary medical, legal and psychological help is not all that is needed. As Aidan Kavanagh writes, 'Liberators accomplish only half their task when they liberate. The other half of their labor is to provide a normal place, a free place, on which the liberation may land.'[39] Those who are working at the terrible and courageous task of freeing themselves from the cycle of domestic violence need a free and normal place on which to land. Those who have not yet found the courage to begin need a place which can show them that such work is both possible and necessary. The liturgy can be that place, and the words of Alice Walker can also be the words of the church:

> I am the woman
> offering two flowers
> whose roots are twin
> Justice and Hope
> Let us begin.

– from 'Remember?', in *Horses Make a Landscape Look More Beautiful*[40]

Notes

1. New York: W.W. Norton, 1981, pp. 3–7.
2. For statistics on domestic violence in the United Methodist context, see the study done by the National Divisions of the Board of Global Ministries' Program on Ministries with Women in Crisis, by Peggy Halsey and Lee Coppernoll: *Crisis: Women's Experience and the Church's Response. Final Report on a Crisis Survey of United Methodists*, March 1982.
3. See especially Marie Marshall Fortune, *Sexual Violence: The Unmentionable Sin* (NY: the Pilgrim Press, 1983), and Mary Pellauer, 'Moral Callousness and Moral Sensitivity,' in Barbara Hilkert Andolsen, Christine E. Gudorf, and Mary D. Pellauer, eds., *Women's Consciousness, Women's Conscience* (NY: Winston Press, 1985), for thorough discussions of the extent and results of this silence, especially for the church.
5. For the sources on these statistics and others, see Pellauer, 'Moral Callousness and Moral Sensitivity,' pp. 37–41.
4. Elisabeth Schüssler Fiorenza, *In Memory of Her* (NY: Crossroad, 1983), p. 344.
6. See for example, 'Liturgies,' *The Westminster Dictionary of Worship*.
7. See Susan Moller Okin, *Women in Western Political Thought* (Princeton: Princeton University Press, 1979), pp. 15–96; see Schüssler Fiorenza, *In Memory of Her*, pp. 88–91, for an analysis of the relationship of this structure to Christianity.
8. The term 'liturgy' will be used throughout this essay to refer to the corporate worship of the church in whatever form it may appear. The worship of so-called 'non-liturgical' churches is not excluded, although, practically speaking, the worship of churches which use published orders or worship and prayers is obviously more accessible for analysis.
9. The most recent liturgical commentaries and handbooks emphasize that during the reading of Scripture and preaching, 'God's life-giving Word, ... comes to us through Scripture.' See

The Service for the Lord's Day, Supplemental Liturgical Resource 1, Joint Office of Worship for the Presbyterian Church (U.S.A.) and Cumberland Presbyterian Church (Philadelphia: Westminster Press, 1984), p. 16. See also: *Word and Table: A Basic Pattern of Sunday Worship for United Methodists* (Nashville: Abingdon, 1980), pp. 29-32; Ray Lonergan, *A Well-Trained Tongue* (Chicago: Liturgy Training Publications, 1982), pp. 5-6; James A. Wallace, C.S.S.R., *The Ministry of Lectors* (Collegeville: Liturgical Press, 1981), pp. 7-15.

10. 'The Will to Choose or to Reject; Continuing our Critical Work,' in Letty Russell, ed., *Feminist Interpretation of the Bible* (Philadelphia: Fortress Press, 1985), p. 130.

11. Fortune, p. 194; Susan Brooks Thistlethwaite, 'Every Two Minutes: Battered Women and Feminist Interpretation,' in *Feminist Interpretation of the Bible*, pp. 99, 106.

12. Thistlethwaite, p. 105.

13. Schüssler Fiorenza, 'The Will to Choose or to Reject,' p. 132.

14. Thistlethwaite, pp. 101-102. See also my analysis of the CCT lectionary, 'Images of Women in the Lectionary,' in *Women: Invisible in Church and Theology (Concilium* 182).

15. See, for example, Casey Miller and Kate Swift, *Words and Women* (NY: Anchor Press, 1986), Robin Lakoff, *Language and Woman's Place* (NY: Harper and Row, 1985), for general introductions. In relation to Christianity see, for example, Letty Russell, ed., *The Liberating Word* (Philadelphia: Westminster Press, 1976).

16. Pellauer, 'Moral Callousness and Moral Sensitivity,' p. 42.

17. See also Fortune, pp. 202-204.

18. *Systematic Theology* I (Chicago: University of Chicago Press, 1951), p. 240.

19. *Beyond God the Father* (Boston: Beacon Press, 1973), p. 13.

20. *The Shaker*, June, 1892.

21. 'The Sacrament of the Lord's Supper: An Alternative Text' (Nashville: The United Methodist Publishing House, 1972), p. 1, my emphasis. This prayer, with a different invitation and with 'Merciful God' in place of the address 'Eternal Father,' has been recently published in the *Book of Services* (Nashville: The United Methodist Publishing House, 1985), which contains services now approved for official (rather than trial) use in churches.

22. Although it is allowed as an option in the 1979 Book of Common Prayer, it is forbidden in the Lutheran Book of Worship (Minister's Desk Edition, p. 36.)

23. 'Weddings consist essentially of a public contract freely and mutually assented to before witnesses. The traditional language – "to have and to hold" – is language still used in conveyance of property. "From this day forward" dates the contract. Then follows the unconditional nature of said contract: "for better or worse." "Till death us to part" terminates the above, and "I give thee my troth' is the pledge of faithfulness to it ... Almost identical words appear in English in fourteenth-century manuscripts, long before other liturgical documents were translated into the vernacular.' James E White, *Introduction to Christian Worship* (Nashville: Abingdon Press, 1980), p. 240.

24. *A Service of Christian Marriage* (Supplemental Worship Resource 5; Nashville: Abingdon, 1979), p.iii. This phrase has been removed from the text printed in the *Book of Services*; see p. 64.

25. *The Sacramentary*, 766. (Collegeville: The Liturgical Press, 1971), p. 763; cf. pp. 760-761. Note, however, this phrase in the blessing of Rite A: 'May her husband put his trust in her and recognize that she is his equal and the heir with him of the life of grace.' The androcentrism of the prayer, however, while only implied here is made explicit in the beginning of the prayer: 'You (i.e. God) gave man the constant help of woman.'

26. This verse was not part of the medieval marriage rites. It first appeared in Luther's 'Order of Marriage,' in 1592. It has been adopted by most Protestants.

27. *Beginnings in Ritual Studies* (Lanham, MD: University Press of America, 1982). See Victor Turner, *The Ritual Process: Structure and Anti-Structure* (NY: Cornell Univ. Press, 1977); Victor Turner and Edith Turner, *Image and Pilgrimage in Christian Culture* (NY: Columbia Univ. Press, 1978); Mary Douglas, *Natural Symbols* (NY: Pantheon, 1973); Ronald Grimes, *Beginnings in Ritual Studies* (Lanham, MD: University Press of America, 1982).

28 For the complete text, see, for example, Arlene and Leonard Swidler, eds., *Women Priests: A Catholic Commentary on the Vatican Declaration* (NY: Paulist Press, 1977), pp. 37-49.

29. This representative function is certainly one of the major barriers encountered by women clergy, who find that people often fail to respond to them as clergy because they do not look, sound, or act like the 'normal' male clergy.

30. See especially Erving Goffman, *International Ritual: Essays on Face-to-Face Behavior* (NY: Anchor Books, 1967); *Encounters: Two Studies in the Sociology of Interaction* (NY: Bobbs-Merrill, 1961); and *Relations in Public: Microstudies of the Public Order* (NY: Basic Books, 1971).

31. NY: Harcourt, Brace, Jovanovich, 1982, pp. 175-176.
32. Schüssler Fiorenza, pp. 126-129. See also *Bread Not Stone: The Challenge of Feminist Biblical Interpretation* (Boston: Beacon Press, 1984), 'Women-Church: the Hermeneutical Center of Feminist Biblical Interpretation,' pp. 1-22, and *In Memory of Her* (NY: Crossroad, 1983), 'Toward a Feminist Biblical Spirituality: the *Ekklesia* of Women,' pp. 343-351.
33. Aidan Kavanagh, *On Liturgical Theology* (NY Pueblo Press, 1984), pp. 146-147.
34. Schüssler Fiorenza, 'The Will to Choose or to Reject,' p. 133.
35. Phyllis Trible, *Texts of Terror* (Philadelphia: Fortress Press, 1984). See especially pp. 1-7.
36. See further J. Frank Henderson, 'Discrimination Against the Laity in Liturgical Texts and Rites,' paper presented at the North American Academy of Liturgy, January, 1985.
37. See also Mark Searle, 'Serving the Lord with Justice,' in Mark Searle, ed., *Liturgy and Social Justice*, pp. 28-29.
38. See Fortune, pp. 221-224; Carolyn E. Shaffer, 'Spiritual Techniques for Re-Powering Survivors of Sexual Assault,' in Charlene Spretnak, ed., *The Politics of Women's Spirituality* (NY: Doubleday/Anchor Press, 1982), pp. 462-469
39. Kavanagh, p. 170.
40. NY: Harcourt, Brace, Jovanovich, 1984.

9.2 Child Sexual Abuse: A Rich Context for Thinking About God, Community, and Ministry

James N. Poling

I first became interested in child sexual abuse when I was a pastor. A member of a church family called me and said that a fifteen year old girl was complaining about sexual advances from her father. With consultation I confronted the parents and counseled with the daughter and probably prevented further harm. But the theological issues of the case haunted me. What was wrong in this family and for these parents that such destructive behavior was possible? Why was the church so inadequate that I knew they couldn't even be trusted with the information? Why did I feel so inadequate as a pastor and a theologian to handle the dynamics of this case?

During my sabbatical in 1985–86 I returned to the issue of child sexual abuse as a pastoral problem and continued my theological reflection. For almost two years I worked with child molesters to continue my training as a pastoral counselor and to stimulate my reflection about the nature of evil in persons and in society. I have questions about the human condition, the doctrine of God and the nature of community.

The Nature of the Human Self

The first set of questions concerns the nature of the human self. What view of the human self can account for the human potential for violence, rage, hatred, sin and evil represented by child sexual abuse? I believe that the human self is a fragile construction of power and meaning. Such a self arises out of empathic bonding with other selves within a web of community. Empathic bonding describes a process of interaction between individuals in which each has access to the interior experience of the other. Access to the interior experience of another is absolutely essential for the emergence of the human self, and deprivation of such bonding prevents a cohesive self from emerging. Evil, then, is the injury to the human self caused by disruptions of bonding. Such disruptions are signs of the failure of community.

The common characteristic of the child molesters I have known in depth is the lack of a cohesive self of power and meaning. Bob grew up in a home where his father was missing most of the time and was physically abusive when he was present. The drama of the home life was dominated by physical fights between his mother and grandmother who were both alcoholic. Somehow Bob survived to age nine when he was befriended by an uncle. This was the first positive relationship Bob remembers. Unfortunately the uncle was also a child molester and took sexual advantage of this needy little boy in exchange for some semblance of care. The result of this early childhood trauma on Bob's self was severe injury to his ability to relate to people and chronic narcissistic rage; that is, a pervasive sensitivity to any chance of being hurt again and intense anger directed at any perception of interpersonal danger.

As an adult Bob is a damaged self who needs protection from himself and others. Whenever he is injured again, his childhood rage is triggered and he becomes destructive. As a truck driver, he was a risk to other drivers when he felt angry. But the worst thing that happened was the repetition of his own childhood trauma in relation to a young female relative. He started molesting her when she was nine years old.

Such behavior is evil because it is injury to another human self who cannot provide her own protection. This is also a failure of community: for the girl because there was a lack of protection; and for Bob, because no one understood him as a fragile adult self that was capable of such destruction.

Bob is an example of a person with extreme injury to the self. But to some extent we all are injured selves, and thus we all need, at times, the compassion and firm limits of the community. The inability of leaders to face their own injuries and the resulting tendency to use power for violence and evil is one of the factors that leads to community failure.

The Nature of Human Community

My second set of questions concerns the nature of human community. What is wrong in our society that such a widespread evil as child sexual abuse has gone unacknowledged for so long? Even now society's responses are often inadequate and inappropriate. In one case, a man who was having intercourse with two daughters over a five-year-period was sentenced in court to probation with no required treatment, partly because his pastor was there as a character witness. In another case, an eighteen year old boy was sentenced to six years in jail because he molested a young boy while babysitting. Such inconsistency is common.

Failure of community occurs in two ways. First, the community is responsible for the nurture of its members. Whenever there is inadequate bonding for a child, the community must respond with corrective action – protection for the child and effective limits on adults who are destructive. Disregard for aggressors and victims is a sign of community failure.

Second, community is responsible to be a center of power and meaning within the larger society and world for the formation of personal identity. A community which lacks a firm identity itself often turns against its marginal subgroups and blames them for its difficulties. Child molesters often serve as objects of public rage and thus serve to detract from society's failure to care for its children and other persons without social power. On the other hand, a fragmented community often externalizes its inadequacies and projects them into an enemy group. Thus anticommunism serves the same social function as hatred of child molesters – it helps the society avoid the pain of seeing its own defects and failures. Every community is inadequate in significant ways and the inability to address these deficiencies leads to evil.

The Doctrine of God

A third set of questions concerns the doctrine of God. Is there an ambiguity in the character of God that makes evil so widespread? Remember that I define evil as injury to the human self caused by disruptions of empathic bonding because of the failure of community. My work with child molesters has given me first-hand experience with what seems a significant flaw in creation – the immense amount of pain and unrelieved suffering in our individual and corporate lives. The cycle of violence and injury seems endless over the generations. Victims become aggressors who create new victims. Is there any way for the cycle to end? Here I am indebted to Bernard Loomer who says that all are involved in a web of interconnected life.[1] The cycle of violence can only be stopped by those whose character can tolerate the knowledge of good and evil in themselves and thus can have compassion for others in their ambiguity. I am essentially no different than Bob the child molester. We are both persons who are good and evil, and it is only if I can tolerate the full knowledge of the good and evil in myself that I can fully accept the evil in Bob without hating him. According to Loomer, Jesus was this kind of human – he could accept good and evil in himself without losing his integrity. And thus Jesus reveals a God who is both good and evil without being destroyed. This brings God near to my experience, though it scares me to try to worship such a radically ambiguous God.

But what does it mean to know about both good and evil in myself, or to contemplate a God who is both good and evil? A part of my struggle in my work with child molesters is what to do with their destructive aggression. What is required is the ability to set limits with compassion. But this means feeling their pain as they confront their destructive patterns. As I have developed a sense of solidarity with them as aggressors, I have been forced to confront my own potential for destructive aggression. Bob has cried out and asked me, both directly and indirectly, for limits on his destructive rage. And he has forced me to confront my fears of anger and my destructive fantasies. As I have struggled, Bob has accepted the limits I have set and has responded to the compassion I have developed for him as I have felt a sense of compassion for myself.

This ministry experience led me to wonder what it would mean to have a God who is in solidarity with aggressors such as me. Is there a God who has struggled with aggression and thus can have compassion for me in my struggle? A god who knows something about destructive aggression? It seems almost a contradiction in terms. I have been taught that God is a suffering God, a God who rejects power in this world and whose son became a victim to reveal God's identification with the victims of the world. What does such a God know of aggression? I don't know what it means to have a God who is not only acquainted with grief, but also knows the pain of destructive aggression.

This question led me to the text of Genesis 6-8. According to this story God indulged in a most terrible rage – the total destruction of the whole creation except for a boatload of people and animals. Later, God saw the mistake and promised never again to be so destructive, even though human evil continued. One interpretation is that God learned a lesson and was never again tempted. But time and again, the Bible reports the same struggle. In Hosea 11, God threatens to send a sword to rage through the towns of Israel, wiping out their children (Hosea 11:6). There are texts throughout the Bible about God's destructiveness.

True, this insight may not be comforting to everyone – to find a split in God between compassion and destruction. But perhaps God's struggle can be useful for us who struggle with the same split. Is God one who knows the pain of destructive aggression? Then perhaps God can be compassionate toward my struggle with my destructive aggression and its evil consequences. Is God one who has agonized over destructive power and thus can set limits on me with firmness and compassion? Perhaps God's ability to confront the destructive side of God's own character can be spiritual resource for the church as it tries to confront its own defects and respond to a world caught in an orgy of violent disaster.

These reflections are inspired by Bob, a child molester who is courageously facing evil in his own life. Working with him has given me the courage to face my own destructive feelings and behaviors. As a result I see community in a different way, and ask forbidden questions about God. My thoughts lead me to an image of the church as a community that can examine its own experiences with evil and aggression. Is there a Christian faith community who knows the pain of its own violent power out of control, and thus can respond with compassion to a world where uncontrolled aggression is a moral crisis? I would like to be challenged by a church like this.

Notes
1.   William Dean and Larry E. Axel (eds.), *The Size of God: The Theology of Bernard Loomer in Context* (Macon, GA: Mercer University Press, 1987).

9.3 Sex and Violence in the Family and Church

Loren Broadus

'You shall know the truth and it will make you flinch, then it will set you free.'

It was eight-thirty in the morning. I was in my study at the church, admiring my To-Do List. A timid knock at the door interrupted my thought. When I opened the door, Ms. Sims was standing there. Her eyes were red and puffed, her shoulders slumped, and her hands were quivering.

When we were seated, I assumed my Carl Rogers' non-directive, understanding, accepting, reflective position and attitude. I had not been out of seminary long enough not to do that. (Carl Rogers was a counseling Guru in the sixties.)

Ms. Sims described a relationship with her husband, who was a deacon in the church I served, that was difficult to believe. 'He beats me,' she whispered, as if ashamed of something.

'What do you mean, he beats you?' I replied.

'He hits me with his fist, knocks me down, picks me up, throws me against the wall or a table and ... and then he kicks me several times.' She sobbed and sobbed and sobbed. She sobbed not so much as one who had been beaten physically, but as someone who had been abandoned, or rejected, or degraded. It was the cry of disappointment, much as one hears from a child who feels betrayed by a parent's love.

'He hits me mostly in the stomach, legs, chest; places that won't show the next day.'

I listened to this sophisticated, professional person, with whom I served on the Library Board, talk about a deacon, a respected citizen of the community. He was the leader of the Boy Scout troop that met in 'our' church building. He was an Eagle Scout.

'He's trying to kill me,' she said.

'Do you mean that he is trying to beat you to death?'

'No! He wants to kill me but make it look like an accident, so he can have our five-year-old daughter.'

'How do you know that?'

I listened while she described 'accidents' that had indeed almost killed her. The latest incident being a tire blow-out that occurred just before she was to enter an interstate highway. According to the service station attendant, the tire had been cut so as to cause a blow-out at a high rate of speed. This was the final act that caused her to seek help. If she died, her daughter would be raised by her brutal spouse.

'What should I do?' she asked.

'Do you have relatives or friends who live out of town where you can go?'

'Yes! In Louisville.'

'Go home,' I said. 'Pack clothes for you and your daughter, and leave town immediately, before Carl returns home.'

She left the office. About thirty minutes later she phoned. 'Brother Broadus, my husband's pastor is here at the house. Carl called him. Brother Smith said I can't leave Carl, and that if I leave Carl I will go to hell. He said I should stay home and try harder to make Carl happy. He said that's God's will.'

'No' I replied. 'It is *not* God's will that you be beaten and for you and Jamie to live in constant fear. Tell your husband's pastor I said that, and then you leave the house immediately before Carl arrives.' She did. And I wondered why she had lived with Carl and endured those beatings for seven years.

The most common response the church and community has made to battered women throughout history is reflected in the advice of Brother Smith. The church and societies have generally endorsed a 'conspiracy of silence' with respect to men battering women.

Throughout history there have been laws (made by men) about spouse abuse. Rosemary Radford Ruether uncovered the following information. 'A decree of the Council of Toledo in A.D. 400 decrees that if a wife of the clergy transgresses his commands, the husband may beat his wife, keep her bound in their home, and force her to Fast, but "not unto death".'[1]

Later, the 'Rule of Thumb' principle appeared in British law, that said that a man may not use a rod larger than his thumb to beat his wife. 'Barbaric, archaic laws,' one might say. But at the time of writing this, March 11, 1990, the Commonwealth of Kentucky legislature is debating and will by *vote* decide whether it is illegal for a man to rape his wife. As of this date, a man may rape his wife and she has no legal recourse.

In February 1990, a conference was held that addressed this issue of violence against women. It was a part of the World Council of Churches' 'Decade of Churches in Solidarity with Women,' with the aim 'to awaken the whole church to assure women the recognition that their struggle for full humanity is not only understood but also shared by men in the life of the Church.'[2]

The following is a touch of what I learned at this Conference and from over twenty years of experience dealing with sex and violence in the family and church.

But first, listen to a few more incidents of violence against women, and also relive your experiences with it. Then the causes and effects will be explored.

When I was eight, nine, ten, eleven, twelve years of age my bedroom was about ten yards from Mr. and Mrs. Lemmons' bedroom next door. In the summer, our windows were open in Jacksonville, Florida. Often, late at night I would be awakened by loud cursing, crying, furniture being knocked about, and pleadings from Mrs. Lemmons. That would go on for what seemed an eternity. Sometimes the police would come to their house. Things would then become quiet.

'Al, take it easy. Calm down. Now go to bed and sleep it off,' or 'Take a walk to cool off,' I would hear. The police would leave. And then, all too often, Mr. Lemmons would resume beating Mrs. Lemmons. I don't think Mr. Lemmons ever went to jail.

As a child, I wondered why Mrs. Lemmons put up with these beatings. Why doesn't she do something to stop this, I thought. But nothing would be done; until one night, Mr. Lemmons hit Buddy, his son, who had become adult-sized since anyone had noticed. But Buddy turned and beat his father brutally. The violence escalated. And I wondered, why do Mrs. Lemmons and Mary Lemmons, her daughter, who was also beaten regularly, stay in that house of horror. That was a long time ago.

Now, an update! Beacon Hill Road, Lexington, Kentucky, two a.m., the doorbell rang. It was the ten-year-old daughter of one of our neighbors and friends.

'Call the police,' she said. 'Daddy's killing mama.'

While I put on my topcoat, dress hat, house shoes, and gloves, Catherine phoned the police. It was cold, so I drove the one block, parked in front of the house, and waited for the police. After four or five minutes, it occurred to me that Carol could be killed before the police arrived. I dashed to the front door, opened the screen door, and rang the doorbell. No answer. I rang the bell again. No answer. On the fourth ring, the door was yanked open. I stepped into the living room and quickly glanced at his hands to see if he had a weapon. No weapons, other than his clenched fist. Our faces were about twelve inches apart.

'I've come to visit.' Picture this. Two a.m. A man dressed in pajamas, topcoat, dress hat, house shoes and gloves, saying to a neighbor 'I've come to visit!'

He stared at me for what seemed a long, long time. 'I'll have nothing to do with this,' he said, as he retreated to the basement den.

I stood in the living room, waiting for something to happen. Was he going after a weapon? Where was Carol? Suddenly I realized that I was interferring in a private, family matter, and trespassing on private property. I would probably be the only person to go to jail if more conflict ensued. Five minutes later, Carol appeared, properly dressed, hair combed, with make-up neatly applied.

'Are you alright?' I asked.

'Yes,' she replied. She was embarrassed. Carol was a professional person, a community leader in Lexington, an intelligent, assertive individual who caused things to happen. Yet she endured these beatings. I sat in a chair and she sat on the couch while she talked about work, her daughters, Catherine and our sons; she talked about everything, except the real subject at hand – her letting Al beat her.

I wondered, why does an intelligent, confident, competitive, compassionate, strong woman stay in a marriage that abuses and humiliates her?

What do you think? *Why* do women stay in such abusive relationships?

From my study of this matter, I've learned that women stay in abusive relationships for the following reasons:

1. They think they do not have any place to go. Moving back into their parents' house is often humiliating and not welcomed. Also, a week at a friend's home with one's children can strain a friendship.
2. They do not have enough money to support themselves and their children. In addition to the estimated thirty per cent cut in income (often more) after separation or divorce, the cost for lawyers is often high and the court proceedings slow.
3. They rationalize that the financial advantages of home, food, credit cards, and car are worth putting up with the beatings. Dr. Theodore Shapiro, editor of the *Journal of the American Psychoanalytic Association* and professor of psychiatry at Cornell University Medical College, points out that the period of rising tension and hostility between couples is frequently followed, after acts of abuse, by contrite reconciliation – which can have its rewards.[3]
4. Because they were raised in families where their fathers beat their mothers, these women assume that this is how people live; therefore, it does not occur to them that they have an option.

   In the American *Journal of Obstetrics and Gynecology*, Dr. Ronald Chez, M.D., writes:

   > There are economic, emotional, and societal interdependencies and constraints for most women. There is also the relative predictability of the known versus the fear of the unknown, including fear of reprisal. There are also cultural and religious constraints, continued hope for change, and the fact that many women love the man who is the batterer.[4]

5. Abused women may stay in such relationships because they think they can change the man. Robin Norwood expressed the thought: 'When we don't like many of his basic characteristics, values, and behaviors, but we put up with him, thinking that if we are only more attractive and loving enough he'll want to change for us, we are loving too much.'[5]

For additional details on why women stay in abusive relationships, see *Battered Wives* by Del Martin.[6]

One startling fact is that some women blame themselves for the battering. This self-blame is the result of the biggest con-game in the history of womankind, which is the societal and psychological conditioning that makes women feel responsible for men's moods, for men's emotional well-being. Wives are supposed to 'make the world right' for their husbands. If something goes wrong at the office, or if a traffic jam throws them off schedule, or if anything makes the man unhappy, a woman is somehow to blame. The hostility evoked elsewhere by failure, or disappointment, or guilt feelings gets displaced onto the woman.

Can you believe that some women and some men believe that when a woman does not fix his broken world, it's her fault that he is unhappy.[7] So, he beats her. Is this rare?

Marie Fortune, a United Church of Christ minister and Director of the Center for the Prevention of Sexual and Domestic Violence, writes:

> Violence against women is a fact of life in the United States. It is the common thread of women's existence which binds us together across race, age, class, sexual orientation and religious preference. This violence is not random; it is not accidental. It is directed at us by men, strangers or intimates, simply because we are women. Because of our gender, we are perceived to be available victims: powerless, vulnerable, deserving of abuse. Statistically, we are most likely to be assaulted by a family member or acquaintance: hence the most dangerous place for a woman to be is in a relationship.
>
> Nearly 1 out of 2 women has suffered rape or attempted rape, 1 out of 5 women has been a victim of physical abuse by a husband, 59% of battered women have been raped by the batterer, 1 out of 3 girl children is sexually abused before she is 18 years old. Simply because of our gender, we are viewed as legitimate targets for male aggression and violence. Every woman carries either the fear of violence or the memory of violence in her life.[8]

Why do men abuse women?

There are four general reasons, and many variations of the four.

The first reason men abuse women is simply that it 'works,' in most cases. It intimidates women. A beating is the punishment for not fixing a man's world. After the battering, the woman tries harder to please the man. She not only does not want to disappoint him, she is afraid to 'make him angry' and she often believes it's her fault that he is angry. (Reader, I am not making this up!) Also – as absurd as it sounds – beating a woman gives the batterer a sense of power. The rewards of 'working off' feelings of anger, disappointment or impotency give temporary relief from frustration and failure. Power, control, and self-esteem have been reported as rewards for beating up women.

A second reason men abuse women is that all too often men can get away with it. In their work *Intimate Violence*, Richard J. Gelles and Murray A. Straus contend that being arrested for family violence is relatively rare. They write:

Our most recent national survey of family violence found that fewer than one in ten police interventions ended in the arrest of the offender. Thus, the cost of arrest, which is very real for public violence, is nearly nonexistent in cases of intimate violence and abuse ... We can expand our first proposition that people hit family members because they can get away with it into three basic propositions:

1. Family members are more likely to use violence in the home when they expect the costs of being violent to be less than the rewards.
2. The absence of effective social controls (e.g., police intervention) over family relations decreases the cost of one family member being violent toward another.
3. Certain social and family structures reduce social controls in family relations and, therefore, reduce the costs and increase the rewards of being violent.[9]

A third reason men abuse women is that society tacitly approves of the behavior. The battering of women by men has been called the 'silent conspiracy.' Marie Fortune points out that we detest the idea of battering women (and children) in the abstract but tolerate it in reality. The American idolization of individual freedom for Bubba contributes to the violence. The man proudly proclaims and believes that, 'It's my house and my spouse, my car and my kid, and what I do with them is my business and nobody else's.' And the laws and actions of our 'good ole' boy' society say 'nobody tells Bubba, or George, or James, or Reginald, what to do.' It is difficult for a woman to get justice in spouse abuse cases. Can you imagine what would happen to a man who suddenly turned on his co-worker and beat her in the office? He would get five to ten years in prison. Yet, the Kentucky legislature, dressed in their three-piece suits, debated whether to make it illegal for Bubba or Reginald to rape his wife. What a man does behind closed doors of *his* domain is his business, so the system supports.

The fourth reason men abuse women is due to the social training that conditions us to believe that violence is a legitimate way to solve problems. During the last presidential campaign George Bush was called a 'wimp.' What did he do and say in response? He paraded Willie Horton, a violent criminal, before the public and promised to deal violently with violent people. George Bush was going to 'kick some ...': People cheered his tough guy pledge of violence.

Violence is part of our patriarchal system. We promote it, practice it, and praise it. We pay Mike Tyson ten million dollars to fight James 'Buster' Douglas. We elect a president, at least partially, because he promises to be as violent as necessary to protect us from violent people. Incidentally, the most frequency of violence against women by men occurs in the following vocations: Most frequently – military personnel, next – police officers, followed by clergy. Our patriarchal system discriminates against women, thereby endorsing violence against them physically, emotionally, financially, and sexually.[10]

Let us now turn to another form of abuse – sexual abuse. In his

Original Blessing, Matthew Fox points out that 'the fear of passion prevents lovers from celebrating their experiences as spiritual and mystical.'[11] I agree with Fox, and would add that one of God's most creative, satisfying, renewing, spiritual acts is intimate sex that affirms people and celebrates the oneness, the at-one-ment of two people.

But the indiscriminate use of passion to use and abuse others sexually is a sad sign of spiritually starved people and a sick society. In addition to the obvious instances of rape as sexual assault, sexual abuse of women often also occurs in more subtle ways. A most common way is the manipulation of women into intercourse who have placed their emotional and physical and intellectual and spiritual lives in the control of men they trust to help them solve their problems.

Catherine, my spouse, and I were scheduled to give some lectures in a distant city. When we arrived at the Ministers and Spouses Conference we discovered that we were in the middle of a major conflict. The minister, who was program chair of the conference, had been accused of having sex with eight different women who were 'his' parishioners. The eight had the courage to come forward with the complaint. The ministers and spouses at the conference were divided over the issue. Some were pastorally concerned for the seductive minister and thought that the church judicatory had no business in the minister's personal business. Others disagreed and thought the minister should be held accountable. The people in the congregation were also divided over the issue. The women who risked their reputations to expose the minister were ostracized: *they* were blamed for causing the trouble. The minister is still the pastor of a church.

We men protect out own. Can you imagine what people would do to the Reverend Betty if she were accused of having sex with eight of her parishioners?

Recently, a church executive responsible for 'placing' ministers in churches was asked what he did when clergy are caught having an affair with a parishioner.

'My first consideration is that I do not want to ruin a minister's career' was his response.

This executive demonstrated understanding, acceptance, forgiveness, and compassions towards the clergyman – all admirable Christian qualities. But he never said a word about the women. Yet, when a minister has sex with a parishioner who is seeking psychological or spiritual help from him (her) the parishioner, the parishioner's family, and the whole congregation are affected significantly. Sexual manipulation of emotionally and spiritually wounded people by clergy comprises the integrity of the church and may damage forever the victim's ability to trust and believe in so-called altruistic spiritual directors and counselors.

This type of abuse is more common than most think. In *Sex in the Forbidden Zone*, Peter Rutter examines how men in power – therapists, doctors, clergy, teachers, and others – often use their power to seduce women. He reports that seventy per cent of psychotherapists have had at least one patient who had a forbidden zone relationship with a former therapist. Twenty to thirty per cent of female university students have been approached sexually by their professors. Thirteen per cent of physicians have sexual involvement with patients.[12]

The eventual emotional damage to a woman who has been sexually manipulated by a man she trusted to help her solve problems is enormous.

> Although it may take decades for her to appreciate fully the betrayal, loss, and damage emanating from the moment of sexual contact in the forbidden zone, she has in that moment been returned to the state of woundedness in which she entered the man's presence. Furthermore, she has been returned to it with hope itself destroyed. Many women never recover.[13]

Because our lives are tied in with those of others, a violation of anyone in a community or society is a violation of all people. For instance, at the time of this writing someone is making obscene telephone calls to women who are a part of our seminary community; that is not simply a private matter between the caller and the women he phones. It is a community concern, for all of us are affected by the obscene calls. When one is violated, all are violated in the community.

What is the solution to this violence of men abusing women? We can start with men working with women to do justice, to correct this gross injustice. Women working with men must address the systemic situations that perpetuate this problem. One consideration in this 'attack' on systems is to realize that simply being 'fair' in an unjust system actually in effect perpetuates the system. That is the dilemma with which we have to wrestle when examining ways to change the rules of the establishment. Yet, in dealing with this problem, we must address our small and large systems, congregations, church bodies, places of employment and families. Policies and procedures for dealing with clergy and others who abuse people sexually by misusing their power must be developed by judicatories and congregations. Wherever we have an ounce of influence we are called to use it for justice.

Specific ways to assist in reducing the abuse of women follows.

1. Locate, support and use the spouse abuse centers. The Domestic Violence Hotline is (800) 333-7233.
2. Help people get counseling when they decide to deal with their abuse, whether they were abused as children or adults.
3. Through the legal system, put abusers out of reach of children.
4. Get sexual abusers of the forbidden zone professional counseling or eliminate their opportunity to abuse.

Diane Eisler, in *The Chalice and the Blade*, describes two basic models for society. The first one is the dominator model, popularly termed patriarchy or matriarchy – the ranking of one half of humankind over the other. The second model is based on the principle of 'linking,' rather than 'ranking.' It is a partnership model in which diversity is not equated with either inferiority or superiority.[14]

It is possible to develop that partnership approach to living and working together.

Men working with women 'to awaken the whole church (and society) to assure women the recognition that their struggle for full humanity is not only understood but also shared by men in the life of the church.'

We will never get it perfect, but we *can* make it better.

There are few happy endings to violence against women stories. But here is one.

Two years ago, I was sitting in a restaurant, having lunch. A woman approached the table and addressed me as 'Brother Broadus.' She was from a special place in my life – a former pastorate.

'I just want to tell you that I am doing great,' she said, while smiling almost slyly. She described her current job, which she enjoys greatly. She is a top executive, managing a few hundred people who conduct social programs to help people. Her daughter has graduated from college and is a professional person.

'I have had a great, free, joyous life since we last talked twenty-four years ago.'

She was the former spouse of that deacon in the church I served – Ms. Sims.

In my further study of this matter, I am interested in hearing from readers of this article concerning comments and experiences relating to family violence and how the church may constructively address this issue. Write me in care of Lexington Theological Seminary, 631 S. Limestone Street, Lexington, Kentucky 40508.

Notes

1. Rosemary Radford Ruether, 'The Western Religious Tradition and Violence Against Women in the Home,' in *Christianity, Patriarchy and Abuse*, eds. Joanne Carlson Brown and Carole R. Bohn (New York: Pilgrim Press, 1989).
2. This conference was co-sponsored by the National Council of Churches of Christ's Commission on Family Life and Human Sexuality, and by the Center for the Prevention of Sexual and Domestic Abuse. The theme of the conference focused on 'Violence Against Women.' While recognizing that men are also sometimes victims of domestic violence, this article focuses on the widespread problem of violence against women.
3. Quoted in 'Battered Wives,' by Stephanie Harrington, *Cosmopolitan* (April 1990).
4. Quoted in ibid.
5. Robin Norwood, *Women Who Love Too Much* (New York: Pocket Books, 1985).
6. Del Martin, *Battered Wives* (San Francisco: Glide Publications, 1976).
7. For an interesting interpretation of this interpersonal dynamic, see Lillian B. Rubin, *Intimate Strangers* (New York: Harper and Row, 1983).
8. Marie M. Fortune, 'Violence Against Women: The Way Things Are Is Not The Way They Have To Be,' Unpublished essay. See also her work *Sexual Violence: The Unmentionable Sin* (New York: Pilgrim Press, 1983).
9. Richard J. Gelles and Murray A. Straus, *Intimate Violence* (New York: Simon and Schuster Inc., 1988), 24–25.
10. For an insightful critique of the partriarchal system in this regard and what is perceived to be the emerging alternative female system, see Anne Wilson Schaff, *Women's Reality* (Minneapolis: Oak Grove, 1981).

11. Matthew Fox, *Original Blessing* (Santa Fe: Bear and Company, 1983), 11.
12. Peter Rutter, *Sex in the Forbidden Zone* (Los Angeles: Jeremy P. Tarcher, 1989). See my review of this volume in the *Lexington Theological Quarterly* 25 (October 1990), 122–23.
13. Ibid.
14. Diane Eisler, *The Chalice and the Blade* (New York: Harper and Row, 1988), xvii.

10. Sexuality and Singleness

About half of the adult populations of the 'first' world are unmarried. A majority of those marrying do not do so until about fifteen years after puberty. Yet pre-married, post-married, and un-married people, and lesbian and gay people, still find themselves defined against a norm which denies them sexual intercourse, if not all sexual activity. Conversely priests and men and women under the vow of celibacy generally report that they are lamentably ill-prepared for the adventure which is celibate life, while those theologies endorsing celibacy are likely to be dualistic and deficient. Can there be a sexual ethic for singles? Can celibate women and men integrate their sexuality and their vocation honestly and creatively?

The first two essays in this section are addressed to single people who may be, or who are open to be, sexually active, while the third is addressed specifically to men and women under the vow of celibacy. They have much in common, all of them being single and sexual, with sexual desires and needs. Douglas Rosenau, in 'Sexuality and the Single Person' sets out to help Christian single people who are seeking 'positive sexual expression'. He describes seven common ways of 'sabotaging sexuality' or using our bodies wrongly. These are followed by 'sexual values' which are subject to clarification and implementation. Finally a range of possibilities for 'single sexual expression' is listed. While avoiding sabotage 'helps', and clarifying values 'protects', the extent of sexual activity (if any) is to be governed by responsible choice within boundaries, including biblical ones. Rosenau's essay is criticisable at several points. It is unclear how the Bible is to be a resource; his language assumes that Christians can work with very individualistic understandings of the person and very secular understandings of moral endeavour. Nonetheless it touches the experiences of single men and women directly, honestly and openly, and brings theological considerations to bear upon them.

Karen Lebacqz, in her essay 'Appropriate Vulnerability: A Sexual Ethic for Singles', observes how 'the two redeeming purposes of sexuality have always been understood as procreation

and union' within marriage. While there has been 'some acceptance of non-marital sexual expression', Lebacqz proposes
to add to procreation and union a third purpose of sexuality which
is, like the others, 'God-given'. It is 'appropriate vulnerability'.
Being vulnerable is grounded in the comfortable nakedness of
Adam and Eve, and is an 'antidote' to the desire for domination
and control. Vulnerability is found in Jesus Christ. There is an
appropriate expression of it which is sexual, and not confined to
marriage. Vulnerability also provides a new principle for making
theological judgments about sexual activity: 'any exercise of sexuality that violates appropriate vulnerability is wrong'. A theology
of vulnerability is called for (and taken up elsewhere).[1]

Ben Kimmerling's starting point is the contradiction she experienced between faithful love for her husband and the command
of Christ to love our neighbours. In 'Celibacy and Intimacy' she
describes how 'the call to universal love lies at the heart of – is
in fact an outcome of – the personal experience of love'. Intimacy
learned in private is continuous with the broader intimacy
required for relationships with others. 'We cannot leave our
bodies outside of our relationships.' She finds two 'enduring
elements' of sexual intercourse, 'the knowledge of a persons's
loveliness' and the physical body-language which is the means of
intimate communication. Kimmerling argues that many celibate
people need to rediscover their bodily loveliness, and that celibate friendships are opportunities for this to happen. The point
at which a celibate friendship becomes an aching desire for
sexual intercourse is experienced as 'the tyranny of a physical
human need'. This predicament then becomes the opportunity for
solidarity with other people who experience the tyranny of other
equally insistent human needs, e.g. for food and shelter. It is
also the opportunity for the discovery that 'while the need for
love has to be met, the desire for sex does not'.

Douglas E.P. Rosenau's essay 'Sexuality and the Single
Person' was first published in the *Journal of Psychology and
Christianity*, 1, 4, 1982, pp.30–36. Karen Lebacqz is Professor
of Social Ethics at McGill University, Montreal, Canada. Her
essay 'Appropriate Vulnerability: A Sexual Ethic for Singles'
first appeared in *Christianity and Crisis*, 43, Oct 31, 1983, pp.
399–404. Ben Kimmerling is a freelance lecturer living in
County Mayo, Ireland. Her essay 'Celibacy and Intimacy' first
appeared in *The Way Supplement*, 77, Summer, 1993, pp.
88–96.

Notes
1. See Adrian Thatcher, *Liberating Sex: A Christian Sexual Theology* (London: SPCK, 1993), pp. 167–8, 173–4.

10.1 Sexuality and the Single Person

Douglas E.P. Rosenau

One Christian psychologist when asked to conduct a workshop on helping singles in their sexual struggles stated, 'Why have a workshop when it can be summarized in one word: DON'T.' Don't, cold showers, remarry have often been the ineffective and calloused advice given to singles on coping with their sexuality. They deserve better than this – both because sexuality should be a dynamic and positive part of every person's life, and because people asking honest questions deserve honest and cogent answers.

The questions are myriad that singles are forced to explore on their sexual journey. Singles leader Jason Towner (Smith, 1979, p. 20) comments:

> How does one go back to holding hands after meaningful marital intimacy? How does one explain to friends that terms like 'swinging single' or 'gay divorcee' are sterotypes? How does one say 'no' in a singles subculture that always seems to say yes?

Masturbation, singles bars, sexual intercourse, skin hunger, dating, curiosity, previous scars, hornyness – and the list goes on and on of the questions and issues that the single person must face in attaining positive sexual expression.

This is not a hopeless scene, for many singles are finding meaningful sexual expression. There are guidelines and appropriate boundaries; there are practical but not easy answers. This paper seeks to help singles and the Christian community find answers as it explores three important areas: common sabotages of positive sexuality, sexual values, and avenues for fulfilling sexual expression.

Sabotaging Sexuality

Certain beliefs and behaviors short-circuit both the enjoyment of personal sexuality and the development of a positive sexual relationship. Seven common and destructive means of sabotaging sexuality follow. If they can be eliminated, the struggle for realizing effective sexual expression is much easier.

Denying or repressing sexuality or sexual desires

'My sexual urges shouldn't hurt me if I can keep from doing anything.' 'Sex just isn't important anymore.' Sexuality is a gift from God. It is as destructive and self-defeating to repress this part of our personality as it is to overemphasize and misuse it. There is a difference between having sexual feelings and fantasies and acting upon them. Honestly surfacing and understanding sexual desires is an important part of the process of controlling them.

Walter Trobisch (1964, pp. 70–71) likens personal sexuality to a tiger. If it is allowed to roam free without any guidelines, it can be extremely dangerous. But, if the tiger of sexual desires is caged up and repressed, it will roar and break out eventually in an even more destructive manner. Denial, repression, fear, and ignorance imperil any type of healthy sexual expression. Acknowledge the tiger and tame it.

Viewing sexuality as simply a biological drive and recreation

'Sex is like eating.' 'Sex is such a great way to combat boredom.' Sexual expression is so much more complex than a simple bodily desire and its gratification. Masters and Johnson (1975, pp. 111–112) write that people all too often are:

> ... victims of the idea that sex and sexual intercourse is a separate function of the total human being, quite apart from the rest of their existence. They act as though the analogy of sex and food is meant to be taken literally ... It is a regrettable confusion because, despite the legitimate ways in which the sexual appetite can be compared to hunger, sexual satisfaction depends on more than the mere availability of a physical partner.

Sexual activity is entered into through the body but it also involves the mind (fantasy, memory, planning), the emotions (caring, feelings, playful), the will (choices, commitment) and the spirit (meaning, purpose, Faith). Treating sexuality as simply friction or recreation will insure diminishing returns. Sex becomes just another high needing increasing stimulation unless the total personality and relationship are involved. As one single stated, 'I am doing it more and enjoying it less.'

Using sexuality in an attempt to meet legitimate nonsexual needs

'I need a friend.' 'I wonder if I am still attractice?' 'I want to feel a warm body close to me.' Human beings have many emotional and physical needs: to love and be loved, friendship, feelings of self-worth and esteem, and skin hunger. Research (Simon, 1976) shows that people self-destruct without mutual physical contact through touching and being touched. Each of the above needs are legitimate; people are not 'islands' and must have meaningful interaction and affirmation.

The problem occurs because many of these nonsexual needs are often met in sexual relationships. In fact many people know of no other way to satisfy them except through sex. It is easy to understand how this confuses sexual and non-sexual desires and can sabotage the ability to meet either in an effective way. The single hopes that sex will equal friendship or fears that skin hunger can only be met through intercourse. Frustration and guilt are so often the results of this confusion of sexual and nonsexual with both areas of legitimate need short-circuited.

Mobilizing sexuality as a weapon

'I'll show him/her.' 'Why do I always fall for the guys who hurt me?' 'I can get him/her to do anything.' Sex can so easily be employed for revenge, rebellion, manipulation, sabotage and punishment with extremely damaging consequences. It is unfortunate but sexually acting out is a convenient and powerful means of rebellion against parents, a rigid religious background or a restrictive relationship. Sexual behavior is also convenient as self-punishment as people allow themselves to be used sexually to prove they are indeed worthless or to expiate guilt.

Sex can quickly become a club with the giving and withdrawing of sexual activity employed as a threat or power ploy. These uses of sex as a weapon demean and destroy the basic purposes of sexuality: enjoyment, communication, playfulness, and building deeper relationship. Sexual potential is wasted and the saboteurs end up 'cutting off their noses to spite their faces'.

Prostituting sexuality to gain romance or sexual affirmation

'If I don't put out, they drop me.' 'My ex said I was a lousy love.' 'I'm curious as to what's out there.' In our society there is a barter system set up. If a date takes a person to Krystals for a hamburger it is a good night kiss, to a movie it's snuggling at her place, to a steak dinner and a show it's all the way. Another variety of this barter is the comment, 'My body is not getting younger, I've got to trap someone now.' Barter can so effectively sabotage any attempt at exciting and growth-producing sexual expression.

Like bartering, curiosity and affirming one's sexiness are poor motivations for sexual expression. Sexual encounters on these bases usually lack self-esteem, commitment and intimacy – important items in dynamic sexual relationships.

Focusing on one aspect of sexuality or sexual expression

'Sex equals intercourse.' 'It's so much easier just to masturbate.' 'Clothes are the important thing.' Variety is the spice of life. People need balance in the many areas of sexuality if they are to harness all the potential available.

It is easy to get sidetracked on one type of sexual expression (intercourse, hair style) to the detriment of others (cuddling, flirting). A person can feel so safe and involved in personal sexual feelings (masturbation) that they neglect relationships, or vice versa. Variety and balance are active antidotes against destructive focusing and ensure sexual growth.

Stunting sexuality through inappropriate values and boundaries

'Even the bad love is better than no love at all.' 'I can't hurt his/her feelings.' 'Everybody is doing it.' 'It feels good.' Actually, the six ways of sabotaging sexuality that have already been explored are caused by inappropriate values and boundaries. It seemed crucial to include ineffective values as a separate sabotage because of certain myths that are posing as sexual values; four of the most common are listed at the beginning of this paragraph.

Wise and effective values (with the necessary boundaries they create) are vital for positive sexuality. Boundaries that grow out of personal values should not be looked upon as restrictive. They are guidelines to protect the single person's values and to free them up for meaningful sexual interaction.

Effective values may include such attitudes and behaviors as self-control, love, practising patience, being honest and open, making commitments, and knowing how to say 'no'. Without appropriate values and boundaries sexual expression can become unfulfilling and self-defeating; the happiness sought is undermined by guilt, anger, confusion and frenetic activity. The next section will further stress the importance of sexual values – how to clarify and implement them.

Sexual Values

Personal sexuality can be divided into three different aspects: *genital* sexuality (erotic arousal, friction, romantic interest, love play), *gender* sexuality (gender identity, Platonic, general male and female interaction) and sexual *values* (prizing, priorities, boundaries). Of these three, sexual values are the *sine qua non* of positive sexuality. They are the fertilizer and weedkiller that keep the garden of genital and gender sexual expression blooming.

All of the sexual sabotages can be prevented if the single person builds an effective values system. Growth and fulfillment can be ensured. This section will explore the two-fold process of clarifying and implementing appropriate sexual values.

Clarifying values

Values-clarification, sorting out what is prized and personally incorporating it as a priority, is a different process for the Christian and non-Christian single. The non-Christian will view this procedure much as the *Values Clarification* (Simon, Howe, & Kirschenbaum, 1972,

p. 20) book develops it: 'the values-clarification approach does not aim to instill any particular set of values,' rather it wishes to help people 'become aware of the beliefs and behaviors they prize' and consistently act on them.

Sexual values-clarification for Christian singles has an added dimension. They, too, are clarifying the sexual attitudes and behaviors that they prize, but they are doing this with the input of Biblical values that apply to sexuality. They do have a 'particular set of values' that they can utilize in building their personal sexual values system.

This does not make the values-clarification process easier for the Christian single. Few Biblical injunctions circumscribe specific sexual behaviors (thou shalt not commit adultery). Rather, general principles are unfolded that must be creatively applied to personal sexuality (love your neighbor as yourself). There is no short-cut to the arduous task of sorting out *what* is values and *why*, whether it is Biblical principles or the final step of creating a sexual values system that is one's own and is working.

It may be useful, without citing specific Biblical references, to lay out several Christian sexual values that need to be considered in clarifying and building a personal sexual values system.

Keeping sex in perspective.   Sexuality is an important part of one's life but it is not the whole. To keep sex enjoyable, all areas of the single person's life must be developing. Also, sexual expression of any kind should include involvement of every part of the personality to maintain satisfaction and excitement. Making out should involve body, mind, emotions, will and spirit:

> Body: friction, sex drive, physical attraction, senses.
> Mind: fantasies, memories, planning, sorting sensory input.
> Emotions: playful, feeling of love, excitement, hurt.
> Will: choices, commitment and follow through, motivation.
> Spirit: meaning and purpose, God, agape love, values, trust.

If sexual expression is simply a physical buzz, it will quickly have diminishing returns.

Balancing self and relationship.   In all areas of life an individual should be aware of and express personal feelings and needs, while remembering that without the context of a relationship this expression becomes quite meaningless and limiting. Especially in sexuality, self (esteem, acceptance, masturbation) and others (relationship, mutuality, love play) need a healthy intermixture.

Developing intimacy.   Sexual expression is an outgrowth of friendship, trust and commitment. Though it often is hoped that the reverse will happen – instant sex does not guarantee instant intimacy. Developing friendship takes time, knowledge, trust, risks and much honest communication, but can help insure fulfilling and positive sexual interaction.

Building character traits. Cultivating certain personal virtues increases the likelihood of a dynamic sexuality. Learn to be childlike with curiosity and playfulness; become a romantic; incorporate patience, honesty and joy; practice love, forgiveness, and respect for oneself and others.

Learning the skills of romance.   The ability to be romantic and a good lover extend much beyond a knowledge of male and female physiology. These skills include effective verbal and nonverbal communication, empathy, gentleness, awareness of feelings, sensuality and openness. The lover in Song of Solomon had these skills plus a healthy fantasy life, a spirit of adventure, and a maturity evidenced by understanding and commitment. The single person should learn to give and receive sexual pleasure within a relationship.

Clarifying values, as has already been stated, is a process. The Christian attitudes and behaviors above must be merged with personal likes and dislikes as a sexual values system evolves. It is not enough for singles to simply clarify and personalize their values – they must also be implemented.

Implementing values

Implementing the sexual values the single person has clarified takes strategic planning, will power and affirmation.

Strategic planning.   After a sexual value has been clarified with the concomitant personalizing and prioritizing, planning must be done on how to carry it into action. Part of this process is deciding on boundaries. Stemming from one's values, boundaries are the line between meaningful and destructive sexual relating. Setting limits is a crucial but not easy part of planning.

The next step is a strategy for positively carrying out one's values. For example: if friendship is an important value in sexual expression, then a plan can be devised to develop open communication from the first date, and perhaps the boundary will be no sexual contact on the first few dates. Some values will be harder than others to find a workable boundary and strategy. Viable plans will have to be specific and realistic as they are tailored to the people and situations involved.

Will power. The bottom line on any value and strategy is choosing to act on it. Singles have to mobilize their will power and choose to practice in their sexual lifestyle the attitudes and behaviors that they prize. This action will be less difficult if they have followed the preceding steps of clarifying their values and creating a specific and realistic strategy for implementation. Putting values into action is also reinforced with affirmation.

Affirmation.   After singles have put their values into practice, they should evaluate and affirm the wisdom and effectiveness of their actions. They need to consider and savor the rewards they are getting from clarifying good values and following through on them. If they are not receiving sufficient affirmation, a given value may need reconsideration. It may be the value is unclear, the strategy is poor, or other variables need to be changed.

Effective values lead to satisfying sexual expression. The final section of this paper will explore sexual activity under the guidelines of a Christian values system.

Single Sexual Expression

The common misconception that sex equals intercourse greatly obstructs enjoyable sexual activity and leads to the equally destructive corollary that the only sexual boundary one needs is a prohibition of intercourse outside of marriage. There are many meaningful expressions of sexuality with requisite values and boundaries for each.

The following list will help emphasize the variety that is involved when single sexual expression is mentioned:

masturbation	wink	French kissing
joking	dreams	girl/guy watching
casual kiss	massage	petting to orgasm
dancing	cuddling	holding hands
caress	pinch	messages
hug	spooning	sitting close
clothing	fantasies	playful teasing
flirting	making out	stroking
touching	compliment	walk and posture
sparking	eye contact	fondling breast
hickey	talking	types of nudity

It would be impossible to individually explore such a large variety of sexual expressions. Instead, gender sexuality, homosexuality, masturbation, intercourse, and relational sexual activity other than intercourse will be briefly examined.

Gender sexuality

Gender sexuality is personal identity with maleness and femaleness and the general interaction of the sexes. Clothing, jewelry, posture and walk, flirting, eye contact are examples of gender sexual expression. Interaction and personal affirmation emerge as vital elements – not sexual arousal. This can be a lively and interesting area of sexual statement.

Homosexuality

Homosexuality, from a consistent Biblical viewpoint, varies from God's moral and sexual ideals, but so often this normative Christian stance has been accompanied by condemnation, disgust, and fear. This is unChristian. It is important to distinguish between the worth of individuals and the self-defeating, inappropriate nature of certain actions. Regardless of whether a Christian single believes being gay is right or wrong, there are several givens: people are more than their sexual preference, sexual preference is learned and can be changed, love and acceptance are not conditional on sexual preference, effective sexual values are needed whether one is gay or straight.

Masturbation

No other sexual activity is surrounded by more controversy and guilt than masturbation. Though there are no specific Biblical injunctions and it causes no physical harm, it is deemed unacceptable because of: fantasies involved, selfishness – good sex is relational, being childish and simply a release, encouraging other wrong sexual activity and personal stimulation.

All sexual expressions include both intrapersonal and interpersonal elements whether engaged in alone or with someone else. Masturbation, orgasm, and a variety of sexual feelings and sensations are experienced intrapersonally but are given context and meaning by the heterosexual interplay and imagery. The issue is not personal (masturbation) versus relational (kissing) activity, but rather a healthy awareness and experiencing in either type of expression both personal (what feels good) and relational (heterosexual interplay and fantasy) aspects.

Concerning fantasy, most of sexuality is in one's mind – the emotional and physical reactions that the mind has learned to trigger when various stimuli are present. Fantasy does not equal lust and there is a difference between thinking about something and doing it. In fact, fantasy keeps the relational factor within masturbation.

Masturbation then is legitimate sexual expression, not simply a release, with mental imagery an integral part. Several keys to enjoyment are making it just one of many types of sexual expression, keeping a balance of personal and relational, maintaining self-control (as in any area of sexuality) and not allowing fantasy to lead into violation of one's sexual values.

Sexual intercourse

The Bible quite clearly prohibits coitus outside of the marital commitment. An easier stance would be that intercourse should be within a committed relationship that is characterized by respect, playfulness, love and patience. Though the latter is also Biblical, the prohibition still seems clear.

This boundary, like any boundary, protects crucial values. Intercourse is an important seal upon and an ongoing renewal of the covenant of marriage. Chastity and fidelity protect coitus as a sacrament within marriage and witness to the value God places on marriage and the process of becoming 'one flesh.' It also seems that God is teaching healthy sexual self-control. In a symbolic manner He is saying, 'Boundaries are vital, I'll set up one significant boundary as a reminder that you need them in every area of your sexual expression.'

Relational sexual activity

Precluding sexual intercourse, the single person still faces a complex task of sorting through appropriate sexual expression. Lewis Smedes (1976, p. 152) states:

> Sexual relationships have many meanings, and they are not all preludes to intercourse ... There is room within the large variety of sexual relationships for mutual exploration, mutual expression of affection, mutual discovery of the meaning and depth of the sexual relationship, each as an end in itself at the time.

Relating this to specific behaviors – what about oral sex, petting to orgasm, deep kissing, keeping clothes on, etc., etc. What sometimes seems the desired and easiest solution is a list of what is right and what is wrong, but that is impossible because right sexual activity is relative to the person (who), the situation (when), and level of relationship (why).

There are no easy answers. Avoiding the common sexual sabotages helps, and clarifying values and boundaries protects. It still comes down to the process of personally making choices and remembering that 'mature individuals assume responsibility for their sexual expression; response always has consequences' (Smith, pp. 128, 131) and 'God will hold us accountable for every permitted pleasure that we forfeit' (Talmud, reference unknown).

In conclusion, two words are very relevant in summarizing sexuality and the single person: *process* and *forgiveness*. All people are pilgrims in the sexual area of life – struggling, growing, defeated, victorious, trying to achieve meaning and fulfillment. An essential part of this process is remembering that to lose a battle is not to lose the war. Take responsibility for today and tomorrow. Forgive, make choices and move on!

References

Masters, W. and Johnson, V. *Pleasure bond*. New York: Bantam Press, 1975.

Simon, S. *Caring, feeling, touching*. Niles, Illinois: Argus Communications, 1976.

Simon, S., Howe, L. and Kirschenbaum, H. *Values clarification*. New York: Hart Publishing Company, Inc., 1972.

Smedes, L. *Sex for Christians*. Grand Rapids, Michigan: William B. Eerdmans Publishing Company, 1976.

Smith, I. *A part of me is missing*. Irvine, California: Harvest House Publishers, 1979.

Trobisch, W. *I loved a girl*. New York: Harper & Row, Publishers, 1964.

10.2 Appropriate Vulnerability: A Sexual Ethic for Singles

Karen Lebacqz

All of us spend our first years single. Most of us spend out last years single. As adults, we are single by circumstance or by deliberate choice. Given these simple facts, it is surprising how little attention and how precious little support the churches have given to singleness (except for the monastic tradition, with its very particular demands and charisms). The scriptural witness on singleness is virtually ignored, despite the fact that Jesus never married and Paul preferred singleness. Throughout history, churches have simply assumed that marriage is the norm for Christians.

Single sexuality, when it is discussed at all, falls under the category of 'premarital sex'. Churches clearly expect that those who are single will get married and that those who have been married and are now single through divorce or widowhood will simply disappear into the closet until they marry again. The slogan recently adopted by the United Methodist Church must stand as a summary of the traditional Christian view of sexuality: 'celibacy in singleness, fidelity in marriage.'

A new ethic for single sexuality is needed, for the tradition that requires celibacy in singleness is not adequate. This situation does not mean that anything goes or that the church has nothing to offer by way of a positive ethic for single people. The task is to thread our way between two views of sexuality: the 'old testament' or 'thou shalt not' approach exemplified by much of church tradition, and the 'new testament' or 'thou shalt' approach evident in much of our current culture.

The 'old testament' or legalistic approach to single sexuality is well summed up in a delightful limerick by Joseph Fletcher (in *Moral Responsibility: Situation Ethics at Work* [Westminster, 1967], p. 88):

> There was a young lady name Wilde
> Who kept herself quite undefiled
> by thinking of Jesus
> and social diseases
> And the fear of having a child.

The 'thou shalt not' ethic was characterized by fear – fear of pregnancy and venereal disease – and by a series of 'dont's': don't have sex, don't take pleasure in it (at least, not if you are a woman) and don't talk about it. As the limerick suggests, sexual involvement was regarded as 'defiling.' 'Bad girls' and 'good girls' were defined according to their willingness to be sexual or not. There was no discussion of the sexuality of divorced or widowed men and women, and gay men and lesbian women simply stayed in the closet.

With the advent of the so-called 'sexual revolution' and the birth control pill, fear of pregnancy was gone. After the 'thou shalt not' of Christian tradition, we encountered the 'thou shalt' of contemporary culture. Here, 'love' was all that counted. Women were 'liberated' and virginity was redefined as 'bad'. Now people talked about sex all the time, with everyone. Far from being defiling, sexual involvement was regarded as mandatory. Sex was supposed to be pleasurable, and 'how-to' manuals abounded. Finally, everyone knew how – but had forgotten why. In short, fear was replaced by pressure – pressure to engage in sex, to do it right, to enjoy it, and to let the world know how much and how well you were doing it.

The result is a clash often internalized into a 'Catch 22.' In the wonderfully perceptive comic strip *Cathy*, Cathy Guisewite captures the confusion of many. As the almost-but-not-quite-liberated 'Cathy' is getting dressed to go out on a date, she reflects: 'I'm wearing the 'heirloom lace' of my grandmother's generation ... with the conscience of my mother's generation ... coping with the morals of my generation ... No matter what I do tonight, I'm going to offend myself.'

Neither the legalistic approach of earlier Christian morality nor the permissive approach of contemporary culture provides a satisfactory sexual ethic for singles. And without a good sexual ethic for singles, there cannot be a good sexual ethic for couples either.

Can we construct a positive, Christian sexual ethic for single people? I think so. Let us begin with Christian tradition, which affirms that sex is a gift from God. It is to be used within the boundaries of God's purposes. As part of God's creation, sex is good. Like all of creation, however, it is tainted by the fall, and therefore becomes distorted in human history. It needs redemption. Such redemption is achieved by using sexuality in accordance with God's purposes and through God's grace.

The two redeeming purposes of sexuality have always been understood as procreation and union. With these purposes in mind, Christian tradition maintained that marriage was the proper context for sex, since it was the proper context for raising children and for achieving a true union. Catholics have tended to stress procreation as the primary purpose while Protestants have stressed union, but both agree on the fundamental purposes of sexual expression.

This tradition has had enormous practical implications for singles. The tradition condemns all genital sexual expression outside marriage, on the assumption that it violates the procreative and unitive purposes of sexuality. Nongenital sexual expression is also suspect, because it is thought to lead inexorably to genital expression. Given such a view of sexuality, it is difficult for single people to claim their sexuality or to develop a positive ethic for that sexuality.

Standards within both Catholic and Protestant traditions have recently loosened, but there has been no fundamental challenge to this basic paradigm. Today some Catholics and most Protestants accept 'preceremonial' sex between responsible and committed adults. (Paul Ramsey argues that this is marriage in the moral sense. See his 'On Taking Sexual Responsibility Seriously Enough,' in Gibson Winter, editor, *Social Ethics* [Harper & Row, 1968], p. 45 ff.) Both traditions have moved toward affirming union as primary, while still upholding the importance of procreation. The meaning of the two fundamental purposes has been expanded by replacing the terms 'procreative' with 'creative' and the term 'unitive' with 'integrative'. (See Catholic Theological Society of America, *Human Sexuality: New Directions in American Catholic Thought* [Paulist Press, 1977], p. 86.) Thus, there is some acceptance of non-marital sexual expression, provided it is in the context of deep interpersonal commitment. .

But however important such revisions may be, they do not really accept sexuality outside marriage. Single sexuality is still difficult to claim. Neither Catholic nor Protestant tradition provides a totally satisfactory explanation of why sexuality should be fully expressed only in marriage or in a 'preceremonial' relationship that will eventuate in marriage. Both traditions still uphold marriage as the ideal, but give no satisfactory reasons for that ideal.

I accept part of the *method* that has led to the traditional interpretation, but wish to offer an additional insight into the nature of sexuality that might provide a fuller appreciation of the ethical context in which sexuality is expressed. I agree with the traditional understanding that sex is a gift from God to be used within the confines of God's purposes. However, I would add to the traditional purposes of union and procreation another God-given purpose of sexuality that I believe opens up a different understanding of human sexuality and of a sexual ethic for singles (as well as couples).

Sexuality has to do with vulnerability. Eros, the desire for another, the passion that accompanies the wish for sexual expression, makes one vulnerable. It creates possibilities for great joy but also for great suffering. To desire another, to feel passion, is to be vulnerable, capable of being wounded.

There is evidence in Scripture for this view of sexuality. Consider the Song of Songs (the 'holy of holies'), which displays in glowing detail the immense passion and vulnerability of lovers. This is not married or 'preceremonial' sexuality, nor are children the justification for the sexual encounter. It is passion pure and simple. And it is graphic sex. The Stoic fear of passion is not biblical. From the Song of Songs we can recover the importance of sexual desire as part of God's creation.

It is equally important to recover the creation stories in Genesis.

These are so often the grounds for our interpretation of what God intends human sexuality to be. It is from these stories that we take the phrase 'be fruitful and multiply' and turn it into a mandate for procreation. It is from these stories that we hear the deep call for union between sexual partners: 'This at last is bone of my bones and flesh of my flesh ... and the two shall become one flesh.'

Without denying the importance of these phrases and their traditional interpretation, I would stress another passage – one that has been ignored but is crucial for completing the picture. The very last line in the creation story in Genesis 2 reads: 'And the man and wife were both naked, and they felt no shame' (Gen. 2:25). In ancient Hebrew, 'nakedness' was a metaphor for vulnerability, and 'feeling no shame' was a metaphor for appropriateness. (On this topic I am indebted to the work of Stephen Breck Reid of Pacific School of Religion.) We can therefore retranslate the passage as follows: 'And the man and his wife experienced appropriate vulnerability.' As the summation and closure of the creation story, the verse tells us that the net result of sexual encounter – the purpose of the creation of man and woman as sexual beings who unite with one another to form 'one flesh' – is that there be appropriate vulnerability.

Vulnerability may be the precondition for both union and procreation: without a willingness to be vulnerable, to be exposed, to be wounded, there can be no union. To be 'known,' as Scripture so often describes the sexual encounter, is to be vulnerable, exposed, open.

Sexuality is therefore a form of vulnerability and is to be valued as such. Sex, eros, passion are antidotes to the human sin of wanting to be in control or to have power over another. 'Appropriate vulnerability' may describe the basic intention for human life – which may be experienced in part through the gift of sexuality.

If this is so, then a new approach to sexual ethics follows. If humans are intended to have appropriate vulnerability, then the desire to have power or control over another is a hardening of the heart against vulnerability. When Adam and Eve chose power, they lost their appropriate vulnerability and were set against each other in their sexuality. Loss of vulnerability is paradigmatic of the fall. Jesus shows us the way to redemption by choosing not power but vulnerability and relationship.

The implications for a sexual ethic are profound. Any exercise of sexuality that violates appropriate vulnerability is wrong. This includes violations of the partner's vulnerability and violations of one's own vulnerability. Rape is wrong not only because it violates the vulnerability of the one raped, but also because the rapist guards his own power and refuses to be vulnerable.

Similarly, seduction is wrong, for the seducer guards her or his own vulnerability and uses sex as a weapon to gain power over another. Any sexual encounter that hurts another, so that she or he either guards against vulnerability in the future or is unduly vulnerable in the future, violates the 'appropriate vulnerability' which is part of the true meaning and purpose of our God-given sexuality. Prostitution and promiscuity are also generally wrong. In each there tends to be either a shutting down of eros or a form of masochism in which the vulnerability is not equal and therefore not appropriate. Sex is not 'just for fun' or for play or for physical release, for showing off, or for any of a host of other human emotions and expressions that are often attached to sexuality. It is for the appropriate expression of vulnerability, and to the extent that that expression is missing, the sexual expression is not proper.

Nothing in what has been said so far suggests that the only appropriate expressions of vulnerability are in marriage. Premarital and postmarital sexuality might express appropriate vulnerability. Gay and lesbian unions, long condemned by the church because of their failure to be procreative, might also express appropriate vulnerability. At the same time, some sexual expression within marriage might not be an appropriate expression of vulnerability – for example, spousal rape or unloving sexual encounter. We must beware of the deceptions through which we reduce or deny vulnerability in sexuality – both the 'swinging singles' image and notions of sexual 'duty' in marriage deny appropriate vulnerability.

But what about singleness specifically? Is there any need for a special sexual ethic for single people? Precisely because sexuality involves vulnerability, it needs protective structures. A few years ago, the United Church of Christ proposed a 'principle of proportionality' for single sexuality. According to this principle, the level of sexual expression should be commensurate with the level of commitment in the relationship. While I have some problems with this principle, it does have the merit of suggesting that the vulnerability involved in sexual encounter requires protection. The more sexual involvement there is to be, the more there needs to be a context that protects and safeguards that vulnerability. As Stanley Hauerwas puts it, 'genuine love is so capable of destruction that we need a structure to sustain us' (*A Community of Character: Toward a Constructive Christian Social Ethic* [University of Notre Dame Press, 1981], p. 181).

Traditionally, monogamous marriage has been understood to provide that needed context. Whatever the actual pitfalls and failures of marriage in practice, certainly in theory the commitment of a stable and monogamous marriage provides a supportive context for vulnerable expressions of the self. Marriage at its best ensures that the vulnerability of sexuality is private and that our failures remain protected in a mutually vulnerable and committed relationship.

Singleness carries no such protections. It is an unsafe environment for the expression of vulnerability. No covenant of fidelity ensures that my vulnerability will not lead to my being hurt, foolish, exposed, wounded. In short, in singleness the vulnerability that naturally accompanies sexuality is also coupled with a vulnerability of context.

Thus, singleness is a politically more explosive arena for the expression of vulnerability in sex because it lacks the protections of marriage. It heightens vulnerability.

An adequate sexual ethic for singles must therefore attend to what is needed for appropriate vulnerability in sexuality. Attention must be paid to the structural elements in the particular situation that heighten or protect vulnerability. For example, a sexual ethic for singles might take one form for those who are very young and another for those who are older. The protections of age and experience may make it sensible to permit sexual encounter for those who are older and single, while restricting it for the very young. Unequal vulnerability is not appropriate. In a culture, therefore, where men tend to have more power than women and women are more vulnerable than men, great care will be needed to provide an adequate context for the expression of sexuality.

We need a theology of vulnerability. Until such a theology is forthcoming, we can only struggle toward a proper sexual ethic. Single people will have to explore their own vulnerability to find its appropriate expression in sexuality. Neither the 'thou shalt not' of traditional prohibitions nor the 'thou shalt' of contemporary culture provides an adequate sexual ethic for singles. 'Celibacy in singleness' is not the answer. An appreciation of the link between sexuality and vulnerability is the precondition for an adequate sexual ethic.

10.3 Celibacy and Intimacy

Ben Kimmerling

In the Roman Catholic church over the centuries celibate people have offered married people their perspective on the meaning of marriage. In this article I hope to reverse this trend by offering my perspective as a married woman on the meaning of celibacy! But first let me explain how my interest in celibacy came about.

When I got married I promised to love my partner and to be faithful to him for life. For many years I assumed that this promise of fidelity meant that I should love only one man. While I was busy having a family I had no reason to question this assumption. However as years went by I became involved in community life. I began to see that there was a contradiction between my assumption about loving only one man and Christ's instruction to love my neighbor. So I asked myself – how can I be true to my commitment to my husband and yet relate in a meaningful and loving – rather than a superficial or remote – way to other men? Finally after a great deal of questioning I found what was – in theory at least – a simple solution. I could love others – but I have to love them in a celibate way. It was at that point that my interest in celibacy began!

Since then I have run many workshops on celibacy and related subjects for religious and priests. Consequently I have become convinced that the experience of sacramental married love can help to illuminate vowed celibacy.

As I understand it each of these vocations witnesses to a particular dimension of God's love. Marriage witnesses to the personal dimension. Celibacy witnesses to the universal dimension.

Having reflected on my own journey I realize that the call to universal love lies at the heart of – is in fact an outcome of – the personal experience of love. Having journeyed deeply into a vocation of personal love I found that I eventually arrived at the point where the vowed celibate vocation begins. Personal love had evolved towards love of neighbour. So my lived experience of married love corroborated the celibates' conviction that love is universal. I began to understand that this conviction underlies vowed celibacy when it is voluntarily assumed. My task now – and it is a lifelong one – is to integrate the personal and the universal dimensions of love into my married life.

As I continued my exploration I asked myself, does the same process happen in reverse for the celibate person? Does the celibate also, at some point, have to integrate the universal and personal dimensions of love into her or his life? Having struggled – perhaps for years – to love people without discrimination and thus witness to God's universal love, does the celibate journey ·eventually lead a person to a point where she or he is called to love some one particular individual in a deeply personal way? Does the journey of celibate into universal love eventually corroborate the married person's experience that all love – of its very nature – must also be deeply personal? Can a celibate person love everyone universally if she or he has never struggled to give love to, and receive love from, one significant person in an intimate and personal way?

How effective is the witness of a celibate person if he or she never faces the issue of intimacy which is inherently present in every human relationship? How can a celibate person become aware of this issue and learn to resolve it, unless it surfaces in a concrete and specific form in relationship with particular human beings?

In the rest of this article I will try to address this issue of intimacy and friendship in the life of the celibate. As space is limited I will focus on one specific and often problematic aspect of intimacy i.e. physical intimacy. I will discuss whether such intimacy is appropriate for the celibate; if so what form it might take, and what role it might play in the celibate's life.

Intimacy

I believe that anyone who wishes to minister to others needs to be able to create and to tolerate a wholesome form of intimacy with others. Intimacy is a way of being with oneself and others. It is a stance one adopts in the whole of one's life. It is an attitude of truth and authenticity: an open space between oneself and others which is free of physical distaste, emotional blocks and intellectual prejudice. It is about availability. It is about appropriate, relevant and truthful disclosure in every relationship. It is about revealing vulnerability as well as strength. It is about transparency. It can exist not only in private relationships – though that is usually where one first learns about it – it can exist in public relationships too. In its presence people feel deeply moved: they feel invited to change and to grow. In this kind of intimacy a person is fully present to others and so God is present too. Unfortunately, however, the formation for ministry which was offered to most celibate people until recently did not encourage this kind of intimacy.

The Formation of Celibate People

Human beings are incarnate spirits. The human spirit manifests itself through the body and the emotions as well as through the intellect. So in order to be fully present to others – in order that spirit may touch spirit – people should not deliberately exclude any one of these dimensions of their personality from their relationships. Instead they must search for truthful and appropriate ways of being present to others on all these levels. If they exclude and deny aspects of themselves, their presence may end up being destructive rather than growthful for others.

This destructiveness is obvious in pornographic relationships. The emotional and to a large degree the intellectual dimension are omitted and the pornographer relates to another person on the physical level only. This dehumanizes both the other person and the pornographer himself.

Until quite recently many candidates for the religious life were encouraged by formation programmes to neglect or suspect the physical and emotional dimensions of relationships and to relate to others in a purely intellectual way. It seems to me that this advice – if taken seriously – was just as dehumanizing as pornographic relating. Indeed in many ways it was more damaging, because it was more insidious. If questioned, people could become self-righteous and could justify their behaviour by the use of religious arguments. Therefore the destructiveness was much more difficult to expose.

The emotional dimension must not be excluded because emotion can modify, civilize and humanize physical desire. The physical dimension cannot be excluded either. We cannot leave our bodies outside of our relationships and so, one way or another, our bodies speak. Therefore instead of excluding these dimensions of the personality from relationships, the celibate must find ways of integrating them into her or his life.

In order to suggest how this might be done I would like to look now at the physical dimension of the married relationship – specifically at sexual intercourse, which is one of the more obvious things which a vowed celibate gives up. If we can understand what is happening during intercourse we can then ask – can the same effect(s) be brought about by other means in celibate friendship?

Physical Intimacy in Marriage

The very word intercourse implies some kind of communication between two people. So what is being communicated during sexual intercourse? Obviously there is the communication of physical pleasure or at least there is the possibility of this. Physical pleasure is very important because it puts a couple in touch with the goodness/Godness of their own sexuality – of their own bodiliness.

However, although physical pleasure is important, it is only a transitory sensation. It cannot be grasped and retained. So is there something more enduring being conveyed? I believe that in addition to the transitory element of pleasure there are two enduring elements in the experience.

The First Enduring Element

Sexual intercourse which forms part of a loving relationship is a very powerful way of accepting the physical being of another person. In the sexual act this acceptance is communicated to the other through touch. Loving intercourse is an affirming experience, in which each partner by delighting in the other reveals to the other the wholesomeness and beauty of his or her body. The message which is communicated is this: you and your body are good, you and your body are acceptable, you and your body are lovable. This knowledge is stored in the body – it is lodged in the bones and in the flesh. It becomes an intrinsic part of that person's being and so he or she acts in accordance with that knowledge when relating with people from then on.

This knowledge of a person's own loveliness which is taught in a loving intimate relationship is one enduring element of the experience.

The Second Enduring Element

The knowledge about a person's own loveliness and acceptability is transmitted – not in the language of words but in the language of touch. This message is received by a partner – not first and foremost in his or her mind, but in her or his body. So a person gradually learns that the body is a centre of intelligence – that it can receive, store and interpret messages. And that it can be used – quite consciously – to transmit messages too. So a new means of communicating – a new language – is gradually learned. This language is then permanently at the person's disposal.

This language – the language of the adult body – builds on the rudimentary physical language learned in childhood. And if the language which was taught in childhood was damaging it can help to neutralize and counteract this. This language of the body is the second element which endures.

So while the element of physical pleasure does not endure, these other two elements – (*a*) the knowledge of one's own loveliness and (*b*) the means – i.e. the physical language – whereby a person can communicate to others their loveliness – do endure.

If the experience of a sexual relationship is reflected upon by couples at a later date, all of this new awareness can be translated into ideas and words. This articulation is important for the Church so that the theology of human sexuality may be enriched. However, the important thing for each individual – the thing which brings about a personal transformation – is that this information is now stored in the body. It has become part of the person. It is now physically known.

When the fact of a person's own loveliness is known, hang-ups about the adult sexual body disappear. The body can then be used to communicate with others in a more natural and spontaneous way. Body language then begins to mirror and enhance verbal language – there need be no contradiction between the two. When two languages are at a person's disposal he or she can be more fully present to others. Consequently a more profound, more nuanced and therefore more truthful communication of the self takes place.

So loving physical intimacy is a freeing experience. It is a redemptive experience: God through a couple's most intimate gestures frees them to reach out, not only to one another but to others, in self-giving love.

The first few lines of the poem 'Saint Francis and the sow' expresses this idea beautifully:[1]

> The bud
> stands for all things.
> Even for those things that don't flower.
> For everything flowers, from within, of self blessing;
> though sometimes it is necessary
> to reteach a thing its loveliness,
> to put a hand on the brow of the flower
> and retell it in words and in touch
> it is lovely
> until it flowers again from within, of self-blessing: ...

Celibate Life

Celibate people too need to be 'retaught their own loveliness' because they too must reach out to others in self-giving love. Let us look now at celibate friendship to see how this re-teaching and learning might take place.

If a child lives in a loving environment it is taught that its childish body is lovely. But if adult sexuality is to be fully integrated this teaching needs to continue in adult life.

If celibate people live in total physical isolation, they cannot discover the goodness/Godness of the human body because there is no one there to mirror back that goodness to them. Those who remain physically remote from others often tend to think of the body as somehow troublesome, unclean, a nuisance – perhaps even as disgusting. They can feel ashamed, bothered or unaccepting of the manifestations of their adult sexuality. They can sometimes even want to marginalize or disown their own bodies altogether. When people reject or deny certain physical aspects of themselves they are not fully present to themselves. Consequently they cannot be fully present to others either.

Celibate friendship offers an opportunity to correct this situation. In friendship celibate people can learn experientially that their sexual body is wholesome and lovable. And they can learn to speak a new language too. However, as the context of this learning is often fraught with pain and dissatisfaction, one must look beneath the surface of a friendship to see how this learning occurs.

Some celibate friendships remain straightforward and uncompli-
cated. In other friendships sexual attraction and desire enters the
picture. Most celibate people – whether heterosexual or homosexual –
find it difficult at first to deal with this. Physical desire can be a fairly
relentless force. It tends to grow stronger and stronger. It generates an
ever increasing interest in, and curiosity about, the physical being of
the other person.

This desire is usually something which happens to people rather
than something they consciously decide to cultivate. Consequently
there should be no moral guilt attached to it. However, many celibates
do in fact feel inordinate guilt when they first find themselves in this
situation.

Flight is not necessarily the right way to deal with attraction and the
desire associated with it – although this of course is a matter for
discernment. I believe that the way in which we define an experience
determines our options. So if this experience is interpreted as a God-
given gift/invitation, rather than as a temptation, it may open up a
wider range of choice.

Physical attraction and desire are generally welcomed and enjoyed
when both partners are free to pursue their physical interest in one
another. Even in celibate friendship it can be a source of joy and
excitement to begin with. As physical desire gathers momentum both
partners feel an urge to express it in some way. To begin with they may
be satisfied with small gestures. However as desire grows the urge to
go further grows too. Eventually the only form of expression which
seems adequate or satisfactory is sexual intercourse.

In celibate friendship difficulties arise at this stage. Unexpressed
physical desire creates a sense of restlessness which is just about toler-
able when there is some hope of it being eventually met. However in a
friendship where both partners decide to refrain from full sexual
expression, there is no hope of it being met.

Then the sense of restlessness becomes almost unbearable. Sexuality
can then be experienced almost as an addiction or an obsession. This
in turn leads to a sense of powerlessness in the face of this force and to
a feeling that one is no longer in control of one's life in the way in
which one used to be. It is an intensely painful and disturbing experience of unfreedom. It is experienced as the tyranny of a physical
human need.

Darkness

In First World countries many people never experience the tyranny of
other physical needs – such as hunger or the need for shelter. Certainly
most vowed celibates – in spite of their vows of poverty – do not. So
until this happens to them they may have little idea how physical needs
can drive a person to behave in a destructive and less than human way.
In friendship a celibate person is invited to look honestly into his or

her own heart – to face all the darkness as well as the light that is there. If this is done, then this experience of physical need can generate compassion and deepen a person's understanding of others. And having faced the dark side of his or her own sexuality the celibate person is better able to counteract and be counter-witness to these same dark forces which are loose in the world.

Furthermore, if a person can live with this pain long enough to experience it fully and then reflect upon it, she or he will discover that the desire for sex is rooted in the need to be loved. Time – and the painful confrontation with one's own sexual longing – allows this distinction between desire and need to emerge. So the celibate person discovers that while the need for love has to be met, the desire for sex does not. Sexual intercourse is then no longer equated with love. It is seen for what it really is i.e. just one means of expressing love. When this distinction has been discovered experientially, a search can then begin for other forms – celibate forms – of expressing love. This search for celibate forms of expression is very important because the person gradually learns a way of celibate relating which becomes part of his or her public life.

A consummated relationship can show the bright, joyful and pleasurable side of human sexuality – though not all such relationships do. A celibate friendship can make a person aware of the dark, untamed, uncivilized side of the personality. In a very particular way celibate friendship can make a person aware of the need for redemption – of the need to be set free. It can make him or her aware too that she or he cannot just snap fingers and bring this freedom about. This process of becoming free cannot be controlled in the way other processes were previously controlled. In fact at this stage a person cannot even imagine how such freedom can ever come about. And so for a long time a deep sense of helplessness and despair is felt about the future and about the management of the person's own sexuality.

However I believe that slowly and painfully with a mixture of what may be thought of as success and failure – although in celibate friendship these concepts have to be fundamentally redefined – physical desire can gradually lose some of its stridency. Sexual responses and behaviour become more the subject of choice. This can only happen if efforts are made to cultivate the emotional and intellectual dimensions of the relationship. It will not happen if, whenever strong desire is experienced in a relationship, the relationship with that particular person is given up.

In a long-term and loving friendship where there is some degree of physical intimacy without full sexual intercourse, friends can teach one another about their physical loveliness. Friends can also learn the language of the body so that in their ministry they can be less inhibited and therefore communicate with others in a more natural, loving, self-giving yet celibate way. So these two elements which are brought about and endure in a consummated relationship, can be brought about and endure in a celibate friendship too.

The challenge in celibate friendship is for each partner to accept the whole truth – the full reality of who she or he is – i.e. that she or he is both celibate and sexual. This acceptance of the whole truth of the adult sexual celibate body does not come about easily. It may be a long time before a person stops regarding the body as a threatening enemy who may suddenly betray him or her, and instead learns to smile benignly on its biological responses. I believe that this struggle to achieve a personal civilization can be conducted within a celibate friendship where there is mutual understanding and acceptance. Yet an even greater part of that struggle must be conducted when one is alone with one's conscience or in conversation with God.

Sometimes it takes years of painful struggle between a person's sexuality and celibacy before the two can be integrated. I believe that this integration is helped by the attitude of a friend. If a friend struggles to accept the whole truth of who that person is – that she or he is both sexual and celibate – then I believe that the celibate person is helped to integrate these two seemingly contradictory aspects into his or her life.

Suggested Criteria in Sexual Morality

Physical communication, whether small gestures or full sexual intercourse, is never only a surface physical statement. It is – or can be – a depth experience too. If we are touched in a caring way, we are touched not just on the surface, but in the depths of our being as well. I think that it is tragic, if – in responding to, or assessing the meaning of gestures which we give to and receive from others – we concentrate only on the physical responses they arouse. We can miss the real meaning of a gesture if we interpret it too narrowly – in terms only of involuntary bodily response. We must not rely only on biological and intellectual criteria, to judge the meaning, the truthfulness or the morality of physical communication. To establish whether a physical gesture is a truthful and authentic statement of who a person is, we must submit all gestures to the criteria, not only of the head but of the heart as well. The heart – which is the seat of the emotions – has its own wisdom, its own language. And if there is a conflict between the two, perhaps we must in the long run learn to listen to the heart. If we have the courage to do so, we may move beyond the letter of the law, to the spirit of the law – and in doing so find that 'new heart' which has been promised to us by Christ.

I believe that each of us has the inherent capacity to interpret the real meaning of a gesture no matter how confusing the context within which it is made. We see a beautiful example of this heart criteria in operation in Jesus as he publicly accepted Mary's sensuous and loving anointing of his feet. Though sexual intercourse may be the most intense form of touch it is not the only form of touch which can transform, liberate and redeem us. Any caring touch can heal us and open us up more fully to God and to others.

In childhood we learn the rudiments of the language of touch. In adulthood we must continually build upon what we have learned. A consummated sexual relationship is one obvious place where a person can learn the subtleties and nuances of the language of touch. But the basic grammar of that language can be learned in celibate friendship too. Through a stumbling process of trial and error, celibate people can gradually learn to distinguish between different kinds of touch. They can learn that while loving touch is always affectionate it is not always sexual. They can learn that loving sexual touch is not always invitational; and that sexual touch which is invitational is not coercive because it does not rob another of the freedom to decline.

It is particularly important when discussing celibate friendship to remember that loving sexual touch is not necessarily an invitation to sexual intercourse. It may simply be a very honest and truthful statement to another person of who one really is. And most people – including celibate people – need to make that statement of who they really are, at some time in their adult lives to someone who can listen, accept and understand.

Such a statement may be made through the medium of gestures – for example in an embrace. And if listened to carefully with one's heart, it might sound something like this. 'I am a man (woman). Although I am celibate I still have all the longings of a man (woman). I cannot hide (deny) this truth from you or myself any more. Can you accept me as I really am?'

Such a statement can be truthful because it acknowledges the reality of human/sexual longing without demanding or forcing a response. If such a statement can be heard and accepted by another person for what it really is – as a confession rather than as an invitation – then I believe that a celibate person can begin to own his or her own body, his or her own sexuality, his or her own humanity in a new, more accepting, less driven way. And so gradually, in the safety of an intimate loving and accepting friendship the celibate is enabled to reclaim his or her own sexuality – the sexual celibate is enabled to 'come out'.

There is no doubt that in celibate friendship there are lonely moments and painful moments. But there are joyful moments too – moments when another reality is fleetingly glimpsed. In the life of the vowed celibate such joyful moments.

> ... are only hints and guesses,
> Hints followed by guesses; and the rest
> Is prayer, observance, discipline, thought and action.
> The hint half guessed, the gift half understood, is Incarnation.[2]

Notes
1.   Galway Kinnell, *the rattle bag* (London: Faber and Faber, 1982).
2.   T.S. Eliot, *The Dry Salvages* V, *The Four Quartets* (London: Faber and Faber, 1944).

11. Families

The topic of 'the family' has received much attention in the 1980s and 90s, both inside and outside the churches. There is alarm at the frequent breakdown of marriages, the rising numbers of children born to unmarried mothers, and the rise in juvenile crime. Families are contexts where male violence against women, and the abuse of children are increasingly found. Families are criticised for having confined wives to the private, domestic sphere where they are subservient to the needs and demands of husbands and children. From a conservative stance the weakening of the conventional nuclear family must be defended at all costs. Those who live outside it are potentially subversive of the social order and potential contributors to its breakdown. If family breakdown can be attributable to individual moral weakness, then the contribution of socioeconomic conditions to the plight of many families can be bracketed out. If the breakdown can be attributable instead to the decline of religious faith, then its patriarchal shape can be ignored. Those families where all the members flourish, are ignored in the maelstrom of these controversies. The single issue raised in this chapter is: what, if anything, can Christian theology contribute to the contemporary discourse of 'the family'? Or, to put it slightly differently; is there a credible theology of the family?

Rosemary Ruether's essay 'An Unrealized Revolution – Searching Scripture for a Model of the Family' shows that 'the Bible presents several different perspectives on the family'. Defenders of the patriarchal nuclear family show appreciation neither of the polygamous slave-holding clan of the early biblical narratives, nor of the 'good wife' of the book of Proverbs who is a 'powerful economic manager'. Neither can uncritical support for the ties of close kinship be sustained by an appeal to the teaching of Jesus, since 'the Christian community is seen as a new kind of family, a voluntary community gathered by personal faith, which stands in tension with the natural family or kinship group'. Ruether analyses the unresolved tension between the community of faith and the patriarchal households of the Graeco-Roman world. These tensions persist, yet even in our own day 'the church remains the main depository in our culture for the values of community life'. That is why she holds that it has 'a new opportunity to reinterpret this ancient Christian vision of the redeemed society as a new community of equals'.

Two out of three contributions to a recent series of articles on a theology of the family appear next. Stephen C. Barton's essay 'Towards a Theology of the Family' shows why 'the family' has become a moral and political symbol, ideologically charged. Theological reflection will need to begin with 'the experience of families and family members who are impoverished, marginalized, victimized or violated'. Families can be 'life-enhancing' or 'life-destroying' and the Church has colluded oppressively and uncritically with 'the family' by endorsing versions of it which are patriarchal, sexist and marginalising. While there are many discontinuities between the biblical social orders and our own, the Bible, according to Barton, remains an essential 'fount and well-spring' for a theology of the family. It provides 'a corrective against being falsely sentimental about family life'. It reveals 'a social pattern marred by sin and human frailty'. It 'offers a powerful *corrective* to any tendency to give the family an inflated importance'. The different traditions of theology within the churches are said collectively to 'constitute a theoretical and practical wisdom of great potential value'. The family can be an institution 'where God's grace is experienced and where people can find nurture and healing', but there is nothing essential to the family as an institution which, in advance of the actual relationships comprising it, make it so. To think otherwise would be to indulge in 'bourgeois idolatry'.

Susan Parsons, in her 'Towards a Theology of the Family – A Response' identifies Barton's approach as 'social constructionist'. The lack of any abiding essence which defines the family, she argues, signals our power to change inherited patterns. Whether families are channels of God's grace has a lot to do with the way in which power is exercised in family groups. We are to expect our experience of families to be conditioned by 'structural sin', i.e. by 'the ways in which good people are fixed by institutions ...' The third essay (by Alan Billings and not reproduced here) represents an alternative 'essentialist' approach to the family based on natural law and founded transcendentally. Parsons summarises this approach and states difficulties both with natural law and the supposition that a fixed human nature is essential to it. She finds agreement between the three writers in their common assumption that 'a theology ... of the family is a critical location for contemporary apologetics, as we seek to demonstrate how the knowledge and love of God is intrinsically bound up with the fullness of our humanity'.

Rosemary Ruether is Professor of Theology at Garrett Evangelical Seminary in Evanston, Illinois, USA. Her article, 'An Unrealised Revolution: Searching Scripture for a Model of the Family', first appeared in *Christianity and Crisis: A Christian Journal of Opinion*, 43, Oct. 31, 1983, pp. 399–404. Stephen C. Barton is Lecturer in New Testament in the University of Durham, England, and was a member of the Church of England Board for Social Responsibility Working Party on the Family. His article, 'Towards a Theology of the Family' is a revised version of a paper prepared for the Working Party and published in *Crucible*, Jan.–Mar. 1993, pp.4–13. Susan Parsons is Principal of the East Midlands Ministry Training Course, England. Her article, 'Towards a Theology of the Family – A Response' first appeared in *Crucible*, July–Sept. 1993, pp. 123–132, and has been slightly revised for publication in the present volume.

11.1 An Unrealized Revolution: Searching Scripture for a Model of the Family

Rosemary Radford Ruether

Conservative American Christians are very concerned about the need to restore what they say is the biblical view of the family: a male-dominated nuclear family consisting of a working husband, a nonworking wife who is a full-time mother, and several dependent children. It is as if the Bible endorses a version of the late Victorian, Anglo-Saxon patriarchal family as the model of family life proposed in the Scriptures. It is taken for granted that this Victorian ideal of the patriarchal nuclear family was created in the Garden of Eden and remained static until a recent, and unhappy, period in the 20th century when it began to be 'undermined' by feminists, gay people, and delinquent children. Since conservative rhetoric about the 'biblical view of the family' lacks any sense of the socioeconomic history of the family over the past three to four thousand years, it is not necessary for its proponents to reflect upon the norm itself or the forces that are challenging it, but simply to restore what is presumed to have always been, as the expression of God's will.

In reality, in biblical times no such nuclear family existed. Rather, the Bible presents several different perspectives on the family, none of which readily corresponds to the modern nuclear family, a relatively recent development in history.

If by the biblical view of the family one means, for example, the sort of family envisioned in the earliest strata of the Old Testament, restoring it would mean restoring an entire tribal form of economics. Such a family, in fact, a clan or small tribe, consisted of several hundred people headed by a patriarch who was the clan sheik. His family consisted of several wives, as well as concubines, their children, his slaves, and their children, other relatives such as his mother, and friends, and hangers-on. His authority also extended over his married sons and his daughters-in-law, his sons' concubines and slaves and their children and married daughters and sons-in-law and their dependents. Such a large clan unit was first based on desert nomadic shepherding, and later adapted itself to settled agricultural life.

Although dependent in legal matters, women of this Hebrew family were by no means shut up in a harem, nor did their role consist solely in child nurture and housekeeping. Rather, they were valued as economic workers who produced much of the goods consumed by the family. In the book of Proverbs, the 'good wife' is praised, not for her good looks or her mothering qualities, but for her efficiency as the manager of this domestic industry. She is described as like 'a merchant vessel who brings her goods from afar.' She considers a field and buys it, and plants a vineyard from her own earnings. She manages a large household of servants who spin and weave the clothes worn by the family. The wife also sells the goods produced in her household to merchants and derives further income. She is clothed in fine linen and purple. Her arms are strong, and she is filled with dignity and strength so that she can laugh at the days ahead.

Nothing is said about her husband's activities, except that he is 'known at the city gates where he takes his place with the elders of the land.' The wife is, in effect, the primary income producer, whose work frees her husband for political activity. Such a woman was indeed a formidable personality, so much so that the book of Proverbs constructs a theological metaphor that compares her to God. She is like God's immanent wisdom which creates, rules, and reconciles the universe. Presumably when our contemporary, conservative Christians talk about restoring the biblical model of the family, they do not have in mind the polygamous slave-holding clan of the partriarchal narratives nor the powerful economic manager of the book of Proverbs.

When we turn to the New Testament, written over a far shorter period of time than the Hebrew Scriptures, the situation is no less complex. Many of the New Testament writings, particularly the Gospels and the historical Paul, were subversive toward the patriarchal family as it existed in Jewish and Greco-Roman cultures. In the Christianity reflected in these texts the church functioned as a countercultural community that claimed priority in the lives of its members and dissolved the primacy of commitment to the family. In order to follow Jesus, one must 'hate,' or put aside the primary commitment to one's mother and father, spouse and children. As Matthew puts it:

> He (or she) who loves father or mother more than me is not worthy of me, and he (or she) who loves son or daughter more than me is not worthy of me. (Mt. 10:37-39)

Or in Luke's version of the saying:

> If anyone comes to me and does not hate his (or her) own father, mother, spouse and children, brothers and sisters, he cannot be my disciple. (Lk. 14:26-27)

In a story found in all three synoptic Gospels, the church, as the true family of Jesus' followers, is contrasted with the blood-related family and kinship group. In this story, Jesus' mother and brothers come to where he is preaching and demand to speak to him. But Jesus repudiates this claim of the kinship family upon him with the words:

> 'Who are my mother and my brothers?' And looking around on those who sat about him, he said, 'Here are my mother and my brothers! Whoever does the will of God is my brother and sister and mother.' (Mk. 3:31-35; cf. Lk. 8:19-21 and Mt. 12:46-50)

Here the Christian community is seen as a new kind of family, a voluntary community gathered by personal faith, which stands in tension with the natural family or kinship group.

The Tension Between Kingdoms

This tension between church and family continues in Paul. Paul does not demand that his followers remain unmarried, but he would prefer that all Christians remain as he is; namely, unmarried (I Cor. 7:7). For Paul, the appointed time of world history is drawing to a close and the kingdom of God is at hand. Concern about the business of marriage and procreation, which are the affairs of the world, draws primary attention away from one's relationship to God. In the coming Kingdom all family relations will be dissolved, so they should not claim primacy in Christian concerns in the here and now. Paul is also concerned with the problems of households divided when one spouse becomes Christian while the other remains an unbeliever.

In both the Jewish and the Greco-Roman worlds, it was axiomatic that the religion of the household was that of the head of the family. A family was not simply a social unit, but also a religious entity united around its household ancestral gods. The family religion, in turn, tied the household to the public order of the state. The public cult, rooted in the household gods of the tribes that came together to make the city or the nation, represented a joint household religion linking all the families together in one community. Therefore, for a person to depart from his or her family religion, the religion of ancestors and the nation, was to engage in an act of subversion toward the family and the public order. This was doubly heinous when dependents in the patriarchal family, a wife, daughter or son, or a slave, departed from the family cult and followed a different religion.

Christianity heightened this conflict since it did not allow its followers to be initiated into its cult and still follow the old religion, as the mystery religions did. As an exclusive faith, Christianity declared other religions to be false and their gods mere idols or even demons. Such exclusivity was also found in Judaism, but, for the people of the Greco-Roman world, Judaism was the ancestral religion of a particular ethos, or nation. So its particularities could be tolerated within its own community, provided that it did not take the form of political rebellion against the Roman superstate. Christianity was different; it was both exclusive and universal. It had rejected its ethnic roots. The religion of no particular national group, it made its claims upon individuals regardless of family or nation. This concept of religion was inherently subversive, disrupting the order of both household and state.

It is important to see the close connection between the family and the state. We are familiar with the idea that Christianity was persecuted as a religion subversive to the state, although we tend to think of this as a mistake, since Christianity's claim was spiritual, not political.

But we have failed to see the equally important fact that Christianity disrupted the family, because household and state were so closely linked in ancient society. To follow a religion contrary to that of the family – a religion, moreover, which declared the official religion to be false and demonic – was to strike at the heart of the social order of both the family and the state. It meant that wives could dissolve their allegiance to their households, children to their parents, slaves to their masters. These persons, in turn, no longer reverenced the state whose prosperity was founded on the favor of the ancestral gods. Thus we should not minimize the seriousness of the assault on society posed by early Christianity.

Most Christians in the first and second century believed that this conflict between Christian faith and the family and state should be expressed boldly and unequivocally. The Christian should be ready to die, if necessary, rather than to concede the claims of the household and state gods. The literature celebrating this position is found in the story line of the Gospels, as well as the popular martyr narratives and the apocryphal Acts of the Apostles. In this literature, rejection of the claims of the family and that of the state are closely tied together, particularly when the Christian believer is a woman, a wife or a daughter. For example, in the mid-second century *Passion of Sts. Perpetua and Felicitas*, two women, one nobly born and another a slave of her household, are united as sisters in their common determination to die for their faith. Perpetua has just had a child, while Felicitas delivers a child in prison. Perpetua is begged by her aged father to consider her duty to her infant son, but she spurns these demands upon her in order to express the primacy of her loyalty to Christ.

In the *Acts of Paul and Thecla*, a young woman of Iconium, engaged to be married, is converted by Paul. She immediately rejects the claims of her fiance and family upon her and takes off to follow Paul. Her enraged husband-to-be complains to the governor that the Christian faith has subverted his marriage rights. For the rest of the narrative, representatives of Thecla's family, her mother and her fiance, as well as agents of the state, pursue her and try to punish her for her rebellion against the combined authority of family and state. She is thrown twice to the lions and miraculously escapes unharmed. At the conclusion of the narrative, she is commissioned by Paul to preach. For Christians well into the Middle Ages the figure of Thecla remained the authority for women's right to preach and claim a religious vocation independent of the demands of the family and public authority.

It is likely that this story of Thecla goes back in oral form to the late first century. (See Dennis R. MacDonald, *The Legend of Paul and the Apostle. The Battle for Paul in Story and Canon*. Philadelphia: Westminster Press, 1983.) Along with the martyr narratives, the story of Thecla represents a form of radical Christianity that goes back to earliest Christianity. It was simultaneously ascetic and apocalyptic. It firmly believed that the present social order was soon to come to an end, and that this coming event demanded a dissolution of one's allegiance to the state, as well as a rejection of sexuality and the ties of marriage. This Christianity was also charismatic and prophetic, believing in the living presence of the Holy Spirit expressed in charismatic speaking and miracles of healing. Its heroes and heroines were prophets and martyrs. Although it is militantly ascetic, it should not be confused with gnosticism, which moved in a different, quietistic, and spiritualist direction. Unlike gnosticism, it has never been regarded as heretical. Rather, the official church claimed its literature and heroes, while trying to dampen its enthusiasm and relegate its martyrs safely to the past.

In I Corinthians 7, Paul replies to a series of questions occasioned by this kind of ascetic and apocalyptic Christianity. Should Christians not yet married get married? Should those who are married abstain from sexual relations? Should the wife or husband married to an unbeliever separate and divorce? Paul is hard put to reply to these questions since, in fact, he shares much of the perspective of the militant ascetic and apocalyptic faith from which these questions come. But he is also concerned to modify the confrontation between this faith and the family. So he suggests a series of compromises, often tentatively and eschewing full claims of authority. It would be better for married Christians to abstain from sex, but, since this might lead to immorality by the non-believing partner, one should concede to the demands of sex, although also allowing for times of abstinence as well. Still, complete celibacy would be the ideal. If one is unmarried, better not to marry. If yoked to an unbeliever, stay with him or her, if the spouse consents. However, if the nonbelieving partner desires to separate, it is right to do so. A sister or brother is not bound to the nonbelieving spouse.

Post-Pauline Polarizations

Paul's efforts to find a middle ground between the claims of family and the claims of faith were not successful. Instead, we see in Christian literature of the next several generations a polarization between two positions, one exalting the claims of faith against family and state, and the other increasingly modifying the early radical vision of faith in order to accommodate the claims of the family and the state.

The first or radical position is reflected in the Gospels as well as in the martyr literature and the popular Acts of the Apostles that I have just mentioned. This literature, as we have seen, affirmed the primacy of the claims of the faith against those of the family and the state. The individual is absolved of his or her dependency and loyalty to these institutions in order to be faithful to a higher loyalty. The mother may deny the claims of an infant son upon her; a daughter may repudiate the demands of a father; a bride-to-be those of her parents and her husband. In some of these popular stories women who are already married are depicted as leaving their husbands in order to follow Christ.

Having departed from the family and the conventional social institutions, women, youth, and slaves join a new community of equals. The hierarchical ties of family and society are done away with. There is no more master and slave, no more dominance of male over female. The differences among ethnic groups, Jew and Greek, Greek and Scythian, are dissolved. All are one in a new family, a new humanity defined by Christ. Thus not only is the Roman matron, Perpetua, praised for rejecting her family and the state, but the social gap between her and her slave woman is overcome as well. The free-born Perpetua and the slave woman, Felicitas, became equals and sisters.

It is not accidental that many of these stories revolve around women, women as wives, as daughters, and as slaves. For the first four centuries of its existence Christianity moved up the social ladder primarily through women, children, and slaves. Male heads of families were the last to be converted precisely because, for them, the claims of ancestral religion of city and state were the religious base of their authority and public offices. Families in which all members were Christian began to develop in the lower ranks of society; in contrast, among the upper classes, even in the fourth century, it was common for the women and female children to be Christian, while the husband and older son remained pagan. Thus the conflict between the Christian faith and the pagan world continued to divide, not just Christians as a group from the outside world, but households as well, separating Christian wives, daughters, and slaves, from pagan heads of family. The pagan paranoia toward Christianity, which flared up in waves of persecution in these centuries, was rooted in this fear that Christianity subverted the social order, not just in its public political form, but at its most intimate base in the family.

Over against that radical Christianity, which affirmed and even exalted in this conflict, urging Christians to remain firm against state and family even to death, there arose a more conservative view which sought to modify the conflict. Not surprisingly, this more conservative view reflects the position of a growing established leadership associated with bishops and with a patriarchal conception of established order in both society and the church. One finds this conservative voice of the institutional church reflected in the apologists of the second century and also in the household codes of the post-Pauline strata of the New Testament.

The apologists seek to modify the confrontation with the state by lifting up an ideal of Christians as ideal private citizens. The Christian is docile and obedient to the state. The Christian is scrupulously moral in all business dealings. He or she observes the strictest code of sexual morality. Therefore, the state should not see the Christian as subversive, but as the ideal citizen whose good private morality is the ideal base of public virtue. The apologists do not deny that Christians reject the public cult and its gods as false and demonic, but they seek to privatize this religious difference. They veil or conceal the apocalpytic vision of Christianity which saw the present world order as soon to be overthrown by God.

This effort to privatize the religious differences between pagan and Christian, while claiming personal morality as public virtue, did not entirely succeed. The pagan world continued to believe that Christianity was politically subversive precisely because it did not separate the private from the public. For pagans, religious belief was a public political act of allegiance to the gods upon whom the prosperity of the state rested. To deny the existence or divinity of those gods was to subvert the transcendent foundations of the state. Moreover, the stance of the apologists contained a kind of concealed contradiction, since they continued, privately, to hold on to an apocalyptic faith that denied the official gods and hoped for an imminent intervention of God to overthrow the pagan state.

The household codes of the New Testament attempt a similar compromise between the claims of faith and the claims of family. It is important to recognize that the original context of these codes did not have in mind the Christian family, but rather the divided household in which a Christian wife, daughter, son, or slave was in potential conflict with the claims of authority of the non-Christian head of the household as father, husband, and master. Like the apologists, the household codes seek to modify this conflict by depoliticizing or spiritualizing it. The Christian woman or slave is seen as inwardly free. The equality of male and female, slave and free, is exalted to the spiritual and eschatological plane. But, on the social level, the wife, daughter, or slave should express this new spiritual freedom by redoubled submission to the patriarchal authority of husband, father, or master.

As the First Epistle of Peter puts it, Christians, although aliens and exiles in this world, should all the more maintain the strictest conformity to outward standards of conduct so that the gentiles (or pagans) will not accuse them of wrongdoing. 'Be subject for the Lord's sake to every human institution,' whether emperor or governor. Servants be submissive to your masters, not only to the kind and gentle, but also those who are harsh and cruel. Likewise, wives obey your husbands, so that those who are unbelievers may be won over by the good behavior of their wives. Clearly what is in view in these texts is not the Christian household, but the household divided and potentially disrupted by Christian wives and slaves asserting their liberty against pagan masters and husbands.

However, like the apologists, the efforts of the household codes to privatize and spiritualize the radical character of the Christian vision were only partially successful. No matter how docile and submissive the wife or slave might be outwardly, she was nevertheless in spiritual revolt against the authority of her master or husband by choosing a religion which was not only different from his, but which made her regard herself as an alien and an exile in this world awaiting an imminent overthrow of his social system. Good outward moral behavior could assuage this contradiction, but not ultimately change the perception of pagan society that such a Christian faith struck at the root of its authority. The wife or slave who conceded, however assiduously, the outward claims of obedience, had nevertheless removed herself inwardly from all claims of this authority upon her life.

Resolutions Unresolved

As Christianity moved from the late first to the fourth century, this conflict between faith and family resolved in opposite, but complementary ways. On the one hand, the radical vision of an egalitarian Christian counterculture is institutionalized in monastic Christianity. Here Christian women, as well as men, continue to claim that faith takes precedence over all worldly institutions of state and family. They dissolve the ties of marriage, reject procreation or worldly occupations, and live apart in a separate community where all become equal and share in a communal lifestyle. But such an ideal of life is no longer proposed to all Christians, but only to an ascetic elite.

On the other hand, we see in the household codes of the New Testament, and in the political theology of the Constantinian state, the Christianization of the patriarchal family and the Roman empire. The hierarchy of husband over wife, master over slave, emperor over subject, is taken into the Christian community itself and sanctified by Christian theology. In Ephesians 5, the headship of husband over wife becomes a symbol of the headship of Christ over the church. The wife should submit to her husband, as to Christ. The husband should love his wife as Christ loves the church. Such 'love patriarchalism,' while it modifies traditional patriarchy by proposing a high ideal of husbandly benevolence towards dependents, nevertheless fundamentally discards the original Christian vision of equality in Christ. Its pattern is paternalistic, not mutual. The exhortation to the husband to 'love your wife as Christ loves the church,' is not paralleled by the exhortation to the wife to love her husband in like manner, but rather by a command to submit to her husband as the church submits to Christ.

A similar pattern is suggested in the relationship of slaves to masters. If the husband and master is not kind and loving, but harsh and cruel, this does not allow his dependents to criticize or rebel against his authority. Rather, the sufferings of Christ now become a model for patient endurance of unjust violence:

> For one is approved if, mindful of God, he or she endures pain while suffering unjustly ... For to this you have been called, because Christ also suffered for you, leaving you an example, that you should follow in his steps. (1 Pet. 2:18–25)

In these texts we see the revolutionary suffering of the cross of Christ converted into a theology of voluntary victimization. The cross of Christ is no longer a symbol of truth and justice which enables the Christian to stand against an unjust world, but it has become an example of patient and unprotesting acceptance of unjust suffering. This corruption of the theology of the cross into a theology of victimization takes place at the most intimate level, in the relationship of women and slaves to the patriarchal head of the family. Starting with the most intimate of relationships, and then moving out to all social relationships, the cross becomes a symbol of unprotesting submission to unjust violence and oppression, rather than a protest against it in the name of an alternative human community. The Kingdom of God becomes an antidote and compensation for this endurance of suffering, rather than a vision of an alternative world.

In a similar way, Eusebius of Caesarea, in the fourth century, Christianized the relationship of emperor and subjects. The emperor becomes the political representative of the Word of God, the vicar of Christ on earth. The Christian should obey the emperor as a visible embodiment of the reign of Christ over the world. In this Christianization of the patriarchal family and the Roman emperor, the Christian church ceases to stand against the dominant social order as a representative of an alternative human community where 'God's will shall be done on earth'. The radical egalitarianism of early Christianity is spiritualized in the first circumstance, as a reward to be enjoyed after death, or it is marginalized in the second into a separate, elite, monastic community set apart from the historical order of family and state.

Thus the hierarchical patterns of power of family, state, and social class fail to be transformed by Christianity, but rather are resacralized as expressions of obedience to Christ. By making the Christian egalitarian counterculture a monastic elite, outside of and unrelated to the family, the Christian church retrenched from the possibility that this radical vision itself could lay claims upon and transform the power relationships of society and family.

And yet, despite conservative efforts to appropriate *the* biblical view of the family, the church remains the main depository in our culture for the values of community life; for the ethic of mutuality and mutual service. In its Scriptures, the church enshrines the early Christian vision of the church as a new kind of community, a new kind of humanity, overcoming the divisions of patriarchal society, of male over female, master over slave, racial group against racial group. But this vision of the church as a new community, a new family, has either been interpreted as a celibate community over against the family, or else distorted into sacralizing the traditional patriarchal family. The challenge to create a new understanding of family as committed communities of mutual service, taking a variety of forms, can also offer the church a new opportunity to reinterpret this ancient Christian vision of the redeemed society as a new community of equals.

11.2 Towards a Theology of the Family

Stephen C. Barton

Introduction: Social and Political Considerations

The relation between religion and 'the family' is (and always has been) intimate and complex. In terms of functionalist sociology, for example, religion sanctifies the family and provides a moral order into which family members are socialized – hence the importance, in the Judeo-Christian tradition, of the fifth commandment of the Decalogue. On the other hand, the family is the most intimate and rudimentary context for the practice of religion and for the passing on of the tradition, as well as providing potent metaphors for articulating religious beliefs (e.g. in Christianity, where God is 'Father' and Jesus is 'the Son', or where the relation of Christ and the Church is likened to that of bridegroom and bride). Given this intimate and longstanding connection, it is not surprising that the Church should feel that it has a stake in the family, and that threats (real or perceived) to the family are seen as threats to the Church. Conversely, changes in Church polity may be perceived as having implications for family life – as, for example, when the ordination of women to the priesthood is seen as a threat to male 'headship' in the family and in society-at-large.

Following on from this, it is important to be aware of the ways in which 'the family' tends to become a moral and political symbol. Whenever there is a 'war over the family', we need to exercise a hermeneutic of suspicion in order to try to discern whether the family is being used as a weapon to serve the interests of a broader (and sometimes hidden) agenda – for example, a conservative agenda to do with maintaining or re-establishing a desired *status quo* of (androcentric and patriarchal) 'family values' and free-market economics; or a liberal agenda to do with social reform aimed at protecting the rights of the individual; or a feminist agenda to do with changing the social *status quo* in the interests of women's liberation; and so on. Putting this another way, statements about the family are moral and political statements. They are not value-neutral, but are part of a world view. This comes to the fore not least in the rhetorical practice of referring in monolithic terms to '*the* family', as if the term is normative and has one meaning only, or as if the statistical norm necessarily constitutes the moral norm. From a Christian perspective, attaining a proper sensitivity to oppressive, manipulative ways of talking about the family, and opening up more liberating and

452 *Christian Perspectives on Sexuality and Gender*

empowering ways of talking about the family must be a major goal.

That the family has enormous symbolic potential derives from at least the following factors: (i) It is perceived to be a traditional social pattern and thereby comes to represent what is held as 'traditional' on a wider front, including the fabric of society as a whole. From classical antiquity on, the family has been seen as a fundamental building-block of the civic community, and threats to the family have been interpreted as undermining the wider political and economic order. (ii) It is an intimate form of social organization – for many, though by no means all, the most intimate one – and therefore carries a high emotional voltage which makes it especially prone to rhetorical manipulation. This is exacerbated by the vulnerability of members of families, such as the unwaged, women, children, the elderly and the handicapped. (iii) It is a ubiquitous form of social organization, so that what is said about the family has a potential for affecting everyone in some way or other. (iv) It is a complex and dynamic social pattern linked inextricably to a correspondingly complex and dynamic set of moral-political concerns to do with male-female sexual identity and role relations, children, the elderly, the disabled, questions of work, property and inheritance, developments in biotechnology, and the role of the state. (v) Finally, it is (as pointed out earlier) a social pattern intimately linked with religion and therefore a potent symbol of a higher order of things.

It is not at all coincidental, therefore, that in England, so much media attention is paid to 'the royal family' as somehow symbolic and representative, since every one of these five factors is concentrated there to a quintessential degree. Nor is it coincidental that the 'soap', with its typical and mdelodramatic focus on family relations, is the most popular form of entertainment on both radio ('The Archers') and television ('Coronation Street', EastEnders', 'Neighbours', etc.). Soaps *appear* to speak to and for Everyman and Everywoman, but they do so in a way which often contains powerful hidden persuaders about 'normal family life', as well as constituting a culturally pervasive distraction from political criticism and reformative action.

It is important to emphasize that to talk of 'the family' is to talk of an abstraction (however powerful that abstraction is!). From an historical and anthropological point of view, it is too simplistic to talk about 'the natural family' in a monolithic way. What we have instead are ways of talking about particular kinds of small-scale, intimate social organization. Two kinds of observation are relevant here. First, familial and household patterns have changed significantly over time and vary greatly from one part of the world to another. Some types of 'family' are defined in primarily biological terms, others in primarily social or legal or religious terms. Also, people speak of 'extended' families as distinct from 'nuclear' families. In Western society, we often hear reference to working class families, middle class families, and aristocratic families. In multi-cultural contexts. Asian or African families live side-by-side with European families. Within those families, authority relations may be patriarchal, matriarchal, egalitarian, or some other pattern. An increasing number of families are single-parent. In many families, the adults cohabit rather than marry. And so on. The variety is enormous.

Second, people's experience of family life varies enormously, as well. Social historians point to changes over time in notions of family sentiment, changes in the rate of infant mortality, the relative lack of privacy in family life before the modern period, the change from arranged marriage to ties of romance, the 'discovery' of childhood as a separate developmental stage, the effects of the advent of effective contraception, and most recently, the trend in middle-class families towards 'androgynization' in marital roles. Feminism, with its roots (partly) in the suffragette movement, has drawn to our attention women's experiences of oppression, constraint, sexual abuse and sheer violence in the context of the family – and this is borne out on an almost daily basis in press reports about battered women. Marxism has highlighted the deleterious effects of free-market capitalism on the family, viewed merely as a unit of consumption and a unit for the production and reproduction of labour. A recent report (cited in *The Guardian* 16.7.1992) indicates that one quarter of children in Britain today are living below the poverty line. Social workers and lawyers are engaged constantly in attempts to protect children from parental abuse, sometimes of the most brutal kind. Approximately one in three marriages in Britain end in divorce, with the impact that that has on both parents and their children.

In the face of this variety in both the form of (what people call) 'the family' and in people's experience, it is essential, in dealing with claims about the family, to ask, Who is making the claims and for whom? and Why are these claims being made? Unless these questions are asked, we are likely to be carried away by a powerful 'family' rhetoric which assumes that 'everyone knows' what the family is and agrees that it should be so.

Theological Reflection

Christian theology is a critical and constructive discipline which tries to articulate the nature of Christian faith and life in a rational and coherent way. As such, it has to engage, not only with the Christian heritage of Bible, tradition and experience, but with modernity as well. Failure to engage with the tradition will produce a theology which is unrecognizable as Christian; failure to engage with modernity will produce a theology which is obscurantist, out-of-touch and incoherent.

The task of theological reflection on the family is a difficult one, therefore. Not only is the family a very complex reality conceived of and experienced differently by different people, but Christian experience and the Christian tradition on the family are complex and varied too. The crucial point ought to be added here that, from the perspective of liberation and feminist theologies, a Christian theology of the family will only begin to be true if it takes very seriously the experience of families and family members who are improverished, marginalized, victimized or violated. There is a proper sense in which theological reflection needs to learn to be partial (in the sense of 'taking sides'). Otherwise, we become prone to being blinded by a very powerful rhetoric of warm sentiment about the family. Part of this process of discernment may be the open acknowledgement that, although from a faith-perspective the family is God-given in some fundamental sense, nevertheless life together in families may be blessed and life-enhancing or demonic and life-destroying according to a great variety of factors, an awareness of which is part of the theological task for the purposes of encouraging the practice of just society.

It is important, theologically, not to reduce religion to matters of the family and family life. This is a natural and understandable tendency given the common and traditional perception of the fundamental role of the family in society and in the Church and given the symbolic potential of the family, mentioned already. It is understandable also in view of the major contribution of the Church to life-cycle rites of passage: baptisms, marriages and funerals. Such contributions – of family to Church and Church to family – are not to be gainsaid. Theologically and existentially, they spring from a recognition of the goodness of God at work in creation and in human society, and from a sense that there are moments in the natural life of human beings which have a 'graced' or sacramental quality about them.

Nevertheless, the effects of reducing religion to matters of the family are serious. In theological terms, there is the danger of idolatry, where the worship of God is supplanted by devotion to the family, and where God becomes a household god and no more. This kind of reduction contributes also to the privatization of religion, to the withdrawal of religion from the public domain into the 'safe' sphere of the domestic and the realm of personal preference or taste. This is a recipe for the secularization of religion. It also places an intolerable burden on the family as the only place of goodness and true religion, when often families are nothing of the kind and (just as important) are not in a position – for all manner of psychological, socio-political and economic reasons – to be so.

An ecclesiological corollary of this reduction is that the Church models itself uncritically on the family – more precisely, on one version of the family – in such a way that whereas the Church should be a structure of grace open to all and contributing to the full humanity of all, it becomes instead another bastion of 'the family' and 'family values' as defined by the dominant interest group. Historically, this tendency is reflected in the way in which a patriarchal society and a patriarchal Church have functioned in a mutually legitimating way with (what many today would see as) disastrous consequences for men themselves, for women, children, single people and sexual minorities, as well as for our very understanding of God. As examples of this process of mutual legitimation, one need think only of various ways in which Church and 'the family' collude in an oppressive way: (i) the image of 'Mother Church' puts women – mothers in particular – on a pedestal, while paradoxically keeping them from exercising formal power in a male dominated institution and society; (ii) the rhetoric of caring and relationality which envelops 'the family of the Church' conceals a heavy moral idealism and emotional load which families – let alone the Church – are often unable to bear; (iii) traditional ecclesiastical sensibilities about sexual impurity and menstruating women go hand-in-hand with a patriarchal society which maintains the social order in part by the control of women's bodies; and (iv) the recognized liturgies of the Church for human rites of passage reinforce the high ideal of life-long, heterosexual marriage, but offer next-to-nothing to single people, the divorced, the handicapped, and sexual minorities. Such examples could be multiplied. They certainly justify a hermeneutic of suspicion of attempts to exalt the ideal of the Church as family – which, of course, is not to deny the value of thinking of the Church as a 'family' or 'household' of some kind!

Reading the Bible Wisely

The biblical tradition provides much food for thought in relation to a theology of the family; but we cannot take over the tradition 'neat'. A process of 'translation' and critical-theological reappropriation is required. Reasons for this include the following.

First, the nuclear family as we know it is primarily a modern, urban development of the industrial revolution, whereas the biblical tradition has to do with tribes, clans and extended families (including slaves) in ancient agrarian civilizations. This raises the question of the relevance of the biblical material to the modern, nuclear family unit. Second, the Bible presupposes a social order quite at odds with what most people assume is right for today. For in the Bible, society is organized along lines which are both hierarchical and patriarchal: husbands, wives, children and slaves – in descending order of authority. In practice, this way of ordering society resulted in arrangements which are no longer morally acceptable – for example, polygamous marriage, slave-owning, and the household head having the power of life and death over his dependants. Today, we live in a more egalitarian and individualistic society where significant attention is at last being given to the rights both of women and of children. So interpreting the Bible wisely has to take this more egalitarian social ethos into account. Third, there is (for some) the 'problem' of world-view arising out of the Bible's eschatological hope for the coming of God's messiah and (in early Christianity) for his imminent return. This raises the question of relevance in another form. How, it is asked, can the Bible's messianic and eschatological ethos provide a viable basis for a theology of the family twenty centuries on? None of these difficulties is unsuperable, but awareness of them is crucial if we are to take modernity seriously and if we are to avoid the danger of creating a fundamentalist ghetto based on deceptively simple slogans like, 'The Bible says'.

The Bible remains then an essential 'fount and well-spring' for a Christian theology of the family. At one level, it contains a rich repository of *narrative* about tribes, clans, households and relationships which offer enormous potential for Christian reflection on the social dimension of personhood: Adam and Eve, Cain and Abel, Abraham and Isaac, Sarah and Hagar, Esau and Jacob, Joseph and his brothers. Naomi and Ruth, and so on – the list is almost endless, and continues into the new Testament, with the birth and infancy narratives of the gospels, stories of family members healed by Jesus or rent asunder by his call to follow, and stories of the conversion of whole households like that of Cornelius in Acts. It is especially noteworthy that such biblical stories do not present a particularly 'rosy' picture of the family. There is fratricide, rape, incest, adultery and murder – as well as love, fidelity and self-sacrifice, both within households and beyond them. This intense realism and 'worldliness' is itself a major contribution to the theological task. Among other things, it is a corrective against being falsely sentimental about family life. If the family is a crucial context for human growth and mutual care, it is also a social pattern marred by sin and human frailty and – like all relationships – in need of God's redeeming grace.

At a second level, the Bible contains a rich repository of *law, custom, poetry and proverbial wisdom* pertaining to kinship, marriage and household order. This repository includes the commandment in the decalogue to 'honour your father and your mother'; the books of Proverbs and Ecclesiastes with their traditional wisdom about good relationships; the celebration of sexual desire and human intimacy in the Song of Songs; Jesus' teaching on the good of marriage in the gospels; and the codes of behaviour for the good ordering of Christian households in the epistles. Again, none of this rich biblical tradition can be taken over neat since it all comes from places and times far distant from our own. But all of it points in various ways to God's care for people's growth and happiness in their common (including sexual and domestic) life. It also points to the importance of wholehearted obedience to God and love of neighbour in response.

At yet another level, the Bible offers what we might call '*prototypes*' for a Christian theology of the family. (I say 'prototypes' rather than 'archetypes', because archetypes have a more static, definitive quality, which leaves little room for change and development.) We may cite, for example, the integrity of the 'one flesh' relation of Adam and Eve in the garden before the Fall; the loyalty of Ruth to Naomi which allows Ruth to forsake her kinsfolk and native land; the use of marital imagery to represent the covenantal love-relation between Israel and

God in the Book of Hosea; the extravagant love of the father for the prodigal son in Luke 15; and the friendship of Jesus with his followers in the Gospel of John. We may cite also the attempt at a more balanced reciprocity which Paul expects of relations between wives and husbands in 1 Cor. 7; and the attempt of other early Christian writers to set conventional, pagan patterns of household order on a higher, christological and ecclesiological plane - e.g. 'Husbands, love your wives, *as Christ loved the church and gave himself up for her*' (Eph. 6:25). Today, the latter kind of exhortation may be seen - with some justification - as a pretext for the subtle perpetuation of male dominance in the form of divinely-ordained condescension towards women. In its original context, however, it marks an important protest against the arbitrary exercise of power by men over women in a patriarchal society, and an attempt to put husband-wife relations on a new, 'agapeistic' plane.

Finally, in its consistent monotheism, its abhorrence of idolatry, and its advocacy of the headship of Christ, the Bible offers a powerful *corrective* to any tendency to give the family an inflated importance. The gospel stories of Jesus calling disciples to leave their kinship and household ties to follow him are a dramatic and hyperbolic expression of this (cf. Mk.1:16-20; Matt.10:34-37; Lk.9:57-62). The fact that the Church so readily adopts a 'familist' ethos and ethic is surely surprising in view of the evidence that Jesus himself did not marry, that he expected disciples (where necessary) to subordinate family ties for his sake, and that he spoke in quite pessimistic terms about what his followers ought to expect from their natural kin (cf. Mk.10:28-30; 13:12-13).

Attending to Christian Tradition

The Christian heritage has many different strands and the Church exists in many different institutional forms each with its own identity, tradition and doctrine. Because of this it is impossible to set out one single and definitive theology of the family. But several of the separate and often overlapping traditions are worth summarizing.

In *Roman Catholicism*, marriage and the family have enormous practical and symbolic significance as part of the natural order given by God for the good of the marriage partners and for the procreation of children. According to Catholic theology, marriage is a sacrament. It is a means through which a man and a woman become a blessing and a source of divine grace to each other. In order to preserve this sacramental understanding, there is a strict marriage discipline. Marriage is for life; and divorce and remarriage are permitted on only very limited grounds. Sexual relations outside of marriage are understood as going against the will of God, on the grounds that the procreative potential of sexual intercourse presupposes the undergirding of the marriage bond. Central to Catholic teaching on the family is the equal dignity of every member, children as well as husband and wife. The family is understood as the foundation of society. In its own right it is a special kind of community where moral and religious formation takes place. The Christian family, in particular, is thought of as a 'domestic church'. Its common life expresses the communion within the life of the Trinity, and involves the practice of the faith and life that is characteristic of the Church as a whole.

The understanding of marriage and the family in classical and contemporary *Anglicanism* is indistinguishable in many ways from developing Roman Catholic doctrine. This is because there has always been a sense in which the Church of England does not have its own doctrine but seeks instead to be the English expression of 'the one holy catholic and apostolic church'. The prayer books of Anglicanism testify to the importance of marriage as a gift of God in creation both for the enrichment of the lives of the marriage partners and for the procreation of children. Although marriage is not generally held to be a sacrament in the strict sense, it is still regarded as 'a holy mystery' and a means of divine grace. On the question of divorce and remarriage, Anglican teaching and practice tends to give more weight to pastoral and practical considerations than to the demands of Christian casuistry. This has meant that Anglican marriage discipline is flexible and pragmatic. What needs to be emphasized here, however, is that, as in Catholicism, Anglican thought about the family is a corollary of the Anglican doctrine of marriage. For this reason, the way into a theology of the family is most likely to have a theology of marriage as its starting-point.

In a broader movement such as *Evangelical Protestantism*, the family is also seen as part of the natural order, the will of God for which is revealed in the Bible. For Evangelicalism as for Catholicism, the family is very important as the intimate community where parents and children are nurtured physically and spiritually. But the family is also important as a symbol of social stability and moral virtue. It is a divinely ordained guard against the ambiguities, individualism and experimentation of a modern world which has lost its way morally and religiously. Characteristically, strong emphasis is placed on the responsible exercise of parental authority in the nurture of children. The family is seen, alongside the Church, as the basic institution for the induction of children into the beliefs, values and skills necessary for good and godly living. Indeed, for some Evangelicals, the family is so important as the locus for Christian nurture and holy living that it tends to displace more institutionalized forms of religion. As in Catholicism – but on biblical rather than sacramental grounds – marriage is understood as monogamous and lifelong, and sexual relations outside marriage are prohibited. Sexual fidelity within marriage is seen as one of the ways that Christians mark themselves off from a secular world gone morally astray.

Significantly different in certain respects is the approach of *Liberal*

Protestantism. In part the heir of a Reformation theology which eliminated the sacramental interpretation of marriage and family in favour of a more civic interpretation, the tendency here is to celebrate modernity and to reinterpret and renegotiate traditional notions accordingly. Here, the family is above all a focus for the development of human individuality, religious sensibility and mature personhood, and strong emphasis is placed on the rights of the individual, including and especially those of the child. In this tradition more than in the Roman Catholic and Evangelical Protestant traditions, there is a more flexible marriage discipline and considerably greater openness to accepting cohabitation as a legitimate context for a developing sexual relationship. This greater openness is due in part to a re-evaluation of Christian tradition and traditional notions of authority, including the respective authority of marriage partners. It is due also to a greater sympathy towards developments in modern knowledge, including developments in the social sciences and the various schools of psychotherapeutic thought and practice.

Liberation theology is a more recent development in Christian thought and practice which is only just beginning to make an impact in Britain. It is a protest against what is perceived to be the injustice perpetrated by Western capitalist individualism (with its paradoxically corporatist manifestations) in its oppression of the poor, especially in the Third World. Where liberal theology gives centre-stage to the individual, liberation theology focuses on the need for solidarity with oppressed classes and groups, not least impoverished families and exploited men, women and children. An important contribution from this corner is the challenge to see how much family life and family values in the West are shaped by prior and often hidden commitments of race, class, property and political economics. Liberation theology also helps us to recognize that the patterns of household consumption in the West have a direct impact on standards of living in the Third World, an impact which impinges immediately and catastrophically on Third World families. In the light of this approach, the Church has been helped to see more clearly that it is not possible to separate matters to do with personal spirituality from matters of social justice. A true understanding of the kind of justice God wants only comes by listening to the voices of the poor and identifying with them in their struggle to live. Furthermore, education in social justice and radical discipleship is a process of spiritual formation which has to begin in homes and families if it is to have lasting effect.

Feminist theology shares with liberation theology the character of a theology of protest and a commitment to unmask injustice in Church, society and the family. But whereas liberation theology focuses on the experiences of the poor, feminist theology focuses on gender oppression and the experiences of women. In feminist theology, the traditional, bourgeois, nuclear family tends to be seen as an instrument of the patriarchal oppression of women. On this view, the family is not a sacred haven from the 'macho' world of work and politics, but a context where issues of gender, work and politics have a major impact in quite profound – though usually unacknowledged – ways. Important as a starting-point for this type of theology is the experience of women, including women's experience of systematic exclusion from the public domain and their horrific history of oppression and sexual abuse. As sources of empowerment and solidarity, 'sisterhood' replaces the 'traditional family', and 'women church' or 'the discipleship of equals' replaces patriarchal, hierarchical ecclesiastical institutions. In feminist theology, the protest of the biblical prophets against social injustice becomes a paradigm for the protest of women today. In relation to the family, this protest focuses on the unequal distribution of power in relations between the sexes and on the traditional confinement of women to the home and to the tasks of shopping, cooking and child-rearing.

It would be a mistake to try to harmonize such various theologies of the family, just as it would be to belittle or neglect them – or to hold uncritically to one while discounting the others. Far better to recognize that, like the various biblical traditions discussed earlier, these church and theological traditions constitute a theoretical and practical wisdom of great potential value. They represent the attempts of Christian individuals and communities in times past and present to develop a good and more godly family and social order.

Building-blocks

Nevertheless, at a general level, it might be claimed that a Christian theology of the family, household or domestic group is likely to be deficient if it does not build on foundations like the following.

God is triune love and God's desire is for human beings to participate in that love by growing to maturity as embodied, historical and interdependent persons, according to the pattern of Christ. On this basis, the family – understood in a relatively plural and inclusive way – has an important role to play. Theologically, it can be a relationship and an institution where God's grace is experienced and where people can find nurture and healing, and thereby grow as persons in their individuality, their social relations, and their relations with God. There is no sense in simplistic distinctions between the Church as a structure of grace and the family as one of nature. This is to claim too much for the Church and too little for the family. It also fails to do justice to the widely held view that the Church itself is a kind of family, and conversely, that the family has a sacramental quality.

However, like any intimate relationship and social institution, the family can become demonic, its potential as a source of grace and mature personhood perverted by sin – men and women behaving in disloyal ways or becoming rivals in a hostile competition for power, parents neglecting their responsibilities to their children and *vice versa*, Church and society falling into the idolatry of 'familism', and so on. Of particular relevance at this point is the way in which theological images from the Bible and tradition may have become interpreted in ways whose effect on domestic relations has been (and remains) pernicious, *even if they were not intended to be so*. In Catholic Christianity, Mary as Virgin Mother may be one such, if it functions to oppress women by upholding an impossible, unattainable ideal. In Protestant Christianity, the metaphor of 'headship' as applied to the man in the household may be another instance, if it functions as a warrant for hierarchical power relations whose consequence is the manipulation, abuse and oppression of women and children.

Consequently, it should be the task of the Church to be itself a solidarity of fallible followers of Christ, seeking in their social-political-economic-ecological relations to be an example of the kind of institution and community which families and domestic groups, in their own way(s), might be also. It should also be the task of the Church to support and (where necessary) help re-form families in ways which enable them, along with other social structures, to be a context where justice and neighbourly love are fostered and where men, women and children can grow into the image of God. This task ought to include the refashioning of the Church and of theology itself in ways which provide liturgies, symbols, models and forms of discourse more conducive to life-enhancing domestic patterns. Important at the level of theology would be a reassessment of the theology of marriage in relation to a renewed theology of friendship, as well as further exploration of the theology of play and the theology of rest. For in all of these areas there are the seeds for creative reflection and practice where patterns of domination in Church, society and family make way for patterns of nurture, cooperation and interdependence.

But the process cannot only be one way, from Church to family or domestic group. For if the small-scale society of the family can be a source of nurture, healing and grace, then it must be the case that such families and groups have a lot to offer to the Church about the nature of loving relationships and the practice of mutual acceptance, interdependence, and neighbourly love. If the Church is able to offer the sacraments of baptism and eucharist to families and domestic groups, they in turn can offer to the Church (what might be termed) the sacraments of hospitality, seasoned friendship and wisdom honed by the pain and joy of intimate relations. Without such reciprocity, families lose their ties to the wider society and the transcendant dimension of our common life, and the Church loses its rootedness in small-scale human sociability and the sacraments of everyday life.

In all this, it is important neither to demean the family nor to exalt it, nor to assume that any particular form of the family is God-given. To demean the family is to be irresponsible socially and 'docetic' theologically – as if the domestic life and bonds of kinship which many people consider fundamental doesn't really matter in God's sight. To exalt the family tends toward the perpetuation of a particular form of bourgeois idolatry, as well as placing the family itself under a sometimes intolerable burden of social, moral and sentimental expectation. It is also to ignore the cries for justice and change from those whom many traditional notions of the family leave marginalized, abused and powerless.

References

H. Anderson, *The Family and Pastoral Care* (Philadelphia: Fortress, 1984).

S.C. Barton, essays on 'Child/Children' and 'Family', in J.B. Green and S. McKnight, eds., *Dictionary of Jesus and the Gospels* (Leicester: IVP, 1992).

B. & P. Berger, *The War over the Family* (Harmondsworth: Penguin, 1984).

R. Bondi, 'Family', in J Macquarrie and J. Childress, eds., *A New Dictionary of Christian Ethics* (London: SCM, 1986), 224–226.

P. Brown, *The Body and Society* (London: Faber, 1989).

R. Clapp, *Families at the Crossroads. Beyond Traditional and Modern Options* (Downers Grove: InterVarsity Press, 1993).

J.B. Elshtain, ed., *The Family in Political Thought* (Amherst: University of Massachusetts Press, 1982).

M. Furlong, ed., *Mirror to the Church, Reflections on Sexism* (London: SPCK, 1988).

W.J. Goode, *The Family* (Englewood Cliffs, N.J.: Prentice-Hall, 1964).

J. Goody, *The Development of the Family and Marriage in Europe* (Cambridge: CUP, 1983).

A. Greeley, ed., *The Family in Crisis or in Transition* (=*Concilium*, 121; New York: Seabury, 1979).

A.E. Harvey, *Promise or Pretence? A Christian's Guide to Sexual Morals* (London: SCM, 1994).

S. Hauerwas, *A Community of Character* (Notre Dame: University of Notre Dame, 1981), Part Three.

J.D. Hunter, *Evangelicalism, The Coming Generation* (Chicago: University of Chicago Press, 1987), ch.4.

A. Joseph, ed., *Through the Devil's Gateway, Women, Religion and Taboo* (London: SPCK, 1990).

R.R. Ruether, essays on 'Church and Family', in *New Blackfriars*, 65 (Jan.–May, 1984), 4–14, 77–85, 110–118, 170–179, 202–212.

A. Thatcher, *Liberating Sex. A Christian Sexual Theology* (London: SPCK, 1993).

S. Walrond-Skinner, *The Fulcrum and the Fire, Wrestling with Family Life* (London: DLT, 1993).

C.J.H. Wright, *God's People in God's Land. Family, Land, and Property in the Old Testament* (Grand Rapids: Eerdmans, 1990).

11.3 Towards a Theology of the Family – A Response

Susan Parsons

The two recent pieces by Stephen Barton and Alan Billings regarding a theology of the family reopen an important debate in Christian ethics. In 1958, in a report commissioned by the Archbishop of Canterbury for the Lambeth Conference, 'The Theology of Marriage and the Family' was considered.[1] At that time, which was acknowledged to be one of 'rapid social change', several important assumptions informed the Commission's work. One of these was that understanding the treatment of issues by the social sciences had become necessary preparation for theological statements, an acknowledgement of the impact which these studies of humanness were to continue to have upon metaphysics and theology (p. 341). The second was the recognition of several, quite distinctive, Christian approaches to issues, like the definition of what is 'natural', revealing a diversity of Christian ethical standpoints entangled with one another. Unravelling some of these, and enabling us to make intelligent decisions between them, was a significant part of the Commission's task (pp. 348–376).

As a result of these two assumptions, the Report came to the conclusion that theology

> does not supply a single unalterable pattern for married and family life. This life has found expression in different patterns in different places at different times. Therefore the scope for generalization about the form it should take in situations of rapid social change is very limited indeed (p. 343).

Diversity then too was a reality of Christian discourse, and the Commission urged, not 'pronouncements', but wise and careful counsel in particular circumstances. Things have changed yet again since this Report. Writing from the perspective only of 'man', with reference to his wife and offspring, is theologically more problematic than it was in 1958. In addition, the language of ideology, and of the power of social myth, has penetrated the modern consciousness more deeply. There is nevertheless a remarkable consistency in recognition of the issues that need to be addressed, since these have come to life again in the recent papers.

In the introduction to his paper, 'Towards a Theology of the Family,' Stephen Barton suggests that '"the family" tends to become a moral and political symbol' and later that 'statements about "the family" are moral and political statements' (p.4).[2] He proceeds to analyse in detail the ways in which this may be recognized in contemporary Britain, using this analysis to suggest that 'the family' does not refer to any *thing*. There is no 'essence' at the heart of the word 'family', but it is 'an abstraction' (p. 6). This helps to explain some aspects of our social relations, to see ways in which these are justified ideologically, and to understand the power of this 'rhetoric' in our society.

He then suggests that as Christians explore the theological tradition, the same thing appears to be true. 'The family' here too may be discerned as 'moral and political symbol'. Theological resources are 'partial,' which seems to mean both 'partisan' and 'limited by perspective'. When we examine these resources, we discover that the precise sense in which 'the family' may be believed to be God-given is not consistent through the tradition, and further, that attempts to argue for its God-givenness without closer examination of one's own limited perspective can lead to idolatry. This may happen in the history of the Church as it seeks to model itself on 'family,' thereby highlighting only certain features and elevating these to a 'sacred' status. The result is a collusion between the Church and one model of 'family,' which the diversity within the Christian tradition itself belies (p. 10).

The approach Barton takes through the main body of the paper, which I would call social constructionist, reveals something of the continuing impact of the social sciences upon theological ethics. It encourages us to be aware, in this case, of the ways in which the nature of the family is already constructed and determined for us by the social context and political institutions in which we find ourselves, and by the tradition in which those things are rooted. We are drawn to the recognition that families, and family life and relationships, are a cultural phenomenon. Thus while the family may emerge as a natural expression of our physicality and sociability, the particular form this expression may take differs by political realities and other historical contingencies. Families change as circumstances change, and so therefore does our language and understanding, and theology, of the family.

This approach may also highlight some of the ways in which we can shape the reality of the family, thus taking our own involvement in history seriously. The family, with regard to its own internal structure of relationships, and its position amongst other social structures, is not a natural 'given', and is not fixed for all time as a pre-set pattern into which our lives are to be poured. There are therefore important ways in which we can have a hand in reforming, or rethinking, or reconstructing the nature of family life and its patterns of relationship. Indeed it would be an essential expression of our responsibility for history, for discerning the precise way in which the love of God may be manifest in our particular personal and cultural circumstances, that we do so.

It is to suggest a framework for such reconstruction that Barton offers his own recommendations, or 'Building-blocks'. He proposes that out of diversity may emerge the 'significant points' which any adequate Christian theology of the family should contain (pp. 11–12). There is much to be gained from these points, but I would want to see them enriched specifically with insights from feminism, insights which reveal the need for some careful thinking about the nature of our humanness.

Barton firstly suggests that the domestic group may be a place for experiencing God's grace, finding nurture and healing, and thereby being able to grow as persons. Exactly *how* one is nurtured and *how* God's grace is experienced are important matters. It is essential to ensure that serious consideration is given to the place of power within domestic groups. There is a tendency to shy away from speaking of the importance and reality of power in family relationships, and yet unless we speak at exactly this point about the person as a centre of responsible decision, of feeling and of thinking, as well as of the 'power to be' expressed in biological drives, we will too easily romanticize what happens in human relationships.[3]

An important principle of feminist thinking – that the personal is the political – may be felt at this point. Our sense of self emerges from the dynamics of human interactions in which power is significant. We become gendered persons within the domestic group, and this process is accompanied by messages about our human possibilities and value. What we become as men and as women is shaped, physically, morally and socially, within these groups. Such roles are learned through divisions of labour and spheres of influence, and through power relations in which different messages are given to boys and to girls regarding the extent and nature of their freedom and responsibilities. As a result, men are encouraged in autonomy and self-definition, while women are ruled by the needs, desires, and projects of others. What is painful to us today is the realization that the power of some is paid for by the powerlessness of others, and that within such relationships, expressions of individual power may be incompatible with one another. We need imagination to envision new possibilities for relationship in which full human maturity is possible.

From these experiences of human relationships, our knowledge of God is formed. An analysis of power will thus need to take account of arguments that our relation to the divine too is learned within the dynamics of a domestic division of labour and of unequal sexual relations. In this way, religious belief is received as an imposition of conventional mores, reinforcing their influence and acceptability. The feminist critique of the family has some important points to make about re-patterning the family so that we may also re-image the divine appropriately. This points to the importance of the marginalized, to the empowering of those who may criticize and transform social relations, which is also essential to full human life.[4]

Barton's second point about the perversion of the family by sin is interesting to me, as a reflection of what is, I think, a rather negative view of human nature which the social constructionist approach generally hides in its heart. I am intrigued by this, and Barton's section here is an example of the theological presupposition which undergirds this more 'political' approach. The 'will to power' is here perverted, and I do wonder whether this is being used as the paradigm of power for Barton, rather than the positive and creative way in which I would want to speak of power above.

Why is there no reference to *structural* sin? As I understand the concept, it refers to the ways in which good people are fixed by institutions, to behave and to think and to relate according to certain patterns of possibility and acceptability. The most important area which here needs to be explored is the division between the public and the private realms. In the west, we stand in a modern tradition which divides the public world of politics and work, from the private realm of personal moral values, religious beliefs and practices, and sexual behaviour. The private realm is taken to be a secret and untouchable space for the free expression and development of each individual, outside the rule of public law unless that law is explicitly transgressed in interfering with the freedom of others, and untouched by considerations of justice which are the measure of the moral in the wider sphere. The family tends to be the symbolic and functional focus of this privacy, being the space within which it is learned and protected. The reality of the family thus allows the public realm to thrive through the nurture, care and support given to individuals within families. This may be even more important in our day, as the public realm becomes increasingly alien – hard – quantitative – aggressive – conflictual – stressful, and as there are fewer satisfactory ways for people to be seriously involved as citizens in the decision-making processes of their own communities.

This division also marks the distinction of men from women, so that women are responsible for the ethic of care in our society, and men for the ethic of individual achievement. The family mirrors this larger structure in its own living arrangements and style of personal interactions, and sets the stage for the future of boys and girls within its ethos. There will thus be very different responses from men and from women when language of love or of sacrifice is emphasized for domestic groups. A critique of double standards of all kinds is important here, not because it illuminates some kind of innate sinful tendency to be unfair to our fellows, but because it reveals social patterns which the church needs to address practically and theologically.

Thus, I would want to emphasize in a critique of the metaphor of 'headship' within Protestant Christianity, for example, its role in supporting the public/private division, and its function in preventing questions of justice from even being raised in the private realm. It is at points like this that a particular kind of collusion of the Church with the wider cultural ethos is keenly felt. On the whole, I would not want to speak in personal terms in this section at all, until a more thorough structural analysis has been undertaken.[5]

Important in Barton's third building-block is a discussion of the role of Church 'as example' to domestic groups. I warm to this section very much. It points to ways in which the Church may embody alternative community, and may itself be a non-traditional group for the encouragement of new possibilities of relationship. Theologically, this suggests the inbreaking of the kingdom, as well as the real need in contemporary society for signs of hope in human relationships and for significant community involvement. The call for a theology of friendship is so important.

Again, in Barton's encouragement of the two-way relation between church and domestic group, is affirmed the theological principle of the interrelation of nature and grace with which I am in basic agreement. This will inevitably involve the Church in politics, through reciprocity with the realities of family life, and will tend to undermine what I consider to be an unhelpful distinction between the sacred and the secular (as also implied in section 2).[6]

There is a dual focus in Barton's final point, which returns us to the concerns of the 1958 report, reminding us that we need to pay attention to the boundaries of ethical considerations. These must involve some statement of what is considered to be natural to human life, and of the transcendent dimension of life which allows for critique and reconstruction. Some attention to natural law is important for Barton's theology of the family.

It is at this point, that a consideration of the response by Alan Billings, in which he criticizes Barton's basic assumptions, could be illuminating.[7] Billings first questions the historico-political approach of Barton's paper, arguing that the belief that the family is historically shaped is itself the product of modern myths, by which scholars have sought to debunk the ideological hold that 'the family' has on the modern mind. Attempts to prove that the nuclear family is a purely modern phenomenon, by means of literary or historical evidence, fail to convince Billings. He believes that it is possible to examine this evidence without contemporary 'myths', either the myth of modern inferiority which seeks a better society through the abolition of the bougeois family (p. 69–70), or the myth of modern superiority which elevates the contemporary family as the site of, previously undervalued, nurturing love (p. 71–72).

When one does so, Billings considers it possible to discover a substratum of nature which consistently underlies history, and which is foundational for a theology of the family. He believes that we are led precisely to what Barton had denied, to 'a permanent moral order within which God (sic) intended human life to be lived and so to flourish' (p. 73). This 'natural law' provides for the Christian family a timeless pattern, which is believed to be part of the God-given order of creation, by reference to which we may both explain the 'universality of the family', and from which we may derive moral guidelines that emphasise intimacy, privacy, and the importance of two parents

(p. 74–75). Since he believes that this foundation of morality is not touched or built upon by Barton, Billings claims that the former work either does not deserve to be called a 'theology', or it is not about 'the family' (p. 67). Billings presents an attempt at theology without the 'myths' of the social sciences.

I am not convinced that the choice he presents to us, between the acceptance of a morality which is historically determined, and of a natural law morality which is founded beyond history, is either necessary or morally justifiable. I question the necessity of this choice because I do not believe that it is possible for us to divide ourselves in two parts in this way – one part fixed nature, another part changeable history. We cannot describe what belongs to our human nature without using vocabulary and concepts revealing the influence of our time and our place and our society upon us. We speak in public language; our images of our humanness and of our bodies are shaped according to prevailing notions of what constitutes good health, and of what contributes to overall human satisfaction. Our moral understanding is developed from within history, from inside culture, and is all the more difficult and challenging to discern as a result.

One need not conclude from this that there is no natural law at all. There is some measure of consistency in our reflections, such that we recognise human beings in other times and places, quite different from our own, as sharing with us in some basic humanness, with which we empathise and find common cause. But exactly which features of human life we emphasise, and precisely how we describe our common human nature, need not be pre-determined in order for us to draw meaningful implications for our own lives. We need not posit the existence of a timeless universal which is made specific in particular instances in order to appreciate what we share. Our human nature just *is* historical, and efforts to bump some part of it out of history, out of the particularities and uncertainties and changes which characterize the human condition, contribute to a dualism which has certainly had a powerful hold on the Christian tradition, but is not its only manifestation.

To be fair, it is unclear precisely which version of natural law ethics Billings supports, since he puts together Scripture, the Fathers and the Reformers, between whom there is considerable and significant theological disagreement about what is natural. For this reason, the reader is led to believe that things are more simple than they are, that there actually is a moral foundation, given and ordered by God, beyond the contingencies of history, and that perceived threats of social disorder and moral decline may be met by application of right authority. The claim that this is so provides a moral high ground, a 'God's-eye' view of the world, from which it is believed Christians may offer a significant and distinctive message to contemporary society. In this way, Billings seeks to affirm the transcendent dimension of Christian ethics.

Two brief comments about this will have to suffice. The first is that the notion of a fixed human nature is not essential to natural law morality. For many Christians, the task of such morality is to apprehend the continuous creative work of God in the present and the future, not to reflect upon the once-given and ordained. This apprehension suggests that there is something to be discovered, to be found, but precisely what this consists in, may not be completely known in advance. New moral principles may yet be discovered. There is adventure and risk in this approach which is the result of the awesome complexity we encounter in the creation.

This further implies that natural law morality does not depend upon a God's-eye view, but is rather a human reflection upon the lived experience of human beings. Recognition of our historicity is the starting point, description of the personal relationships and structural realities by which our lives are formed is the raw material of reflection, and fulfilment of the deepest longings of the human heart is the end for which we hope. That the divine presence is known in the shapes of our humanness is the mystery of our faith.[8]

In conclusion, I would agree that Barton's approach needs for its own sustenance a re-description of human nature, including some statement of aspects of our humanness in which power and friendship may firmly take root. Without this, involvement in domestic groups will appear to be another consumer option in modern society, complete with designer labels and private insurance policies.

I am also suggesting however, that the description of natural law ethics illustrated by Billings, is not the best way to proceed with this. The transcendent dimension of our moral life is more elusive than his straightforward setting out of divine ordinance implies, more heartbreaking than his description of failing to live up to an ideal can possibly suggest, and so very much more flexible and pliant than his claim of universality can accommodate.

Presumably we are all in agreement that a theology and ethics of the family is a critical location for contemporary apologetics, as we seek to demonstrate how the knowledge and love of God is intrinsically bound up with the fullness of our humanity.

Notes

1. 'The Family in Contemporary Society' A Report to the Archbishop of Canterbury before the Lambeth Conference of 1958, by a Commission chaired by Dr. M.A.C. Warren, reprinted in Ian T. Ramsey, ed.: *Christian Ethics and Contemporary Philosophy* (London, SCM Press, 1966) chapter 19. All page numbers refer to this edition.
2. Stephen Barton: 'Towards a Theology of the Family' (CRUCIBLE, Jan./Mar. 1993) pp. 4–13.
3. Paul Tillich: *Love, Power and Justice*, see particularly his insistence on the ontological unity and interdependence of these concepts. (London, Oxford University Press, 1954).
4. Sharon D. Welch: *A Feminist Ethic of Risk*, see especially chapter 4 in which persistence, imagination and solidarity are emphasised as the important signs of human maturity (Minneapolis, Fortress Press, 1990).
5. Susan Moller Okin: *Justice, Gender, and the Family*, see especially chapter 6 in which the public/domestic dichotomy is challenged on the grounds of justice (USA, Basic Books, Inc., 1989).
6. Rosemary Radford Ruether: *Women-Church*, see especially the historical and theological

reflections on church in Part I (New York, Harper Row, 1985).

7.   Alan Billings: 'Christian Reflections on the Family: A Reply to Stephen Barton' (CRUCIBLE, Apr./June 1993), pp. 67–76.

8.   See Charles E. Currant: 'Absolute Norms in Moral Theology' in Outka & Ramsey: *Norm and Context in Christian Ethics*, chapter 5 (London, SCM Press, 1968); Kevin T. Kelly: *New Directions in Moral Theology: The Challenge of Being Human*, see particularly chapter 3 (London, G. Chapman, 1992); Ian T. Ramsey: 'Towards a Rehabilitation of Natural Law,' in Ramsey, *Op. Cit.,* chapter 20.

Acknowledgements

The editors and publisher gratefully acknowledge the following permissions to reproduce copyright material. All possible attempts have been made to contact copyright holders and to acknowledge their copyright correctly. We are grateful to: *Africa Theological Journal*, for Emmanuel Martey, Church and Marriage in African Society: A Theological Appraisal, 20.2, 136–147, 1991; *American Baptist Quarterly*, for William Stayton, A Theology of Sexual Pleasure, 8, 94–108, 1989; *Anglican Theological Review*, for Robert Williams, Toward a Theology for Lesbian and Gay Marriage, 72.2, 134–157, 1990; *Christian Century Foundation*, for James Nelson, Reuniting Sexuality and Spirituality – Copyright 1987, reprinted by permission from the February 25, 1987 issue of *The Christian Century*; and for Karen Lebacqz, Appropriate Vulnerability: A Sexual Ethic for Singles – Copyright 1987, reprinted by permission from the May 6, 1987 issue of *The Christian Century*, and for William Willimon, The People We're Stuck With – Copyright 1990, reprinted by permission from the October 17, 1990 issue of *The Christian Century*; *Christianity and Crisis: A Christian Journal of Opinion*, for Rosemary Radford Ruether, An Unrealised Revolution: Searching Scripture for a Model of the Family, 43, 399–404, 1983; *Church and Society* Magazine, Presbyterian Church (U.S.A.), for Marvin Ellison, Sexuality and Spirituality: An Intimate and Intimidating Connection, 80, 26–34, 1989; *Contact, The Interdisciplinary Journal for Pastoral Care*, for Alison Webster, Revolutionizing Christian Sexual Ethics: A Feminist Perspective, 107.1, 25–29, 1992; *Cross Currents*, for Sandra Friedman & Alexander Irwin, Christian Feminism, Eros and Power in Right Relation, 40, 387–405, 1990; *Crucible*, for Stephen C. Barton, Towards a Theology of the Family, 4–13, 1993, and for Susan Parsons, Towards a Theology of the Family – A Response, 123–132, 1993; *Encounter*, for Jennifer L. Rike, The Lion and the Unicorn: Feminist Perspectives on Christian Love as Care, 51, 247–255, 1990; *Heythrop Journal* (Blackwell Publishers), for Richard Price, The Distinctiveness of Early Christian Sexual Ethics, 31,

257–276, 1990; *Journal of Feminist Studies in Religion*, for Mary Grey, Claiming Power-in-Relation: Exploring the Ethics of Connection, 7, 7–18, 1991; and for Sally Purvis, Mothers, Neighbors and Strangers: Another Look at Agape, 7, 19–34, 1991; *Journal of Pastoral Care*, for James Poling, Child Sex Abuse: A Rich Context for Thinking about God, Community and Ministry, 42, 58–61, 1988, and for James B. Ashbrooke, Different Voices, Different Genes, 46, 174–183, 1992; *Journal of Psychology and Christianity*, for Douglas E.P. Rosenau, Sexuality and the Single Person, 1.4, 30–36, 1982; *Journal of Religion and Ageing*, for Barbara Payne, Sex and the Elderly: No Laughing Matter in Religion, 3, 141–152, 1986; *Journal of Theology and Sexuality*, for Stephen C. Barton, Is the Bible Good News for Human Sexuality? Reflections on Method in Biblical Interpretation, 1.1, 42–54, 1994, and for William D. Lindsey, The AIDS Crisis and the Church: A Time to Heal, 1.2, 11–37, 995; *Lexington Theological Quarterly*, for Loren Broadus, Sex and Violence in the Family and Church, 26, 13–23, 1991; *Modern Theology* (Blackwell Publishers), for Daphne Hampson, On Power and Gender, 4, 235–250, 1988; *Pastoral Psychology*, for Daniel Helminiak, The Trinitarian Vocations of the Gay Community, 36, 100–111, 1987; *Perkins Journal*, for Marjorie Procter-Smith, Reorganising Victimisation: The Intersection Between Liturgy and Domestic Violence, 40, 17–27, 1987; *The Reformed Journal*, for Stanley Hauerwas & Allen Verhey, From Conduct to Character: A Guide to Sexual Adventure, 36.11, 12–16, 1986; *Religion and Intellectual Life*, for Carter Heyward, Is a Self-Respecting Christian Woman an Oxymoron: Reflections on a Feminist Spirituality for Justice, 3.2, 45–62, 1986; the Religious Education Assocation, 409 Prospect St., New Haven, CT 06511–2177 U.S.A. (membership information available on request), for *Religious Education*, Karen Lebacqz and Deborah Blake, Safe Sex and Lost Love, 83.2, 201–210, 1988; *Review and Expositor*, for J. Michael Hester, Men in Relationships: Redeeming Masculinity, 87, 107–119, 1990; Elizabeth Stuart, for Lesbian and Gay Relationships: A Lesbian Feminist Perspective; *Themelios**, for Astri Hauge, Feminist Theology as Critique and Renewal of Theology; *The Way (Supplement 77)*, for Ben Kimmerling, Celibacy and Intimacy, 87–96, 1993; *Westminster Theological Journal*, for Daniel Doriani, The Puritans, Sex and Pleasure, 53, 125–143, 1991; *Word and World: Theology for Christian Ministry*, for Roland Martinson, Androgyny and Beyond,

5, 370–379, 1985; and *Worship*, for German Martinez, Marriage as Worship: A Theological Analogy, 62, 332–352, 1988.

* *Themelios* is an international journal for theological and religious studies students, expounding and defending the historic Christian faith. It is published by the Religious and Theological Studies Fellowship, a constituent part of the Universities and Colleges Christian Fellowship, and the International Fellowship of Evangelical Students.

Index of Names

Index of Subjects